# WHO BETRAYED THE JEWS?

# WHO BETRAYED THE JEWS?

## THE REALITIES OF NAZI PERSECUTION IN THE HOLOCAUST

### AGNES GRUNWALD-SPIER

*For my beloved sons Daniel, Benjamin and Simon*

First published 2016

The History Press
The Mill, Brimscombe Port
Stroud, Gloucestershire, GL5 2QG
www.thehistorypress.co.uk

British Library Cataloguing in Publication Data.
A catalogue record for this book is available from the British Library.

ISBN 978 0 7509 5364 1

Typesetting and origination by The History Press
Printed in Great Britain

The Somme is like the Holocaust. It revealed things about mankind that we cannot come to terms with and cannot forget. It can never become the past.

Pat Barker, November 1995, on winning the Booker Prize

Tell your children of it, and let your children tell their children, and their children another generation.

Joel 1:3

# CONTENTS

# FOREWORD

There is a saying in the Talmud that the saving of a single life is the equivalent of saving the entire world. It might well be said that the converse is also true, that the betrayal to death of a single person is equal to the death of an entire world. It might seem inconceivable, but the story of the destruction of the Jews of Europe is as much the story of a large number of such individual betrayals as of the mass murder of entire communities. This is the story of such betrayals.

In her earlier work Agnes Grunwald-Spier publicised a number of men and women whose actions, echoing those of the better-known Oscar Schindler, saved a number of Jews, seeking neither rewards nor recognition but merely doing what they felt to be right. Grunwald-Spier showed how there were many as deserving of praise as those who did what they felt was right out of high moral purpose, out of their own humanity. But in the progress of this study she uncovered another side of the Holocaust, which, as she says, shocked her. This was the realisation that there were groups and individuals who acted in the directly opposite manner, who in one way or another betrayed the trust of others who might well have escaped the fate of their fellow Jews.

Betrayal can take many forms; some people were entrusted with the cherished belongings of Jews who hoped that they might be able to return to claim them; later they denied that they had ever received them. To some extent such greed is explicable and falls into the same category as the conduct of those who would not themselves take action against their Jewish neighbours, but were fully prepared to take advantage of the opportunities that the removal of those neighbours offered them. Those who employed concentration camp labour knowing the conditions under which these slaves were working are equally culpable. The railway companies who profited from transporting Jews from the further points of Europe to the gas chambers of Auschwitz cannot complain if attention is drawn to their behaviour. And there are still art galleries housing objets d'art, the provenance of which is still far from clear.

What however many would agree as shocking and almost unbelievable is the conduct of those who knowingly handed over information about individuals who had gone into hiding, those who not merely profited casually but who actively sought to profit. Everywhere there were rewards for those who disclosed the whereabouts of those sought by the Gestapo. It is easy to forget that, for example, the hiding place of the Frank family was not found by the Gestapo but had been revealed to them.

The story that Grunwald-Spier tells is of a wide range of such circumstances, stretching from the employee at Auschwitz whose duties were limited to checking the cash and valuables of the inmates to the girls walking the streets of Rome and pointing out those Jews who might otherwise have escaped detection. What she has found during the course of her research might well be considered even more shocking – that those girls betraying their clients were Jewish girls. Sometimes such actions were for a financial reward; more often it was out of fear and desperation, the hope that they might at least save themselves.

These are betrayals by individuals, but they are what might be considered as collective betrayals. Most would consider the actions by doctors in the camps as a clear betrayal of the Hippocratic oaths that they had taken on qualification.

The account of *The Other Schindlers* was one of praise, and Agnes Grunwald-Spier was right to tell us of it. But this account has also to be told. It is a story which must make us all pause, for it involves even those who might well consider themselves as bystanders. No one can be sure what they might do under such circumstances; no one can know that they would be able to resist the ultimate temptation. What Grunwald-Spier teaches us is that we can never stand aloof.

Professor Aubrey Newman

# ACKNOWLEDGEMENTS

Inevitably a book like this requires the assistance of many people. I have acknowledged many different individuals' assistance in the text and the footnotes – the people who gave me their stories, the academics and experts who patiently answered my questions and the institutions who sent me their documents and publications free of charge.

I would also like to thank the staff of the Wiener Library and the British Library in London. They were always very helpful. However, at the time I had my hip-replacement operation they were both especially accommodating in reserving books and desks and carrying piles of books for me. It was much appreciated.

I would particularly like to thank Hildegard Abraham for her endless help with German translation and her enthusiastic support for my work. Without her, the book would have taken even longer and I would never have heard Annelore's remarkable story about being a Mischling. I would also like to thank my mentor Emeritus professor Aubrey Newman for the insightful foreword and reading the draft when I was wrestling with my editor Mark Beynon over the length of the book. Mark was always most encouraging and eventually gave in and agreed to publish the whole book intact, which Juanita Zoë Hall edited with great patience and understanding. Sir Martin Gilbert, who wrote the foreword to my first book, died in February 2015; I am grateful for his kind support over several years.

Inevitably, my dear parents, Leona and Philipp Grunwald, and my grandfather, Armin Klein, were often in my mind as I worked and I hope they would have been proud.

Finally, I would like to thank my three precious sons for their support, as ever. Other 71-year-old mothers play bridge or golf and have their nails done. I pestered Daniel for help with the sportspeople and Olympians and Benjamin for help with the international law. Simon helped with the glossary and abbreviations. As with the build-up to publication of my first book, my daughter-in-law Michelle was expecting a baby and this time a sister for Jamie was born, named Sophie Leona Anne. Unfortunately the members of my family have been neglected as a result of my labours, but I hope they will regard it as having been worthwhile.

In spite of all this help and support, the book's faults and imperfections are mine alone.

Agnes Grunwald-Spier

2016

# GLOSSARY

| | |
|---|---|
| AJR | Association of Jewish Refugees. |
| Bar Mitzvah | Ceremony of coming of age for a boy aged 13. Afterwards he is regarded as an adult and can be part of a minyan – see below. |
| Barneveld List | Barneveld was the site of a camp where about 700 prominent Dutch Jews were interned. Most of these Jews survived the war and were referred to as the 'Barneveld Group'. This group was created when K. L. Frederiks, then the permanent secretary of the Dutch Ministry of Home Affairs, compiled a list of 'deserving Dutch Jews'. Artists, doctors and industrialists found a much-coveted place on 'Frederiks' list', but hundreds were refused. |
| Bat Mitzvah | Coming of age for a girl. |
| Blockältester | Barracks chief. |
| Blockwaerter | Block warden. |
| Brit Milah | Male Circumcision – on the eighth day after birth, if the boy is well enough. |
| Bucket List | A list of things you decide you want to do before you die. Comes from the colloquial phrase for death – 'he kicked the bucket'. |
| Cantor/Chazan | A person who leads a Jewish congregation in prayer (usually in song). |
| Chanukah | Festival of the Lights – usually in December when lights are lit for eight nights. |
| Chuppa | Canopy under which a Jewish marriage takes place. It represents the new home of the young couple. |
| DOB | Deutscher Offizier Bund, or German veterans' association. |
| DP | Displaced person. |
| ERR | Einsatzab Reichsleiter Rosenberg – Nazi organisation dedicated to appropriating cultural property. |
| Gau | A region or county in Germany. |
| Gauleiter | A political official governing a gau under the Nazis. |
| Gymnasium | Not a gym – a grammar school in Europe. |
| *Hatikvah* | The Israeli National Anthem. *Hatikvah* means 'The Hope' and was written in 1886 with a theme found in Smetana's *Moldau*. Translation of the words:<br>As long as the Jewish spirit is yearning deep in the heart, |

With eyes turned toward the East, looking toward Zion,
Then our hope – the two-thousand-year-old hope – will not be lost:
To be a free people in our land,
The land of Zion and Jerusalem.

| | |
|---|---|
| HEART | Holocaust Education and Archive Research Team. |
| HJ | Hitler Jugend – Hitler Youth. |
| IMAJ | Israeli Medical Association Journal. |
| Incunabula | Printed books dated from before 1501. |
| JHI | Jewish Historical Institute. |
| JRP | Jewish Renaissance Project. |
| JTA | Jewish Telegraphic Agency, founded in 1917. Not-for-profit source of reporting on issues and events of Jewish interest. |
| Judenältester | Jewish Elder, leader of the Judenrät. |
| Judenfrei | Free of Jews – Nazi term. |
| Judenrät | Jewish Council (plural – Judenräte). |
| JuPo | Judenpolizei, Jewish police. |
| Kaddish | Prayer for the dead. |
| Kapo | Used to describe a Jew assigned to oversee others in the camps. |
| KZ | Konzentrationslager – concentration camp. |
| Landrat | Person in charge of a German district or administrative area. |
| 'Mazeltov!' | Translates literally as 'Good Luck!'; however, used to convey congratulations. |
| Mikvah | Ritual bath to be taken at prescribed times. |
| Minyan | Ten Jewish adults (only men in Orthodox communities) are required to say certain prayers. 'Minyan' is the word for the assembly of ten. |
| Mischling | Nazi term for 'cross-breed' – someone with Jewish and Aryan ancestry (plural Mischlinge). |
| NSDAP | Acronym for the Nazi Party (Nationalsozialistische Deutsche Arbeiterpartei, or National Socialist German Labour Party). |
| OdF | Opfer des Faschismus – 'Victim of Fascism'. |
| Oneg Shabbat | A celebratory gathering to mark the Sabbath. Not to be confused with the collection of documents buried in the Warsaw Ghetto to record life in the ghetto by Emanuel Ringelblum. |
| POW | Prisoner of war. |
| Revier | Sick bay/camp hospital for concentration camp prisoners. |
| Righteous Among the Nations | An honour applied by Israel to non-Jews who risked their lives during the Holocaust to save Jews. |
| RjF | Association of Jewish war veterans. |
| RKK | Reichskulturkammer – Reich Chamber of Culture. |
| RM | Reichsmark(s) – Nazi unit of currency. |

| | |
|---|---|
| RSHA transports | Reichssicherheitszentralstelle. Transports of Jews organised by Eichmann's office, Jewish Section IV-B4, of the Reich Central Security Office. |
| SA | Sturmabteilung – paramilitary wing of the Nazi Party. Called the 'brownshirts' because of the colour of their uniforms and also known as 'storm troopers'. Initially led by Ernst Röhm. Eventually lost power to the SS. |
| Schutzpass | Letter of protection from Swedish legation in Budapest. |
| SD | Sicherheitsdienst – the intelligence agency of the SS, headed by Reinhard Heydrich. |
| Shoah | The Holocaust – literally 'destruction' in Hebrew. |
| SNCF | Société Nationale des Chemins de Fer – French national state-owned railway. |
| SS | Schutzstaffel – 'protection squadron'. A paramilitary group which took over from SA. |
| Succot | A Jewish festival commemorating the Israelites' journey in the desert. |
| Sutler | A camp follower, selling food, etc. |
| Tallit | Jewish prayer shawl. |
| Talmud | A central text of Jewish law, philosophy, ethics and customs. The basis of the Jewish legal framework. |
| TB | Tuberculosis. |
| Torah | The five books of Moses given by God to the Jewish nation at Mount Sinai. |
| TUB | Technische Universität Berlin – Technical University of Berlin. |
| UNRRA | United Nations Relief & Rehabilitation Administration. |
| USHMM | United States Holocaust Memorial Museum. |
| Voivodeship | A voivode is a governor general in Poland. The voivodeship is the area he administers. |
| Volksdeutsche | Nazi term to describe ethnic Germans as a race. |
| Volksgemeinschaft | 'National Community'. Nazi social concept implying a harmonious society free from class conflict and class divisions (Ian Kershaw). |
| Waffen-SS | Armed force of the SS created in 1939. Headed by Heinrich Himmler. |
| Wehrmacht | The German armed forces. |
| WJC | World Jewish Congress. |
| W&N | Weidenfeld and Nicolson (publisher). |
| Yeshiva | Jewish educational institution that focuses on the study of traditional religious texts, primarily the Talmud and Torah study. |
| Zionist | Someone who regards Israel as the homeland of the Jews. |

# INTRODUCTION

No one is born hating another person because of the colour of his skin, or his background, or his religion. People must learn to hate, and if they can learn to hate, they can be taught to love, for love comes more naturally to the human heart than its opposite.

Nelson Mandela (1918–2013), *Long Walk to Freedom*

Brothers, don't forget. Recount what you hear and see! Brothers, make a record of it all!

Reported last words of the 81-year-old historian, Simon Dubnow, on 7 December 1941 in Riga, Latvia, when he was dragged out of his home to the execution site.

When I was writing about Holocaust rescuers in *The Other Schindlers* I was overwhelmed by their courage and generosity of spirit. However, there was one person who really shocked me, and that was a Belgian traitor called Prosper de Zitter who betrayed members of the Resistance and allied airmen trying to get home. I wondered how he could deliberately lead someone into a Gestapo trap knowing he was leading them to their probable death. I began to ponder the meaning of betrayal and treachery.

The most famous traitor in history is Judas, who betrayed Jesus for thirty pieces of silver. Many were betrayed in the Holocaust for money, paltry sums or a bag of sugar, but many were not. The neighbours who snitched to the Gestapo because they suspected someone of being Jewish received no reward but still chose to betray, and I wondered why.

I thought about my maternal grandfather, Armin Klein, who refused to leave Hungary. He asked my mother, 'Why should I leave my native land?' He had a misplaced faith that his native land would be safe. The answer, that only came later, was 'You are a Jew and you will die in Auschwitz in 1944 without even a chance to know your fate and say goodbye to your family. You will die around the time your first grandchild is born – the birth you were so excited about.' Armin was sitting on a bus in Budapest in mid-1944 when it was stopped and all the Jews were taken off and sent to Auschwitz. There, he is believed to have died almost immediately.

As I, his first grandchild, investigated the field, I was shocked by what I found. I have lived with the Holocaust all my life, seventy-one years, but I was unaware of the economic aspects of the Holocaust. An exhibition organised by the Leipzig City Museum in 2009 was entitled '"Aryanization" in Leipzig. Driven out. Robbed. Murdered.' How true that was, because the Jews were robbed before they were killed and the variety of ways devised by the Nazis to do this were numerous and innovative.

Hitler had not hidden his views. Their earliest expression is believed to be the Gemlich letter of 1919. It appears that after Germany's defeat in the First World War, Hitler was attached to the Bavarian Army's military propaganda unit in Munich. Its role was to stamp out Bolshevik views brought home by POWs from Russia. Hitler's ability to hold his listeners' attention impressed his superior officer, Captain Karl Mayr. When a soldier called Adolf Gemlich, who was doing similar propaganda work in Ulm, wanted clarification on 'the Jewish Question', he wrote to Captain Mayr, who suggested Hitler should draft a reply.

In the letter Hitler is very clear about the need to get rid of the Jews from Germany, but as Sir Ian Kershaw has commented, it is unlikely that at that stage Hitler could have 'envisioned the industrialised extermination of the Jews that he would pursue'. He added, 'Not even Hitler was capable of imagining in 1919 that could be done.' But the letter clearly shows that 'already in 1919 Hitler had a clear notion of the removal of the Jews altogether'.[1]

Was the Holocaust a surprise to the Jews? As early as January 1923 the 'pitiless extermination' of Austrian Jews was threatened in letters being widely distributed with the help of district officials of lower Austria, demanding the Jews leave Austria voluntarily. The penalty for not complying with the threat would be all manner of violent deaths. A letter handed over to the authorities by the *Wiener Morgenzeitung* (WM) declared:

> In the near future the Aryan people will arise and mercilessly put an end to the Jewish domination. The Jews will first of all be stricken down, then indiscriminately murdered, exterminated and hung, their bodies being thrown in the Danube. Then and then only shall Vienna be free of this vampire. Help us, oh God of the Germans, in this task.[2]

In the 1930s, the politician Vladimir Jabotinsky (1880–1940) realised that the Jews were in danger. Perhaps he had more sensitive antennae than most, because he remembered the Kishinev pogrom of 7 April 1903 in which forty-nine Jews were killed and 500 were wounded. He had an ambitious plan to evacuate the Jews of Poland, Hungary and Rumania to Palestine over a ten-year period, but the British would not agree and Chaim Weizmann dismissed the idea. Imagine how different the history of the twentieth century might have been …[3]

Someone who never underestimated Hitler was Carl von Ossietsky (1889–1935), who won the Nobel Peace Prize in 1935 for his courageous work as a journalist. He realised the strong appeal Hitler had among the German middle classes who had never really been interested in 'real liberalism' and whose 'inner crudity, crass hostility to culture and hard ambition' had been clearly demonstrated during the economic difficulties. As early as 1931 he wrote about the likelihood of proletarian aspirations being set aside in a crisis under the influence of: 'reactionary bourgeois politicians who would rather have the right to bloodshed monopolised by executioners and the armed forces'.[4]

In the Old Testament[5] we read of King Ahab coveting Naboth's vineyard. When Naboth refuses to give up his vineyard, which was a family inheritance, King Ahab, encouraged by his wife, Jezebel, arranges for Naboth to be killed so he can have the vineyard. The Lord condemns both the murderer and the thief using the phrase, 'Gam ratsachta, vegam yarashta' – 'You have both murdered and inherited'. This emphasises that the act of murder is compounded by looting the victim's property.[6] The Jews of Europe were murdered and their goods, whether merely their old clothes or priceless art collections, were stolen from them without pity or mercy.

These issues have only been seriously addressed in the twenty-first century. The lawyers have toiled:

> The restitution campaign that closed the twentieth century has contributed to an evolving jurisprudence on human rights and war crimes regarding loot and spoils. Drawing lessons from its exposure provided an expansion of a moral pedagogy, for this issue is not exclusive to Jewish claimants. As so often in history, the treatment of Jews is a moral barometer that can serve as a measure of societal well-being and an early warning system for more universal scourges. During Kabila's march on Kinshasa, Congo, CNN financial analyst Myron Kandell wryly commented that 'it took a Holocaust banking scandal to prise open Mobutu's Swiss accounts'.
>
> Thus, the spoliation of Jewish property, both during and after the war, as a serious violation of human rights, provides lessons for jurists in their treatment of war crimes and crimes against humanity in other theatres of genocidal behaviour. The Holocaust, in its focus on the total extermination of the Jews, is not only *primus inter pares* among genocides but also a benchmark for the atrocities wrought upon *all* of the victims of Nazism, and for current and future excesses in man's inhumanity.[7]

Israel Gutman, a survivor of the Warsaw Ghetto Uprising, became a major historian of the Holocaust. He was a witness at Adolf Eichmann's trial in Jerusalem in 1961 – the architect of the Holocaust tried in an independent Jewish state: 'His testimony was personal and anguished. He recalled glimpses of the procession of naked Jews being marched toward the gas chambers by laughing Schutzstaffel (SS) guards. I sometimes tried to look into the eyes of the SS brutes. I wanted to see if I could see a spark of humanity but they were elated when we were tortured. They were drunk with blood.'[8]

The Nazis were meticulous in creating a legal framework for their persecution of the Jews. This was gradually built up from 1933 with increasing burdens laid on the Jews. Thus, the faithful citizen or member of the Volk had no good cause to question what was being done because there was valid legislation to justify every step.

No one has rejected such an approach more succinctly than Edmund Burke who, in 1775, spoke for three hours in the House of Commons on 'Conciliation with America'. The significant concept is, 'It is not what a lawyer tells me I may do; but what humanity, reason and justice tell me I ought to do.' Under the Nazis these were often two very different paths.

This book is not intended to be, nor can it be, a comprehensive narrative of the Holocaust. It is almost a scrapbook of the Holocaust. Its intention is to give readers an insight into the horrors of the Holocaust – by looking at the different forms of betrayal that took place – how the noose was tightened round the neck of the poor, trapped Jews. The physical and economic strangulation took place over years, and finally those who survived to get to the camps were depersonalised and starved, tortured and worked to death.

There is no shortage of information and I was snowed under with it all. However, some people, even at this late stage, chose not to divulge their stories, which is sad because if not recorded they will be lost – less ammunition against the Holocaust deniers. Some stories I received were very brief – from child survivors who knew very little. A lifetime's tragedy in half a sentence – and no one else left to ask.

My friend Renée Fink from America told me, 'My parents were hiding in Holland and were betrayed.' The only information she had was that they were living on a boat on the Loosdrechtse Plasse in 1942. Their names were Edit and Fritz Laser and they had come to Holland from Germany in 1933.[9] Fritz was born in Königsberg on 30 May 1896 and Edit in Breslau on 15 July 1911. Edit was sent to Auschwitz via Westerbork where she was killed on 19 May 1943, aged 32. Fritz died on 31 March 1944, but the town where he died is not known.[10]

Fortunately they were farsighted and brave enough to hand their precious daughter over to the Dutch underground:

> I was placed with a Catholic family of eight children (I made the ninth). They took me for the duration of the war, sharing what little they had with me and endangering every one of them each and every day for hiding me. I loved them all and wanted to stay. And you know, I'm sure they would have continued to make a home for me.[11]

The scale of the horrors is unimaginable – at its height the Auschwitz extermination camp was devouring 6,000 Hungarian Jews per day in mid-1944[12]. I have no desire to embark on 'my tragedy is greater than yours', but as I write this introduction the radio is broadcasting news on the Syrian tragedy. The announcer says that around 150,000 have been killed in the three years the Syrians have been fighting. Seventy years ago, as the gas chambers at Auschwitz *alone* consumed their daily supply of 6,000 Jews, it would take just twenty-five days to kill 150,000 Jews.

Auschwitz was just one extermination camp. For instance, it is also recorded that, in the so-called 'Harvest Festival' killings of November 1943 at the Majdanek camp, 17,000 Jews were shot in one day.[13]

I am not an academic. I am, at 71, one of the youngest Holocaust survivors. I embarked on this book because I am horrified by what I see around me today – those who deny the Holocaust ever happened, or those who denigrate what it actually was; those who have no idea of the intricacies of its conception or implementation.

I was first awoken to this detail in the 1990s by my dear mentor, Professor Aubrey Newman, who spoke at a conference about men in suits looking at plans for the crematoria and calculating the throughput to be processed per day. Not counting boxes of baked beans, nor packets of rice, but gassed Jews whose bodies were to be burnt leaving only the ashes of whole communities. This book is meant for those who compare the Holocaust to relatively trivial events, which bear no comparison – because *no* other genocide bears comparison. It was even responsible for the development of the word 'genocide'.

Recent archaeological work has been undertaken at Treblinka by the forensic archaeologist, Caroline Sturdy Colls, who searched for the gas chambers which were destroyed by the Nazis in 1943 to hide the evidence of their misdeeds. What she found corroborated the witness testimonies – the mendacity of the Nazis that, right at the end of people's terrible journey to the gas chambers, they placed orange tiles with embossed stars of David in them so that the victims were tricked into thinking they were going into a Jewish bathhouse for delousing.[14]

I see the rise of right-wing parties everywhere, particularly in Hungary which tried to eliminate my parents and me and deprived me of the siblings I might have had. In March 2014, there was a stand-off in Hungary between the Jewish community and the government because of the emphasis of the proposed commemoration of the seventieth anniversary of the Hungarian Holocaust. I dread to think what my parents, whose lives were so bitterly damaged by their persecution, would think if they were alive today.

When we look at Europe today, particularly many of the countries that were occupied by the Nazis, many of us would shudder at the current political situation as outlined in *The Times* on 3 March 2014: The Golden Dawn party in Greece; Jobbik, the third largest party in Hungary, with its uniforms like those of the Arrow Cross in the Holocaust, has two seats in the European Parliament; in Slovakia, Marian Kotleba, leader of the 'Our Slovakia' Party, who wear Nazi-style uniforms and call the Roma 'parasites', and so on. In January 2014, in a protest against Hollande in Paris, among the 20,000 crowd there were shouts of 'Jew, France does not belong to you' and 'The Holocaust is just a hoax.'[15]

In the March 2014 elections there was a rise in the vote of the father and daughter Le Pens' National Front, giving them eleven elected municipal mayors instead of the four elected in 1997.[16] In the mayhem in Ukraine in early March 2014, the synagogue in the Crimean city of Simferopol was sprayed with swastikas and the words, 'Death to the Jews'. On 9 May 2014 it was reported from Riga that a nursery school 'owned by a traditionalist lawmaker featured a German-language sign advertising the establishment as being 'Jew-free' [Judenfrei]'.[17]

In Iran, denial of the Holocaust was strident and persistent under the previous president, Mahmoud Ahmadinejad, and better was hoped for with his successor, Hassan Rouhani. However, the Iranian Supreme Leader, Ali Khamenei, marked Nowruz, the New Year holiday on 21 March 2014, by stating, 'The Holocaust is an event whose reality is uncertain and if it has happened, it's uncertain how it has happened.'[18]

Following the *Charlie Hebdo* tragedy, the Iranians announced their second Holocaust cartoon contest with a closing date of 1 April 2015 and a first prize of $12,000. A total of 839 entries were received from 312 'artists'. Apparently there was a special category for cartoons with the Israeli prime minister and Hitler.[19]

But closer to home there is the English clergyman, Richard Williamson, who in spite of international condemnation has for many years denied that Jews were gassed in the Holocaust. He is joined by another Anglican cleric, Reverend Stephen Sizer of Virginia Water, who, as the world marked the seventieth anniversary of the liberation of Auschwitz, suggested that Israel was behind the 11 September 2001 attacks in America.[20] A vegan, Peta Watson-Smith, recently appointed to the ruling council of the animal protection charity the RSPCA, compared farming to the Holocaust.[21]

For all these reasons, I wanted to give the reader a flavour of what the Holocaust really meant and how truly dreadful life was for the persecuted Jews. Many others were persecuted, and Roma, homosexuals, Freemasons, Jehovah's Witnesses, Communists and Trade Unionists suffered dreadfully, but the Jews were the principal target of the Nazis and unfortunately formed the largest number of victims. I have also used information from other subsequent genocides such as Bosnia, Cambodia and Rwanda, and the activities of the Japanese during the Second World War.

I have deliberately used the word 'betray' in the broadest sense. I have shown the betrayal by the individual but I have also shown the major betrayal by states and governments, by the police and the railway companies who colluded and benefitted from the Holocaust. We have expectations of behaviour from these bodies which are enshrined in our own perceptions of what is just and fair, what is enshrined in national law and what was enshrined in international law by 1939. The behaviour the Jews were subjected to was a betrayal of all these norms and the bulk of international legislation which followed 1945 is a testament to the degree that existing constraints were found wanting and were seen to have failed.

Classifying the information was difficult and in some cases different aspects of an individual's story appear in different chapters, with cross references. In other cases the whole story appears in one chapter, depending on the basis of the original betrayal. If the reader finds the system difficult, I apologise, but I had to make a judgement and this seemed the best approach. There was never going to be an ideal approach because any individual's story has various aspects.

I decided very early on that I wanted to deal with topics rather than merely presenting a lengthy collection of unfocussed narrative memoirs which would leave the reader exhausted and confused. I became especially interested in betrayals by friends and neighbours, which were particularly painful, but are common to all genocides.

As I finished writing this book, the shocking events in France in January 2015, with the *Charlie Hebdo* murders, transfixed us all. We saw the cartoonists and journalists shot dead because people disapproved of their work and opinions, and saw Jews, shopping for the Sabbath in a kosher supermarket in Paris, cherry-picked to be gunned down. Visiting Neath & Port Talbot College prior to Holocaust Memorial Day 2015, I discussed with a large group of students the enormous parallels with the behaviour of the Nazis. Those whose views did not conform with Nazi ideology were destroyed and Jews were specifically chosen for destruction. These modern parallels make understanding the Holocaust even more imperative.

The tragedies in this book are testimony to the true horrors of the Holocaust and the many notes (listed at the back of this book) demonstrate that I have not made it up. I hope that the soul of Simon Dubnow would approve. I was destined for death as a baby before I was aware of life itself. Therefore, at 71, I am content that, with all its flaws, I have made my own small contribution to recounting what I have heard and read and have, to the best of my ability, recorded it all.

# 1

# IMAGINE ...

Imagine you wake up one morning and you are no longer able to keep your job, your university place or your place in your profession. You are not guilty of any sackable offence; you are merely no longer acceptable. There is no recourse to law or a tribunal.

Then you are told you have to register your family and all your goods and possessions. You may be very poor with very little of intrinsic value, you may be very rich with fine paintings and porcelain – either inherited or as the result of your own efforts. It makes no difference, it will all be taken from you. Again, there is no recourse to law or any tribunal.

You may be dragged out into the street to perform some humiliating task like scrubbing the streets with a toothbrush, with a crowd of your fellow townspeople laughing and jeering at you – you may recognise former schoolmates, neighbours or work colleagues in the crowd. You may be beaten up as you try to get home. There is no recourse to law or tribunal.

Having been deprived of 'luxuries' like your radio or bicycle, you will be forced to exist on a limited diet because your ration cards no longer permit you to buy certain foods. You are only allowed to shop at certain hours, late in the day, when stocks are low. Your children are excluded from school. There is nothing you can do and the local police to whom you might have gone for help are part of the enforcement process, so there is no recourse to law or tribunal.

You are then told that you have to leave your home and most of your possessions. You are sent to a ghetto where your family share a room with other families, or you may endure a terrible journey in a cattle truck to a transit camp or to a death camp. On arrival you will endure filth, starvation, diseases or medical experiments. In some cases you might be worked to death, or endure death by shooting so you fall into the trench in front of you, or by being gassed when you were expecting a shower. You have no recourse to law or tribunal.

You may have been a doctor, you may have won Olympic medals for your country, or perhaps you have been awarded an Iron Cross for fighting for your country in the First World War. You may have been a professor, you may have run the local shop and looked after your customers well – it didn't matter. You were not wanted by your country and you had to be eliminated with maximum cruelty.

Look out of your window – look down your street. Think about this happening in your town, to you and your family – your children. One and a half million children were murdered in the Holocaust. Think about the houses in your street being cleared of the families, with their goods looted or sold off to fund the Nazi machine. This is the reality of what happened to Jews in the Holocaust.

Who was responsible for such a betrayal?

## Background

Anti-Semitism did not suddenly appear in Germany, or the rest of Europe, with the electoral success of the Nazis in 1933.

Kaiser Wilhelm II (1859–1941) was the son of Queen Victoria's eldest daughter and it is alleged he had an incestuous obsession with her. He was a dysfunctional man – Simon Sebag Montefiore called him 'a dangerous clown'. Reviewing a new book by John Röhl about the Kaiser, Montefiore described him as:

> … hysterical, bombastic, weak, vacillating, petty, selfish, possessed of a total lack of judgement. He enjoyed himself by tickling his generals and by smacking foreign royal bottoms, including King Ferdinand of Bulgaria and Grand Duke Vladimir of Russia, sometimes with his Field Marshal's baton. He loved farting, anal and transvestite jokes, but he was also a vicious anti-Semite. (After his abdication, he declared the need to cleanse Germany of Jews by gassing them; there is a link from the opera bouffe of the Kaiser to the crimes of Hitler.)[1]

John Röhl deals with his anti-Semitism, and his close friend, Count Philipp zu Eulenburg, and his circle of homosexuals. Indeed, Röhl comments, 'It is indeed disturbing to reflect that the generals who took Germany and Europe into the Armageddon of 1914 not infrequently owed their career to the Kaiser's admiration for their height and good looks in their splendid uniforms.' Lord Salisbury thought him 'not quite normal', Sir Edward Grey, 'not quite sane'. Other European dignitaries thought him 'mentally ill', or having 'a screw loose'. Leading German princes and statesmen felt the same, with Bismarck explaining that he had only wanted to remain in office after 1888 because he knew of Wilhelm's 'abnormal mental condition', something which even Eulenburg was shocked and frightened by. His Hitler-like rages made Eulenburg predict an imperial nervous breakdown, which did not happen.

Fits of rage, unfortunately, were not the only characteristic that the Kaiser shared with Hitler. Full-blooded anti-Semitism was another, and Röhl makes it perfectly clear that Wilhelm II had nothing to learn in this respect from the Führer. If, like Hitler, he had Jewish friends as a youth, he later turned on the Jews as Germany's most deadly enemy, informing Sir Edward Grey, for example, in 1907 that 'They want stamping out'. He also believed in an international conspiracy of Jewish capitalists and communists – the 'Golden International', blaming the First World War, Germany's defeat and his own abdication on an international conspiracy of Jewish freemasons, so that in exile in Holland his anti-Semitism reached fever pitch.

In 1919 he wrote to General von Mackensen, 'Let no German ... rest until these parasites have been destroyed and exterminated.' He called for an international, Russian-style pogrom against them, condemning them as a 'nuisance' that humanity must in some way destroy. Then, in his own hand, he added, 'I believe the best would be gas.' It was altogether natural, therefore, that before he died in June 1941 he welcomed Hitler's victories as confirmation of the fighting qualities of the troops of 1914–1918. He boasted:

> The hand of God is creating a new World and working miracles ... We are becoming a US of Europe under German leadership, a united European Continent, nobody ever hoped to see ... The Jews are being thrust out of their nefarious positions in all countries, whom they have driven to hostility for centuries.[2]

Alfred Wiener (1885–1964) founded the Wiener Library, first in his hometown of Vienna and then, when he had to leave, taking it to Holland in 1933 and finally to London in 1939. He was an avid collector of newspaper cuttings and pamphlets all his life. The library marked its eightieth anniversary on 7 November 2013 and it led his grandson, Daniel Finkelstein, to write about a pamphlet Alfred had written in 1919 entitled *Vor Progromen?*, which means 'Prelude to Pogroms?'. He opened the pamphlet with the words, 'A mighty anti-Semitic flood has broken over our heads', and went on to describe the spread of hatred against the Jews that existed in German society. Finkelstein underlines that his grandfather noted that the trends which led to the Holocaust were apparent fourteen years before the Nazis came to power.[3]

Paul Mühsam (1876–1960) was born during the time known as the German Empire (1870–1914 or 1918). He described his childhood growing up in Chemnitz and Zwittau (Schindler's hometown). He detailed the activities on Sedentag (Sedan Day), celebrated every year from 1870 on 2 September. Sedentag marked the final victory of the Franco-Prussian war in 1870 when the French, under their Emperor Napoleon III, surrendered. It was important because as a result Bismarck was able to unify Germany.

He compares his lot as a Jewish boy with his school chum Bernhard, who had consoled him after an unpleasant incident on the way home from school. Paul reflected:

> I also knew that narrow bounds were set to my future activities, while all doors
> were open to every non-Jew. In spite of the emancipation secured by law, a Jew
> at that time could become neither an officer nor a judge, nor any other kind of
> official, especially in Saxony, where the emancipation had gained acceptance only
> a few decades earlier. And even though I was far from striving for such positions,
> the mere impossibility of attaining them was a heavy fetter on my sense of justice
> and self-esteem.[4]

He wrote of his family's participation in local events:

> At every patriotic commemoration we were all assembled in the [school] audi-
> torium. On Sedan Day the entire school marched as a body three quarters of an
> hour to Kaltenstein, where gymnastics were performed and a dance followed.
> And when this day of remembrance took place for the twenty-fifth time, after
> a solemn church worship service there was even a parade for all citizens and
> schools, in which we seniors were the standard bearers. Bernhard in front with
> sash and sword, my father too, marched along among the veterans – the only time
> that I remember him putting on his medals.

(If he was writing about the twenty-fifth anniversary of the Battle of Sedan in
1870, it must have been 1895). He commented that even though the Jews had
been emancipated for decades, neither then nor later were they regarded as full
members of the community. This should have 'given every Jew food for thought'.
He described the Jews as being mesmerised by the freedom they now enjoyed and
'the radiance of European-Christian culture':

> … they thought only of ridding themselves as completely as possible of the
> slackening fetters of being a Jew and thoroughly assimilating to the Christian
> world about them, in the belief that in this way, be it with or without baptism,
> they would be able to escape their Jewish fate once and for all. This was a funda-
> mental error, which would yet prove to be very disastrous. For within a Christian
> national totality, formed by a non-Jewish race, the Jew, for reasons of religion and
> origin, is a foreign element and does not cease to be regarded as such no matter
> how much he, having fully assimilated, believes himself to have been absorbed
> without distinction by the organism into which he intruded.
>
>  Certainly, it could be otherwise. Religion and race could completely recede as
> decisive factors in the life of a people and of nations in favor of humanity, which
> alone determines the value and essence of the person.[5]

Paul was a lawyer, and when he lost his practice as a result of Nazi legislation he left for Palestine (now Israel). These thoughts come from a manuscript written in 1956 – *I was once a Human Being*. He became a very successful writer admired by many, including Stefan Zweig, and died in Jerusalem in 1960.

Life was difficult for Jews in Poland and Rumania in the 1930s and other countries were launching anti-Jewish attacks, both physical and legislative. Of course, no one expected the Holocaust – who could envisage it? Victor Klemperer, a language professor in Dresden, who was a convert to Protestantism and married to an Aryan, wrote in his diary on 5 September 1944, 'The Jewish problem is the poison gland of the swastika viper.'

... the precariousness of Jews' existence on the soil of Europe could not be denied. Their options for survival decreased dramatically once Great Britain curtailed entry to the obvious haven of Palestine, joined by other nations who also closed their hearts and their doors to Jews in desperate need. Moreover, Roosevelt, Chamberlain, and other leaders masked the Jewish people's unique calamity. With ever thickening shadows of war clearly visible on the horizon, réal-politik reigned supreme in these corridors of power. As a consequence, Europe's defenseless Jews, facing unprecedented anguish, would find few allies to answer the call of conscience.[6]

# 2

# BETRAYAL BY FRIENDS

The shifts of fortune test the reliability of friends.

(Cicero, Roman philosopher, 106–43 BC)

A friend is someone who stabs you in the front.

Oscar Wilde (1854–1900)

I may be wrong, but I have never found deserting friends conciliates enemies.

Margot Asquith (1864–1945)

The tribulations of war strained all relationships, and friendships of many years were stretched to the extreme. Many survived the tribulations, but many did not, and it was not possible to know who would be true. As Joachim Fest wrote about his father, Johannes Fest, 'One of the most shocking things for him had been to realise that it was completely unpredictable how a neighbour, colleague or even a friend might behave when it came to moral decisions.'

Jupp Weiss (1893–1976), a Dutch Jew who survived Westerbork and then Bergen-Belsen, told his family about his experiences in a long report dated 25 July 1945, written when he had returned to Amsterdam. He wrote the following:

We had sold our furniture. Everything else, such as clothing and linens, I had given for safe keeping to one of my employees. Unfortunately, as happened to many, many others, nothing can be found. The following joke circulates here: every returning Jew [only 5 per cent of those who left] visits his 'safe keeper' and apologises that he was not 'gassed' and therefore is back.[1]

The persecution of the Jews created stresses with non-Jewish friends and contacts, as indeed was intended. Marta Appel (1894–1980), who lived in Dortmund
with her husband Rabbi Ernest Appel, wrote about this in the days following
the 1933 boycott:

> Our gentile friends and neighbours, even people we had scarcely known before,
> came to assure us of their friendship and to tell us these horrors could not last
> very long. But after some months of a regime of terror, fidelity and friendship
> had lost their meaning, and fear and treachery had replaced them. For the sake
> of our gentile friends, we turned our heads so as not to greet them in the streets,
> for we did not want to bring upon them the danger of imprisonment for being
> considered a friend of Jews.
>
> With each day of the Nazi regime, the abyss between us and our fellow citizens
> grew larger. Friends whom we had loved for years did not know us anymore.
> They suddenly saw that we were different from themselves. Of course we were
> different, since we were bearing the stigma of Nazi hatred, since we were hunted
> like deer. … We were no longer safe, wherever we went.

Marta came from Metz, and had met old friends, teachers and pupils at her old high
school in Metz, every four weeks at a café since she had been living in Dortmund.
After the Nazis came to power, she had stopped going because she did not want
her friends to be compromised by being seen in public with a Jew. One day she
met one of her old teachers who, with tears in her eyes, begged Marta to return.
'Come back to us; we miss you; we feel ashamed that you must think we do not
want you anymore. Not one of us has changed in her feeling towards you.' Marta
decided to go to the next meeting, but it was a hard decision and she did not sleep
the night before. She was fearful for her gentile friends. However, when she arrived:

> It was not necessary for me to read their eyes or listen to the change in their
> voices. The empty table in the little alcove which had always been reserved for
> us spoke the clearest language. It was even unnecessary for the waiter to come
> and say that a lady had phoned that morning not to reserve the table thereafter.
> I could not blame them. Why should they risk losing a position only to prove to
> me that we still had friends in Germany?[2]

Ernest Levy, formerly Löwy (1925–2009), was the youngest of eight children. He
was 13 on 4 November 1938, when his family were forced out of their home with
ten minutes to pack by a German Nazi and a Slovakian policeman. His home was
in Bratislava in Czechoslovakia, although his father, Leopold Löwy, was actually
Hungarian. As they clambered on the bus the police started to board up and seal
the house. Leopold Löwy was the last on the bus:

He seemed to stop, hesitate momentarily in the rain and stare across the road. I craned my neck to see what he was so engrossed with. When he got on the bus he was shaking. Tears were running down his face, mingling with the streaks of rain. 'You won't believe this,' he said to mother, his voice trembling, 'but Kraijchirovich is standing in the doorway of his shop – smiling. The man is actually smiling'.

Kraijchirovich, the German barber who had cut our hair and made jokes about school, was glad to see us leave. We had provided him with some of his best custom, but he must always have envied us, having to listen to the music and laughter coming from our windows.[3]

Later, Ernest experienced a similar reaction in Budapest. In April 1944 Ernest was being deported from Budapest. They were driven through the streets by the Hungarian mounted police lashing them with whips. He looked into the crowd for someone he knew – perhaps a friendly face. 'As Kraijchirovich had done in Bratislava, the people thronging the streets of Budapest to get a good view of our humiliation smiled as we were taken away.' He added that the only person showing any pity was a young Hungarian prostitute called Klari he had shared a cell with earlier.[4]

I remember my mother telling me that when my father was being taken away as a forced labourer in Budapest in 1943 she went with him to see him off. She said there were people standing around jeering and one said, 'Like the monkeys going to the zoo'. She told me she fixed him with a look and he shut up. My mother had guts – she also had a fearsome 'look'.

Otto Deutsch was born in Vienna on 12 July 1928. He lived with his parents, Victor, born 1888, and Wilma, born 1900. His sister Adele was born in 1921. Photo No. 2 shows Victor and Wilma on their wedding day on 18 May 1920 in the Schiffschul.[5] Otto was a young boy of 10 in Vienna on 9–10 November 1938 when Kristallnacht took place. Even now, aged 87, he still carries the shock and confusion over the action of the man he knew as 'Uncle Kurt' who had taken him to his first football match when he was about 6.

Otto told me how the family's apartment was broken into by a group of Hitler Youth. Some of them were not much older than Otto himself. Leading these young thugs was the man whom Otto called 'Uncle Kurt', for he was not only their neighbour, he was Otto's father's best friend. Both Victor and Kurt had been soldiers in the Imperial Austrian Army and shared the same trenches in the Great War. They were both decorated soldiers and were very proud of this bond which had made them even closer. By sheer coincidence, they married around the same time, and young Kurt was born a few months before Otto.

After the war, during the Depression, both men were unemployed and went out together in the morning to seek work. They lived in the 10th Municipal

District known as Favoriten in a large council block – Otto's family at No. 15 and Kurt's opposite at No. 13. They all lived like one family and the two women cooked together, because it was cheaper to do so. The fact that they were Catholic and Otto's family was Jewish was something that they did not talk about. Otto had regarded Kurt Kowatsch as his hero because he took him to his first football match.

However, on that night all their joint history was forgotten when Kurt burst into Otto's parents' bedroom and pointed at Otto's father in bed. He told the youngsters, 'That is the Jew in his bed.' His father was taken away that night and Otto never saw him again.

After Kristallnacht, that part of Vienna was declared 'Judenfrei' and they had to move out. Otto says one of the few areas where Jewish life was still acceptable was Leopoldstadt and they therefore had to move there at very short notice. They moved their few possessions through the centre of the city on a cart. Otto says he remembers this vividly – he was less than 10 years old and was very excited. He helped with pushing the cart but reflects, 'I was probably more hindrance than help.'[6]

Otto subsequently discovered that his father had first been taken to Dachau concentration camp and from there to a destination in Saxony, to enlist in the Forced Labour Battalion which was building Germany's first autobahns (motorways). Eventually he was allowed to return home. However, almost twenty-four years to the day after their marriage, on 22 May 1942, he and Wilma, together with Otto's sister, were deported. They were taken to an isolated forest near Minsk known as Maly Trostinec and, on arrival, were shot on 24 May 1942.[7]

Maly Trostinec was where many Austrian Jews were sent. It is not a well-known Nazi site and was used on Reinhard Heydrich's orders between May and October 1942. More than 15,000 people from Vienna, Königsberg, Theresienstadt and Cologne were sent by train to Minsk. They were then moved off to an assembly point where their valuables and money were taken from them. Any deemed suitable for forced labour were selected, but this was usually a small number. The remainder were then transported by lorry about 18km to where trenches had been prepared in the pine forest, and they were shot. Only seventeen people are known to have survived from the Austrian Jews sent to Maly Trostinec.[8] Even Austrians know very little about this particular Nazi murder site, and accordingly a conference was held in November 2011 in Vienna to inform people about the events and read extracts from the books of writers killed there.[9]

Otto told me, 'I visited this site in June 2011, and was able to say Kaddish by the crematorium, where the bodies were burned.' Otto came to England with the Kindertransport on 5 July 1939 just before his eleventh birthday. Tragically his beloved sister Adele, at 17, stayed behind at home to care for their mother who was quite unwell. Photo No. 3 was taken the day before he travelled.

Otto was placed with a devout Christian family in Morpeth. They were called Mr and Mrs Ferguson, but Otto called them Auntie Nell and Uncle Jim. Otto has stressed that they:

> … made no attempt to convert us to their religion – on the contrary – in order for us not to forget our Jewishness it was arranged that once a month we were visited by students from an Orthodox Jewish college in nearby Gateshead.
>
> I spent two happy years in Morpeth learning the English language and becoming a little 'Geordie' lad. To this day, I still have great affinity with the North-East of England.[10]

Like many of the Kinder Otto regularly speaks about his experiences, and for Passover 2009 he was interviewed for a BBC programme about 'The Kindertransport'. Otto told the interviewer he was very excited when he found out he was leaving Vienna. He asked his mother, 'When are we going?' She replied, 'No, Otto, not we, only you are going away.'[11]

Otto added later that, afterwards, Kurt was not friendly but did not do anything else as far as Otto knows. Otto elaborated that although they saw Kurt senior he did not speak to them and Otto assumes he was embarrassed, but he was also very busy with his SS work. Otto still saw Kurt junior; after all they were only 10 and didn't really understand what was going on. He told me that in November 2012 he had advertised for Kurt junior in a Viennese newspaper because they had been such very good friends but never heard anything. Otto reiterated what a shock that incident had been because Kurt and his father had been such good friends for twenty years.[12]

Some friends were more supportive. Werner J. Cahnman (1902–1980) recalls his mother getting a phone call around 7.00 a.m. on 9 November 1938. It was from a family friend, a retired doctor, who said he had just been warned that mass arrests of Jews were imminent. His informant was a former patient who was now an official in the Gestapo. Accordingly Werner and his mother urged Cahnman senior to leave for work as soon as possible.[13]

Zeef Eisikovic (1924–) wrote about his father's arrest in Bockov in Czechoslovakia (now Ukraine). His father was called Asher Oskar and had joined the Communist Party in 1924. He had been born in 1891 and married Frieda in 1923. In the spring of 1942 he had been anxious the night before when he went for a walk with his wife and she sensed his anxiety. Two friends of his had already been arrested:

> The next day two men from the Hungarian secret police came to the door. They were former school friends of my father's, with whom he had grown up. They ordered him to come along at once. Because they were old friends, he was allowed to take along a blanket.[14]

He was tortured so badly for four weeks in Mukatschewo (Mucačevo) that he died. The counter-espionage unit was in the seventeenth-century Kohner Castle and they specialised in liquidating spies. There were probably about six people there from his father's circle, but also non-Jews, including the Communist leader, Lokota, who is commemorated by a statue in Bockov today. Half the prisoners taken to the castle did not come out.

Zeef heard from survivors that they were made to squat, rather than stand or sit, for days and were beaten with sticks. The section thrived on discovering spies and when none were available, they had to 'find' some. Zeef discovered:

> My father survived four weeks of interrogations; then he was brought to the hospital. A soldier lying in the next bed reported to my mother that he saw my father had suffered a haemorrhage. He had suffocated from internal bleeding. The soldier asked him whether he had a family. 'Yes, a wife and three sons,' my father replied. These were probably his last words. He was buried in the Jewish cemetery in Mukatschewo in his clothes under police escort. He was not allowed to be undressed, so that nobody could see the swellings on his body. He was black with bruises, but they wanted to keep it secret that he had been beaten to death. A few weeks later, my mother was informed by the authorities that my father had died of an illness. They sent her a vial of medicine as evidence. Apparently at that time they still tried to preserve appearances to some extent. It was not yet a routine matter, so to speak, to kill someone off.[15]

It seems sad that Oskar's old school chums didn't feel they could give him a hint of what was to come and therefore a chance to flee. Sadly, Zeef's mother, Frieda, and his youngest brother, Chaim, born 1930, were deported to Auschwitz in 1944, where they were both killed.

Alfred Schwerin (1892–1977) had lived in Pirmasens, which is near the border with France. Its synagogue was destroyed on Kristallnacht and he only moved to Ludwigshafen when all the Jews were evacuated at the beginning of the war. He describes in some detail what happened when, in October 1939, he went to Frankfurt to collect his suitcase which he had left with old friends. The daughter of the family had treated him very kindly when he had left the case a few weeks earlier, but his reception on this visit was:

> … one of the most disgraceful things that happened to me in Germany throughout the entire Hitler period. I had been close friends with this family for thirty-one years. I was the godfather of one son, who was then twenty-five. When my friend and I said goodbye to one another on the first mobilization day in the year 1914, he had embraced me emotionally, had said I should call him 'Du' and

had asked me to look after his wife and children in case he did not return. Since then we had stuck together in perfect friendship.

Now, as I was going up the stairs to the apartment, my friend, who had just come from the cellar and saw me from above, hurried ahead of me without giving a sign of greeting and alerted his family. His wife asked me from a distance to wait for them in the living room. As I walked past the kitchen, through the crack of the door I saw the sons and the sons-in-law hide behind the door and move closer together in order not to be seen by me or have to greet me. Then, after a few minutes, the couple greatly embarrassed, came into the room where I was, and for the moment they were unable to utter a word, although we hadn't spoken with one another for a long time. Also, neither one of the two had the courage to ask me to sit down.

Finally, they reported that they had already taken the luggage to the station, supposedly to make it easier for me to transport it; but probably the truth was that out of cowardly fear they no longer wanted to store Jewish property. Also, from a remark I had to conclude that they had gone through the suitcases to see for themselves that they did not contain any suspicious objects.[16]

Throughout his visit the couple 'hurried back and forth excitedly, without figuring out how to tell me to disappear from the scene as soon as possible'. Alfred wrote that he did not say a word as they lamented their situation and he deliberately refused to leave quickly to ease their 'wretched role'. He concluded, 'After I had finally taken my leave, I once again could not come to grips with the fact that these last years could have changed the Germans so much.'[17]

A suitcase triggered Gilbert Michlin's reflections on two mothers – his own, Riwka, who was to die at Auschwitz, last seen by him climbing into a truck, and Madame Culet, his best friend Maurice's mother. He described their life in Paris with his father already away:

A few months before our arrest in 1944, my mother had a strong premonition of the danger we were in. She asked Maurice's parents if they would keep a little suitcase filled with our important documents in their country house in Saint-Maur. She filled it with my papers, my awards, our diplomas, photographs, my parents' passports, their kettubah [marriage contract] and other important documents. When I got out of the camps after the war, I went to pick up the precious suitcase. I remember being ecstatically grateful to Maurice's parents for having kept these treasures. However, later on when I thought it over, I radically changed my view. I was slightly disgusted. Why this drastic change? I remember those days when the dread was horrible for us, the round-ups were more frequent and people were disappearing. My mother felt that something terrible was going to happen. I think back to her, in the country house where we went to drop off the suitcase, and I am certain today that she was secretly hoping that my friend's parents would offer to hide us there. But silenced by pride and not wanting to trouble them, she did not say anything. Yet it would have been easy for them to keep us in this isolated suburb. They did not have the presence of mind to make the offer, which would have doubtless saved her life.[18]

Michlin reflected on the situation and pondered Maurice's mother's behaviour. He surmised:

Maurice's mother understood that my mother was in dire straits. The very fact of bringing the suitcase was proof of it. The risk of hiding my mother in this house was virtually non-existent. Maurice's mother preferred not to take any risk. Our problems were not hers, and perhaps her anti-Semitism was the real reason. I remember she later talked to my wife about my mother, giving her a compliment, 'Your mother-in-law was Jewish, but she was *clean*.'[19]

Reading this story made me feel really uncomfortable – in such a situation would I have been able to ask for help? I also just wondered about Madame Culet. What would she have said if Gilbert's mother had swallowed her pride and asked her to hide them? Some research on this subject is illuminating – apparently it showed that most Jews turned to friends and family for help and mostly the initiative came from the asker – which presumably was how the suitcase came to be left in the first place, although Michlin doesn't say.

The researchers found a refusal rate of 4 per cent, which is surprisingly low.[20] The researchers also found that two-thirds of the rescuers were asked for help and agreed. One-third initiated the rescue. Surprisingly, those asked to help then went on to perform other rescues.[21] In their conclusions the researchers underlined 'acts of altruism are all the more likely when the request comes from known people, and people in need are more likely to ask people they trust'.[22]

Sadly, this research suggests that had Mrs Michlin asked Madame Culet to hide them, she would have agreed and Gilbert's mother would not have been killed at Auschwitz.

Elaine Sinclair told me about her family's experience in a village called Brnik, close to a town called Dabrowa Tarnowska, which was part of the Austro-Hungarian Empire but is now in Poland. Elaine's grandmother left to go Wiesbaden around 1911, just after she married, because they thought the prospects would be better in Germany. Several of her sisters followed. In October 1938 one of them, Esther Weiser, returned to Brnik with her three children, Adolf, Doris and Julius, and her husband, Hermann. They held Polish passports and were part of a large group of Poles who had been resident in Germany and were forcibly returned to Poland by train.

After the war, another sister whose husband was Esther's husband's brother went back to find out what happened to them. She was told by the mayor of Dabrowa Tarnowska that the family had hidden in the woods supported by neighbours until 1942. They were then betrayed by a school friend of another member of the family. The Germans sent sniffer dogs into the woods to find them and they were shot in the woods. They were hiding with other members of the grandmother's family.[23]

It seems they were part of the Polenaktion of 1938. After the *Anschluss* in 1938, Austria ceased to be a refuge for those fleeing the Nazis. Other countries therefore became worried about a surge of Jewish refugees, but Poland's actions were directed against its own people, unlike elsewhere. On 31 March 1938 the Polish Parliament passed a law permitting the withdrawal of Polish citizenship rights from Poles who had lived abroad for five years without a break. This affected 30,000 Polish Jews in the German Reich and 20,000 Polish Jews in Austria.

In an attempt to avoid a mass exit, people were asked to go the nearest Polish consulate to have their passports stamped. If they failed to do so, the passport would expire on 30 October 1938 and they would become stateless with no right of entry to Poland. As soon as this became known in Berlin from the German Embassy in Warsaw, thousands of Polish Jews received expulsion orders as of 27 October 1938. Others were arrested and expelled on foot or in mass transports across the German–Polish border in great haste.

Because the order did not reach all parts of the Reich at the same time, the departure date ranged from 27–29 October 1938. Additionally local authorities had some flexibility in handling the expulsion and who was involved. In some areas whole families were affected and were pulled out of their homes by the police; in other places only men were taken. In some areas only adults were involved; in other places infants and toddlers were also removed.

The routes of German railway lines influenced the mass transports, and so the three border towns with railway connections received mass transports – Bentschen (now Zbaszyn), Konitz (now Chojnice) and Beuthen (now Bytom).

It is important to recall that the Polenaktion of October 1938 has a direct connection with the other major catastrophe of 1938 – Kristallnacht. Herschel Grünspan, who shot the German diplomat Ernst Eduard vom Rath at the German Embassy in Paris, was trying to make people aware that his parents had been expelled to Bentschen. This shooting gave the Nazis their excuse for the catastrophic events of 9–10 November 1938.[24]

However, another young girl had a very different experience. Gerta Vrbová (1926–), who grew up in Trnava in Slovakia, wrote about her childhood and her gradual realisation that the world about her was changing. As a young girl of 12 in 1938 she was friendly with the girl next door called Marushka Šimončič. On the last day of the summer holidays Gerta had invited Marushka to cycle with her to Gerta's uncle's farm for lunch and then go fishing in the nearby stream. It was some distance to the farm. Even in mid-morning it was very warm and they stopped for a rest under some trees, 'lying there in the shade next to each other felt good, and I had a comforting sense of trust and friendship between us'. [25] Just then Marushka interrupted 'the peaceful silence and sleepy relaxed mood' by saying, 'My father said I shouldn't have come out with you today.' Gerta was surprised because he had always been so friendly and kind to her. When Gerta asked Marushka 'Why not?', she had the grace to blush and said:

> He said that because you are Jews, you will soon be taken away, and then we will be able to take over your father's shop and we will move into your house. But we must show that we do not like mixing with Jews and that we approve of the National Socialist principles. My father joined the Hlinka Party a month ago, so he knows about these things.

Gerta's pleasure in the outing was quite gone, and after a while she tried to find out what Marushka, herself, thought about it. Marushka wouldn't look her in the eyes. 'I don't know what to think, I'm confused and I will miss you, but if it's going to make it difficult for my family that I have a Jewish friend, I'll have to stop seeing you.' Gerta clarified what she really meant was, how did she feel about the plans that the Jews should be sent away and others would take over their property? Marushka, who was a year older than Gerta, was clearly embarrassed but said:

> Everyone says that you had too much money, that you exploited us and that it's time for the people to take over everything. Well, you are richer than my family, aren't you? They will send you to a work camp, and everyone thinks that it will be good for you to learn to work hard, whilst the people you exploited enjoy themselves. I think that this is just, and although I'll miss you, it will be nice to live in your house.

Gerta wrote how stunned she was by 'Marushka's total lack of compassion, feeling of justice and crude greed'. Life would be much better for her – why should she care about Gerta and her family?

Gerta did not want to go anywhere with her. Marushka was quite surprised when Gerta told her she could stop seeing her Jewish friend then and there. She seemed to think they could carry on with their afternoon trip as normal, saying, 'But we could have enjoyed ourselves', quite oblivious to the pain her words had caused her 'friend'. Gerta got on her bicycle and went home. At home the comfort eased her hurt somewhat, but when her parents asked her what was the matter she said she didn't feel well. She went up to her room and wrote about the events of the day in her diary, concluding, 'This morning is the end of not only my summer holiday but also of many other good things and dreams of my happy carefree childhood. It is probably the end of my childhood.'

The next day she went back to school for the autumn 1939 term. The school was a gymnasium, with a mixed intake including Catholics and Jews, Czechs and Slovaks. On the first day, it was warm and pleasant. The non-Catholics went in an hour later to avoid the religious instruction. When Gerta arrived she saw some Jews and Czechs outside the closed gates. On the gate was a large notice saying, 'Jews and Czechs are excluded from school'. There were about twelve children aged 11–18 hanging about outside, not knowing what to do. They rang the bell, but no one came out – there was a chorus from the other children, 'Jews out, Czechs out.' They also shouted obscenities without hindrance.

Some of the older children had been at the school for many years, with friends among the pupils and good relations with the teachers. No one came to talk to them and they stood outside the school feeling 'betrayed and confused'.[26]

Some time later, Gerta was still surprised at the equanimity with which the adults accepted what was happening – they believed it would pass soon and they could continue 'living amidst those who had betrayed and humiliated them as though nothing had happened'. Much to Gerta's surprise not everyone abandoned them. One day her father's friend, Mr Pavelka, came to visit – a cheerful farmer in his forties with kind eyes. He was a large man and when he sat in the cane chair it creaked with his weight. He said to Gerta's father:

> If you want us to keep any of your possessions for you, my wife and I have decided that we will hide them and when all this is over we will return them to you. In case you have to leave suddenly, or if the Slovak Hlinka Guard wants to confiscate Jewish property, at least they will not find much.

Pavelka was correct, and he was 'a true and honest friend'. Her mother, like so many others, wrapped up her silver, jewellery and a few cherished items into a brown parcel which she handed to Pavelka. After he had gone, she asked her mother whether they would need those things when 'all this is over?' She replied that they would need something to start again and also something to trade in the next difficult years. 'How very right she was!'[27]

Her family gradually began to be aware of what was happening and what their fate might be. One day they were discussing being 'resettled', their doubts about it and whether they should tell other families what was planned. Her father, Max, was sceptical:

> We can try but will they believe us? Look, we had the cattle trucks filled with Austrian Jews passing through our town, the people inside were screaming, they were hungry, thirsty and crowded and we all heard their screams yet none of us believes even now that this will happen to us.

Uncle Hans said quietly, 'Can you blame us that we have more trust in human dignity than is justified?'[28]

Later, in April 1942, kindly Mr Pavelka turned up. When Gerta opened the door, 'his nice warm brown eyes smiled at me and I thought he could be trusted'. Even though her father was asleep, he was very insistent about seeing him, but he must have heard as he appeared in the doorway. They both went into the living room, leaving Gerta feeling apprehensive that they would have to leave. After some time, he came out:

> His shoulders were slumped, his hazel eyes were sad, and the smile was gone from his face. I knew then for certain that the news was bad. I put my arms around his shoulders and tried to comfort him. He looked pale, sad and somehow defeated. I understood that his grief was due to the realization that he could not protect us from what was to come.

Mr Pavelka had told him the Jews would be rounded up the next day by the local government and no one knew where they were going. He was going to make plans, but he told her to get ready. Her mother was incredibly calm, telling her to pack only what she needed and what she could carry a long way.[29]

It would be three years before Gerta returned to Trnava in May 1945, alone. As she walked from the station to her old family home in the main square she reflected:

> At first glance little had changed in Trnava since I left more than three years ago in April 1942 yet I felt a stranger in my home town. As I walked towards our house, which I knew was now occupied by the family who had taken over my parents' shop and appropriated all our possessions, the memory of the betrayal by my former friend Marushka suddenly hit me and opened wounds I thought had healed.[30]

With these thoughts, she reached the house and stood outside, thinking about how hard her parents had worked to provide that home. Her mother had got up at six each morning to do two jobs which included travelling to Bratislava each day to run her own business, after helping as a cashier in the family's butcher shop. When she came home in the evening she always had time for Gerta and the family. So much for Marushka's accusations of exploitation:

> I opened the gate and entered the courtyard which I remembered housed many beautiful plants when we lived in the house, but there were none there now. As a child the courtyard was a place where I played out many of my fantasies: with my grandmother Jeanette's help, I wrote and organized plays which my friends and I performed in front of an audience of our parents and their friends. Here

I learned to ride a bicycle, sat on a stool in the sun and dreamed about the future. Now I stood here alone in a place that had become barren and considered my own present situation. I went outside and headed towards the butcher's shop that used to be my father's.

She must have had some trepidation as she went to the shop:

I knew I had to talk to Mr Šimončič, the man who threw our family out of our home. The entrance to what used to be our shop was wide open and I found Mr Šimončič in the almost empty shop sitting behind the counter. I noticed that he had become quite fat and looked uglier than I remembered. The shop which used to be neat and tidy was now dirty and empty. When I entered the shop and Mr Šimončič saw me he exclaimed with horror: 'You are still alive.'[31]

She asked, very politely, for a room in the house which was her family home. He was quite dismayed:

'You cannot stay here, we have nowhere else to go and we need the whole house. You will have to find accommodation elsewhere. You can't just turn up and expect us to move out.' He refused to let me into the house and I knew that there was no point in arguing with Mr Šimončič who still didn't understand that the fascist lawlessness was now finished and that he would have to return the stolen property.

The Russians were administering the area at the time and she went to see the Russian authorities for help. The smartly dressed Russian officer was called Sergej, and he listened to her story. They went back to the house together and Sergej explained to Mr Šimončič that he had to provide accommodation for Gerta and asked her which room she wanted:

At first I thought I would like to have my old room back. I ran up the stairs and headed towards the room that used to be mine, but when I opened the door, my heart stopped for a minute, for now it was Šimončič's daughter Marushka's room, and there was nothing in it that reminded me of my old room. I didn't recognize it at all and felt it would be too painful to move into this room.

Instead she chose her parents' room and Sergej sorted out the paperwork with Marushka's father and told him to vacate the room at once and give Gerta the keys for her room and the house.[32]

One day, she went back to her old school and saw her former schoolmates leaving at the end of the day – she recognised some of them but they all walked past her. Not one even acknowledged her, let alone spoke to her. To cheer herself up she went to see Mr Pavelka:

> He and his family received me with open arms and were pleased to see me and Mr Pavelka was anxious to know what had happened to my parents, but I had no news for him. In spite of the warm welcome I felt that my visit had caused embarrassment, and that the family was ashamed for the behaviour of their fellow Slovak citizens. They offered to return to me all our things they had kept for us, but I only took one towel as a souvenir. I had nowhere to take the rest, the fur coats, carpets and jewellery. I didn't visit again. How could I care about furs, jewellery and other possessions when my family might be dead?[33]

She waited for her parents to return, eventually realising it would not happen. In September 1945 she was ready to move on and exchanged her family's house with a neighbour who had always been good to her, in return for a Leica camera, a typewriter and a gold watch. The house sale had one condition, which he accepted – the Šimončič family would have to leave.[34]

I was put in touch with Gerta in London and she told me, 'My father died in [a] work camp in Hungary in December '44, and my mother in Ravensbrück in March '45. It is very tragic that they died just a few weeks before liberation, and difficult to get to terms with it.'[35]

Lilli Aischberg-Bing (1885–1985) was a German-Jewish woman from a wealthy family who, by her own admission, lived a charmed life in Nuremberg before the Nazis. In 1983 she wrote a memoir about her experiences of the Nazis. She was 48 years old on 1 April 1933.

Almost immediately after Hitler was elected she had a terrible shock. She had been a member of the local Classical Choral Society since she was 16:

> Every Thursday evening for 32 years I went to our rehearsals. I sang in Bach's *Passion of St Matthew* perhaps 20 times. We sang Mozart, Handel, Haydn and many more.
>
> On this first of April we gave a concert of Beethoven's 9th Symphony, the *Choral Symphony*. It was Schiller's *Ode to Joy*, praising in the noblest words, in the most beautiful music, equality of all mankind, love of all human beings, belief in a loving God, praising friendship as the greatest virtue; that was for me the end of it. Next morning the wife of the conductor came to our house, tears running down her cheeks, begging me to resign. If they would not expel me, as only Aryans could belong to it from now on, her husband would lose his job. To me it was like an explosion, it was so unforgettable to me, because it was my first experience and my mind was unprepared.[36]

Marianne Meyerhoff was 22 when she visited her mother's friend, Erica, in Berlin in 1963. Her mother, Lotte, was still alive. Erica was one of her mother's three close non-Jewish friends who cared for her parents after Lotte was sent away in 1939 (see pages 419–420 in Chapter 16). Erica told Marianne how her mother was hurt by the friends who abandoned her in 1933 and her father, Professor Wachsner, suffered too.

One day in 1934, he held a student seminar on Ludwig Wittgenstein at home. One student, Maximilian Thiel, arrived late, and at the ring of the doorbell Lotte and Erica looked out of the window. They saw Thiel carefully remove a swastika pin from his lapel before entering the house:

> Lotte's jaw dropped, literally, I could have killed him. I felt betrayed. Max, who was one of Professor Wachsner's own students and one of the best, came into the dining room, apologising no end for his tardiness. It was a contradiction neither of us could get out of our minds, giving himself and his talent and energy over to a system that hated the Jews while sustaining the profoundest respect for the professor, all bound in one. In those days there often were such opposing ideologies oddly coexisting in the same person. Didn't they see how conflicted that was?[37]

Four years later, after Kristallnacht, Lotte was with her father helping him clear his office when he finally had to leave teaching:

> Max Thiel appeared, his former student and his best, strode right in, sinister in his black SS uniform, spit-polished jackboots, and death's head insignia on his cap. Years had passed since Max had applied to my father to be his mentor and guide him through the preparation of his doctoral thesis. Together they had discoursed long hours in awe and reverence for the marvels of life in its myriad forms. How could such an intellectual as Max fall prey to ersatz Nazi racial policy?

He had apparently come to see his old professor to say how sorry he was about the situation. He claimed, 'I thought it more respectful if I came myself.' Her father responded, 'Respect? Where has your logic fled? You think you can spit us out like vomit and come in here and talk of respect? Thank you for your concern. Now if you will excuse us, this is still my office until I clear my things out of here.'[38]

Dr Michael Siegel (1882–1978) and his wife, Mathilde, had a fine collection of Nymphenburg porcelain. Dr Siegel was a partner in the law firm, Kanzlei Siegel, in Munich. The firm had represented the famous Nymphenburg porcelain company in its legal affairs since the 1890s. The Siegels were friends of the Bäuml family who owned the company at that time. Each Christmas they received a highly prized Nymphenburg porcelain figurine and these were displayed in their home in a glass cabinet.

When they were leaving for Peru in August 1940, they asked a non-Jewish acquaintance to keep the collection safe for them. When Dr Siegel went back to Munich after the war he contacted the gentleman concerned. Unfortunately he had an attack of amnesia and had no recollection of a Nymphenburg porcelain collection. Their daughter Bea told me that she believed it had gone to a Nazi,[39] but knew no more. Certainly, whenever the subject 'was mentioned in the family it was always with disdain'.[40] There was nothing they could do about it, and at least they were alive. Some time later, Bäuml enquired about their collection and was told the sorry tale. 'Without telling my parents anything, Curt Bäuml arranged to reconstruct and pack a duplicate collection for shipment to Peru, based on pre-war records still in existence at the factory. My parents were speechless and greatly moved by this extraordinary gesture of kindness and compassion.'[41] What a very different reaction from two men who were known to the Siegel family in the good times. Some of the pieces were brought back from Peru and were given to Bea and her brother, Peter.[42]

Porcelain is a great love of mine and perhaps this is why an article entitled 'History of a Tea Service' caught my eye in July 2013. Sara Kirby-Nieweg described how, during the Holocaust, a tea service had been entrusted to a neighbour by Gholina Nieweg who was Sara's father's first cousin. The family lived in Appingedam in Groningen in northern Netherlands, where Sara was born. When her father, Meijer Nieweg, was deported to Auschwitz on the first transport from the Netherlands on 15 July 1942, she and her mother went into hiding separately. At the end of the war, only six Jews from the Jewish community of eighty-two had survived.

Sara is now the only Jewish survivor, returning many times in recent years to find people who remember her family. She wrote:

> It's an emotional search but an enriching one. I have learned that the deportation was, and still is, a traumatic experience for most of the deportees' former friends and neighbours and that offers of help were sometimes not accepted due to the family's wish to stay together.

An exhibition about the former Jewish inhabitants held in the city museum early in 2013 resulted in Sara being contacted by a woman called Zus Nolden. She brought the tea service her family had guarded for seventy years, as she was the daughter of the neighbour to whom Gholina entrusted her teaset. They had never used it because it didn't belong to them, but had carefully protected it in a cabinet behind closed doors. The exhibition gave the history of Jews in north-east Groningen from the sixteenth century. With Sara living in England that long history concludes with no Jews living in Appingedam.[43]

Gholina and her husband Benjamin had a tobacco shop on the ground floor of a house in Farmsum and the Nolden family lived on the first floor. The Noldens had three daughters and two sons and Zus was the middle child. On the eve of their deportation, the Niewegs gave each of the Nolden children a little present to remember them and entrusted the parents with the tea service and a few little vases and a cream and sugar set.[44]

Sara told me Zus was about 6 when the Nieweg family were deported in 1943 and she remembers Gholina giving them the gifts. She also remembers Gholina's mother, Kaatje Klein.[45] Sara said, 'For this family the deportation of the Niewegs was obviously a traumatising experience.' Gholina and her husband, Benjamin, had one child Herman, who was born in 1924, and her mother who was born in 1869. Apparently the Noldens had offered to help Herman escape to England, as the husband worked in a shipyard, but Herman wanted to stay with his parents. (Farmsum is a small village close to Delfzijl on the northern coast of Groningen, very close to the border. Sara says this is why the Jewish men were deported so quickly, so that they could not escape by boat.)

Sara's own father, who arrived at Auschwitz on 17 July 1942, died there on 18 August of 'intestinal problems'. 'My father apparently had a ticket to England, but his mother was fearful of letting him go, and asked him what would happen to them if he went. If they had known what lay ahead for them, she would probably not have held him back.'

In June 2013, Sara and Zus visited Farmsum and the house where the families had lived. Zus had asked for permission from the current resident of the Nieweg flat, who wasn't initially very keen but agreed. Zus found it a very emotional experience.[46] Gholina, her husband, son and mother were all deported to Sobibór on 17 March 1943, where they were gassed on 20 March 1943.

The tea service was not an expensive one – not in the Nymphenburg collection league. Although Sara told me it says 'Meissen' underneath, there are no crossed swords – the Meissen sign. It was transfer printed and the pattern is quite badly worn in places.[47] But it was valuable to Gholina and she wanted it to be safe. The Nolden family held faith with the trust she had placed in them at her most desperate time for exactly seventy years and justified that trust by returning the items to Sara at the earliest opportunity. Now the tea service and the other items finally sit in a glass cabinet in a Nieweg home once more.

Sara told me she has no photographs of Gholina and her family:

I was overawed by the huge responsibility. My main worry had been to get the service home safely, since I was terrified that something would get broken in my care, on the way home, when it had been kept safe for 70 years by the Nolden family.

It was not until I was home and had unwrapped and washed each item carefully, and placed it on a dedicated shelf in my glass cupboard, that I could relax and feel that the tea service had come home.

Thanks to the care, honesty and generosity of Zus Nolden and her family, I now have something tangible to remember my father's family by.[48]

Charlotte Salomon (1917–1943) was a young artist from Berlin. When life became difficult for Jews her family persuaded her to go to the South of France before she was 21 and needed a passport. Her paternal grandparents were living in Villefranche and she lived with them and started painting her famous series of small paintings. When war broke out her grandmother committed suicide out of fear for the future. In May 1940 Nazi Germany declared war on France, and in June, after Italy joined in, the South of France was cleared of 'foreigners'. Charlotte and her grandfather were sent to the Gurs camp in the Pyrenees, but in view of their age they were released in July.

Charlotte was quite traumatised by these events and a doctor suggested she should start painting again. She painted 1,300 small gouache pictures, about A4 size. They were autobiographical. The series, called *Life? Or Theatre?* was completed in 1942. An Austrian Jew, Alexander Nagler, was living in the house, and following the departure of the owner for America, Charlotte was left alone with Nagler. Jews' identity documents were being stamped with 'Jew'. Alexander became Charlotte's only regular contact because Jews were being picked up in the street and it was dangerous to go out.

They had a good friend, Dr Moridis, a neighbour. After the death of her grandfather, Charlotte and Alexander decided to get married. Dr Moridis, who was always a helpful friend and neighbour, obtained an Aryan set of papers without 'Jew' for him. When he went to the police station to get the marriage licence, he was told that as an Aryan he was not permitted to marry a Jew. He blurted out that he was Jewish. Permission to marry was granted, but he had to leave behind the fake papers with his address on. They were married on 17 June 1943 at Nice Town Hall, with Dr and Mme Moridis as the witnesses.

When they told Dr Moridis about the documents he was shocked, telling them to leave the area – he even offered them a flat he owned in Nice rent-free. They went there for a bit, but preferred the house in Villefranche and returned to enjoy the summer there.

On 8 September 1943, when the Italians signed an armistice with the Allies, the German troops took over the whole coast and the Gestapo was in control. At seven o'clock on the evening of 24 September 1943, a Gestapo truck drew up outside their home. Charlotte and her husband were dragged out of the house and thrown into the truck. Charlotte was then four months pregnant. On 7 October they were transported to Auschwitz. On their arrival, 10 October 1943, Charlotte was killed. Nagler was killed on 1 January 1944.[49]

Toivi Blatt (1927–) came from Izbica in eastern Poland – a town with 3,600 Jews before the war. It had been established in 1750 by Anton Granowski as a town for

Jews dispossessed by their Christian neighbours. Until 1914 it was occupied almost entirely by Jews, and even today it is the only town in Poland without a parish church. Some Polish families came between the wars but the Jews still represented 92 per cent, with about 200 Christians.

Blatt told Laurence Rees in 2003 how, in April 1943, the Germans were rounding up the remaining Jews in Izbica. Toivi was a fit 15 year old running away from the Germans when he saw an old school friend, Janek, who was a Catholic Pole. Toivi said he shouted, 'Janek! Please save me!'

'Sure!' Janek replied. 'Run to the barn not far past our house.' So Toivi rushed to the barn, only to discover that the door was padlocked:

> So I walked around the barn and then a little Polish woman started to yell at me, 'Run, Toivi, run! Janek is coming!' So if Janek is coming why should I run? He will open the gate. But why is she so panicky? And when I turned around I saw Janek coming with a Nazi – the rifle pointed at me. And Janek said to the Nazi, 'This is the Jew.' I said, 'Janek, tell him that you are joking!' And Janek says, 'He's a Jew. Take him.' Janek then said goodbye to me in a way which is difficult even now for me to repeat … he said, 'Goodbye, Toivi. I will see you on a shelf in a soap store.' And this was his goodbye – the rumours were that the Nazis were making soap from human bodies.[50]

Blatt was sent to Sobibór, but escaped in the 1943 uprising. (Sadly, Toivi died in the US on 31 October 2015.)

Jacques Helbronner (1873–1943) was a successful lawyer who became a leader of French Jewry. During the 1930s he was an active member of the Central Consistory of French Jews (Consistoire Central des Israélites de France) in Paris and he became vice president. Helbronner was an establishment figure, deeply rooted in French society and culture, and was well suited to representing the native French Jews with his close contacts with the French bureaucracy. In June 1933 he stated, 'French Jews are French before being Jewish.'[51]

After the fall of Paris in June 1940, the consistory joined other Jewish organisations in going south to the unoccupied zone, and as the president had escaped from France, Helbronner became president. His close personal relations with the head of state, Marshal Philippe Pétain, were no doubt influential in his success. Their relationship went back to the First World War and Helbronner was said to have strong admiration for him and named his son after Pétain. It is recorded that in the first year and a half of the occupation the two men met twenty-seven times. Helbronner's trust in Pétain and his principles led him to lead the consistory on the basis of Judaism being a religion, defying the racial and national definitions promoted by Vichy.

However, he was regarded as timid and he disregarded the plight of foreign-born Jews. He only changed his position when, in January 1943, there was a round-up of

French and foreign Jews in Marseilles. Helbronner continually complained to the French authorities against the decline in French life and the arrest of the Union Générale des Israélites de France (UGIF) leaders in the summer of 1943.

He was arrested on 19 October with his wife and they were deported to Auschwitz a month later, where they both died. His good friend did nothing to help save him. His effectiveness had been hindered by his view of himself as spokesman of the Jews de vieille souche (of old vintage) and his trust and confidence in France and its head of state.[52]

Roman Halter (1927–2012) was born in Chodecz in Poland. The Eszners were 'German' Poles like the Halters were 'Jewish' Poles. The Eszners were their neighbours and were separated from the Halters by the timber fence Roman's father had put up between the two properties. His father stacked logs against the fence and Roman used to climb up the logs and from the top he could see the Eszners' property and call his best friend, Karol. They went to the same school, but Karol was in the class above as he was nearly two years older – their birthdays were a week apart. They would often walk to school together, chatting all the way. 'My parents were selective about my playmates, but even though Karol was a German Pole, he seemed well-bred and friendly enough and he never called me anti-Semitic names, so they were not averse to our spending time together.'[53]

In 1939 there were almost 800 Jews in Chodecz – there were 1,200 German Poles (Volksdeutsche) and 2,200 Poles. In the twelve months between September 1939 and September 1940, half the Jewish population was either murdered or sent to forced labour camps on the Berlin–Poznan Highway. Chodecz was in the part of north-west Poland which had been marked as integral to the Reich and so without delay it was being made Judenrein.

A few days after the start of the war a brigade of Polish soldiers came and rounded up the German Polish people and took them away. Two days later, they marched back in a long column which stopped on the street where the Halters lived. It was a warm day and the people looked tired and dusty from the roads. They knew these Volksdeutsche well and Roman's mother sent him out with a bucket of drinking water, a ladle and a cup to offer people a drink. Among the people there were the Eszners and his 'great friend' Karol. Suddenly he was kicked from behind by a soldier with a rifle. He fell on his face, spilling the remaining water. He was quite indignant about this act of brutality and asked the top-ranking officer about giving the people water. He said yes to water, 'but no food'. Other people came out offering water too:

> When I returned home, my mother wept.
> In mid-September Hitler's armies arrived in Chodecz and all the Germans turned out to welcome the 'liberators'. They lined the streets through which the troops passed and they shouted 'Sieg Heil', giving the Nazi salute and the young

girls hugged and kissed the soldiers. Some even made swastika flags, which they waved with great enthusiasm. My family and I watched through netted curtains.

Only three months before, Karol had finished at the local primary school and would be going to high school in Wloclawek. Both families attended the prize-giving and afterwards, 'His parents and mine walked home proudly together after the prize-giving. Karol and I followed them and we all chatted together happily.'

The SS settled into the town and with the help of the Volksdeutsche drew up a list of potential leaders and troublemakers among the Jews and the Poles. They rounded up Polish and Jewish leaders and they were shot as in other nearby towns. Those taken included their Jewish doctor, Dr Baron, and the old Polish doctor. They requisitioned any house that took their fancy and that included the rather elegant house that the local blacksmith, Mietek, lived in with his family. The Germans thought it would be ideal for the officers, so they just evicted the blacksmith's family. They were Roman Catholics and were taken to the forest and shot. 'The Germans behaved with brutality not just toward the Jews in the town, but also toward the local population who were Polish and not Volksdeutsche.'

Within two months, Roman's family were evicted from their home, next to the Eszners, and put in three rooms on the edge of the town. They had to leave most of their possessions behind and everything else was taken – their land, house, horses and timber yard.

New proclamations were announced each day on the noticeboard of the SS police station, which Jews were ordered to read. There was the notice about wearing the yellow star on the front and back of a coat or outer garment. Any Jew seen outside the perimeter of the Chodecz without a permit would be shot. Jews could not walk on the pavements. There were to be no gatherings in people's homes and his school was now only open to German Poles. Roman wrote that 'every day, new, humiliating and dreadful things were demanded of us'.

Then one day the lovely old wooden synagogue, the precious Torah scrolls and all the prayer books were torched and everything was burnt to the ground. His grandfather was stopped in the street by young local 'Germans' who cut off his beard with a knife, and when 'Karol passed me, he walked along the pavement, while I had to walk along the road. He looked away.'

The town was being run by a man called Major Oberst. He and his family lived in the largest Jewish house which had been confiscated from a cousin of Roman's father, who was a corn and grain merchant. At the end of October 1939, Roman was summoned to report at the police station and was told he was to begin work at the Oberst house, starting at 6.00 a.m. He was 12 years old. One of his tasks was to carry two full buckets of buttermilk on a yoke from the dairy to the Obersts' home – he had to walk about a mile and it took him about half an hour. He really struggled with the full buckets.

Around this time, Oberst started training the young Volksdeutsche – Roman knew most of them from coming to buy timber from his father. As he struggled with his pails early in the morning he would see the recruits jogging with Oberst. When he saw them, he carefully put his pails down and took his cap off, as the kitchen maid had told him.

> Karol Eszner also took part in these early morning runs and toughening-up exercises and marches, although he was only just past fourteen years old. He was not the only German fourteen-year-old in the group to do so. One morning, as I stood to attention by the kerb, my cap in hand, the buckets carefully placed next to me, the yoke on the ground in front of me, waiting for the singing recruits to march past, Oberst halted the column. He motioned me to come closer to him. He then asked these SS volunteers if one of them knew this young Jew.

Roman said he knew nearly all of them, either from school or from coming to buy wood, building materials or even coal from his father. Some of them were the sons of the men who had carted coal from the railway station to their yard in Chodecz:

> Karol Eszner stepped forward and said in good German [Roman said he had never heard him speak German before] that their house was next to where we used to live and he knew me well.
>     Oberst then said to Karol, 'Come over here and knock this Jew to the ground'.
>     Karol came close to me and, and with absolutely no hesitation, he hit me hard with his fist on the side of my face. It hurt. I swayed, tripped and fell backwards to the ground. And as I lay there on my back, the Oberst ordered Karol to drag me to the kerb and to tell me to look down at the ground next time. As I lay there dazed by the experience, the group started singing 'Gagmen England' – 'We're off to England soon!' as they marched off.[54]

Roman Halter's father and grandfather died of starvation in the Lödź Ghetto. His mother, half-sister, her two children and Roman were selected for the Chelmno Ghetto. His mother told him to run away. 'She said, "Run in a zigzag and don't stop when they shoot or shout, 'Halt'". I did as she asked and escaped that selection, but my mother, half-sister and her children all perished there.'

The story of Rudi Lek (1917–2007) is included as a contrast to all the friends who became betrayers, and demonstrates what a difference loyal friends could make. The Lek family from Antwerp moved to Amsterdam for the duration of the First World War and then returned to Antwerp. Rudolf was the youngest of five children born in Amsterdam. He had a girlfriend when he was in his early twenties called Ida De Ridder. Her father, Alfons De Ridder, a well-known Belgian writer and poet, wrote under the name Willem Elsschot. They met through her brother, who was Rudi's best friend at school.

Alfons offered to hide Rudi by getting false papers saying that Rudi was his son. Rudi was very tempted, but his parents contacted him and pressed him to leave while he could. He was very reluctant to leave Ida and his family but decided to go. He walked along the beach from the De Ridders' summer villa at Kerkepanne to Dunkirk and got on a boat. Ida said his last words to her were 'Look after my piano for me!' He left Holland on 17 May 1940 during the German invasion of 10–28 May. He told his daughters that he escaped with other civilians on the last civilian boat to leave Dunkirk.

Rudi was able to come to England because he had a British passport. It appears his grandfather had been given the Freedom of the City of London. The family story is that Wolf Lek was a famous diamond polisher living in Amsterdam. In the middle of the nineteenth century he was invited to London to do some work on the diamonds for Queen Victoria's crown and he moved to London with his family. As a result he was given British nationality and the Freedom of the City.[55] Unfortunately, the rather faded document, dated 25 January 1874, granting the freedom, gives his name as 'Wolf Lack' but it probably saved Rudi's life and that of his parents.[56]

So, this is not a story of hiding anyone in an attic. Ida wrote a book called *The Piano*, and she wrote that they didn't save any people, 'just a piano'. However, the De Ridder family were prepared to 'adopt' a Jew, which was very courageous. Ida died in 2009.

Rudi was able to join the British Army and during training he met his wife, Decima Joan (1922–2004), who was in the Land Army at Bicton. They had two daughters, Anna and Maria. After the war he trained as a teacher and in 1956 they moved to the Isle of Wight where he became a French teacher. Rudi returned to look up the De Ridders in 1946 and found they had indeed looked after his precious piano. Apparently it had been left in the Lek family home and the De Ridders arranged to have it taken to their home in Antwerp.

When I asked what happened to the rest of the contents, Rudi's daughter, Marie, said she thought their maid's family looked after them and returned them after the war but was uncertain as the house was used by Nazi soldiers after the Leks' departure.

Rudi made arrangements to ship the piano to London, and he can be seen playing his beloved piano in 1999 in photo No. 6. You can see it was a Bechstein, which was a premier make – Queen Victoria was an early customer. The Holocaust had a big impact on the company because so many music-loving customers were lost.[57] He returned to Belgium and Holland several times after the war.[58] The piano was moved to the Isle of Wight and later back to the mainland to reside today in Marie's home – a memorial to her father and his faithful friends. Rudi died in 2007.

# 3

# ACQUAINTANCES, CONCIERGES AND NEIGHBOURS

... we cannot understand what is happening to our neighbours.

Joseph Chamberlain, 18 January 1906

Thou shalt love thy neighbour as thyself.

Matthew 19:18

One of the most shocking things for him had been to realise that it was completely unpredictable how a neighbour, colleague or even a friend might behave when it came to moral decisions.

Joachim Fest, on his father, Johannes

This chapter deals with betrayals by people who would have known about the Jews in their vicinity. They may have had a financial arrangement, as with a tenant or a concierge, but mostly it was a question of just living in proximity.

Robert Gellately, a professor of history at Florida State University, discovered a collection of 19,000 Gestapo files in Munich in the 1980s – he was in a library when the archivist suggested he might be interested in them. They covered Würzburg, Speyer and Düsseldorf, and gave details of denunciations by members of the public. Most of this sort of file were destroyed by the Gestapo at the end of the war, but these survived somehow.

Before his discovery the Gestapo and secret police were assumed to have been responsible for snooping, but he was able to show it was also the ordinary citizens. He found that, instead of the denunciations being based on high ideals about the Third Reich or fear of authority, their motives were banal – greed, jealousy and petty differences. He found business partners turning in associates for their own benefit and, likewise, jealous boyfriends betraying rivals. Neighbours would betray families who did not keep the bathroom clean or had a nicer property.

He told me:

> I always counted as 'denouncers' only those not in the Party or police – when it might have been their 'duty'. I wanted to get at the civilian, non-official people, but of course young men and women in the youth organizations or members of the party, acted as denouncers in a formal sense as well. However, I did not want to be seen as exaggerating the social co-operation – though many of my academic foes accuse me of that anyway. In fact, I suspect that nearly all the cases of breaking Nazi laws by Jews were denounced by those outside the police, which simply did not have the resources to enforce racial policy on their own.
>
> Years ago I spoke to a Jewish women's organization that included women from all over Europe. They had survived. When I got onto to the subject of denunciations, they all started nodding their heads in agreement. One, from France, asked me about 'the Gestapo' in France that came for her and her family – they hid and escaped. I asked a few questions and soon showed that it was not the Gestapo at all, but the French gendarmes who came for them, tipped off by neighbors.
>
> And so denunciations represent a potent tool of the system, used voluntarily by individuals for reasons of their own, from deeply selfish ones to 'idealism' and faith in racism. This was one of the main concrete forms that betrayal of the Jews – and others – took during the era of the Third Reich.[1]

One of the people whose experience Gellately unravelled was Ilse Sonja Totzke, who was born in Strasburg in Alsace-Lorraine in 1913. She came from a musical family and moved to Würzburg in 1932 to go to the local music conservatoire. She had many Jewish friends and maintained them after 1933. She was repeatedly denounced to the Gestapo for her friendliness to Jews, but nothing concrete was found against her. In 1941 the Gestapo warned her to stop associating with Jews and she was forced to sign a declaration that repetition of the offence would lead to her being sent to a camp.

She had a Jewish friend in Berlin, Ruth Basinski, another musician. They attempted, unsuccessfully, to flee to Switzerland together in February 1943. Basinski was sent to Auschwitz, where as a gifted recorder player, she was placed in the orchestra and survived. Totzke was taken back to Würzburg for questioning and made the following statement:

> The thought of fleeing from Germany has already been with me for a long time, as I do not feel well under the rule of Hitler. In particular, I have found the Nuremberg Laws to be incomprehensible and this is the reason why I continue to keep up contact with the Jews who were my acquaintances.

On 12 May 1943 she was sent to Ravensbrück, a women's concentration camp north of Berlin, and is recorded as being liberated on 26 April 1945 but has never been located since. No one knows what happened to her, but Yad Vashem recognised her as 'Righteous Among the Nations' on 23 March 1995.[2]

Marta Elian (née Steiner) was a young girl when her family was taken to the Nagyvárad Ghetto with just a few hours' notice on 3 May 1944. Her father, Laszlo Steiner, owned a large bakery employing seventy people in Nagyvárad (at this time part of Hungary). They lived on the top floor of a family house and her father's brother and family lived on the first floor. In the basement lived the caretaker and his wife. He maintained the heating system and she helped out with domestic work a few times a month. They were a Hungarian non-Jewish couple and had their flat rent-free as part of their contract.

Marta now lives in London and she told me of two incidents that happened, the first in 1944 and the second in 1945.[3]

When the family was ordered to go to the ghetto, they were not allowed to take suitcases and instead they put clothing and food supplies in bundles made out of bed sheets. Sometime later, Marta observed the caretaker's wife, who had always been pleasant, opening the bundles and removing some of the food. Marta was really shocked, but decided to say nothing. The caretaker and his wife remained in the flat when the family left for the ghetto. The Steiner family escaped from the ghetto into Rumania and they returned to the flat in 1945. The flat had been completely stripped of everything except one single shoulder pad left on the floor. Marta did not know what had happened to the caretaker and his wife.

The second incident concerned a close female friend of the family who had survived Auschwitz. On returning to Nagyvárad (now Oradea) she stayed with the Steiner family, sharing a bedroom with Marta, while waiting for news of her family. When she visited her house, which she found had also been stripped of all possessions, she met her former neighbour, who embraced her. He expressed his sympathy that no possessions were left. Looking at the neighbour, she commented that not everything had gone as she observed her husband's monogram on his shirt.

Another employee who could not resist temptation was described by Norbert Barclay:

> A maid who had been with my paralyzed uncle and his wife for many years took all their jewelry and silver. When my aunt tried to stop her; she pushed her to the floor and, cursing Jews, left. And my family and I lived in fear of Mitzi, who had turned into an ardent Nazi.[4]

Steven Fenves (*b.* 1931) was from Subotica, Yugoslavia, the town my maternal grandparents had come from. In an interview at the United States Holocaust Memorial Museum (USHMM) on 8 June 2010, he described how after his father, Lajos, was deported to Auschwitz in April 1944, Steven, his mother, maternal grandmother and sister were forced into the ghetto in May. He said the day they had to leave their home was one of the grimmest days of his life. Fenves went on:

> We lived on the second floor and word was out, I don't know how the word got out, but the word was out and people were lined up all along the stairway waiting to ransack the apartment, cursing us, yelling at us, spitting at us as we were leaving.

The interviewer asked him, 'These were people who had been your neighbours?' and Fenves confirmed that was right.[5]

On 18 November at UCL, I heard about the lives of the Jews of Shavl in Lithuania. Keith Morgan, a Canadian journalist born in Blackpool, worked with a Lithuanian survivor, Ruth Kron Sigal, writing her story for many years. He said Ruth's mother, Gita Kron, had left various valuables with neighbours when they were sent to the ghetto. This was a kind of insurance for future barter. In July 1941 restrictions began to be imposed, such as the one on 18 July requiring the wearing the yellow Star of David and observing a curfew. In addition, 'all Jewish property was to be registered and real estate sold so that the Jewish community might be moved to a designated area of town – in other words, a ghetto'. They also had to hand over their valuables when the 'legal looters' burst into their home.

The couple had a bag ready to hand over, though their most valuable possessions were already long gone. The official announcement of intent had forewarned and forearmed the community. Many, like the Krons, had found places to secrete their belongings for collection, 'when all of this nonsense is over'. Some had buried their treasures while others had lodged their valuables with neighbours and gentile friends. The Krons more realistically saw their stash as a means of bartering in the future, for whatever they might need to get them through the inevitable hard times ahead.

They were surprised to find the men were not satisfied with their offering and conducted a search for more booty which actually proved fruitless.[6] As Gita was blonde she could pass as a gentile, so periodically she would leave the ghetto without her star. She visited former neighbours and friends to retrieve goods for barter, sometimes hiding eggs in the fur trim of her long coat. It was not always a successful exercise. Some so-called friends offered little in return for the more valuable jewellery Gita presented. Then there were those who wanted nothing more to do with their Jewish neighbour. They threatened to call in the Gestapo – the occupational police force – if she did not get out of their sight. It was the same story many of her ghetto neighbours would tell.[7]

Dr Siegel and his wife Mathilde (Tilde) from Munich were keen walkers, and in 1926 they built a small log cabin in a village called Dorf Walchensee in Upper Bavaria. They often spent the summer there and Siegel gave free legal advice if needed. They called their cabin the Häusl. Their son remembered travelling by train until 1936 when they bought an Opel car. However, this pleasure was short-lived, as in December 1938 Jews were no longer allowed to hold driving licences.

Their rural idyll was further spoilt by the local Nazi (Mr B) who ran a café. Before 1933 he had been happy to consult Dr Siegel several times about legal matters, but once the Nazis were in power his behaviour changed. He even spat in Siegel's face on one occasion. Siegel's son recalls that in 1937–1938 a notice was nailed to the Häusl, warning that if they opened the door, the Häusl would be blown up together with the family. They didn't try. In 1939 they had to sell the property to an Aryan. The person who bought it was known to the family and behaved correctly. However, after the war he offered to pay the true value rather than the derisory amount Aryanization permitted. Dr Siegel declined.[8]

As Gellately found, some people had 'suspicions' which they reported to officials with disastrous results for the victims. Others kept their suspicions to themselves. Henri Obstfeld, who was a hidden child in Arnhem, told me about two stories concerning him.[9] On the first occasion, in 1944, aged about 4, he was out for a walk with the daughter of his foster mother who had her own child in a pram. They met an acquaintance, who looked at Henri and said, 'Is that a Jewish child?' The daughter replied, 'Oh no, he is a nephew.'

Later, after the war in 1945, Henri's foster mother visited a delicatessen near their home in Arnhem. The shopkeeper recognised her and said, 'You used to come here with a little boy. Was that a Jewish child?' When she admitted that he was, he replied, 'That's what I thought.'[10] Neither of these two people reported their suspicions. Had either of them done so, the consequences for Henri, and the kindly Klerk family who looked after him for two and a half years, would have been dire as they would probably have been picked up by the police.[11]

Robert Krell (*b.* 1940) was also a hidden child in Holland. He described an incident in 1961 when he returned to The Hague, to visit his step family, 'my Christian angels' Violette and Albert Munnik, and his 'sister' Nora. His parents had survived and took him to Canada in 1951. He went up the stairs at Loenenschestraat 147 and knocked on the door:

> The neighbour opened his door. 'Robbie?' he asked. 'Here to see your Moeder?'
> 'Yes, Meneer deVries.'
> 'Robbie, I've always meant to ask you why you never thanked me for not betraying you?'
> So from the ages 2–5, I had lived next door to death, a neighbour with the thought of betrayal in mind. Fortunately he did not act on it. Thousands of Dutch men and women did. And Jews and neighbours died.[12]

Howard Smith (1914–2002) was an American journalist based in Berlin for CBS from January 1940 until December 1941, when he was thrown out of the country for refusing to include Nazi propaganda in his reports. Later, he found worldwide fame as the chair of the first ever televised presidential debate between Richard Nixon and John F. Kennedy in 1960.

He described the life of elderly Jews who were his neighbours in Wittenberg Platz. He wrote about the Jews who were left behind after the wealthy and influential had gone and the young had fled or been imprisoned:

> Those who remained were old, decrepit, pathetic creatures whose spirit of resistance had been broken long ago, and whose bodies were almost broken. The Bernsteins – Frau Bernstein about fifty and her aged mother-in-law – who lived in the apartment next to mine, were typical examples. The husband and son, respectively, was arrested in 1938 and was still in prison. The daughter of Frau Bernstein, the younger, had escaped to Czechoslovakia early in the Nazi regime, and had not been heard of since. For the first two years of the war, the old couple lived unobtrusively in their three-room apartment on Wittenberg Platz. I knew them and spoke to them daily, but our familiarity never overstepped a smile and a casual greeting. They did not want to attract attention by having too close a friendship with me, a foreigner and – through no fault or virtue of mine – an Aryan.[13]

Howard Smith detailed the difficulties of those Jews still living in Berlin. In October 1941, a Jewish friend of his, Fritz Heppler, called on him, telling him the Gestapo were raiding Jewish homes because of rumours that Jews were hoarding food. Howard offered to help Fritz, but a few days later he came home to find:

> The door of the Bernsteins' apartment next to mine was sealed to the doorpost with six little white stamps, and another little white stamp covered the keyhole. On each little stamp was a spread eagle, gripping a swastika in its claws and around it in a circle, the words: 'closed by the Geheime Staatspolizei'. Fritz, and the Bernsteins, and thousands of others had gone colonising in the East.[14]

On the other hand, a Jewish worker from Hamburg who was able to emigrate fairly late, told of the support he received from his neighbours. In London, he told the press that his non-Jewish neighbours left food, which Jews were not allowed to buy, outside his room on a fire bucket of sand. During harvest time, a neighbour who owned an orchard would pile fruit into the bucket which was labelled, 'Windfall – without value', although the fruit was in very good condition. This was being done in spite of the severe punishment imposed on those caught in pro-Jewish activity.[15]

Hedi Fried (b.1924) grew up in Sighet, Rumania, with her parents and little sister, Livi. She was 15 in 1939. In 1944 they were forced into a ghetto with 3,000 other local Jews. She wrote about their preparations for the ghetto. Hedi described how she hid her favourite books and her diaries under the beam in the roof, hoping she would be able to come back soon to collect them:

> We had already handed our valuables to our neighbour, Mrs Fekete, who had volunteered to hide them. She had visited us one day in March and told us that her husband, an officer in the Hungarian Army, had heard that we were to be moved. She thought we should have difficulty in hiding our valuables; they should have been handed in to the authorities long ago. When a family was moved, the house would be searched, and if any valuables were found, severe punishment would follow. So she offered to help us and keep the jewels and everything until we came back. I kept only my thin necklace with its heart and clover, and the little pewter ring which my boyfriend Puiu had given me.[16]

In the ghetto, they were running short of money and food and Hedi thought they should get some money from Mrs Fekete. However, the only way they could get out of the ghetto was by volunteering for outside work clearing away the rubbish from homes vacated by Jews. She noted that the homes that had been so carefully locked did not remain locked very long. 'As soon as we were in the ghetto, they were expropriated and handed over to German and Hungarian officers. But before the new owners moved in, they had to be emptied of all "unnecessary rubbish".'[17]

She volunteered, and had to be ready the next day at eight o'clock. Her parents tried to discourage her but agreed finally. The next day she was put to sort the contents and make an inventory at a small villa:

> … furniture in one pile, china in another, clothes in a third, ornaments in a fourth. What would be done with it all we did not know, though I assumed that it would be taken to Germany. Anything that was worth anything.
>
> It was horrible to root around in other people's homes, emptying drawers of photographs into the dustbins, photographs that meant so much to those that had owned them. I began to feel sick and was glad I did not know any of the people who had lived there. It was hard to imagine that the same thing was happening in our home …[18]

It was nearly time to go back to the ghetto – finally Hedi plucked up courage and asked the guard if she could pop home to collect a love token she had left behind. He told her to be quick and she ran off to Mrs Fekete's home and rang the bell:

> She opened the door. When she saw me, she stiffened. 'What are you doing here?'
> 'I need a little money.'
> 'I have no money. Why should I give you money?'
> 'But we left a lot of money with you before we went away.'

'What money? I haven't had any money from you. You'd best be off before my husband returns. If he finds you here, it'll be the worse for you.'

There was nothing to do but turn and go. I ran back, my heart in my shoes. I had not expected this. Now I understood why she had been so 'nice', this Hungarian officer's wife who had secretly warned us. I should have guessed she had such a motive. Why not get something out of the Jews, since everyone else was? We were still naïve. How long would it be before we dared to look truth in the face?[19]

When I first read this, I had a nagging feeling about what 'Fekete' meant in Hungarian – I have never spoken Hungarian, but when I was little my parents used to speak it to each other which gave me some understanding. I looked it up and I was right – it means 'black'. How appropriate for a black-hearted woman.

Hildegard Abraham told me about her parents-in-laws' experience with their Dutch neighbours in Amsterdam. Like many families, including Anne Frank's, they fled Germany for the Netherlands. They were Siegfried (1899–1974) and Gerda Abraham (1911–2000), who lived in Amsterdam from 1935 until they were sent to the Amsterdam Ghetto area in May 1944. From there they went to Westerbork transit camp until 19 May 1944 when they were sent to Bergen-Belsen. Miraculously, they both survived with their son Henry (1933–2006), and were taken from Belsen on 21 January 1945 and exchanged at the Swiss border. From there the Americans, who had organised the exchange, put them on a train to Marseille. They arrived in Algeria and they spent a year there, mostly in an UNRRA camp. They arrived in America in January 1946 and settled in New York.

Hildegard told me she never understood about the American exchange until she read Max Paul Friedman's book, *Nazis and Good Neighbors*. Apparently Siegfried had obtained false passports from Haiti and claimed his mother lived there, although she had actually died at Theresienstadt, when they were arrested by the Gestapo on 8 May 1944. Accordingly, they were sent to Bergen-Belsen instead of Auschwitz.

Early in 1945, the commandant said some prisoners would be put on a Red Cross train to Switzerland and exchanged for German nationals whom the Americans had in custody. The Americans had arrested more than 4,000 German nationals from fifteen South American countries and interned them in the desert in Texas. The Americans were fearful that the 1.5 million ethnic Germans based particularly in Southern Brazil, Argentina and Chile but also in other countries could be mobilised for a Nazi takeover. Apparently, President Roosevelt believed this might happen and so the military prepared for such an eventuality. This activity ran counter to his 'Good Neighbor' policy, meant to ensure the Latin American countries were given diplomatic independence.

Friedman claims this policy was airbrushed from history. He particularly noted the difference in approach to Germans in North America, who had hearings and were often released, while the South American Germans were denied hearings by Washington. Friedman asks:

> Why were less than one percent of all German citizens in the United States interned, while the US orchestrated deportation program led to the expulsion of perhaps 30 per cent of the Germans in Guatemala, 25 per cent in Costa Rica, 20 per cent in Columbia, more than half in Honduras?

There is no space to deal with this issue further, but this extremely misguided policy did result in the saving of a few Jews, and Hildegard's husband and parents were among them.[20]

Hildegard told me they had given silverware and other valuables to their neighbours before their arrest. After the war they were told by some people when they were trying to retrieve these items, 'No, we don't have these things any more, we thought you were all dead!' Others, however, did return the items to them.[21] The Abrahams never returned to live in Amsterdam and Hildegard thinks this exchange took place on a visit two or three years after the war.

Another lying Dutch neighbour was Mrs Hendricks. John Fransman (*b.* 1939) has described how his parents realised in mid-1942 that Jews were being rounded up and so they made preparations. One day, 3-year-old John and his father went up their garden with his money box which contained silver rijksdaalders (crowns) and buried it at the bottom of the garden. John didn't understand why they were doing this, but was happy to do it with his father. As his parents felt the net closing in:

> They had also given some precious items and some jewellery to different neighbours for safekeeping. I only found out about this after the war when my mother told me about it and I saw some of the items. One of them was a Persian lamb fur coat which one day we saw being worn by the neighbour, Mrs Hendricks, whom she had trusted to look after it. She had lied to my mother on our return, telling her she had had to sell it for food during the war. She had not expected us to return.[22]

John has never returned to that first home and the coins may still be buried there.[23]

Robert Fraser wrote to me from Australia with his grandmother's story from Vienna. The story is as told by Robert's mother, Erna Fraser, so Mama, Robert's grandmother, was Malwine (Nagel) Nowak:

> Early in 1942, Mama and Hanni [her daughter], as well as my Aunts Berta and Therese [Wortmann] and my Uncle Emil Sternschein [by marriage], were still

living in the one room of our once comfortable apartment. Our faithful maid, Käthe, who was still working for Mama at that time and receiving no pay, heard a rumour that a new wave of terror was in the offing. She offered Mama and Hanni an attic in some remote house in Ottakring, and so Mama and Hanni went into hiding in this attic. Käthe had taken charge of our dog, Sissi, since Mama was not allowed to keep a dog. How Käthe found enough food for Mama and Hanni I could not find out, but Emmy and Hans also contributed. This attic had a little window overlooking the street, and on occasions, Emmy or Käthe would walk past with Sissi, so that Mama could have at least a glimpse of her beloved pet.

One day Sissi saw Mama looking out of the window, recognised her, and started to bark and wag her tail. Sissi couldn't understand why she had to be parted from Mama. Now there at last was her old mistress, on whose lap she used to lie for hours, and it is understandable that she wanted to run to her, and wanted everyone to know that she had found Mama again. Sissi barked furiously, and pulled on her lead, but unfortunately all this was observed by an informer, who immediately reported this incident to the Gestapo. I had known this man well; he had lived in one of our apartments.

Even then, he had been hostile towards us, because he was a Tenants' Representative and had made life unpleasant for us, even when my father was alive. He had changed his political colour many times; at one time he was a Communist, then he became a member of the 'Fatherland Front', and now he was a Nazi. He found an opportunity to perform his 'duty' by denouncing and betraying Jewish people.

His 'victims' were arrested and eventually died in Terezin (Czech name for Theresienstadt Ghetto) and Auschwitz. Sissi died of a heart attack some time later during a bombing raid on Vienna.

I thought this was just such a tragic story – in effect they were betrayed by the little dog Sissi giving away their hiding place. The background to the family is that Mama's father, Robert's great-grandfather, Moritz Nowak, went to Vienna from Moravia in the mid-1860s. He was a pharmacist, but in Vienna he became wealthy through property transactions. He involved himself in Jewish communal activities and helped to found the Hubertempel synagogue in Ottakring. His son Oskar was born in Vienna and was a businessman – he was Robert's mother's father.

Robert's father was one of the Jewish men rounded up on Kristallnacht and sent to Dachau. He was released on condition he left the country. He came to London and then to the Kitchener refugee camp in Kent. His wife, Erna Finkelstein, Robert's mother, did not want to leave her ill mother but finally had to leave in late summer 1939, arriving in England four days before Germany invaded Poland.

Erna's siblings were Emma (Emmy), Paul, Fred, Fritz, Johanna (Hanni) and Erna. Fritz escaped to America, while Fred lived in Belgium and France and went to America after the war. Paul died young. Emmy was married to Johann (Hans) August Krumm, who was not Jewish and was therefore fairly safe, but Emmy was nearly arrested once. Hans was able to rescue her. He had converted to Judaism to marry Emmy in 1924. However, under the Nazis he buried his Jewish marriage documents and passed himself off as a non-Jew. He was instead punished for being married to a Jewish woman by being called a Rassenschänder (race defiler) and taken as a forced labourer on the 'Westwall'. He was invalided out and allowed to return to Vienna. He died in 1924.[24]

The family were arrested in 1942 – Emmy witnessed the arrest but could do nothing to help. They were sent to Theresienstadt where Malwine, Mama in the story, died on 5 December 1942. The two aunts, Berta and Therese Wortmann, died in Treblinka – Berta on 1 September 1942 and Therese probably in August 1943. Johanna Nowak (Hanni), Erna's sister, was sent initially sent to Theresienstadt, but was then sent to Auschwitz on 12 October 1944 and no more is known. Robert says only one member of that generation survived, apart from his mother, and she went to Israel. Nothing more is known of the faithful maid, Käthe – not even her surname.[25]

The Jews of Ponevezh in Lithuania lived not far from Shavl – 40 miles east. Meyer Kron's older sister, Tzilia Schatz, lived there and they had stayed put when they could have joined Meyer and his family. Her husband, Abraham, was a respected lawyer and they had foolishly assumed his profession would protect them. The Germans invaded both towns on the same day, 26 June 1941, but Ponevezh had a Jewish population of 10,000 – the third largest in Lithuania. Shavl had 8,000 Jews.

Terrible pogroms were undertaken by the Fascists among them. Among the ringleaders were prominent local people – including the high school principal, the school inspector, the deputy provincial prosecutor and the secretary to the provincial court. The local Fascists did not wait for the German Army to arrive before they attacked the Jews – the Jews were marched round the town and beaten on the way, while the local people stood around watching in large numbers. Some just watched and stayed silent while others hurled stones at their Jewish neighbours.

Many of the Jews' persecutors would consider themselves good and faithful Christians. In many parts of Central and Eastern Europe, particularly in rural areas, medieval myths and prejudices still dominated religious teachings. Jews were Christ's killers. They were the physical incarnation of evil on earth.

Some of the Jews had to do slave labour on local farms. Abraham and Tzilia heard a terrible story about a farmer who was not satisfied with the work done by the Jews. He arranged for his sadistic cronies to take the Jews to a cement factory nearby. Inside there were vats of concentrated lime, to which the Jews were made to add water. When it was all frothing and bubbling, they were ordered to jump in and swim around. Those who refused were pushed in and anyone who tried to climb out was beaten ferociously with rifle butts. Eventually they let them get out, but they were not allowed to go home because they were proof of the terrible savagery. However, the story was leaked by one of the participants over a beer in a local pub.

On 23 August 1941 the remaining Jews of Ponevezh were marched out of the town in various contingents of about 200 Jews – hundreds of police and locals lined the route so no one could escape. Tzilia and her daughter, Betty, followed the path that her husband and son Nathan had taken earlier in the day. There were no official orders for killing the Jews at this stage – the SS and its local helpers were just using their initiative.

The SS had employed Lithuanian shooters to do their dirty work. They were red-faced because of the vodka they had been given for breakfast. The SS knew that some of those tasked with the final duties would show a weakness of spirit without a belly full of liquid courage. The mainly young riflemen dutifully ordered their victims to take off their clothes and pile them in the clearing. They would later be collected and doled out to the 'poor' in Ponevezh. The naked Jews had to approach the recently dug 60-yard-long trenches, some of which were half full.

The stench was unbearable. Faeces mixed with urine everywhere. Bodies lay contorted, frozen during their owners' death throes. The faces of some were missing … The group filed down the earth ramp at the end of the trench. The latest batch of victims lay flat on the corpses as ordered. Some stared down into people they had known all of their lives, while others were cheek-to-cheek with the grotesquely contorted faces of complete strangers.

The eighty-plus guards armed with rifles fired a hail of bullets into the Jews from both sides of the pit. Those who appeared to be still alive afterwards were given a single shot in the head by an SS officer. This went on all day until there were no Jews left standing.

The last group included patients from the Jewish hospital and all the medical staff. The doctors and the nurses were still wearing their medical whites when they arrived at the pits. Witnesses later reported that a surgeon, Dr Theodore Gutman, was among them. He addressed his team, encouraging them to accept their death with dignity. Rather too confidently, he assured them that future generations would avenge their deaths.

Meanwhile, back at the ghetto another group of the local folk had a final run through to check nothing of value belonging 'to their now deceased neighbours' was left behind. The Nazis did their bookkeeping and recorded a total of 7,523 Jews killed on that one day (1,312 men, 4,602 women and 1,609 children). I wonder whether that included the small child who was rescued alive from the pit and who some tried to save? The commander insisted, 'The child cannot be permitted to get away. Better to kill him and so ensure that there is no one left to avenge the blood of the Jews.' He then aimed his pistol at the child, shot him through the head and walked away.

Such events usually ended with an evening's festivities hosted by the local community in a local hall – often a church building. Sometimes priests were involved in some of the squads – they often recruited executioners and sometimes even pulled the trigger themselves. They might suspect that they had the blessing of the Archbishop of Kaunas, Juozapas Skvireckas, whose diary records his approval of Hitler's anti-Semitic policies, although he did protest about converted Jews being persecuted.[26]

My Polish friend Aleksandra Kopystynska (*b.* 1937), known as Ola, told me her father's tragic story. Ola was born in Warsaw and her Jewish mother, Irene Waksenbaum, was also born in Warsaw. At the end of the 1920s she converted to Catholicism to marry Ola's father, Jozef Smietanowski. Ola's brother, Stefan, was born in 1930. Her grandfather died in 1935 and her grandmother, Matylda Centnerszwer, was killed in her bed in the Warsaw Ghetto around 1942.

In late 1939 or early 1940 the family, including the father, were ordered to the Warsaw Ghetto. However, her father decided to escape and they went to a small village, Zyczyn, about 100km from Warsaw. The village was remote, lost among large forests with no electricity. It was 5km to the nearest main road and the railway station. They went as relatives of the wealthy owners of the land, forests and watermill. This was not a lie, as the wife of the owner, Mrs Maria Pac, was a distant cousin of Ola's father.

The Germans had prohibited use of the mill, so it was illegally used at night. Jozef was made manager of the mill and there was a younger worker called Zygmunt Pietrzak. Before long, Jozef realised that Zygmunt was behaving dishonestly toward both the owner and local peasants. Jozef warned Zygmunt that he knew what he was up to and even mentioned it to his wife. This did not endear him to the lad. Apparently, one day Zygmunt's sister, Krystyna, met a boy in the forest who was going to the post office housed in the railway station, to post a letter for Zygmunt. She offered to post the letter for him. She noticed it was addressed to the Gestapo so she kept it instead. It stated that in the village there was a Jewess with two children.

Some time later, during the night of 24–25 February 1942, Jozef was called to the mill, which was unexpected. The mill was working but only Zygmunt was there. Ola, who was 4 at the time, has no knowledge of what happened, but they had a fight and Zygmunt pushed Jozef, aged 43, into the cog-wheels of the mill. Zygmunt went home and told his sister, 'I killed Smietanowski', and he disappeared the same night. Her poor brother, aged only 12, was left to collect the bodyparts of his father the next day. Irene had to leave the village with her two children and went back to Warsaw. Just before the Warsaw uprising they returned to the village and stayed until the end of the war.

There was a trial after the war. When Pietrzak came back with a wife and two children, Krystyna accused him, not Ola's mother. She still had the letter to the Gestapo and it is believed that they had a dispute over land. At his trial he was condemned to death for killing Jozef and collaborating with the Germans. However, that was commuted to twenty-five years and he was freed after fifteen. Ola has attempted unsuccessfully to see the documents from the trial.

Ola believes the crime was based on deep hatred and a desire for revenge. She refers to the existence of very strong anti-Semitism and the 'moral licence' the Germans gave the Poles to kill Jews.[27] She also told me that the Germans, often with the collaboration of the Polish police, paid for each denounced Jew. The reward varied from money or goods to alcohol, sugar or cigarettes. The country was very poor, so apart from money the peasants could also take advantage of the abandoned Jewish properties and, even in Warsaw, people just moved into flats abandoned by people sent to the ghetto. 'In one moment they became owners of the flat with everything inside unscrupulously. In villages peasants even wore the clothes of killed or arrested Jews.'[28]

Samuel Morgenstern (1875–1943) was born in Budapest, but in 1903 he opened a glazier's shop with a workshop in Liechtenstein Strasse near downtown Vienna. Sigmund Freud lived quite close by. He married Emma Pragan, a Jewish woman four years younger in 1904, and in 1911 a son, their only child, was born. It was in Skokie, Chicago, at the Conference of Child Holocaust Survivors in November 2010 that I came across one of the most extraordinary stories in this book when I met Samuel Morgenstern's niece, Ilse Loeb.

In 1937, Morgenstern recalled that Hitler first came into his shop in 1911 or 1912 offering him three paintings, which were historical views in the style of Rudolf van Alt (1812–1905), an Austrian landscape painter. He had sold other pictures because he sold frames and 'in my experience it is easier to sell frames if they contain pictures'. He became a loyal purchaser of Hitler's pictures, and Hitler brought them in regularly, not using an agent. Peter Jahn met Morgenstern between 1937 and 1939 when searching for Hitler's paintings for the German archives with Dr August Priesack, a Munich professor, who authenticated Hitler's signature on the pictures:

> Priesack was a Nazi who, in the 1930s, worked for the central archive of the party, authenticating paintings attributed to the Führer, and then flooding the market. After the war he put himself about as a Hitler expert. In the early 1980s, he was called in by a collector of Hitler paintings. According to Robert Harris's book *Selling Hitler*, the man who had really painted them, Konrad Kujau, was there. He laughed inwardly, he said, when Priesack looked at one of his works and fondly recalled seeing it back in the days of the Reich.

Knowingly or unknowingly, Priesack became one of the most enthusiastic champions of Kujau's forgeries as authentic Hitlers. He collaborated with the American collector Billy F Price to compile the only attempt at a catalogue of Hitler's paintings, published in 1983. (The cultural historian Frederic Spotts estimates that two-thirds of its contents are forgeries.) Priesack is the 'document expert' who contributes to authenticating the paintings on sale in Cornwall. His very presence is an alarm bell.[29]

Jahn said their relationship was extremely friendly and Morgenstern was very fair to Hitler. Jahn said in his deposition that 'Morgenstern was the first person to pay a good price for the paintings, which is how their business contact was established'. Morgenstern was a meticulous record keeper and therefore Jahn was able to locate many of the owners of Hitler's paintings. It appeared that most of them were Jews – the Morgensterns' ordinary customers who lived in the new buildings around the shop. One of them was Dr Josef Feingold, a lawyer. He was interviewed in May 1938, presumably by Peter Jahn, a Nazi, who noted he was 'apparently not entirely Aryan, but certainly leaving the impression of being respectable, a war veteran'. His law offices were downtown in the Stephenplatz and he had supported a number of artists whom Morgenstern had sent to him. He bought a series of views of old Vienna painted by Hitler and had one framed by Samuel in the Biedermeier style.

Surprisingly, when Peter Jahn was exploring Hitler's output he found unsold pieces in both Morgenstern's shop and Altenberg's, after more than twenty-five years. Hitler told his chum Reinhold Hanisch, 'it was only with the Jews that one can do business, because only they were willing to take chances'.[30] Hamann calls him Karl but elsewhere he is called Reinhold. He acted as Hitler's salesman, selling the paintings and sharing the profits. Hitler had him tracked down and killed in 1938, according to Joachim Fest, because he did not want his miserable early years to become common knowledge.[31] He must have been really pleased to know that Hanisch's memoirs of those years were published in the USA under the title, *I was Hitler's Buddy*, in 1939.

In the second article, dated 12 April 1939, Hanisch described Hitler's views about Jews and acknowledged their charitable spirit. He also praised the writer Heine:

> Hitler argued that it was sad that Heine's fatherland did not … recognize his merit. Hitler himself didn't agree with Heine's views but his poetry deserved respect.
>
> But he admired the Jews most for their resistance to all persecutions. He remarked of Rothschild that he might have had the right of admission to court but refused because it would have meant changing his religion. Hitler thought that was decent, and all Jews should behave likewise.[32]

There is no way of knowing when these articles were actually written, but Hanisch concluded the second one:

> Perhaps many people will doubt the truth of these statements, and point to the German Reich today. But I have often noticed myself that anti-Semitism took cruder forms in Germany than in our country. This is due to the character of

the Germans, especially the Prussians. I am convinced that Hitler himself doesn't
agree with many of these insanities, but is the prisoner of his circle.[33]

However, when Hitler became the country's leader after the *Anschluss*, the
Morgensterns' luck ran out. In autumn 1938 their business was Aryanized – the
stores, the fully stocked warehouse and the workshop were all taken over by a Nazi.
The 'purchase price' had been set at 620 marks but this was never paid. Additionally,
as Samuel had lost his commercial licence, he could not work. So the couple had
no source of income and, aged 63 and 59, they were really stuck. They couldn't
even leave the country because they could not afford either the travel costs, the
visa or the obligatory 'Reich flight tax'. Like so many thousands of Jews, they felt
the noose tightening around their necks.

The Morgensterns could only think of one solution – to write to Hitler himself,
whom they had known and helped all those years ago. The letter was typed and
addressed to:

His Excellency the Reich Chancellor and the Führer of the German Reich Adolf
Hitler in Berchtesgaden:

Vienna, 10 August 1939

Excellency!
I humbly ask your indulgence for daring to write to you, Mr Reich Chancellor,
and submitting a request.

For thirty-five years, I had my own business as a glazier and frame manufacturer in Vienna, at 9 Liechtensteinerstrasse, and in the years before the war Mr
Chancellor was frequently in my store and had the opportunity to judge me to
be a correct and honest man.

I have no police record and for eight years served as a non-commissioned
officer in the Austrian army and was on the Romanian front, plus my industrial
association twice gave me a diploma for running an exemplary company.

On November 10 my store was closed in the course of legal measures and
my commercial license was revoked at the same time which made me totally
indigent since to this day I have not received from the Department of Property
the slightest compensation for my store which was worth Reichsmark 7,000 and
was Aryanized on 24 November 1938.

I am sixty-four, my wife is sixty years old, we have for many months depended
on welfare and intend to emigrate and to look for work abroad.

It is my most humble request to Your Excellency to please direct the
Department of Property to give me in return for handing over to the State my
un-mortgaged estate in the XXI St District which according to an official esti-

mate is valued at Reichsmark 4,000, a small compensation in the form of foreign currency so I have the necessary disembarkation money and my wife and I can live modestly until we have found work.

Please have my application checked and please approve it.

Faithfully yours,

Samuel Morgenstern Glazier

Vienna, 9.4 Liechtensteinerstrasse

[Note: Somebody had written 'Jew!' in the margin.]

However, getting a letter to Hitler was difficult, especially in August 1939 just before war started. Hitler himself mentioned this to his old childhood friend from Linz, August Kubizek, whose letter reached him months late. He said, 'Writing to him directly was not advisable, as he often never even saw mail addressed to him, because it first had to be sorted to relieve him in his work.'

The journey of the Morgensterns' letter has been tracked – it was mailed in Vienna on 11 August. It arrived in Hitler's secretary's office at Berchtesgaden on 12 August and was forwarded to the 'Führer's Chancellery' in Berlin on 14 August and opened on 15 August. The word 'Jew!' may have been added then. In any event, the secretary's office did not pass the letter to Hitler but sent it back to Vienna on 19 August to the Finance Ministry. Unfortunately for the poor Morgensterns, waiting anxiously for a reply, it was merely filed away and 'forgotten for the next fifty-six years'.

While they waited in vain for the reply that would never come, the noose was tightened further when their house was confiscated and they were relocated to Leopoldstadt. On 28 October 1941 they were deported to the Litzmannstadt Ghetto. Their deportation order was stamped in red ink, 'To Poland'.

Litzmannstadt (formerly Lódź was named after a German First World War general. It was the second largest ghetto, after Warsaw, in Poland. After the first resettlements, another 160,000 Jews were forced into this ghetto. They lived in very poor conditions and had to work on making textiles, shoes and furniture for the German Army and industries. The Morgensterns were among 25,000 Jews deported to Litzmannstadt from central Europe, and 5,000 Gypsies from Burgenland were also sent there and later sent to Auschwitz.

The western Jews lived uneasily with the unfamiliar eastern Jews, which of course was intentional. It added to the complete misery of the inhabitants:

… their painfully cramped situation, constant hunger, and physical exhaustion through excruciatingly hard work, was meant to rob them of their human dignity.

Especially the lack of hygiene proved to be a highly effective means of 'corroborating' the old anti–Semitic prejudice about the 'filthy Jews'. One of the survivors from Łódź, Leon Zelman, has reported details:'The latrines were constantly plugged. People pulled carts loaded with excrement through the streets, passing wagons filled with corpses to which horses had not been put either, but half–starved Jews. Pulling excrement carts … equalled a death sentence, because the human draft animals invariably caught infections by breathing in the fecal vapors … In the summer, swarms of mosquitoes came down on the ghetto, spreading epidemics.[34]

Little is known of what happened to the Morgensterns, except that Samuel died of exhaustion in August 1943 and was buried in the ghetto cemetery. Emma's brother-in-law confirmed later that Emma was with him until he died. It is believed that Emma was deported to Auschwitz in August 1944 when the ghetto was cleared. Nothing else is recorded, but her brother, Major Max Pragan, applied to a Viennese court after the war and she was declared dead in December 1946. The fate of their son is not known.[35]

The Morgensterns' tragedy is increased by reading about Dr Bloch, the Hitler family's doctor in Linz. In 1907 he had to inform the family that Klara Hitler, Adolf's mother, was in a hopeless condition. Hitler was very upset and slept alongside his mother on the sofa, staying with her day and night. Dr Bloch visited every day from 6 November 1907, administering morphine. Adolf really suffered during his mother's terminal illness and everyone commented on his appearance. On 21 December 1907, 47-year-old Klara Hitler died.

Dr Bloch completed the death certificate and wrote, 'Adolf, his face showing the weariness of a sleepless night, sat beside his mother. In order to preserve a last impression, he had sketched her as she lay on her deathbed.'

Later, on 24 December, when the family called on him after the funeral to express their thanks he noted that of all the bereaved families he had seen, 'In all my career I have never seen anyone so prostrate with grief as Adolf Hitler.' He received many gifts and postcards from Adolf always expressing his gratitude and best wishes. Dr Bloch in turn had special fondness for the family.

He too was devastated by the *Anschluss*. He was 66 when his practice was closed on 1 October 1938. His colleague, Dr Franz Kren, had married his daughter, and they fled abroad. Bloch was confident in Hitler's affection as, in 1937, the Führer had asked the Linz Nazi Party members about him and called him a 'noble Jew'. However, he made several attempts to contact him – the Morgensterns only wrote once.

On 16 November 1938 he wrote saying he was convinced that Hitler 'had not forgotten his mother's doctor, whose professional conduct was always determined by ethical, never material, considerations; but I am also convinced that thousands of those who share my faith and, like me, are suffering so much torment of the soul, are governed by the same principles!'

Hitler responded to Dr Bloch very promptly and put him under the protection of the Gestapo as Linz's only Jew. Doctor and Mrs Bloch were allowed to stay in their home quite undisturbed while the arrangements for emigration were made. They were then able to sell their beautiful home for a fair price and allowed to keep the proceeds – an extremely privileged position. However, the *Anschluss* destroyed Dr Bloch:

> After so many years of respect and comfort, he lost the basis of his existence, his friends, his house and his homeland. In 1940 he and his wife emigrated to the United States. Because his medical degree was not recognised there, he could no longer practise his profession. In 1945 Dr Bloch died a broken man in New York.[36]

Ilse told me that she was unaware of the story until Brigitte Hamann contacted her, and she did not know if her father knew the story – he certainly never mentioned it. She told me that tragically her parents had a terrible death at Belzec concentration camp.[37]

It must be remembered that Hitler wrote his letter to Gemlich only twelve years after his mother's death and seven or eight years after he first starting selling pictures to Samuel. It is clear from the literature that, at the time Hitler was selling his pictures to Samuel and Feingold, he had a lot of Jewish contacts and many Jewish friends in the men's hostel where he lived. His best friend was a religious Jew – Neumann, a trained copper polisher. Neumann gave him a coat when he had nothing to wear and lent him money. He also discussed anti-Semitism and Zionism with Neumann in a joking but friendly manner. He also defended Heine, who was under anti-Semitic attack at the time, and acknowledged the achievements of Jewish composers like Mendelssohn and Offenbach.

Other Jews provided financial support to him, such as the Jewish locksmith, Simon Robinson, from Galicia, who received a small invalid's pension and helped Hitler financially. In the days when he was homeless in 1909 he profited from Jewish social institutions, from the public Warmestuben to soup kitchens and Jewish citizens' donations to the homeless shelter in Meidling and the Brigittenau men's hostel.[38]

But, in the intervening years he changed his outlook – Joachim Fest wrote that Hitler 'had felt an exaggerated sense of obligation' to Neumann. However, during the progress of change all these figures from his youth began to recede into the background, replaced by 'the apparition in a long caftan and black hair locks', which once struck him 'as I was strolling through the Inner City'. He described in *Mein Kampf* how the Jews became unlike the rest of humanity and 'had lost all resemblance to Germans':

Was there any form of filth or profligacy, particularly in cultural life, without at least one Jew involved in it? If you cut even cautiously into such an abscess, you found, like a maggot in a rotting body, often dazzled by the sudden light – a kike! … Gradually I began to hate them.

This chance impression became 'twisted' in his brain and it gradually became an obsession which lasted to his final hour.[39]

## Concierges

It appears that before the days of electronic observation (CCTV) the Nazis had their own stooges. There was a person appointed or paid to be a blockwaerte or blockwaerterin who reported on what happened in their block. This was confirmed by a former student at Heidelberg University in 1991–1992 who lived in a fraternity house for one semester. He said that he was told the housekeeper who lived on the ground floor of the fraternity's mansion with her husband, in the centre of Heidelberg, had apparently been a blockwaerterin during the Nazi period. He added that it was 'an open secret – all the fraternity members knew but were presumably not meant to. They seemed to find it darkly amusing and a little disturbing …' Apparently each block had one who would have reported to a higher official.[40] Joachim Fest refers to the one who spied on his parents and their family.

Benjamin Fondaine (1898–1944) was a successful Rumanian poet born as Benjamin Wexler in Jassy, Rumania. He emigrated to France in 1923.[41] He was living in Paris with his sister, Line, who had some health issues. Neither Benjamin nor Line had declared themselves Jews to the authorities. An attempt was made to get him to Argentina, but with all the arrangements made he chose not to leave his wife and sister.

In March 1944 he and his sister were denounced to the Gestapo:

Although the facts were never brought to light, it appears that they were denounced by the concierge of their house at 6, Rue Rollin, in Paris. This hypothesis is based on the evidence that, shortly after the liberation, the concierge in question hanged himself, without, however, leaving any explanation of his final act.

Line's fate is unknown but Fondaine's is recorded:

He was sent to Drancy and managed to get a letter to his wife Geneviève, in which he gave precise instructions on dealing with his manuscripts. Late in

May 1944 he was deported to Auschwitz. His last days were recorded by a fellow prisoner and published in a literary newspaper. He was gassed and his body cremated in Auschwitz on 3 October 1944.[42]

In contrast, Krystyna Chiger wrote about their loyal concierge, Galewski. His daughter Danusha was the same age as her and they played together and her mother looked after Krystyna during the German invasion when she was 4.[43] When the Germans came to the building, as they did frequently, Galewski would stall them until her father could get out through the back entrance:

> He was a good man, Danusha's father. He helped us many times. The Gestapo and the SS, they would come for inspection and ask, 'Are there any Jews living here?' Galewski would shake his head, *Nein!* Then he would engage the Germans in conversation, knowing my father would have seen them approaching from our upstairs window. Galewski kept them talking, to give my father time to hide or to escape.[44]

Mieczyslaw Centnerszwer (1874–1943) was Ola's great uncle and a famous scientist. Because he was well known he was allowed out of the Warsaw Ghetto before its final liquidation on 22 July 1942. Ola's mother was born in 1904 in Warsaw. Her mother was Matylda Centnerszwer and Mieczyslaw was her cousin. He studied chemistry at the University of Leipzig and met a German girl called Franciszka Anne Beck. She converted to Judaism and they married in Berlin in 1900.

In 1917–1919 he was professor of chemistry at Riga Polytechnic. From there he went to the University of Latvia in Riga from 1919 to 1929, again as professor of chemistry. In 1932 he was appointed as head of division of chemical physics at the University of Warsaw. On 19 September 1935 the foundation stone was laid for the new buildings for the Faculty of Chemistry. (See Photo No.7)

At the start of the war he formally divorced his wife (presumably to protect her) and was forced into the Warsaw Ghetto. His wife remained on the Aryan side. While in the ghetto he wrote a textbook on inorganic chemistry and taught physics and chemistry. When he was allowed to leave the ghetto, he went into hiding with his former wife. Unfortunately, he was betrayed to the Gestapo by the concierge's son and they came and shot him in front of his wife. She was about 70 at the time and was sent to a labour camp in Germany after his death.[45] His daughter, Jadwiga (Hedwig) Grohman, wrote a deposition after the war, dated 16 February 1972.[46] This explains more of the background of her father's life.

His parents ran a famous bookshop and publishing house in Warsaw. However, the scientific brain came perhaps from his grandfather who was a mathematics professor at the Berlin Rabbinical School. When Mieczyslaw matriculated he went to Leipzig to study bookselling, presumably with a view to joining the family firm.

However, he did not like this and decided to study chemistry. The Riga University was transferred to Moscow during the First World War where he was made a full professor. He lectured in inorganic and physical chemistry. As professor of chemistry in Warsaw he published hundreds of scientific papers and two volumes of *Physical Chemistry*. He received honorary doctorates from the Universities of Riga and Madrid and was awarded the order of Officier de Sciences at the Sorbonne.

At the beginning of the war in 1939 his private library of several thousand books was completely burnt down as a result of bombing. He was in the ghetto at Ogrodowa Street 5, but just before its liquidation he escaped by going through the court building which gave him access to Leszno Street in the Aryan quarter. He hid with his wife for a few days while he obtained false documents in the name of Mr Wierzbicki. He moved from place to place and in the end returned to his wife, staying with her for a few months until he was betrayed by the concierge's son. According to his daughter the betrayer brought the Gestapo into the apartment block and they asked him for his documents. Without waiting to see the documents, they shot him in the neck in front of his wife. Although he never renounced his Judaism, he was buried in the Catholic cemetery with a priest conducting the service.

Thanks to her father's friends the concierge's son was arrested after the war, but at the trial the key witness was missing – his widow. This was because, after being sent to Germany as a forced labourer with many other citizens of Warsaw, she stayed in Germany because it was her birthplace. Accordingly, the case was dismissed. The testimony concludes, 'When my mother received the letter stating the caretaker's son had been released "due to lack of evidence" she suffered a stroke and died a few days later.' Thus, the concierge's son was ultimately responsible for the deaths of both husband and wife.

I have been unable to find any more information about Hedwig, except that the JHI told me the testimony was sent from Germany.[47] Ola was unaware of this testimony when she drafted her record of her uncle's tragedy. She has followed the family's scientific inclinations. She is a retired professor of physics at Warsaw University. Up to retirement, besides teaching, she conducted research in atomic spectroscopy and laser physics.[48]

Diane Webber's great-grandparents, Rachel and Fishel Klepfisch, were betrayed by the porter in their block of flats in Antwerp. It was probably quite soon after the Germans arrived – late 1940 or early 1941. They were sent to Auschwitz. Their daughter, Esther Helszajn (Diane's great aunt) was in hiding, so only found out after the war and told her sister in London, who was Diane's grandmother.[49]

'Miss Bluebell' (1910–2004) was really Margaret Kelly. She had been born with wonderful blue eyes in Dublin's Rotunda Hospital and brought up by an ageing spinster in Liverpool. She learnt to dance, aged 14, to strengthen her frail legs on a doctor's advice. After dancing in Berlin for five years, where she met Marlene Dietrich and Christopher Isherwood, she went to Paris where she danced at the

Folies Bergère. When she was 22 she created her own group, the Bluebell Girls, which in 1948 moved to the Lido on the Champs-Elysées. The troupe was unique because the dancers were tall, at least 5ft 10in (1.75m), with long legs.

In 1939, Margaret married the pianist and composer at the Folies. He was Marcel Leibovici, a Rumanian Jew, who came to Paris to study classical music but found working at the Folies more interesting. He also wrote songs for Edith Piaf. In 1940, Margaret was arrested and held at Besançon, an internment camp for 3,000–4,000 holders of British passports, all women and children. The awful conditions caused many hundreds of internees to die of pneumonia, diarrhoea, food poisoning, dysentery and frostbite. Margaret managed to get back to Paris when she proved to the Irish Chargé d'Affaires, Count O'Kelly, that she was Irish – a member of a neutral nation.[50]

In 1942, it was Marcel's turn. He was arrested and sent to the dreaded camp at Gurs where 1,000 Jews died in two months from diseases such as typhoid and TB. However, Marcel did quite well because he acted as an interpreter and was sent to the town to buy food, which involved a lot of sampling.[51] The Resistance helped him escape and return home, where Margaret found a hiding place. After a few months, he had to move again because of the risk of betrayal. She had a friend with an empty apartment they could use on Rue Bertholet on the left bank. 'The concierge, a delightful elderly woman, was both helpful and kind, and readily agreed to look after the new tenant.' Within an hour Marcel was installed.

Some months later in July 1943, when she was pregnant with their third child, she had to go to Gestapo HQ on 84 Avenue Foch – a terrifying prospect. However, her good German from her Berlin days stood her in good stead and she was able to go home.[52]

In the autumn, she was rehearsing a new show when two French plain clothes policemen told her there had been a report that she was an English Jewess and she was to go with them. Very firmly, she said:

'I'm not English – I'm Irish. And I'm not Jewish. I'm a Catholic, like you.' She presented them with her documents including the letter which secured her release from Besançon and eventually they were satisfied. 'We are sorry we have troubled you. But you see, we have to follow up every call we get, and this is what had been said about you!'

Margaret never found out who had been responsible for giving the police false information about her, but since the consequences, had she been unable to prove its falsehood, would have been deportation and death, she concluded that it must have been someone who held a strong grudge against her.[53]

Although the Allies were making good progress in 1944, Marcel was very fed up in his hideaway, after two years' confinement. The concierge kept him safe by getting rid of unwelcome strangers and snoopers and dealt with tasks like the payment of his utility bills. He was still careful, and there were no lights visible at night and fortunately no plumbers or suchlike were needed during this period.

Bluebell came when she could, bringing his fresh laundry on her bicycle, and she made sure to arrive at different times to avoid creating a routine. She also made sure she gave the concierge around 60 francs a week for Marcel's food and other comforts. The period after D-Day on 6 June was difficult because the Germans were still fighting and food supplies became very limited. Eventually Paris was liberated on 25 August and Marcel was able to phone Bluebell with the magic words, 'I'm coming home'.

He saw the children he had not seen for two years, and the little daughter he had never met, who was 1¼ years old. For Marcel and Bluebell the ever present fear of denunciation was at last gone and family life could return to normal. However, the joy of liberation was tempered by recriminations on collaborators, who were attacked by crowds and some were literally hacked to death in the streets. Women who had fraternised with the enemy had their heads shaved right to the skin and they were unable to go out until it grew back because it was such a badge of shame.

Surprisingly, one woman who had her head shaved was Marcel's concierge who had looked after him so carefully. The concierge's granddaughter phoned Bluebell, saying the old lady was in police custody. Bluebell was indignant. She went to the police station and told the officer that the concierge had hidden her husband and had been kind to him. Bluebell's testimony was so powerful that the concierge was allowed to go back home. Two hours later, the granddaughter rang again, even more distressed. Bluebell returned to the police station. This time she had to listen to the officer:

> It seemed that the apparently sweet old lady, far from being an unjustly accused innocent had been responsible for betraying several loyal Frenchmen who had spent time hiding in the rooms of her apartment building. In each instance where she had betrayed someone she was paid a reward of fifty francs. Therein lay the reason why Marcel had been saved from denunciation. Bluebell had been paying her sixty francs a week, plus various gifts of scarce food such as eggs or condensed milk which she had bought from Frederic Apcar. A mere ten francs had therefore saved her husband's life. Bluebell was aghast, never having suspected that such disgraceful perfidy had reached out so closely to her, while Marcel, perhaps less astonished, accepted his good fortune. It was a reinforcement of the unofficial rule of the occupation years – that no one should be trusted. The woman was eventually tried for her crimes and given a long sentence which in view of her age she could never complete, for Bluebell heard not long afterwards that she had died in prison.[54]

The Bluebell Girls flourished – there have been about 14,000 and they still entertain visitors to Paris. Sadly, Marcel was killed in a car crash in 1961. Margaret Kelly

Leibovici died on 11 September 2004, aged 94, and is buried in Montmartre Cemetery. She received many honours, including an OBE from the Queen and the Chevalier de la Légion d'Honneur for her seventy-two year career from her adopted country.[55]

Finally, it is salutary to compare the reactions of these neighbours with those of Linda Besso's (née Bentata, 1903–1942) neighbour in La Baule in south Brittany on the Atlantic coast. Linda was a Manchester girl who married a man from Milan, where they first lived.[56] Later they moved to Brussels where she had three children, Jacqueline, Janine and Freddy. All was well until her husband died unexpectedly in 1937. When war seemed imminent, her parents begged her to return to Manchester, which she did for a while. However, in 1938 the prime minister, Neville Chamberlain, met Hitler and announced 'Peace in our time', and Linda returned to Brussels so the children could continue their education.

When Belgium fell in May 1940, they fled to La Baule in France where she rented a villa. She became very friendly with her neighbour, Madame Yvonne Despretz, who wrote an eyewitness account of Linda's arrest with her children by the German police on 16 July 1942. Linda and her three young children were gassed at Auschwitz in December 1942. Her brother, Victor Bentata, knew something was wrong because, until July 1942, he had regularly received cards from her. She sent them via relatives in Morocco, so that if the Germans invaded England they would not have a Jewish family's address in Manchester.

After the war, the Red Cross told Victor that his beloved sister and her children had been gassed at Auschwitz. He died prematurely in 1961 – his daughter believes as a result of this major tragedy. When his widow was 90 she spoke for the first time about the tragedy of the Besso family's murder.[57]

My mother continued, saying that before they were taken, Linda must have realised the danger she was in and entrusted her valuable collection of jewels to a lady who must have been a close friend. After the war, this Catholic French lady contacted my father and said she had something of importance to give him, and asked him to meet her in London. My mother related how she gave him a suede bag containing beautiful jewels with a list written by my aunt – every item was there. My mother spoke of this lady as having the highest degree of honesty as no one would have known if she had not returned them. As my mother said, no amount of jewels could replace the loved ones who had been killed so cruelly, but the fact that in the midst of all that horror there was a noble soul was a comfort. My parents had no idea who this lady was, and because of the distraught state they were in, they had not kept a record of her name.[58]

Yvonne had died in 1988, aged 98, leaving four children, all then in their eighties. However, Linda's family in England knew nothing about the neighbour and the valuable package until it was handed over. Perhaps her Manchester family did not know about Linda's collection of jewellery? Had Madame Despretz chosen to keep the jewels no one would have known and she would never have been found out. She must have been a remarkable woman to make that visit to London to keep faith with her promise. One item was so valuable that Victor sold it in the early 1950s to buy a property for a relative fleeing persecution.

When Victor's widow died, his daughter, Jackie, and son, Jack, determined to go to France to find the family to thank them. A local French newspaper covered the story and consequently they were contacted by Albert Gamignon, aged 81, a school friend of Freddy. He told them that he remembered the Jewish children being taken out of school in February 1942 and then returning, very embarrassed, wearing yellow stars with the word 'Juif'.

At the local town hall they saw a document covering the requisition of Linda's villa by the Germans after her arrest, and an eyewitness account of the arrest:

Mme Yvonne Despretz born 11 July 1890, living in the Villa Les Opales, Avenue Saumur tells us: I witnessed in the capacity of neighbour the arrest of the Besso Family 16th July 1942. The doors of the Villa Martine were locked in my presence by a German soldier. About 3 weeks ago accompanied by a German officer I entered the VM where I packed some things, sheets and clothes to send to MM Besso to the transit camp in Angers, she having been given permission to receive some of her belongings. The Villa Martine was in a state of inexpressible disorder when I left. Cupboards emptied, drawers opened. Since then I have seen no one enter the villa. Apart from the furniture there is nothing worth taking.[59]

Jackie commented:

It appeared that the Germans had been searching for the jewellery.
    ... the Gestapo had wind of the collection of jewels and arrested Mme Despretz who saw the police coming down the road. She threw the jewels out of the window [into the garden] denying she was in possession of them. She was interrogated for 24 hours before being released.[60]

Jackie and Jack finally tracked down the Despretz family in 2010 and met the surviving children. They all remembered the family and their story – the three eldest had been classmates to the Besso children, so the events must have had a big impact on them. Jackie and Jack brought certificates of acknowledgement from Yad Vashem for what their mother had done, for each of her children. Touchingly they, in turn, returned a small pill box marked 'Mm Besso', which contained trinkets and a child's pearl necklace. They had kept it safe for sixty-eight years.[61] With its return, the family had fulfilled the agreement made in 1942 and kept faith with Linda

Besso and her trust in her friend and neighbour, Yvonne Despretz. How different would the history of the Jews in the Holocaust have been, if there had been more people like Mme Despretz?

A more realistic postscript was related by Herta Nathorff who was a niece of Albert Einstein and was a doctor in Berlin. She managed to leave in 1939, but recorded Nazi activities during the 1930s in her diary. She was particularly pained by the behaviour of someone she had helped, and recorded on 9 October 1935:

> I met my former secretary today. She fixed me sharply with her short-sighted eyes, and then turned away. I was so nauseated I spat into my handkerchief. She was once a patient of mine. Later I met her in the street. Her boyfriend had left her and she was out of work and without money. I took her on, trained her for years and employed her in my clinic until the last day. Now she has changed so much that she can no longer greet me; me, who rescued her from the gutter![62]

# 4

# BETRAYAL BY JEWS

---

Some rise by sin, and some by virtue fall.

Shakespeare – *Measure for Measure*

---

I hesitated about including this chapter because it seems such an embarrassment to reveal that Jews betrayed other Jews for money and other reasons. A novel by Giuseppe Pederiali described the real events in the Rome Ghetto during the Holocaust. This was the oldest Jewish community in Italy and suffered most with the round-up of 1,000 Jews on 16 October 1943 by the SS, and on 24 March 1944 with the massacre of Fosse Ardeatine. In the massacre 335 men, seventy-five of whom were Jewish, were murdered by the SS in revenge for the Resistance's bombing in the Via Rasella which had killed thirty-two German soldiers – the victims had been chosen at random and had not been involved in the bombing.

Pederiali wrote about a Jewish girl from the ghetto called Celeste Di Porto, known as 'La Pantera Nera' – the 'Black Panther'. After becoming involved with a Roman Fascist she betrayed over fifty fellow Jews to the Nazis, presumably for financial reward (5,000 lire for every Jew arrested). Apparently, she walked the streets of her neighbourhood greeting various acquaintances warmly by name and was followed by Fascists or SS men who immediately arrested the person concerned. Dan Kurzman, a historian, wrote that if the arrested man 'denied he was a Jew, as he usually did, Celeste would come to testify and, to the laughter of her Fascist friends, would personally pull down the victim's trousers to show that he was circumcised'.[1] She was tried in 1947 and sentenced to twelve years in prison.

Pederiali gave his character Vittorio the following words:

He had spoken about it even publicly at his book launch in Rome at the Campidoglio, and in newspapers, some of which had criticised his aggressiveness in penetrating Celeste's world and her character … 'It seemed unfair to me to hide the facts. If there were some rotten apples among the Jews of Rome, why not say so? It would be racist to describe them only as heroes and victims …'[2]

Further information on Celeste's activities was given by the Jewish DiVeroli family who were first mentioned in Rome's city records in 1539 as itinerant pedlars. In 1944 the family became itinerant again, hiding in different places to avoid arrest. Attilio, the father of the family, returned to his itinerant life of buying and selling and because he was blind in one eye he took his 15-year-old son, Michele, with him while the women stayed with an acquaintance. Rosa said they had arranged to meet the two men on 18 March 1944, but they did not arrive. The next day Rosa and her sister Silvia went to the Nazi HQ and, rather courageously, asked to see their father and brother. They were told to go to the prison called Regina Coeli. Although they were afraid, they took some food, but Rosa admitted she was always reckless.

They went every day with food to supplement the meagre prison rations, but when they arrived on 24 March the guards told them that the men had been taken away and they did not know where. Rosa had her misgivings, which proved correct – they had been taken to the Ardeatine Caves and shot. Afterwards the Germans dynamited the entrance to hide the evidence. However, the sisters did not know until later.

A few days later Rosa and Silvia, at some risk, went back to the ghetto to a baker they knew would sell them some bread. There Rosa saw an old school friend known as 'Stella' (Star) because she was beautiful. She was from another old ghetto family. When Rosa saw her she was frightened she would betray them, as she knew of her reputation. However, she asked her if she knew what had happened to her father and brother. Stella (Celeste, the Black Panther) said they were fine and were with her own cousin. As they walked away she called Rosa and again they were afraid, but she just warned her to stay out of sight for a few days.

Rosa contacted her cousin, Renato DiVeroli, who, having seen a list of the victims, confirmed both Attilio and Michele were listed. Michele was the youngest victim. Celeste's own cousin died there too, so she had told the truth to some extent. Of the seventy-five Jews killed there, it is believed that twenty-six were betrayed by La Pantera Nera.

Lazzaro Anticoli, a young street peddler arrested on the morning of the massacre, managed to scribble a note before being dragged off to the caves, 'If I never see my family again, it is the fault of that sellout Celeste Di Porto. Avenge me.' According to Italian historian, Silvio Bertoldi, Anticoli's name was added at the last minute, replacing that of Celeste Di Porto's brother. Her own father was so deeply ashamed by his daughter's betrayal that he turned himself in to the Germans; he died in a concentration camp.[3]

We have no means of knowing what drove Celeste to betray her fellow Jews. Susan Zuccotti, an Italian historian, has speculated whether the informers would have been as ready to denounce Jews if they had known what was going to happen to them and if they had realised what was actually occurring in the camps. There is no consensus among historians about the level of awareness, but Zuccotti thinks many Jews were unwilling to believe the Allied reports about atrocities in the camps and dismissed them as propaganda, refusing to hide or get false papers and thus putting themselves at severe risk. It also raises the issue of what Celeste knew, and whether she would have behaved differently had she known she was sending Jews to inevitable death.

Zygmunt Bauman has pondered the question of Jewish complicity. He maintained that many Jews co-operated because they were presented with choices that made it seem like the only rational option. He also discusses the position of the heads of Jewish communities, often coerced into running the Judenrät (Jewish Council), who handed over a limited number of names, believing the Nazis' lies and mistakenly thinking that would save the majority. Bauman says the Nazis relied on this. 'While in full command of the means of coercion, the Nazis saw to it that *rationality meant co-operation*; that everything the Jews did to serve their own interest brought the Nazi objective somewhat nearer to full success.'[4]

The Fosse Ardeatine Massacre, regarded as a major war crime, is symbolic of German atrocities in Italy during the Third Reich. A major commemoration is held every year, with Italian politicians laying wreaths. During the massacre, five men were sent into the cave together and their names were crossed off by an SS officer – Erich Priebke. As five men were shot by the SS, the next five were brought in. As the afternoon wore on, the victims had to climb over the bodies of those already dead. Apparently, the executioners were drinking heavily throughout the afternoon and therefore the shooting became more erratic. 'Several victims survived the initial shots. Some suffocated under the weight of the dead lying on top of them.' The only person punished was Herbert Kappler, the SS officer in charge of German police and security services in Rome – he was given life imprisonment in 1948.[5]

Priebke died in Rome in October 2013, aged 100. His wish to be buried next to his wife in Argentina was refused and the Vatican opposed a Catholic funeral. His hometown in Germany also objected for fear of a neo-Nazi shrine being created. Finally, a funeral in Rome was disrupted by rioters and the local authorities buried him in an unknown place. He had never expressed any remorse for the massacre.

Boris Smolar (1897–1986) was a Russian-born American journalist, working for the Jewish Telegraphic Agency (JTA). He was based in Berlin from the spring of 1932, when the Nazis were already 'creating a stir'. There were regular bloody fights between the Nazis and the Communists with the use of revolvers and knives. The moderates hoped the extremists would destroy each other.[6]

The Nazis were already 'thundering against the Jews', even though they then represented less than 1 per cent of the total population, with 500,000 Jews in Germany. However, German Jews, especially the leaders, did not consider the Nazis a serious threat because they did not think Hitler would be elected. In any event, they were convinced that even if the Nazis came to power they would not implement the anti-Jewish measures threatened in their propaganda.

Significantly, this relatively complacent view was not shared by the foreign diplomats based in Berlin who had been following developments closely. Soon after his arrival, Smolar had a series of talks with these people as well as high officials in the German Foreign Ministry. This resulted in him deciding to dispatch a series of cables to New York to 'draw attention to the danger looming for German Jewry'.

His first cable, which predicted the possibility of Hitler taking power, appeared in the general American press and had a large impact. The second one warned American Jewry to be prepared for Hitler taking over and warned that the Jewish leadership in Germany did not have the foresight to see this. 'I added that American Jewish organisations should not lose time but should do something – directly or through Washington – to let the Nazis know the world was watching what was happening to German Jewry.'

His policy worked and Dr Cyrus Adler, then president of the American-Jewish Committee, went to Washington to talk to officials in the State Department, the Chairman of the Senate Foreign Relations Committee, Senator Borah, and other powerful congressmen. The American correspondents of the Berlin papers also took notice and the *Berliner Tageblatt*, one of the most important newspapers in Germany, printed an article on the impact of Smolar's report on the US Government's officials. It also influenced the foreign journalists in Berlin:

> American correspondents in that city, who had heretofore paid scant attention to strident Nazi anti-Semitic propaganda – they considered it to be only a minor aspect of Nazi propaganda – were instructed by cable to send detailed reports on the Nazis' anti-Jewish agitation. They contacted me immediately for details. The State Department asked the American Embassy to send a detailed report on Nazi Jew-baiting.

The interest spread to the German Foreign Ministry, not yet in Nazi hands. Many of the officials were interested to know why Smolar thought Hitler would gain power, and he sensed they were quite pleased that he had stirred things up in Washington and encouraged the USA to intervene to counter the Nazis' tactics. However, the German-Jewish leaders were not pleased with the 'interference'.

Smolar wrote, 'They simply refused to believe that Hitler could come to power and that he would carry out his anti-Jewish program.' He was stunned by their behaviour and wrote that, in view of what happened a year later, he was aghast that the leading German-Jewish organisation the Central Verein Deutscher Staatsbürger Jüdischen Glaubens (Central Association of German Citizens of Jewish Faith) chose to make a public statement after Dr Adler's visit to Washington, saying that German Jewry was not in danger.

He was also invited to a meeting with the Central Verein's executive committee at which 'I was expressedly asked not to alarm the world over the danger to German Jews should Hitler gain power'. He refused, not surprisingly, and said he would sooner leave Germany, and again reiterated his view about:

> ... the terrible danger in store for German Jews should Hitler gain power, to which they, the leaders were closing their eyes – until it would be too late!
> The leaders of the Central Verein certainly did not expect that a year later, in April of 1933, they would be asking me to return to Germany to be the only Jewish foreign correspondent who could report to the world on Nazi persecution of the Jews and on the extreme terror in which they were living.

After this meeting, he received a call from a senior official, Dr Sobernheim, in the German Foreign Ministry, where they knew of this disagreement. Smolar was invited to his home for dinner. He knew of Smolar's meeting and asked about it. Smolar explained that the leaders did not appreciate the threat to the Jewish community and that it was important to raise awareness in America and Britain to take measures to prevent the Nazis implementing their anti-Jewish policies. This should be done even before they came to power. He was therefore leaving Germany as he was not prepared to do what the Jewish leaders wanted.

Dr Sobernheim considered this and then said, 'They are fools. They don't know what's good for them.' He himself was an assimilated Jew and a member of inner government circles. He knew the leaders and respected them. However, they didn't want Hitler to succeed and refused to accept it was possible. He knew the true situation with great unrest among thousands of unemployed. The government was very weak, and the workers and the unemployed were divided into the Social Democrats, Communists and Nazis. The Social Democrats' numbers were falling.

'Perhaps worst of all were a number of big German industrialists like Krupp, Thyssen and Hugenberg, who were secretly financing the Nazis. They reckoned that if the Nazi Party gained control, they could exert influence in their own favour. They were terribly afraid of Communism, which was growing just as fast as Nazism was because of the great economic crisis.'

At the end of the evening they both hoped that they were wrong and the German-Jewish leaders were right. This has resonances with the Hungarian Jews' reaction to international interference on the *numerus clausus* legislation in 1920. However, when they were proved wrong the Jewish leadership called him back to Berlin. He went just for a few weeks but stayed for several years. As an American

Jew, he was the only journalist the Nazis could not touch and his ambassador protected him too. Additionally, the Nazis knew that their man in New York would be vulnerable if they expelled Smolar from Berlin.

Smolar did not give details about Dr Sobernheim, but I think he was Professor Moritz Sebastian Sobernheim, a noted Orientalist and rapporteur on Jewish political affairs in the Ministry of Foreign Affairs from 1918. He had been born in Berlin in 1872 and had two very distinguished brothers. He himself wrote several books and from 1924 he was the president of the German Federation of Israelite Communities. His early death in Berlin, on 5 January 1933, aged only 61, saved him from the horrors to come.[7]

Leonard (Leo) David Frank (1903–1943) was an eminent Amsterdam lawyer married to an English woman, Beatrix. They had three sons – Steven, Nick and Carel.[8] He was involved in many organisations as his legal expertise was much in demand and he was a legal advisor to the mental hospital, Het Apeldoornse Bos. He was also a founder-member of the first 'legal aid' scheme (Ons Huis), giving free legal advice to the poor of Amsterdam.

Aged only 33, he was awarded the Ridder van Oranje Nassau (the Dutch equivalent of a knighthood) by Queen Wilhelmina of the Netherlands in 1936 – at that time the youngest person to receive that honour. With the rise of the Nazis in Germany many Jews, including Anne Frank's family, fled to Holland thinking they would be safe there. Holland was neutral during the First World War. Leo Frank became the head of a Jewish welfare organisation funded by the government that helped these refugees find work and a home.

Following the invasion of Holland, the government finance was withdrawn, leaving Jews to fund it. Leo was instrumental in getting funding for refugees from many reluctant Dutch Jews. In due course this welfare organisation was absorbed into the Jewish Council of Amsterdam where Leo was, reluctantly, made to continue this valuable work. He used this cover to help the Dutch Resistance get Jews with false papers to the Alps, where a mountain guide led them into neutral Switzerland avoiding all the border guards.

On another occasion, he pleaded with the German authorities to spare a man due to be deported to Auschwitz. He also helped Jews to find hiding places in Holland. Tragically, it was this activity that led to his betrayal, inexplicably, by two Jews whom he had helped to hide. The Gestapo raided his office and arrested him one morning in December 1942.

Now that Leo's wife was on her own she demonstrated the courage and ingenuity that helped her later in the camps. She disguised herself as a man and changed places two or three times with a cleaner in the prison so she could see Leo. Three good non-Jewish friends petitioned the Nazis to show clemency and cited all the organisations he had been involved with. This was a very courageous thing for them to do, as they all had responsibilities and families. The Nazis would not relent about Leo's fate, but agreed to put his wife and sons on the Barneveld List, which ensured they would not be sent 'east'.

Leo had been sent to Amersfoort Prison, tortured there and then sent to Westerbork on 23 December 1942. He was deported to Auschwitz on 18 January 1943 where he was gassed on 21 January, aged just 39 years. He is listed in the Erelijst van Gevallen 1940–1945 (Roll of Honour for War Patriots) in the lower house of the Dutch Parliament, along with 17,000 others, including three of his nephews. A ceremony is held each day with a new page turned over.

The promises made to the family about their future were not kept – yet another betrayal. In March 1943, Leo's widow and three sons were ordered to leave their home and go to the railway station to travel to Barneveld. They lived in the castle with 660 people until the Germans entered the camp in September 1943, giving them twenty minutes to prepare for departure to Westerbork.

Westerbork was enclosed by a moat and 6ft high barbed wire fences with watch towers on stilts. Guards with machine guns and searchlights looked down on the prisoners. There were about 15,000 inmates there at any time. The hygiene conditions were terrible. There were lice everywhere and dysentery, scarlet fever, polio and hepatitis, although people did not starve. However, 8-year-old Steven said he learnt to be self-sufficient and streetwise there.

Transports left Westerbork every Tuesday to take the Jews to the 'east', as organised by Adolf Eichmann. Transports were clearly labelled – mostly cattle trucks going to either Auschwitz or Sobibór, both death camps in Poland. If you were lucky you might get to Bergen-Belsen or Theresienstadt, near Prague. After a year in Westerbork, Beatrix and the boys were sent to Theresienstadt in September 1944.

The journey was memorable and Steven said he would never forget it:

> 39 hours in a crammed cattle truck, no food, no water, no sleep, but what I remember the most was the stench that built up of human sweat, of vomit, of urine, of faeces and the gradual depletion of oxygen. One was gasping for breath. Then the train stopped. There was a rumble as the door was slid open and I remember this waft of ice cool air which invaded the cattle truck and suddenly I could breathe again.[9]

Theresienstadt was a garrison town built in 1780 to house 8,000 soldiers and their families. The Germans crammed 40,000 Jews in the same space. Steven's family starved there and Steven wrote, 'that feeling of hunger, the pain is something that I shall never forget'.

When the typhus epidemic started, Beatrix Frank volunteered to work in the camp's hospital laundry where she had access to hot water – the only place in the camp. She washed her children's clothes there, well out of the sight of the camp authorities, and this helped keep the typhus at bay. Tens of thousands of Jews died of typhus through the dreadful conditions they were forced to live in. Other diseases and starvation were also killers. Beatrix washed other people's clothes too, trading her labour for food – mostly a bitter bread which she mixed with hot water to make a kind of bread porridge – 'broodpap'. She fed this to the children in the children's home from an old aluminium saucepan – one spoonful for each child.

At this time, Steven and his brothers, Nick and Carel, were separated from their mother and put in a children's home. They spent their time inventing games to play – they made a pack of fifty-two cards and torches from bulbs, wire and used batteries that the guards had thrown away. Steven said, 'if you put the batteries between your thighs at night you could regenerate them sufficiently to light your torch bulb briefly, when it got dark. And it shone like a bright star in the dark sky, so comforting.' Steven still remembers the selection of the children in their home – the guards deliberately split siblings; one to stay and one to go. That was all they had left, with other members of the family long gone. The screaming and wailing is still in his memory.

As the Allies were closing in, open cattle trucks came from Auschwitz with mostly corpses, but the few survivors told them about the gas chambers. He witnessed the bombing of Dresden and rumours of liberation began. Early one morning, the children were woken and made to get dressed and taken to a dimly lit tunnel at the crematorium. They were made to line the tunnel and soon a box was passed to him by a little girl on the right and he passed it to the little girl on his left. The boxes contained the ashes of the dead. However, in true German efficiency each box had a label which bore the name of the person whose ashes they were – their date and places of birth and death. You could hear, every now and then, a quiet sobbing as a child held the ashes of their mother or father or other family members – they had to be nudged to pass it on. The ashes were being thrown in the river to hide the evidence.

Soon after this, on 9 May 1945, the Soviet Army arrived to liberate the camp, but left very quickly, fearing infection from the typhus epidemic. The Red Cross came and everyone was quarantined and unable to leave for a month until they were fitter. Beatrix Frank was determined to get to England. In Pilzen, Steven writes, 'I witnessed a DP camp and a sight I shall never forget of utter of human misery.'[10] Through his mother's persuasive powers, she got her children to England. 'Two RAF pilots flew us completely illegally to Croydon Airport where they "dumped" us on the runway and took off again.[11] We were home.'[12]

Beatrix died in 2001, aged 90. Steven and Carel live in London and Nick is in Adelaide.

Howard Boyers (1915–2010) was a much respected Sheffield solicitor. During the Second World War he became a pilot officer in the RAF and was awarded the DFC in 1945. After the war he returned to the law and was senior partner in Boyers, Howson & Co. 1946–1972. He served as Clerk of the Peace at the Sheffield

Magistrates' Courts 1964–1971, chairman of the VAT Tribunals 1972–1975, chairman of the Industrial Tribunals 1975–1980 and acting regional chair 1980–1984 and regional chairman 1984–1987. He was also chairman of the Employment Tribunals from 1964 until he retired in 1980.

Howard was a close friend of my late father-in-law, Gustav Spier, and many years ago he told me about something he experienced during his time in the RAF which shocked him considerably. He wrote me a letter in 1997 detailing the incident:

> The RAF started a moral leadership course for Jewish personnel in October 1944 but I could not be released for it because I was on operational duties. I was available for the second course in February 1945, held in Manchester under the aegis of Rabbi Israel Brodie, who was then Senior Jewish Chaplain to the Armed Forces. One of our meetings, attended by about 3 dozen airmen and women, was addressed by Neville Laski KC who had been President of the Board of Deputies 1933–39. We were shocked at his prolonged diatribe directed at many targets but largely against 'foreign' Jews, mainly East European Jews, the most immediate victims of the Nazis. He and his friends had nothing in common with them, with their foreign dress, appearance and habits, he said. He complained (inter alia) that no Jewish solicitor had ever given him a brief (I remember thinking, 'You'll never get one from me and I'm not surprised you've never had one'.) He told his captive audience that the Grand Dukes of British Jewry (of whom he was one) would govern the community in the future as they had in the past. He was clearly an embittered man and one of yesterday's men.
>
> He did not expect any question or reaction at the end of his address, but we were all so obviously of one mind that at the end, as senior officer present, I took it upon myself to say what I believed was the unanimous view of his audience. I asked him what he thought we were fighting for and on behalf of those present I expressed profound disagreement with his views. It was his turn to look shocked. It was really a Jewish dry run for the 1945 General Election when in the wider community the Armed Forces and civilians alike threw off the yoke of people who were 'born to govern'.
>
> At the end of the meeting I was surrounded by the whole course, all thanking me and congratulating me. Brodie joined in, and on the several occasions on which I subsequently met him, showed me the greatest friendship.[13]

Howard Boyers died in May 2010, aged 94. As an immigrant Jew from central Europe, I always found this incident remarkable and I think the Jews of Europe would have expected their co-religionists to endeavour to support them – the view expressed, for example, by Werner Cahnman when he was in Dachau.

It appears that the members of the British Jewish Establishment had a fear that if they made strident demands to the government on behalf of the persecuted

European Jews, it would demonstrate that their loyalty lay more strongly with their co-religionists abroad than with their fellow citizens here in Britain.

> The spectre of the cosmopolitan Jew, loyal to international Jewry but to nothing else, haunted Jewish communal leaders (and many of those whom they led) as much as it haunted British purveyors of anti-Jewish prejudice, of whom there was a growing number in the 1930s. It was precisely for this reason that Neville Laski turned his back on the World Jewish Congress (WJC), formed in 1936 on the initiative of the American Zionist Rabbi Stephen Wise and the Lithuanian-German Zionist Nahum Goldmann. The WJC was designed as the Diaspora counterpart of the World Zionist Organisation, and the complement to it. Laski consistently and successfully argued against the affiliation of the Board of Deputies to the WJC and tried (in vain) to persuade the Foreign Office to have no dealing with it. Jews in different countries, he told his colleagues in the board, possessed 'differences of outlook, very largely the analogous differences of the general communities of which they form part'; 'the semblance of internationalism and unified action in the World Jewish Congress has therefore no basis in fact', and could only provide ammunition for those who peddled the frequent and unfounded charge against Jews by the anti-Semites, 'that there existed an international Jewry'.[14]

However, on 9 April 1936 Laski had written to Felix Warburg, a leading American non-Zionist, 'The bogey of the international Jew which finds its crudest form in the Protocols [of Zion], is if you will bear with me, definitely assisted both by Zionism and by its offshoot, – or, as I have termed it, facet, – the World Jewish Congress.'[15]

He was so opposed to the concept of Jews as an international united people that:

> Early in the history of the Congress, Neville Laski, President of the Board of Deputies between 1933 and 1939, had privately approached a Foreign Office official and informed him that mistaken 'conceptions of the Jewish people as a united national organisation' and 'ideas of Jewish nationhood' were a danger to the civic rights of Jews in all countries.[16]

A similar view was expressed by another Jewish leader in March 1936. He was also a lawyer, Jacques Helbronner, who was vice president of the Central Consistory. The French Jews shared:

> … the French animus against foreigners. They called for a restrictive policy, and for caution about the distribution of relief or the opening of French borders. At its harshest, as in the speech of Jacques Helbronner, vice president of the Central Consistory, in March 1936, refugees whom he termed 'riffraff', the rejects of society, the elements who could not possibly have been of any use to their own

country should not be allowed to stay in France. He lobbied the government to close the French borders to refugees from Germany.[17]

The issue of Jewish indifference to the situation of the European Jews was discussed in Richard Bolchover's book, and he deals with the problems that arose with British Jewish institutions failing to appreciate the situation. It seemed that individuals were more successful in perceiving what was required. For instance, Rabbi Dr Solomon Schonfeld personally lobbied MPs and peers over a parliamentary motion regarding the conditions of Jews in Europe with great success, as he reported in the *Jewish Chronicle* on 29 January 1943 (p. 37).

This was later also reflected at the end of the war – in late 1944 Norman Bentwich wanted people to volunteer to go Europe to help the Jews as they were liberated, but the response was disappointing, as was the response for people to meet Jews released from camps when they arrived at British ports.

Dayan Grunfeld reported to the *Jewish Chronicle* on the Kindertransport, on 31 December 1943:

> When the children were brought over in 1938 the Jewish community, which had shown such great generosity when it was a question of donating money for the refugee organisation, showed themselves very reluctant to take Jewish refugee children into their homes. Grunfeld described many of these children as 'lost souls' brought up by non-Jews. He cited many cases of conversions. Most of the children had lost their parents and had been entirely dependent on the Jewish community for any form of Jewish education.[18]

A request for rabbis to go as temporary chaplains to the liberated concentration camps also met with little response. The secretary of the United Synagogue, which had appealed to the Amersham & District Synagogue to release their rabbi, the Reverend Indech, for a two month attachment at Bergen-Belsen, wrote a memorandum on 7 May 1945. It recorded his conversation with the synagogue's treasurer, Mr A. Winer. Apparently Mr Winer had shouted at him down the telephone for ten minutes, insisting 'that it was more important for Mr Indech to remain in Amersham than it was for him to go to the concentration camps'.

On 9 May 1945 the executive officers of Amersham Synagogue, including Mr Winer, wrote to the United Synagogue:

> While we realise to the full the importance of Welfare and Rehabilitation work among the survivors of our Continental brethren, the members of our committee whom we have consulted on this matter unanimously agree with us that the position of this community renders the service to it of the Rev. J. Indech of greater importance.[19]

Kitty Hart-Moxon still remembers her distress at the remark made by her uncle, Otto Muller, who met her and her mother at Dover in September 1946. They arrived in England having survived mock executions, Auschwitz and all manner of other horrors:[20]

> My uncle was my mother's brother-in-law. In other words my mother's sister's husband thus my uncle. (They came over from Vienna in 1938). He, my uncle, collected us from Dover and was driving us to Birmingham (where they were living). In the car on the way he announced the following: 'I want you to remember that in my house I do not want you to talk about anything that happened to you, I don't want to know and I don't want my girls (my cousins) upset'.
>
> That in effect set the scene that I encountered wherever I went – including the Birmingham Jewish Community – who completely ignored survivors and offered no support whatsoever. There were no welfare benefits from the government or support from local authorities. In fact restrictions were imposed on the occupations we were allowed to follow.[21]

Kitty had told a *Guardian* reporter, Stuart Jeffries, in 2010 that 'My mother and I became very angry at being silenced'.[22]

Dianne Webber told me about a Jew in Brussels who went by the name of Jacques and drove around the city in a black Citroën identifying Jews and taking them to Gestapo HQ. He was eventually killed by members of the Resistance.[23] One family who were betrayed by him were the Blums – the testimony below by Nicole Helszajn is a translation from the French:[24]

> My Aunt, Antoinette Blum, known as Toni (my mother's sister) was arrested in the street because this Jacques was patrolling in his black Citroën and was arresting people to check their papers. He would do this because of people's appearances and racial 'exterior physical signs' that he recognised. This probably happened in 1942. My grandfather Maurice Blum was arrested at home where he was hidden with my aunt. After my aunt's arrest, the Gestapo had the address. My grandfather was deported to Auschwitz and immediately gassed as soon as he got off the train (according to the information I received from the museum, as well as with his identity card). My aunt was an experienced seamstress and she worked in a workshop making uniforms for German soldiers at the Kazerne Dossin in Malines not far from Brussels all the war. She would have seen her father get on to the train along with the others on the convoy (the windows of the workshop overlooked the platforms). I have a letter from the museum with the number of the convoy. The museum was established in the same Kazerne Dossin which was the assembly point in Belgium for Jews who had been arrested to be sent to the camps in convoys.

Toni Blum was obviously a slave labourer in the factory for the rest of the war. Malines (Mechelin) was a transit camp for Belgian Jews. USHMM states:

> A German military administration coexisted with the Belgian civil service …
>
> Belgian Jews were also rounded up for forced labor. They worked primarily in the construction of military fortifications in northern France, and also in construction projects, clothing and armaments factories, and stone quarries in Belgium.[25]

Manfred Landau (*b.* 1923) grew up in Berlin, attending the Jewish Kaiser Strasse School near the Alexander Platz. The headmaster there, Rektor Reschke, was Jewish but hated the Ostjuden – the Eastern European Jews, which included Manfred's family. Manfred told me that during the war Reschke worked for the Gestapo and used to pick Jews who were hiding in Berlin out in the street. He was protected by the Nazis all through the war.[26] The only other fact that Manfred was able to tell me about his headmaster was that six months after he left school in March 1937 he asked Reschke for a reference. He refused, saying he didn't know what he had been doing for the last six months.[27] Manfred came to England on the Kindertransport on 2 December 1938 and lives in London.

Through the internet I found quite a few references to Reschke. The first was of a sighting by Lothar Orbach (now Larry, born 22 May 1924), who was interrogated by the Gestapo in the summer of 1944 after being betrayed by a colleague, Siegfried Goldstein. He was taken to the former Jewish Hospital on the Iranische Strasse – it was known as 'the last stop before Auschwitz'. He was taken to the office of Kommissar Walter Dubberke who ran both the camp and the Search Section:

> Sitting at a desk in the reception area outside Dubberke's office, I saw a man who looked familiar. I said a name aloud, and was stunned when he actually glanced up at me. 'Rektor Reschke? Is that Rektor Reschke?' He was the former principal of the Jewish Grammar School on Kaiserstrasse. Could it be true that he was now collaborating with the Gestapo, trying to save his own skin by destroying the children he had taught? He kept shuffling his papers. When they dragged me past him, he tried to look right through me. I leaned over and spat in his face. He said nothing, just wiped the saliva with his sleeve. Didn't he know they were going to kill him anyway?[28]

It appears Larry was wrong about Rektor Reschke's fate. In fact, although he was imprisoned after the war he died, presumably peacefully, in his bed in August 1964, unlike most of those he betrayed. However, he was part of a major Gestapo organisation in Berlin – the Search Service – Fahndungsdienst.

A report to the WJC in Geneva declared:

The headquarters of the network of Jewish informants run by the Gestapo is located in Iranische Strasse. Some of the Jews are allowed to roam the streets without the yellow star and look for Jews who are in hiding, in disguise, or who have false papers. These patrols roam through the city streets and look for people they know. If they meet such and such a person they seem really delighted [to see them], but in the hours that follow – or the next day at the latest – the victims have already been picked up by the Gestapo and taken to Iranische Strasse, where there is a camp and where [deportation] transports are organised.[29]

This was the first mention of the Search Service, which was created after the round-up of the remaining Berlin 'non-privileged' Jews on 27 February 1943. This led many Jews into hiding, and thus there were only three groups of Jews left in the capital. They were those regarded as first-degree Mischlinge those in 'privileged mixed marriages' to non-Jewish partners, and those living in hiding illegally. They were known as 'U-Boote' – submarines.

When Propaganda Minister Joseph Goebbels declared Berlin Judenfrei in June 1943 several thousand Jews were hiding in the city and they were to be targeted by the Berlin Gestapo. In the summer of 1943 they were estimated to number between 3,000 and 4,000. By February 1944 there were about 2,000 left and 1,400 survived until the end of the Third Reich.

Following the example of the Viennese SS, who came to Berlin at the end of 1942, the use of Jewish police was established. They were called the Judenpolizei, or JuPo. In Vienna, the JuPo were forced to help with deportations and make sure no one tried to escape. They also had to establish where Jews who had failed to report for deportation had gone. In exchange, JuPo members were exempt from wearing the yellow star and given special papers.

When they brought the 'Viennese methods' to Berlin, three JuPo men came to initiate the Berlin Jewish community. The search patrol was set up in the assembly camp on Grosse Hamburger Strasse in the Mitte district, a former Jewish community home for the elderly – the building mostly held Berlin Jews waiting to be deported. The whole operation, including the Search Service, was run by the Gestapo Chief Commissioner Walter Dobberke, who was always looking for new Jewish informers in the camp:

His promise to potential informers was a powerful one: that he would make sure that they their [*sic*] families would go to Theresienstadt instead of Auschwitz. Members of the Search Service had their own rooms on the premises, which were furnished rather luxuriously, according to eyewitness accounts. They were granted green permanent certificates of passage that allowed them to leave the camp day and night, unsupervised and without the yellow star.

Harry Schnapp reported being invited by Dobberke to help. Many refused, others committed suicide. Those who accepted the offer hoped to help their families and improve their own chances. According to a 1946 list the Search Service consisted of eighteen people – the Jews in hiding called them 'greifer' (catchers, or snatchers).

Günther Abrahamson was one of the first to join up as Dobberke had asked the Jewish head of the camp, the ex-headmaster Reschke, to assign two people for special tasks. Abrahamson had to locate the addresses of hiding Jews, investigate and write short memos for Dobberke and also report verbally to him each day. He claimed:

> I seized [the offer] immediately, firstly because I saw it as the chance to get out of the hell of the camp system. But secondly [because] I had the instinctive feeling that here, in contrast to having to look on powerlessly as usual, there would be a chance to do something positive against the Gestapo.

In the summer a 'first-degree Mischling' and former First World War flak officer, Heinz Gottschalk, was assigned to work with him. Soon there was a third – Stella Kübler. Stella was undoubtedly the most famous and notorious greiferin, who roamed the streets of Berlin with Rolf Isaaksohn, whom she later married. Born in 1922, she was very attractive and intelligent, but also cruel and unscrupulous. At the end of 1941 she was called up for 'forced labour' at the Siemens-Schuckert firm in Fürstenbrunn. Her first husband, Manfred Kübler, was sent to work at the Wilhelm Banzhaf firm in the Pankow district and Stella's parents were forced to work at the firm of Erich & Graetz in the Treptow district. Stella was transferred there in early 1942 but, as a forced labourer, she received about half the normal pay for her shifts.

Stella and her mother were at work when the big February 1943 raid took place, and they hid in the cellar under a large cardboard box. They then had to go 'underground', but Stella's husband was arrested and sent to Auschwitz on the thirty-third transport and died a few weeks later.

To go underground you needed to organise an illegal existence, obtaining food and false papers and renting some half-safe accommodation. It was when getting her documents that Stella met Isaaksohn, but she was arrested by the Gestapo when she met him in a pub on 2 July 1943. She was badly tortured and although she later escaped she was recaptured. Again she was tortured, and as a result she made her first betrayal of an old college friend, Hellmann, around August 1943.

But another chum from college was a notorious passport forger the Gestapo were desperate to find, and Dobberke was in charge of the hunt. Just before she was due to be deported Dobberke made her an offer – he said he would spare her and her parents from the next transport if she delivered the forger. Thus, Stella became a member of the Search Service and her parents were held in the camp as hostages. However, she failed to deliver but was given further names and addresses. She was working on this for three months that took the victims to the assembly camp. When Jews were picked up, an infamous furniture van was used. The van had 'Silberstein' on the outside – 'Move out, Move in with Silberstein'.

She was empowered to work with the Gestapo and make arrests:

> As Max Reschke, the Jewish leader of the assembly camp, later recalled, Dobberke instructed him that Kübler could 'go to the camp leadership at any time without disturbance, may not be stopped by any camp, may not be stopped by marshals'. Reschke understood immediately what this 'extraordinary instruction' meant. 'After that we knew the score.' Stella was allowed to enter and leave the camp at all times, and had constant access to the SS and a special room on the premises.

After this Stella and Rolf hunted down Jews based on tips the Gestapo received from informants, both within and outside the assembly camps. They also had a card index at their regional HQ on Burgstrasse. These two were authorised to check the papers of people on the street. They would point out people to be bundled into the bogus furniture van lurking in the street nearby. Sometimes Stella offered to provide food or accommodation and if they accepted the offer she would bring the Gestapo to the arranged meeting place.

Since the 'searchers' had themselves lived illegally, they were familiar with the special difficulties facing the U-Boote. It was precisely this intimate knowledge of the living conditions of underground Jews that made them so useful as informants. They knew that many Jews went to public places in the evening, blending into the crowd in cinemas, theatres and opera houses, even though this was forbidden to Jews. On 16 December 1943 Stella and Rolf went to the Staatsoper Unter den Linden, where Rolf recognised members of the Zajdman family in the orchestra. They arrested Abrahm Zajdman and his son Moritz after the performance. Moritz tried to get away but Stella shouted, 'Keep him! Jew!' and passers-by caught him and dragged him back to the opera house by his hair. The Gestapo were already waiting, and father and son were taken to Grosse Hamburger Strasse.

The greifer lined their pockets with the possessions of the hiding Jews and, together with the Gestapo, they received food, tobacco and money as bribes for exemptions from deportations. It appears that considerable sums changed hands. Arnold Gerson reported in 1956 that he paid sums of RM15,000, RM35,000 and RM60,000 as bribes to Möller and Dobberke – the 'searchers' had RM10,000 for themselves. At Stella's trial on 9 October 1972, mention was made of how Rolf Isaaksohn enriched himself.[30]

Stella was spectacularly successful – she became the leading Nazi informer. She led the Gestapo to over 300 U-Boote, most of whom were former classmates or co-workers. It is reported that sometimes the authorities promised to save a relative off the deportation list every time the greifer brought in a new name.[31]

By the end of 1943 Stella was known as a Gestapo spy by the Jews in hiding and everyone warned friends about the 'blonde poison'. Acts of revenge were always a threat to the greifer. A resistance group was set up called the Society for Peace and Reconstruction (Gemeinschaft für Frieden und Aufbau – GFA) which was well informed about their activities. They wanted to stop Rolf and Stella, and a couple of plans to kill them, including poisoning Stella's coffee, were hatched but proved unsuccessful. So, in February 1944 the GFA turned to intimidation:

> Using a form from the Luckenwalde District Court, they prepared a phony death sentence for her, 'in the name of the German people', to be carried out by hanging. She was anonymously warned about continuing to work for the Gestapo and told that if she was seen on the street, she would be killed instantly. Hans Winkler and Hildegard Bromberg sent the letter by registered mail, with a copy to the Gestapo. The 'death sentence' had an immediate effect; Dobberke banned his agents from leaving the assembly camp for fourteen days. In late 1944, in response to the increased danger faced by members of the Search Service, the Gestapo apparently issued them with pistols.

The last transport to Theresienstadt on 23 February 1944 included many who had worked for the Search Service, employees of the Jewish Community and Stella's parents, Tony and Gerhard Goldschlag. Stella tried desperately to save her parents. She pleaded with Obersturmbannführer Möller to intervene but he refused, although he did promise she would be appointed an 'honorary Aryan' (Ehren-Arierin) after the Germans had won the war. However, Stella's parents were deported to Auschwitz and died there. Meanwhile, at the beginning of March 1944, the assembly camp (Sammmellanger) and Search Service were moved to a former Jewish hospital in the district of Wedding.

Stella's position became difficult and she wanted to stop, but Rolf wanted to carry on. To bind her to him, they were married with special Gestapo permission on October 1944 at the registry office in the Wedding district. Rolf carried on with his rounds with two other colleagues, as Stella was now regarded with suspicion in the team.

In April 1945, rumours about the liquidation of the camp circulated as Dobberke had received orders from Möller by telephone which had been overheard by the shoeshine boy – a 14-year-old detainee. The prisoners tried to persuade Dobberke that if he released them they would intervene on his behalf after the war. On 21 April 1945 Dobberke signed release papers for all the inmates. Meanwhile Stella and Rolf, with Kurt Bolz, fled with false papers using dead Gestapo officials' names on 17 April 1945.

In December 1945 Stella applied in Liebenwalde for recognition as a 'victim of fascism' (Opfer des Faschismus – OdF):

Her cover was blown during a check by the Berlin Jewish Community ... The person responsible for processing OdF applications in the Jewish Community was Alexander Rotholz, the very man who had once been commissioned by the GFA to observe Stella in the assembly camp and had been involved in drawing up the bogus death sentence against her.

Many people turned out to see her brought to the Jewish Community centre and the staff had trouble protecting her from vigilantes. The police handed her over to the Soviet secret police and she was tried at a Soviet military tribunal in May 1946 in Lichtenberg. She was charged with crimes against humanity and for distributing anti-Soviet propaganda. She was sentenced to ten years in prison. She said in her defence:

> When I read in the papers that I had allegedly brought tragedy to so many men, women and children, that really disturbed me. Then I spoke to my own conscience and I came to the conclusion that my only crime and the only thing I was guilty of was to have let myself be engaged as a Jew in an external service of the Gestapo. But I note that I entered this Gestapo service against my will.

However, a 'wanted' poster for both Rolf and Stella issued in March 1946 claimed they had betrayed 2,000 Jews between them.

Stella was imprisoned in various camps, where the conditions were poor and she caught TB. She was released in January 1956, but a further trial took place in 1957 because so many witnesses contacted the Jewish community wanting to testify. Stella was charged with accessory to murder as well as wrongful deprivation of personal liberty resulting in death. She was given another ten year sentence but it was not served because of time in custody and her previous sentence. A 1972 appeal confirmed the 1957 guilty verdict.

She committed suicide in 1994, aged 72. She never really showed any signs of remorse or guilt about what she had done and saw herself as a victim. She is quoted as saying late in life, 'The Jews said, furthermore, that they would much rather be picked up by Jews than by the Gestapo, since the Gestapo was far more drastic.'

Between 1943 and 1945 some twenty Jews spied for the Gestapo in Berlin in return for promises that they and their families would receive special treatment. Stella Kübler-Isaaksohn was the most feared and most well known. However, the Gestapo did keep some of their promises to the greifer. Some family members were sent to Theresienstadt Ghetto rather than straight to Auschwitz. However, they did not realise that the ghetto was merely a 'waiting room of death'. Usually the spies were deported to Theresienstadt first and then to Auschwitz. Only a few were protected until the end of the war and only three were tried. Others, like Rolf, disappeared without trace.

What can be concluded from these unpleasant activities?

> They were themselves subject to Nazi persecution, and certainly, many sought to improve their own situations by working with the Gestapo. But a whole range of other motives may have applied as well. The 'searchers' enjoyed some power in the camps and may have been able to influence the Gestapo's persecution policy in certain areas. They could, moreover, warn people of impending arrest and were even in a position to strike the names of some camp detainees from the transport lists. At the same time, they were authorised to make arrests on their own initiative; in most cases, this amounted to nothing short of the power to issue death sentences. An insidious feature of the National Socialist persecution was its ability to turn victims into the agents of their own destruction.[32]

Such activities were not unique to Berlin. In Amsterdam the Dutch police worked with the Bureau of Jewish Affairs to arrest Jews and take them from their homes – they were set up in February 1942 and wore black uniforms. One of them was Pieter Schaap, who arrested the Jewish Ans van Dijk (1905–1948) on 16 April 1943 at her hiding place. He pressed her to work for him as an informer. She accepted Schaap's offer and one of the first people she betrayed was her brother, Jacob. As a result, Jacob with his wife and three children were sent to Sobibór extermination camp where they were all killed on 9 July 1943. Following this, she betrayed a further 150 people. Eyewitness reports indicated that she liked the work and enjoyed the benefits – she had a regular salary from the Nazis plus 'head-money' for each person she betrayed. She also received presents from the bosses and they all stole from the people they betrayed. She is believed to have been on the periphery of the betrayal of Anne Frank's family.[33]

The *modus operandi* was the same as in Berlin. She was given a list of names and she tried to earn their trust by saying she was working for the Free Netherlands resistance organisation. She promised them a safe house to hide in, ID papers and ration cards to get food. She then arranged to meet them at the safe house where the arrest took place.

Ans also trained other Jewish women working under Pieter Schaap. After the war he declared, 'She was the best one I had!' Ans was executed on 14 January 1948 and Pieter Schaap on 29 June 1949 – both by firing squad.[34]

Additional information on Reschke was provided by Uwe Steinoff, who runs the Muehlberg Camp website. Reschke was born on 18 January 1894 and died on 30 August 1964. He was the son of a merchant and went to the Jewish Teacher Training Institute in Berlin 1911–1920. Those studies were interrupted by service in the First World War and time in captivity during 1914–1919. He became a teacher in Berlin 1920–1925 and from 1927–1942 he was the rektor at the Jewish school on Kaiserstrasse in Berlin. When the school was closed by the Nazis in July 1942 he went to work as a manager for the Reich's Association of Jews in Germany, which was part of the Nazi administration. In this capacity he became involved in the deportation of Jews and was dealing with the deportation of the stepmother and siblings of his wife. From July 1943 he was made a steward at the Grosse Hamburger Strasse assembly camp. In January 1944 he was made the leader when the previous leader, Werner Simon, was deported.

Apparently Reschke was brutally beaten up by SS officer Alois Brunner who was Eichmann's top aide. His anti-Semitism was so extreme that, as a young party member, he was picked to be Eichmann's secretary. Brunner is believed to have been directly responsible for the deaths of at least 130,000 Jews – he was the officer involved in deporting the Izieu children. After operating in Austria and Berlin, he was transferred to Greece, where he deported all 43,000 Jews in Salonika within just two months. In June 1943, he was sent to France to take over the Drancy transit camp near Paris from the French administrators. During fourteen months in France, Brunner sent an estimated 25,000 men, women and children to their deaths.

He escaped capture after the war and was never found, although he was known to be living in Syria, acting as an advisor to the Syrian Government with the alias Dr Georg Fischer. He had absolutely no remorse for his actions – many years ago he told the Austrian magazine *Bunte* that he had no qualms 'about getting rid of that garbage' and his one regret was that he had not killed more Jews. In a telephone interview in 1987 he told the *Chicago Sun Times*, 'The Jews deserved to die. I have no regrets. If I had the chance I would do it again …'[35]

Witnesses reported that Reschke ran the Grosse Hamburger Strasse camp with a rod of iron, insisted on discipline and was particularly harsh on escape attempts. The camp was moved to Iranische Street and he still had the same post. He had special permission to go home each evening to his own apartment at the Hackescher Market to stay with his wife and son, Daniel, born in 1930. Somehow, he managed to get him sent to a Jewish children's home, 'Beit Ahawah', run by Beate Berger in Berlin. These children were saved to go to Palestine (Israel), but after the war people knew what Daniel's father had done. Although no one blamed him, it was a burden for him.

On 22 April 1945 Reschke escaped from Berlin and taught in the Potsdam area in May–June 1945. He was arrested by the Soviet administration and sent to special camps. From March 1947 he was in Special Camp No. 1, Muehlberg, and in September 1948 he was sent to Special Camp No. 2, Buchenwald – the Soviets ran these camps on the site of the concentration camps. He was finally tried in 1950 and sentenced by the District Court of Chemnitz in Waldheim to twenty-five years in prison because, out of selfish ambition, he actively collaborated with the Gestapo and 'contributed to the persecution of enemies and victims of Nazi tyranny'.

In 1951, Rabbi Leo Baeck pleaded with Otto Nuschke, Deputy Prime Minister of East Germany, for clemency. Accordingly, Reschke's sentence was reduced to ten years and he was released on 31 December 1955. However, the BVN (the Union of Persecuted under Nazi Regime) were seeking witnesses to his actions in 1956 but nothing seems to have happened. He appears to have said at his trial that the camp leaders were 'bad representatives of the Jewish race with respect to moral and character'.[36] 'I just wanted to help my fellow Jews', he said at his trial in 1950.

In Greece, there were two Jewish brothers – the Recanati brothers from Athens, who were the most important Jewish traitors to the Germans. Only traitors could recognise the peculiar accent of the Ladino-speaking Jews of Salonika and the Recanati brothers were trusted by the Greek Jews because they spoke to them in Ladino. They could also identify Jews by their appearance and stopped them in the street, demanding items such as money, gold, watches and even shoes. Over 200 Jews were caught and handed to the Germans to go to the Haidari concentration camp in Athens.[37]

Maurice Soriano from Rhodes reported on Costa Recanati, whom he saw when all the Jewish men over 16 were told to report on 19 July 1944 to Gestapo HQ which was in the Hotel Soleil:

> A group of Germans accompanied by an interpreter, Costa Recanati, questioned us, examined us, took away our papers and finally imprisoned us in the same building. I noticed that the interpreter spoke Ladino fluently. Since I was the director of the Jewish community, I asked him how he had learned this language so well. He said that he had Jewish friends who spoke Ladino.

Maurice did not believe him. After they had been imprisoned overnight without food or water, Recanati and the Germans reappeared and they were told all families were to report the next day at 4.00 p.m. Recanati gave the instructions in Ladino:

> My dear friends, it is for your own good, if you don't want to suffer, to take with you all your savings. Savings in money, jewelry and gold so you will not die of hunger. I don't want you to reproach me afterwards for not having told you.

Maurice bribed Recanati to get him out because his wife was Turkish, but it is unclear whether Recanati did, as his wife had contacted the Turkish consul and he intervened for them and they managed to get away to Turkey.[38]

The activities of the Recanati brothers were corroborated by Lela Salmona (1918–2008, née Amiel) from Salonika, living in Athens in 1944. Her husband, Joseph Salmona, had been betrayed to Recanati by someone who owed him money and he came looking for Lela and her daughter, Marcelle, born in 1938. Lela was hiding with a Christian family called Halyvopoulos when one of the brothers (it is not known which) came for her. She said she did not wish to take her daughter and her host family were keen to keep Marcelle with them. But Recanati said, 'What sort of mother are you? Take her. She will be in a nursery whilst you are working.'

So the two of them went with Recanati, taking just blankets, to the German office in a former embassy where she saw her husband, who was crying and said 'Sorry.' The women were put in different rooms to the men and she saw a woman with a small boy. She had black lips and hands as she had been tortured to reveal the whereabouts of her husband but she did not know where he was.

The next day they were all sent on trucks, having to stand because they were so crowded, to the Haidari camp where they waited to travel on the last transport to Auschwitz with Jews from Corfu. Marcelle was killed at once and her husband also died. Lela survived and eventually found her way back to Athens in May 1945 when the cherry blossom was in flower. She eventually came to England in May 1946 where she married again and had another daughter, called Marcelle in memory of her first murdered 6-year-old daughter. It was that Marcelle who gave me the information on the Recanatis.[39]

I asked if she was still in touch with the Halyvopoulos family who tried to save her namesake. Marcelle said:

> Quite apart from the fact that all my childhood summer holidays were spent with them, my own 2 daughters have also spent time with them. In fact the entire Halyvopoulos family have been invited to both of my daughters' weddings. In reality, it would be true to say that they have become the Greek family that my mother so tragically lost in Auschwitz.[40]

Armando Aaron's testimony states that the Recanati brothers were sentenced to life imprisonment after the war. He was from Corfu and said that the last Greek transport arrived at Auschwitz on 16 August 1944.[41]

The final Jew in this chapter is Mordechai Chaim Rumkowski (1877–1944), the elder of the Lódź Ghetto. Lódź was the first Jewish ghetto in Nazi Europe, established in April 1940, six months earlier than the Warsaw Ghetto. It lasted four years and four months, until its final liquidation in July–August 1944. It was famous for having the most dictatorial Jewish Council, the most notorious elder, Mordechai Chaim Rumkowski, and an especially hated chief of police, Leon Rosenblatt.

Rumkowski was an unsuccessful businessman and a former orphanage director when, on 13 October 1939, the Nazis appointed him chairman of the Judenrät. All the holders of such office were in the same dilemma of trying to meet the Nazis' demands while endeavouring to protect the Jews as much as was possible.

Rumkowski was 66 when Lucille Eichengreen (born 1925 as Cecilia Landau), a German Jew, first met him. She had arrived in October 1941 with her mother, who starved to death in July 1942, and her sister Karin, who was taken away on a truck and murdered aged 12. The German Jews were a minority among the Polish Jews, who had been there some time. Jacob Zylberstein (1922–2012) explained that the German Jews found life in the ghetto hard because they came from more comfortable backgrounds. The Polish Jews like Jacob were used to a very low standard and coped better.[42]

The Nazis allowed the Jewish Council, known as the Ältestenrat or Council of Elders in Lódź, considerable freedom in running the Ghetto. They ran the factories, food distribution, the ghetto police and other services. Zylberstein explained:

> They got a special ration. They had special shops to go to and pick up their food, which was very nice. Enough to live quite comfortably. I was very angry that a selective part of people in the ghetto was supplied [that way] and the rest just ignored.[43]

Rumkowski looked like everyone's grandfather, but he had a bad reputation and Lucille was 'terrified'. She later found herself working in the kitchen with several other young women of her age. She was put to working out portion control in an adjoining office, which meant she got extra food. She had been warned by her previous boss using the Polish word for pig to describe Rumkowski.

Her boss was right. In almost every ghetto that the Nazis established the Jewish leaders behaved responsibly – but not in Lódź. Rumkowski was known to put people on the deportation list because he himself wanted to be rid of them, and he committed still more personal offences, as Lucille was about to discover.[44]

He came to visit the kitchen every evening and was very strict. If something was not right he would hit the waitress with his cane. He would then visit Lucille in the office and molest her. He wanted her to be his mistress and to put her in a private apartment. Lucille was distraught: 'I started to cry – I didn't want to move. I couldn't understand why anyone would want to do that ... But sex in the ghetto was very valuable – it was traded like you would trade anything else.'

Lucille was most definitely not a willing participant in this 'trade', but she was certain that if she did not let Rumkowski abuse her, then her 'life was at stake'. 'If I had run away, he would have had me deported, I mean that was very clear.'

Her story was corroborated by Jacob Zylberstein, who described Rumkowski's technique and confirmed he took advantage of young women. He described how he behaved when he saw another woman he fancied. 'We were all in the dining room and he just comes in, took a hand around her and just walks out with her. I saw that. Not anybody told me, but I saw that.' Zylberstein also believes that a woman's life might very well have been 'in danger' if she did not consent to Rumkowski's wishes. 'Personally I didn't like the man, I didn't like what he represents.'[45]

The kitchen was soon closed and Lucille was sent to a leather factory in the ghetto, making belts for the German Army. She never saw Rumkowski again but was left feeling damaged: 'I felt disgusted and I felt angry and I felt abused.' When the Lódź Ghetto was finally closed in 1944 Lucille and Rumkowski were sent to Auschwitz. Lucille, as a young woman, was sent to work and was saved by the defeat of the Nazis.

Rumkowski was regarded very unfavourably in the immediate post-war period, mainly as a result of survivors' memoirs such as that of Yehuda Leib Gerst, who wrote:

> Toward his fellow Jews, he was an incomparable tyrant who behaved just like a Führer and cast deathly terror on anyone who dared to oppose his lowly ways. Towards the perpetrators, however, he was as tender as a lamb and there was no limit to his base submission to all their demands, even if their purpose was to wipe us out totally.[46]

The general condemnation of members of the Judenräte during the early post-war period was exemplified by President Shamar in 1967 when he described him as being 'delighted to be in power' and 'gave the impression of a degenerate who drank up his power as a drunkard drinks his wine'. However, later research has been kinder to the Judenräte and Rumkowski.[47] In assessing him it is important to remember that he had three choices – to obey the Nazis' orders, to disobey, or to commit suicide, but the deportations would have continued whatever he chose.

However, where he had choices he often made harsh decisions without involving others and treated the ghetto Jews with 'arrogance and contempt'. It is suggested that his role in organising the labour in the camp has been exaggerated, as nothing would have been allowed without German approval. In addition, the Jews knew that the labour provided them with a lifeline and food and were therefore accepting it.

Primo Levi described him as in a grey zone:

> There are, however some extenuating circumstances. An infernal order such as Nazism exercises a dreadful power of seduction, which it is difficult to guard against. Instead of satisfying its victims, it degrades and corrupts them, makes them similar to itself, surrounds itself with great and small complicities. In order to resist, one needs a very solid moral framework, and the one available to Chaim Rumkowski, the merchant of Łódź … was fragile. His is the regrettable and disquieting story of … functionaries who sign everything, those who shake their heads in denial but consent, those who say 'if I didn't do this, somebody worse than I would'. It is typical of regimes in which all power rains down from above and no criticism can rise from below, to weaken and confound people's capacity for judgement, to create a vast zone of gray consciences that stands between the great men of evil and the pure victims. This is the zone in which Rumkowski must be placed …[48]

Even Rumkowski's death is controversial. Various versions are recorded. One version is that the Nazi command gave him a sealed letter for the head of the camp, assuring him he would receive special treatment. When they arrived, Rumkowski and his family were the first into the gas chamber.[49] Others report that a special car met the train and drove him and his family to the gas chambers. A final version is that he was beaten to death at the entrance to Crematorium No. 2 at the request of Jews from Lódź.[50]

Very few of the Jews who betrayed their co-religionists did ultimately save themselves, as most ended up as Nazi victims when they had served their purpose – betrayed in turn. The people who were thrust into roles of authority as a member of a Judenrät had little choice and mostly did what they could to alleviate their community's predicament to the best of their ability. None of us know how we would have reacted in their shoes.

# 5

# ATTACKS BY MEMBERS OF THE PUBLIC

Whoever avoids the Jewish Question is my enemy.

Dietrich Eckart (1868–1923), Hitler's mentor

As persecution spread Jews were vulnerable to attacks from members of the public – some were merely verbal but others were physical to varying extents. They could be attacks on them physically or on their homes, or even full-scale pogroms. The aspect that all have in common was that the person attacked had no recourse to any protection from the normal authorities such as the police or the law. The persecuted Jews were without the normal rights of a citizen and had no redress – this was a major betrayal.

Elizabeth Freund (1898–1982), an economist from Breslau, recorded her life in Nazi Germany while waiting for her emigration papers. After they had to start wearing the yellow star she was told about an experience on the city train in Berlin, where a mother saw that her little girl was sitting beside a Jew. 'Lieschen, sit down on the other bench, you don't need to sit beside a Jew.' At that, an Aryan worker stood up, saying, 'And I don't need to sit next to Lieschen!'[1]

Jews had not been allowed to own telephones at home for over a year, and Elizabeth wrote:

I go to the post office to make a call from a telephone booth there. I am scarcely in the booth when a woman rips open the door and drags me out screeching: 'We Aryans have to wait. The Jews are always in the booths. Out with the Jews! Out with all Jews from Germany!' It is such a terrible scene that I don't know how I got out onto the dark streets again. I was afraid she would rip the clothes from my body.[2]

In the autumn of 1941, Elizabeth and her husband finally got their exit permits, but they had a summons to the Gestapo in Alexanderplatz. They went to present their passports with the exit permits. The Gestapo official got their file and took out a piece of paper with writing on it – he tore it up. Her husband asked what it was and they were told it was their expulsion to Poland. The official then said, 'I'm glad you are getting out of it!' Elizabeth commented, 'So, Gestapo men are sometimes also human beings.' That was a Thursday, and they were due to leave on the Sunday.

Meanwhile, the first expulsion of Jews from Berlin took place during the night of Thursday–Friday. The police came around at eleven so that ordinary Germans did not see what happened. They were only allowed one small suitcase and were taken to a transit centre at the Levetzowstrasse synagogue. The Jewish Community had to provide nurses, doctors and aides as well as food, because food from home was not allowed. Elizabeth heard these details from eyewitnesses afterwards:

> It is a terrible night, with rain and thunderstorms. The synagogue is not big enough. The people have to stand in the yard for hours in the rain. The scenes that took place there are supposed to have been indescribable. Families were separated, married couples were torn apart, children dragged away, parents left behind. Already during the arrests, in the apartments, people took their lives. There in the synagogue it goes on. Body searches take place, suitcases are ransacked. All must turn in their identification papers, birth certificates, passports. Etc. Everything is taken from them that has monetary value, as well as soap, combs, shaving gear, scissors, brushes, everything that a civilised person needs in order to look clean and neat. They are supposed to become as neglected as the unfortunate Jews of the Polish ghettos, whose caricatures appear in the *Stürmer*.[3]

(This narrative was confirmed by Bert Lewyn in his memoir *Holocaust Memoirs: On the Run in Nazi Berlin*, where he described the terrible situation inside the synagogue and how he was forcibly separated from his parents.)

Polish Jews were used to being abused by members of the public. As early as June 1934, the following report came from Warsaw, Poland:

> A crowd of Jews were returning from the banks of the Vistula River after alighting from the ferry. They were surrounded by a larger group of hostile peasants, who proceeded to attack them in a brutal fashion. Later all Jewish shops in the township were targets for vandals, who destroyed windows and doors. In recent weeks raids on the Jewish population over Poland by Nara[4] anti-Semitic mobs have increased in frequency and intensity. Police action against them has been of little avail, and the number of Jewish victims is mounting. Today's edition of *Haint*, Yiddish daily, was confiscated by authorities for unstated reasons.[5]

*Haint* was a Polish Yiddish daily newspaper. It was founded in Warsaw in 1908 by Samuel Jacob Jackan, who was its first editor. From 1920 it was edited by Abraham Goldberg, and after 1933 by an editorial board. During the First World War it became a Zionist organ. It ceased publication when the Germans invaded Poland in 1939.[6]

Later in the year on 21 August there was a further report:

> Police today arrested twenty-four Naras, National Radical anti-Semites, operating illegally under the name 'National Revolutionary Camp'. The group, which included students and women, was believed by police officials to have been planning to continue the proscribed Nara activities on a large scale, particularly its anti-Jewish activities.
>
> The Naras, an offshoot of the older Endek anti-Semitic group, withdrew from the Endek party on the ground that the older group was not sufficiently anti-Jewish.[7]

Lilli Aischberg-Bing (1886–1983) was a resident of Nuremberg all her life until 1938. After the events of Kristallnacht, three phone calls from an anonymous friend warned them of danger and told them to leave. Fortunately, her two grown-up children were already in America. In her memoir she describes how she and her husband went for a walk one evening in December 1938 burdened by the need to leave Germany as soon as possible:

> I still see the beautiful city of Nürnberg, the ancient castle, the medieval walls and towers of the old fortifications covered with snow. When we were returning home and came close to our house, we saw three boys about 17 years old, standing across the street, throwing heavy, hard snowballs at our middle window.
>
> I have to explain that this window was quite beautiful. An artist had designed it when my father built the house, with the idea that it should be the home for the family for many generations to come. This is how we planned before Hitler came to power, never thinking how transitory everything is that man creates. The window was of stained glass, little pieces put together like in an old church window. The colors were white roses and green leaves. Well, as I said, they threw those snowballs at it and my husband wanted to go over and stop them, when I made it clear to him that they would beat him to death, that he must understand, that we stood outside the law and had no protection by the law. So we went into the house, went to bed, lying quietly nearly breathlessly, listening for a long time always a snowball followed by some shattered glass. I just mentioned that we stood outside the protection of the law. Can you imagine what that means? It took us a long time to understand, because the German judges before Hitler were unquestionably just and uncorrupted. It is unbelievable how quickly a hundred percent civilized institution can be changed.[8]

This story has resonance with one from the family of Rabbi Ernest Levy (1925–2009) in a small town in Hungary. His daughter, Judy Russell, gave me the story as her father told it to her:

> After the family was reunited in Budapest and they settled and made the best of their new lives. My father and his next older brother Alex, known in the family as Munky, occasionally went to visit their grandparents in the small Hungarian town of Papa. The boys were in their early to mid-teens.
>
> The grandfather was the Cantor in the Synagogue there and was a well-respected man in the village. He had been held in high esteem by not only the members of his own congregation but by the townsfolk. They still lived well in the early 1940s and had a maid who came in daily. The rumblings were beginning to affect them a little and by that time the Hungarian army had billeted a regiment of soldiers in the town.
>
> On this occasion Dad and Munky went to Papa for a few days and they slept in a small spare bedroom at the front of the house. The room was only big enough to hold the two single beds, the boys slept in with a passage between the bed into which the door opened. One evening the boys went to bed as usual as did the grandparents whose bedroom was in another part of the house. My father and his brother were woken up by a crash in the middle of the night and when they came to their senses they were aware of a draught and as they sat up cautiously in their beds they realised that a large stone had been thrown through the window. Fortunately it had landed on the floor between the beds and not on one of them but the window was completely shattered and there was fragments of glass everywhere. It was dark and they could see little but could feel the glass on their bed clothes etc. they were terrified to move as they did not have shoes in the room and the floor was covered in glass and yet they were wondering if more missiles would come through the window, What should they do stay or try to get out the room.
>
> Having chosen to stay they were afraid to call out and no one else had heard the crash and it was silent around them. They lay in the beds afraid to move until the sun began to rise and they knew that the maid would be arriving very shortly. As soon as they heard movement they started to call out and the maid opened their door to find them prone in the beds and glass and wood fragments everywhere and a very large rough stone lying on the floor.
>
> Had circumstances been different, as soon as the grandparents were aware of what happened they would have called the police. As it was the room was tidied, the beds were stripped, washed and well aired, the window was made safe and the incident was ignored. The grandparents and the boys were pretty sure that the stone had been thrown by young men going back to the barracks at the end of a night out. They also knew that even if the incident was reported nothing

would be done by the local police. They also felt it was better 'not to make a fuss' or 'keep their heads down and not complain'. Everyone was aware that it was not a good idea to put your head above the parapet even in this situation.

Dad mentioned other incidents having occurred and again the grandparents supporting this non-confrontational attitude. I perhaps am not expressing this well, as it was not a confrontation but things being left. I don't think he ever really expanded on the specifics of other incidents that befell his grandparents but I got the impression there were others.[9]

Boris Smolar (1897–1986) was an American journalist living in Berlin in the early days of the Nazi takeover. He sent regular reports to America for the Jewish Telegraphic Association (JTA). The Italian Ambassador in Berlin, Vittori Cerruti, was very popular with the Nazis. His wife, Elizabetta, was of Jewish descent, but she was convinced his status would protect her. One night, she was to meet him for dinner at Kempinski's – a fashionable restaurant. When her taxi arrived at the restaurant, the meter showed 2 marks and she gave the driver a 5 mark note expecting some change. When the driver didn't give her any she asked for it. He responded, 'You want 3 marks, you damn Jewess,' he yelled. 'You dirty Jews, first you suck our German blood and then you want our money!'

When she demanded he drive to the police station so she could make a complaint, he said the captain of the precinct was his best friend. 'He'll show you how dirty Jews have to behave.' He said to his chum, 'Look I've brought you a fresh Jewess who dares to demand money from me when she has certainly been exploiting us Germans all her life.'

The captain promptly began calling her names and when she asked if she could use the telephone, he said, 'We have no phone for Jews'. Even when she said her husband was the Italian Ambassador, they just laughed. Eventually, they did let her use the phone, thinking she was bluffing. They were stunned when shortly afterwards the ambassador arrived and phoned the German Foreign Ministry. The Chief of Protocol arrived and apologised profusely but the ambassador's wife wanted them punished. In the end it was agreed, each man would pay a fine to the Red Cross. Smolar commented, 'This was the happy end of the incident for Mrs Cerruti, the wife of Mussolini's ambassador to Germany. Had she been a German Jew, she would certainly have suffered a different fate. Sheer terror had been unleashed against the helpless German Jews.'[10]

Elizabetta Cerruti wrote a memoir and I searched it in vain for her version of this story. However, her insights on meeting, and sometimes entertaining, Hitler were fascinating. On 12 June 1934 Hitler made a state visit to Venice to meet Mussolini and was to stay at the Grand Hotel. The hotel manager asked her how best to please him. She told him to concentrate on the desserts because that was what Hitler really enjoyed. However, she told the manager that with the hotel's cordon bleu her instructions were somewhat superfluous. The manager, blushing, looked embarrassed, so she asked him what was wrong. He replied:

> 'As a matter of fact, our chef is a Jew; so I thought it would be better to send him to the Excelsior at the Lido for three days. Foreigners often have upset stomachs in Venice and if anything like that happened to Hitler here, we might be accused of paying a Jew to poison him!' He paled at the very thought.[11]

The meeting to discuss Austria's fate, held in Sra near Padua, was not a success. Hitler and Mussolini travelled together by car, but Hitler was uncomfortable in his brown gabardine and limp fedora, against Mussolini's smart gold-braided uniform. Opposition brought out the maniacal aspects of Hitler. 'It is my will, and the indomitable will of the German people,' screeched the Führer, 'that Austria become an integral part of the Reich!' Il Duce blasted back with Italy's equally indomitable resolve that Austria remain independent. Anxious attendants heard fists thumping, and increasingly frenzied rantings. Finally the door flew open and both men tramped through, not looking at each other, and they travelled back in separate cars.[12]

Lisa Tyre (1929–) from Vienna, wrote about the one incident that particularly upset her father the day after the *Anschluss*. Viennese always go to coffee houses, having their own coffee house with their own table and their waiter. Her father had a coffee house that he had been going to for twenty or thirty years, where he had his table and his waiter. The day after the *Anschluss*, when he went to his coffee house as usual the waiter looked at him and pretended not to know him. Her father said, 'Hello, Franz.' The waiter just looked at him, looked him up and down, turned over the lapel of his coat and showed a long-time Nazi membership button, saying, 'I don't wait on dirty Jews.'[13]

The Chiger family lived in Lvov, Poland, and the mother, Paulina, was made to work in the Janowska labour camp, making uniforms for the German Army for twelve hours a day in return for just two bowls of soup. They had to march several miles along the Janowska Road each way. She told her daughter, Krystyna, that was the worst part of the day. They had to march in rows flanked by Germans with rifles. If anyone fell out of the line they would be hit or shot.

One evening Paulina came back covered in mud and crying. Her daughter got a wet cloth and helped clean her up, asking who had done it. Paulina always tried to protect her daughter and merely referred to some 'bad people'. Later Krystyna discovered:

> … there was a group of Ukrainian children making mud balls and throwing them at the Jews. This was a game to these children! And my poor mother was made to suffer this torment without stepping out of line.
>
> 'Dirty Jew!' they shouted, 'Dirty Jew! Good for you!'

One by one, step by step, she was hit by wet clumps of mud. The mud was hard and filled with small rocks and other debris and it must have stung terribly when it hit her, but more than the pain was the anguish of the moment, the humiliation. Of course, my mother was not alone in this indignity; the other Jewish workers in the line was also under attack. But my heart ached only for her. More than once this happened. It made me very angry. My father, too. But what could he do about it? Shake his fists and shout? What could any of us do about it but continue on?[14]

In Vienna, following the 1938 *Anschluss*, Jews were attacked in the street in anti-Semitic riots. Jews were publicly attacked and beaten by pro-Nazi gangs. Elderly men were forced to strip naked and crawl about on all fours. Orthodox women were made to dance on desecrated Torah scrolls. One young Austrian Jew, Leah Sachs, reported seeing storm troopers urinating in a Jew's face before they savagely beat him. Others were seized by Nazi troops, forced to their hands and knees and ordered to wash the city streets, to the delight of jeering crowds of otherwise proper Viennese.[15]

Such behaviour was not limited to Vienna. Laa an der Thaya was a little town in northern Austria on the Czech border, with an established Jewish community. The first record of Jews in Laa was on '8 July 1277 when Emperor Rudolf affirmed the decision of Duke Leopold that the Jews in Laa needed not to be the servants of the other inhabitants of the town'. This makes it clear that there was a Jewish community in Laa even before 1277.[16]

Accordingly, in spite of some anti-Semitic incidents in the early 1930s they did not expect much trouble from the Nazis because it was their home. After the *Anschluss* Jewish shops were targeted, with Nazis blocking the entrances and posters declaring, 'Don't buy at Jewish stores'. Karola Österreicher wrote, 'A so-called Aryan took over our shop. Everything of value – the jewellery of my mother and the money from the shop – had to be handed over to our neighbour. Another neighbour removed the supplies from our stockroom for days and days.'

It was alleged that a woman from a farm outside Laa, unaware of the new restrictions, came to town and tried to go into one of the Jewish shops to buy something. 'The Nazis put a sign around her neck and marched her through the streets of Laa calling her names. The woman who told me about this in an interview is still too afraid to tell what was written on that sign.'

Before long, local newspapers were publishing rules on interaction with Jews. The following extract comes from an article dealing with correspondence and business dealings, published in *Laaer Nachrichten* on 13 May 1938:

### On public relations to Jews.

It has been observed that people from the farms do not know how to behave in relations with Jews of any kind. The following has to be said about this:

Regarding correspondence with Jews – which might be still necessary for any reasons – one should only write the address, but no formal greeting like 'honored colleague' or even 'dear business partner'. The factual part of the letter is to begin directly after the address and the name. At the end there should be no formal closing like 'yours sincerely' or 'sieg heil' or similar formulations. One should just sign the letter without any formal greeting. One should also not write 'dear Mr Pig-Jew' as was recently recommended. Regarding business dealings, there is one rule: members of the party are not allowed to have business dealings of any kind with Jews. This means that the Jewish merchant must be pushed out of business with all our might.

The notorious 'toothbrush cleaning' of streets also occurred:

Also in Laa the Jews had to clean the streets with toothbrushes. Caustic chemicals were mixed into the water so that the Jews' hands would be injured. And it happened more than one time that Jewish people had to clean the streets. Felix J. remembers such a situation: 'Shortly after the *Anschluss* all Jewish women were forced to clean all political anti-Nazi slogans painted on roads and walls. I understand that young Nazis, the pride of the new Austria, were looking on and jeering.

Felix, however, comments that there was a tiny ray of hope. His mother was forced to participate:

… in this outrage … but just beforehand one of my good friends invited me to a bike ride, and was rather insistent that I join him. I now wonder whether he tried to keep me away. It turns out, that this friend of mine became an SS-Untersturmführer [equivalent to a 2nd Lieutenant in the British Army] and died in Yugoslavia during the war. He may have known what was going to happen.[17]

The matter of Jews being forced to clean the Viennese streets has a surprising link with Margaret Thatcher. After her death in April 2013, I read in *The Times* obituary how her family had saved an Austrian Jewish girl in 1938. In her book, *The Path to Power*, she had written:

My family understood particularly clearly Hitler's brutal treatment of the Jews. At school we were encouraged to have foreign penfriends. Mine was a French girl called Colette: alas I did not keep up contact with her. But my sister, Muriel, had an Austrian Jewish penfriend called Edith. After the *Anschluss* in March 1938, when Hitler annexed Austria, Edith's father, a banker, wrote to mine asking whether we could take his daughter, since he very clearly foresaw the way events were leading. We had neither the time – having to run the shops – nor the money to accept such a responsibility alone; but my father won the support of the Grantham Rotarians for the idea, and Edith came to stay with each of our families in turn until she went to live with relatives in South America. She was seventeen, tall, beautiful. Well-dressed, evidently from a well-to-do family, and spoke good English. She told us what it was like to live as a Jew under an anti-Semitic regime. One thing Edith reported particularly stuck in my mind: the Jews, she said, were being made to scrub the streets.[18]

The girl's name was Edith Muhlbauer and, after living in Grantham for two years, she went to Brazil to live with her uncle in 1940. Fortunately her parents managed to get to Brazil too, but the rest of her family were exterminated, mostly at Auschwitz. When the story was published in 1995, the *Sunday Times* tracked Edith down – she was married with two children. Edith told the journalist, 'If Muriel had said "I am sorry, my father says no" I would have stayed in Vienna and they would have killed me.' In fact, Edith lived a long life – she died in 2005 aged 84.

Edith's daughter, Betina Nokleby, sent her condolences to Mark Thatcher when his mother died, so Mark responded with an invitation to the funeral. Betina made an eleven hour journey from São Paulo to London to be at the funeral and to visit Grantham, Thatcher's hometown. She said, 'It was an honour to be invited, but more than that it was an honour for my mum. Lady Thatcher and her sister saved her life, and she was always grateful to them. I would not be here, if they did not help.'[19]

In his funeral oration, the Bishop of London referred to Margaret Thatcher's religious upbringing. She had given a lecture at a nearby church and told her audience, 'We often went to church twice on a Sunday, as well as on other occasions during the week … We were taught there, always to make up our own minds and never take the easy way of following the crowd.'[20]

Another English woman, Christabel Bielenberg (1909–2003), married a good-looking young German lawyer in 1934 and lived in Germany throughout the Nazi period. Neither Bielenberg nor his girlfriend were interested in politics, and when they attended an open-air Nazi rally he led her away as Hitler rose to speak. 'You may think that Germans are political idiots,' he confided, 'but I can assure you that they won't be so stupid as to fall for that clown.' We know he was wrong.

The marriage took place as Anglo-German relations were deteriorating fast, and even on the way to the wedding Christabel's father stopped the car to offer her the chance to go to America. Afterwards, when she exchanged her British passport for a German one, an official at the London Embassy said, 'You have not made a very good swap, I'm afraid; except of course that this handsome fellow is included in the deal.'[21]

In 1933, Christabel and her husband-to-be were having a quiet drink in a country inn. There were three young Jews quietly drinking wine and talking at the next table. There were some storm troopers leaning against the bar who looked drunk and truculent. 'This place stinks,' said one. 'And I know why,' said another. Christabel sensed trouble and looked around for allies and realised there were none.

> The other citizens present were either gulping down their wine, hurriedly paying their bills or already halfway to the door. The Jews left quickly and Peter made sure they could get away whilst roars of beery laughter came from the bar.
>
> It was just another incident, and it was not the picture of the drunken buffoons in brown shirts which stuck in my mind for they were a sight we had got used to: it was rather the hurried scrambling to depart, the jostle of gutbürgerliche [middle-class] backsides, the sudden void. It was not the agitation but the acquiescence that shocked me … It was then that I too had the uncomfortable suspicion that something very nasty indeed might have come to stay.[22]

Some ten years later a woman whom she used to help with food ration coupons appeared at the front door with an extremely blonde young woman who was too hesitant to enter the house. Ilse explained that she was Jewish. The Gestapo had hammered on her door and she and her husband had removed the compulsory yellow star and fled down the fire escape. Since then they had been living in attics and cellars. A hairdresser had dyed her hair and recently a priest had given them space in his attic. However, 'some members of his flock, pious Catholics all, had recently been making discreet, but pointed enquiries. Since yesterday the good Father had felt himself and his house to be under surveillance.' He had not actually asked them to leave, but they knew they had to leave but had nowhere to go. The woman could pass as an Aryan but the husband looked very Jewish, so he would have to live in a cellar and only go out at night. Christabel did offer them help.[23]

In Budapest, Anna Sondhelm (1927–1997, married name Markus) said that during one night there had been a raid and a friend of hers had a terrible experience. She was staying with her parents and grandmother in a Swiss schutzpass house which should have been protected. She told Anna's grandmother and aunt in the morning that there had been an Arrow Cross raid at the house. She was 'lucky' because she was 'only raped' by the Arrow Cross men, but her parents and grandmother were taken to the Danube and shot. Anna's family were hit very hard by this as they had all lived together before and knew the victims well:

> She was absolutely beside herself and told us how it happened and told us how she could escape through a light shaft after she had been raped and she ran over in her nightgown to my aunt and uncle, Swedish House, whom she knew in the area. And ran and ran and ran.[24]

This is most significant testimony because about 20,000 Jews were shot into the Danube by the Arrow Cross, mostly taken from the ghetto during December 1944–January 1945. Sometimes they were tied together in pairs, so one bullet would take both into the icy water where they died because of the extreme cold in the harsh Hungarian winter. My mother had relatives and friends who were killed in this way and she always said, 'the Blue Danube turned red'. Today there are sixty pairs of metal shoes concreted to the banks of the Danube to mark where the Jews were shot into the river, leaving their shoes on the banks. The memorial was erected in 2005 on the Pest side of the Danube below the Hungarian Parliament. The fact that we all wear shoes makes this memorial both personal and universal. However, significantly, the plaque does not specify that the victims were Jewish and states, 'To the memory of the victims shot into the Danube by Arrow Cross militiamen in 1944–45'.

Another Hungarian, Mozes Schön (Mosche Shen in Israel), was born in Sighet in 1930 but in 1937 his family moved to Nagyvárad, my father's birthplace, in Hungary (now Oradea in Rumania). He described life in Hungary in the interwar period in an interview on 5 May 2004:

> Anti-Semitism was also apparent in Nagyvárad. Jews had been banned from certain professions; for example, they were no longer allowed to be lawyers, and the Jewish public servants were made redundant. Universities were given Jewish quotas. On top of the many legal restrictions, there was also hostility from the general population. As far as I could see, the Hungarians were more inclined towards anti-Semitism than the Romanians. Romania turned its back on its Jewish population, but the Hungarians themselves actually organised deportations to forced labour camps in Germany and to the death camps in what is now in Poland. I had already come across anti-Semitism as a child, 'Nice young boys' were always trying to pick a fight with us Jews. They used to abuse us by saying 'dirty Jews' or other curses like that. It was nothing out of the ordinary at the time.[25]

An incident in St Étienne in central France is more encouraging. St Étienne is 60km south of Lyons. It was an important manufacturing town surrounded by coal mines. One evening, a young woman, Marcelle Garnier (now Aune, *b.* 1925), was accosted by a young Jewish man after the curfew hour. He said there was a German patrol coming down the road and if they pretended to be a courting couple the Germans might ignore them. This is exactly what happened and while the patrol saw them, they did not stop.

Marcelle's father, Paul Remy Garnier, was a Communist and union leader in the local mines. He was known to the authorities because during the Spanish Civil War (1936–1939) he had taken supplies to the Communists. Marcelle was the eldest of five children and there were eight years between her and the next sibling. Her mother had died during a sixth pregnancy and Marcelle was left to look after the other four children.

Paul Garnier had already been questioned and imprisoned for short periods by the Vichy Government and the Gestapo, so he was concerned for the future. He had the younger children fostered and told Marcelle to find a job with accommodation as he expected to be taken away. She worked for a doctor, until he was taken away by the Germans – he was probably a member of the French underground. She then had a job at the Kursaal, a cinema owned by Jews. As she often finished work late, she had a curfew pass.

That was how she came to be walking home late when the young Jew saw her. He was being hidden by a chemist and she went back there with him because it would have been dangerous for her to be seen on her own after the incident. Additionally, by then her father was imprisoned in the Fort Mon Luc, run by Klaus Barbie, and was subsequently deported to Buchenwald, so she was very vulnerable. Her father died, but she never knew the date or the circumstances and only knew of his death when his fellow prisoners returned to St Étienne after the war.

The next morning, she went back to where she lived and never saw the young man again until after the war. One day when she was working at the cinema, he turned up with a small delegation of friends and some flowers to thank her for what she did for him that night. Marcelle was 88 when she told the story to her son, Jean Jacques. He believes a representative of the Jewish Community came with the young man. She cannot remember his name or that of the chemist but recalls that many of the shops around the Place du Peuple were owned by Jews.[26]

When I asked about the local attitude to Jews, I was told it was quite positive, but Jean Jacques said, 'she did say that they were unaware of the number of Jews until the beginning of the war when the deportations started'.[27]

However, the young Jewish man was lucky in his choice. Marcelle was used to her father's anti-Nazi activities and she was, therefore, perhaps more willing to help him than another young woman might have been. Had she not agreed, he might not have survived the war to walk round the town with his chums. Moreover, had the Germans chosen not to ignore the courting couple, things could have been very difficult for both of them. (See Photo No. 9)

My Polish friend, Aleksandra Kopystynska, 'Ola', told me this snippet – no names are known. A young Polish man found a Jew hiding in the forest. He was obviously hungry and so the Pole gave him something to eat, probably a piece of bread. He then killed the Jew because he thought it was his duty. The Pole was very young and thought he had been a good man because he fed the Jew first.[28]

Another betrayed Jew didn't even get fed. Max Dessau (1927–2003) recalled the story of the 'dog-catcher' whose name is unknown. One day around August–October 1940, the Poles rounded up the local Jews and took them to the woods to shoot them.

All were killed except for one man. He was almost naked but he managed to hide in a hole overnight and the next morning he approached the nearest home, which was the dog-catcher's, and asked for help. He covered him with a blanket and then tied him up and put him on his wagon. The dog-catcher handed the Jew over and he was killed – the dog-catcher's reward was about 1lb (500g) of sugar.[29]

'One day I was practically dead,' Max Dessau recalled of his time in the dreaded concentration camp, Dora. 'They had put me in a bag near the crematorium. Then there was bombing, and they went away. I was left alone.'[30] These stories demonstrate how large a part luck played in any Jew's survival. Had the dog-catcher been of a different disposition, the Jew who approached him might have been safe.

Jan Gross listed three curious incidents of Poles asking for items which they realised would be available once the current Jewish owner was killed. The speakers demonstrate a complete lack of sensitivity to the situation and do not show shame or embarrassment:

> ... a prosperous miller's wife from Radzilow, Chaja Finkelsztajn, describes [an incident] at the same moment as the mass killing of Jews was unfolding in her native village on July 7, 1941. Someone approached her with a suggestion that she turn over what she owned, since she would certainly be killed together with her family. And it was only right, Chaja's interlocutor argued without malice, for the good people who knew the Finkelsztajns to get their possessions, or else the killers would be rewarded.
>
> To a Jewish man trying to find a hiding place with a peasant acquaintance near Wegrów, the latter's son-in-law said matter-of-factly, 'Since you are going to die anyway, why should someone else get your boots? Why not give them to me so I will remember you?'
>
> Miriam Rosenkranz ... said that they were deporting us for sure: and then this [Polish] woman acquaintance looked at my feet [and the following exchange took place].
> 'Really you could leave me your boots, Missy.'
> 'But Mrs Joseph, I am still alive.'
> 'Well, I wasn't saying anything, only that those are nice boots.'[31]

There is a footnote to the Rosenkranz story. 'While still alive Jews were treated as if they were the temporary custodians of "post-Jewish" property.' These three stories exemplify a change in perception about the Jews and their property and suggest that there was a change in the views of private property rights. Gross comments that there is:

> ... a shift in shared norms concerning acceptable behaviour toward the Jews.
> To take Emanuel Ringelblum's formulation, it illustrates how the inhabitants of

Polish towns and villages ceased to perceive their Jewish neighbours as human beings and began to treat them as if they were 'the deceased on leave'.

The question of Jews and their property was addressed by Emanuel Ringelblum (1900–1944). He was a professional teacher of Polish-Jewish history. I was surprised to find that a man who was murdered in 1944 in Warsaw had addressed this issue, which I had considered mostly a post-war issue for obvious reasons. Although as a Pole he was writing about the situation in Poland, as we have seen, this situation was not unique to Poland:

> One of the most important economic matters in the field of Polish-Jewish relations was the problem of Jewish possessions and goods left with Poles for safe-keeping. This practice dated from before the formation of the Ghetto and was prompted by constant searches made by the Germans in Jewish flats. Then the only resort was to hand over these belongings to Aryans for safekeeping. At this time it was done on a mass scale. Belongings were given for safekeeping to former clients, partners and to Christian acquaintances in general. Goods had to be given to Aryans for safekeeping because of several anti-Jewish decrees – registration of all textiles, leather goods, etc. In many cases, the Jews entered into partnership with the Christians, handing over their warehouses and stocks on condition that the Jew should be a partner in the business. It usually turned out badly for the Jew. The war had demoralized people who had been honest and decent all their lives; now they appropriated the Jews' possessions unscrupulously, in most cases not wanting to share even part of them. The Jews were treated as 'the deceased on leave' about to die sooner or later … In an overwhelming majority of cases, perhaps 95%, neither goods nor personal belongings were returned. Stock explanations were usually given that the things had been taken away by the Germans, stolen etc. These Jewish belongings more than once supplied a motive for blackmail and denunciation. In order to eliminate an unwanted claimant, someone would turn him over to the 'competent authorities'.[32]

Gross adds to this what Ringelblum tragically could not have known, since he was arrested with his family on 7 March 1944, then tortured and murdered. It is believed he was betrayed by Jan Lakinski, a well-known informer who was later killed by the Polish Resistance. Ironically, Ringelblum could have been helped to escape by the Resistance but he would not leave his wife and son behind. Julian Hirszhaut, who saw him in prison with his handsome son, Uri (1932–1944), said Emmanuel asked, 'What is this little boy guilty of?'[33]

It was a common occurrence still, after the war, that Holocaust survivors would have to file suit in order to retrieve property that they had left for safekeeping with friends and acquaintances.[34]

It is also apparent that during the Holocaust many Jews were killed by Poles merely to get their hands on their property. Gross writes:

> Mass killings in the Podlasie region, of which the murder in Jedwabne was but one episode, were accompanied by widespread and thorough plunder of Jewish property. It would be more difficult to name those townspeople who did *not* plunder Jewish houses while their inhabitants were being incarcerated in a large barn on the outskirts of Radziłów, an eyewitness to the murders told a journalist sixty years later. Everybody seemed to be in the street grabbing what they could. Symbolically most evocative in this respect were probably the calls of pogrom organizers in Wasilków, who were running around and screaming: 'Don't break anything, don't rip it up. All this is already ours.'[35]

Radziłów was situated 10km from Jedwabne, and on 7 July 1941 (three days before the Jedwabne murders) several hundred local Jews were murdered by the local Polish people. It can be perceived that Jedwabne was a copycat crime, following the example of Radziłów. In both cases the local residents forced their Jewish neighbours into a barn which was then burnt with the Jews trapped inside.

In August 1941, Helena Klimaszewska moved from the Goniądz to Radziłów 'to get an apartment for her husband's parents because she knew that after the liquidation of the Jews there are empty apartments'. When she arrived, she was told that Godlewski decided what happened to 'post-Jewish' apartments. She went to see him and made her request. She later testified in court:

> Godlewski replied, 'don't even think about it'. When I said that Mr Godlewski has four houses at his disposal and I don't even have one he replied, 'This is none of your business, I am awaiting a brother returning from Russia where the Soviets deported him and he has to have a house.' When I insisted that I need an apartment, he replied, 'When people were needed to kill the Jews you weren't here, and now you want an apartment.' An argument that met with a strong rebuttal from Klimaszewska's mother-in-law: 'They don't want to give an apartment, but they sent my grandson to douse the barn with gasoline' [referring to the barn in Radziłów].

And so we are witnessing a conversation between an older woman and other adults that is premised on the assumption that one gains a right to valuable goods by taking part in the murder of their owners.

It appears that the grandson in question, Józef Ekstowicz, together with another youth, clambered onto the roof of the Radziłów barn into which several Jews had been herded by their neighbours. They then doused the barn with gasoline and it was set on fire with the Jews trapped inside.[36]

A smalltown schoolteacher from Luków was travelling on 5 November 1942 through the Siedliska village. 'I went into a co-operative store,' he wrote:

> Peasants were buying scythes. The saleswoman says, 'you'll need them for today's round-up'. 'What round-up?' I ask. 'Of Jews.' 'And how much do you get for a caught Jew?' I asked. Embarrassed silence. So I went on, 'for Jesus Christ 30 silver coins were paid, you should request as much.' Nobody answered anything.

As was noted in the case of Max Dessau's 'dog-catcher', the reward received by peasants for betraying Jews was a few pounds of sugar, some vodka or, most often, the victims' clothes. Sometimes the Poles could not even wait for the Jews to be killed.

The *Biuletyn Informacyjny* (Information Bulletin) dated 13 November 1942 carried a poignant article called 'Disgrace':

> From various localities, actually from all places where bestial murders of Jews had occurred, one hears that the Polish population participated in the plunder of victims of German killings alongside the Hitlerites … It turns out that frequently 'solid' citizens, 'serious' farmers, participated in these criminal displays … In some instances fights broke out between those human beasts who were awaiting their turn until miserable Jews got killed, so they could strip still warm bodies of their clothes and underwear. In a few cases, the cordon of Hitlerite murderers was broken, as people couldn't wait till the execution, and proceeded to undress Jews condemned to death while pulling from each other's hand pieces of clothing.[37]

*Biuletyn Informacyjny* was the main underground publication and was exceptional in that, throughout the occupation, there was not a single line with anti-Semitic overtones.[38]

In some places, the killing of Jews became a spectator sport. One man wrote about his experience in Liepaja in Latvia in July 1941 – he was the head of 2nd Company, Reserve Police Battalion 13. When he arrived in Liepaja, he heard about the execution of Jews. One day, they were still clearing up their quarters when some marines from the naval unit came past. They said they had heard that Jews were always being shot in the town and they wanted to see for themselves.

Later, on Saturday, 24 July 1941, he was out carrying out searches in the town when he saw a lorry with Jews crouching in the back being guarded by uniformed Latvians. He could tell they were Jews because of the yellow patches on their clothes. Out of curiosity he followed the lorry. He ended up near the naval port near the beach. He saw SS-Untersturmführer Kügler with some SD (intelligence branch of the SS) men and a number of Jews. The Jews were crouching on the ground. Then they had to walk in groups of about ten to the edge of a pit where they were shot by Latvian civilians:

> The execution area was visited by scores of German spectators from the navy and the reichsbahn [railway]. I turned to Kügler and said in no uncertain terms that it was intolerable that shootings were being carried out in front of spectators.[39]

## Post-Holocaust Attacks

Alice Herz-Sommer (1903–2014), who died at the age of 110, was the oldest Holocaust survivor. She was a victim of anti-Semitism in her home town *after* the war. When she returned to Prague with her son who had been ill, she discovered she was not welcome. She had come from a German-speaking family and after the war she found the native Germans had gone, having been beaten and, in some cases, killed. Herz-Sommer was forced to lie. She told the civil servant that they had spoken Czech at home, read Czech newspapers and her friends were all Czech-speaking.

They let her stay, but she couldn't move back to her home or retrieve her possessions. Everywhere she encountered terrible anti-Semitism and consequently she decided to leave and go to Palestine (Israel). The Czech authorities would not give her permission to take her new piano. It was only after she contacted her old friend Max Brod, the musician, that the President Klement Gottwald allowed her to ship the concert grand piano. However, when it finally arrived in Jerusalem, she found it had been left in the rain and the hammers had gone rusty.[40]

Her co-religionists in Poland were less fortunate, particularly in non-urban areas. Mejer Cytrynbaum was trying to recover a house and a large three-door oak armoire he had left for safekeeping with Polish peasants during the war. The efforts kept him near his native village. A memo from the Ostrowiec branch of the Jewish Committee to the voivodeship Jewish Committee in Lublin described the circumstances of the:

> … four children of citizen Mejer Cytrynbaum aged twelve, ten, eight and seven. For two and a half years these children hid in an underground bunker, without light or fresh air; one of them is sick with joint inflammation. After liberation they settled in Denków [where the family was from] but because of the hostile attitude of the local population [threats to their life] they were compelled to move to Ostrowiec. Because there are no [Jewish] schools in this district, the children cannot study. Sending them to a Polish school is totally out of the question. This state of affairs has a negative influence on the children's health and intellectual development but the committee has no chance whatsoever of doing anything about this.[41]

There were also issues over finding work, where Polish Jews found they were still being discriminated against. They were still being branded as Jews by local bureaucrats. One of the flagship weeklies of the periodical *Kuźnica* carried the following article on 14 October 1945:

> The Third Reich is no more. Nobody knows what happened to Hitler. Himmler and Goebbels took poison. But Jewish identity cards have reappeared – in the reborn, democratic Poland. Let's be precise. It's not so much identity cards as labor certificates issued by the Regional Labor Office in Dąbrowa Górnicza City Government, a round stamp is visible with the letter 'J' – Jew ... Who are the people responsible for this horrendous Hitlerite scandal in a Polish state institution?

Dr Shlomo Herszenhorn, then in charge of the government office to help Jews, made a tour in February 1945 to inspect attitudes to Jews by local officials:

> In Kraków, he reported the top echelon of the administration was well disposed toward the Jews but 'the attitude of subordinate authorities was bad'. In Łódź the attitude of local authorities was 'not bad'. In Radom, despite pressure from the higher-ups, the executive organs of the administration 'were not friendly, [were] even hostile'. In Lublin voivodeship the local administration appeared to Herszenhorn 'generally correct' in its attitude except in Chelm Lubelski and Krzczonów, where 'street round-ups of Jews for compulsory labor were a frequent occurrence'.[42]

Mrs Nassowa, who was taking care of Jewish orphans, received a ration coupon from the head medical officer in Lublin, Dr Rupniewski, for 20 litres of cod liver oil. When she went to collect the oil, which was a precious supplement for the vitamin-deficient winter diet, the woman in the health centre refused to give her the oil when she gave her the coupon. She said, 'So this is why I was trudging for three months to collect fish oil, so that Jewish children would get it. I won't give them any fish oil.' Mrs Nassowa reported the incident the day it happened – on 9 December 1945.[43]

However, none of this prepared the Holocaust survivors for the events of 4 July 1946 in Kielce. The Kielce Pogrom consisted of a mob of Polish soldiers, police officers and civilians who attacked and murdered Jews. It is regarded as the worst outburst of anti-Jewish violence in Poland after the Holocaust.

A particularly sinister aspect was the accusation that Jews used the blood of Christian children for ritual purposes, often with reference to making matzo (unleavened bread) for the Passover. This is known as the 'blood libel' and dates from twelfth-century England. On 1 July 1946, a 9-year-old boy, Henryk Blaszczyk, had left home without telling his parents. When he came back on 3 July, he told his parents and the police, presumably to avoid punishment, that he had been kidnapped by Jews and hidden in the basement of the local Jewish Committee building on 7 Planty Street.

That building provided shelter to 180 Jews, as well as housing various local Jewish institutions. As local police went to investigate, the story began to unravel because the building had no basement. However, a large group of angry Poles collected outside, including 1,000 workers from the Ludwikow steel mill. People fired at the Jews in the building, killing some of them. Outside the angry crowd beat Jews trying to escape the shooting or driven onto the street by the attackers; again some were killed. At the end of the day the mob had killed forty-two Jews and injured forty others. Two non-Jews died as well.

Three days later, the Jews buried the victims in a mass grave in the Jewish cemetery. The government ordered members of the military and local residents to attend the funeral as a sign of respect. Although the government executed nine of the attackers on 14 July following a hasty judicial investigation, the Kielce Pogrom created enormous fear in the post-war Polish-Jewish community. In the three months afterwards 75,000 Jews left Poland in the mass westward migration called the 'Brihah', meaning 'flight' or 'escape' in Hebrew.

In autumn 1946 the Polish authorities tried civilians, soldiers and police for participation and complicity in the killings. Among the defendants were the commander of the Kielce office of the security service, Major Wladyslaw Sobczynski, and the chief of police, Colonel Wiktor Kuznicki, as well as his deputy, Major Kazimierz Gwiazdowicz. Of the three only Kuznicki received a one year sentence and the other two were acquitted. Shamefully, the Kielce Pogrom became a symbol of how precarious Jewish life was in Eastern Europe in the period after the Holocaust.[44]

What happened to Jews in Poland after the war may not be, intrinsically, much of a story. That a quarter of a million people were no longer welcomed by the majority population in the country their ancestors had lived in for centuries was not very unusual by the standards of the epoch. As ethnic cleansing goes, the murder of some 500–1,500 people should not have raised many eyebrows, either. As to flight into exile, those Jews who ran away from Poland, for the most part successfully resumed their lives in Israel, Canada, the United States, Australia and various countries in Western Europe and South America – certainly a lucky denouement by twentieth-century criteria. And yet, half a century later, we ask ourselves, 'How could there be anti-Semitism in Poland, of all places, after Auschwitz?'[45]

# 6

# INDIRECT OR DIRECT COMPLICITY

Should one make accountable only the visible political and military figures of the regime who are now assembled in the hotel-prisons? What about the thoroughly guilty stratum of intellectuals who stood and served National Socialism?

Thomas Mann, writing to Joseph Pulitzer, newspaper publisher, summer 1945

All who knowingly take part in deportation of Jews to their death in Poland or Norwegians and French to their death in Germany are equally guilty with the executioner. All who share the guilt shall share the punishment.

President Franklin Delano Roosevelt, 1944

Professor Dr Hugo Sinzheimer (1875–1945) was a successful assimilated academic lawyer who had escaped to Holland in 1933 with his wife. They spent the war in hiding, nearly starving to death. In 1945, he wrote to his colleague Dr Ernst Fraenkel (1898–1975):

We would never have thought possible the bestiality, the loathsome meanness and genuine anti-humanity the Germans were capable of. What we experienced here and saw before our eyes was a new variety of Man, a variety whose nature is determined by the fact that it has expelled the notion of 'fellow human being' [nebenmensch] from its inner self. Naturally, I would never think of blaming the entire German people. I believe that the main responsibility for what happened lies with those circles which form the so-called German elites: officers, professors, teachers, doctors, advocates ...[1]

Raul Hilberg's (1926–2007) Jewish family fled Austria for America just in time in 1939. He became the pre-eminent Holocaust historian in the immediate post-war period and devised the categories of 'perpetrators', 'bystanders' and 'victims'. He wrote:

> The Holocaust was not the product of a single will, not the work of a single monolithic organization. Nothing is so astonishing about this event as the fact that in its component parts it was ordinary as could be. It is only the configuration that stands unprecedented in history.
>
> The participants in the destruction process were lawyers, accountants, physicians, engineers, diplomats, bankers, clerks. They ran the gamut of modern, organised, specialised society. In my research over nearly 30 years, I have met them through their documents. But there has been a precarious lack of documentation about an integral part of the destructive machine, the German railroads ...[2]

Hilberg was studying chemistry when he was called up to the US Army and in 1945, aged only 19, he found himself in Munich confronting Hitler's crated personal library. It changed his life, and he went home to study the Holocaust at a time when very few were doing so. He was the first to claim that the Holocaust resulted from a huge bureaucratic machine with thousands of cogs, not just one preconceived plan or single order from Hitler:

> As unaccountable separate instructions were passed on, formally and informally, to a range of actors who included train schedulers and gas chamber architects, responsibility became ever more diluted, he argued, even as the machinery of death churned inexorably ahead.[3]

Hilberg was interviewed in 1992 by *The Chicago Tribune* when his book, *Perpetrators, Victims and Bystanders*, was published. It contained:

> ... a collection of word portraits of otherwise anonymous men and women upon whose labours the Holocaust depended. Among them were not just the street thugs who provided Hitler with his original following, but educated people and professionals. Accountants and bookkeepers drew up the contracts by which Jews were forced to surrender their property before being sent to the concentration camps. Architects and engineers worked on blueprints for the gas chambers.

Hilberg commented:

> The work was diffused in a widespread bureaucracy, and each man could feel that his contribution was a small part of an immense undertaking. For these reasons, an administrator, clerk or uniformed guard never referred to himself as a

perpetrator. He realised, however, that the process of destruction was deliberate, and that once he had stepped into this maelstrom, his deed would be indelible.[4]

Commenting on Oskar Gröning's admission of responsibility at his 2015 trial, Efraim Zuroff said he was the first Nazi he had heard admit remorse. Zuroff, who has spent thirty-five years at the Simon Wiesenthal Centre tracking down suspected Nazi war criminals, continued that there is 'no difference' between those who actually physically killed Jews and those who were in an administrative role:

> The person who directly committed a physical murder is far more easily iden-tifiable as someone who is culpable, but we know from history that Holocaust victims were the victims of desk murderers. Bureaucracy went to work to help carry out the Final Solution.[5]

However, Gröning made a distinction between his admitted 'moral guilt' and 'legal guilt', which he did not accept. Zuroff, commenting during the course of the trial, said:

> … since his role was of an accountant, a conviction will validate the important fact that one did not have to pull a trigger or push someone into a gas chamber to be considered complicit in Nazi war crimes, and that the revised German prosecution strategy also applies even to those like Groening, whose hands may not literally be full of blood, but whose actions nevertheless facilitated the shred-ding of rivers of blood by others.[6]

However, ten years earlier Gröning had admitted that as a member of the Hitler Youth in the 1930s he was involved in the book burning. He also described his time in Auschwitz with great joy. Apparently he enjoyed the facilities provided for the SS – the canteen, cinema and theatre. Gröning stated that, when he left Auschwitz in 1944:

> There were dances – all fun and entertainment …
>  I'd left a circle of friends who I'd got familiar with, I'd got fond of, and that was very difficult. The special situation at Auschwitz led to friendships which, I still say today, I think back on with joy.[7]

I wonder whether he ever thought about what his jolly friends had been doing all day, or the starving Jews a few yards away?

His trial concluded on 15 July 2015 with a sentence of four years in prison. Judge Kompisch stated, 'Mr Gröning knew exactly what was going on at Auschwitz, he stated very honestly that he never expected anyone to survive.' He then said to him, 'What you, Mr Gröning, described as moral culpability and being a cog in the machine, this is exactly what the law means when talking about aiding and abetting.' He was found guilty of aiding and abetting in the murder of 300,000 Jews from Hungary from May to July 1944. My grandfather, Armin Klein, was probably among them.[8]

# Railways

## German Railways

Hilberg became obsessed with the railways' role in the Holocaust. In 1976 he published an article in which he stated:

> The railroads, however, were involved not on the fringe of the operation, but were indispensable at its core. Year after year they transported millions of Jews to the mysterious 'east' where the victims could be annihilated quietly, out of range of peering bystanders and prying cameras. The Reichsbahn carried on under increasingly difficult conditions, almost without letup.[9]

However, the stash of documents he expected to find covering all these millions of journeys could not be found by the Allies and so the role of the Reichsbahn was never raised during the Nuremberg Trials:

> Among the many hundreds of defendants and witnesses – SS officers, generals, bankers, civil servants, diplomats and doctors – not one was a railroad man. The very subject of the Reichsbahn was hardly even recognized in the thousands of transcript pages accumulated in the trials.

The German railways employed 1.4 million German employees in 1942 plus 400,000 in occupied Poland and Russia. In 1977 Hilberg described a meeting with two railroad workers in the railway HQ in Frankfurt. He met them in 1976 and the older one was 60 or so – he told Hilberg that he started in 1938. He was very patient and considerate as he explained the system. Hilberg asked, 'Did he know anything about Auschwitz? "Yes." Had he been there? "Yes." On one of the pilgrimages? "No it was during the war. I put up the signal equipment, the lights." There he stood, courteous, well-mannered, considerate. He was the perpetrator!'[10]

The fact was that decent men like this chap created the Holocaust by making decisions and moving bits of paper. They were not psychotics, they were law-abiding family men. Hilberg said the railways did their task of moving Jews from their home towns to the killing centres and, by carrying on as usual, nothing was changed:

The SS had to order the trains and pay for the passengers, so much per track Kilometre, children under ten at half fare, children under four went free, one way to Auschwitz, Treblinka, Bergen-Belsen. The SS chafed under the cost and elaborate organisation which had to be set up to fund these transports. Jewish community funds were siphoned off, deposited into special bank accounts and used by the SS to make the payments. Finally, the railroad said all right, if you will send a minimum of 400 people, we will charge you half price fare. It was the railroads, not the camps, that did the body counts to calculate the fare![11]

The Reichsbahn would transport anyone for payment – the price was based on the number of travellers and distance covered. In 1942 the third class was 4 pfennig per kilometre of track. Children under 10 were half fare and under 4 were free. The trains were requisitioned by the SS and the Police, through the Main Office where 'resettlements' were headed by Adolf Eichmann. However there was a minimum charge of 200RM (Reichsmark).

Generally there were about 1,000 to fill a deportation train, but this was later increased to 2,000.[12]

There were issues when trains had to cross different currency zones. The first railway on the first segment of the journey was responsible for payment for the whole journey and had to get the money back from the other countries. There were particular problems with the deportation of the 46,000 Jews from Salonika which cost nearly 2 million RM, and confiscated Jewish property was to be used to back the payment, but the situation was complicated by the need to use RMs which were limited in Greece.[13]

Hilberg said that in mid-1942 there were 850,000 freight cars in the network and 130,000 were moved each day for different purposes, with the army having priority. Passenger trains ran to a timetable but freight ran as required. The Jewish transports were special trains, but under the jurisdiction of the passenger trains they had no priority, particularly with military transport. The conditions were terrible – suffocating stench in summer or freezing in winter.

'A German guard captain on his part complained when his men had to ride in an unheated coach. He had high praise, however, for Red Cross ladies who handed hot beef soup to the police as the train passed through icy Lithuania.'[14]

The Jews crowded into locked trains with no water may have remembered the words of Isaiah 41:17, 'When the poor and needy seek water, and there is none, and their tongue faileth for thirst, I the Lord will hear them, I the God of Israel will not forsake them.' As Hilberg wrote:

In the locked cars, mothers cried out for water for their parched children. But the trains were shunted aside every time an armed forces train rode by … So the train would arrive, five or ten percent of its 'cargo' dead. Payment was still the same, live or dead. Not one railroad worker was ever tried ...[15]

Everyone was complicit, yet no one accepted responsibility.

## French Railways: SNCF

Between March 1942 and August 1944, SNCF transported 76,000 Jews and other 'undesirables' through France to Nazi concentration camps. This included US and Canadian pilots who had been shot down in France – they were put on SNCF trains and set to Buchenwald and Auschwitz, rather than the prisoner-of-war camps.

The carriages were packed in tightly to maximise the number of passengers and therefore the revenue. The SNCF employees forced everyone – including young children and the elderly – to stand for the whole trip, which would last several days. There was no food or drink and no sanitary facilities – these were terrible, inhuman conditions. One SNCF train left the French concentration camp at Compiègne on 2 July 1944 with 2,166 passengers. When it arrived at Dachau three days later, 536 people had already died. The SNCF employees cleaned the carriages and disposed of the bodies.

In America there are many survivors and their relatives who can protest about SNCF, but they are diminishing each day and SNCF has never acknowledged its role nor made any restitution. Even though the Nuremberg Principles made it clear that coercion is not a valid defence, SNCF claimed that it was coerced into operating the deportation trains. This is not supported by the facts or historians. Recent studies and tribunals have found that SNCF collaborated with the Nazis. Christian Bachelier's 1996 report for SNCF found that it retained responsibility and for control of the deportations, including the technical conditions.

The Lipietz court case confirmed that SNCF made no objection or protest about the convoys. The court pointed out that SNCF's own agents had blocked the openings of the cars, made no provision for any water, food or minimal hygienic conditions, and presented no evidence that it was under any duress whatsoever that might have excused such acts.

SNCF even submitted invoices for the deportations after the liberation of Paris (and after which any conceivable 'defence' of coercion would have been nullified). SNCF's willing collaboration is particularly tragic because, according to an article by Jochen Guckes entitled 'Le Role de chemins de fer dans la deportation des Juifs en France' (*Revue d'histoire de la Shoah*, January–April 1999), SNCF's refusal to co-operate, even by means of passive resistance, would have been a catastrophe for Germany.

It appears that only one SNCF employee ever refused to participate in the deportations. He was a train driver called Léon Bronchard (1896–1986). On 31 October 1942 he refused to take a train with Jewish deportees from Montauban to Germany, and about two months later he refused to take a trainload of German soldiers. He was arrested and deported to a concentration camp with his oldest son, who was aged 20. Léon survived and returned to France after the war. He died in 1986 and was recognised as Righteous Among the Nations in 1994. Yad Vashem stated, 'To the best of our knowledge, Léon Bronchard was the only railway worker in all of France who dared refuse to transport Jewish deportees.'[16] He was also awarded the Legion of Honour.

It is clear to say that Bronchard was not a typical train driver. In June 1940 when the armistice was signed, Bronchard was living in Brive-la-Gaillarde, a town in the Vichy-controlled zone. Bronchard was opposed to the Vichy regime for both ideological and humanitarian reasons.

In November 1942 Bronchard was living next door to a family of Polish Jews called Rosenberg. They had emigrated to Paris in 1920 and three of their four children were born in France, but they had not acquired French citizenship. They fled from Paris to Brive. Rosenberg and his son joined the Resistance, leaving Mme Rosenberg and her three daughters at home in Brive. Bronchard saved their lives by providing forged identity cards that were so convincing that the 17-year-old daughter, Paulette, was able to work as a courier for the Resistance, carrying documents and information. Bronchard also helped Adolphe Strykowsky, a Polish-born Jewish friend of the Rosenbergs who was being hunted by the Gestapo. Bronchard lent him a railway uniform and then took a train to pick up Strykowsky about 3km from town and took him to safety in Grenoble, which was under Italian control:

I think the incarceration in the camp with his son was as a result of his Resistance activities. The records say that the punishment from SNCF was a brief suspension and loss of his Christmas bonus. It would therefore appear that SNCF could easily have refused to collaborate in the murder of Jews. Instead as Georges Lipietz stated, they went out of their way to help the Nazis with unprecedented 'misplaced relentless professionalism'. During the war, despite all the shortages of everything 'there were always trains available in France to deport the Jews'.[17]

Alain Lipietz reiterated his father's views that SNCF's actions were based on 'inhumanity, opportunism and misplaced professional devotion'. He refers to a document from the winter of 1942–1943, in which a German railway official wrote that, as trains were in such short supply, the orders for deporting the Jews were to be halted temporarily. However, an SNCF official wrote back that 'local arrangements' could be made so that the all-important removal of the Jews could continue at the usual rapid pace. Lipietz also draws attention to a plaque at Clermont-Ferrand commemorating the last convoy on 20 August 1944. It reminds posterity of the terrible truth that, more than two months after D-Day,

French railway personnel were still hurrying Jews out of France even when German troops were no longer there enforcing deportations.

The Lipietz family tried to sue the SNCF based on the experience of Georges Lipietz, a French civil engineer who died in 2003, and his half-brother, Guy. In 1944, the Lipietz family was transported from Toulouse to the camp at Drancy. From there they were sent to concentration camps where many of them died. Georges Lipietz had been born in Gdansk in Poland and had come to France in the 1920s with his family to escape Polish anti-Semitism. His son, Alain, was born in 1947 – he is a former member of the European Parliament and an economist.

It needs to be remembered that SNCF was charging the Nazis the cost of a third-class ticket for each Jew transported to Auschwitz. Not only does this have a whiff of immorality about it, it is also fraud. The quality of the cattle trucks and the horrendous conditions meant that SNCF was defrauding the Nazis in their accounting – the charge should have been considerably less than a third-class ticket. As Georges Lipietz said of his journey from Toulouse with his family in 'jam-packed wagons usually employed for livestock', they were shunted to the Gare d'Austerlitz in Paris on a journey lasting thirty-six hours without food or water. Georges Lipietz later described it as 'how the SNCF turned us into cattle'.

Quarterly bills for the transport were presented from the SNCF to the 'Transportation Ministry of the Interior'. Invoices show that the company was demanding payment for 'Provision of transportation to Camps of Internment, Centers of Supervised Stays, Interned and Expelled Persons, etc.' On 24 October 1944, Invoice 45,313 demanded 210,385.9 francs for the first quarter of 1944 from the prefecture of Haute-Garonne. This invoice was being presented *after* France had been liberated, but the SNCF was not going to miss out.[18]

Justice was achieved for the family when they were awarded €61,000 in June 2006. Justice was denied, however, in 2007, when it was dismissed on appeal through a technicality.

In 2010 SNCF took itself across the pond and bid for a $45 million contract for a new 800 mile high-speed railway in California. The same year, a public apology for SNCF's wartime deeds was made by the chairman, Guillaume Pepy. In 2011 he made another apology. However, in December 2011 it was announced that Holocaust survivors in Florida had succeeded in getting the state's education committee to refuse a donation of $80,000 from SNCF America for a programme on France's role in the Holocaust. They had argued that since SNCF had refused to pay reparations to its victims, this donation was merely a PR ploy to get the valuable contract.

Austrian-born Governor of California Arnold Schwarzenegger vetoed legislation brought by Bob Blumenfield which would have forced SNCF to disclose fully its role in transporting Jews to the death camps. However, Maryland has introduced such legislation, the first in the USA, and that would please the soul of Georges Lipietz who died in 2003.

In 2012 Blumenfield reported that an SNCF representative told him firmly that:

> 'SNCF will never pay the survivors anything' and that that [*sic*] 'would rather not do business in California' than take any such actions.
>
> Rather than finally take responsibility for its role in the Holocaust and in the death of tens of thousands of people and to finally pay reparations it owes its victims, it appears SNCF has decided to do just the opposite. This type of conduct … is shocking and alarming.[19]

Leo Bretholz, born in Vienna, Austria, in March 1921 to Polish-Jewish parents, gave testimony to the US House Foreign Relations Committee on the conditions on the train. He said:

> For the entire journey, SNCF provided what was one piece of triangle cheese, one stale piece of bread and no water. There was hardly room to stand or sit or squat in the cattle car. There was one bucket for us to relieve ourselves. Within that cattle car, people were sitting and standing and praying and weeping, fighting.

In a recorded interview held by USHMM, Bretholz recalled his escape through a cattle car window. It was 6 November 1942 when he was on Convoy 42 – a train bound for Auschwitz, with 1,000 people including children. After twenty-four hours of the wretched journey, an elderly woman waved her crutch at Leo and persuaded him and another young man, Manfred Silberwasser, to escape from the train – she said that at least if they escaped they could tell their story. Using spare clothes soaked in the human waste on the floor to strengthen the fabric, it took them a whole day to work on the rusty iron bars. They were desperate to escape before they got into German territory, Bretholz later explained. Eventually they escaped through a window and jumped off the train.[20] Having escaped seven times during the Holocaust, he survived to go to the USA in 1947 and was actively involved in the fight against SNCF's US subsidiaries:

'In the name of the SNCF, I bow down before the victims, the survivors, the children of those deported, and before the suffering that still lives,' said Guillaume Pepy, SNCF's chairman, during a ceremony at a railway station in Bobigny, a Paris suburb on 25 January 2011. The company was giving the station to the local authorities for a memorial to the 20,000 Jews deported from there to Nazi camps, between 1943 and 1944.[21]

On 20 June 2012, Samuel Rosenberg (Sandy) spoke at the hearing of the US Senate Committee on the Judiciary about 'Holocaust-Era Claims in the 21st Century', in favour of the Holocaust Rail Justice Act (S.634). He referred to his pride in the law passed in Maryland which should result in 'long awaited transparency from SNCF'. He also stressed that ten years had passed since SNCF's victims had sought accountability:

> So far, SNCF has been successful in escaping responsibility by claiming it is an arm of the French Government entitled to foreign sovereign immunity.
>
> I was shocked to learn that SNCF succeeded in evading jurisdiction and had a suit dismissed from French Administrative court based on the argument that it was performing a *private* function when it deported countless thousands toward their certain death. In the US, however, SNCF argues just the opposite – that it is an arm of the French Government, to once again evade the jurisdiction of the courts. That SNCF has succeeded in ducking accountability by advancing these contradictory arguments is unconscionable.
>
> Leo Bretholz and his fellow survivors deserve truth, justice and accountability from SNCF. It is appalling that some 67 years after the Holocaust, SNCF still refuses to accept full responsibility for its actions.[22]

At 93, Leo was still waiting – the elderly woman who encouraged him to escape chose well. He did her and the other 1,000 people on Convoy 42 proud. Sadly, Leo died on 8 March 2014 after I had written this section, but the fight continued. In December 2014 agreement was finally reached between the USA and France on compensation for the SNCF involvement in deporting 76,000 Jews to the French–German border in seventy-six cattle cars from 1941 to 1944. German trains later took the deportees to Nazi death camps.

Stuart Eizenstat, the US Special Advisor on Holocaust Issues, said, 'This is another measure of justice for the harms of one of history's darkest eras', after he had spent three years negotiating with the French.[23]

## Hungarian Holocaust Victims Sue Nation's Railways

In 2010 an American lawyer launched a lawsuit on behalf of Hungarian Holocaust survivors – the suit targets the Hungarian State Railways for transporting hundreds of thousands of Jews to their deaths, charging it with 'complicity in genocide'. Anthony D'Amato, who specialises in international law, sued the railway for the theft of victims' property and not their deaths. At the federal court, he stated the Jewish deportees had to leave their belongings in their suitcases at the trackside when they were taken to Auschwitz. 'As soon as the train left the station, railroad employees and their friends leaped upon the piles of suitcases, tearing them open with knives and pliers, and grabbing every valuable item,' according to the suit.

Apparently, international law limited America's ability to sue foreign governments or a state-owned railway, as in this case, for the death or suffering of loved ones. However, this doesn't apply to property. The lawyers sought $240 million in damages based on 5 per cent of the estimated wealth of Hungarian Jews on the eve of the Holocaust – an educated guess of how much victims could have put in their suitcases en route for the camps.

Peter Black, senior historian at USHMM, commented that although Germany paid reparations after the war, other countries, particularly those like Hungary which were under Soviet control, were reluctant to acknowledge a moral responsibility and financial one. While many questioned the likely success of such a case, Black thought the case had merit. 'It makes the point of how many people profited by the Holocaust – moving into victims' apartments, taking over their businesses. It was a tragedy that brought benefits to many bystanders.'[24]

The case was heard, with others concerning banks, on 27 August 2012. Its decision referred to the fact that although the genocide in Hungary didn't start until 1944 the country had already introduced a series of laws to limit Jewish economic influence. Jews had to hand property over to government officials and a special account was created to centralise and pool funds from frozen Jewish accounts. It stated, 'Hungarian banks – both private and public – allegedly froze Jewish assets to prevent their escape from the country. Those who survived death camps returned to find that their homes had been sold and safety deposit boxes looted.'

The plaintiffs were seeking to hold the banks and the railways liable under American law for 'genocide, aiding and abetting genocide, bailment, conversion, constructive trust and accounting'. The court accepted that genocide was a violation of international law and the alleged actions of the banks and the railways clearly qualified. Judge David Hamilton's opinion was that:

> Expropriating property from the targets of genocide has the ghoulishly efficient result of both paying for the costs associated with the systematic attempt to murder an entire people and leaving destitute any who manage to survive.
>
> The freezing of bank accounts, the straw-man control of corporations, the looting of safe deposit boxes and suitcases brought by Jews to the train stations, and even charging third-class train fares to victims being sent to death camps – should be viewed, at least on the pleadings, as an integral part of the genocidal plan to depopulate Hungary of its Jews.

However, in the seventy-six page decision it was stated that domestic remedies needed to have been exhausted before the case came to a US court. Alternatively, it needed to be demonstrated why this could not be done.

Whether these cases stand a chance of achieving any success is not known, but they serve the purpose of airing the issues of culpability of the unknown faces behind the Holocaust and reminding the world of what was done to the victims at the time, and subsequently.[25]

Recent research on 'Escapes from Deportation Trains' shows that 764 people escaped like Leo Bretholz. They had to contend with other issues – such as other Jews in the train fearing being shot as a reprisal for an escape, or leaving family members behind. Many people never spoke about their escapes.

One Belgian woman, a member of a Trotskyite Resistance group, Claire Prowizur (*b.* 1923), was with her husband, Philippe Szyper, when they escaped from the train stopped by Robert Maistriau.[26] She felt guilty because she had left her terminally ill father on the train. She only found peace twenty years later when she met a woman who had been in the same cattle truck. She told Claire that her father opened his eyes and whispered, 'I'm the happiest man because my daughter left and is free.' He died before they arrived at Auschwitz.[27] When she landed from the train with her husband, she felt terribly calm. 'I closed my eyes … I simply allowed myself to live without moving for a few moments, fearing to inhale too much the breath of freedom.'[28]

## Police

The role of the police in assisting with the round-up of Jews will always be controversial. We should remember that when three Jewish women were ordered to report for deportation on Guernsey in April 1942, that order was made by policemen wearing the traditional uniform of the trusted British 'bobby'. Therese Steiner told the officer she would never see him again and burst into tears – she knew her fate. Nevertheless, the three Jewish women were deported and died in Auschwitz.[29]

After the war, Gilbert Michlin returned to France and tried to explain his experiences following his arrest by the French police:

All the government employees who had signed arrest orders, police officers who implemented them without any compunction, railroad workers who transported people to their deaths, all carried on their lives after the war without even a second thought. I was ashamed of this country that refused to face up to its past, and I knew that the anti-Semitism that had promoted these infamous laws was not dead.

For all these reasons, leaving became imperative.[30]

After the war Gilbert found the papers relating to both his arrest and his mother's, during the night of 3 February 1944. The papers were held at the Center of Contemporary Jewish Documentation. They were signed by a man called Hennequin who was the director of the 'infamous municipal police' – Gilbert called him 'France's version of Adolf Eichmann'. The policemen given this task were told they were arresting 'Jews and Jewesses who were foreign or without a country whose information was attached'. However, there was an additional comment – Gilbert noted it thus:

> But a slight subtlety was added: among those who were to be arrested were 'all Jewish members of the family, particularly children under the age of sixteen, even if there was no file card on them'. In other words French Jews as well. This was my case.[31]

Another French boy also experienced his mother dying at Auschwitz. In 1989 Isaac Levendel contacted Serge Klarsfeld, who helped him contact Gaston Vernet, an old neighbour from his childhood who told him about his mother's arrest:

> Gaston had reiterated several times that my mother had been arrested by *two Frenchmen!* They had spoken perfect French with the southern accent of Marseille, and had worn leather jackets and fancy felt hats … This was a shock because, for all these years, I had believed that my mother's arrest was the work of the Germans, thanks in part to Claire Steltzer's bitter words to her mother after our return to Carpentras: 'There is nothing you can do. The Germans did it.'[32]

His mother had a friend, Madame Sokolowski, who was orphaned in a Russian pogrom as a girl. She had a strong survival instinct and a healthy mistrust of gentiles. Her husband was well educated and initially believed that 'here in civilised France, there will be no danger for us'.[33]

Kristallnacht, in November 1938, forced people to reconsider their own position. Were there non-Jews willing to oppose and intervene? 'Similarly, we must consider the role played by local government officials – be they police, firefighters or other civil servants – who often struggled to balance professional integrity against the pressure to carry out orders that they recognised to be immoral and illegal.'[34]

Kristallnacht forced German civil servants, especially policemen and firemen, onto the horns of a dilemma. Trained and sworn to uphold the law and to keep the community safe, they received explicit orders during the pogrom to refrain from doing their jobs. Throughout Germany on 9 and 10 November, most German policemen did exactly as they had been ordered, which was to stand by and do nothing. The same held true for firemen, though some of them were called into action only when the flames from a burning synagogue threatened surrounding structures. In at least one case, in Heldenbergen, firemen were called in to dismantle a synagogue because a fire would have been too dangerous. Civil servants responded to their orders with obedience, if not necessarily always with enthusiasm.[35]

Around 9.30 p.m. on Kristallnacht, after Hitler had left the Old Town Hall, Goebbels stood up and spoke to the Nazi officials present. No record of his instructions exists, but afterwards it was reported that he said Jewish businesses were to be targeted and synagogues set on fire. The police were not to interfere and firemen were only to protect Aryan property.[36] Later, at 11.59, the Munich Fire Department recorded the first case of arson on a Jewish site, a clothing store owned by Hans Weber.

Willie Nowak (*b.* 1908) from Berlin wrote about Kristallnacht:

> I was called in the morning by a German Christian friend who told me that I shouldn't go out on the street … I told him that I will because I want to see what's going on. So he went with me and we were standing right on the other side of the street, looking at the burning synagogue, at the prayer books laying on the street, the Torah scrolls laying on the street burning … On both ends of the synagogue on the street were policemen standing and firemen. Nobody did anything to kill the fire. They just let it burn …
>
> They didn't do anything to save the synagogue or anything else. I listened to the comments, the laughter of the people among whom I was standing. I was very upset. My friend had to hold me back because I wanted to jump in and save at least the Torahs, or a prayer book, anything. But he held me on both arms … trying to calm me down, not to start anything.[37]

Willie does not specify which synagogue he was watching, but we do know about the saving of the beautiful Oranienburger Strasse Synagogue in Berlin, built during 1859–1866 in the Moorish style as the main synagogue for Berlin, seating 3,000. Bismarck attended its inauguration in 1866. Albert Einstein, a fine musician, gave a violin concert there in 1930.

During Kristallnacht the synagogue was set on fire – the sacred Torah scrolls were desecrated and furniture was smashed. Many Germans were in the street watching and a psychologist, Joachim Krueger, speculated how easy it would have been for them to put the fires out if they were minded to, but putting out fires was the job of the fire departments. 'Most fire departments did appear on the scene, but instead of putting out the flames, they idly stood by, simply making sure the fires did not spread to non-Jewish buildings.'

Kaiser Wilhelm I had granted the synagogue legal protection. Wilhelm Krützfeld was the chief of police for the synagogue's area and he held the document. He knew what the Nazis were doing and when the fire started in the synagogue, he appeared with his men with the Kaiser's grant in one hand and his pistol in the other. He ordered the Nazis to leave and told the fire department to put the fire out. Both groups obeyed.[38]

It is a fine story of courage and moral behaviour – except Krützfeld wasn't the hero – it was Lieutenant Otto Bellgardt, a junior police officer. According to Regina Scheer, the story was based on an eyewitness report. Hans Hirschberg was 27 when he watched events with his father, a tailor. He remembered that his father, Siegmund, and the police officer discussed their time in the First World War, while the policeman supervised the fire brigade. Hans assumed it was Krützfeld, but he was not in the army during that war. Later, Inge Held, a neighbour and Hirschberg's sister, confirmed that the hero was Bellgardt. Afterwards, Krützfeld protected Bellgardt for what he had done, instead of reprimanding him as the Nazis demanded, and took the blame himself. Perhaps this is why Krützfeld is normally identified as the rescuer. Otto Bellgardt was killed during the war on the Eastern Front.

Some years ago a Baltic cruise took me to Riga and I found the synagogue by accident. The décor consisted of palm trees, which I had never seen before. An elderly gentleman who spoke some English showed me round. I asked how the synagogue survived during the Holocaust. He said that the back wall of the synagogue was shared with the church behind. The Nazis intended to destroy that synagogue, but the priest protested it would damage his church and so the Nazis desisted. There had been 40,000 Jews in Riga before the Holocaust but only about 150 survived.

Back home, I found it was called the Peitav Synagogue, because it is on Peitavas Street. Built in 1903–1905, it was decorated in the Art Nouveau style with ancient Egyptian motifs – stylised palm branches and lotus flowers. All the other synagogues in Riga were burnt down on 4 July 1941. The Jewish Community's website says:

> The Peitav Shul was the only synagogue in Riga to escape the common fate because it was located in the Old Town and there was a risk that the fire would spread to nearby buildings. During the war the synagogue was used as a ware-house. After the war it was learned that the eastern wall of the synagogue, where the bookcase with Torah scrolls (*Aron Kodesh*) was located had been concealed. This deed, which saved the Torah scrolls from destruction, is attributed to Gustavs Shaurums, a priest from the nearby Reformist church.

He must have been the one who stayed the Nazi arsonists' hands and prevented a complete betrayal of that community.[39]

## Polish 'Blue' Police

Jan Grabowski wanted to establish what happened in Poland away from the main factories of death. He undertook research in Dabrowa Tarnowska, a rural Polish county. He found German court files that had never been opened. There were 66,678 people in the county in 1939, of whom 4,807 were Jews – nearly 2,000 were farmers, but the rest lived in the town of the same name. The rural Jews lived with the non-Jews until 1942 when they were deported to Belzec, leaving behind 337.

Grabowski's research found that a further 286 were killed. Only fifty-one Jews survived, less than 1 per cent.[40]

A hunt for the Jews (Judenjagd) was organised to winkle out the remaining Jews by offering incentives – sometimes sugar or clothes, often stripped from dead Jews. Grabowski described the untold story of the Polish 'blue' police. This was the only uniformed, armed Polish police force working under the Nazis, using its local knowledge and its networks of informants to track down Jews.

A Polish doctor, Zygmunt Klukowski (1885–1959), kept a diary for 1939–1944. He noted that, when the SS left after the liquidations:

> … today it is the turn of 'our' gendarmes and our 'blue' policemen, who were told to kill every Jew on the spot. They follow these orders with great joy. Throughout the day, they pulled the Jews from various hideouts and, after robbing them, finished them off in plain sight of everyone.

If a Pole was fed up with hiding a Jew, he could hand him to the 'blues' who would rob and then shoot him and then tell the Germans. Grabowski found that while the Germans found and murdered seven Jews, 220 were denounced and killed by the locals or the Polish 'blue' police. When he started his research, the local synagogue was in ruins. It has now been restored by EU funding – however, no Jews are left.[41]

Klukowski's diary is famous because of his meticulous records. He was the director of the hospital in Szczebrzeszyn for twenty-five years. On 26 November 1942 he noted:

> The farmers are seizing the Jews in the villages, out of fear of possible reprisals, and are taking them to the town, or sometimes simply killing them on the spot. In general, there has been a strange brutalisation in relation to the Jews. A psychosis has seized hold of people, and following the German example, they do not consider Jews to be human, regarding them rather as an injurious pest that must be exterminated using all available means …[42]

Otto von Wächter (1901–1949) was the Nazi governor of Lemberg (now Lviv in Ukraine) and in 1942 sent the Jews of Galicia to the Belzec camp. His son, Horst (1939–), refuses to accept his father's responsibility, claiming, 'My father was a good man, a liberal who did his best. Others would have been worse.'

Philippe Sands is a professor of law at University College London, as well as a practising QC. He visited Horst in his home of twenty-five years – the 'Schloss Haggenberg', a seventeenth-century baroque castle north of Vienna. There Sands saw mementos of the Hitler years, including a book dedicated to SS-Gruppenführer Dr Otto Wächter 'with best wishes on your birthday', signed in deep blue 'H. Himmler, 8 July 1944'. A family heirloom – a token of appreciation for services rendered – 'a direct line between Horst's family and the Nazi leadership'. There are other photographs of the Nazi hierarchy including Hans Frank, Hitler's lawyer, who was Governor General of Poland and who was hanged at Nuremberg for the murder of 3 million Jews. These photos place Otto at the heart of the greatest international crime – and they are in Horst's family album.

Sands went to Lemberg to research his own family's story – his grandfather was born there in 1904. Lemberg was also the birthplace of two lawyers from the Nuremberg Trials: Hersch Lauterpacht, who created the concept of 'crimes against humanity', and Rafael Lemkin who invented the term 'genocide'.

Niklas Frank (1939–), son of Hans Frank (1900–1946), wrote a controversial book, *Der Vater* (The Father), published in 1987. He asserted that it was right to hang his father. This was the first time a high-ranking Nazi's child had condemned his father. Niklas suggested that Philippe might wish to meet Horst von Wächter. 'Horst takes a rather different attitude to mine.' They met a few weeks later at the schloss.

While Sands liked Horst, he realised that he struggled to come to terms with Otto's actions 'in a way akin to Austria's failure to fully recognise its role in that period'. Wächter worked closely with the SS policing the Jewish ghetto. Over eighteen months he supported the deportation and murder of just about every Jew in the area. The *New York Times* listed him as among the 'unholy ten', following the Polish Government in exile, as his speciality was 'the extermination of the Polish intelligentsia'. In August 1942 Hersch Lauterpacht's entire family were victims, excepting his 12-year-old niece, Inka, who told Sands how they were taken by the Germans, assisted by Ukrainians. Simon Wiesenthal claimed that Wächter was 'personally in charge' when his mother was sent to her death, but this is disputed.

Horst's father has blighted his life – the family were ostracised in Salzburg and this led to feelings of insecurity and the question, 'Was my father really a criminal?' Horst has coped by distinguishing between the system and his father, the individual and the group. 'I know that the whole system was criminal and that he was part of it, but I don't think he was a criminal. He didn't act like a criminal.' He had a list of excuses for his father and even claimed he saved Jews.

Horst claimed Otto 'knew that if he left Lemberg they would put some brutalist there, instead of him'. When Sands asks, 'More brutal than killing every Jew?' Horst has no reply. A document referred to the operation which sent 40,000 Jews to Belzec. Horst still could not condemn his father. Didn't this perpetuate his father's wrongs, asked Sands. Horst replied merely, 'No', blaming others – Himmler, the SS and Hans Frank, 'But not Otto von Wächter,' reflected Sands. However, Horst concluded, 'Indirectly he was responsible for everything that happened in Lemberg.'[43]

How very different from Niklas Frank. Interviewed by Andrew Nagorski of *Newsweek*, he said his father was a 'monster'. He added:

I'm against the death penalty, but I believe my father's execution was totally justified.

There isn't a day when I don't think about my father and everything the Germans did. The world will never forget this. Wherever I go abroad, and say that I'm German, people think 'Auschwitz'. And I think that's absolutely just.[44]

These two sons of leading Nazis met in London in February 2014 to debate the impact of their father's crimes – Philippe Sands was referee. Niklas lost his patience with Horst several times. However, Horst did acknowledge such a conversation could not happen in Austria, '[There] we don't want to know anything.' Coincidentally, both men were born in 1939, but Frank sees his father as evil and Wächter sees his father as a victim of circumstance. Apparently Horst wrote to Niklas saying it was time he came to peace with his father, but Mr Frank is haunted by photographs of the victims. 'It is my duty as a son to put things right.'[45]

Another relative of a Nazi took a different approach. Bettina Göring, Hermann's grand-niece, followed her brother and had herself sterilised at the age of 30, to end the bloodline. Her brother said 'I cut the line.'[46]

As a footnote, it appears that Richard Strauss, whose racial position was disputed, wrote a 'lost' piece of music in Hans Frank's honour in 1943 and it was recently reconstructed and played in the UK. Frank was praised as 'our friend' and 'saviour of Poland'.[47]

## Channel Islands

The Holocaust in occupied Europe demonstrated the Jews' betrayal by their fellow countrymen. This was done as enthusiastically in the Channel Islands, with its handful of Jews, as with the millions on mainland Europe. An August 1945 British Intelligence report recorded, 'When the Germans proposed to put their anti-Jewish measures into force, no protest whatever was raised by any of the Guernsey officials and they hastened to give the Germans every assistance.'[48]

Older readers in the UK will recall the 1980s television series *Bergerac*, in which John Nettles (later to find worldwide fame in *Midsomer Murders*) played a policeman on the island of Jersey. He made his home there and was embraced as Jersey's adopted son. This all changed in 2010 when he made three documentaries about the Nazi occupation of the Channel Islands (the islands of Jersey, Guernsey, Alderney, Sark and Herm) – the only part of Britain occupied by the Nazis. Nettles, a history graduate, had been previously unaware of the details of the occupation and only knew about a few German bunkers.

The adopted son was shocked when he received abusive letters and warnings not to set foot on the islands again. 'The islanders didn't like the way we talked about the Resistance, didn't like the way we talked about the collaboration or allegations of it and they didn't like the way we talked about the treatment of the Jews by the administration.' Aged 69, he published a book on the subject in 2012, even though he knew that 'you can't write about the occupation without upsetting somebody'. He realised, 'either I don't tell this story and keep my friends or I tell it and lose them all'.

The Nazis arrived in 1940 to islands with no defences, because Churchill thought the islands were impossible to defend, so no struggle occurred. The Germans decided to run the occupation through the existing government infrastructure as in France and were keen to pursue any Jews. In October 1941 notices were put in the newspapers in Jersey and Guernsey asking Jews to register with Clifford Orange, the Chief Aliens Officer in Jersey, and the police in Guernsey. Most Jews had already fled to the British mainland but twelve Jews registered in Jersey and four on Guernsey.[49]

The entire population of Alderney had fled, leaving 'half-eaten meals on the tables and pet dogs and cats running in the road'. Half of Guernsey's population fled, as did 20 per cent of Jersey's. Nettles dispelled the myths about the five-year occupation being 'a rather gentle, even benign affair', 'that the Germans kept within the terms of the Geneva Convention', and 'It was certainly uncomfortable but not horrendous. Unpleasant but not unendurable.'[50]

As elsewhere, registration was the first step to systemised persecution. Jewish businesses had to advertise themselves with a notice, 'Jewish Undertaking'. The businesses were then Aryanized – compulsorily sold to non-Jews. The Channel Island authorities didn't merely co-operate with this process, they actually administered it. Later orders, as elsewhere, restricted the Jews' permitted shopping hours and imposed a curfew on them. The only order which was contested in Jersey was the yellow Star of David with 'Jew' rather than 'Jude', which were ordered by Dr Casper, the German commandant, but never arrived. No one protested on Guernsey.

Nettles asserts that the truth was different. 'It is more morally complex, ambiguous and difficult. It is the story of a sustained and wholesale attack on human values, of great suffering, venality and violence.' The occupation resulted in curfews being imposed. Identity cards were issued and food shortages threatened starvation. Radios were forbidden, as elsewhere in Europe, which made islanders very isolated.

Sybil Hathaway, the Dame of Sark, invited the invading German officers to her home for a lobster dinner. Immediately after the war the British Government investigated all claims of collaboration and pointed to this as evidence of fraternisation and collaboration. In Guernsey, where Victor Carey was bailiff, the British didn't know 'whether to hang him or knight him, so mired in controversy was his tenure of office'. Nettles has defended many of the leaders who offered 'wise and resourceful leadership' but, as one Guernsey politician pointed out, the Germans always had a gun, so they had to obey. They did not encourage resistance because of fear of vicious reprisals.

However, the islanders doing the Germans' bidding in making lists of the birthplace of all residents had fatal consequences for some, as they allowed the Germans to arrest thousands who were sent away to camps and enabled them to identify the Jews. Nettles highlights:

> The Jewish question in the Channel Islands is one of the most difficult to address. People are deeply, deeply hurt by accusations that they are anti-Semitic, or that they were too much inclined to load the Jews onto the transporters.
>
> Their defence that 'we didn't know what was going to happen to them' seems to betray a lack of awareness that the Jews were a special case in the Nazi ideology. They were there to be killed and they were deserving, therefore, of the protection of the civil authorities. This is something they did not receive.[51]

Local lawyers had to determine the status of firms like Marks & Riches. If the majority shareholding was not in Jewish hands then the firm was not declared Jewish. The Attorney General became involved in examining the status of Harry Leopold Marks, as his holdings were only 49 per cent of the total number of shares issued and Mr Arthur Riches was managing director. The Attorney General decreed that, in view of this balance of ownership, 'then the business does not, in my opinion, require to be marked as Jewish. If, however, there are other Jewish interests therein to over 50 per cent, then, in my opinion, the business, should be marked as Jewish.'

David Fraser, a law professor specialising in the Holocaust, condemned these deliberations:

> The Attorney General here establishes and confirms the legalised normality of anti-Semitism in Jersey. The Aryanization process becomes, in the correspondence between Aubin and Briard, nothing more than another legal question to which traditional interpretive skills and mechanisms are to be applied. The question is whether, in addition to Mr Harry Marks, there might be some other Jewish shareholder whose interest would bring the legal mathematics of Nazi anti-Semitism into operation under Jersey Law.

The Attorney General further clarified how normal legal rules should operate by stating the relevant date was 1 July 1940, the date of the German occupation of the island, 'unless the German Field Command otherwise directs'. In the end the firm of Marks & Riches was declared a non-Jewish undertaking and was able to function all through the Occupation.

More important than the determination of the legal question of the owner-ship of Marks & Riches, however, is the tenor and tone of this correspondence between a leading island lawyer and the Law Officer. Legal rules apply, technical professional skills are to be deployed, operative dates to be determined, etc. There is no indication here, or elsewhere, in the extensive legal correspondence on the Aryanization process, that anyone stopped to question the moral and ethical basis and consequences of engaging themselves within a world of legalised evil.[52]

Nathan Davidson was born in Rumania in 1881 and spent time in Egypt where he was naturalised. When he had to register he had been living in Jersey for five years.[53] On 11 December 1940 the Bailiff of Jersey had to provide a list of 'Jewish undertakings' within seven days, providing 'the name of the proprietor, the nature of the business, a list of branches or sidelines, turnover and value of stock'. Clifford Orange provided the information on 18 December 1940 and Davidson's business was listed as: 'Mr Nathan Davidson, Groceries, fruit and vegetable store, 38 Stopford Road, St Helier; Sidelines newspapers; Turnover £250; Stock £10.'[54]

It was the most modest of the six businesses listed. He was offered the option of appointing an administrator or closing the business. He declared to Clifford Orange on 23 November that he was closing the business and that 'beyond a small banking account I have no other assets or property whatever'. On 11 January 1941 he was told by the bailiff that it had to be closed by 25 January. On 23 January he wrote to the Attorney General:

> In accordance with your instructions I beg to inform you that I have finished the winding up of my business … the blind on the window pulled down and a notice CLOSED displayed.

Mr and Mrs Davidson had to leave their home at the same time, since they lived above the shop. They moved to 59 Oxford Road.[55] Like the other registered Jews, he was under terrible financial strain because he had no income and no means of maintaining his family. On 18 January 1943 he notified Clifford Orange that he had sold his radio, confiscated on 11 September 1941, and asked Orange to hand it to the purchaser, a German officer. Jews had to give up their radios a year before the rest of the population.

The Davidsons were told they were to be deported imminently – the date was 13 February 1943. 'But the strain was clearly too much, and Nathan Davidson was admitted to St Saviour's Mental Institution on 25 February 1943. He died there on 29 February 1944, the St Saviour's Parish Register listing his cause of death as "maniacal exhaustion, insanity".'

On Jersey, Victor Emanuel (1870–1944), born in Germany, committed suicide by hanging in his home on 9 April 1944 and the coroner recorded, 'suicide whilst of unsound mind'.[56]

Nathan Davidson's story was tragic, but the postscript is worse because Clifford Orange was overzealous:

> Clifford Orange required a number of individuals to complete Jewish registration forms under the First Order of 1940 who did not strictly fit the definition of a Jew as specified in the German order. The order required that the civilian authorities register only those with more than two Jewish grandparents or who had belonged to the Jewish religion. Davidson had informed Orange that only one of his grandparents was to his knowledge a Jew ...

Orange completed the form and asked Davidson to sign it. Tragically, the fact of the matter is that Davidson did not need to register because under the Nazi classification, he was not a Jew.[57]

Additionally, it subsequently emerged that an order dated February 1942 stated that Egyptian subjects were nationals of the British Empire, and that too exempted Davidson.[58] It could be argued that an overzealous, or merely careless, civil servant killed Nathan Davidson as surely as if he had shot him with a gun. He was only 63 when he died – presumably not included in the 6 million. As with most victims of the Holocaust, Nathan Davidson and his wife suffered months and years of fear, humiliation, privation and stress before the end finally came.

## Będzin

Mary Fulbrook has written about Będzin (German name – Bendsburg), a small town some 25 miles from Auschwitz. The local civilian administrator was Udo Klausa whose wife, Alexandra, was a close friend of Fulbrook's mother. Both women were born in Berlin and were friends as teenagers but parted in the 1930s. Fulbrook's mother was a committed Christian of Jewish descent and left Germany where she had no future as she was married to a Jew. They ended up in England, but she corresponded with Alexandra until one of them died. 'Alexandra' is one of Mary's names and Udo's mother was her godmother.[59]

Mary Fulbrook is professor of German history at University College London. In her mother's papers, after her death, she discovered an unpublished memoir by Udo Klausa who had been the landrat (chief executive) of the landkreis (county) of Będzin. She admitted that although she was a German historian, she did not know what a landrat's functions were. Her family had always regarded him as involved in ordinary local government during the war.

In 1939, when the Germans invaded Poland, there was a population of 54,000 in Będzin, nearly half of whom (24,495 or more) were Jewish. Less than four years later nearly all the Jews were dead. Thus, a Jewish community which had existed in

Będzin since the beginning of the thirteenth century, following the gift of privilege from Casimir the Great to work as merchants, was virtually annihilated by the Nazis. After the war, Mordecai Lichtenstein, a survivor from Auschwitz, found only 160 Jews were registered on 15 February 1945 – he assumed even that figure was too high.[60]

Arno Lustiger recalled in 2008 that the Jewish high school of Będzin, the Fürstenberg Grammar School, proudly started each academic year with a procession led by their brass band to the Great Synagogue where they would be blessed by the rabbi. But not in 1939 – on 10 September:

> Within days, the Great Synagogue was set on fire, and, locked inside it and the surrounding houses, several hundred Jews were burnt alive, or shot dead as they jumped out of windows or sought to flee their burning homes. Local Polish people could hear the screams as Jews plunged into the water of the nearby river, in a vain effort to put out the flames, but were shot at if their heads popped up to get some air. Others were luckier, and found sanctuary in the nearby Catholic church. For days, the river ran red with blood; and people had to step over dead bodies in the streets between the ruins of the burnt-out houses.[61]

In Klausa's 1945 memoir, written when he was in hiding, fearing that he might be interned by the Allies, he claimed he only learnt gradually what was happening in concentration camps, and in fact it was the victors, the Allies, who told them. He felt he had not done anything wrong, nor had he any reason to be ashamed.

> Whatever Klausa's self-confessed motives may have been, it is also certain that many people did indeed just go along with Nazism out of a diffuse sense of not wanting to stand out against the herd, not wanting to miss career opportunities, not wanting to draw adverse attention to themselves.[62]

Klausa, as Landrat, was in overall charge of the gendarmerie under the leadership of Heinrich Mentgen, whom he supported. One former prisoner, David Auerbach, born in 1925, remembered Mentgen as one of the most violent men.[63] Fulbrook lists many of the activities he was involved in, which included the search for escapees from Auschwitz – which Klausa claimed not to know about. Although Klausa admitted he was around at the time of the Losien murders:

> There can be no doubt on the archival evidence that Klausa was both physically present and in charge of the area at the time of the Losien murders and highly appreciative of the way the gendarmerie was performing. Indeed, on file there is even a letter of 20 November 1942 from Klausa to the district leadership [Kreisleitung] of the NSDAP praising Mentgen and his work, which Klausa personally signed using the Nazi 'Heil Hitler' salutation.[64]

Klausa was also responsible for the forced labour camp at Golonog where the railway was being built. Three hundred Jewish workers were held here, guarded by police officers and members of the Sturmabteilung (SA) who reported to the landrat. Mentgen reported to Klausa about conditions on 18 April 1942:

> The camp is still without drinking water. The wash barracks is still being built. Sanitary and toilet facilities are available ... The Jews deployed here remain under constant guard. The camp is surrounded by a high wire fence to prevent anyone from escaping.

A survivor, Boruch Wadowski, reported soon after the war:

> Jews had been held together in primitive barracks, for a long time with no cooking equipment or facilities and very little to eat – small portions of bread, margarine and bitter black coffee, supplemented by a watery soup – and forced to do hard labour on railroad construction for eleven hours a day, from six in the morning until five in the evening.

However, Klausa never mentioned guarding the inmates and overseeing the operations at the labour camp in his memoir. It didn't affect his view of Mentgen as a 'decent' police official who 'would not tolerate any excess or transgression'. Again, overseeing a small camp of forced labourers was clearly just a routine part of what, in the Third Reich, was deemed to be 'only administration'.[65]

The Jews were put into a ghetto prior to 'evacuation' which would render Będzin Judenrein. During these plans the Jews were made 'self-sufficient' by relying on their own resources and distribution channels for the food they were still permitted:

> As Klausa noted in his report of October 1942: 'All *Jewish food shops* have been closed. The distribution of foodstuffs now takes place through larger distribution points that the Jewish Community has itself set up.' But there was not a great deal of food to be distributed. The Reich Minister for Food and Agriculture took a decision to cut rations for Jews even further, with effect from 19 October 1942, to near starvation levels. Jews were clearly now deemed to be barely worth feeding for very much longer.[66]

In her conclusions, Professor Fulbrook examines the events that Alexandra observed and/or was aware of – even wrote to Fulbrook's mother about – yet seemed in some way unable or unwilling to join up the dots about:

> Is my godmother's apparent incapacity to register the significance of what she

undoubtedly saw with her own eyes – effectively an 'eyewitness' while yet failing to 'bear witness' – in itself a critical clue, helping us to understand both how the Holocaust was possible and how so many Germans lived with the knowledge afterwards.[67]

She was 26 when she left Będzin in the late summer of 1943 – a relatively young woman. However, she was five years older than Sophie Scholl, who was killed at the age of 21 on 22 February 1943 for her opposition to the Nazis in the White Rose resistance group. The observation is made that Sophie at 21:

> ... had been able to perceive the fundamental immorality of Nazism even from her distant vantage point in the University of Munich, in a southern region of Germany, Bavaria, a quiet backwater far away from the eastern front. My god-mother had apparently not been able to register it fully, even though she lived in the very epicentre of the Holocaust, resident a mere marathon's distance away from Auschwitz.[68]

The horrors perpetrated on the local Jews in the area make tough reading, but they highlight the true nature of what the Jews experienced and the sheer sadism of the perpetrators. A book review confirms my judgement:

> Many of the stories she tells are gruesome, and reading them is not easy, but they are absolutely necessary to the understanding – even if a tentative and limited one – of what happened then and there, and why the likes of Udo Klausa, decent though they may have been at heart, cannot be permitted to escape the judgment of history.[69]

Even though I have lived with the Holocaust all my life – seventy-one years – I find the events of 31 July 1940, known as 'bloody Wednesday', in the little town of Olkusz (German name – Ilkenau) which was south-east of Będzin, extraordinarily sadistic and terrifying. It may have been a reprisal for the death of one or two German gendarmes. All the available men, both Jews and Poles, were gathered together. Jacob Schwarzfitter was interviewed in 1946 in a 'displaced persons camp', by an American psychology professor, David Boder. He said:

> We were led out at day break, with our hands up, they jabbed us with bayonets and we were compelled to run. When we arrived at the square, we had to pass a cordon. On both sides stood SS men, with [metal] rods, belts, rubber truncheons, clubs and they beat us. Every one had to go through. People went through the cordon and emerged covered with blood.

Poles and Jews had suffered this, but then the Jews were singled out and made to lie as though making up the paving stones of a path and they were walked over by the German soldiers and the police in their big heavy boots. Jacob said:

> Out of the Jews who had been brought there a living pathway was created, over which the Germans walked. After lying for eight hours we were ordered to get up. Everyone was pale and black. We all looked like dead men.

Another eyewitness, Henryk Otuch, recalled:

> One Jew by the name of Glajtman [Gleitmann] was maltreated by a German to the point where he lost consciousness, with the German standing on the face of the Jew, who was lying down, and seeking to keep his balance, and continuing until the face of this Jew was squashed to pieces. After this water was poured over the Jew. Another Jew was forced to beat his colleague etc. After this all the Jews were transported somewhere.

Some sources say boys as young as 13 were made to lie in the pathway, others say 16.[70] I really cannot think of anything appropriate to write after this ...

# 7

# PULSEN – LOOTING AND PLUNDER

---

Both are thieves, the receiver as well as the stealer.

> Phocylides, sixth century BCE poet, *Moral Epigrams*

To the victor belong the spoils of the enemy.

> William L. Marcy, 1786–1857

---

Ian Kershaw found indifference to the fate of the Jews and silence when the deportations were taking place. However:

> … where real interest was awakened on the part of the non-Jewish population it was less a product of human concern or moral principle than self-interest and the hope of material advantage. Such was the case when a complainant in Fürth near Nuremberg wrote to the Reich Governor of Bavaria in 1942 on behalf of the co-tenants of her apartment block protesting at the sequestration of Jewish property by the local Finance Office when so many were crying out for it. 'Where is the justice and Volksgemeinschaft in that?' she lamented.[1]

Boris Smolar wrote of his return to Berlin after the Reichstag fire on 27 February 1933, saying he did not recognise the city. He described the Nazi flags hanging everywhere, including the entrances of many of the stores:

> Groups of Nazis, in brown and black uniforms would march behind huge Nazi flags through the streets singing Nazi songs. The whole city seemed to be engulfed in a sea of thousands of swastika flags.
>
> In the evening, after work, the hordes of Nazi marchers became even larger. Like divisions of an army they would march singing behind their flags to squares

where 'unwanted' books would be burned. Nazi trucks would pull up to the bonfires every few minutes and dump several thousand books into the flames, with wild 'victory' yells from the uniformed Nazi storm troopers.

The Jewish population was in utter terror. Jews were afraid to appear on the streets. Jewish businesses on the Kurfürstendamm – the liveliest section of Berlin – had been pillaged; the doors had been ripped out and the windows smashed. Big black swastikas and the word 'Jude' in large, crude letters were daubed on the walls. Nazi gangs burst into Jewish homes and ransacked them. It turned out that the Nazi leaders in every neighbourhood had long before assembled lists of Jewish homes worth plundering.[2]

In the Netherlands, the Nazi-led Dutch police employed a firm called Abraham Puls & Sons to pillage and empty the homes of 140,000 Jews who had been deported or had fled. From this firm a new word entered the Dutch language – 'pulsen', meaning 'to rob'.

Ad van Liempt wrote that:

Of the more than 100,000 Jews living in the Netherlands who were murdered in the Second World War, a substantial number were arrested on the basis of an incentive system. There were two distinct groups eligible for a bonus of seven guilders and fifty cents [7.50fl.] – about $47.50 [2005] – for every Jew brought in: certain members of the Amsterdam police force and some officials working at the Zentralstelle für jüdische Auswanderung [Central Bureau for Jewish Emigration]. The role of the latter group, the so-called Colonne Henneicke, has never been studied in any depth.[3]

He gives two reasons why – 'One obvious explanation for this would be that it is typical of the Dutch character to turn a blind eye to the very blackest pages of our nation's history.' However, the information only emerged during the perpetrators' trials and these records were only made available to the National Archives in 2000. Liempt writes that his interest was aroused in 1989, when a historian, Loe de Jong, showed him 'a receipt that proved that premiums were collected for arrested Jews. That slip of paper has haunted me ever since, and the result was, ultimately, this book.'

When Germany invaded the Netherlands on 10 May 1940 the 160,000 people of Jewish descent were more worried than most – 200 committed suicide. AVRO, the Dutch broadcasting company, dismissed its nine Jewish employees on 21 May 1940, as it was 'company policy', but at this point there was no pressure from the Germans.[4]

The journalist Philip Mechanicus was dismissed from his newspaper in May 1940. Two months later the Air Raid Defence had to be purged of Jews by 15 July.

The regulations kept coming and the Jews became increasingly isolated. A letter sent by F. Wimmer, General Commissioner for Justice and Government Affairs, demanded that no more Jews should be hired and those in place were not to be promoted. In October 1940 they were all to be dismissed. Yad Vashem has described Wimmer as both 'a seasoned lawyer' and 'a rabid anti-Semite'.[5]

Subsequently, all officials had to complete a 'Declaration of Aryan origin' and anyone with three or four Jewish grandparents was dismissed – this affected about 2,500 people. On 22 October a further decree said all Jewish businesses had to be registered and so the grisly process rolled on like a juggernaut. Ordinance 6, of 10 January 1941, decreed that all Jews, even those with only one grandparent, had to register with the Office of Public Records so everyone knew who they were and where they lived. This was because 'the Jewish influence on Dutch life as a whole has become intolerable', reported the *Deutsche Zeitung in den Niederlanden*. This was a German-language nationwide newspaper which was published during almost the entire occupation of the Netherlands.

It was intended to create a ghetto in Amsterdam but it never proved practical because of the demography of the city. In February 1941 the Nazis began arresting Jews in Amsterdam, most of whom were never seen again. This led to the only anti-pogrom strike during the Second World War. In spite of the strike, the anti-Jewish measures continued, and coupled with that was another favourite Nazi tactic – the creation of a Jewish Council (Joodse Raad) which meant the Jews had to do the Nazis' dirty work for them. So the Jews had to stop protests and choose victims.

They also had a newspaper, the *Joodsch Weekblad*, which would announce the week's bad news to the Jewish community. Jews had to turn in their radios. They were no longer allowed in swimming pools and parks, cafés and restaurants, museums and theatres. Jewish children were forced to attend different schools. Jews had to resign from any clubs of which they were members. By mid-1941 they all had a 'J' on their identity cards. All told, there were 160,820 Jews in the Netherlands, including 15,549 half-Jews and 5,719 quarter-Jews. The registration was complete, and the mass plunder could now begin.

Underlying all these anti-Jewish measures was a single, steadfast principle: the extermination of the Jews would be financed entirely with Jewish money. It was not to cost the state and its Aryan citizens a penny.[6] To achieve this a 'roofbank' (literally, a 'plunder bank') was required. The Germans chose an old Jewish bank, Lippmann, Rosenthal & Co., which was split in two for the purpose. One office remained a bank even though it was under German control. The other office at 47–55 Sarphatistraat, previously a branch of the Bank of Amsterdam, became the roofbank. The original Lippmann, Rosenthal & Co. had been trading at 6–8 Nieuwe Spiegelstraat in Amsterdam since 1859 (the building is now occupied by a contemporary art centre). The Nazis' choice of this well-known Jewish bank was intentional as it lulled Jews into a false sense of security that their property would be safe. In 1941 and 1942 all Dutch Jews had to hand over all their valuables – securities, cash, art objects, precious metals and jewellery – to the Sarphatistraat branch; the two banks were administered quite separately.

In reality, it was more like a storage depot/sales office for stolen Jewish property than a regular bank. It was an executive agency under the direct supervision of Seyss-Inquart's Reich Commissariat. Its main task was actually to sell off Jewish possessions as they came in. Many of the staff were ordinary bank employees and twenty-five accepted a post at that branch. This reorganisation was based on ordinance VO 148/1941, dated 8 August 1941, and entitled 'Ordnance on the Handling of Jewish Capital'. This is generally known as the First LiRo Decree – LiRo being the normal abbreviation of Lippman, Rosenthal & Co. The decree's purpose was to seize the Jews' private property and was based on wholesale deception:

> … all Jews were required to report and surrender control over their money and securities to the bank. In return, they were given receipts and proofs of transfer, and they had the option of withdrawing money to cover the basic costs of living. Interest was calculated; costs were declared. In short everybody thought this was a temporary measure, and very few Jews seemed to suspect their money was gone for good.

The Germans were good psychologists and the scheme worked well. As soon as the decree was announced the securities and money flooded in and the system struggled to cope.

The second LiRo decree was dated May 1942, and this required Jews to hand over valuables, in packages, to the office on Sarphatistraat:

> Once this ordinance went into effect, there was no holding back the tidal wave of goods. Hundreds of thousands of articles were dropped off at LiRo; sometimes the owners' names were not even recorded. LiRo was forced to rent extra facilities to store it all, including two floors of the immense diamond exchange. There was also plenty of junk mixed in with the rest, from Jews who were not willing to part with their possessions without a fight. They sought out other possibilities and, for form's sake, turned in various trinkets.[7]

The role of Lippmann, Rosenthal & Co. came to light recently in a report about a painting held by the Dutch royal family. Apparently, in 1960 Queen Juliana bought the painting by Joris van der Haagen (1615–1669) without being aware of its history. The Dutch museums have been criticised for failing to give back plundered art, as some 20,000 works are still missing. The palace agreed to return the work to the original Jewish heirs, with the subtle comment, 'One painting was found where there were indications of involuntary loss of possession during the German occupation.'[8]

By the end of 1941 the Jews had been isolated – they could no longer travel anywhere, nor could they change address. The first stage of the deportations came on 5 December 1941 when non-Dutch Jews had to report to the Central Bureau for Jewish Emigration for 'voluntary emigration'. They would be sent to Westerbork, a transit and detention camp 500m square, about 100 miles from Amsterdam, and at times it became overcrowded. The Dutch railways laid a single track from the nearby village of Hooghalen to the camp.

Jews from villages and towns in north Holland and some from the south were told to leave their homes and go to the capital and find accommodation. They could only take what they could carry and the houses were sealed. This caused great panic and chaos, which was aggravated by men and boys being sent to forced labour camps.

The structure for deportations was created with quotas set by Adolf Eichmann. The Netherlands had to send 15,000 Jews to Poland in the year 1942, and the authorities were confident that this would be met with non-Dutch Jews. However, there was a slight hiccup in the planning in the summer. France was behind in its quota of 100,000 for 1942. The numbers would be made up by increasing Holland's quota to 40,000 – a mere bookkeeping entry! Accordingly on 19 June 1942 all Dutch-born Jews would now be listed with names and addresses by the Office of Public Records.

From 2 May 1942 the Dutch Jews had to wear the yellow star so they could be identified. Those who refused were threatened with Mauthausen camp and non-Jews who opposed the measure or wore the star in protest were briefly sent to Amersfoort camp. In the meantime, the noose was tightened even more – bicycles had to be handed in, a curfew was imposed between 8.00 p.m. and 6.00 a.m. and Jews had to be in their own homes. Restrictions on food shopping were also imposed as the greengrocer, butcher and fishmonger were all forbidden to Jews.

On Friday 26 June 1942 at 10.00 p.m. the Jewish Council was summoned to Ferdinand Aus der Fünten's office. He was in charge in Amsterdam. Apparently this was the Germans' favourite day for important meetings as it meant the Jews had the start of the Sabbath on Friday evening completely disrupted. At that meeting it was announced that forced labour, supervised by the police, was imminent. David Cohen (1882–1967), one of the co-chairs of the Jewish Council and a classics professor, said forced labour was a violation of international law and was told by Aus der Fünten, 'We'll decide international law' and the council could choose who would be exempt.[9]

This intentionally put the members of the council in an invidious situation, as if they did not co-operate the police would make the choices. They chose to co-operate, but the conduct of members of Jewish Councils will always be debatable and there is no way of knowing what would have happened if they had refused to co-operate with the Nazis. Would things have been worse or better?

The first deportations to Westerbork took place on 15 July 1942 on two trains, on the same day the first train of Dutch Jews went to Auschwitz. For those in Westerbork the weekly train to the east, 'the venomous snake', was the main focus. A journalist formerly with the *Algemeen Handelsblad*, Philip Mechanicus (1889–1944), who was on one of the last transports to Auschwitz, described it as such in his chronicle covering the eighteen months he spent in Westerbork – a most important source on conditions in Westerbork.[10]

Holland met its quota, but the system was refined, with the Dutch Theatre on Plantage Middenlaan made into a new depot for arrested Jews and those going for forced labour (arbeitseinsatz). A new police unit, the Amsterdam Police Battalion, was sent into action. They had been trained by the Nazis so the Germans knew they could be relied on in mass round-ups where the ordinary Amsterdam policeman was unreliable. However, a Bureau of Jewish Affairs was being set up within the police force, consisting of mainly NSB (Dutch National Socialist Movement) men, and it was to be led by the fanatical Nazi, R. Dahmen von Buchholz. This force would be important in the major operation Amsterdam was about to undertake – the deportation of about 10 per cent of its population.

At the beginning of August 1942 there were a couple of raids which caused panic and, although the Zentralstelle (Jewish Emigration Bureau) stated the Germans preferred not to break up families:

> … old people were being dragged out of nursing homes and children out of orphanages, entirely independently of their families. There was only one law that counted: the quota sent by Berlin. When a disabled veteran who had lost one of his legs asked to be exempted, his request was denied on the grounds that 'a Jew is a Jew, with or without legs'.[11]

On 2 and 3 October 1942 the Germans assembled all available men and the Amsterdam police force for a large raid, and within a few days 15,000 Jews had been arrested and taken to Westerbork where the crowded conditions became indescribable. At the end of 1942 the new commandant, Konrad Gemmeker, organised a social evening at the camp. No one knew why – the 40,000th Jew had been deported – Westerbork had complied with Berlin's quota.

To pacify the terrified families left behind, the Nazis created another sham – the postal correspondence. On the one hand, tens of thousands of letters were written by the families of deported Jews, collected by the Jewish Council, translated ostensibly for the German censor and then sent to the Emigration Bureau and destroyed by burning. On the other hand, letters came from Auschwitz and other camps full of reassurance:

… the food was good, and there were enough blankets; the work was hard but bearable, and there was a nice shower at the end of the day. All of this was written under duress, by Jews about to be gassed. The Jewish Council received thousands of such letters and by distributing them to families, they helped perpetuate the Great Lie.

In March 1943 the letters came from a new Nazi resort – Sobibór – a new camp created in 1942 near Lublin in Poland. It was truly a death camp as hardly anyone survived. Of the 34,313 Dutch Jews sent there only nineteen came back. Most of the trains from Westerbork bypassed Auschwitz at this time and went to Sobibór. Auschwitz was busy dealing with a higher priority – the murder of the Greek Jews.[12]

There was only one remaining issue to be dealt with – the Jews who had avoided capture. In the spring of 1943 it was calculated that about 25,000 Jews had escaped, perhaps by going into hiding. This could not be allowed and the Nazis decided to stimulate the search for these remaining Jews by offering a premium per head of 7.5fl. This sum could be doubled if the person was a 'penal case' – a Jew who had violated one of the ordinances.

> The possibility of earning such bonuses was offered to policemen at the Bureau of Jewish Affairs, but also to the civil servants working for the various subdivisions of the Zentralstelle. In addition, there was also a sizable budget for informants. And thus in its final phases the hunt for Jews in the Netherlands acquired a new dimension: for a few dozen highly motivated men, it became a money-making enterprise.[13]

At the same time the seizure of Jewish goods was well under way, involving many organisations who bickered while completing the task. The houses vacated by the deported Jews were stripped of their contents which were taken away. The contents mostly went to German cities where, because of allied bombing, household goods were increasingly required. Many items were stolen, but clearing 29,000 homes within a year was a major achievement.

The difficulties of moving the goods were solved by sending them to Amsterdam Harbour where, in the autumn of 1943, no fewer than 666 canal boats and 100 train cars travelled to the Ruhr Valley filled with Jewish possessions moved by Puls. However, before Puls arrived the Office for the Registration of Household Effects (Hausraterfassungsstelle), established in spring 1942, had to list all the Jewish goods. Although manned by Dutchmen, the concept was German and very precise. Every single item – every cup, table and lamp – was recorded in lists by a small army of inventory clerks in all the houses vacated by the deported Jews. Copies of the lists went to the 'roofbank', the ERR and the Zentralstelle. It appears that the registration office's inventory system had been set up even before the deportations began.

There was a central card system, on which each item was individually registered and each Jew had one or more cards sorted according to the office's number. There were different sections and warehouses for carpets, paintings, antiques, furniture and bronze, gold, silver and jewellery, and bric-a-brac. The records from the warehouses did not survive, but the card index survived with its thousands of cards. There were four subdivisions called 'Colonnes', named after their leaders. The fourth one, Colonne Harmans, was given the task of investigating stolen or misappropriated Jewish possessions. Like everywhere under the Nazis, many Jews gave their valuables to friends and acquaintances to avoid confiscation. The Colonne Harmans was meant to recover these items and hand the guilty to the police. The people who did this work were not trained detectives but often unemployed men from the local job centre.[14] Harmans was sacked in late 1942 for theft and he was replaced by Wim Henneicke, aged 33, with no police background and in spite of a criminal record from running an unlicensed taxi service, but he controlled his Colonne with firm discipline.

The Registration Office came under the Zentralstelle and its staff increased quickly. The employment contracts with Lippman, Rosenthal & Co. have survived. Thus, the Jew hunters were paid out of the proceeds of stolen Jewish property. The deviousness of the system takes time to absorb – the Dutch Jews paid for their own deaths.

Henneicke was hired in June 1942 and paid 270fl per month while the normal employee earned 230fl. Henneicke's salary was worth $1,675 in 2002. However, there were perks. The only inventory specialists were based in Amsterdam and therefore when other parts of the country needed inventories, the men went off to spend a week in other areas and this time out of town earned generous expenses.

The work was often done while the occupants were still present, awaiting deportation. This process had its own bureaucratic procedure too, as one operative admitted after the war:

> I gave one receipt to the Jews whose belongings I had confiscated, while another copy was dropped off at the offices of the *Zentralstelle*. One copy went with the seized property, and another copy stayed in the book, and that one I kept until the book was full, at which time it was turned over to the *Zentralstelle*.[15]

The work was based on tip-offs – Henneicke had a vast network of informants who fed him information by post and telephone. They were rewarded fairly generously and these funds also came from the roofbank. He soon acquired a colleague, William Briedé, a trained bookkeeper. He was hired on 1 April 1942 at a salary of 290fl per month, because his job was confidential. Once a month he collected a suitcase from the LiRo branch at Sarphatistraat and used it to pay all the salaries of the staff at the Register Office.[16]

In March 1943 their work had an added dimension – they were to hunt for Jews, as well as their property. The payment was a bonus of 7.5fl (equivalent to £30 in 2015) of kopgeld (head-money) for each Jew brought in. It was calculated that fifty-four Dutchmen actually rounded people up and brought them in to get their bonus. However, they really had no authority to arrest unless a policeman was present.

Little was known about this until 1948 and it appears that Colonne Henneicke arrested about 8,000–9,000 victims during 1943.[17] It should be remembered that this figure included hundreds of toddlers who were snatched from their hiding places with foster families and sent to their deaths. The elderly and infirm were also rounded up, sometimes in ambulances because, at the end of the day, each Jew was worth 7.5fl regardless of who they were. In September 1943 there was a final raid during which the two chairmen of the Jewish Council, David Cohen and Abraham Asscher (1880–1950), were sent to Westerbork. The theatre was empty and the nursery was closed. The colonne were dissolved.[18] Both men survived.

The members of the colonne showed a lot of initiative. Under interrogation Henk Hopman told the detectives of his own wheeze when, as an inventory clerk in Jewish homes, he would receive money from Jewish owners if he helped them rent out their properties. After the goods were stored in one sealed room, the rest of the property could be rented out. The clerk got a reward for being so helpful. He was the only one to mention this income as he put an explanatory note on his income tax return for 1943 when he declared 6,000fl – an enormous amount.[19] Most of the men in the Colonne Henneicke claimed to have been reluctant to move to tracking down Jews, rather than just their goods, and on interrogation minimised the numbers they had hauled in – in most cases the paperwork proved otherwise.[20]

Since I first wrote this section, some new research has appeared which demonstrates that in one special area of the Netherlands, Limburg, like Albania, there were more Jews at the end of the war than at the beginning. Herman van Rens and his wife discovered that 10 per cent of Jews hiding in Limberg were caught, one-third of the rate in Amsterdam. In 1933 there were 800 Jews, but by 1945 there were 2,200. In the rest of Holland 75 per cent of the Jews were killed. Van Rens stated that people of Limberg have a unique dialect and a very close-knit community. 'When you betrayed someone to death in Limburg, everybody knew and it carried different social implications than in Amsterdam.' At the time the Henneicke Column was active, the Limburg police had almost given up proactive attempts to find Jews in 1943.[21]

The area was different geographically – not so flat, and with limestone caves leading into Belgium. It is estimated about 3,000 people escaped to Spain and Switzerland through the area. Additionally, Van Rens stated that, whereas in Amsterdam the police rounded people up without notice, in Limberg in 1942 Jews under 60 were given twenty-four hours' notice to report. More than half did not report as they went into hiding. Later, older Jews were given a week's notice, and they too went into hiding in the same numbers.

Van Rens concluded:

> So the perception of Dutch Jews being too docile, too obedient, clearly doesn't hold up because when they were given a chance, even if it was just 24 hours, to save themselves, most made serious attempts to escape the Nazis' claws. For me it was an encouraging discovery.[22]

Philip Mechanicus (1899–1944), the journalist incarcerated in Westerbork from November 1942 to March 1944, commented on other activities by Lippman & Rosenthal that he observed. On 8 August 1943 he wrote about the censorship of letters being sent to prisoners in Westerbork:

> Everyone in the camp is complaining that he has been receiving hardly any letters recently. The agents of Lippmann & Rosenthal carry out the censorship. It is asserted that letters on which the address of the sender is not shown are simply burned. Hardly credible. I myself have only received two letters in the past fortnight, with the sender's address shown. Again and again people who receive letters are called to account by the agents because of some cryptic reference to money or persons in hiding. In this way they help the German authorities to recover money from Jews or to find Jews.

On the same day, he writes about the arrival of some 'S-cases' (punishment cases – the lowest form of life):

> Yesterday night another small transport came in from Amsterdam, including about a hundred S-cases who had been in hiding. Their heads were shaved and they were given prison clothing. The agents of Lippmann & Rosenthal are also playing a new part in relation to these Jews. They pump them to find out the addresses where they have been hiding. The Jews are behaving worse than shamefully – nearly all of them give the names and addresses of their hosts and benefactors quite readily.[23]

Later he reported other activities by Lippman & Rosenthal. On 7 October 1943 he noted:

> The Barnevelders received their luggage today, some of it ransacked. Lippmann & Rosenthal had stolen linen, tobacco, toilet soap and articles of value from the cases. Some cases reached their owners completely empty. What the Barnevelders left behind at Barneveld has been brought here in lorries. The Commandant and

his staff are picking out what they fancy and are reserving the rest for purposes as yet unknown.

Two days later, on 9 October, he noted:

> The agents of Lippmann & Rosenthal left today, carrying in their pockets many fountain pens which they had appropriated for their own use; they also had gleaming briefcases (ditto) and in their suitcases articles which they had filched from Jews. They released the letters still in their possession, all more or less unopened. Tens of thousands of letters were poured out over the huts like an avalanche. Some people got ten letters at once, the oldest of which dated back to the beginning of August.[24]

## The One that Got Away

Very few Jews managed to beat the Nazis' financial net when emigrating, but one nameless Berlin Jew did. Boris Smolar reported his story and how he advertised for a secretary in Hitler's most important newspaper, the *Völkischer Beobachter*. He listed the skills required and the salary he would pay. He also asked for references to be sent with the application, which were to be sent to a box number at the newspaper. A few days after the advertisement had appeared thick envelopes began arriving for the postbox in question. They began piling up and the advertiser failed to collect or provide a forwarding address.

A week later, the newspaper received a letter from the advertiser from a Geneva hotel. In the letter he explained that he had to go to Geneva at short notice for business reasons and he would have to stay for a week. He asked the newspaper to forward any replies to the Geneva address and had courteously provided confirmation of his address and signature by a Swiss lawyer. The people in the office of the chief Nazi newspaper were delighted to show him how successful his advertisement had been and posted all the replies in a large package.

> The package bore, of course, the return address of the *Völkischer Beobachter*. Who in Nazi Germany would have dared to open it? Neither the post office censors nor the customs officials. Letters and packages from the *Völkischer Beobachter* were beyond suspicion, and this was what the Jewish advertiser was expecting.

The parcel arrived safely in Geneva. He carefully opened each letter and found the stock certificates he had sent himself. He would have been unable to take them out of Germany on his person because they would have been confiscated, so he thought he would let the Nazi newspaper deal with the problem and get his stocks and bonds out of Germany for him.

The trick worked, and as a joke he sent the *Völkischer Beobachter* a thank you note for helping him get his fortune out of Germany. He was, of course, not at all in need of a secretary.[25]

Krystyna Chiger (*b.* 1935), the *Girl in the Green Sweater*, living in Lvov, poignantly described the topsy-turvy world of Nazi theft. In 1942 her family were living in a building close to one requisitioned by the Germans for high-ranking officers. They would wander into their apartment and pick up art, silver or furniture and inspect them:

> One by one the officers came to our apartment and one by one they left with our nice things. It must have been heartbreaking for my parents to see all their worldly possessions being taken from them, but at the same time they were thankful that we were not being taken out into the street along with our things. Soon, all of our furniture was gone, except a fine Auguste Förster, one of the best pianos ever made. My mother used to play for us, very beautifully, but the piano had been silent since the German occupation. Still it pained her that this wonderful instrument would be taken from our apartment and that she would never play it again. The piano was claimed by a German officer named Wepke, a man who was acting as the interim governor of Lvov. The only solace was that Wepke seemed to appreciate how fine a piano he was about to receive and that he could also play it beautifully. It was the poetic way to look at the injustice, to see that at least the piano would be enjoyed and put to beautiful use.
>
> I have kept a picture in my mind of my brother and me sitting on the floor of our apartment, our furniture all but gone, the walls checkered with bright squares where our paintings used to hang. In another time, in another place, it would have been a picture of any two children, their household packed for a move out of town. I sat on the floor and watched and listened. I could see the shine of the piano pedals against the polish of the officer's boots. Watching him play, listening to him, you would never think he was capable of cruelty. The splendor that spilled from his fingers. The joy! When he was finished he stood and complimented my father on the piano. Then he made arrangements for the instrument to be transported to his apartment across the street. Before it was taken away, my father wrapped the piano carefully with a blanket pulled from our linen closet. It pained him to lose the piano, but it pained him more to see it damaged. He stamped it with his name – IGNACY CHIGER – on the small hope that he would someday get it back, after the war. Always, he was thinking ahead to the end of the war. Always, he was hopeful, and so he put his stamp on everything.

In fact their piano proved very popular and another officer came wanting it. Her father told him that Officer Wepke had already claimed it. The second officer was very angry, no doubt because Wepke outranked him and also because he had seen the piano first. He could have shot Krystyna's father, but he accepted it and contented himself with taking some of their remaining items:

> The next day, the piano delivered, Wepke sent an officer back to our apartment
> with a package for my father. It was our blanket, along with a bottle of wine and
> a note of thanks for the piano. I was six years old, still a child, and even I could
> recognize the absurd mix of humanity and inhumanity. It was a curious gesture of
> civility, we all thought. My father wrote about it after the war, how it was strange
> to find decent people among such animals. That such a people, with such a high
> culture, could do such terrible things … it was unthinkable.[26]

Very few managed to protest, but in Vienna one young blond Jewish man made his point. He entered a large, well-known department store and spent more than an hour trying on hats, suits and jackets. He waited until the assistant had carefully packed everything when he announced, 'I'm sorry, I forgot you don't sell to Jews.' The young man, named Teddy Kollek, then left the shop and soon left for Palestine. In due course he became a much loved Mayor of Jerusalem.[27]

Kitty Hart-Moxon (b. 1926) was born in Bielsko in Poland. She is a survivor of Auschwitz. I asked her why the Germans continued with the 'Final Solution' when they knew they were losing the war. Kitty told me the Jews actually financed the German war effort through the looting because nothing that was found was wasted.

As a young girl Kitty spent two years in Auschwitz-Birkenau. For eight months she worked in the 'Canada Kommando' in the vicinity of the gas chambers, sorting men's jackets. She had to open up all seams and remove all valuables that were hidden inside. They found enormous quantities of valuables – diamonds, gold, various currencies – on each shift, and often it took four people to carry the loot away in blankets or buckets. The currency was of no use in the camp and was used as toilet paper. Huge quantities of items were found sewn into corsets.

Kitty told me she buried valuables in a gap behind the toilet hut and next to Gas Chamber No. 4. It was not possible to keep a single item of value as this was punishable by death. On one occasion she dropped a whole pouch of diamonds into a large container of soup being carried by men, in the hope they could later rescue them from the soup.

Kitty buried items hoping they could be used to bribe technicians in ammunition factories where prisoners worked to obtain explosives. On 7 October 1944, the prisoners known as 'sonderkommando', who worked inside the gas chambers, blew up and destroyed crematoria Nos II and IV. Kitty was evacuated on 11 November 1944 – all the male prisoners and some of the girls were killed after the uprising.[28]

Few of the inmates of Auschwitz had the chance to be personally involved in bringing a Nazi to justice. Sonja Fritz (b. 1921) wrote about her return to Vienna and gave an eyewitness report on Auschwitz to her old friend, Anton Jakl, whose

Jewish mother-in-law had been gassed at Birkenau. Later, Jakl mentioned that a man had been 'assigned to live on my estate'. Vienna was being bombed and people were evacuated to the countryside:

> Jakl went on telling me that this man frequently received boxes from Upper Silesia. Now, I started to get interested because Auschwitz was situated in Upper Silesia and the SS had acquired many possessions which the inmates had brought with them to Auschwitz. They would send home to their families everything they could lay their hands on. Since I had worked in the Commandant's office and issued the identity cards for the SS men, I knew practically all their names.

Jakl mentioned 'Grabner' and she was 'flabbergasted'. SS-Untersturmführer Maximilian Grabner was the dreaded chief of the Political Section. The Auschwitz Gestapo 'was anathema to all of us in Auschwitz', and they were terribly afraid of him. The chief of the Austrian police was Dr Duermayer, who was a former Auschwitz inmate. She told Jakl to contact him at Police HQ and Jakl and Duermayer both went to Jakl's estate where Grabner was arrested.[29] It was recorded in the *Auschwitz Chronicle* on 1 December 1943 that Grabner was returning to his former Gestapo post in Kattowitz (now Katowice in Poland), but in fact he was arrested 'for repeated abuse of office in Auschwitz'.[30]

On 9 December further skulduggery was revealed. A member of the Resistance in the camp wrote a secret letter to Teresa Lasocka, a member of the Kraków underground, known as 'Assistance for Concentration Camp Prisoners'. He explained that pressure from abroad had brought changes, such as shooting being forbidden. He went on:

> Our greatest murderers – Grabner, Boger, Woźnica, Palitzsch – are relieved of their duties: dismissed and transferred. They are being investigated because of thievery in Canada. On the night of seventh–eighth, they set fire to a barracks of the Political Department where the evidence of their thievery was deposited. They destroyed this material. Lachman did it. In this way, they want to prevent Berlin from learning of the evidence of their guilt. Publish. The new Commandant has eased tension. The Political Department has fallen from its leading positioning the camp and plays only a subordinate role.[31]

The Polish Resistance was concerned that, as a result of this sabotage and the destruction of the evidence of the individuals' guilt, the investigation would cease and the accused be acquitted. Accordingly the leader sent instructions for a 'letter to be put into good German *as soon as possible* in 3 copies on a German typewriter'. It was to be sent as soon as possible to the director of the Special Commission in Auschwitz, commandant of Auschwitz 1 and the camp commander of Auschwitz 1.

These letters were to be sent in carefully sealed envelopes as quickly as possible, preferably from Auschwitz rather than Upper Silesia.

Grabner had been moved from the Political Department in October 1943 and was investigated by Dr Konrad Morgen, an SS judge, as he was accused of being responsible for killing 2,000 prisoners 'beyond the general [guide] lines'. The story becomes quite confusing, because another letter from the Resistance on 6 October 1944 reports on Grabner being tried in Buchenwald 'for exceeding authority and arbitrary shooting to death in approximately 40 cases'. He was sentenced to death, which was commuted to twelve years.[32] A trial against him began in Weimar in 1944 but was never finished. However, in 1947 he was condemned by the Supreme War Tribunal in Kraków and executed.[33]

The trial of the so-called 'Auschwitz bookkeeper', Oskar Gröning, in April 2015, brought to light details of the theft of Jewish goods from the poor souls arriving at Auschwitz. The 93-year-old said his job was to guard the luggage left by the Jews sent to the gas chambers or for work. Trained as a bank clerk, he had volunteered for the SS and was given the job of counting the money taken from the Jews.[34] The charge against him was that he 'provided assistance to others in the deliberate collective murder' of 'at least 300,000 people', mainly Hungarian Jews, in a two month period between May and June 1944. He said there was a lot of food and vodka for the SS soldiers – while the Jews were starved. He appeared to have no misgivings about his role collecting the Jews' money. He said, 'It belonged to the state and the Jews had to turn it in.'

Once the Jews had been gassed, any teeth with gold crowns were pulled out and 86-year-old Max Eisen testified that his job was to break the gold crowns out of the teeth. His father's last words to him in Auschwitz were begging him to tell the world about Auschwitz if he survived. He was the only survivor out of his family – his parents, his grandparents, two little brothers and baby sister, aunt and uncle. They had been rounded up by the Hungarian police and pushed in a cattle truck with only standing room for three days. He travelled from Toronto to give his testimony at the trial with a photo of his murdered family.[35]

## Golden Harvest

The recent case of the art hoard of Gurlitt highlighted the cases of Jewish stolen art (see *The Monuments Men* film). No doubt given the obsession with Jewish wealth, people would not consider that the theft of everyday items, especially clothes from murdered Jews, was a significant reading item. The truth is that the Nazi genocide was given consent by most Europeans in the occupied countries – as Gross concluded, the people acted 'according to norms that were then in place'.[36]

Saul Friedlander, himself a survivor, wrote:

Not one social group, not one religious community, not one scholarly community or professional association in Germany and throughout Europe declared its solidarity with the Jews [some of the Christian churches declared that converted Jews were part of the flock, up to a point]; to the contrary, many social constituencies, many power groups were directly involved in the expropriation of the Jews and eager, be it out of greed, for their wholesale disappearance. Thus Nazi and related anti-Jewish policies could unfold to their most extreme levels without the interference of any major countervailing interests.[37]

The plunder of Jewish property was a common experience in occupied Europe.

From the Dnieper to the Channel, from Paris to Corfu, no social stratum could resist the temptation. And if one were to ask what a Swiss banker and a Polish peasant had in common (besides that each has an immortal soul), the answer, with only a little bit of exaggeration, could be a gold tooth ripped from the jaw of a Jewish corpse.[38]

On 8 January 2008 a photograph was published for the first time in the largest Polish daily newspaper, *Gazeta Wyborcza*. It illustrated an article about digging through mass graves at the site of the Treblinka extermination camp:

Gleaners, or, as they were called at the time, 'diggers' (kopacze), sifted through the ashes and remains of murdered Jews at sites of all the Nazi extermination camps in Poland (Treblinka, Belzec, Sobibór, Chelmno and Auschwitz) for many years after the war, looking for pieces of jewelry and dental gold overlooked by the Nazis. Occasionally local police would chase them away.

The photo came from Tadeusz Kiryluk, a former director of the Treblinka Museum. He explained that it showed a group of peasants caught by the police just after the war whilst digging at Treblinka.[39] The photo looks quite normal, until you notice the pile of skulls and bones at the peasants' feet. This was not normal agricultural labour because the peasants are standing on the ashes of the 800,000 Jews gassed and cremated in Treblinka between July 1942 and October 1943. The peasants had been digging through these remains looking for gold and jewels.

Gitta Sereny asked Franz Stangl, who, after being commander of Sobibór, was reassigned to Treblinka, why the Jews were exterminated. He said it was their money, and asked, 'Have you any ideas of the fantastic sums that were involved?' It seems that the profitability of the whole enterprise was high on the agenda of the perpetrators.

As with Auschwitz, transports left Treblinka – over 1,000 train wagons filled with the possessions of murdered Jews. Money, jewellery and all other goods were listed by the SS and checked by the railway employees at the Treblinka railway station. The stationmaster, Franciszek Zabecki (1907–1987), listed the goods transported:

Into freight-cars separately male coats tied in bundles were loaded, separately,
men's suits, jackets, trousers; again separately, children's clothing and women's
wardrobe – dresses, blouses, sweaters, old and new, caps, hats; men's tall boots,
and male, female and children's shoes. Men's, women's and children's underwear,
separately, used and new items, swaddle cloths, pillows, cushions … Suitcases
filled with pencils, fountain pens, and glasses, umbrellas and canes tied in separate
bundles. They also shipped spools of thread of all kinds and colors. Leather for
the production of shoes was tied in separate bundles, hard sheets for manufacture
of soles, leather bags, clothes. In cardboard boxes shaving utensils were packed,
razors, hair-cutting clippers, mirrors, even pots and pans, wash-basins, carpentry tools, saws, planes, hammers, in general everything that could be brought
over by several hundred thousand people … They also shipped shaved women's
hair. The load was described as a military cargo: Gut der Waffen-SS [Property
of Waffen-SS] Freight cars were dispatched to Germany and sometimes to
SS-Arbeitslager in Lublin.[40]

Zabecki had been a railway worker before the war and was sent to Treblinka
on 22 May 1941. In reality he was part of the Polish Resistance and had to keep
notes of the movements of the German rail transports. He was one of the few
non-Germans to see all the Jewish transports from the beginning to the end in
October 1943. He gave evidence at post-war trials, including Franz Stangl's, on
the crammed trains leaving again quite empty. He also described horrific incidents, noting that there were such terrible scenes at Treblinka station that the
passenger trains were no longer allowed to stop there from September 1942.[41]
He wrote a book of his memoirs in 1977 which is still a leading source on the
deportations to Treblinka.

The impact on a local economy of the siting of death camps was something new
to me. It seems that at Treblinka there was a relatively small staff of SS men and
the rest were Soviet POWs, mostly Ukrainians, trained to be guards. There were
about 100 of them and they were very welcome to the locals because they had
money and valuables. They traded with locals, buying alcohol, tasty food and sex.
They brought a flow of capital to the area never seen before or since. In Treblinka,
Belzec and Sobibór over a million and a half Jews were murdered, including Jews
from several large cities. These Jews had taken money and valuables with them in
the vain hope that they might survive. The locals benefitted from this loot.

A Warsaw engineer living in the village of Treblinka during the building of a
railroad bridge, Jerzy Krówlikowski, remembered that 'wrist watches were sold by
the dozens, for pennies, and local peasants carried them in egg baskets offering
them to whomever was interested'.[42] Prostitutes from local towns, or even Warsaw,
turned up to take advantage and local houses sold vodka and food.

Another informant said:

The village Wólka Okraglik is situated near Treblinka. Peasants from there used to send their wives and daughters to meet with Ukrainian guards employed at the camp. They were beside themselves if the women did not bring, in exchange for personal services, enough jewelry and valuables that belonged to the Jews. Theirs was a very profitable business.

Often the trains were waiting in the station or were split up and waited for several hours or even overnight. Krówlikowski, whose memoirs echo those of Zabecki, wrote that when trains arrived people came to the station from neighbouring villages:

> When I saw people near the train for the first time I thought that they came out with a noble intent to feed the hungry and bring water to the thirsty. But I was quickly told by the workers with whom I spoke that this was regular commercial activity, selling food and water at very profitable prices. And indeed this is what it was, as I later found out. When transports were not guarded by German gendarmerie, which didn't allow anybody to approach the trains, but by one of the auxiliary police formations crowds would assemble, bringing pails of water and bottles of moonshine. Water was for the people locked up in freight cars, while liquor was used to bribe the convoy guards, so they would allow the locals to approach the train. When there was no liquor, or convoy guards would not be satisfied with this form of payment, girls would come forward, put their arms round their necks and cover them with kisses – anything in order to come close to their wagons.
>
> After permission was granted, trade with the unfortunate prisoners dying of thirst and willing to pay 100 zlotys for a cup of water began. Apparently, it happened occasionally that people took the money but did not hand over the water. In the meantime the convoy guards would drink their hooch and then engage in 'their games' with trapped and suffering prisoners.

The 'games' consisted of the drunk guards accepting a bribe from the Jews to let them escape and then shooting them as they tried to run away.[43]

Very similar goings on with water and food are described at Lublin, with trains to Majdanek and near Targówek. Locals collected a few thousand zlotys each time.[44] A woman wrote after the war that it had been very difficult for people in her area to 'keep their decency' during the German occupation.

Such profiteering was not limited to Poland. In Lithuania, 100,000 people were shot in the Ponary Forest (Paneriai in Lithuanian) near Vilnius. About 80 per cent of the victims were Jews. Kazimierz Sakowicz (1894–1944), a former journalist, lived on the edge of the forest recording the activity in his diary from 1941–1943. He worked at the train station near where the mass murders occurred during Nazi occupation. On 11 July 1941, he began recording what he saw in very brief entries:

Since July 14 [the victims] have been stripped to their underwear. Brisk business in clothing.

August 1–2 For the Germans 300 Jews are 300 enemies of humanity: for the Lithuanians they are 300 pairs of shoes, trousers and the like.

Since August 22 the Germans have been taking the valuable, leaving the Lithuanians with the clothes and the like.

November 21st ... A Shaulist [Lithuanian volunteer working with the Nazis] with a rifle left the base and on the road (it was market day ... Friday) he began to sell women's clothing: a few topcoats, dresses and galoshes. He sold the last pair of coats, navy blue and brown, for 120 rubles and as a 'bonus' he also threw in a pair of galoshes. When one of the peasants (Waclaw Tankun) asked whether he would still sell [him something for his wife] the Shaulist replied. 'Let them wait' and he would 'choose' a Jewish woman exactly her size.

    Tankun and his wife were horrified, and when the Shaulist left they went away quickly. The Shaulist reappeared with the clothing. He was angry that the 'yokels' weren't there because he had 'gone to the trouble' of choosing a Jewish woman from the fourth line whose height was about that of the villager's.

October 7 1943 Since the morning, near the crossing, a market for the effects of yesterday's victims ...

October 11 The constant shootings, practically every day, have caused the Lithuanians who trade effects to be at the crossing permanently, day and night. They drink entire nights away.

October 13 The Shaulists are waiting for something, because there will be a group ... And the merchants also wait. They are not disappointed. At about 12 in the afternoon a truck.[45]

Sakowicz was shot on his bicycle on 15 July 1944. His diary was edited and published posthumously.

The Jews of Greece also suffered terribly but their story is rarely told. In 2000, Heinz Kounio, the president of the assembly of the Jewish Community of Thessaloniki (formerly Salonika), explained what happened to the Jews and the

Wehrmacht officer, Max Merten's role. He said Merten, the most powerful man
in the city, told the Jews, 'Bars of gold are the price [of survival].'

Several days before being sent to Auschwitz, the Jews were confined in a temporary camp.

> There they were required to hand over everything, including jewellery and all items
> of gold. From that moment on, the jewellery was gone. Merten and his assistants
> collected it in sacks. Andreas Sefihas, president of the Jewish Council in Thessaloniki,
> told a similar story, also in 2000: 'I alone had to pay [Merten] 1,000 gold British
> sterling in hope of winning my father's release from one of those camps.'

On 17 October 1942 Merten demanded that the Jewish Community hand over
10,000 gold pounds in return for the release of Jewish male forced labourers. In
July he had selected several thousand Jews for construction work for roads, airstrips,
railways and mining for ore. They were supervised by the Todt Organisation – the
Nazi public works authority using slave labour because inflation meant they could
not afford to pay Greek workers. The conditions were bad, with no accommodation,
so they had to sleep outside with very little food. Many of the Jews became ill with
lung infections and died. As this was a very inefficient way to undertake construction,
Merten abandoned forced labour and instead demanded a ransom of gold which
had appreciated in value during the war. He could sell it when wages were required.

Accordingly, in November he demanded 3.5 million drachmas from the Jews
which he reduced to 2.5 million, but it had to be gold and paid in £5,000 instalments by 15 December 1942. The Wehrmacht squeezed £25,000 out of the Jews
of Salonika to meet its operating costs in November and December 1942 which
equalled RM500,000. The coins were sold on the gold exchange for paper money
to pay the wages of German soldiers and Greek workers. This was no secret. On
11 January 1943, a Todt official reported on construction projects, 'As I have already
stated, the military commander has promised Salonika-Aegean [divisions] a half
billion drachmas, as soon as the sum has been raised by the Jewish community.
He was not, however, able to name a precise date.'

Additionally, after the war Merten admitted using the proceeds from the sale of
Salonika's Jewish cemetery to pay Greek workers. The ancient cemetery in the centre
of Salonika was obliterated when Jewish associations and institutions were dispossessed. The site was 357,796 square metres and was divided up into lots and auctioned
– even the headstones were sold off. In 1943 the Reich Economics Ministry said
that in late 1942 wages for the road construction and the mining of ore in northern
Greece 'had been made available from what was then an unknown source. It later
emerged that these funds were money that had been raised from Greek Jews.'[46]

The experience of the Jews of Rhodes is another example of how the death of
Jews was intertwined with the plunder of their goods and valuables. Rhodes came

under Italian control after the collapse of the Ottoman Empire, as the Italians captured Rhodes around 1912, and the Jews came under Rome's Chief Rabbi. It was confirmed in 1923 by the Treaty of Lausanne. The Jews were very happy and the Italians favoured the speaking of Ladino. After Mussolini fell in 1943, the Germans, arriving in September, were keen to conquer Rhodes before the British.[47]

On 8 June 1944 a Greek tanker, the *Tanias*, which had been commandeered by the Germans was torpedoed by the British submarine HMS *Vivid*, west of Heraklion. Aboard were all the 265 Jews of Crete, many of them children, who had been rounded up and were en route to Piraeus for their ultimate destiny in the death camps of Poland. There were also about 200 Greek and Italian POWs destined for the Nazi labour camps. All died in a watery grave as a result of the policy to attack all enemy ships coming out of Crete as they were used to transport German troops back to the mainland. All that was left of the Cretan Jewish community who worshipped in a fifteenth-century synagogue, vandalised by the Germans in 1941 and looted by their neighbours, was a community of seven men and three women in 2009.[48]

No anti-Jewish measures had been introduced in September 1943 because they had no interest in doing so. By July 1944 the troops needed funds. It was then that Lieutenant General Ulrich Kleemann, commandant of the eastern Aegean based in Rhodes, ordered Jews to be detained. Three ships arrived on the night of 20–21 July bringing plenty of fresh supplies of food.

It is recorded that the soldiers on Rhodes protested about the deportation order. However, Kleemann issued an order on 16 July aimed at combating 'doubts' and explaining the need for a 'radical solution to the Jewish question' on which ordinary soldiers could not pass judgement. The Jews were all rounded up in a few days.

In the summer of 1944, 1,673 Jews from Rhodes and ninety-four from nearby Kos were deported on ships to the port of Piraeus – the journey began on 23 July. It took eight days to reach Piraeus, arriving at Auschwitz-Birkenau on 16 August. Jews from Rhodes commemorate 23 July 1944 all over the world and it is a date of pilgrimage. Jews remember life in Rhodes like a 'paradise lost' – there was nothing negative until the anti-Jewish legislation. Interfaith relations were so good that Jewish books were given to the Mufti when the Jews were deported.[49]

Laura Varon (1926–) grew up in Rhodes and wrote about her family's deportation in July 1944. They were assembled in a building where she saw two SS men standing next to large sacks of money and four wooden barrels filled with jewellery – someone took her purse from her. She found her Auntie Diana in the toilets:

> She was flushing a special bracelet down the toilet. I gasped at first, but she just turned to me and smiled wryly. 'Somehow I don't think they are taking our valuables for safekeeping.' Auntie turned briefly, tossing a small ring into the toilet. 'I'll not have these German using *my* jewellery for their fun.'

Laura described how 2,000 of them had to walk through the town in the heat in a 'long, shuffling line', carrying belongings or small children. There were people in groups watching them and some of them shouted, 'It's good they are taking you from Rhodes. Go away. Do not come back.' She was suddenly aware that 'in a single afternoon, home had become a foreign place'.[50]

Afterwards, she told Yad Vashem that her mother was gassed at Auschwitz as soon as they arrived. Her father then was ill with diarrhoea and gave up:

> My Uncle Rachamim one day was coming from work and he saw a line of men going toward the gas chamber and my father was there among them. And the last thing my father said to my Uncle Rachamim was, 'Take care of the children.' Me and my brothers and my sister.

Later she realised the rest of the men had gone:

> And I found out after that my brother, Asher, with my Uncle Rachamim, went to Buchenwald. My brother Joseph and my Uncle Shmuel went to Mauthausen, and my friends Jacko and Salvo went to Dachau.[51]

The historian Michael Molho described the Jews' journey to Piraeus:

> On 24 June, the detainees are crammed into three transport barges towed by a schooner. After a journey reminiscent of Dante's Inferno they arrive in Piraeus, where they are handled roughly. Those who in the opinion of the navy watchmen are slow to disembark are brutally mistreated. An elderly woman is beaten so badly with a revolver that her brains splatter the surrounding detainees. Seven deportees have died at sea, twelve more are in the process of dying and the rest are starved, thirsty, helpless and exhausted. In Piraeus they are robbed of everything they have on them. Belts and shoe soles are searched and whatever is concealed there confiscated. The brutish guards go so far as to search the private parts of helpless, horrified women. False teeth, bridges and crowns are ripped from people's mouths. The booty is collected on four crates usually used for transporting cans of petroleum. The crates, suddenly converted into treasure chests, are filled to the top with jewelry, bars of gold, gold coins, and valuables of all kinds.

Shortly afterwards they were put on trains to Auschwitz. Twenty-one Jews died in transit, 1,145 died at Auschwitz and 437 died in labour camps. Only 151 Jews from Rhodes and twelve from Kos survived. In 1947 Rhodes had sixty Jews and Kos one. It is said that the Jews had lived on these islands since biblical times.

The Jews of Rhodes travelled further than any other group of deported Jews – at first it seems like the 'insane ideology of racial genocide'. However, there was a currency problem as Italian liras were legal tender on Rhodes while drachma were used elsewhere. That made gold desirable, so it was being ripped out of mouths.

The valuables stolen at Piraeus were only a small part of their possessions as the remainder had been left on the island. When they were rounded up, a Greek-Jewish collaborator told them to take a lot of provisions and valuables with them. The Wehrmacht confiscated all these items and then, as Molho wrote:

> Accompanied by informants, the Security Police searched the abandoned houses for hidden treasures. Whatever could be transported – household items, linens, furniture, glass, books – was carefully packed. Immediately after the Jews were gone, Ulrich Kleemann formed a 'committee for securing Jewish estates'.

Violette Fintz, a survivor, said the Jews were taken to a military airfield where a German officer seized their valuables on 20 July. There was a translator sitting next to him (probably the collaborator Recanati) who spoke Ladino. Four sacks were full of jewellery and the deportees were told it was being confiscated 'to pay for the maintenance of the Jewish population'. In fact it funded the Germans' expenses locally. Erwin Lenz, a German soldier on Rhodes, testified that malnutrition on the island was spreading to the troops by the autumn of 1944. He said the head of the Nazi Party ordered the 'exchange of belongings confiscated and secured from Jews, who had been deported several months previously, for food from local merchants'. He stressed the transactions should be done delicately and everyone was told to maintain 'strict silence about the source of the goods', but German soldiers knew these transactions were taking place.[52]

The Museum of Greek Jews in Athens holds a proclamation from 9 June 1944 to the people of the Greek island of Corfu, signed jointly by the prefect, the mayor and chief of police:

> As is also the case in the remainder of Greece, the Jews have been rounded up in the island of Corfu, and are waiting to be shipped off to labor camps. This meas-ure is bound to be greeted with approval by the law-abiding native population of Corfu, and will also be of great benefit to our dear, beloved island.
>
> Fellow countrymen, Citizens of Corfu!
> Now commerce is in our hands!
> Now we will be the ones to reap the fruits of our labor!
> Now food supplies and the economic situation will prove to be to our advan-tage, and ours alone!
>
> Jewish property as a whole rightfully belongs to the Greek State and, as a result, to each and every one of us. It will be taken over and managed by the Prefecture.[53]

In Salonika, when the oldest Greek-Jewish community was deported it was noted:

> ... as soon as they were marched away, people rushed into their houses, tore up floorboards and battered down walls and ceiling, hoping to find hidden valuables. There was a 'complete breakdown of order' wrote an official at the time, and the second-hand shops of the city began to fill up with stolen goods.[54]

It is tragic to read on 30 May 2014 that the Jewish cemetery in Thessalonika was very recently desecrated. A recent Anti-Defamation League report said that 69 per cent of Greeks had anti-Semitic views – the highest in Europe.[55]

## Corruption

Heinz Kuhn's flight from Germany at the age of 19 in 1939 was nearly thwarted by a greedy Nazi. Even though he had been baptised in 1927, his life was not safe. His parents planned for him to leave Berlin for Britain and join his older sister in what is now Namibia. All was well until 'A Nazi official suddenly demanded an extra bribe, which the family could not pay; a French couple, overhearing, offered them the money.'[56]

He never got to Africa, but became the outstanding representative of Coptic studies in the UK, based at Durham University.

We do not know how many young Jews' flights were thwarted by such greed, but obviously desperate Jews were sitting ducks for such exploitation. Corruption was a central structural problem of National Socialism. This was partly because the normal supervisory bodies no longer existed. The abolition of a free press meant there was no critical independent press and there was no parliamentary control, just mere rubber-stamping. The judicial system was under the Nazis and bodies like auditing offices were limited in their powers.

There was competition for material resources through the Aryanization processes, and the competition and rivalry between different organisations also led to corruption. The Nazis operated through cliques and camaraderie so that individuals did not get posts or positions by election but by patronage and by 'networking' on the old boy network. This meant there was little or no accountability and few limitations on power.

Additionally, many Nazis regarded themselves as having been 'victims' of the Weimar period run by the Jews and Social Democrats and were looking for compensation after 1933. Frank Bajohr categorised the Nazis as a party of 'organised self-pity'.

Another aspect was the nepotism. The old-time members of the party had their own chums and contacts which added to the corruption, so that a gauleiter's (local

official) chauffeur could have better opportunities for self-enrichment than someone more senior in the hierarchy. Additionally, the Nazi ideology of 'the master race'
gave the Nazis in occupied countries a superior attitude to the native population.

Political corruption is usually defined as 'misuse of public offices for private
ends'. It is not limited to bribery and corruptibility but extends to improper use
of office, fraud, embezzlement, nepotism, patronage etc. However, a major problem
was that, although corruption was officially condemned, in fact nothing was done
to deal with it. There were three aspects of the Nazi attitude to corruption:

1        Some corrupt practices were officially encouraged, and this represented
an organised system of abuse of power – examples were privileging party members, especially party veterans, with special Employment Office measures and the
opulent gifts and endowments that Hitler provided for members of the military,
political and scientific elites.

2        Tolerated corruption included black market activities, especially in occupied countries. The creeping replacement of public budgets with special funds and
illegal bank accounts and foundations was also accepted, above all by the gauleiters
who were not subject to any control in their finances or power.

3        Corruption that was not tolerated affected the Nazi Party, like the embezzlement of membership dues and contributions.

The boundaries were also blurred by rank, so more senior officials were less likely
to be rebuked. The seriousness of matters such as black market activities varied at
different times, and this was symptomatic of the whole culture.

The numerous forms of bureaucracy and the fluid boundaries of corruption
characterised the creeping loss of rights by Jews, their financial and economic ruin,
their forced expulsion and finally their deportation and murder. In this process the
state's claim to dispose of Jewish property could only be partially established. There
was also a tension between the financial and foreign exchange policy interests of
the Reich and the desire for personal enrichment or the promotion of the interests of the party and its members. There was tension over the disposal of Jewish
property linked to questions of power and institutional influence which touched
the relationship of state and party. But the right was claimed by the anti-Semites
in the party, and its offshoots were unwilling to subordinate their personal claims
to the Reich's sole rights of disposition. They all claimed they had made sacrifices
during the 'time of struggle' and demanded a fair share of the expected booty as
soon as the party came to power.

The anti-Semitic aspect of the Nazi seizure of power was not just apparent
through violent attacks on Jews, but was also directed at their material assets,
which the Nazis did not perceive as the Jews' personal property but as 'fraudulently
acquired' or 'stolen assets of the people'.

Many activists launched their 'hunt for booty' as early as 1933. In Hamburg, the
SA made sham searches of Jewish homes, seizing jewellery and cash and abusing

the members of the Jewish community who were summoned to hand over keys to safes. In Munich the SS robbed the Jews, often exploiting the opportunity to commit private acts of revenge. In one case, a dismissed employee attacked his former Jewish employer and forced him to hand over a large sum of money from the firm's safe. In Pillau and Elbing members of the SS obtained an ID card with the gauleiter's signature, visited the homes of wealthy Jews and extorted increasing sums of money with threats each time they came.

An SA lieutenant colonel forced the owners of a Jewish department store in Breslau to make a 'donation' of RM15,000, most of which he put in his wife's savings account. Also in Breslau they specialised in blackmailing Jews to hand over funds, and this was described as 'excessive National Socialist zeal' at the District Court of Breslau. The criminal acts were pardoned on the basis of the Amnesty Law of August 1934 – common practice in sentencing persons guilty of anti-Semitic theft and violence.

During the *Anschluss* in Austria about 25,000 self-appointed 'commissars' had occupied Jewish businesses, and once the Jewish owners had been removed had helped themselves freely. Josef Bürckel, Commissioner for the Reunification of Austria with the German Reich, commented that many of the commissars had got 'mine' confused with 'thine'.

In Germany during Kristallnacht 'wild confiscation' and plundering took place. In the South Hanover-Braunschweig gau the SS forced its way into businesses and homes and confiscated money, valuables, typewriters and cars. The NSDAP (Nazi Party) Reich Treasurer reported on similar activities in Stettin:

> A few party comrades from District Headquarters went to the Jews and first cut their telephone lines. Then they presented the Jews with 'deeds of gift' prepared by a notary informing them that they were being given an opportunity to make a donation. Occasional bold replies were answered with threats of shooting.

The NSDAP gau leadership in Berlin combined pogroms and enrichment with particular cynicism. The gau head of propaganda, Chief Wächter, forced the leaders of the Berlin Jews, which included Rabbi Leo Baeck, to make a 'voluntary contribution' of RM5 million as 'reparations' for the damage caused by Kristallnacht. This was called 'scherbenfonds' (debris funds) and RM300,000 was used for the state funeral of vom Rath. The Berlin party organisation received RM200,000 and the SA and SS received RM70,000 'for day-long service, including night duty'. Nazi Party leaders who had torn or damaged their shirts and coats during their nights of plundering and destruction also received compensation from the 'debris funds'; likewise, the widow of an SA officer whose sudden death was perceived as due to his 'superhuman exertions' in arranging the state funeral.

## *Aryanization – Focus of Corruption*

Robbery and wild confiscations of Jewish property demonstrated not only the precarious legal status of the Jews under the Nazis and the arbitrary nature of their treatment, but also the pressure from Nazi activists who expected the party to redistribute the Jewish assets to them personally, rather than letting the state dispose of them. This view is exemplified by the letter from the deputy leader of the Weser-Ems gau to the Führer's deputy. He expressed the opinion that 'Jewish assets will accrue to the state', and party comrades could 'go away empty-handed' and, therefore, 'the Party [must] assert its claims'.

Christian Weber spoke for those in the party who had earned the 'Blood Order' (Blutordensträger), which was awarded to participants in the 1923 putsch, and those who had been members of the party since 1932. He demanded that the proceeds of the 'Jewish wealth levy' (Judenvermögensabgabe), imposed in November 1938, should be distributed to benefit party veterans. He suggested that RM10 million should be diverted to help the Blutordensträger who wanted to buy Aryanized Jewish property – a fine scheme; Jewish money to be spent on buying Jewish property – a double theft, a double betrayal.

The Nazis had great expectations from the Aryanization of Jewish property, which started in 1933 and was legally enforced after 1938. The party ensured its role in the process, as after 1936/1937 all purchase contracts between Jews and the Aryan buyers had to be authorised by the NSDAP gau economic advisors. The process was exploited by party members because of their key roles in the Aryanization process. Apparently, many gau headquarters and regional party organisations used Aryanization to set up secret, unauthorised funds separate from the party and public budgets. These funds could be disposed of without any accountability and came mostly from extorted 'contributions' forced from former Jewish owners, and also from Aryan buyers as a condition for authorising their Aryanization contracts.

Some people were really organised. In the gau of Saar-Pfalz, Gauleiter Bürckel founded the Saar-Pfalz Property Company (Saarpfälzische Vermögensgesellschaft) specifically for this purpose. It forced Jewish owners, even those already in camps, to Aryanize their property, and 40 per cent of the sales proceeds went into a special account in the gau's coffers.

The Franconian gau's demands were remarkably modest by comparison, as the buyers were merely asked for 1.5 to 3 per cent of the purchase price – they collected a mere RM350,000. In Hamburg, Gauleiter Kauffman benefitted by at least RM854,000 in compulsory 'donations'. Gauleiter Murr, of the Württemberg-Hohenzollern gau put the requisitioned donations in a special fund called 'financial thanks' which was used to purchase businesses previously owned by Jews.

The Thuringian economic advisor collected 10 per cent of the purchase price of all Aryanizations, which he declared to be necessary to cover alleged 'expenses'. These funds were transferred to a special account in the gau which was originally intended to provide old-age benefits for 'party veterans'. However, the money was used to provide 'loans' to party members to acquire Jewish businesses being Aryanized. Many other gaus followed the same policies as in East Prussia, where the SS Security Service (SD) noted in an Annual Report, 'the NSDAP had helped many party members achieve economic security by providing loans from its funds'.

Thus we can see that party members benefitted from this organised system of expropriation of property from the Jews. It was excused by 'economic hardships' suffered during the earlier 'time of struggle'. This institutional privileging of party members reached its peak in 1938–1939 when Aryanization was being forcibly imposed and the party was so influential that the Aryanization of the retail trade was openly exploited as a fully blown benefits programme for NSDAP members. A report on the 'dejewification' (entjudung) of the Berlin retail trade endorsed the policy that 'old and meritorious party comrades who suffered hardships during the time of struggle should be at the head of the line'. This was supported by preferential loans from banks and savings and loan associations to these 'valuable applicants' to help them purchase Jewish assets.[57]

## Sale of Deported Jews' Possessions

Deported Jews were deprived of all their possessions before death. The early stages consisted of giving up bicycles, radios, pets and countless other items of convenience and pleasure. On deportation most of their remaining possessions were left in their property. We should not be surprised to know that the Nazis had a very efficient system for dealing with these goods.

A retired Hamburg librarian, Gertrud Seydelmann, recorded her feelings on the response to the auctioning of Jewish property:

> We still had no supply problems. Stolen goods or goods paid for with worthless paper money still poured in to us from the whole of Europe we had occupied and plundered. Our food cards, clothing cards, and shoe-purchase credits were still properly redeemed. Men on leave still brought meat, wine, clothes and tobacco home from the occupied territories. Ships still lay docked in the port with Jewish property that had been seized in Holland. Simple housewives from the Veddel quarter [a working-class district] were suddenly wearing fur coats, trading in coffee and jewellery, had old furniture and carpets from the port, from Holland or from France ... Some of my readers also asked me to stock up at the harbour with carpets, furniture, jewellery and furs. It was the stolen property of Dutch Jews who – as I was to learn after the war – had already been carried off to the gas chambers. I wanted to have nothing to do with it. Even in rejecting this I had to beware of the primitive, greedy, money-grubbing people, particularly women.

I could not express my true thoughts. Only some, less euphoric women whose husbands I knew to be confessed Social Democrats could I carefully influence, in that I made clear to them where these shiploads full of the best household effects came from and told them the old proverb: 'Ill-gotten gains never prosper'. And they took note of this.[58]

There was an indifference to the fate of the Jews which was generally put down to the impact of the war and the bombing on the German population, particularly in the later years of the war. However, this is not always true:

One investigation based on life-history interviews about the Swabian community of Baisingen, which had been unaffected by bombing, showed that the residents there overwhelmingly showed no moral scruples about taking part in the auctioneering of the property of their Jewish neighbours, and some even went to the authorities and to Jewish villagers before the deportations to secure particularly lucrative goods for themselves.[59]

There was also the fact the auctions were organised by the German Reich, which therefore appeared to be the owner of the goods. Accordingly the purchasers could:

... nurture the fiction that this was not the property of deported and murdered Jews, but state property that they were buying, particularly since a majority of the goods offered had belonged to foreign Jews, facilitating the anonymisation and depersonalization of their property further.[60]

Hans and Karl Klemm ran their auction house in Leipzig and in 1933 they had a very good year. The sales rooms and warehouse were located in a large building at 19 Grosse Fleischer Lane. As early as 1933 Jews were leaving as a result of the Nazis' anti-Jewish policies and the Klemm brothers were asked to sell their goods. Karl Klemm joined the NSDAP on 1 May 1937.

A couple of weeks before Kristallnacht, Polish Jews living in Germany were subject to expulsion and theft. This became known as the 'Polenaktion' of 27–29 October 1938. It resulted from the Polish Government's anxiety about the possible return of 60,000–100,000 Polish Jews from Germany to escape Nazi persecution. On 6 October 1938 it issued a decree requiring all Polish citizens living abroad to renew their passports by the end of that month. Accordingly, the Germans arrested about 17,000 Polish Jews who were forcibly transported to the Polish border on 29 October. This included approximately 1,600 Polish Jews from Leipzig whose household goods were confiscated. The Gestapo and the Chief Finance President of Leipzig contracted the Klemm Auction House to dispose of the Poles' property. Examination of the company's books from 1939 shows they were primarily filled with contracts from the Gestapo and the Chief Finance President. It must be remembered that these contracts to sell confiscated Jewish property led to an enormous increase in profits for the company, thus making the Klemm brothers profiteers of Jewish persecution.

The deported Polish Jews were in limbo for some weeks as the Polish authorities thought refusal to allow them into Poland would force the Germans to take them back. The Jews were left to camp in appalling conditions until 24 January 1939 when Poland finally agreed to admit them. They were allowed to liquidate any businesses, but were forced to pay the money into accounts which never paid out – further theft and betrayal. One of the expelled families were the Grynszpans, whose son Herszel was living in France. It was this treatment of his family that led him to shoot a German diplomat in Paris – the action the Nazis used as the excuse for Kristallnacht.[61]

The Klemms kept a commission of 10 per cent of the auction price and their costs for delivery and advertising were reimbursed. Klemm auctioned off belongings that had been confiscated by the authorities, as well as household goods that had been stored with moving companies. Moreover, when Jews were forced to move to the cramped quarters of the Jewish houses (Judenhäuser) they had to auction many belongings because there was no room in the cramped new accommodation. From 1942 until the end of the Nazi regime, the Klemm Auction House was kept busy auctioning off the last worldly goods of Leipzig's deported Jews.

Before the auctions, Hans and Karl Klemm would have removed the most valuable and desirable objects for themselves, which were given to friends and acquaintances or sold at discounted prices. The Klemms continued their auctions after 1945. In 1946 their past caught up with them when accusations about their activities under the Nazis began to pile up. On 26 May 1948 they were arrested by the Leipzig police and investigations began. In February 1949 they were tried in the Leipzig District Court. Their activities were judged to constitute active support of the Nazi regime, along with illicit personal enrichment. Hans Klemm received a prison sentence of two years and six months, his brother Karl got two years. They were incarcerated in the Brandenburg-Görden penitentiary and their private assets became the property of the Free State of Saxony.[62]

The Klemm brothers had also held auctions *in situ*. After the deportation of the inhabitants of the Jewish Home for the Elderly in Leipzig, based at Humboldtstrasse 13, the former occupants' belongings were sold to the citizens of Leipzig at an auction on site.[63] I think it might have been hard for the purchasers to be ignorant of the source of their purchases on this occasion.

A postscript to the Klemm brothers' activities arose on 10 November 1946, when Laura (Lore) Sonntag contacted Hans Klemm from New York. She wanted his help in reclaiming property, confiscated in 1940 by the Leipzig Gestapo. Laura, a Jew, had fled with her children during 1939–1940 and eventually emigrated to the USA. She wanted the return of her husband's books. He was the renowned bookbinder and artist Carl Sonntag (1883–1930), whose book covers had made him famous well beyond Leipzig.

Hans Klemm himself had auctioned off the goods, taken from her home in Großdeuben (near Leipzig), at a public auction on 21 August 1941. The directors of Leipzig's libraries and museums had shown great interest in the valuable books and works of art. In 1994, a restitution agreement returned certain works of art, which the city of Leipzig itself had purchased for the Museum of Fine Arts, to the heirs of Laura Sonntag, who had died in 1979. On 18 August 1941, Leipzig's own City History Museum (Stadtgeschichtliche Museum) had purchased various works of art, valued at RM30, from the Klemms. They included three watercolour paintings, one wood engraving, one copper engraving, one colour lithograph and two photos showing various views of Leipzig and environs. It was only during research for the exhibition, 'Aryanization in Leipzig', that these items were found in the museum's stores and it was realised they belonged to Laura Sonntag.[64]

It is important to consider two aspects of the theft of Jews' property. Many people were very eager to put their sticky little hands into the pot. However, there was also the official theft, sanctioned by the state through its various laws. It is noted that, in Leipzig, the Chief Finance Ministry (Oberfinanzpräsidium) was headed by Friedrich Sobe, who had a legal background and had been a judge before 1915, when he moved into finance. Beginning in 1935, the Oberfinanzpräsidium steadily increased its surveillance of financial transactions involving Jews. From 1938 onwards, at the direction of the Reich Finance Ministry, Sobe, as Chief Finance President, was directly responsible for the pilferage of property from Jews who emigrated or were deported. With Sobe's verbal approval, Chief Finance Ministry employees could, at no cost, remove articles from the Klemm Auction House – the proceeds from which were intended for the municipal treasury – and sell them at the appraised price for their own personal profit.[65]

It seems as though anyone could take anything they fancied and either keep it or sell it and pocket the proceeds.

## The Camondo Family in Paris

The story of the Camondo family of Paris is not one strictly of looting, as the family had given away enormous amounts of art objects, but were deported nevertheless.

The website of the Musées des Arts Décoratifs in Paris has a short paragraph about one of its gems – the Musée Nissim de Camondo. It is reproduced below:[66]

A family's tragic destiny:
Comte Moïse de Camondo was born in Istanbul in 1860 into a Sephardic Jewish family that owned one of the largest banks in the Ottoman Empire, established in France since 1869. Moïse de Camondo meant to give his mansion and collec-

tion to his son Nissim. But World War I broke out, and Nissim was killed in an air battle June 1917. After this tragic loss, he decided to bequeath his property to the 'Arts Décoratifs', in memory of his son. The museum opened the year after Moïse de Camondo died, in 1935. During World War II, his daughter, Béatrice, his son-of-law Léon Reinach and their children, Fanny and Bertrand, died in the Nazi camps. The Camondo family died out.

The website words have a remoteness about what happened to these people and implies an inevitability to it all. However, I believe their destiny could have been changed, they could have been saved from the camps and the family need not have died out.

The family was of Sephardic Jewish origins, which means they originated from Spain and would have been expelled in 1492 as a result of the Spanish Inquisition. Abraham-Salomon Camondo (1781–1873) was born in Constantinople (Istanbul) into a family already financially prominent and influential with the sultan. He became a spokesman for the Jewish community both at home and abroad. In 1840, when the great Jewish leader, Moses Montefiore, came to seek the sultan's help over a famous blood libel case in Damascus, his host was Abraham-Salomon.[67]

In 1865 the family took Italian nationality. King Victor Emmanuel II rewarded their support for his unification plans by making Abraham-Salomon a count, and this title was transmitted through the male line. The family moved to France in 1868 and became bankers to Empress Eugenie. In 1873 Count Abraham-Salomon Camondo's death was marked by a state funeral in Constantinople.[68]

Count Moïse de Camondo (1860–1934) was married briefly to Irène Cahen d'Anvers, before she ran off with the family stable manager, Italian Count Charles Sampieri, and converted to Catholicism. As a child she was painted by Renoir and the picture was universally disliked by the family, but it came with her on her marriage. It was stuffed in a cupboard and forgotten until Béatrice found it and returned it to her. Irène managed to survive the Nazis, perhaps because of her religion and Italian name, but the Nazis confiscated the Renoir. It was owned briefly by Göring and then sold to the Swiss arms dealer, Georg Bürhle.

After the war, Irène saw the picture in an exhibition and sought its return. She later sold it to Georg Bürhle and his foundation still own it. She was the sole heir to the Camondo fortune and it is said she squandered it in the casinos of the south of France.[69]

There were two children, Nissim (1892–1917) and Béatrice (1894–1944), and it was the count's intention to leave his sumptuous home to the son, but he was a pilot who died in 1917 in an air battle.

Somehow the saddest part of the tale is the death of young Nissim, the gifted, courageous son who was a much-decorated flyer in the First World War. He was killed after an air battle on the German front and the Germans so admired his

bravery that they paid him the honour of burying him in one of their cemeteries.
After the war Moïse had to move heaven and earth to bring Nissim's body home.
He is buried in the family tomb in Montmartre and the golden stone palace,
modelled after the Petit Trianon, is his memorial.[70]

The devastated count decided to leave his home to the French state as a museum
in his son's name. He specified that he wanted to 'preserve in France, in a setting
peculiarly appropriate to them, the finest objects I have been able to find of that
decorative art which was one of the glories of France during the period that I have
loved above all others'.

The Holocaust came to France and there is a letter from Béatrice's ex-husband,
Leon Reinach (1893–1944), a composer, telling her to leave Paris with their children,
Fanny (1920–1944) and Bertrand (1923–1944). However, after her divorce she had
converted to Catholicism and thought her wealth, following her father's death, and
the influential people she rode horses with in the Parc Monceau would protect her.

> In a small back room in the museum, a video tells the history of the Camondo
> family. There are stills of Béatrice on horseback as late as 1942, the year the family
> was arrested. She had believed, until it was too late, that her family would be safe.
> They had given so much to France: the museum, her brother's heroic life. They
> were prominent, loyal citizens. They were French; surely that mattered more than
> whether or not they were Jewish?[71]

This was written by an American-Jewish woman whose mother had French relatives
murdered in the Holocaust. I think she captures that feeling of bewilderment that so
many cultivated and assimilated Jews had about their position in their country.
Another visitor, Kate Hedges, commented in 2005:

> But finally, it is the de Camondos' glittering rise and terrible fall which defines
> one's visit to this museum. Like the family in the 'Garden of the Finzi-Contini',
> the de Camondos had every reason to believe that they were secure in this
> fabulous world they had created. In the end, neither their immense wealth, their
> exquisite taste not their powerful friends could save them.[72]

Surely this has sadly missed the point – surely their powerful friends *chose* not to
help them. Was this ultimately so surprising – their sojourn in Paris over the last
century had not been all easy.
Benjamin Ivry wrote about the exhibition held in 2010 in the Museum of Jewish
Art and History in Paris – he referred to the 'typically Gallic bile that seems to
have surrounded most of the family's philanthropy'. Isaac de Camondo (1851–1911)
bequeathed at his death:

... a massive number of great Impressionist and post-Impressionist paintings to the Musée du Louvre (dozens of which are on view at the Musée d'Orsay). These include seven Manets, fourteen Monets and five Cezannes – all masterworks and, even at the time he purchased them, high-priced treasures. To ensure that the doors of the archconservative Louvre would be opened to these artists, some of whom, like Degas, Renoir and Monet were still living at the time, Isaac added a hefty donation to pay for their 'installation'. Even so, after this staggering gift, the Louvre refused to accord Isaac a place on its Acquisitions Committee, on the ground that he was a 'foreigner'.[73]

It was also known that the people who profited from him (like the art dealer Ambroise Vollard) also bad-mouthed him. Vollard wrote a rather nasty description:

M. de Camondo's forefathers had not hesitated, on entering Europe, to abandon slippers and fezzes for boots, bowler hats and, in course of time, the nobiliary particle. But neither jacket, bowler hat, nor even a subscription to the Opera and a racing-stable sufficed to exhaust M. Isaac de Camondo's zest for the career of a gentleman. He felt bound to exhibit a taste for art. And with that *flair* that he showed not only in affairs of finance, the banker of the rue Gluck realised that the connoisseur of painting who would not appear out of date, owed it to himself to take notice of the Impressionists.[74]

Isaac was, in fact, extremely knowledgeable about French painting and also Asian art and he donated hundreds of pieces to the Louvre which are now on display at the Musée Guimet in Paris. He collected not just the popular printmaker Hokusai but also Sharaku. He persuaded the Louvre to accept living painters, thus breaking the tradition that artists had to have died at least fifty years before they could be hung in the Louvre.

His younger cousin, Moïse de Camondo, was also a keen collector and he was the creator of the Nissim Museum. The family were unstinting in their generosity yet were careful about their position. They took no stance over the Dreyfus affair, perhaps conscious of their position as outsiders, but also collected Degas, who was a notorious anti-Semite, and Isaac, a keen Wagnerian, attended the first Bayreuth Festival in 1876.

In spite of these liberal attitudes, when the cards were down they were Jews and, as such, not worthy of support by non-Jews. Moïse's daughter Béatrice must have been surprised:

Béatrice was an obsessive horsewoman who implicitly trusted in her upper-crust riding friends. She continued to compete in equestrian events even after the Nazi Occupation of France, and was eventually deported to her death, along with her young son and daughter and her ex-husband Leon Reinach. So much for French equestrian friends.[75]

Béatrice and her daughter, Fanny, were interned in Drancy in 1942. In 1943 her ex-husband, whose uncle had defended Dreyfus, and her son, Bertrand, were arrested trying to cross into Spain. On 17 November 1943 the two children and their father were sent to Auschwitz on Convoy 62 and on 17 March 1944 Béatrice went on Convoy 69 and she died on 4 January 1945, four months after Paris was liberated.[76]

The 2010 exhibition had various documents from the period of the occupation, including a Gestapo file entry dated 24 March 1943, referring to Leon Reinach, a composer and son of a distinguished scholar, Theodore Reinach, who had also given a magnificent home to the French state, in the following manner – 'possesses typical Jewish characteristics (crooked nose, thick lips and circumcised and apparently unreligious). Moreover, he behaves in [Drancy detention camp] in an insolent and pretentious manner and we recommend that he and his family be assigned soon to one of the transports of Jews.'

The indifference to the fate of these arch-patriots, if not the anti-Semitic vitriol aimed at them by French society and the government, led one Frenchman to respond to the exhibition angrily. Art critic Philippe Dagen wrote acidulously in the newspaper *Le Monde*, 'This is how the French government expressed its gratitude to the descendants of those who had overwhelmed it with priceless donations':

*Le Monde*, November 2009

Les rares interventions tentées pour les protéger n'ont rien pesé face à la préfecture de police et à la Gestapo. Toutes les mesures nécessaires afin de s'approprier leurs biens et leur fortune ont été prises dès 1941 avec un complet cynisme. Le parcours finit donc devant la longue vitrine où s'alignent les ignobles correspondances du temps de Vichy. C'est ainsi que l'Etat français a témoigné sa reconnaissance aux descendants de ceux qui l'avaient comblé de dons inestimables.

[The rare attempts to protect them were useless against the power of the police and the Gestapo. All the measures required to appropriate their possessions and wealth were taken, with perfect cynicism, from 1941. The path leads to the 'long window' where the vile correspondence of the Vichy period is on display. It is thus that the French State has shown its gratitude to the descendants of those who heaped incalculable gifts on it.][77]

# 8

# PEOPLE OF THE BOOK

There's nothing in the world for which a poet will give up writing, not even when he is a Jew and the language of his poems is German.

Paul Celan (poet) 1920–1970

Wherever books are burned, men also, in the end, are burned.

Heinrich Heine, 1797–1856 (written in 1820–21)

The Jews have been known as the 'people of the book' and literacy has been a vital component of Jewish life for centuries. Moses Maimonides (1138–1204), the greatest Jewish philosopher, wrote:

Every Jew is obligated to study Torah, whether he is poor or rich, healthy or ill, young or old. Even if he is a pauper who derives his livelihood from charity, or if he has family obligations to his wife and children, he must still establish fixed times for Torah study – both day and night, as it says (Joshua 1:8), 'You shall think about it day and night.'

The great Sages of Israel included wood choppers, water drawers and blind men. Despite these [difficulties], they were occupied with Torah study day and night, and were amongst those who transmitted Torah in the unbroken chain dating back to Moses.[1]

The unnamed librarian of the Sholem Aleichem Library in Radomsko, Poland, wrote, 'From days immemorial books played an important, even vital role in our nation's life. Rightly we were considered in the Diaspora the people of the book when the book served as a loyal companion of our nation.'[2] Accordingly, every Jewish home, however impoverished, would have a few prayer books, but most would have more than that because of a love of learning and the prioritising of the education of the next generation.

Book burning was not a Nazi invention. Milton wrote in 1644, 'he who destroys a good book kills reason itself', while Heinrich Heine correctly predicted that the burners of books would burn people as long ago as 1823. When Goebbels took over control of books, among other cultural matters, lists of books regarded as not suitable to be read by Germans were drawn up by Nazi student organisations, professors and librarians.

On the night of 10 May 1933 Nazis raided libraries and bookshops across Germany. They marched on night-time parades lit by torchlight, sang chants and threw books onto bonfires. That night over 25,000 books were destroyed by burning. Some had been written by Jewish writers, including Albert Einstein and Sigmund Freud. However, most of the books were by non-Jewish writers whose views were different to the Nazis, and therefore not deemed suitable for Germans to read.[3]

Book destruction continues even in 2015. The library of the Mar Matti Monastery in Iraq, with eighty historic manuscripts mostly around 500 years old, has been rescued from the monastery and stored in a flat in the Khurdish city of Dohuk. The 'Islamic State' militants were a threat to these valued manuscripts.[4] Speaking of an earlier attack on the Mosul Library and book burnings, UNESCO (United Nations Educational, Scientific & Cultural Organisation) director general, Irina Bokova, spoke of 'an attack on the culture, knowledge and memory', and said it was evidence of 'a fanatical project, targeting both human lives and intellectual creation'.[5] Nothing new here then …

One of the ironies of the Nazis' approach to the Jews was their schizophrenic attitude to Jews and their love of culture, be it their books or their art collections. In 1938 in Turin, the Italian Fascists burnt Jewish books. There were only about 4,000 Jews in Turin but the local Fascists forced their way into the Jewish Community Library before the Nazis arrived, and took most of the collection to create a bonfire in Piazza Carlina.[6]

The German Nazis arrived in Italy in July 1943, as soon as King Victor Emmanuel III had removed Mussolini from office. The Fascists had been in power since October 1922 without official anti-Semitism and had been supported by many Italian Jews. Anti-Jewish legislation was only introduced in 1938 and shocked many Italians, as Christopher Duggan observed.

Maria Teresa Rossetti, born in 1914 in Padua, wrote in her diary on 10 September 1938:

> The most beautiful sentiments (love of the fatherland, of the family, of work, of humanity) have vanished beneath false ideas. Freedom – of thought and the press – is a meaningless word. Books and works of art must have one theme only: fascism and Duce. The newspapers sing one chorus: adulation … Mussolini

himself, whom I once admired as the most complete genius, seems to me to have lost his sense of equilibrium. Pity has been banished and cruelty, in the form of the campaign against the Jews, has been elevated into patriotism.[7]

She noticed that as a result of the anti-Jewish laws several of her physics teachers were being expelled, but a few days later she showed her unbounded enthusiasm for Mussolini when he visited Padua, and wrote in her diary on 24 September:

I did not miss a word of the speech or an expression on his face and came away with a marvellous impression. He is an exceptional man who emanates an immense force, capable of shackling endless multitudes. His face is unique and inimitable, full of strength and sweetness, hard and human. You should have seen how he smiled at the cheering crowd and with what perfect style he made the Roman salute! To behold that face is to feel ready for anything, for any sacrifice, for any struggle ...[8]

## The Einsatzsab Reichsleiter Rosenberg (ERR)

The history of the Paris satellite camps of Drancy was dominated by Alfred Rosenberg – he wrote a great deal, but his 'great work' was *The Myth of the Twentieth Century*, which was published in 1930. It was widely translated and disseminated. In it he set out his theory of history which he saw as driven by the confrontation between the Aryan and Semites.

He was born in Tallinn, Estonia, in 1893 and studied in Riga and Moscow both as an engineer and as an architect. In 1919 he moved from Moscow to Munich and joined the Nazi Party as soon as it was created, having become a naturalised German in 1923. When Hitler was in prison after the Munich Beer Hall Putsch of 9 November 1923, Rosenberg took over the running of the party.

'This pioneer of Nazism, who had a particular penchant for lengthy theoretical disquisitions of a pseudoscientific character, also developed a theory of art that explained that Jews were incapable of any real artistic creativity, and that their possession of Aryan works of art was therefore an act of usurpation.'[9]

In April 1933, Rosenberg was put in charge of the Nazi Party's foreign policy bureau. On 24 January 1934 he became the 'Führer's representative for the supervision of the intellectual and moral instruction and education of the Nazi party'. While Hitler was the spiritual leader of the German people, Rosenberg had official control of cultural policy. In June 1934 he created the Rosenberg Bureau (Amt Rosenberg), which would oversee various administrative bodies, the most important of which was the ERR. It was dedicated to the plunder of Jewish cultural goods, first in the Reich, and subsequently across occupied Europe.

Later, on 10 November 1938, he created an ambitious project called 'Hohe Schule', which is translated as 'High School' but was intended to be a new university system. They had realised that the Nazification of the existing historic German universities was unrealistic – although the concept of the Heidelberg myth seems to contradict this.

> Rosenberg was thus a great creator of ideological agencies that together pro-
> duced dozens of reports on the occupied countries, on the United States, on
> England, on the Jewish question and on the education of the 'New Man'. The
> need of these administrative bodies, the Hohe Schule in particular, for teaching
> materials furnished a permanent pretext for operations involving the looting of
> documents, archives, artworks, books and the like.[10]

Later, Rosenberg's empire expanded with the creation of the new Sonderstab, or Kommandos, which were in effect organisations for theft. In July 1940 a branch of the ERR was created in Paris intended to supply books for the Hohe Schule, in the first instance by appropriating collections from major libraries. It was at this point that the question of the transportation of these stolen goods to the Reich became a consideration. However, in August 1940 the ERR had to submit to the orders of both the high command in Paris and the embassy, who insisted that they were only to take items from individuals and not from libraries and public collections.

In September, the ERR's mission was extended to cover works of art, and they organised depots in which to store and sort goods as well as making inventories and assigning new owners. Göring visited regularly, and most of the goods had come from Jewish collections. In 1941, the ERR moved from the Hotel Commodore to a town house at 54, Avenue D'Iéna. It was a very fine horseshoe-shaped building which had belonged to Émile Deutsch de la Meurthe, who had been a pioneer of the French oil industry with his brother. It had been built in 1890 with fifty rooms over five floors. Living there was Yvonne, the daughter of Émile, who had given her the house as her dowry when she married Pierre de Günzburg. The house was occupied by members of the family on each floor when the Germans requisitioned it with its contents. Apparently Pierre and Yvonne spent the war in New York.[11]

There is no denying that the bulk of the art treasures of Europe were in Paris – and Göring was involved with Rosenberg, together with General Wilhelm Keitel. Keitel sent an order to the army in France which stated that Rosenberg was 'enti-tled to transport to Germany cultural goods which appear valuable to him and to safeguard them there. The Fuehrer has reserved for himself the decision as to their use.' This was clarified in a secret order issued by Göring on 5 November 1940, specifying the distribution of the art objects being collected in Paris:

1      Those art objects about which the Führer has reserved for himself the
decision as to their use.

2    Those ... which serve the completion of the Reich Marshal's [Göring's] collection.

3    Those ... that are suited to be sent to German museums.

The French Government protested about the looting of the country's art, which it claimed was against the Hague Convention. In spite of this, the Nazis decreed that the art objects to go to Hitler's collection and those which the Reich Marshal claimed for himself would be loaded onto two railroad cars to be attached to the Reich Marshal's special train to go to Berlin. This was followed by other carloads. A secret official German report recorded that 137 freight cars loaded with 4,174 cases of artworks, and comprising 21,903 objects including 10,890 paintings, were sent from the west to Germany until 1944. As early as January 1941, Rosenberg estimated the art loot from France was worth a billion marks. [12]

The looting of art in occupied lands was a specific policy of both Hitler and Göring according to captured Nazi documents, reported Shirer in 1962. Both men increased their own private art collections. Göring, the Reich Marshal, calculated his own collection was worth RM50 million, with the looted goods.

> Indeed Göring was the driving force in the particular field of looting. Immediately upon the conquest of Poland he issued orders for the seizure of art treasures there and within six months the special commissioner appointed to carry out his command could report that he had taken over 'almost the entire art treasury of the country'. [13]

In Italy, Alfred Rosenberg's ERR people appeared at the synagogue in Rome on 30 September 1943. Many Nazis did not agree with preserving Jewish culture and would have agreed with the gleeful Nazi comments on the 1939 destruction of the Lublin Yeshiva Library in the *Frankfurter Zeitung* on 28 March 1941:

> For us it was a matter of special pride to destroy the Talmudic Academy, which was known as the greatest in Poland ... We threw the huge Talmudic library out of the building and carried the books to the marketplace where we set fire to them. The fire lasted twenty hours. The Lublin Jews assembled around and wept bitterly, almost silencing us with their cries. We summoned the military band, and with joyful shouts the soldiers drowned out the sounds of Jewish cries.

I had assumed the Lublin Yeshiva Libray was an ancient establishment and was surprised to read that it was only built as the inspiration of Rabbi Meir Schapira (1887–1933). In August 1924 the rabbi came to London to promote the yeshiva and seek funds – he was only 37 at the time. In an interview for *The Jewish Chronicle* on 29 August 1924, he explained the thinking behind creating the large yeshiva (study centre for Jewish theology):

> The upheaval of the war saw the gathering in Poland of a new generation which felt the need of advanced Jewish study, and there was no adequate institution for the purpose. It was felt that it would be better to have one large Yeshivah rather than a number of small ones.

He described the laying of the foundation stone on 30 May 1924:

> The foundation-stone was laid in the spring, and was the occasion of one of the largest Jewish gatherings ever held in Poland, no less than 50,000 being present, including the Chief Rabbi of Poland and the great Chassidic leaders. No less than one hundred and twenty Rabbis were present. So imposing was this demonstration that it gave uneasiness to the anti-Semites who were discomforted by this sign of the vitality of Judaism in Poland. They deemed it necessary to organise a counter-demonstration in Lublin calling upon the Government to prohibit the establishment of the Yeshivah in the city. Of course the Government, which had been represented at our function, took no notice. [14]

On 19 December 1930, a film was shown about the yeshiva at the Regent Cinema, Stamford Hill. The chief rabbi was represented by Dayan Feldman. The Polish Embassy was represented by Mr Xavier Zalefki, an attaché who spoke of the Polish Government's interest in the Jews of Poland. He said, 'The Government gave the Lublin Yeshiva every possible support because the building stood for Culture and without Culture no nation could live on.' [15]

Sadly, Rabbi Schapira became ill and died in 1933 aged only 46. Perhaps it was timely for him: this premature death meant he did not live to witness what happened to the 3 million Polish Jews and his precious library. When it was desecrated, the library consisted of 20,000 books, although he had aimed for 100,000 volumes. Some students were killed, and the elegant building served as the HQ of the German Military Police during the war.

However, it appears that Alfred Rosenberg was particularly interested in libraries for his pet project – a high school (hohe schule) for the NSDAP (Nazi Party). It was to be the Central National Socialist University, dedicated to advanced academic study. By 1943 several institutions had already been established: in Hamburg they would study colonial research; in Halle it would be religion; in Kiel the study of lebensraum (literally, 'living space'); in Stuttgart, biology and race; and a centre for the 'Jewish Question'.

This project had the impressive name of the Institut der NSDAP zur Erforschung der Judenfrage, based in Frankfurt, where the mayor had already confiscated the

Jewish books from the local municipal library. The institute was intended to be critical in 'teaching the spiritual basis and tactics of our ideological adversary'. Jewish scholars were brought from the liquidated Vilna Ghetto (now Vilnius) to work at the Frankfurt centre, where eventually over 6 million books were accumulated.

Rosina Sorani, the secretary at the Rome synagogue, kept a diary of this period and that is why so much detail is available to us seventy years after the events. We know that on 30 September 1943 about twenty officials searched the premises of the synagogue in Rome and, as Rosina noted, they paid particular attention to the two libraries – the Biblioteca Comunale and Biblioteca del Collegio Rabbinico. These libraries, like those of other ghettos in Europe, were the communal centres of both spiritual and secular life. The next day, 1 October 1943, two men from the ERR came to the synagogue and introduced themselves to Ugo Foá, president of the Jewish community, as orientalists. One of them, in a captain's uniform, claimed to be a specialist in Hebrew from Berlin. Permission was sought to examine the community's libraries.

These were not typical synagogue libraries and it must be remembered that the Jewish Community in Rome was the oldest in Europe, having existed since 161 BC when Judah Maccabee sent delegates. Consequently, the libraries had amazing treasures:

> The Biblioteca Comunale had a magnificent collection, one of the richest in Europe, not only for the study of Judaica, but also of early Christianity. A heritage of 2,000 years of Jewish presence in Rome, the library contained vast treasures that had not yet been catalogued ... Among the known material were the only copies of books and manuscripts dating from before the birth of Christ, from the time of the Caesars, the emperors, and the early popes. There were engravings from the Middle Ages, books from the earliest printers and papers and documents handed down through the ages.[16]

The collection was considerably enlarged in 1492 when many of the Jews expelled from Spain arrived. Unfortunately, the catalogue was based on the date of acquisition which made research very difficult. Undeterred, the ERR officers told Foá that he was to hand over the catalogues. A few days later another officer arrived. This was a lieutenant, who claimed to be a palaeographer (one who studies ancient writing) and a specialist in Semitic philology. His men rifled through the libraries, while the witness watched the Nazi intellectual and described what she saw:

> ... the officer, with artful and meticulous hands like fine embroidery, touched softly, caressed, fondled the papyrus and incunabula; he turned the pages of manuscripts and rare editions and leafed through membranaceous codices and palimpsests. The varying attention of his touch, the differing artfulness of his

gestures were at once proportionate to the volume's worth. Those works, for the most part, were written on obscure alphabets. But in opening their pages, the officer's eyes would fix on them, widening and brightening, in the same way that some readers who are particularly familiar with a subject know where to find the desired part, the revealing passage. In those elegant hands, as if under keen and bloodless torture, a kind of very subtle sadism, the ancient books had spoken.[17]

Rosina Sorani was present when the officer telephoned an international shipping company and arranged for the books to be transported out of Rome. Rosina noted in her diary on 11 October 1943:

> … they turned to me and told me that they had seen very well how many books there were in the libraries, and in what order; they declared the libraries under sequester, that within a few days they would come to get the books and that all was to be as they left it; if not, I would have to pay with my life.[18]

Sorani informed Foá, who contacted the president of the Union of Jewish Communities, Dante Almansi. Together the two men drafted a letter sent to four offices within the regime. Perhaps they were not surprised that none of the Fascist officials were willing to intercede, especially since three of the offices were run by Guido Buffarini-Guidi. He was a notorious anti-Semite and war criminal and was busy drafting further anti-Jewish legislation far fiercer than that of 1938.

On 13 October two large freight containers pulled up in front of the synagogue. Foá and Almansi were frantic and were especially worried about priceless gold and silver religious items they held. However, a genius decided to use the mikvah, which had been drained and a workman was brought in to hide the precious items within the walls. Some books were hidden in a municipal library, Biblioteca Vallicelliana, which was nearby.

Promptly at 8.30 a.m. the next day the ERR officials came back with transport – it was 14 October, the first day of the festival of Succoth. It took all day to load the contents of the two libraries, while the workman continued hiding valuables in the mikvah walls. Later, large pieces were hidden in gardens and homes all over Rome. The remaining items were collected on 22 December – this time it was the first day of Chanukah. The Nazis confiscated 10,000 books from the Jewish community of Rome.

These activities rightly caused panic among the Jews of Rome, who were less protected than their books. Most of the books were returned from Frankfurt after the war, but most of the Jews did not return. By the autumn of 1943 the diplomats, the military and the Vatican, including Pius XII, knew the Germans were preparing to deport the Jews.

The SS commander in Rome, Herbert Kappler, had received orders from Berlin to seize Rome's 8,000 Jews and transport them to 'northern Italy where they are to be liquidated'. It is claimed this is the only Nazi document that makes direct reference to 'liquidating' the Jews rather than 'special handling'. Only two days after the book raid, on 16 October 1943 and early on the Sabbath, over 1,000 Jews were seized in the ghetto and held over the weekend very close to the Vatican – but the Pope did not interfere. One poor woman, Marcella, captured with two children, gave birth overnight in the courtyard after the Germans refused to let her go to hospital.

On Monday morning they were herded onto the railway for their journey to Auschwitz, which involved terrible suffering. They arrived on the evening of 22 October but because several other trains were already there they had to wait until the following morning for their fate. The *Auschwitz Chronicle* for 23 October records:

> 1,035 Jewish men, women and children arrive with an RSHA [Reich Security HQ] transport from Rome. After the selection 149 men and 47 women are admitted to the camp and receive Nos. 158491–158639 and 66172–66218. The remaining 839 people are killed in the gas chambers.[19]

Presumably Marcella and her three little ones would not have been suitable as workers. 'The Germans expended far more consideration for the safety of the books than the Jews. Of the 1,041 Jews deported that day, only fifteen returned to Rome after the war.'[20]

The books stored in Frankfurt were threatened by the allied bombs, and consequently the ERR's vast holdings were moved to six separate repositories in a small village called Hungen after 1943. The books from Rome were joined by the Rosenthaliana Library from the University of Amsterdam and Jewish ritual silver and other Judaica from the Jewish Historical Museum and many other Dutch-Jewish collections (see page xxx).

Patricia Kennedy Grimstead from the International Institute of Social History (IISH) in Amsterdam has been researching this subject for over twenty years and, even after nearly seventy years, researchers like her are seeking to find further archives of the ERR activities. Many of the books were returned from the Offenbach depot, created for housing plundered books and restoring them.

The IISH was created in the 1920s by a pioneer of modern economic history, Nicolaas W. Posthumus (1880–1960), who set up the Netherlands Economic History Archive (NEHA) which concentrated on collecting archives. The political developments of the 1930s made Posthumus realise that a separate institution was required.[21] The IISH itself was a victim of the ERR's avarice, and the seizures from its archives in the Netherlands and Paris 'were among the largest so ruthlessly removed during occupation from any Western Institution'.[22]

After the war the Rothschild Library in Frankfurt was used to house the vast collections. On 3 January 1888 the Rothschild Library was given by Hannah Louise von Rothschild (1850–1892) in memory of her father, Mayer Carl von Rothschild. It was created on the English model of the free public library and offered free access to academic literature and modern fiction for all.

It started with a collection of about 3,500 books and the library grew steadily and numbered 75,000 books in 1913 and 130,000 in 1945, specialising in art, music, literature and modern fiction in various European languages. In 1928–1929 the library was incorporated into the Frankfurt University Library. Under the Nazis the library was renamed 'The Library for Modern Languages and Music' with every effort made to remove name of Rothschild. The extensive collection was preserved, however, and still serves today as an indispensable academic resource.

In October, a young American officer in the Monuments, Fine Arts & Archives Section of the Allied Military Government was asked to make a survey of the collections with a view to restitution, and he recommended that these operations should be moved to a better site at Offenbach. Ironically it was located at an abandoned IG Farben plant. The United States Archival Depot was run by Major Seymour J. Pomeranze, who was a Jew and a former archivist at the National Archives. They eventually processed millions of books (See photo No. 12).

The collection from the Collegio Rabbinico of Rome was returned in 1947. A total of 26,568 items were returned by two railroad cars. Of this number, 159 crates (6,579 books) belonged to the Collegio Rabbinico, fifty-seven crates of books (6,112) and six crates of archives belonged to the Instituto Austriaco di studi storici in Rome, and twenty-four crates of books (4,585) and fifteen crates of archives were returned to the Instituto Italiano di Speleologia-Postumia.

Stanislao Pugliese concluded:

> I had begun this study assuming that the books of the Roman Ghetto had 'merely' been sacrificed in a burnt offering to racial hatred; a holocaust enveloped in the Holocaust. But the real fate of the books proved in many ways even more disturbing: pseudoscience and corrupted scholarship at the service of a deviant and diabolical ideology. Here is but one small – yet bitterly ironic – example of the immense perversity of the Nazi project; a people whose entire existence was bound and symbolized in the Book were systematically destroyed, while their precious works were given lavish and even loving attention from the very people who sought their destruction.[23]

However, the second stolen library – the Jewish Communal Library – has never been found. Various investigations have been conducted, the latest under the Anselmi Commission on the Confiscation of Jewish Assets in 1999–2001. A few volumes turned up in Amsterdam and New York, but nothing concrete. As recently as 9 February 2015, a panel discussion was held in New York at the Primo Levi Centre, entitled 'The Lost Jewish Library of Rome', to analyse the investigations and discuss future efforts to recover the library.[24] After the discovery of the Gurlitt hoard of paintings in 2012, anything is possible.

Another confiscated library is that of Sigmund Seeligmann (1873–1940) a well-known Dutch bibliographer and historian. He had a private library of more than 18,000 books on Jewish subjects and often invited scholars to use what was regarded as one of the most important Jewish libraries in pre-war Europe. Following the invasion of the Netherlands, Seeligmann's Library was confiscated by the Nazis in October 1941 and sent to Berlin.[25]

Ironically, Sigmund's son, Isaac Leo (1907–1982), was sent to Theresienstadt. There he met Leo Baeck and had discussions with him. In Theresienstadt he was assigned to catalogue books confiscated from Jewish libraries, among which he came across books from the seminaries of Berlin and Breslau, and private books, including those owned by his father. Later, he said that seeing his father's books stamped with a swastika had been even worse for him than the usual hardships and humiliations of life in the camp.[26]

Eventually, what was found of the library at Theresienstadt was sent to the Hebrew University in Jerusalem. This was about 1,400 books.

Six years after the end of the Second World War and ten years after Seeligmann's death, his books arrived in the new Jewish state of Israel. Looted by the Nazis in Amsterdam, sent to the RSHA Library in Berlin, evacuated to Czechoslovakia and finally recovered by the Hebrew University, the books bear witness to the fate of European Jewish cultural property in the hands of the Nazis. In this way, Seeligmann's influence upon scholars continues through his books in the National Library of the Jewish people.[27]

From an obituary in the *Amstelodamum* – the journal of the society about Amsterdam, we read Sigmund was born in Karlsruhe on 21 May 1873, but he came to Amsterdam with his parents aged 11, gaining Dutch nationality in 1897. No one would have known he was not born in Amsterdam because of his love and knowledge of Amsterdam.

His library consisted of thousands of volumes which he called 'Hebraica and Judaica'. It was the largest private collection in the country and it had expanded beyond his original intention. The library was the world to him and he clung to it with all his heart and power. His collection was celebrated and praised far beyond the continent of Europe. He was always expanding the collection and adding the latest publications – he had informers all over the world who would tell him about items coming up. He called himself a historian, but he was also a skilled bibliographer. Anyone who asked him about any subject was surprised by his knowledge on not only that subject but also the latest literature on that topic. When he reviewed a book he often demonstrated more knowledge than the writer himself.

He was a modest man, in spite of his considerable knowledge. He corresponded with scholars all over the world, and when they visited Amsterdam he showed them around the city, took them to the museums and offered them dinner in his home. He wrote several memorable publications and anyone wanting to see his comprehension of problems should read his final work, *The History of the Jews in the Netherlands*, for which he corrected the proofs on his sickbed and which appeared 'when the angel of death was knocking on his door'.

He was a man of strong views, likes and dislikes. He easily mocked those he regarded as bungling, with false learning and even flawed Dutch. 'Yet those who could enjoy his friendship and his confidence will cherish as a jewel the memory of his personality.'[28]

Dr Hoogewoud, who has written about Seeligmann, confirmed that his library was the largest private Jewish library in the Netherlands at the time and its seizure was a major goal of the ERR. I was curious how he could amass such a collection, and Dr Hoogewoud said he had wealthy parents so he did not have to do paid work and was able to devote himself to this obsession. He died of natural causes on 31 October 1940. In 1950 his widow, Juliette Veershijm (1897–), emigrated to Israel.[29]

Dr Hoogewoud has written about how books were identified at the Offenbach Archival Depot – this was a large five-storey building along the River Main which was part of the old IG Farben factory in Offenbach, near Frankfurt. The Americans chose this as a sorting site for all the books they found. It was organised by a young Jewish captain, Seymour Pomrenze (1915–2011), who found himself in charge in March 1946.

Colonel Pomrenze (79) spoke about his experiences at a conference in April 1996 held in the Amsterdam Portuguese Synagogue, fifty years after the event. He remembered his co-operation with the Dutch Chief Archivist Dr Dirk Petrus Marius Graswinckel. The first transports were easy, because the Germans had not even opened the Rosenthaliana boxes, transported as late as the summer of 1944, and they could be returned without a detailed inspection. However, the rest was much harder as there were looted books from all over Europe to be sorted and gathered for boxing and crating to be shipped back to their countries of origin.

There were thousands and thousands of books with various types of stamps and markings – they were called semi-identifiables because their country of origin had to be determined. Pomrenze's successor, Isaac Bencowitz, organised eleven sorting units which each had a sorter, three stamp-seekers and one packer. Bencowitz had all the library markings photographed and each sorter had to select the books with the markings and put them in the correct box. They worked on the *ex Libris* book plates and books that merely had personal names either stamped or handwritten. This initiative meant the origins of the book could be established and books returned.[30] (See photo Nos 13a, 13b & 13c)

Martin Dean at the USHMM wrote about the 'Restitution of the Books' from the Offenbach Depot. By 1946 there were 500,000 Jewish volumes whose owners could not be identified. After deliberations they were handed to the Jewish Cultural Reconstruction Organisation (JCRO) which distributed the books to educational establishments in the USA. The basis on which this was done was being investigated as late as March 2000 by the Presidential Advisory Commission on Holocaust Assets in the United States.[31]

The Offenbach Depot was designated as the sole archival depot by the Military Government in the US zone of Germany (OGMUS) and was supervised by the US Army Monuments Fine Arts and Archives officers (*The Monuments Men*). As explained by Dr Hoogewoud, bookplates and markings or stamps were used and the large-scale shipping of books back to Holland, France, Czechoslavakia, the Soviet Union and other countries of origin can be traced through surviving ledgers and photographs.

In addition, between 1945 and 1947 the Library of Congress went to Germany to collect sensitive Nazi material that might otherwise have been destroyed. This included Nazi films and some 60,000 volumes from the Reichskolonialbund Library, which was considered 'a working tool for German expansionism'. It was quite imperative that anything restitutable should not be included by the Library of Congress.

At the end of 1945 a request was made for 25,000 books for use by Jewish refugees in the DP camps. There was particular concern that religious leaders should have access to prayer books and also ordinary books of no historic or artistic merit. In all, 21,000 books were sent but most of these books were lost track of when the DP camps were closed or were outside the US zone.

Most of the remaining unidentifiable books were originally to go to a central Jewish library, but that plan did not materialise. Instead they were distributed to 'public and quasi-public religious, cultural or educational institutions' in Israel and America.

Colonel Seymour Pomrenze gave his personal reminiscences of his days at Offenbach on 30 November 1998. He first saw Offenbach after his colleague, First Lieutenant Leslie Poste, a library and archives specialist, had driven him through a blinding snowstorm. Poste was obsessed with restitution operations being expedited in accordance with military regulations. Since it was established in July 1945 nothing had yet been restituted. Poste had also looked at the ERR's activities and its educational branch – the Institute to Research the Jewish Question. The ERR, backed by the German military, had traced Jewish, Masonic, Socialist and other anti-Nazi cultural objects throughout Germany and Nazi-occupied Europe and deposited them in many places, especially in Frankfurt am Main in the Rothschild Library, Hungen and Hirzenhain in Hesse and all over Bavaria. The ERR targets ranged across Europe from the Ukraine to the French–Spanish border, and from Greece to the British Isle of Man. The ERR even raided Italy which was an ally.

Poste also explained that the staff all felt that the books should be moved to one large secure facility. They chose the IG Farben at Offenbach. The first impression was both overwhelming and amazing at once. There was a seemingly endless sea of crates and books – they needed to be returned to their owners as soon as possible. It was a well-guarded five-storey concrete building suitable as a warehouse, but requiring some repairs. Inside were six or seven Germans led by a US citizen who was a displaced person and did very little. The operation was being run ineffectively and he had to make it work properly.

He set it up under a military directive in conjunction with Monuments, Fine Arts & Archives Wiesbaden on 2 March 1946. As director of the Offenbach Archival Depot (OAD) he was given extensive authority. He was to function as an archivist – he created an organisation chart as a blueprint for action. Three branch chiefs would be responsible for administration, operations and liaisons respectively. He needed hard-working personnel and requested about fifty people a week from the local German employment office. By 28 March there were 180 employees and the building was made suitable and heavy-duty shelving provided. Security had to be imposed and employees were watched for theft, particularly of small books that were easy to hide.

Tons of material was received from the places were the Nazis had left them. By 25 March 1946 the OAD had processed over 1.8 million items in 2,351 crates, stacks, packages and piles. The piles were checked for information on country of origin or language and waited further processing. Other items were studied by real experts and professionals. Many items required preservation or repair and the OAD did not have the necessary materials. One of the employees – a former monk – had worked with documents in a religious order and he was instructed to extemporise care and preservation techniques. He dried out wet books by hanging them up from clothes driers and applying extra heat.

What did the OAD achieve? By August 1947 some 2 million books and other identifiable materials had been restituted and distributed (3 per cent of the Nazi-looted materials were restituted) and the distribution was – Berlin 700,000, the Netherlands 329,000, France 328,000, USSR 232,000 and Italy 225,000.

In addition, the YIVO Institute for Jewish Research, with its HQ in New York, got 92,000 items. This was directed by the US State Department. The American Jewish Joint Distribution Committee (AJJDC) sent 24,000 books to displaced persons, while the Library of Congress had 20,000 books. German institutions received 50,000, Poland 25,000 and Belgium, Czechoslovakia, UK, Greece, Hungary and Yugoslavia each received less than 10,000.

Very conscious of Offenbach's importance, they wrote detailed monthly reports, kept pictorial albums and saved the correspondence, and these items are in twenty archival boxes in the US National Archives in Washington and also at Yad Vashem in Israel. Pomrenze's colleague, Isaac Bencowitz, also kept a diary and Pomrenze quoted this extract:

> I would walk into the loose document room to take a look at the things there and find it impossible to tear myself away from the fascinating pile of letters, folders, and little personal bundles. Not that what you held in your hand was so engross-ing, but rather what the next intriguing item might be. Or in the sorting room, I would come across a box of books which the sorters had brought together, like scattered sheep into one fold – books from a library which once had been in some distant town in Poland, or an extinct Yeshiva. There was something sad and mournful about these volumes … as if they were whispering a tale of yearning and hope since obliterated … I would find myself straightening out these books and arranging them in boxes with a personal sense of tenderness as if they had belonged to someone dear to me, someone recently deceased.

Pomrenze himself was involved in moving the books to YIVO in 1947 and later he was involved in restitution of the Collegio Rabbinico de Firenze's historic library, including the incunabula, to Italy. It was the highpoint of his civilian and military life. He concluded that his work had been with the 'cultural Holocaust'.

Facts and figures on the Offenbach Archival Depot fail to reveal the intensely moving story of this phase of restitution activity. Through the depot passed the remnants of age-old cultures, and particularly of a culture which survived the vicissitudes of interminable persecutions and periodic massacres. These books and objects were what was left of the hundreds of Jewish institutions of learning, of Jewish communities wiped out by the Holocaust. Few can fathom the depth of the Jewish tragedy for which these remnants stood as a sad memorial.[32]

As late as 13 September 2014, Britain was being urged to check in the British Library, Cambridge University Library and the Bodleian Law Library in Oxford. The Conference on Jewish Material Claims against Germany said Britain had not 'been sufficiently vigorous in trying to identify books that were looted from Jews among the volumes that it acquired from Germany'. The British Library holds around 12,000 books seized from German libraries and institutions from 1944–1947, and this may include items formerly owned by Jews. The Jewish Cultural Reconstruction Organisation gave Britain 19,082 books, 245 museum pieces, sixty-six synagogue items and twelve Torah scrolls. However, there were many complaints that inadequate attempts to find the rightful heirs were made.[33] Three days later (16 September 2014) there was a letter from the head of collec-tions and curation at the British Library saying that all the appropriate searches had been made.[34]

# 9

# LIVING CONDITIONS IN CAMPS, GHETTOS AND TRANSPORT

You may write me down in history
With your bitter, twisted lies,
You may trod me in the very dirt
But still, like dust, I'll rise.

Maya Angelou, 'Still I Rise'

On 26 October 1942 there was a shooting party at von Ribbentrop's hunting lodge with Mussolini's foreign minister, Count Galeazzo Ciano, and Himmler's personal doctor, Felix Kersten. When Kersten told Himmler he liked deer stalking, Himmler replied:

> How can you find any pleasure in shooting from behind cover at poor creatures browsing on the edge of a wood, innocent, defenceless and unsuspecting? Properly considered, it's pure murder. I've often bagged a deer, but I must tell you that I've had a bad conscience each time I've looked into its dead eyes.[1]

This chapter looks at the terrible conditions Jews were forced to endure once the Nazis had forcibly removed them from their own homes and includes the vile transports which were usually those designed for cattle. I have not attempted to write a comprehensive review but rely on the descriptions of those who were there and survived the horrors to record these facts.

Isaiah Trunk, who studied the Nazi-imposed Jewish Councils (Judenräte) in occupied Europe, examined the medical situation of the Holocaust victims. He regarded the circumstances the Jews were put in as an intrinsic part of the Nazis' plan to exterminate the Jews. He writes:

The pernicious conditions craftily devised by the Germans to undermine the health of the Jews resulted in the spread of epidemics and in a sharp increase in fatalities, taking a heavy toll of Jewish lives …

It can be safely assumed that the attrition of Jewish lives through the massive fatalities inflicted by diseases and epidemics was part and parcel of the Nazis' diabolical plan to hasten the physical destruction of the Jews. To achieve this goal, the Germans deliberately created unsanitary conditions which could not but spread contagious diseases.[2]

He enumerated the Nazis' methods to aggravate the Jews' health and expedite their deaths. The Governor General of Occupied Poland, Hans Frank, a qualified lawyer, told a group of German physicians on 11 July 1943 that the death of 3 million Jews was down to sanitary conditions. Frank was well aware of what they were doing, as detailed in his diary entry for 9 September 1941:

> The chief of the [Warsaw district] office, Dr Hummel: The danger of typhus has increased, because the resistance of the population, particularly of the youngsters, has decreased. The ghetto inmates get insufficient food. In addition, there is not enough soap and people live in overcrowded quarters. As of today 2,405 cases of typhoid fever were registered; the actual number, however is much larger. The fact that the Jews have been enclosed in the ghettos is a blessing, but the ghettos have to be totally isolated.[3]

Trunk lists the following factors as 'the gravest':

1   The mass expulsions of the Jews from their domiciles in the winter of 1939–1940:

> People who were forcibly moved had their welfare undermined and also suc-cumbed to illnesses and epidemics more than those who were not disturbed. Examples were one of the shelters in the Warsaw Ghetto (at 15 Stakvi Street) 207 of 673 inmates died during March to July 1941 representing 31%. In a children's home at 127 Leszno Street 333 of 600 children died between May and June 1941. Figures from the Łódź Ghetto and Lublin also showed very high mortality rates.[4]

2   Impossible living conditions and the crowding of large numbers of people into dilapidated lodgings:

> In March 1941 in the Warsaw Ghetto there were 1,309 people per hundred square metres with an average of 7.2 people sharing a room, whereas in the Aryan side the figure was 3.2 persons. In some places as many as 20 or 25 people had to

share a room of six by four metres. In the Łódź Ghetto 95% of the accommodation had no sanitation, no water, no toilet facilities, no sewers. When the Ghetto was closed there were 68,000 persons per square kilometre or seven times that in the 1931 census when 10,248 persons lived in the same area. Other ghettos quoted are Odrzywól, in Radom district, where 700 people were crammed into a space recently occupied by five families and in Siauliai Ghetto 2 square metres were allocated per head, although a secret document entitled 'Regulations for Treatment of the Jews in Latvia' said a maximum of 4 square metres were to be allotted per head.

German inter-office correspondence recorded that: 'the apartments allotted [for the ghetto inmates] are as a rule unfit for use … the tenements are so bad that 90% are ripe for demolition.'[5]

3  Hunger and freezing cold:

Hunger was an integral feature in the evil strategy of the occupiers against the Jews. The Governor General entered in his diary under the date of August 24, 1942, the following note: 'Incidentally, I should like to state that we have condemned 1,200,000 Jews to death by hunger. Naturally the fact that [not all] Jews will die of starvation will, it is hoped, precipitate [more] anti-Jewish measures'. Bread was the main item available. The daily ration was 107 grams per person per day in November 1941 but was usually about 83 grams and by 1942 this was reduced to 33 grams. Between January to August 1941 the food received was calculated as about 10% of what was required in calories. The poor who only existed on the food allocated, often sold their food stamps and existed solely on soup distributed once a day by the soup kitchens. Things were so desperate that three mothers ate parts of their babies that had died of hunger – this demonstrates the desperate straits the Nazis had reduced these poor women to.

The hunger also caused an increase in tuberculosis in the Warsaw Ghetto and the number of deaths increased tenfold from 1939 to 1941. Children, refugees and expellees were the main victims. Elsewhere food was only allocated to the Jews when the remaining population had enough – which meant that they would rarely get anything.

Virtually no fuel was allocated and bits of wood were burnt such as old floor boards, doors and stairs from demolished houses and bits of furniture in Łódź. In January 1941, most of the 1,218 deaths were as a result of the cold and both adults and children were found frozen to death. Dead bodies of frozen children were found lying in frozen urine in the children's homes in the Warsaw Ghetto.[6]

4  Poor sanitary conditions in the ghettos:

The facilities for washing bodies and clothes were limited by the resources and therefore hygiene became poor. Lice plagued the population and particularly the refugees and expellees often arrived in the clothes they were wearing when rounded up. The impact varied from place to place and time to time. Where the Councils were allowed to deal with the epidemics they were usually able to reduce the impact.

5  Forced labour's contribution to the rapidly increasing death rate of the Jewish population – this was the policy of 'extermination through work'.

## Conditions in Dachau Camp

On the evening of Kristallnacht, 9 November 1938, two men called at the Cahnman home in Munich asking for Cahnman senior. His agitated wife explained his absence and so their 36-year-old son, Werner (1902–1980), offered himself instead. They accepted Werner's offer, telling him he was going for a brief interrogation and to bring a toothbrush. In his memoir Werner recorded that, as the car sped into the city, he saw 'my father pedalling slowly homeward on his bicycle, looking pensive and downcast'.

He was taken to the Wittelsbacher Palais, a former royal palace and the Gestapo HQ at the time. He found hundreds of other people there queuing through various formalities. After a great deal of waiting, eventually, in the grey and foggy early morning of 10 November, they were loaded onto trucks and buses. After about an hour they had to get off. He knew what to expect so jumped to the ground very quickly, thus avoided being kicked by an SS man standing by the door, 'But older and heavier men were knocked down and kicked repeatedly before they could move on.'

They knew they were in Dachau but the reception was not encouraging:

We were marched around, kept waiting, interrogated, abused, marched around again, kept waiting again, and so forth, ad infinitum. We were deprived of all our belongings, which were, however painstakingly registered. Then our heads were shaved. Finally, stark naked, we were herded into shower rooms. After that, we were ordered to run through a long corridor, around various corners, to another room, for a 'medical examination'. On every corner stood an SS man who kicked each prisoner, as he passed by, with his boot or a stick; if a prisoner was slow, he was kicked repeatedly.

Werner's relative youth helped him escape most of these blows, but the so-called 'medical examination' consisted merely of being asked to turn on one's heels several times, ostensibly for inspection, but in fact it offered another opportunity for kicking and whipping. Elderly men who stumbled were trampled on unmercilessly. They then received prisoners' clothes and waited in a queue, enduring verbal abuse again. The SS amused themselves by asking if they knew why they were in Dachau:

> The reply – 'I do not know' – was another occasion for slaps and kicks. People were made to say: 'Because I am a traitor'; 'because I am a war-monger'; 'because I am a criminal'; and similar remarks.

It was only in the evening that they got to the barracks, about forty-eight hours after most of them had last eaten. But as soon as they reached the barracks they had to queue outside for their meal – two potatoes and a herring. Werner wrote that although he was very hungry he couldn't eat the herring. His brother-in-law, Leo, was in the next barracks and swapped the herring for a potato. It took him less than three minutes to eat his potatoes and a brown 'something called "coffee"'.

Overnight they were packed tightly on thin straw mattresses on a cement floor. Space was so limited they had to sleep on their sides. Before daybreak they were woken and had a lot to do:

> We had to fold the mattresses, store them in certain places in orderly heaps, take towel, soap, and toothbrush from drawers allocated to us, wash ourselves, go to the toilet, and be ready for breakfast within, I believe, fifteen minutes. Since there must have been several hundred persons in each barrack one can imagine the demeaning bedlam that was occasioned by all of this. There was shoving, pushing, yelling and cursing among the prisoners. Especially besieged by the impatient crowds were the toilet seats, which were arranged in an open row along the walls. If I remember correctly, no one was allowed to use the toilet except in the morning and during the night.

People were rushed around and then made to wait endlessly. There was no work to be done and time passed either standing to attention being counted or marching, running, exercising and singing German folk songs. Meanwhile the SS officers yelled, 'Why are you still here?', 'Why don't you get out of the country?', 'You can't exploit innocent goyim any more!', 'No more profiteering permitted!'

The elderly and infirm really suffered. If they broke down they were carried off and seen no more. Showing them compassion was punished, as was moving during standing to attention. On one occasion on a cold, windy evening they had to stand motionless for several hours – dozens who fainted or fell were dragged out of sight by the SS and never seen again. The death toll was appalling – some people were beaten to death, some contracted fatal illnesses and some were tortured.

Werner's diabetic friend Hans died within a day without his insulin. Others died from sheer sadism. The food was very limited and of very poor quality:

> The thin soups, hard bread, stale potatoes and nondescript coffee that used to be the mainstay of our daily diet had reduced us to hungry beasts. People had hunger reveries, daydreaming about roast beef, veal and goose. I was a lanky, skinny, rather underweight fellow when I entered the camp. Still, I lost about twenty pounds during the five weeks of my imprisonment.
>
> There were lots of rumours because no one knew why they were there and for how long. Hardly anybody understood that there was no rhyme or reason in the whole thing. Our families worked for our release, but success or failure was like a game of dice.

Perhaps the largest of all the many shocks the 'Dachau experience' gave its prisoners was over foreign intervention:

> We were quite sure that the 'civilized world' – Britain, France, the United States – would not stand for the mockery of justice and contempt for human rights to which we were exposed. We were even more certain that the statesmen of the world would realize that the Nazi regime was inexorably drifting towards war. It seemed to us that it was a matter of self-preservation for the democratic powers to slay the ugly dragon before he could rise and devour them. Little did we imagine that many influential people in the West lived with the illusion that they could accommodate themselves to Hitler, and that our fate was a matter of extreme unconcern to practically everybody.

Werner was released on 16 December 1938 with a visa for Paraguay and his possessions returned. He was told that if he failed to leave the country in due time he would be rearrested. He returned home just in time for Friday night dinner. He really struggled when he got home, fearing he was verging on mental illness. He pulled himself together and left Germany on 20 June 1939. He reached America via England and became a sociologist. He died in Forest Hills, New York, in 1980.[7]

Jews resorted to desperate measures to survive on the meagrest of rations. The German population had little understanding of what was really happening and that starvation was a deliberate Nazi tool to eliminate Jews. The remarkable fact is not that so many died but the number of people who managed to survive malnutrition and starvation for such long periods.

A young woman called Frau Popist referred to Jews as 'Israeli'. She described an experience on a snowy night in Hamburg in January 1942:

Married, more than eight months pregnant, and home alone, she happened to look out of a window facing the street. Below her she saw 'Israeli' laborers shovelling snow. Among them was a woman who had managed to push aside a small pile of apple cores for herself. Frau Popist cupped her hands to show me how small the pile was. Her voice beginning to shake, she described how a Nazi Brownshirt, riding by on a bicycle, spotted the pile, kicked it away in fury, and screamed obscenities at the woman. Not until that moment, said Frau Popist, did she open her eyes and recognise the basic cruelty of her government.[8]

Many people tried to help, and smuggled food – especially to children. One eyewitness to a horrific incident was George Hammond (1919–2003), a British POW in Poland in Gross Golmkau, working on German farms. George was with the Royal West Kent Regiment when captured at Oudenarde in Belgium in 1940:

The weather bitterly cold during January and February 1945 I saw about 2 to 3 hundred Jewish women and children being marched and pushed along the road towards Danzig about 30 miles away. They were all in a bad state suffering from the cold, very poorly clothed and very week and hungry.

Two young girls who I could see were suffering from starvation broke away from the column and ran into the farm yard where I was working and picked up a mangle worsel[9] which was animal fodder. The guard shot one and the farmer axed the other through the head. Their bodies were thrown into a tow cart at the rear of the column.

George later told his nephew Chris Hammond that the family who owned the farm where he worked had looked after him, giving him food, so he was shocked when the farmer killed the girl.[10]

The guards were shooting anyone who fell out of file, I felt sick and sorry for them, unable to do anything to help them as one of the guards held his rifle at me and made threatening gestures if I dared to give any of the children food.

I was remembering the time in 1940 when I was walking, marching on and starving. I was told later that these poor wretches ended up in one of the concentration camps where they went to the gas chamber.

When I returned to my camp that same evening I was told by my mates that they had someone hiding in the cupboard.[11]

She was a 16-year-old Jewish girl from Shavli (Siauliai). Lithuanian-born Sara Rigler (née Mutuson) was prisoner No. 58,384 at Stutthof concentration camp in Poland.

She was on a death march from Stutthof to the Baltic coast in January 1945, in advance of the arrival of the Soviet Army:

> The group of 1,200 women, including her sister, Hannah, and her mother, Gita, was staggering in the snow, dressed in rags, with only wooden clogs on their feet, with no food, and under the heavy blows of the SS guards. Hundreds of women perished on the way and only about 300 reached the village of Gross Golmkau (Golebiewo in Polish) 30 kilometres south of Gdansk.[12]

Sara left her mother to try to find food because they were so desperate. Stan Wells, who found her, was one of George's chums and gave her some food, wrapped her in an old army coat and took her to the rest of the group. They were so shocked by her condition they decided to help her and hid her in a hayloft in their barracks – Stalag 20B in Gross Golmkau. This was very dangerous because there was a nearby police station whose horses were housed in the barn under Sara's hiding place.

One of the gang, William Fisher, kept a diary on scraps of paper, which he transcribed after the war:

> 26 January 1945. God punish Germany ... I have seen today the filthiest foulest and most cruel sight of my life ... At 9 a.m. this morning a column straggled down the road towards Danzig – a column far beyond the words of which I am capable to describe. I was struck dumb with a miserable rage, a blind coldness which nearly resulted in my being shot ... They came straggling through the bitter cold, about 300 of them, limping, dragging footsteps, slipping and falling, to rise and stagger under the blows of the guards – SS swine. Crying loudly for bread, screaming for food, 300 matted haired, filthy objects that had once been Jewesses! A rush into a nearby house for bread resulted in one being clubbed down with a rifle butt, but even as she fell in a desperate movement she shoved the bread she'd got into her blouse ...[13]

The next day, 27 January 1945, William recorded the temperature as 15 below and saw more Jewesses in the same condition as before. Stan told him one of them got away and that they were hiding her. They enabled her to have a wash and feed her while one of the lads minded the horses. 'Take all clothing off kid, give her paraffin for lice in her hair.'

The next day everyone brought her food – she overate and was ill. On 29 January he noted:

> We had a good look at her. Her eyes are large as is usual with starvation, sunken cheeks, no breasts. Hair has not been cut, body badly marked with sores caused by scratching lice bites. Head still a bit matted and lice still obviously in ... Feet

blue and raw with frostbite, the right heel is eaten away by frost and constant rubbing of badly fitting clog.[14]

The men were being sent to Germany soon, but they managed to leave Sara with a local woman until the Soviets arrived. After the war, Sara found that no one else from her family had survived. She added 'Hannah' to her name in memory of her sister and settled in America. It took her twenty-five years to find her saviours. The ten have all been recognised by Yad Vashem as Righteous Among the Nations and as British Heroes of the Holocaust in April 2013.

Chris Hammond told George's regimental journal, 'George was affected by what he saw out there. It upset him all his life and he could never talk about it but I think he would have been very pleased with the medal and that things had been recognised.'[15]

Sara's camp, Stutthof, opened on 2 September 1939, the day before the war started, was the first camp to be established outside Germany. From the beginning it was noted for its cruelty – the first inmates were dead within a week from sheer brutality.[16]

Another woman in Stutthof, Marian Kampinski (*b*. 1925), was almost 14 when the Nazis invaded Poland. She was sent to Auschwitz with her mother, older sister, Etka, and younger brother, Icek, from the Łódź Ghetto in June–July 1944. Sadly her brother died in Auschwitz and later the three women were moved to Stutthof. She described the terrible conditions in horrific detail:

I never thought that such conditions like those I experienced first in the ghetto, then at Auschwitz, then at Stutthof, could exist or that they could get progressively worse. We went from one state of inhuman conditions to a further state of inhuman conditions. It was like going from one level of hell to a deeper level of hell. The stench, the crowding, the disease, the hunger, the cold was unbearable, but I kept the challenge of survival foremost in my mind and did my best to endure.

People started dying more frequently; the death toll went up daily. Every night we lay shoulder-to-shoulder with the dead and the dying. We listened to the sobs and the earnest prayers to God and other mutterings for somebody to help, somebody to stay close. The dying people always wanted someone to be there with them, to hold them as they went. They were scared. Each morning there were new dead bodies. Mother and Etka and others would take them outside or, after the doors were locked, place them in the rear of the barracks. As the days passed, those of us still alive grew ever more withdrawn. The pain and suffering continued on its endless path and it was like we had given up on words. Talking could do nothing. Our bodies had been tortured by hunger and disease, deprived to their very limits. With this torture, more and more people began to lose their minds …

> We were transferred to a third barrack on a block called 31st block. It was known as the worst in the camp. Illness, hallucination-inducing fever, and death were rampant. Not even the Germans wanted to come near this place. It was no surprise when typhus took hold. It had already taken hold of the entire camp and people were suffering unimaginable pain. It was the middle of winter. Snow was lining the frozen ground of our barracks. Our bodies were ridden with lice and crowded together. The disease spread like wildfire from person to person and the order came to quarantine our block. We couldn't leave and nobody outside could come in. Food and water distribution was halted. People died in the hundreds and were left to lie where they died. Nobody came anymore to remove the dead in order to burn or bury them. Outside and inside the barracks, it became an open graveyard of corpses.[17]

The sheer horror of the way these Jews were treated defies our understanding. Three centuries earlier, in 1665 London experienced the Great Plague, brought by rat fleas. Those infected were confined to their houses with a red cross painted on the door. As the plague took hold of London, the famous diarist Samuel Pepys wrote on 7 June 1665:

> This day, much against my will, I did in Drury Lane see two or three houses marked with a red cross upon the doors, and 'Lord Have Mercy upon Us' writ there – which was a sad sight to me, being the first of the kind … that I ever saw. It put me into an ill conception of myself and my smell, so that I was forced to buy some roll tobacco to smell and chew, which took away the apprehension.[18]

It is quite astonishing that 300 years later infected people were being locked up without food and water in the manner described above. At least in the London of 1665 carts went round each night collecting the dead and ensuring burial of the corpses. Additionally, the Great Plague was a natural tragedy. The deaths that Kampinski describes were the result of the Nazis' deliberate policy and their creation of such conditions where these deaths occurred is a complete betrayal of their victims.

## Transport to Treblinka

Franciszek Zabecki (1907–1987), the stationmaster at Treblinka Station, kept records of the trains as they came into the station. He is one of the main sources of information on the running of Treblinka, as he was there all the time. Additionally, as a member of the Polish Resistance he was trained to report on the movement of troops and equipment. He described the first train's arrival on 23 July 1942:

... the train was made up of sixty covered wagons, crammed with people. There were old people, young people, men, women, children and infants in quilts. The doors of the wagons were bolted, the air gaps had a grating of barbed wire. Several SS men with automatic weapons ready to shoot, stood on the foot-boards of the wagons on both sides of the trains and even lay on the roofs. It was a hot day, people in the wagons were fainting ... Without a word, we understood the tragedy, since 'settling' people coming to work would not have required such a strict guard, whereas these people were being transported like dangerous criminals.

On the wagons we could see chalk marks giving the number of people in the wagon, viz: 120, 150, 180 and 200 people. We worked out later that the total number of people in the train must have been about eight to ten thousand.

The 'settlers' were strangely huddled together in the wagons. All of them had to stand, without sufficient air and without access to toilet facilities. It was like travelling in hot ovens. The high temperature, lack of air and the hot weather created conditions that not even healthy, young strong organisms could stand. Moans, shouts, weeping, calls for water or for a doctor issued from the wagons. And protests: 'How can people be treated so inhumanely? When will they let us leave the wagons altogether?' Through some air gaps terrified people looked out, asking hopefully: 'How far is it to the agricultural estates where we're going to work?'

Twenty wagons were uncoupled from the train, and a shunting engine began to push them along the spur-line into the camp. A short while later it returned empty. The procedure was repeated twice more, until all sixty wagons had been shunted into the camp and out again. Empty they returned to Warsaw for more 'settlers'.[19]

Much has been written about the brutality of the Ukrainian guards. Zabecki expressed the view that the Lithuanians, who mostly guarded the trains, were much worse:

They really were sadists; they used to shoot at people, blind, through the windows of the cars, when they begged for doctors, water and to be allowed to relieve themselves. They did it as a sport – they laughed and joked and bet while they did it. Amongst the Ukrainians there were several who we knew wanted to get away. But you see, that too was dangerous. They were in just as much danger as everybody else.

It should also be remembered that trains that arrived late in the day often had to wait overnight in the station with all those people packed in like sardines.

Those who survived became hardened to what happened around them. Gitta Sereny interviewed one Treblinka survivor from Prague, Richard Glazar

(1920–1997), who told her about his time sorting the goods taken from people coming to Treblinka on the transports. (Kitty Hart-Moxon was doing similar work in Auschwitz.) He stressed that these Jewish workers (and the German guards) lived on the supplies stripped from the new arrivals, including the food they had brought with them. He described what happened when the transports ceased briefly:

> Things went from bad to worse that month of March … There were no transports – in February just a few, remnants from here and there, then a few hundred gypsies – *they* were really poor; they brought nothing. In the storehouses everything had been packed up and shipped – we had never seen all the space because it had always been so full … You can't imagine what we felt when there was nothing there. You see, the *things* were our justification for being alive. If there were no *things* to administer, why would they let us stay alive? On top of that we were, for the first time, hungry. We were eating the camp food now, and it was terrible and, of course totally inadequate (300 grammes of coarse black bread and one plate of thin soup a day). In the six weeks of almost no transports, all of us had lost an incredible amount of weight and energy. And many had already succumbed to all kinds of illness – especially typhus. It was the strain of anxiety which increased with every day, the lack of food, and the constant fear of the Germans who appeared to us to be getting as panic-stricken as we were.
>
> It was just about when we had reached the lowest ebb in our morale that, one day towards the end of March, Kurt Franz walked into our barracks, a wide grin on his face. 'As of tomorrow,' he said 'transports will be rolling in again.' And do you know what we did? We shouted, 'Hurrah, hurrah.' It seems impossible now. Every time I think of it I die a small death; but it's the truth. This is what we did; that is where we had got to. And sure enough, the next morning they arrived. We had spent all of the preceding evening in an excited, expectant mood; it meant life – you see, don't you? – safety and life. The fact that it was their death, whoever they were, which meant our life, was no longer relevant …[20]

He related how, the next morning, they all stood about, together with the Nazis, waiting and wondering where the people would be from – it proved to be 'the Balkans'. It was, in fact, a very special transport of 24,000 rich Bulgarians from Salonika. They came with special supplies for the long journey and when the doors of the carriage were opened:

> … we nearly fainted at the sight of huge pieces of meat, thousands of tins with vegetables, fats and fish, jars of fruit and jams, and cakes – the black earth of the ramp was yellow and white with cakes. Later, after the Bulgarians had been taken away, the Ukrainians fought us for the food.[21]

Glazar went on to speculate what would have happened if the Bulgarians had been aware of their fate. He said, 'They wouldn't have stood for it. It would have been a bloodbath.' He was amazed that people still arrived without a clue – that was in late March 1943. Already nearly a million had been killed in Treblinka, Richard and Zabecki agreed, and 3 million or so in other camps. Yet these people were as full of illusions 'as we Czechs had been six months before'. 'How could they not have known?' He went on:

> Marvellous-looking people they were; beautiful women, lovely children; stocky and strong-looking men; marvellous specimens. It took three days to kill them all. And ten days later we had processed all their belongings. Imagine, at fifty kilograms a person – that's what each was 'allowed' to bring for this 'resettlement' – there were 720,000 kilograms of *things*; incredible, how the machine proved itself in those ten days.
>
> This is something, you know, the world has never understood; how perfect the machine was. It was only lack of transport because of the Germans' war requirements that prevented them from dealing with far vaster numbers that they did; Treblinka alone could have dealt with the 6,000,000 Jews and more besides. Given adequate rail transport, the German extermination camps in Poland could have killed all the Poles, Russians and other East Europeans the Nazis planned eventually to kill.[22]

He had a good friend, Karl Unger, and the two of them were the only successful escapees from the camp on 2 August 1943 – the rest were recaptured near the camp. Unger and Glazar made their way to Poland and survived. After the war he attended many of the trials of the Nazis concerned with Treblinka, including Fritz Stangl. Glazar committed suicide by jumping out of a window in Prague on 20 December 1997, the day after his wife had died.

## Auschwitz-Birkenau

Glazar's comments on the supply of provisions are supported by Rudolf Vrba (1924–2006), famed for his escape from Auschwitz with Alfred Wetzler in April 1944. They confirmed to the outside world what was really happening inside Auschwitz.

> At the beginning of 1944, he noticed that preparations were under way for an additional railway line, for an expected transport of Jews who, in the SS camp language, were called 'Hungarian salami'. Transports from different countries, Vrba would later explain, were characterised by certain long-lasting provisions packed in the prisoners' luggage for the final journey into the unknown. As he subsequently wrote:

When a series of transports of Jews from the Netherlands arrived, cheeses enriched the wartime rations. It was sardines when a series of transports of French Jews arrived, halva and olives when transports of Jews from Greece reached the camp, and now the SS were talking of 'Hungarian salami', a well-known Hungarian provision suitable for taking along on a long journey.[23]

Jan Krugier's (1928–2008) father was a manufacturer and a modest art collector. His mother died when he was 5. His father was a Polish patriot and, at the age of 14, Jan was a courier delivering his first bomb in a rucksack to blow up the toilets at the Hotel Bristol in Warsaw. His father was killed fighting the Germans and in 1942 Jan and his family were arrested. His stepmother and younger brother were sent to Treblinka to be killed, but Jan escaped twice. After hiding in the woods for some months he was sent to Auschwitz-Birkenau to work as a slave labourer in the IG Farben chemical plant. He was then sent to Mittlebau-Dora where they made VE rockets.[24] From there, he survived a death march to Bergen-Belsen where he was liberated by the British in April 1945.

He was tormented by his experiences all his life but his wife, Marie-Anne, said in 2008 that he only spoke about them in the last fifteen years of his life and he was 80 when he died. She said he often disbelieved his own memories of the horrors he had witnessed. One of the incidents was the murder of 8,000 gypsies in one night.

> I remember one thing that [he told me] – when he arrived at Auschwitz, his group, they put them in a sort of big barracks, and there were people sitting there talking and playing, it was a very strange atmosphere. They were gypsies. And during the night they woke up and they heard screams and yells and trucks and dogs barking and so on and the next morning there wasn't anybody left. And his group was put in the barracks where [the gypsies] had been. And as time went on, he said, 'Do you think it was true? I wonder often, could I have had a vision or some sort of nightmare?'[25]

His recollection was correct – the gypsies were 'liquidated' during that night. It was the night of 2 August 1944. On 1 August, 1,400 gypsies were taken out of Auschwitz and sent to Buchenwald, including one little 8-year-old girl who had been snatched from her adoptive parents in Hamburg, because her real mother was half-gypsy.

On the night of 2 August after evening roll call all the gypsies were moved. Many people witnessed the terrible scenes, including Wladyslaw Szmyt. He was a gypsy himself, but he had been misclassified as a Polish political prisoner and was imprisoned in Birkenau next to the gypsy camp where many of his relatives were incarcerated.

On the night of 2 August he watched as gypsy children were smashed against the side of trucks and he heard automatic machine-gun fire and pistol shots. He saw the gypsies fight back with whatever makeshift weapons they could find, often spoons or knives, but soon they were overwhelmed. 'I started yelling,' he says. 'I knew they were taken to be destroyed. That's the end. Must be the worst feeling in the world.'

That night, according to the *Auschwitz Chronicle*, 2,897 gypsies were taken and gassed. Most of their bodies were burnt in open pits because the crematoria were not working at the time.[26]

Jan had wanted to be an artist, but ended up as an art dealer on the advice of the sculptor Giacometti. He became a friend of the Picasso family and amassed an amazing art collection at his home in Geneva which sold at Sotheby's in London on 6 and 7 February 2014.

It is very hard to understand the life in Auschwitz – it is beyond our comprehension, as is the arbitrary nature of life or death. This is demonstrated by an extract from the *Auschwitz Chronicle* for 23 April 1941 when a prisoner had escaped:

> Commandant Höss chooses 10 prisoners from Block 2 as hostages and condemns them to starve to death in retaliation for the escape of a prisoner. The ten prisoners are listed with their numbers, but it appears that there was a very young prisoner born in October 1924 who was so paralysed with fear when he was selected that he didn't move. In his place an old man, who was very debilitated and allegedly a high school teacher, came forward. The young man, who was 16 at the time, was Mieczyslaw Pronobis (No. 9313), who told his family and friends after the war. The man who offered himself in his place is listed as a 'physics teacher at the humanistic Odrowaz Gymnasium in Königshütte' and is unnamed. The report concludes:
>
> They are locked up together in a cell in the cellar of Block 11 and receive nothing to eat or drink. The dark cell is opened a few days later and the bodies of the deceased prisoners are taken out. On April 27, Marian Batko is the first to die; the rest die by May 26, 1941.[27]

It is appropriate to consider the conditions in which Jews travelled from place to place – in some cases they were *dying* conditions rather than *living* conditions, but they were in most cases quite horrendous and this needs to be highlighted.

A 19-year-old Hungarian girl, Susan Singerman (née Gerofi), who was deported with her parents, younger sister, grandmothers, aunts, uncles and cousins to Auschwitz. They endured a five day journey in a cattle truck containing 100 people with only one bucket of drinking water and one bucket for sanitation for the whole time. There was a sign on the truck which said, '20 horses or 25 cows'. On arrival most of the women were sent to the left and were gassed within thirty minutes. Her father died at Dachau two weeks before it was liberated. She only discovered these losses after the war.[28]

Sonja Fritz wrote about the arrival of the transports with Greek Jews. Some of the staff from Block 10 had to go to the ramp to help shave the new arrivals' hair. The Greek Jews had the longest journey to Auschwitz of any other prisoners – those from Rhodes had the worst. Sonja noted:

> The poor Greek girls had spent a long time in the cattle cars and their hair was full of lice and so infested that we got blisters on our hands. The first transport of Greek girls went directly to Block 10 and they gave us so many olives that we got indigestion.[29]

Julia Weiss (now Nicholson) was born in Cluj in 1922. Her father was a lawyer. She was arrested in Budapest trying to get back home the day the Nazis invaded – 19 March 1944. She was at the station with her non-Jewish boyfriend and he was allowed to leave with her bags, so she had nothing with her. She had been arrested with Julia Kertész (Uli), a friend from Cluj, also trying to get home. They were taken to Kistarcsa, about an hour from Budapest, where her bits of jewellery, including a little watch she loved, were taken away. Later, they were taken to Auschwitz in a cattle truck, but it was not too crowded.

On arrival they were offered travel in a lorry or walking. Julia and Uli were glad to walk after the long journey. It saved their lives – everyone opting for the lorries was gassed on arrival. A footnote adds that the first transport from Kistarcsa was on 29 April 1944 with 1,800 Jews on board. Most were gassed on arrival as only a third were required for forced labour:

> We then had to endure the whole procedure – our pubic hair and underarm hair was shaved off. We had to hand over our last belongings. I was given a blue suit with sleeves, a kind of dress like a sack, with shiny cuffs, which were covered in dead lice. I didn't know what the things stuck on the cuff were at first. And because I am so tall and have big feet I was given men's shoes, but with no shoelaces. The clothes had been worn by people who had already been murdered, but I didn't realise that at the time. Then, we were tattooed with numbers. Mine was 80,519. Interestingly, the hair on our heads was not shaved completely, just to above the ears. I didn't register anything to start with. I was still afraid for my parents and my brother – not for myself. I just hoped that they were OK. And I wanted to let them know I was OK – well, that I was alive. It helped a great deal to know Uli was with me. We talked about home, about our families, reminiscing about happy, untroubled times. There was one thing we regretted most of all: that we were still virgins and that we might die before we had experienced what it was like to be in love.[30]

Witold Pilecki (1901–1948) was a 39-year-old Polish cavalry officer who, in 1940, deliberately got himself to Auschwitz to find two arrested comrades. At that time it was purely a camp for Poles. He managed to send out reports of the camp which were only published in translation in 2012. When it became a death camp for Jews in 1942 he wrote about Jews being gassed and then burnt in the 'new crematoria'. He was working outside the camp at that time, and wrote:

> When marching along the gray road towards the tannery in a column raising clouds of dust, one saw the beautiful red light of the dawn shining on the white flowers in the orchards and on the trees by the roadside, or on the return journey we would encounter young couples out walking, breathing in the beauty of springtime, or women peacefully pushing their children in prams – then the thought uncomfortably bouncing around one's brain would arise … swirling around, stubbornly seeking some solution to the insoluble question: Were we all … people?[31]

## The Auschwitz Orchestra

Pilecki may have marched to his work hearing the music the Auschwitz women's orchestra played at the main gate as the slave labourers went to work each morning and returned each evening. They were a motley crew of musicians, surprisingly a mixture of Aryans and Jews who lived together in the music block. Some of them did not play, they copied the music, because all the music had to be arranged and reorchestrated for their extraordinary collection of instruments.

Anita Lasker-Wallfisch, a cellist, has described her experiences in *Inherit the Truth*. She describes how the orchestra was run by the violinist Alma Rosé, Gustav Mahler's niece – named after Alma Mahler. Her father was a famous Austrian violinist and both escaped to London after the *Anschluss* in 1938, but Alma returned to Holland. She had married two non-Jewish men and also converted to Christianity but that did not mean that the Gestapo lost interest in her. She was arrested in late 1942, fleeing to Switzerland, and sent to Drancy transit camp, north of Paris. In July 1943, she was sent to Auschwitz. The orchestra was already in existence, but when Alma arrived she was put in charge which gave her the privileges of a kapo – like extra food and a private room. The ordinary orchestra members had better clothing and avoided manual work.

The two professional players were Anita Lasker-Wallfisch and Fania Fénelon, who was a vocalist and pianist. Fania also wrote about her experiences, criticising Rosé and saying that she was concerned with her own self-interests and treated the musicians badly. Anita disagreed, saying Alma had to keep on the right side of the Nazis to protect the musicians' interests. While she was in charge not one member of the orchestra was killed and ill musicians were treated in the hospital, which was unheard of for Jewish prisoners. She herself fell ill and died in 1944, probably as a result of food poisoning, though typhus was also a possible cause.

Thousands of prisoners were marched in and out twice a day to places like the IG Farben factory, with the orchestra there to help them march in time. The musicians had to take out their stools and music stands and sit there in all weathers – sometimes playing in sub-zero temperatures scantily clad. Although they had roll call afterwards, as they were privileged in the winter it was done inside. Afterwards they had a hot drink which was unidentifiable and if they had saved anything from the previous day they ate it – so apparently no food was provided – just the hot drink.

Alma struggled with her 'musicians', as many were unsuited, but she was determined to have a genuine orchestra of very high standards. She had to drill everyone note by note which she did with great fervour, but as Anita writes, 'We must not forget that outside our little world the gas chambers were working non-stop.'[32]

Alma was very strict and imposed severe punishments for playing wrong notes. Anita described one incident:

> I remember that I had to wash the floor of the entire block for a whole week on my knees for playing badly. I had just returned from the Revier [sick bay], where I had miraculously recovered from typhus. It was the type of typhus that was rampant in the camp. Commonly known as 'Flecktyphus', it was transmitted by lice. If you had been fortunate enough to recover from it, or escape the 'selection' which was made regularly in the Revier, it left you unbelievably weak, and usually with impaired eyesight and hearing for a while. I myself returned to the Music Block in such a deplorable state and had duly been punished by Alma for my inadequacies.[33]

Anita wrote this some fifty years after the events – at least, the book was published in 1995. At the time of the incident she 'was furious and hated her', but at the time of writing she spoke of her admiration for Alma's attitude:

> … with this iron discipline she managed to focus our attention away from what was happening outside the block, away from the smoking chimneys and the profound misery of life in the camp, to an F which should have been an F# …

Her standard was her father's and her highest praise was to say, 'this would have been good enough to have been heard by my father'. She always stressed that anyone who survived should go to London to see her father and tell him about the orchestra, which Anita did, but he had died in 1946. Alma was quite aloof and dignified and her attitudes were not dictated by fear of the SS, whom Anita suspected respected her.

Their work also involved concerts on most Sundays – often in the open air between the two camps or in the revier:

> Also we always had to be ready to play for any SS personnel who came into our block for light relief after their exhausting work of determining who should live and who should die. It was on such an occasion that I played Schumann's *Träumerei* for Dr Mengele.[34]

Alma died on 4 April 1944 – she was taken to the revier complaining of blinding headaches and died a few days later. Her special status was signified by the people in the orchestra all being summoned and filing past her body, which was laid out on a white cloth. Even the SS seemed upset, wrote Anita.[35]

Henry Golde (*b.* 1929) was born in Plock in Poland. The transcript of his interview for the Wisconsin Historical Society (1–2 October 1980) runs to 107 pages and he was able to give enormous detail of his experiences in several different types of camps and ghettos. He went from Plock Ghetto, to a ghetto in Chmielnik, then to a munitions factory at Skarzysko-Kamienna in Poland, while his parents and brother were gassed at Treblinka. In the autumn of 1943 he was sent to a slave labour camp at Czestochowa and three months later he was sent to Buchenwald.

Soon he was sent to a munitions factory at Colditz in Germany and, just before the end of the war, the slave labourers were force-marched to Theresienstadt in Czechoslovakia to be liberated on 1 May 1945. In reading his story about being a slave labourer, it must be remembered that for much of the time he was a small boy of 11 years or so, and was only 16 when he was liberated. Amazingly after those terrible experiences, he was still thriving in 2014, according to my sources.

Henry was the younger son to Felix and Gina Golde. His older brother, Marcus, was born in 1925. His father was Polish but his mother was Lithuanian. When the Germans occupied Plock in September 1939, the 2,000 Jews (total population 10,000) were sent to a ghetto where they stayed for about six months. Golde said all the Jewish shops were closed and the goods were confiscated. He spoke of theft by the Volksdeutsch, who were German nationals who lived in Poland and acted as interpreters and informers for the Germans:

> ... they wore swastikas on their arms for identification and they were the most ruthless people that I came across and they would start going into Jewish homes and help themselves to everything. Jewish homes were looted by them, including some of the Germans in uniform. Jews had no rights whatsoever. Rations were given out to the Jews.[36]

He explained that as the Jews were not allowed to go the shops:

I was kind of a cocky kid. I did not wear a yellow badge and because I felt nobody would recognise me. I would go into German stores, I would go into Polish stores and buy all kinds of supplies. I was more or less like a runner for a lot of neighbors because I did have blond hair and blue eyes and I felt that they wouldn't recognize me and I refused to wear yellow badges. And one day I was caught because one Polish Christian recognized me when I went to a dairy to buy milk ... And I was right in front of the line when a Polish woman pointed out to the German that was selling the milk, you know, 'He's a Jew'. So she grabbed the pot from me, the container that I had for the milk, and tipped it back it back into the big container and she told me to get out.

He commented that he was lucky, because if she had taken him to the German HQ he would have been killed. The penalty for not wearing the yellow badge was death.

He also told the interviewer that when the Gestapo first came the schools were closed. They arrested all the intellectuals in the town and they were never seen again. They took both Christians and Jews – people like 'the principles [*sic*] of high schools, principles of all the other schools, the judge, lawyers and so on – whoever they figured that are intellectuals'. When the interviewer asked if anyone raised their voices over what was being done to the Jews Henry replied, 'Oh no, not at all, just the opposite. They were laughing at the Jews.' He referred to the strong Polish anti-Semitism and said the Poles were never pleased with Jews. 'If a Jew was rich then he was making a living off the poor Poles. If a Jew was poor, he was that dumb dirty Jew.'[37]

When the ghetto was liquidated in early 1940 his family was sent to another ghetto in Chmielnik. He described the journey and how the German soldiers came in the night and took everyone away. The soldiers took everything from them and threw them on the trucks. People were being beaten and left with nothing. They were taken to the outskirts of Mlawa and, when they arrived, the guards were lined up and beat people with sticks as they got off the trucks. The only accommodation was a kind of horse barn with straw on the floor. He described how, the next day, everybody was made to go to the building where the Germans were living:

... they would ask everybody if anybody had any valuables or money and so on that they had to give it up. And if they would find anything on the person [he or she would] then be shot. So the Jews gave up all the belongings that they had, all the money and I never seen so many diamonds and money and so on in one pile that I've seen there. They took everything away from people. And then of course we went through a search, too.[38]

They stayed there for a week with soup once a day. However, when they went out to get the soup, there were three people beating people on the head with sticks. All 2,000 from the ghetto were there. 'Sanitary conditions were atrocious. The men and women and children and all they had was a big hole in the ground and that's where you had to go to relieve yourself. It was just terrible.'[39]

From there Golde was taken, with some 3,000–5,000 men and women, to Skarzysko-Kamienna, which was the largest munitions factory in Poland. There were three different sections – Camps A, B and C – and they were all 10 miles apart. The camp was surrounded by a forest.[40]

He was sent to Camp B – 'Conditions were not good at all. There wasn't much food, the work was very hard and the beatings and uncertainty was great.' They were terribly hungry all the time and they knew their time could be limited, because every month there was a fresh transport bringing newcomers who were stronger, and every month there was a 'selection' of those to be eliminated. 'Therefore we knew that we're going to work until we can't work any more and then we're going to die because they always had replacements.' Golde reflected that these replacements had come from home and were strong:

> The funny thing about people is, my feeling is that if you take a person and you don't give him any food, you keep him hungry, you don't give him any clothes, you keep him cold, and you beat him, then you have an animal, and people virtually become animals. The only concern of people was survival and how to get your stomach full.[41]

It was also filthy in the camp. People slept on bunks on straw with no covers or pillows. People slept in their clothes in winter to try to keep warm. There was a stove in the middle of the barracks but unless somebody stole some wood it was not lit, otherwise it was freezing. People huddled together for warmth but no one got undressed. 'The lice were eating you up alive.' Once a month they were allowed to have a shower. However, they had to go to Camp A, which was 10 miles away and meant a round walk of 20 miles. Many people were too weak to walk that far so they never had a shower. Another problem was a lack of towels and hot water. If you went for a shower the water was cold and you couldn't dry yourself, so you would walk out into the cold winter and freeze to death.

A further problem was clothing – everything he had when he left home had fallen apart and for four years he had no underwear. When his shoes fell apart he was given wooden shoes and then, bizarrely, a paper suit:

> ... then they came up with paper suits. Well a paper suit was like, if you could stand it up, it would stand by itself. It was stiff. You looked like a robot walking around. When it rained and it got wet, it got completely soggy. And then of

course it frayed out. The seams would fray out and you looked like an American Indian in a full dress. And they didn't last too long. I would say about six month and the whole thing would fall apart. So I would say every year, they would give out new suits, and they were not very practical. Then one day, apparently from one of the Jewish transports, they brought some clothes in you know, and I was lucky enough to get a jacket and a pair of pants that didn't fit me, but this was much better than a paper suit.[42]

He was a 14-year-old boy when he arrived in Buchenwald, between time in labour camps. He told an USHMM interviewer that there was no work. The only time the Germans came was twice a day to count people. It was boring but when you had work 'you might forget a little bit about all the other troubles like food, hunger and cold and so on'. He went on:

And you seen people and that's the first place that I've seen the walking dead. And you'd ask yourself, 'What were the walking dead?'
   They were the people that were dead, they looked like skeletons, but apparently, their body didn't die down yet. Their minds were gone. They wandered around blindly. They actually were, dead, but they still walked around.[43]

## Shavl Ghetto (Lithuania)

Dr Wulf Peisachowitz, Gita Kron's cousin, was a very popular doctor in Shavl with steely blue eyes – he was 'the physician of choice among a number of the town's gentile elite'. He was head of the ghetto's medical affairs, in charge of medicine in the ghetto. He was more worried about the shortage of medicines than food and used every opportunity to smuggle it in from the Shavl hospital. He brought medicines to fight diphtheria and typhus – as in other ghettos he was supposed to report the outbreak of these diseases to the Nazis but did not because he knew it would be a patient's death sentence. His helper, Nathan Katz, who acted as his 'drug runner', got medication from the pharmacy in the town, sometimes resorting to breaking in.

Joseph Leibovich, brother of the Judenrät chairman, contracted TB and Wulf knew he needed to get him out of the ghetto to cure him. He managed to get him into a quiet side room in the city hospital away from the other patients. Wulf tried to clear his lungs by plunging a syringe into his chest. Just then two members of the Gestapo burst in and dragged Leibovich off the operating table, causing the needle to snap in two. One of the nurses had betrayed Wulf.

They were both taken to police HQ and Leibovich was taken to the cellars. Wulf could hear him screaming as he was tortured. He survived to be cured of his TB later, with further secret treatment. 'Then it was Wulf's turn. To his great surprise, his torturer merely sat him down and issued a succession of threatening orders, hitting everything but Wulf with various instruments of torture. The Nazi's wife was Wulf's patient.'[44]

However, in February 1942, Wulf was confronted with two policemen in the ghetto as their chief, Albinas Grebliunas, was seriously ill with typhoid. Wulf quickly established he did not have typhoid but blood poisoning and when Grebliunas soon rose from his bed, following the prescribing of the correct drug, he was thought to have performed a miracle.

The police chief was so delighted that he asked Wulf what he wanted in return. Wulf and the Judenrät explained that the Nazis had cut back food rations to the ghetto. Accordingly, Grebliunas arranged for a special squad to guard the ghetto's entrance, looking the other way when food was smuggled in. The arrangement only lasted until August 1942 when the Nazis, realising what was going on, stopped the smuggling, demanding the Judenrät hand over fifty smugglers on 2 September to be shot. The Judenrät wrestled again with doing the Nazis' dirty work. They knew that failure to provide the fifty victims would result in the Nazis choosing fifty people randomly. It was too much for them and so the members of the Judenrät turned themselves into Gewecke, the head of regional administration. He was absolutely furious – ranting and raving for some time, but eventually a face-saving plan was agreed. He would accept a payment of RM20,000 to call off the executions. The Judenrät collected the sum with great difficulty from the ghetto Jews – knowing that Hitler's treasury was unlikely to benefit.[45]

## Cluj Ghetto

The Cluj Ghetto in Rumania was created in May 1944 when 16,000 local Jews were rounded up, with 2,000 from the surrounding areas. Between 29 May and 13 June they were deported to Auschwitz where most of them were killed – one survivor was Magdalena Berkovics, née Farkas (1919–). Her father, Mendel, was from Hungary and her mother, Berta, was a local girl. Her brother, Tibor, was six years older and was a doctor and a violinist who died in 1944. In 1937 Magdalena went to a music conservatoire where she played the piano and gave lessons. She had two music degrees. In 1939 she married a singer she had accompanied on the piano.[46]

Magdalena was aware of low level anti-Semitism which caused a difference between her colleagues and herself. When the ghetto was created she stayed in the family home – presumably because it was within the ghetto area. 'The men were taken away for forced labour so only women were left. It was crowded and food was scarce but she was still able to teach piano, even to Christian children who came into the ghetto. With the money she made from teaching she got food on the black market. She seldom got mail and the radios were taken away.' In June 1944 a Hungarian colonel told the Jews they would be going away.

> She took winter clothes, some food, including a jar of jelly, but put everything down because it was too heavy. They left from the railroad station, and were in a train car with seventy others, who were asking for water. Many people died over the three to four day journey. When the train arrived in Auschwitz, which she had not heard of before, Magdalena told people not to worry. Magdalena was then separated from her family except her 25-year-old cousin. She was not able to say goodbye to the other relatives, none of whom survived. She was taken to the baths, had her clothes taken away and her hair removed. She wore others' clothes and was only given soup to eat.
>
> There was no work to do, so she was taken to Stutthof in August 1944 and from there to different camps – Steinort, Ebling and Groudentz – where she dug ditches and worked from 2.00 a.m. until 5.00 p.m. She always had stomach problems and would eat raw potatoes.

She told the interviewer that one day the guards disappeared and people shouted, 'We are free!' She eventually got back to Cluj and found Christians living in the family's house, but said no more about it or what happened to her husband. In 1946, however, she married her second cousin, Zoltan Berkovics, and they stayed in Cluj until they moved to America where their only son was living in the 1980s. She has never returned to Rumania.

As I write, there have been international outcries about a Christmas carol broadcast on Rumanian TV from a regional TV station, TVR Cluj, in which a group in traditional costumes sang a song about 'The kikes, the damn kikes, Holy God would not leave the kike alive, neither in heaven nor on earth, only in the chimney as smoke, this is what the kike is good for, to make kike smoke through the chimney on the street' ('kike' is an American word for Jew). A YouTube video of the performance showed the choir singing the offensive song and then taking questions from a female host who thanked the singers before asking about their choice of music and why it reflects the traditional Cluj culture in Rumania.[47] The TVR company subsequently distanced itself from the choice of song, but at the time was happy to broadcast it. The Rumanian Foreign Minister and other government officials condemned the broadcast and the station was fined US $15,000.[48]

Hedi Fischer (1930–) was parted from her mother and brothers in June 1944, when she was put on a cattle train with a few thousand other Jews from the Debrecen area of Hungary. She has written:

> ... we were loaded into cattle trucks which were then sealed. The temperature in the Hungarian summer was nearly 100 degrees and we were given no water or bread, only a bucket to be used as a toilet. Soldiers with dogs and bayonets

were guarding us all the way on a horrific journey which lasted five days and nights. The stench in our wagon was unbearable. There were 80 people. Old and young, some sick, but none of us had enough space to lie down. The constant heat, hunger, thirst and lack of sleep, made us quite delirious. We had no idea where they were taking us and were convinced that they would kill us when we would get there. I must have been very dehydrated because my whole body had swollen up and I felt ill.

Finally, we reached Strasshof, in Austria, where I was carried out by two inmates and put on the grass. In the wagon two women of about 40 had committed suicide by swallowing poison, three others lost their mind and two older persons died of suffocation. It is hard to describe how we felt after that humiliating trip. We could breathe fresh air and then we were taken into a place to shower with real water. Our clothes were taken into another room, to be disinfected. After another day's hunger we were given a piece of bread and bacon. As I was brought up on kosher food, I refused to eat the pig product.

She was told she was going for forced labour in Vienna. She volunteered to work in an electronics factory with her friend, Alice. They worked for Siemens & Schuckert near Tulln. There were only thirty Jews among the Poles, Ukrainians and Yugoslav workers. Conditions were terrible. Hedi wrote:

Our barracks were bare; our bed had only straw on it and was full of bedbugs. They kept us awake at night. We had to walk 5km to our work place and lived on black coffee, a small piece of bread and a kind of soup. Needless to say, we were hungry all the time and could not think of anything else except getting hold of some real food.[49]

The firm Siemens & Schuckert was founded in 1903 as an electrical engineering company. They supplied electrical parts to all sorts of Nazi camps and used slave labour. In 1966 they were incorporated into Siemens AG. It is important to remember that such companies made profits out of the exploitation and misery imposed on their wretched slave labourers.

## Sobibór

Toivi Blatt was 15 when he and his parents were deported from their home town, Izbica, Poland, to Sobibór. Sobibór was one of the 'Operation Reinhard' camps established in April 1942. About 250,000 people are calculated to have been murdered there in a year – the throughput was calculated by Wirth at around 20,000 a day. Most of the Jews were killed as soon as they arrived, but when Toivi arrived one of the German officers was looking for carpenters and, although he wasn't a carpenter, Toivi volunteered.

He thus became a member of the Jewish Sonderkommando which helped with the running of the camp. Part of his work was to deal with the Jewish transports – many of the Jews from outside Poland had no idea what they were coming to. When a Dutch transport of 3,000 Jews arrived, they had to divide the women and children on one side and the men on the other. They took the women away first. They had to leave their luggage and:

> ... women were told to leave their handbags, just throw them on the side. At that point I noticed their eyes – in the women's eye some kind of anxiety, they were afraid. Because what do you have in a handbag – the most important stuff. One woman didn't want to leave it and the German hit her with a whip. They went to a yard, a big yard, and there was a German we called 'the angel of death', or 'the doctor' or 'the priest' because he was talking to them so nicely. To the group he apologised for the three day travel from Holland but now he said they're in a beautiful place, because always Sobibór was beautiful. It was in a forest. And he said, 'Now for sanitary reasons you need to go have a shower and later you will get orders to leave here'. The people clapped 'bravo' and then they undressed themselves nicely and untied their shoes and they went straight through a room maybe 200 feet long to a barrack and there I was again. I was waiting for them.
>
> Then the women started getting completely nude, young kids, young girls and old ladies and I was a shy boy – I had never seen a nude woman and I didn't know where to look. But I needed to cut their hair. So they gave me long scissors. I didn't know what to do with the shears. So my friend who was many times there in this barrack, he said, 'Just cut the hair, you need to cut it very close.' So I am asked to leave a little bit, especially by the young girls, not to cut much. They didn't know they will die in a few minutes. Once their hair was cut, they were told to go further up from the barracks just a few minutes to the gas chamber. And I am sure that this trap was so perfect, I'm sure when they were in the gas chambers and the gas came out of the shower heads instead of water, probably they were thinking that it was some kind of malfunction. I remember once a transport came from Holland, it came in the middle of the night. 3,000 people arrived and when they were already taken out of the gas chambers to be burnt, I remember thinking it was a beautiful night, the stars – and 3,000 people died. Nothing happened. The stars are in the same place.[50]

In October 1943 he took part in the mass breakout of Sobibór organised by Red Army prisoners. They escaped through a hole in the fence and ran into the forest. Three hundred prisoners escaped and most did not survive, but Toivi did. He acted as a courier for the Polish underground and stayed in Poland after the war. In 1959 he went to the United States.[51]

Julie Orringer's grandfather was a Hungarian forced labourer when he experienced a rare act of compassion. He was caught trying to send letters back to his family, which was prohibited. As he was being punished a very exalted Hungarian army officer came by and asked why he was being beaten. 'When he heard that my grandfather was being punished for trying to send word to his wife and child that he was still alive, the officer punished the people who were beating him and cleared my grandfather of all charges.'[52]

Solomon Radasky (1910–2002) was a furrier in Warsaw with his own shop when Poland was occupied by Germany. He said out of seventy-eight people in his family, he was the only one to survive the Nazis. In the Warsaw Ghetto he worked in a shop called Tobbens'.

On 1 May 1943 he was shot in the right ankle, but it was a flesh wound and the bone was unaffected. However, soon afterwards, although his destination was Treblinka, there were too many people and so half the train went to Majdanek, another death camp south of Warsaw. There his clothes were taken away and he was given a striped shirt and pants with wooden shoes and sent to Barrack 21. He was lying on his bed when an older man asked him how he was and he told him about his ankle:

> He said, 'I can help you'. He had been a doctor in Paris. He took a little pocket knife and operated on me. To this day I do not understand how he could have kept a knife in the camp. There were no medicines or bandages. He said, 'I have no medication, you have to help yourself. When you urinate use some of the urine as an antiseptic on your wound.'

Solomon explained he had to walk 3km to work, and he couldn't be seen to limp as he would have been taken out of the line and punished. 'At Majdanek they hung you for any little thing. I did not know how I would make it. God must have helped me and I was lucky.'[53] Solomon died on 4 August 2002 in America.

Joseph (Jupp) Weiss (1893–1976) was born in Flamersheim, Germany, the second of nine children to Albert and Mathilde Michel. Jupp served in the army from 1912, all through the First World War, rising to sergeant. After the war he settled in Cologne and worked in his uncles' department store, Michel & Company. He married Erna Falk, an opera singer, in 1922. In July 1933 they legally emigrated to Holland and settled in Haarlem with their two sons, Wolfgang (born 1924) and Klaus-Albert (born 1928). They were given permanent residence but were unable to get Dutch citizenship.

An older brother, Jacob (born 1883) known as Köbes, who stayed in Germany, was taken to Dachau during Kristallnacht. He was released on 27 November on condition he left Germany, so he too went to Holland, but left to take his family to America, arriving in New York on 3 December 1939.

Meanwhile Jupp, who planned to emigrate to Palestine (now Israel) placed Wolfgang, aged 14, in an agricultural training school in Gouda. Germany occupied Holland in May 1940 and in September 1940 Jupp and his family were expelled from their home, moving to two furnished rooms in Hilversum. On 29 January 1942 Jupp, Erna and Klaus-Albert (aged 13½) were taken to Westerbork camp in north-east Holland. Wolfgang, who was now 18, went into hiding. On 10 January 1944 they were sent to Bergen-Belsen where Jupp was made a Jewish Elder – the authorised spokesman for Jews with the Germans.

On 10 April 1945, the three were sent east on a train. Jupp became ill with typhus on the second day and when the train was attacked from the air, the passengers were evacuated. However, Jupp was too weak to move and was nursed by his wife and sister, Rosa. After the Russian Army liberated them on 23 June, Jupp was taken to a nearby farmhouse. Two days later, Erna succumbed to typhus and she died on 6 May – two days before VE day. Jupp was too weak to walk or attend his wife's funeral. After being quarantined, Jupp, his sister and Rosa arrived back in Holland on 25 June and were imprisoned by the Dutch as 'Germans and Jews', along with recently arrested Dutch SS men and women – real traitors.

Jupp learnt that Wolfgang was safe and they were reunited on 12 July. The two boys emigrated to Palestine in 1946 and 1947, and Jupp was able to emigrate to Israel in September 1948, with his family multiplied all over the world. He died in Jerusalem in 1976, aged 83.[54]

Jupp described their experiences in a letter to his family, dated 20 June 1945. On 29 January 1942 they were taken from their flat in Hilversum to Westerbork transit camp. All stateless and German Jews were sent there from January 1942. Within a few days Jupp and Erna were asked to look after about 100 orphaned boys, mostly German, aged 14–20. The couple had their own room and their son slept with the boys. They managed to get some supplies sent in from outside. They all ate together in a large dining room and had good relations with the boys, who loved Erna like a mother. Jupp was a Zionist, and had problems with the Jewish camp leaders whom he criticised for carrying out the Germans' orders rather than representing the Jews and acting on their behalf. He thought this attitude nearly got him to Auschwitz many times.

Westerbork changed when they started to deport Dutch Jews to Poland, and the numbers increased from 1,000 to 20,000. Jupp was then in charge of all the barracks. The youngsters were no longer in just one place, the school had to be enlarged and kindergartens created. 'It was gratifying work, and it would have been useful had it not been that children were shipped out to the east every Tuesday.' He tried with other men to improve life by organising regular shipments of food and clothing from Amsterdam. 'Many people arrived here without anything, they were taken from their homes literally out of bed, wearing nothing but a nightshirt or pyjamas and slippers; or they came from other concentration camps.' They had to care for these people, but also deal with the tragedy of the weekly departures to the east.

They organised Jewish activities every evening in their room, sometimes with as many as twenty-five. A Chanukah party for 1,000 children in 1943 tragically shows how many children were incarcerated. They obtained sweets and fruit from outside each time, and had an Oneg Shabbat in the young people's barracks every Friday evening. They marked Jewish festivals with religious services, although the demands of forced labour made this difficult. They had an orchestra and Erna gave recitals of Schubert and Schumann Lieder. However, often 'someone who attended or even participated in an activity happened to be transported out on the following days':

> We Jews are a proud people, we walked into our fate head high. The attitude of the young people was exemplary; on every transport out of Westerbork which included young people, there was singing of the Hatikvah. Everyone departing knew what their fate was going to be, even though no one could imagine the sadistic cruelties which have now come to light. We were proud of their dignity and poise.

Jupp had trouble with Jews working for the SS, who regarded themselves as big shots (gernegrossen), so he and Erna moved to the tinfoil factory in a large barracks with 500 workers. They had to separate foil from chocolate wrappers and electric wires – the work was not hard and the hours were not long. The men sat on the left and the women on the right. Erna sat at the artists' table and Jupp at the Zionists' table. When the coast was clear they sang at Erna's table and men would talk Zionism or practise their Hebrew. They tried to keep optimistic and that kept up their morale.

On the evening of 9 January 1944 they were told they would be sent to Bergen-Belsen the next day. They left Westerbork in the afternoon of 10 January on a transport of 1,100 people singing *Hatikvah*. At Bergen-Belsen they were greeted by the Waffen-SS with dogs. The barracks were much poorer and 'you can imagine the food'. On the third day they were sent to a factory reprocessing old shoes, which was very dirty work. After a few days Erna was ill with rosacea and was sent to the infirmary. Klaus worked in the carpentry shop having learnt the trade in Westerbork.

Jupp determined to avoid any sort of office, but he was soon elected to the newly formed Judenrät and a few days later he was made deputy Judenältester. In December, the SS from Auschwitz took over at Bergen-Belsen. They abolished the Judenrät and Jupp alone was picked out to be Judenältester. He was given all the office work for the nine camps making up Bergen-Belsen.

When Erna recovered she had no work, so she looked after the children and the sick, who all loved her as usual. They created an old-age home in one of the barracks, so men aged 70 and women aged 65 did not have to work any more. They also organised a sick bay, children's quarters, youth workers and sick visitors. The SS tried to sabotage these facilities by taking people away, but they persevered.

Forty-five countries were represented, including Cyrenaica (eastern Libya), Tunisia, Morocco, South Africa, North and South America and every European country. Religious services were forbidden, but a morning service at 5.00 a.m. was held with the African and Balkan Jews in their long tallits – the oldest was an Albanian, who died aged 110. Even though most were not religious, the services gave them great strength. Bar Mitzvahs and Brit Milahs were held and they had some Torah scrolls. Jupp got up about 3.00 a.m. or 5.00 a.m., getting four or five hours' sleep for fifteen months to arrange all these activities. The languages spoken were German, Dutch, French, Ladino, Italian, Hebrew and English. It was surprising that everyone got on so well.

The role of the Jewish Elder has been described as:

> …a 'Jewish Elder' was a working prisoner who usually was a prominent personality … On the other hand, he was also the representative of a 'Jewish Council' and a helper to all those Jews who were threatened by, and who became victims of the Nazi Holocaust. The result of this problem of dual roles was that the 'Jewish Elder' had to engage in a balancing act that was never entirely free of accusations of collaboration and corruption.
>
> This book is not only a biography of one such man in Germany, Josef Weiss, but it is also the beginning of research that has barely begun in Germany. The reputation of the 'Jewish Elders' is still heavily burdened with many reproaches.[55]

Jupp described his beloved wife's death from spotted typhus with complications of encephalitis – there had been a typhus epidemic among them and he was lying sick next to her when she died.

The Germans took them away from Bergen-Belsen on 10 April, even though 85 per cent of them were ill: 'they put us on a disease-ridden train'. He says he was unconscious for much of the journey while Erna nursed him. She died and was buried in Tröbnitz, 50 miles south of Berlin in a new Jewish cemetery, as there had never been a Jewish community there. (Jupp had Erna reinterred in Jerusalem in 1952.)

In the six weeks they were in Tröbnitz they buried 600 of the transport of 2,500. He wrote of his wife's bravery and how she used to worry about him because he 'was Judenältester and always [had] one foot in the grave'.[56]

The German writer, Hans-Dieter Arntz, was responsible for getting a street named after Jupp in his birthplace, Flamersheim, as well as a plaque on the family home. The ceremony was undertaken in the presence of relatives from England, Israel and America in May 2013.[57]

# 10

# COMMERCIAL BETRAYAL

The superior man understands what is right; the inferior man understands what will sell.

Confucius, *c.* 500 BC, Chinese philosopher

Commercial betrayal could occur in many areas – both in normal commercial activities and within Nazi camps and ghettos, which often involved slave labour.

The *Kovno Ghetto Diary*, by Avraham Tory, details the use of Jewish labour from the ghetto.

His diary also gives many examples of how the German authorities not only exploited Jewish labour in Kovno itself but throughout the Kovno region for the personal gain of individual Germans, who would order suits, shoes, even rings and jewellery, to be made for them in the ghetto – always without payment. Both the Gestapo and the German civil administrators, Tory noted early in 1943, 'take advantage of their tour of duty here to get rich. Every day they pack up their parcels and bundles and send them by mail to their homes in Germany.'[1]

## Use of Slave Labour

Many of the well-known German companies employed slave labour at their factories in various camps. Not all the slave workers were Jews, but all were treated very badly and when they died were replaced from the unlimited supplies of 'factory fodder'.

Even as late as 27 May 2014, *The Times* carried a report on Audi's use of slave labour. The company expressed shock at the revelations that Audi, trading then as Auto Union, had contracts with the SS to use more than 3,700 camp inmates, working at seven dedicated concentration camps under inhumane conditions. In addition 16,500 forced labourers worked at vehicle plants in Saxony – about a quarter were Jews. The company was also morally responsible for the conditions at an underground plant outside the camp at Flossenbuerg, where '18,000 concentration camp prisoners were used, of whom 4,500 met their death, without question'. Richard Bruhn, the former CEO of Auto Union, a Nazi Party member, was honoured for his services to Germany. In the 500 page *Times* report, Bruhn is identified as being personally responsible for brutal exploitation of prisoners and working people to death.[2]

### Gilbert Michlin and Siemens

After the war, Gilbert Michlin (1926–2012) had a party each year for his birthday to remember that, in 1944, two days before his eighteenth birthday, he was deported from Paris to a slave labour subcamp at Auschwitz. He worked for Siemens and fought to find out why Siemens kept him and eighty-seven other slaves alive. He was never given access to Siemens' archives but he was told by its director, Frank Wittendorfer, that the Siemens' archive consisted of 2.5 linear miles of files with 400,000 photos and 3,000 films. These archives had been moved from Berlin to Munich before the end of the war to avoid Allied bombing. However, they were proving as difficult to inspect as those of the Vatican.[3]

Gilbert established a relationship with their archivist, the historian Wilfried Feldenkirchen, but he died in June 2010 in the crash of an electric model of a Siemens car. Writing in March 2011, Toby Axelrod, Michlin's cousin, speculated that he might soon get some answers as Siemens was providing files for an exhibition on its Nazi-era operations at the Ravensbrück women's concentration camp.

Dr Wittendorfer had only succeeded in making catalogued items accessible. Why wouldn't the company answer his questions – didn't they owe him that? Sadly, the optimism of the article was of no comfort to Michlin, who died in 2012 without any answers. His cousin is pursing the investigation.[4]

### BMW

Another company whose use of slave labour has received publicity is BMW. The group made munitions, aero engines and batteries for U-boats and V-2 rockets. The company was created by Gunther Quandt who died in 1954. His first wife, Magda, later married the Nazi propaganda leader, Joseph Goebbels. Quandt's great granddaughter is Susanne Klatten, the richest woman in Germany. She was alleged to have been the victim of a major scam by Helg Sgarbi, whose father was a Polish-Jewish slave labourer in a BMW factory. A documentary on German television in October 2007 revealed the facts.[5]

The TV company, NDR, took five years to research the documentary *The Silence of the Quandts*, which was broadcast, unlisted, on a Sunday night at 11.30 p.m. Apparently NDR was fearful of an injunction from the Quandts preventing transmission. One of the participants was a member of the Danish

Resistance – 82-year-old Carl-Adolf Soerensen, who was deported in 1943 to a concentration camp in the Stöcken area of Hanover and was forced to work in the Quandts' Afa battery plant. He explained how he came with forty comrades, six of whom died in the first three months. They were assembling batteries for German submarines, handling toxic heavy metals without protective gear. He was told by the SS men that inmates in Stöcken could only expect to last six months as most died of lead poisoning.

A journalist, Rüdiger Jungbluth, wrote about the Quandt family in 2002 without access to the family's archives. His book failed to have the impact of the documentary because:

> A book is easy to set aside, but images remained permanently etched into one's consciousness. One of the indelible images in the NDR documentary is of former forced labourer Theophilos Mylopoulos, who talks about how the prisoners were whipped at the Quandt family's battery factory, were denied water and were forced to drink out of the toilets.[6]

One member of the family appeared in the documentary: Sven Quandt, who inherited a fortune from Varta, formerly Afa Battery Company. Demonstrating a remarkable lack of insight, he said in the film, 'We must finally try to forget this', and then added, 'Every family has its dark side'.[7]

The dark side of their relationship with the Nazis had begun early, when Magda divorced Gunther in 1929. At her marriage to Goebbels in 1931, Hitler was 'best man'. She is remembered for committing suicide in Hitler's bunker in 1945, having first killed her six children. Magda and Gunther had remained on friendly terms and when he was arrested in May 1933, Goebbels ensured his release by speaking to Hitler. Gunther subsequently became one of the most significant German arms producers and in 1937 was made Leader of the Armament Economy (Wehrwirtschaftsführer) – this title was reserved for industrialists who were leaders in the Nazi economy and profits were correspondingly good.

It is alleged that he was active in appropriating factories in Nazi-occupied countries, in particular Czechoslovakia, and exploiting the Aryanization policy of the Nazis. In Belgium he tried to take over a chemical company whose owner he erroneously believed to be Jewish – had he been Jewish he would have been forced to forfeit the company. Quandt went so far as to formally contact the relevant government body about the matter.

On another occasion in Luxembourg, when a businessman was arrested by the Gestapo in 1943, he asked the Defence Ministry if he could acquire the majority of the shares in the man's company. Even Albert Speer did not support him on this and the episode was included in the film. It is also unclear how much Quandt was involved in Nazi crimes prior to 1939, but Jungbluth claims an Aryanized company was absorbed into his weapons empire and it is also alleged that forced labourers were used in at least one company as early as 1938.

Another historian, Ralf Blank, found slave labourers from concentration camps in at least three Quandt factories – in Hanover, Berlin and Vienna. Hundreds of these slaves died because of the awful conditions, especially in the Afa factory. A satellite concentration camp was created in the Hanover factory, which had an execution area complete with gallows.[8] It cannot be argued that the family was ignorant of these activities because Gunther and Magda's son, Harald, were the directors of Pertrix GmbH, a subsidiary of Afa based in Berlin. That firm used women slave labourers, including Polish women who had come from Auschwitz.

At the end of the war, surprisingly, Gunther was classified as a 'collaborator', as the body dealing with denazification (spruchkammer) did not have the full details of his activities. Benjamin Ferencz, who was a prosecutor at the Nuremberg Trials, claims that if the evidence known today had been presented to the trials, 'Quandt would have been charged with the same offences as [German industrialists] Flick, Krupp and the directors of IG Farben'.[9]

In September 2011 the family's investigation into the Nazi period was published after consulting the family's own files. The 1,200 page report gives details of the firm's activities and use of an estimated 50,000 slave labourers from concentration camps. These labourers endured harsh conditions and some were executed. The Quandt family was also found to have benefitted from taking over dozens of businesses from Jews under the Aryanization policy.[10]

Harald Quandt, the only child of Günter's marriage to Magda, was bought up in the Goebbels' household. In his diary for 21 February 1942, Goebbels wrote, 'Magda returned from her cure at Dresden. She brought Harald with her and our family is now complete again. The children are very happy to have their mother with them again.'[11]

The editor described Mrs Goebbels as 'the comely and presentable Magda'. He added, 'It was a matter of common gossip in Berlin society circles that Joseph Goebbels insisted that his wife deliver one baby a year. The offspring consisted of six children at the end of the Hitler regime.'[12] When Gunther died in 1954, Harald, with his half-brother, inherited Varta, BMW and Altana AG.[13]

## Allianz Insurance Company

Gerry Feldman was an American historian who wrote a devastating official history of the Allianz Insurance Company. 'Gerry also led an international team of researchers in a history of the Deutsche Bank, which uncovered its financing of the construction of Auschwitz and role in processing the gold derived from the dental fillings of Jews killed in the death camps to help fund German armaments.'[14]

The chairman of the board of directors of the Allianz Insurance Company was Dr Schmitt, a trained jurist. He was becoming a recognised leader of the insurance industry during the Weimar Republic and was forging ties with the Nazis in the early 1930s. On 30 June 1933 he was appointed Reich Economy Minister, but in June 1934 Schmitt had a heart attack and ceased to be a minister in 1935. He had the distinction of appearing on the cover of *Time* on 6 August 1934. He was followed at the Economics Ministry by Hjalmar Schacht.

When I started this book I had my car insurance with Allianz, as they offered the best deal. I did not know then that they also offered the best deal to the Nazis. Allianz insured SS factories, motor pools, barracks and death camps. The Munich-based firm, which still offers insurance, banking and financial services, also insured death camps such as Auschwitz and Dachau during the Second World War. A recently sold subsidiary, Dresdner Bank AG, controlled a company that helped build Auschwitz and bankrolled the SS.[15] When I had to renew my insurance, I changed companies.

In response to various legal actions taken by former slave labourers, negotiations between the German and American governments and the companies involved took place during 1998–1999. Consequently, the scale of the use of slave labour by the Nazis was acknowledged in a joint statement issued by several well-known German companies on 16 February 1999. The first paragraph read:

> The companies Allianz AG, BASF AG, Bayer AG, BMW AG, DaimlerChrysler AG, Deutsche Bank AG, Degussa-Hüls AG, Dresdner Bank AG, Fried, Krupp AG Hoesch-Krupp, Hoechst AG, Siemens AG and Volkswagen AG today proposed to the Federal Chancellor the establishment of a 'Foundation Initiative of German Enterprises: Remembrance, Responsibility and Future'. The Federal Chancellor welcomes and commends this Initiative and pledges the Federal Government's support.[16]

It is clear that this list was not regarded as comprehensive, as the final sentence reads, 'Other German companies that are involved but have not have not yet participated in this initiative are called upon in the efforts now under way.'

Since this statement was issued, the foundation has been established, with a budget around $5 billion contributed by the German Government and the companies involved. Final agreement was formalised on 17 July 2000 and President Rau of Germany (1999–2004) asked forgiveness on behalf of the German people for the wrongs committed. The recipients were 1.5 million living former slave and forced labourers, which in itself gives an indication of how many people were enslaved during the war, as so many had already died. Payments were concluded in 2006.[17]

However, the internet revealed the following list, which of course includes non-German companies ... [18]

## Foreign Companies' Role in the Holocaust

### IBM

IBM's role was revealed by Edwin Black's controversial book in 2001. In the introduction he explained that when he first visited the Washington Holocaust Museum in 1993 with his parents, who are both Holocaust survivors, the first thing he saw was an IBM machine. There, in the very first exhibit, an IBM Hollerith D-11 card-sorting machine – riddled with circuits, slots, and wires – was prominently displayed. Clearly affixed to the machine's front panel glistened an IBM nameplate. The exhibit explained little more than that IBM was responsible for organising the census of 1933 that first identified the Jews. [19]

He gradually began to realise that IBM worked hand-in-hand with the Nazis from 1933 and throughout the war. It gave the Hitler regime the technology and the tools needed to expedite and automate Hitler's war against the Jews. The New York office and IBM chairman Thomas Watson (1874–1956) micromanaged every aspect of the German subsidiary (Dehomag) which was their most profitable operation. Thomas Watson was a recipient of one of Hitler's special medals for foreign friends in 1937 (see page 244). IBM custom-designed the machines and custom-designed the applications. Watson ignored the anti-Jewish behaviour and was accused of being obsessed with the profit.

In an interview in 2001, Black was asked what accounted for IBM's involvement with the Nazis. He replied:

> It was never about the Nazism. It was never about the anti-Semitism. It was about the money. They didn't hate the Poles when they opened up a subsidiary in war-torn Poland. They didn't hate the Dutch when they opened up the subsidiary in Holland just before the Nazis moved in, or the French when they ramped up the subsidiary in occupied France. They didn't hate the Brits or the Americans when Hollerith machines were used to target the V2 rockets. It wasn't personal – it was just business.

He also explained the difference between Standard Oil merely supplying goods such as oil or gasoline, and IBM doing more than sell equipment:

> Watson and IBM controlled the unique technical magic of Hollerith machines. They controlled the monopoly on the cards and the technology. And they were the ones that had to custom-design even the paper forms and punch cards – they

were custom-designed for each specific purpose. That included everything from counting Jews to confiscating bank accounts, to coordinating trains going into death camps, to the extermination by labor campaign.

That's why even the paper forms in the prisoner camps had Hollerith notations and numbered fields checked. They were all punched in. For example, IBM had to agree with their Nazi counterparts that Code 6 in the concentration camps was *extermination*. Code 1 was *released*, Code 2 was *transferred*, Code 3 was *natural death*, Code 4 was *formal execution*, Code 5 was *suicide*, Code 7 was *escape*. Code 6 was *extermination*.

All of the money and all the machines from all these operations were claimed by IBM as legitimate business after the war. The company used its connections with the State Department and the Pentagon to recover all the machines and all the bank accounts. They never said, 'We do not want this blood money.' They wanted it all.[20]

### Hugo Boss

The trendy menswear firm Hugo Boss was 'outed' as a Nazi supplier when Hugo Boss's name was found on a list of dormant accounts released by Swiss bankers in July 1997. An Austrian magazine, *Profil*, researched the subject and interviewed Siegfried Boss, who stated, 'Of course my father belonged to the Nazi Party. But who didn't belong back then? The whole industry worked for the Nazi Army.'

However, the issue was not his membership of the Nazi Party, but the fact that the small family-run company, Hugo Boss, founded in 1923, which had made uniforms for the police and postmen, turned to making Nazi uniforms. Hugo had joined the party in 1931 and two years later began making uniforms for the Nazis. According to Eckhard Trox, a military uniform expert, thousands of companies had contracts from the Nazis to provide the black uniforms worn by the SS, the brown shirts worn by SA storm troopers and the black and brown uniforms of the Hitler Youth. The main issue is that, according to *Profil*, the company brought forced labourers from Poland and France to their factory to help increase the output later in the war.[21]

There is some irony that the company spokeswoman said there was nothing about it in their archives. A major contract for a company from 1933 to 1945, which involved bringing extra labour from abroad to boost output, and yet nothing in the firm's archives. As a result, a historian was commissioned to write the history of the firm. It is stated that 'The research and printing costs of this publication were financed by Hugo Boss AG. However no influence whatsoever was brought to bear concerning either its content or form.'

After the war Hugo Boss, himself, was forced to undergo denazification and he was classified as 'incriminated' and fined a sum of RM100,000. That was the second highest punishment imposed in the Reutlingen Chamber of Commerce Precinct.

The reasons for the sentence included his early membership of the Nazi Party and that he benefitted financially from Nazism. Additionally, his friendship with Georg Rath, the notorious local Nazi leader who had made a name for himself in Metzingen with crude and coarse behaviour, was taken into account.[22]

In 1935, the *Kölnisch Zeitung* (*Cologne Gazette*) reported on the scale of Aryanization of larger Jewish firms which was causing concern over a drop in share prices. It also reported on the Aryanization of two large firms in the electrical industry which had been bought by Siemens, and commented on the change in ownership at the heavy industry firm Orenstein & Koppel AG, which had been founded on 1 April 1876 in Berlin by Benno Orenstein and Arthur Koppel. It was estimated that 260 larger Jewish firms had been Aryanized by the autumn of 1936.[23]

Heinrich Wohlwill invented an industrial process for recovering copper in 1903, which was in use until the Second World War. The patent resulted in the creation of a world-class industrial firm called Norddeutsche Affinerie. He was the technical director from 1913 until 1933 and also a member of the board until the Jewish members were removed in 1933. However, he continued his relationship with the company in a less prominent position, having access to the research laboratories while drawing his pension.[24] He was known internationally and was listed as a member of the American Electrochemical Society in their *Transactions* for 1918. He was shown as a member since 29 June 1907, under Columbus University, Ohio[25] (see also page 306).

Otto Wolff (1881–1940) and Ottmar Strauss (1878–1941), who had met as young men at the Cologne firm Nathan Pelzer Wwe, established their own metal company in Cologne in June 1904, having enormous success in the early part of the twentieth century and benefitting from the requirements of the First World War.

Strauss's administrative skills led him into a parallel career in government as a civil servant under the Kaiser and in the early years of the Weimar Republic. He became a Geheimrat Regierungsrat (Privy Councillor) in 1919 and was one of the most successful assimilated German-Jewish industrialists of the time.

Strauss was youngest of eight children to Emmanuel – a successful ironmonger. His success enabled Strauss to become an art collector and he had a very eclectic taste. He and his wife, Eva Emmy, held open house at their home in Cologne for members of the artistic world. He owned a villa in Marienburg, an affluent quarter of Cologne, and a country house in the vineyards overlooking the Rhine near Bonn. The country house was destroyed in the Second World War.

The Nazis' legislation turned this successful businessman and highly regarded civil servant into an outcast simply because he was Jewish. His art collection was dispersed in three sales by the Hugo Helbing Gallery in Frankfurt 1934 and 1935.

He left Germany in December 1936 and died at the Hotel Baur au Lac in Zurich on 25 August 1941. His family also fell foul of the Nazis' legal maze in another manner. Sexual relations between Jews and Aryans were forbidden under the Nuremberg Laws as 'rassenschande' (racial shame) from 1935. Apparently Ottmar's son, Karl Nathan, had an illegitimate son with an Aryan woman which was prohibited by the Nazis. He was convicted of this offence but managed to escape to England with his father's help. From England, he was sent to Australia on the *Dunera*.[26]

One of Ottmar's pictures was restituted to his family in 2004. It had been painted in 1906 by Hans Thoma and was called *Dusk at Lake Garda*. Strauss bought it in 1922, but when it was offered for sale in 1935 as Lot 180 it was not sold. In February 1943 an agent bought the picture on behalf of Martin Bormann. It was transferred to storage in the salt mines of Bad Aussee (Aussee No. 7704) along with enormous amounts of other stolen art between 1944 and 1945, and after the war the picture was put in the Bavarian State Picture Collections (Bayerische Staatsgemäldesammlungen).[27]

On 5 October 2004 Reinhold Baumstark, general director of the Bayerische, returned the painting to Dr Jost von Trott zu Solz, representing the family of the late Ottmar Strauss. Dr Jost is an attorney dealing with restitution. 'Professor Baumstark expressed his pleasure that once again it had been possible to help victims of National Socialist terror receive the justice they had long deserved and, at the same time, to set a reminder of the crimes committed.'[28] The picture was auctioned by Christie's in April 2005 in Amsterdam when it realised €24,000. In 2011 the picture was sold again, this time by Sotheby's, but it only made £13,750. Another picture with a dubious provenance was displayed in London during the winter 2008–2009. It was called *Bridge at Hampton Court*, and was painted by Sisley. The notes from the National Gallery say the picture was owned by Otto Wolff, but add that when their firm was Aryanized he took over Strauss's villa in Cologne and 'probably had a hand in the sale of his collection'. His passion was collecting books but he also collected art.[29]

After Otto Wolff died in 1940 in the USA, his company was run by his adopted son, Otto Wolff von Amerongen, who spent most of the war in Portugal. His war record is dubious and Werner Ruegmer, a director of a 2001 film about the company, said he was a Nazi spy in Portugal. He accused him of selling plundered gold from Nazi-occupied countries' central banks. He was also accused of selling shares stolen from persecuted Jews. He was also exporting tungsten from Portugal to Germany. It was required to harden steel for rifles and artillery and Portugal was Germany's only supplier in the war. Ruegemer also told the journalist, Robin Munro, 'The documents referring to the activities of Wolff in Portugal as head of the Lisbon subsidiary of the industrial concern Otto Wolff, and as representative of an industrial consortium of Wolff, Rheinmetal, Krupp and IG Farben, come from the National Archives in Washington.'

IG Farben was the firm that built and operated the chemical plant at Auschwitz in which Gilbert Michlin found himself. Several of its company executives were imprisoned following the Nuremberg War Crime Trials. Gustav Krupp was too ill to appear before the court, but his son was jailed.

Barbara Bonhage, a Swiss historian who has written about Switzerland's role in financial transactions with the Third Reich, said that the firm Otto Wolff traded tungsten with the Germans between 1941 and 1944. She confirmed IG Farben were also involved. She said, 'The firm Otto Wolff was also mandated by the Third Reich to sell in neutral countries shares stolen by the Nazis.' Otto Wolff, himself, denied dealing in gold or shares but was imprisoned after the war briefly. The documents in which he admitted being a counter-intelligence agent were released by the Clinton administration in 1999.[30] He ran the company for many years and promoted trade with Russia.

Max Uhlfelder's role in Dr Siegel's mistreatment by the Nazis was covered on page 300. Max's business was started in 1878 as a household and haberdashery store by Max's father, Heinrich Uhlfelder (1853–1928). He was so successful, he was honoured as a Privy Councillor of Commerce in 1924 for his charity work. He was also chairman of the supervisory board at Orag AG which made tailoring supplies. He ran the store with his son, Max, but his daughter, Margarethe, was also active in the company.

By the 1930s Kaufhaus Heinrich Uhlfelder GmbH was the second largest store in Munich and had 7,000 square feet of floor area and 1,000 employees. It was very modern and its pride were the escalators which carried customers up to all three floors of the store. No other shop in Munich had escalators, nor provided such good social welfare for its staff.

The Nazis had targeted Jewish residents and companies since the party's origin in Munich after the First World War. This was aggravated after Hitler came to power in January 1933 and, in March 1933, Max Uhlfelder was one of the 280 Jews taken into 'protective custody' at Dachau. He was also targeted on the Boycott Day of 1 April, when Nazi demonstrators protested outside the store. During Kristallnacht, on 9 November 1938, the store was ravaged, plundered and set on fire and the escalators destroyed. It was left for days with the doors open. Max and his son were taken to Dachau again with 1,000 other Jews, where many were badly treated and some even died. In January 1939 the Uhlfelders were released with visas for India, but before they could leave they were stripped of their assets and they even had to pay for the repairs to the store.

The store was Aryanized in December 1938, when it was forcibly sold to Aryans at an outrageously low price. Many people were involved in this 'legal' process:

... the Munich 'Aryanization Office' run by Nazi Gauleiter Adolf Wagner proposed the liquidation of the Uhlfelder store at the Chamber of Industry and Commerce. The request was supported by interested parties in the retail sector and Munich's Mayor Karl Fiehler, and ultimately approved by the Third Reich's Minister of Commerce, Hermann Goering. The warehouse passed into the possession of retailers, with the other properties handed to the Löwenbräu brewery – as a substitute for the Bürgerbräukeller beer cellar which had also been expropriated.

During the 1944 air raids the department store was severely damaged.

Max Uhlfelder had gone from India to the United States. His sister was not so fortunate. Grete Meyer, her husband, Josef, and their son, Alfred, were among the first group of Jews deported to Kaunas on 20 November 1941, where they were murdered.[31] Max returned to Munich in 1953 and after many legal suits he was awarded compensation. His plans to rebuild the store failed, so in 1954 the City of Munich bought the land on which the store stood and it is now the site of the Munich City Museum. There is a neon light on the building with the store's name to act as a memorial.[32] Max died in 1958, aged 72, and in his will he asked for a plaque to be placed at Rosenthal 16 to recall the history of the store and its owner. This was done in 1964.[33]

The reference to the Löwenbräu Brewery receiving property as a substitute for property previously expropriated aroused my curiosity. However, it was difficult to find much information. The famous brewery had started in 1383. By 1863, Löwenbräu was the largest brewery in Munich and by 1900 it was the largest in Germany. In 1921 it merged two other breweries – Unionsbräu Schülein & Cie and Munich Bürgerbräu. As a consequence, the new supervisory board for the new company included Wilhelm von Finck from Bürgerbräu and Joseph Schülein (who was Jewish) from Unionsbräu. In time he became the head of the firm and the Nazis derided the Löwenbräu beer as 'Judenbier' (Jews' beer). In fact, it appears he didn't spend much time at the brewery and was at his farm at Kaltenberg Castle, where he died in 1938. Afterwards his son was held at Dachau briefly and consequently the family fled to the USA when the firm was Aryanized in 1938.[34]

The icon of modern haute couture, Coco Chanel (1883–1971), has been revealed as attempting to betray her Jewish partners to the Gestapo. Two Jewish brothers, Paul and Pierre Wertheimer, had a major share of the company Les Parfums Chanel, which they had set up with her in 1924. The brothers' father, Ernest, came from Alsace during the Franco-Prussian War and invested in Bourjois, a theatrical make-up company. By the 1920s his sons had turned it into the biggest fragrance and cosmetics company in France. As a girl, I remember tiny round black and white boxes of vivid rouge on sale in Woolworth's.

Chanel created No. 5 in 1922 with a perfumer, Ernest Beaux, from Grasse. It was a great success, but they were only able to produce small quantities. The founder of the department store, Galeries Lafayette, Théophile Bader, wanted to sell the popular perfume and accordingly he introduced Chanel to his chum, Pierre Wertheimer.

By 1924 they had incorporated the company Les Parfums Chanel and the Wertheimer brothers had 70 per cent of the profits, Bader got 20 per cent and Coco Chanel 10 per cent. Although she must have agreed, she was subsequently unhappy with this arrangement and sought the help of lawyers. When the Nazis occupied France, Paul and Pierre fled to New York, leaving Coco hoping to take control of the company. Apparently she contacted the Nazis, telling them the company was Jewish-owned and should be Aryanized and returned to her. However, the Wertheimers were one step ahead of her and signed the company over to a French engineer called Félix Amiot. He was a good Aryan who sold arms to the Nazis. After the war the Wertheimers were fortunate to get the company back, and after her death they acquired full control of the company which is held by the family today.[35] Recent news reports indicate that Coco Chanel acted as a German spy from her home in the Ritz Hotel (the German air force's HQ).[36]

It seems as though no company is free from taint – the founder of IKEA, Ingvar Kamprad, was revealed in 1994 as member No. 4013 of the Swedish Nazis – the Svensk Socialistick Samling. In 1943 he was a recruiter for the party as an enthusiastic and active member. This was covered by the press in August 2011.[37] The next month revealed that the Stasi had a file on IKEA, which used political prisoners in East Germany to make sofas during the 1970s. There was a factory in Waldheim standing next to a prison and its inmates were used as unpaid labour. One of the former prisoners, Hans Otto Klare, who was sent to Waldheim for trying to escape to West Germany, made hinges and other parts for IKEA furniture and described the conditions:

> Our labour team lived on the upper floor of the factory with the windows covered. The machines were on the lower floor, and you had little rest. On the factory floor you had no proper seating, no ear protection: no gloves. Conditions were even more primitive there than in the rest of the GDR [German Democratic Republic]. It was slave labour.[38]

Another prisoner said he recognised some of the parts he had made when he went shopping in IKEA after the fall of Communism. The Stasi file quoted Kamprad as saying he had no knowledge of the use of prison labourers. He added, though, that if it did exist, 'in the opinion of IKEA it would be in society's interests'. A later report referred to IKEA having sixty-five workshops in East Germany as well as prisons where IKEA products were made. The popular 'Klippan' sofa was made at

Waldheim, but from the 1960s products were made in many former Communist countries including Poland.[39]

## Ethical Aspects of Holocaust Slave Labour

The use of slave labour, particularly by the Nazis, raises several issues for us today:

Should claims that go back over fifty years still be heard by today's courts?
Should today's stockholders be responsible for human rights abuses committed decades ago?
Should companies be held responsible for events they were ordered to undertake during wartime?

Ethics specialist, Margaret Somerville, from the Centre for Medicine, Ethics & Law at McGill University in Montreal, speaking of present liability for past wrongs, believes:

> It would be wrong to exonerate today's investors of responsibility for past injustices, since to some degree the success of those companies has been built on the suffering of people many years ago.

She told me:

> Complicity in evil is a very important topic in ethics and that complicity can be passive – failing to do anything to try to stop – as well as active, and it can be present in the form of indirectly profiting from evil. In particular, if the same company still exists as was involved in the past wrongdoing, I would argue it's presently liable, especially if criminal or human rights breaching conduct was involved as those wrongs are not subject to a limitation period for prosecution.[40]

## The Car Industry

Philip Mendlowicz (75) wrote a letter to Volkswagen (VW) headquarters which was published in *The Toronto Star* on 28 August 1999:

> My name is Philip Mendlowicz and I was a slave labourer in concentration camp KZ Reichenbach from 1942 until 1945. I worked for your people for 12 hours a day, six days a week. I walked 3 miles every day from the camp to the factory and from the factory to the camp with no food or payment. I was making parts

for the auto industry for the German army. I have no proof; unfortunately they did not give letters of reference in those days.

Do you people think that I deserve some kind of payment from your company for my slave labour?

Looking [forward] to hearing from you.

It is not clear whether he ever had a reply, but the retired furniture salesman from North York, Toronto, was less polite about Volkswagen when interviewed by Lynda Hurst. He told her, 'You were not human to them. They wanted you to be an animal. They didn't care if you fell down sick. They sent you to the death camp. There were always more to take your place.'[41]

Mendlowicz was a Polish Jew – the only one of his family to survive the Holocaust. The problem with the claims is that the average age of the survivors was 81 (in 1999) and, even if they get compensation, it would be only for their labour all those years ago. As another survivor from Poland said, 'Nothing is being said about how they brought you down to a subhuman level, dehumanised you and took away your dignity.' Philip Mendlowicz died on 12 January 2010 – I don't know whether he got his financial compensation, but he survived to have children and grandchildren.

This issue is complex. Volkswagen argued that forced labour was introduced by the Third Reich and therefore the federal German Government as its legal successor should deal with legal petitions. Volkswagen also did not consider itself to be the same company as the Volkswagen factory that created Hitler's 'People's Car'. Roger Boyes, the veteran Berlin-based *Times* foreign correspondent, wrote in 1998, 'Slave labour is fast becoming a hot issue in Germany, partly because more German companies with wartime pasts are moving into the American market and are therefore exposed to lawsuits or at least bad publicity.' Roger Boyes reported:

> Thirty Jewish labourers are preparing a court case to claim back pay from the years 1944–1945. Most of them were taken from ghettos in Hungary at the ages of 15 or 16, singled out as being fit for work in the 'selection' at Auschwitz concentration camp, and then taken to Wolfsburg to work on armaments at the Volkswagen factory.
>
> Although life was certainly better than in Auschwitz, the workers led a miserable existence. They began at 6.30 a.m. and worked until 6 p.m.
>
> The short lunch break and the vast size of the factory meant that many were unable to reach the front of the queue to get their food. The daily ration comprised a potato, a turnip, a ladle of thin soup, three ounces of bread and a portion of margarine.[42]

On 29 August 1999 it was reported that Volkswagen had agreed to pay each of its ex-slaves the equivalent of $3,500 in US funds. If this was agreed by German industry generally then $6 or 7 billion would be required, which is many times more than has been pledged.[43]

VW's spokesman, Bernd Graef, said 7,000 were forced to do unpaid work for them during the war but VW was only one of 12,000 German firms to use slave labour. With some reluctance some voluntary payments were agreed.

The Conference on Material Jewish Claims against Germany, which has been seeking recompense for slave labourers since its creation in 1952, stated, 'Unfortunately VW's decision to recognise historic and moral obligations toward former slave workers took more than 50 years. Many slave workers had already died without compensation or recognition of their suffering.'[44]

In February 1999, VW agreed to go further and join other German companies to compensate victims. William Horsley noted that the 7,000 slave labourers were making mines, V-1 missiles and anti-tank rocket launchers. Many of the overworked and underfed workers died in appalling conditions in hidden military complexes, some of which were underground. It is estimated that one million Jews, Slavs, gypsies and others died from the cruel treatment of slave labourers.[45]

A postscript to the VW story comes from William Shirer, the veteran American foreign correspondent based in Berlin during the war. He describes how VW was funded because Hitler wanted people to have access to a car. At the time, car-ownership was one per fifty people in Germany, against one in five in the USA. Hitler wanted the car to cost RM990 – $396 at the time. The Austrian engineer Dr Porsche designed the car, possibly with help from Hitler. However, private industry could not make a car at that price, so it was decided that the state should build it. In 1938 a factory was started which was to be large enough to produce a million and a half cars a year – 'more than Ford'. Initial funding was 50 million marks but the main funding came from the ingenious 'pay before you get it' instalment plan. Workers would pay a set weekly amount of 5, 10 or 15 marks. When 750 marks had been paid, the purchaser received an order number entitling the purchaser to a car as soon as they were produced:

> Alas for the worker, not a single car was ever turned out for any customer during the Third Reich. Tens of millions of marks were paid in by the German wage earners, not a pfennig of which was ever to be refunded. By the time the war started the Volkswagen factory turned to the manufacture of goods more useful to the Army.[46]

Hitler declared the car was to be called the 'KdF' and the new town being built was called the 'City of the KdF Car', until the British renamed it Wolfsburg in 1945. However, the fraud was maintained:

> Only the Volkswagenwerk management knew that its price would have to be at least twice what was being advertised. Intended to finance production once the plant was completed, the savings scheme was a swindle. The 280 million RM

gathered from the 336,000 subscribers served as the fodder for corrupt dealings within the DAF. Even after the war started, with the VW plant switching to military production and refusing car orders, the propaganda encouraged front soldiers to keep paying into the scheme.[47]

Deborah Sturman, a US expert on slave labour legal issues, has written a very clear explanation of the reason why the issue is so important and so unjust. I have reproduced the whole paragraph because it is so significant.

> Fortunes amassed through slave labour and Aryanization were among the funda-
> mental elements that allowed Germany to become the political and economic
> power it quickly became. Volkswagen's headquarters and main factory, still in
> use today, for example, were built almost entirely by slave labour. Not only was
> slave labour instrumental in maintaining wartime industrial productivity; it also
> permitted extensive investment in production machinery that was dragged to
> safety from Allied bombings (at great cost in slaves' lives) to Autobahn tunnels and
> underground factories (dug and built by concentration camp prisoners). Apart
> from these direct material benefits, the economy West Germany also derived
> significant indirect benefits from the massive modernization in management and
> production methods that had been achieved during the wartime experiences, as
> well as by the tight web of business relationships created by the war effort. These
> were among the most important legacies of Hitler's *Volksgemeinschaft*, the racially
> pure community of Aryans. The 1950s economic miracle, of which post-war
> Germans are so proud, was thus deeply rooted in benefits accrued during the
> war, largely through universally condemned practices.[48]

She is the child of a family affected by the Holocaust, as her grandparents' siblings were murdered. She learnt German, as well as Dutch, French and Italian, after moving to Belgium to study music and make it her career. In Germany, she played for the West German Broadcast Orchestra, married a tax attorney, had a child and got involved in Jewish causes. But she found being a Jew in Germany difficult. Once, when she insisted a grocer give her a receipt for 6lb of coffee she was buying for the orchestra, he refused, saying, 'I haven't seen such pettiness since the Jews left.'[49]

On 4 March 1998, Elsa Iwanowa, a 73-year-old Belgian woman resident in Antwerp, filed an action against the Ford Motor Company and Ford Werke AG. She had been born in 1925 in Rostov in Russia. She was a non-Jewish Slav – the Nazis regarded them as inferior to the Aryans. In June 1942 they began abducting adolescents as young as 14. On 6 October 1942 Elsa was abducted and sent to Germany with about 2,000 other adolescents. When she arrived in Wuppertal, she was bought by Ford Werke with thirty-eight others. She had to do heavy work in the factory and if they failed their quotas the security officers beat them with rubber truncheons.[50]

She was employed as a slave labourer in a Ford manufacturing plant in Cologne, during the Second World War. She was looking for reasonable payment for the work undertaken. The records show that half the workforce were slave labourers and the conditions were terrible. The slave workers lived in:

> ... wooden huts, without running water, heat or storage. Locked in the huts at night, the workers mostly adolescent children, slept in three-tiered wooden bunks without bedding. Food consisted of two paltry meals a day. Workers who became ill were sent to Buchenwald concentration camp. Failure to meet production quotas led to beatings from Ford security officers or other plant workers.

Elsa said in a telephone interview from Belgium, 'It was very cold; they did not pay us at all and scarcely fed us. The only reason that we survived was that we were young and fit.'[51]

The American Ford Motor Company owned the majority of the shares in its subsidiary Ford Werke AG from 1933 to 1945. Two senior executives of the firm, Edsel Ford, Henry's only son, and Robert Sorenson, served as directors of Ford Werke AG throughout the Third Reich. Apart from any other crime this was violating the Trading with the Enemy Act.[52] Ms Iwanowa alleged that:

> ... the company made immense profits providing the German army with tracked vehicles and other trucks. This was because it worked at peak capacity for many years, and did not have to pay wages to many of its workers. Unlike most American facilities in Germany, Ford was not taken over by the German government during the war.[53]

Ford and Hitler seem to have had a friendly relationship since Hitler awarded Henry Ford the 'Great Cross of the German Order of the Eagle' on his 75th birthday in 1938. This was a newly created medal for foreign friends of the Third Reich. It consisted of a Maltese cross bracketed with four eagles and four swastikas and was clearly a Nazi medal. Apparently it was in recognition of Ford's notorious anti-Semitic pamphlet, *The International Jew, a Worldwide Problem.*

Another recipient was Charles Lindbergh in October 1938. James Mooney, General Motors CEO for overseas operations, received a similar medal a month later 'for his distinguished service to the Reich', and Thomas Watson, president of IBM, was also honoured.

Kurt Ludecke was a former associate of Hitler. He claimed he was sent to the USA in 1924 to raise finances for the Nazi Party and met Siegfried and Winifred Wagner, son and daughter-in-law of Richard Wagner. In the 1970s an elderly

Winifred Wagner recalled meeting a very enthusiastic Henry Ford. Although Winifred (1897–1980) was born in Hastings in England, she was an enthusiastic supporter of the Nazis. She recalled that:

> The philosophies of Ford and Hitler were very similar. Ford was very well informed about everything going on in Germany ... He knew all about the National Socialist movement ... Ford told me that he helped to finance Hitler with money from the sales of automobiles and trucks that he sent to Germany.

Frau Wagner claimed that, when she informed Ford that Hitler was still in need of money, he made a remark about being willing to support a man like Hitler who was 'working to free Germany from the Jews'.[54]

It appears that Ford also funded a Hungarian anti-Semite in 1927 with $3,000 – his name was Laszlo Vannay. The *New York Times* for 28 April 1927 described him as 'one of the most fanatical leaders against the Jews during the white terror of 1921'. According to Vannay, Ford wanted to see evidence of his anti-Semitic activities before he sent the money, so he sent him newspaper cuttings and a copy of the charges made by the Hungarian Attorney General for his anti-Semitic activities.

It is not clear how much control Dearborn, Ford's HQ in America, had over the German business after December 1941 – the company claimed there was none, but some sources suggest dividends of $60,000 were received from 1940–1943. American intelligence reported the vehicles made at German Ford and GM (General Motors) plants were the backbone of the German transportation system. Additionally, and perhaps more significantly, after the war Ford demanded reparations from the US Government for damage to the German plants by Allied bombing. It was awarded almost $1 million for damage to the military truck complex in Cologne.[55]

Both GM and Ford refused to allow access to their wartime archives. The Ford spokesman, John Spellich, defended the company's decision to maintain business ties with the Nazis as the US Government had diplomatic relations with Berlin until the Japanese attack on Pearl Harbor in December 1941. However, GM's spokesman, John F. Mueller, said that GM lost day-to-day control over the German plants in September 1939 and insisted they 'did not assist the Nazis in any way during World War II'. According to reports from the US soldiers who liberated the Ford plants in Cologne and Berlin, they found destitute foreign workers behind barbed wire and company papers extolling the 'genius of the Fuehrer'.

Henry Schneider, in a report for the US Army dated 5 September 1945, accused German Ford of serving as 'an arsenal of Nazism at least for military vehicles' with the 'consent' of Dearborn. Spellich claimed that the German subordinates had kept them in the dark about what was happening in Cologne.[56] However, the Schneider report, available in the US National Archives, demonstrates that American Ford agreed a complicated barter deal that gave the Reich increased access to great quantities of strategic raw materials, in particular rubber. Albert Speer, the Nazi armaments chief, told a researcher, Snell, in 1977, that Hitler 'would never have considered invading Poland' without synthetic fuel technology provided by GM. The companies had to work with the Nazis and made their companies seem as German as possible, which is why in April 1939 German Ford gave Hitler a personal present of RM35,000 in honour of his fiftieth birthday, according to a captured Nazi document.

The papers show quite clearly that the companies continued to work with the Nazis rather than get rid of their German assets. In March 1939, less than three weeks after the Nazi invasion of Czechoslovakia, the GM chairman, Alfred P. Sloan, defended the strategy as sound business practice, given the fact that the German operations were 'highly profitable'. A concerned shareholder, who had written to him in the spring of 1939 obviously objecting to this policy, got short shrift from Sloan in a reply of 6 April 1939. He said the internal politics of Nazi Germany were not GM's business and they must conduct themselves like a German company and had no right to close down the plant.

The German GM operation was Adam Opel AG, which had been acquired in March 1929. Documents from both the US Army's post-war investigations and contemporary German files show the significance of Ford and GM to the German military. They show that James Mooney, the GM director in charge of overseas operations, was meeting Hitler for discussions in Berlin two weeks after the invasion of Poland. He too was a recipient of Hitler's special medal.

Typewritten notes by Mooney show that he was involved in the partial conversion of the principal GM automobile plant at Russelsheim to the production of engines and other parts for the Junkers 'Wunderbomber', a key weapon in the German air force, under a government-brokered contract between Opel and the Junkers aeroplane company. Mooney's notes show that he returned to Germany the following February (1940) for further discussions with Luftwaffe commander Hermann Göring and a personal inspection of Russelsheim plant.[57]

This evidence completely undermines GM's claims that American GM had nothing to do with Nazi armaments. It is recorded in congressional testimony in 1974 that GM said that American personnel resigned from management positions in Opel after the war started in 1939, 'rather than participate in the production of war materials'. This is contradicted by the German evidence – the documents from the Reich Commissar for the Treatment of Enemy Property – which show that the American part of GM was having a say in German affairs after 1939 as the company issued a general power of attorney to an American manager, Elis S. Hoglund (known as Pete), in March 1940 and he was also made a director.

When Hoglund left Germany a year later, in February 1941, to return to Detroit, the power of attorney was transferred to Heinrich Richter, a prominent Berlin lawyer. Mueller refused to answer questions about Hoglund, or to allow access to his files and those of other wartime managers. He also declined to comment on the use of French and Belgian prisoners at Russelsheim in the summer of 1940, when Hoglund was still looking after GM's interests in Germany. Both Opel and GM were protecting their investments and an FBI report cites Mooney as saying he would refuse any action that might 'make Hitler mad'. In the autumn of 1940, Mooney told a journalist, Henry Paynter, he would not return his Nazi medal because it might jeopardise GM's $100 million investment in Germany. Paynter quoted Mooney as saying, 'Hitler has all the cards.'

There is some irony that, in spite of converting Russelsheim for aircraft production, they resisted similar conversions at home and a company document cites shareholders being told that the car assembly lines at Detroit were 'not adaptable to the manufacture of other products' such as planes.

In the same way, after the fall of France in June 1940 Henry Ford personally vetoed a US Government-approved plan to produce Rolls-Royce engines for British fighter planes, according to accounts published by his associates. After Pearl Harbor it was illegal for the US motor companies to have any contact with their subsidiaries on German-controlled territory. Ford's spokesman Spellich insists that it had no control over the German firm, but company historians have found documents showing that dividends worth $60,000 for the years 1940–1943 were received. Interviews with the historians were declined.

Indirect contact did occur – in June 1943 the Nazi custodian of the Cologne plant, Robert Schmidt, travelled to Portugal for talks with Ford managers there. There was also a Treasury Department investigation on Ford after Pearl Harbor, for possible illegal contacts with its subsidiary in occupied France which produced German Army trucks. No charges were filed.

US Ford condemned what happened in the Cologne plant during the war, but the managers in charge were still employed. Schmidt was arrested after the war and barred from working for Ford. However, he was reinstated in 1950 after he wrote to Henry Ford II saying he had always 'detested' the Nazis and never been a member of the party. A letter signed by a Cologne Nazi in February 1942 described Schmidt as a trusted party member ...

Mel Weiss, an American attorney for Iwanowa, argues that American Ford received 'indirect' profits from forced labour at its Cologne plant because of the overall increase in the value of German operations during the war. He notes that Ford was eager to demand compensation from the US Government after the war for 'losses' caused by bomb damage to its German plants, and therefore should also be responsible for any benefits derived from forced labour.[58] The same applies to GM – paid $32 million by the US Government for damage resulting from bombing on its German plants.

In 1998 the Ford Motor Company was the sponsor of a commercial-free broadcast of *Schindler's List* by NBC, which led to some cynicism. One blogger drew attention to the report issued in 1974 by the United States Senate Committee on the Judiciary, Subcommittee on Antitrust and Monopoly, which dealt with the activities of General Motors (GM), Ford and Chrysler during the Second World War.[59] Joshua Karliner referred to the power of these three companies, both in the USA and in Germany, which was both economic and political. They were concerned with government relations with these countries that 'maximised corporate global profits'. It continued:

> In short, they were private governments unaccountable to the citizens of any country yet possessing tremendous influence over the course of war and peace in the world. The substantial contribution of these firms to the American war effort in terms of tanks, aircraft components, and other military equipment is widely acknowledged. Less well known are the simultaneous contributions of their foreign subsidiaries to the Axis powers. In sum, they maximized profits by supplying both sides with material needed to conduct the war.

It appears that, during the interwar years, the 'Big Three' carmakers undertook extensive expansion in Europe and the Far East. As a result, by the mid-1930s many of their largest factories were in what were now becoming politically sensitive countries – Germany, Poland, Rumania, Austria, Hungary, Latvia and Japan. They therefore became involved in both the preparation for, and progress of, the war:

> In Germany for example, GM and Ford became an integral part of the Nazi war efforts. GM's plants in Germany built thousands of bomber and jet fighter propulsion systems for the Luftwaffe at the same time that its American plants produced aircraft engines for the US Army Air Corps ...
>      ... In 1938, for instance it [Ford] opened a truck assembly plant in Berlin whose 'real purpose' according to US Army intelligence was producing 'troop transport-type' vehicles for the Wehrmacht.
>      However, in April 1938 when Hitler asked him to build a truck and automobile assembly plant in Berlin, Ford agreed. Construction was soon underway, and in July Henry Ford was awarded his Swastika-studded Cross of the German Eagle Order. In October 1938, another famous American received the Cross–Charles Lindbergh. The outbreak of war resulted in the full conversion of the GM and Ford plants to military production in the Axis countries. It appears that their subsidiaries built nearly 90% of the armoured 'mule' 3 ton half-trucks and more than 70% of the Reich's medium and heavy-duty trucks. These vehicles were 'the backbone of the German Army transportation system' according to American intelligence.

Thus the report concluded that:

… GM and Ford became principal suppliers for the forces of fascism as well as for the forces of democracy. It may, of course, be argued that participating in both sides of an international conflict, like the common corporate practice of investing in both political parties before an election, is an appropriate corporate activity. Had the Nazis won, GM and Ford would have appeared impeccably Nazi; as Hitler lost, these companies were able to re-emerge impeccably American. In either case, the viability of these corporations and the interests of their respective stockholders would have been preserved.

The situation with France was similar. Historian Charles Higham's bitter commentary, forty years later:

No attempt was made to prevent Ford from retaining its interests for the Germans in Occupied France, nor were the Chase Bank or the Morgan Bank expressly forbidden to keep open their branches in Occupied Paris. It is indicated that the Reichsbank and Nazi Ministry of Economics made promises to certain US corporate leaders that their properties would not be injured after the Führer was victorious. Thus, the bosses of the multinationals as we know them today had a six-spot on every side of the dice cube. Whichever side won the war, the powers that really ran nations would not be adversely affected.[60]

Their 'Vicar of Bray' mentality was to the benefit of their profits and their future. It is important to remember that subsequent post-war success was based on the nefarious wartime trade, which no doubt prolonged the war and contributed to the number of deaths, especially of Jews incarcerated in various Nazi camps.

By the mid-1940s, Ford had already suffered two strokes. He had his third and most severe attack in May of 1945. According to witness, Josephine Gomon, he was watching uncut footage of the Majdanek concentration camp in the Ford auditorium. He never recovered his mind or physical strength, Gomon later reported. After this, Ford claimed that government agents were after him and made sure that his chauffeur was armed.

If Ford made any connection between the grisly concentration camp footage and his own actions, it was only reinforced during the Nuremberg Trials. The leader of Hitler's Labour Front, Robert Ley, wrote to Ford from his cell as he awaited trial. In view of their mutual interests, Ley wrote, he would like to work for Ford after he was released. After all, he added, he had done nothing more in the past few years than engage in anti-Semitic activities. Ley was later to hang himself.[61]

# IG Farben

The most powerful German economic corporate emporium in the first half of the twentieth century was the Interessengemeinschaft Farben, or IG Farben, for short. 'Interessengemeinschaft' stands for 'Association of Common Interests', and IG Farben was apparently nothing more than a powerful cartel of BASF, Bayer, Hoechst and other German chemical and pharmaceutical companies.

IG Farben was the single largest donor to the election campaign of Adolf Hitler. One year before Hitler seized power, IG Farben donated 400,000 marks to Hitler and his Nazi Party. Accordingly, after Hitler's seizure of power, IG Farben was the single largest profiteer of the German conquests.

It is important to be aware that Britain's ICI had a cartel agreement with IG Farben, as did Standard Oil of New Jersey. In fact, Farben controlled 500 companies in ninety-two countries.[62] ICI signed an agreement with IG Farben, which established production quotas for nitrogen, the main ingredient in fertiliser. In 1935, the companies agreed that IG Farben would sell nitrogen in all of Europe, except for Spain and Portugal, as well as South and Central America, while ICI would control the markets in the United Kingdom, Spain, Portugal, Indonesia and the Canary Islands. And they agreed to share the Asian market.[63]

Zyklon B was produced by an IG subsidiary called 'Degesch of Frankfurt'. IG Farben controlled 42.4 per cent of the company's stock, which meant they had five seats out of eleven on the supervisory board (aufsichtsrat) and three places on the firm's managing board (vorstand) held by IG vorstand members. One of the three was Wilhelm Mann, who was also the company's chairman. He should have been aware of the sales of Zyklon B because he regularly reviewed Degesch's accounts, although his background was as a chemist rather than as an auditor. It is not known whether he ever queried why the SS needed so much pesticide. It appears that Gerhard Peters, Degesch's general manager, knew about the true use of Zyklon B but kept it secret and never discussed it with anyone other than the SS. Another executive, Bruno Tesch, from the distribution and sales agency, Tesch & Stabenow, mentioned it in a report in July 1942 which was seen by two colleagues, but no one saw fit to give Mann the information – as far as we know.

Mann, a trained chemist, never picked up on the rumours circulating or made the connection. He saw figures showing that consumption of Zyklon B at Auschwitz 1942–1943 was ten times more than at Mauthausen. It could be argued that Auschwitz was so much larger that more fumigation was required. Mann, as chairman of the firm producing Zyklon B, was regarded as a diligent man, so his failure to make the connection is surprising.

The commandant of Auschwitz, Rudolf Höss, said after the war:

I assume with certainty that this firm knew the purpose of the use of the Zyklon B delivered by it. This they would have had to conclude from the fact that the gas for Auschwitz had been ordered continually and in great quantities, while for the other departments of the SS troops etc., orders were only placed once or six-monthly intervals. I cannot recall the exact quantities of Zyklon B which we received from Tesch and Stabenow, however I estimate that at least 10,000 cans, that is 10,000 kilos, had been supplied by them in the course of three years.

These businessmen had no interest in the use of this profitable commodity, but it is vital to be aware of the impact of its use. Dr Münch was described by Lifton as 'a human being in an SS uniform'.[64] He was working as a doctor in Auschwitz from 1943 to 1945. When questioned about the working of the gas chambers by survivor Eva Kor, she noted:

> … he said this was a nightmare he lived with every day. The Zyklon B was dropped to the floor and operated like dry ice, rising up, so people were trying to get away from it and gasping for air. With their last breaths they were climbing on other people, so ended up in a little mountain of intermingled bodies. Dr Munch would look through a peephole and when the people on the top of the pile stopped moving, he knew that everybody was dead and he would sign a death certificate. No names, just a number.[65]

Jozef Paczynski (1920–2015), who survived Auschwitz, tattooed with No. 121 as he arrived in 1940, was Höss's barber. He spoke of his most painful memories about the gas chambers, and the women and children in particular: 'The door slammed shut – there were loud screams, but they got less and less until there were whimpers and then just silence … in Auschwitz you got used to anything.'[66]

In any event, Zyklon B was a financial success – 'According to the accounts, IG's dividends on its Degesch holdings for 1942, 1943 and 1944 (the years of the Final Solution) were double those for 1940 and 1941.'[67] However, Wilhelm Mann did have some idea what was going on at Auschwitz, because he authorised the IG funding and wrote the cheques for SS-Hauptsturmführer Josef Mengele's wages.

Despite the endless supply of guinea pigs Mengele's work didn't come cheap, but IG Farben seems to have been willing to foot the bill. As Wilhelm Mann said in a letter to an SS contact at Auschwitz, 'I have enclosed the first cheque. Dr Mengele's experiments should, as we both agreed, be pursued. Heil Hitler.'[68]

The statement that Mengele's work did not come cheap aroused my curiosity and I wondered what Mengele would have been paid for his demonic work. I found it very difficult to find out, until I was put in touch with Dr Sven Keller who wrote about Mengele. He told me that he had never seen his pay book or tax files and thought they had not survived. He said Mengele was merely a junior officer in the Waffen-SS and he would have earned about RM500 per month gross. Dr Keller suggested that he probably did his 'research' to promote his career and achieve a professorship after the war.[69]

One of Mengele's victims emerged into the public eye in 2009 when he was rushed to an Israeli hospital. He had refused to see doctors for sixty-five years. He had a heart attack and the doctors told his wife, Ahuva, they thought he wouldn't survive because he only had one kidney. Yitzhak Ganon was 85 when he had his second operation in the state-of-the-art hospital in Petach Tikva, near tel Aviv. He told the reporter from *Der Spiegel*, Christoph Schult, how he came to have the first one:

> I come from Arta, a small city in northern Greece. It happened on Saturday, 25 March 1944. We had just lit the candles to celebrate the Sabbath when an SS officer and a Greek policeman burst into the House. They told us we should get ourselves ready for a big trip.

The big trip took two weeks to take them to Auschwitz – his sick father died on the way. On arrival, they had to undress for an inspection. Yitzhak's mother and five siblings were sent straight to the gas chambers. Yitzhak was tattooed with No. 182558 – still visible on his left forearm. He was then sent to the camp's hospital where he was unfortunate to be picked by Mengele.

> Ganon had to lie down on a table and was tied down. Without any anaesthetics, Mengele cut him open and removed his kidney. 'I saw the kidney pulsing in his hand and cried like a crazy man,' Ganon says. 'I screamed the "Shema Yisrael". I begged for death, to stop the suffering.'
>
> After the 'operation' he had to work in the Auschwitz sewing room without painkillers. Among other things, he had to clean bloody medical instruments. Once, he had to spend the whole night in a bath of ice-cold water because Mengele wanted to 'test' his lung function. Altogether, Ganon spent six and a half months in the concentration camp's hospital.
>
> When they had no more use for him they sent him to the gas chamber. He survived only by chance – the gas chamber held only 200 people. Ganon was No. 201.

After liberation he returned to Greece and found a brother and sister who had survived. He went to Israel in 1949 and got married but never, ever, visited a doctor until 2009.[70]

Kitty Hart-Moxon and her mother, Rosa Felix, escaped from the Lublin Ghetto, Poland, and were sent to work for IG Farben. A priest provided them with false documents and told them to mingle with Poles being rounded up for forced labour. They were sent to Germany to an aluminium factory at Bitterfeld with a group of fifty Polish women. Because both Kitty and Rosa spoke good German they were given office jobs. None of the Polish women did, and so they had to work in the factory where there was a lot of aluminium dust and they had no protective masks – the girls were always coughing. They were housed in a shed.

There were many different nationalities working there and they were all given different food – the Poles were treated worst. One girl told Kitty she thought she was Jewish but would not betray her. However, the quality of their German made them suspect and together with another ten from the group they were sent to the Gestapo for interrogation. After a trial and mock execution they were sent to Auschwitz in April 1943.[71]

The Nuremberg War Criminal Tribunal convicted twenty-four IG Farben board members and executives of mass murder, slavery and other crimes against humanity. Amazingly, however, by 1951 all of them had already been released and were continuing to consult for German corporations.

The Nuremberg Tribunal dissolved IG Farben into Bayer, Hoechst and BASF. Today, each of the three 'daughters' of IG Farben is twenty times bigger than IG Farben was at its height in 1944. More importantly, for almost three decades after the Second World War, BASF, Bayer and Hoechst (now Aventis) each filled its highest position, chairman of the board, with former Nazis:

1   Carl Wurster, chairman of the board of BASF until 1974 was, during the war, on the board of the company manufacturing Zyklon B gas.
2   Carl Winnacker, chairman of the board of Hoechst until the late 1970s, was a member of the Sturm Abteilung (SA) and was a member of the board of IG Farben.
3   Curt Hansen, chairman of the board of Bayer until the late 1970s, was co-organiser of the conquest of Europe in the department of 'acquisition of raw materials'.

Under this leadership BASF, Bayer, and Hoechst continued to support politicians representing their interests. During the 1950s and 1960s they invested in the political career of an eager, young representative from a suburb of the BASF town of Ludwigshafen. His name was Helmut Kohl. From 1957 to 1967 young Helmut Kohl was a paid lobbyist of the Verband Chemischer Industrie, the central lobby organisation of the German pharmaceutical and chemical cartel. He became Chancellor of Germany for sixteen years from 1982–1998, and the German pharmaceutical and chemical industry became the world's leading exporter of chemical products, with subsidiaries in over 150 countries, more than IG Farben had ever had.[72]

For many years he argued that German companies that used slave labour should not have to compensate their victims. His argument was that the companies were merely following Nazi Government orders when they employed slave labour. This is the same line of argument that was used at the Nuremberg Trials – that an officer could not be responsible for mass murder because he was merely obeying orders – an argument rejected by the court. Germany is the only country in the entire world in which a former paid lobbyist for the chemical and pharmaceutical cartel became head of the government.

## The Issue of Compulsory Rest Days

In Kovno in 1929 difficulties were reported. The government had lately made ostentatious declarations of friendship to the Jews, as had Prime Minister Valdemaras and Lithuanian representatives abroad especially in America. These people have been making flattering comments about Lithuanian Jewry according to the Yiddish daily, *Yiddishe Stimme*, in an editorial. Unfortunately, the paper declared these fine words were not being paralleled by deeds. Jewish trades and Jewish artisans were still being economically ruined by the compulsory Sunday rest law. Jews were also still barred from government positions. Two Jewish doctors were recently dismissed from their state positions and the few Jews who still held state positions would soon be compelled to leave them. The newspaper commented that the list of complaints against the government could be increased. A conference of Jewish merchants held at Shavle, decided to ask the government to postpone the date when taxes would be collected because of the tradesmen's difficult position. The Jewish merchants said they were facing ruin.[73]

Jews in Salonika also suffered from restrictions on Sunday trading. In 1934 it was reported that a decree ordering strict Sunday observance in Salonika was published, in the official *Greek Gazette*, signed by President Alexander Zaimis. This was a serious blow to the Jewish merchants, who had to close two days a week unless they choose to break the Sabbath. Trading on Saturday is permitted. Sunday was only a partial day of rest in Salonika since 1923 when due to Jewish protests small traders were permitted to open on a Sunday morning. The recent decree was made as a result of protests from non-Jewish grocers who demanded complete observance of Sunday as a rest day.[74]

## Boycotts and Christmas Trading

Boycotts against Jewish businesses and shopkeepers did not start in 1933 but had been a fact of life since the end of the nineteenth century. They took place throughout the years of the Weimar Republic and, as the Jewish Attorney Georg Baum pointed out in 1925, were used as a means of suppressing one's political opponent economically rather than trying to win a political argument.[75]

Over the years the Nazis 'used boycotts as a means both of propaganda and stigmatisation and discrimination'. They were a very effective tool because they created a combat situation and media attention. They intensified the Jews' social and economic segregation. The boycotts were meant to destroy the material basis of Jewish life in Germany and 'as such the pauperisation and social death of the Jewish minority became crucial steps on the way to their physical extermination. Boycotts attacked the position of German Jews in society and their self-perception and self-esteem.'

Boycotts also helped the Nazis create the exclusive German Volksgemeinschaft by forcing the German citizens to live in a 'German' manner. The boycott created a three element scenario – the anti-Semites outside the Jewish shop, Germans doing their shopping, and the targeted Jews. Recent research shows that campaigns against Jewish department stores continued from 1928, and then attempts were made to attack local neighbourhood shops.

The traditional view of the boycott is that of storm troopers outside the Jewish-owned shop, forcing the German citizen to make a choice and exposing themselves, not only to the Nazi activists but also to the milling crowd. However, the activities were not always violent and often used what appeared to be innocuous means of advertising. Anti-Semite activists (but also local business partners and competitors, trade associations and neighbours) used leaflets, pamphlets and stickers to encourage boycotts against Jewish businesses and shops, even promoting boycotts through bonus systems, gift hampers and sweepstakes in order to convince people to buy only from Germans. By means of shop signs, posters and advertising, avowed members of the NSDAP, as well as neighbours, business partners and competitors, tried to label themselves as German and Christian businesses as opposed to Jewish ones. Thus, without taking any action that was violent, or in open violation of existing laws or social mores, German society educated its citizens to recognise the difference between Germans and Jews, and to act accordingly.

Many Jews sought legal action, which was permitted under German law, and there were many successful cases. A political boycott was forbidden by law and so was the public labelling of shops as Jewish by activists. However, in the later years of Weimar it became harder to use the law to fight prejudice and the Nazis used special labelling, like 'German' or 'Christian', which was not illegal. Instead of a slogan such as 'Germans don't buy from Jews', they used 'Germans buy only from Germans'. This usage demonstrated how, already, there was a distinction between 'Jewish' and 'German' and how one could not be both (see Nivea, page 324).

The stereotype of the Jew was part of the modern racist anti-Semitism as well as traditional religious Judeophobia. Jews had been associated with commerce and, in particular, usury through the ages, as demonstrated by the infamous Shakespearian 'Shylock' in the *Merchant of Venice*, and the figure of the money-grabbing Jew developed into the Weimar period. The Nazis added to this figure the concept of Jews as the killers of Christ, particularly at Christmas. When shop owners hoped for good trade they worked on the division between Jews and German Christians.

In 1930 there was a nasty leaflet produced in Königsberg called 'The Golden Calf is Playing Christ Child':

> With real Jewish cynicism the Rabbi says; What a pity that Maria didn't have two Jesus babies. Then OUR FOLKS could make their deals with the Christmas trade twice!!! Take care that the foreign vermin [fremdstämmige volksschädling], the Jewish bloodsucker, does not reap his profit smiling benignly. Every penny you hand over at the department store's pay desk to the Jewish floozy will become a nail used to crucify you and your children.

This short piece combines all the classic Jewish stereotypes. In Christmas 1931 there was reference to 'Christian charity' and how Christmas was the most German of all festivities. In legal cases it was becoming harder to prove that anti-Semitic statements were offensive and harmful. In 1931, two furniture shops in Hagen owned by Sally Lederfeind and Willy Niemeyer had a serious dispute because both had 'Niemeyer' in their names. For many years Willy had placed notices warning that his was the only Christian furniture store in Hagen and added, 'Don't be deceived'. The court's judgement was that there was no harm in showing which shop was Jewish and which was Christian.

Accordingly, shops which were Jewish began to be identified all round the towns, not just in Jewish areas, and maps began to be produced and distributed in the autumn of 1935, when the Nuremberg Laws had defined the differences. Apparently, small booklets were being produced in different towns in the form of a notebook from 1929. They contained postage tariffs, a calendar and most importantly the way to the 'proper' Jewish shops. The one for the small town of Aue was published by NSDAP in 1931 and included a list of German shops, and on the back it had a favoured Nazi phrase, 'Germans, don't buy from Jews'.

Inside the booklet there is no blatant anti-Semitism and the word 'Jew' does not appear, but the language uses words that conjure the anti-Semitic stereotype – such as 'fair prices' as opposed to 'inflated prices' and 'sneaky' and 'unreliable advertising'. Many of the booklets had spaces for advertising which tended to be a bottom-up strategy, such as the 'card of honour of the German mother', created by the Nazi Party in Görlitz. Presumably working like the loyalty cards we have today, the card gave benefits and privileges to German mothers but, of course, it could not be used in Jewish stores.

A further method of indicating which shops were Jewish was devised for Christmas 1933 and 1934, designating suitable styles of window dressing for German shops and objecting to Jews using Nativity scenes, statues of saints and Madonnas in their windows. However, Jews were permitted to use a fir tree, or candles in Breslau, although other towns had different views. In Schneidemühl one Jewish businessman, Saly Eifert, was told that usage of a fir tree might be a problem.

In Leipzig, a cardboard Santa Claus was put on every front door containing a list of desirable gifts, and the same Santa was in the window of all drapers' shops as 'a first-hand signpost to our shops'. In 1933, signs marked 'German Business' began to appear all over Germany in all colours and designs and some began to add swastikas and anti-Semitic caricatures. Labels were being stuck on Jewish shops at night and had to be scraped off each morning, and this even happened in Berlin in March 1935. They had messages like 'Those who buy from Jews are traitors of the people' or 'The Jew is the devil's son'.

In December 1934 it was reported that a high-powered anti-Jewish campaign was in progress throughout Germany in the pre-Christmas period, in spite of repeated orders from the economics minister, Hjalmer Schacht, that Jewish traders should not be molested. Nazi groups were beseeching Christmas shoppers 'not to betray Germany' and to avoid patronising Jewish shops. In many towns they were campaigning against Jewish stores and pickets were in front of the shops. The pickets displayed posters threatening any Aryans who traded with Jews and any prospective purchasers were frequently met by groups of Hitler Youth shouting anti-Jewish slogans. At the same time in Worms, Jewish shops were targeted with yellow handbills with cartoons of the medieval ghetto badge Jews were forced to wear and Nazi slogans.[76]

In December 1936 'posters appeared in Budapest urging the public not to patronise Jewish stores for Christmas shopping'.[77] Later, on 21 January 1942, the Hungarian authorities issued an order prohibiting Jews from selling newspapers and ordered all Jewish news-dealers to return their licences. This deprived 300 Jewish families of their livelihood, reported the Berlin correspondent of the Swedish newspaper, *Svenska Dagbladet*.[78]

In 1941 it was reported from Stockholm on 26 December, 'Huge crowds attending pre-Christmas auctions of confiscated Jewish goods in the leading German cities, paid fantastically high prices after spirited bidding for each article, it is reported by Berlin correspondents …'

Although new house furnishings, when available, cost only a third of the price for many of the articles at the auctions, the reports state, the scarcity of consumer goods and the German people's fear of imminent inflation produced the rush to buy these Jewish-owned furnishings. Ordinary couches brought 1,000 marks, nominally $400; upholstered chairs were sold for 400 marks; 75 marks were paid for ordinary cotton bed sheets.

The government authorities announced that the money realised on the goods, the owners of which had been deported to Poland, would be used to 'pay the costs of evacuating Jews'.[79]

In Trier, people were being forced to put signs up, and in Worms everyone had to complete a form giving Aryan ancestry and any Jewish investments or dealings with Jewish suppliers or salesmen. Those who did not wish to participate were threatened with the publication of their names under a heading 'Shops that do not want to be German!' The police were involved in these activities, even though the government was still officially opposed to boycotts.

The next stage was photographing people who shopped at Jewish shops, or the guards outside would write down their names which were then listed on notice-boards or in newspapers. This became well established by the summer of 1935. The activity continued, even though the party leadership and the government opposed this behaviour. The actions changed according to circumstances, and this made it difficult for the Jews to react as the playing field was continually changing. Their economic situation deteriorated as a result and in small towns Jews became totally isolated as they could be more easily identified.

Neustadt an der Aisch was a town of 10,000 inhabitants – most of them Protestant. The Nazi Party had gained 68 per cent of the vote in July 1932. However, it was still difficult for Jews to identify who was responsible for anti-Semitic activists. Werner Cahnman, who was a correspondent for the Central Verein (CV), noted that there were twenty Jewish families with sixty-five individuals in May 1933, after which time there were violent attacks on these Jews. In addition to all the old posters, there were some saying 'Jews not served here'. Cahnman was told that they were forced to do this, otherwise they were threatened with boycott themselves and would have their name in the newspaper. Cahnman reported that there was serious pressure on gentiles.

Like many local newspapers, the *Neustädter Anzeigenblatt* had a column for pillorying traitors and printed announcements almost every day – 'There are still Germans who buy from Jews. One of them is the schoolteacher Haas from Schauerheim. This is the last warning to him and to everybody who has not yet realised what we are fighting for. The revolution is not over yet.'

That announcement was made on 2 May 1933, and on 3 May there was a notice that Mr Max Geissendörfer, Nürnbergerstrasse 31, was given a ride through the town 'by the Jew Karl Wekkerich in his carriage'. The headmaster Karl Köhler was also pilloried on 5 May because he had greeted Jews. A few days after the CV had contacted the ministry the boycotters became more aggressive: 'in the few cases where customers succeeded in entering a Jewish shop, people with cameras took pictures of them leaving the shop and running the gauntlet of jeering and laughing onlookers in one case, even ushering them out with a drum roll', reported Cahnman. There were crowds outside the shops all day and it was all very threatening.

Two teachers, Hertlein and Riedel, were particularly active with their colleague Schöller, who was a member of the Kreispropagandaleitung (Reich Propaganda Office). It appears that in Neustadt not just the teachers but most of the activists were well known in the town. 'It was a typical element of the Nazi boycotts that in many cases local notables, schoolteachers, officials and even the mayor played an important part in them.'

The situation in Neustadt became even more serious as the Nazis proclaimed a total economic ban on the Jewish population, so that selling to them was banned. It was called a 'passivboycott' and was most effective in small towns or villages with just a few Jews, who became fearful not only of their businesses and income but also of being starved when food was not supplied. One baker told a Jewish family, 'I request your entire family to avoid my shop in future. The party leadership insists on this.' It is important to remember this was happening in May 1933.

Hairdressers no longer served Jewish customers; cars were not repaired by mechanics; one enterprising tailor asked a Jewish customer to collect his finished suit at night; Jews waited for a plumber in vain; an electrician even refused to repair dangerous damage to an installation because he feared disadvantages.

The evidence shows that many were influenced by the Nazi pressure, but some felt guilty. Others showed initiative, like the milkman who told a Jewish family to collect their milk at 5.00 a.m. 'until the crisis is over'. Such support made the Jews feel they could trust their gentile neighbours and colleagues with whom they had lived for decades.

The Jewish partners of the company Gebrüder Schwab wrote to the Reichswirtschaftsministerium on 28 March 1934, 'We belong to Neustadt, we were born in this town, we have become part of the population here, we defended our Heimat [social cohesion], we always played our part and we are convinced that we are just as "good Germans" as anybody else.'

This could have been written by any of the millions of victims of the Nazis. This was a waste of time – their long-time customers were denounced publicly, anyone attempting to visit the business was spat at by children and one woman was pursued with terrible obscenities. The Nazis wanted the town Judenfrei within the year – but they had to wait for Kristallnacht, when the synagogue was set on fire and the old people's home was burnt down, for the last Jews to leave Neustadt in December 1938. The Schwab company was ruined.

Hannah Ahlheim, on whose research this section is based, concludes that the situation in Neustadt was probably unique because it was such an early stronghold of Nazism. For Jewish businessmen, 1935 was a crucial period. They found the economic climate had changed for them and James Grover McDonald, the High Commissioner for Jewish & Other Refugees, of the League of Nations, commented that there was 'no longer a minimal guarantee in any field of commercial activity' for the Jews in Germany.

At the close of 1935 Jewish businesses anticipated heavy losses and some department stores anticipated 50 to 70 per cent losses. In small towns some shops had no income at all. The boycotts, followed by the Nuremberg Laws, led many Jews to decide to leave Germany. The boycotts had erected an invisible wall between Jews and Germans in everyday life. The public's reaction to the boycotts and the stigmatisation of Jews was symptomatic of what was to come. The public was forced to take sides and shopping became a political activity.

The fact that most people chose to remain neutral, at best, was significant. By 1935 James McDonald was writing of the Jews in Germany as 'sentenced to live apart within the four walls of a legal and social ghetto that has been closed behind them now'. Ahlheim concludes that 'the boycott of Jewish businesses finally not only contributed to the social death of German Jews but prepared the ground for their physical extermination'.

Brenda Bailey reported on the 1 April boycott:

Mary decided this was the day for us both (I was six years old) to walk through the town to visit our Jewish friends and all the small Jewish shopkeepers en route. She ignored the warning signs, simply telling the guards she needed to speak to the shop-owner and walked through any doors that were open to talk to the frightened people inside. No doubt Mary's English accent must have afforded some protection. Camera crews were on the streets to record the events of the day. One of the Quakers went to a cinema that evening and saw us both on newsreel, talking to a guard and then walking past him into a Jewish shop. Friends in Meeting were perturbed and felt Mary had taken a great risk, particularly as she was a German citizen by marriage.[80]

# 11

# EDUCATION

There is no education like adversity.

Benjamin Disraeli (1804–1881)

Without a solution to the Jewish Question there will be no solution to humankind.

Fritz Fink, 1937

## Schools

Fritz Fink (1893–1945), who was a poet and a bookseller, wrote *Die Judenfrage in Unterricht* (*The Jewish Question in Education*), which was published in Nuremberg in 1937. It was intended for teachers to encourage them to incorporate anti-Semitism in their teaching in every part of the curriculum.

Julius Streicher was not only involved in publishing *Der Stürmer*, but also produced various other pamphlets. He wrote the introduction to Fink's pamphlet:

The racial and Jewish Question is the central problem of the National Socialist worldview. Solving this problem will ensure the survival of National Socialism and thereby the survival of our people for all time. The enormous significance of the Jewish Question is recognized today by nearly every member of the German people. This knowledge cost our people a long period of misery. To spare coming generations this misery, we want German teachers to plant the knowledge of the Jew deep in the hearts of our youth from their childhood on. No one among our people should or may grow up without learning the true depravity and danger of the Jew.[1]

The introduction continued by encouraging teachers not to spend just an hour a week dealing with the Jewish Question and racial issues as 'an independent subject'. He encouraged them to bring it into every lesson. The pamphlet 'wants to show German teachers simple ways in which the Jewish Question can be incorporated naturally into the curriculum'. He claimed that while adults had lost their racial instinct about Jews, 'A dislike of the Jews is innate in uncorrupted German youth.' They must explain to their charges why they should hate the Jews. Those who fail to tackle the issue:

> … are the weaklings, the cowards, those German teachers ruined by this deadly enemy. The way that animals keep to their own kind either in migration or breeding and this must be learnt between mixing the races 'of blacks or Orientals with white people, or Jews with Gentiles'. Accordingly, 'the children will see in the Nuremburg Laws nothing other than a return to the natural, to the divine, order'.

Streicher then referred to work done by Professor Karl Escherich (1871–1951), a retired forest entomologist, on termite colonies. He explains that where termites allow other insects to come in and disrupt their social patterns and even kill their queen, it created a revolution in the termite state and everyone was murdered. This compared with the impact of the Jews on Germany and he concludes that:

> Such a lesson will help the children understand why the Nuremberg Laws redefined citizenship and excluded the Jews from any influence in political and governmental life. The children must learn that the laws directed against the Jews and the struggle against him is not the result of an arbitrary whim, but an action necessary to defend our people.[2]

While many headmasters were chosen carefully to give a lead and perform elaborate Nazi ceremonies, this was not uniform. In Hamburg the Wilhelm Gymnasium was popular with Jewish parents. In 1936, when Rudolf Heymann was selected, his father was concerned about how his son would be treated. He went to see the headmaster, Dr Bernhard Lundius, who told him, 'As long as I am headmaster I can reassure you.' Rudolf was happy at the school and left in 1938. Mostly the teachers were not Nazis, and the headmaster did what he could without threatening his own position as headmaster. This is not regarded as an uncommon situation.[3]

Early in January 2014, it was announced that a school in Greece had found the graduation certificates of 157 Jewish students who either fled the city or were deported to Nazi death camps. Antonio Crescenzi, a teacher at the Italian School in Thessaloniki (Salonika) found a pile of old documents about ten years ago. When he sorted through them, he realised how important they were. He has managed to track down some of the students and their descendants and intended to present their certificates finally in a special ceremony later in 2014. The documents related to students who were born between 1912 and 1928 who studied at the school, one of two Italian schools that existed in the port city before the war. Salonika was a major centre for Sephardic Jewry in the Balkans and had a pre-war Jewish population of 55,000. The Nazis deported nearly 50,000 to the extermination camps, mostly Auschwitz, of whom only around 2,000 came home.[4]

## The Hitler Youth

The Hitler Youth (Hitler Jugend or HJ) is included here because there were some difficulties with members who had specific duties to perform which often interfered with school work. These created tensions between schools and the party.[5] The HJ was created unofficially by Baldur von Schirach, the son of an aristocratic German father and an American mother. Having joined the Nazi Party in 1924, he proved adept at organising events for youths and students. In 1929 he was put in charge of the Nazis' German Students League and two years later he was made Reich Youth Leader of the NSDAP, a post he held until 1940. He claimed that he became a convinced anti-Semite after reading Henry Ford's book *The International Jew* as a 17-year-old. He later said:

> You have no idea what a great influence this book had on the thinking of German youth. The younger generation looked with envy to the symbols of success and prosperity like Henry Ford, and if he said the Jews were to blame, we naturally believed him.[6]

Although he was an aristocrat, he opposed Christianity and his peers. Once he was in charge of the HJ, he used a mixture of 'pagan romanticism, militarism and naïve patriotism to organise the recruits for Hitler's war machine'. By 1936 there were 6 million members and these were to be trained according to Schirach's book, *Die Hitler-Jugend*, which was published in 1934.

They were to be moulded into a new race of 'supermen'. They were taught that their German blood was better than that of any other nation. By the start of the war there were nearly 9 million members of the HJ and 16,000 formed the 12th SS Panzer Division.

Toward the start of the war, von Schirach was being undermined by Martin Bormann and others, who joked about his effeminate behaviour, claiming that he, personally, failed to live up to HJ ideals. In 1940 he volunteered for the army, serving in France, and then later he was made gauleiter in Vienna. He ultimately lost control of the HJ.

He seemed ambivalent about the Jews – in 1943 he complained about the conditions in which they were being deported, but in 1942 he had said the removal of the Jews to the east would contribute to European culture. The fact that 65,000 Jews had been deported from Vienna to Poland while he was governor went against him at the Nuremberg Trials. It appears that, during his trial, he recognised what he had done in misleading the German youth and poisoning a whole generation. He said, 'I put my morals to the side, out of misplaced faith in the Führer, I took part in this action. I did it. I cannot undo it.' He also acknowledged that 'it was the most all-encompassing and diabolical genocide ever committed by man ... Hitler and Himmler together started this crime against humanity which will remain a blot on our history for centuries.'

Göring's wife (Emmy) claimed they were not really friends with any other Nazi leaders except for Baldur von Schirach, who had lost faith in Hitler. Emmy asked why a previously planned visit had not happened, and Henrietta von Schirach explained:

> The Führer threw out my husband and me. On the day before I had seen a train full of Jews leaving the station, packed like sardines, and I reproached Adolf Hitler for not treating the Jews more humanely. We got into a discussion – and then suddenly it was all finished. 'Get out of my house at once,' he cried to me. And so we naturally left in a hurry.[7]

In 1946, Shirach was sentenced to twenty years' imprisonment, served in Spandau Prison, and he was released in 1966. In his memoirs, published a year after his release, he tried to explain the fatal fascination Hitler had exerted on him and the young. He blamed himself for not having done more to prevent the concentration camps. He died in 1974.[8]

William Shirer gave weekly radio broadcasts for CBS from Berlin, from 1938 until December 1940. He always started, 'This is Berlin ...' On 12 March 1940, he reported:

> Beginning April 20th, all German youngsters between ten and eighteen are compelled to join the Hitler Youth organisations. Conscription of Germany's youth was laid down in a law dated 1936, but will only go into effect now. Boys between seventeen and eighteen will receive preliminary military training.[9]

The dangers of the youngsters trained by the Nazis were skilfully observed in 1941 by the veteran US journalist Howard K. Smith,[10] who lived in Germany from 1936 to 1942. He wrote cynically that:

> The little creatures in their brown shirts and short black trousers could be amusing if they were not so dangerous. They are dangerous; more so than a cholera

epidemic. There is, so far as I know, no demoralization in their ranks. They love the whole show, and are just aching to get big enough to get into the fight themselves. Frankly, I am more afraid, more terrorized, at watching a squad of these little boys, their tender faces screwed in frowns to ape their idolized leaders, on the streets of Berlin, than I am at seeing a panzer brigade of grown-up fighters speeding across the city. The grown-ups we only have to fight; but we shall have to live under the children who are being trained for their role.[11]

Smith explains that previously the Hitler Youth activity took place after school – I suppose, like the Scouts:

Hitler Youth training, drilling and study used to be something which took place after school, extra curricular activities. Now Hitler has decreed it shall be part of the curriculum: mornings must be given over to studying the Nazi version of history and other subjects, and afternoons to Hitler Youth activity. If a boy is a good Hitler Youth, he passes no matter what he knows about anything else. If he has not been a good, vigorous Hitler Youth, he cannot even enter a secondary school, regardless of how intelligent he is or what other talent he has. That is another decree of that year of progress, 1941.[12]

Smith, who had been a Rhodes Scholar at Oxford University in 1937, was obviously shocked by the indoctrination of the next generation:

For nine years now, their malleable little minds have been systematically warped. They are growing up in a mental plaster-cast and they like it with its accompaniment of drums, trumpets, and uniforms and flags. They are enthusiastic; the biggest hauls in the Winter Relief collections are always made by the Hitler Youth and the *Bund Deutscher Maedel*, the League of German Girls. I have never seen so completely military a German as the little seven-year-old boy who knocked at my door one day and, when I had opened it, snapped to rigid attention, shot his arm high and shouted at me a falsetto 'Heil Hitler!' after which he asked me in the clipped sentences of a military command would I donate twenty pfennigs to 'support the Fuehrer and the Fatherland in this, our life-and-death struggle'.[13]

Ian Kershaw found that the anti-Jewish enthusiasm of the Hitler Youth was not always shared by the rural population. In Upper Bavaria the local peasants were concerned that the boards put by the youngsters saying, 'Jews not wanted here' would stop them coming to buy their hops. They took the boards down and replaced them with 'Jews very much wanted here'. Kershaw comments that the continued trade with Jews in rural areas was not based on a pro-Jewish view but merely on a desire to sell all their produce and animals.[14]

The Hitler Youth were trained from an early stage in the dogma of German racial superiority and consequently the inferiority of other people, especially Slavs, Sinti and Roma (known as Gypsies) and Jews. It has been argued that post-1945 apologists deny this indoctrination went systematically from the age of 10. It is also asserted that the HJ boys and girls were not involved in Kristallnacht. They were not dispatched in any organised way – 'they were forced to watch and digest the experience and learn the required racial lessons from it':

> In Alzey (Rhenish Hesse) the SA co-opted the local HJ group and took them to a Jewish family's apartment and with the terrified family watching, the boys demolished the furniture with an axe. In Munich the HJ drove around in abstentious staff cars to the residences of Jews known to be wealthy and took money from some and intimidating others to leaving their homes.

HJ leadership wanted the youngsters to learn from Kristallnacht how to treat Jews, but the responses of the HJ varied from finding the experience fascinating and justified, to some who struggled with it, particularly after discussing it with their parents. Others were disturbed, but closed their eyes to it, regarding it as unavoidable. They were to receive daily propaganda and training sessions on why Jews were different and evil.

They were assembled to hear Reich Economics Minister Walther Funk, in May 1938, who explained to them why Jews had to be expropriated (have their property taken away) – after taking their business and their wealth from them, they could be given some inferior leaseholder while they didn't have the ability to move them completely out of Germany.

HJ children were taught anti-Semitic songs, with texts describing 'Jewish blood dripping from the knife'. They were told to find practical experience in dealing with Jews, and in Vienna during the *Anschluss* they were involved in much of the ill-treatment meted out.

In 1941 a group of HJ were taken to Theresienstadt to see the Jewish enemy first hand:

> They were confronted with one of them who, they were told, had to stand upright for twenty-four hours on end. 'And if he faints?' asked an incredulous visitor. 'Then he gets a bucket of water over his pelt,' replied the swaggering HJ leader, with a laugh. 'And then you will see how quickly he will get on his feet!' And he continued: 'Of course these are no ordinary criminals, they are depraved creatures, detritus, you understand?' An SS guard hastened to add: 'The Jews are our most repulsive cases. One has to approach them like a disease, like an epidemic.'

There was a similar situation in the schools where anti-Semitism was promoted. Some of the teachers were ex-soldiers who resented the Jews for allegedly selling Germany down the river. Some teachers read *Der Stürmer* regularly and drew anti-Semitic cartoons on the blackboard. Even a mathematics exercise book read as follows: 'In Germany the people of foreign race are the Jews. In 1933 the German Reich had 66,060,000 inhabitants. Of those, 499,682 were practising Jews. How much is that in per cent?'

'Jewish children were part of the mainstream education system in the period 1933–1936 until they were gradually squeezed out. The class in one Berlin school shortly before the war was told by its teacher that "all Jews are bad" and, as he pointed to the dark, curly-haired Esau, who had done nothing wrong, "even Esau and the other two Jewish students in this class".'

It was very easy for anti-Semitic teachers to turn a whole class toward hatred of Jews. One pupil remembered a Jewish classmate:

I did not want to have anything to do with him. Of course I ignored him, but then I did not hurt him either. Somehow he had fleas, I did not like him. Not because he was personally unpleasant, I did not relate to him in any way, it's just that he was a Jew, and therefore I could not stand him.

This led to problems for the half-Jews – Mischlinge – who were defined in Nazi law books with special distinctions. The Nuremberg Laws of 15 September 1935 defined Jews as having three Jewish grandparents. The Mischlinge with two grandparents were 'of the first degree' and with one grandparent, 'of the second degree'. They were still allowed in the schools, at their own risk, but were victimised by vicious teachers. The Tübingen neurologist, Jürgen Peiffer, recalls that in Stuttgart in the early 1940s the two Mischlinge in his class had to wear white shirts during school ceremonies, when everybody else wore their uniforms. After October 1941 they had to wear a yellow star as well. A 'half-Jew', Hanns-Peter Herz, reported:

We had a tough, hard-core Nazi as a physical education and swimming teacher. The first day we had to put on our swimming trunks and stand alongside the pool. When we were all lined up, he said: 'Herz, step forward. And you stay there. We won't go into the pool with a half-Jew.' From then on I spent swimming class, two hours every week, standing at the edge of the pool in my trunks. I didn't learn to swim until 1963.

One Aryan-looking girl had a gentile father who had fought in the First World War, but her mother was Jewish. She was ostracised by the whole class when this became known. Former friends would come and touch her and say, 'Ouch, I have come into contact with Steinbrecher, and now I smell of garlic.' She was taken away to a Jewish school, where the pupils couldn't sit too near the windows for fear of the rocks hurled in by German passers-by.

The indoctrination that Jews were Germany's enemies went hand-in-hand with adulation of Hitler and his infallibility. Every school had at least one portrait of Hitler, and his personal and political biography was taught both in school and in the HJ. The important dates for Nazis were Hitler's birthday, on 20 April, and 9 November, which was the approximate day of Germany's First World War defeat. The date was memorialised in both the Munich Beer Hall Putsch of 1923 and Kristallnacht in 1938. Hitler's birthday was used for official HJ initiations and the adulation was encouraged with attendance at the events at which he spoke, culminating in the Nuremberg Reich Party Rally on 8 September 1934, orchestrated by Albert Speer and Leni Riefenstahl and attended by 60,000 members of the HJ. The event was recorded by Riefenstahl in *Triumph of the Will* and shown in cinemas. The HJ were being trained and moulded to be obedient and compliant followers, and leaders who would be required to lead the fight to come.[15]

Lothar Orbach (now Larry) who was born in 1924, from a proud German family who happened to be Jewish. He writes very eloquently of their first realisation that the Nazis were here to stay and life would never be the same. He was very excited because, in the spring of 1934 when he was 10, he had won the school genealogy project. He had managed, with some help from his father, to trace his German ancestors further back than anyone else in the school. He got back to the 1490s when Moses Auerbach (or Orbach or Urbach, since they are spelt the same in Hebrew) was a court Jew to the Bishop of Regensburg. As a result he was given the honour of reciting 'Kaempfe Blute' which was one of his favourite poems. It was written by the man who wrote 'Deutschland Über Alles', the country's anthem, and he was proud of being a German.

He practised in front of his parents and two brothers and everyone was bursting with pride. However, a few weeks later, just before Larry was due to make his recitation, the rektor (headmaster) summoned him and Larry assumed he wanted to check that he was appropriately prepared. The rektor was sitting at his desk, facing Larry, with a portrait of the Führer on the wall behind him:

> In his usual polite tone, the rektor tells me that the administration has decided that it would not be fitting for a Jew to represent the student body by reciting 'Kaempfe Blute'. Because I am a Jew, the indisputable fact that I won the gene-alogy competition is irrelevant. The second-place winner, a surly sixth grader whose German ancestors are all Aryan, will have the honor.
>
> This cultured, intelligent gentleman, this respected pedagogue, relays this news to me in the most matter-of-fact way, as though he is pointing out some obvious anomaly that makes my participation in the commencement a logical impos-

sibility: you have no legs, so you cannot run the race; you have no arms, so you cannot carry the torch; you are a Jew, so you cannot be a German.[16]

Larry managed to keep control until he got home when he sobbed to his mother. His parents were really upset and his father threatened to go to school to beat the rektor up. His mother said the racial hatred came and went. None of them could know that his schoolmates, his chums on the football pitch, 'would soon pledge to destroy' him, and that his father, 'a staunch German patriot, would be sent to die in a concentration camp by the country he had served valiantly'. He was a master sergeant in the Medical Corps in the First World War and was awarded the Iron Cross, Second Class, for bravery after he shot a knife-wielding Frenchman in the barracks near Sedan.

His parents decided to leave Falkenberg because they were having trouble with their shop – smashed windows and customers boycotting them. They sold the store for very little, but had decided to go to Berlin where there were more Jews and they lived with his maternal grandmother. Larry enjoyed his new school where there were four Jewish boys among the class of twenty-four.[17]

In spite of the debacle over his recitation, 'Aryan classmates seemed to want to keep their Jewish friends as long as they could. It was only when their parents began punishing them for associating with us that they turned away and then reluctantly at first.'

Larry's friends all joined the Hitler Youth as it was mandatory for all school children:

> Dressed in perfectly pressed uniforms with ribbons and badges, they marched in big parades far grander than those of my sports club. Some of my class-mates were given the honor of carrying the flags and banners; a few even brandished drill weapons. I watched them go, these classmates and teammates and neighbourhood friends of mine, withdrawing into their own circle and leaving me outside. I was captivated by the pageantry of the Hitler Jugend, jealous of the camaraderie, and would have joined in a minute It never occurred to me that I would be an enemy against whom they were joining forces.

When the Nuremberg Laws were introduced in September 1935, the four 11-year-old Jewish boys of the 228 Volksschule of Berlin became second-class citizens and old friendships were over. They had to sit in a back corner of the room. The Aryan children were told not to associate with them unless absolutely necessary. 'My parents were clearly unhappy about our treatment at school, but they said nothing; it was the law and, after all, we were Germans, we obeyed.'[18]

## Italian Schools

Indoctrination in school was not just found in German schools. In Italy, the school syllabus was altered in 1929, with more references to the Duce and Fascism, when a new text book was brought in with material chosen and approved by a ministerial commission. Coercion certainly helped the enthusiasm, with the introduction of a civil service law in January 1927 which 'exposed any teacher who did not display sufficient enthusiasm for the regime to possible dismissal'. However, there was considerable enthusiasm already, particularly among the young, who saw Mussolini's defence of Catholicism as the main reason to support Fascism. Women, who made up the majority of primary school teachers, were particularly keen. This is exemplified by a teacher from Abruzzi, born in 1901:

> I wanted to become a teacher as I felt attracted by the mission of being an educa-
> tor … I enrolled in Catholic action and taught catechism to the girls … When
> communism started to incite the working classes into hating their employers and
> to spread materialistic and atheist ideas, I was against it and welcomed fascism as
> a liberator, so much so that in 1926 I founded the women's Fascio in Montorio
> al Vomano, and was its secretary until 1929.

Teresa Rossetti from Padua started keeping a diary in 1926, when she was 11. She was stimulated by her teacher's passion about Mussolini and his saving Italy from civil war and she told the girls it was their duty to help build 'the future Italy, great and powerful, worthy daughter of ancient Rome'.

In December 1926, Maria recorded that a shrine was created in the school. It was a memorial to the Unknown Soldier, with a rifle, sword and helmet together with a bronze effigy with a laurel crown. Maria wrote, 'I like that wall so much; it is the holiest in the building.'

The 'education' continued a few months later when the headmaster spoke about the foundation of the Fascism movement. He described how, in March 1919, Mussolini and his group of 'thirty men' had sworn to make Italy 'great and strong'. His stirring words were remembered by Maria: 'With Benito Mussolini the Italy of the centuries of Rome had been restored, the Italy of our fathers, powerful and beautiful!'[19]

## Universities – Withdrawal of Degrees

On 20 July 1939 a Nazi official journal announced that the University of Rostock had withdrawn an honorary degree conferred in 1900. Dr Kurt Rosenfeld, former Prussian Minister of Justice, had an honorary Doctor of Law degree conferred on him, but almost forty years later it was withdrawn. At the time he had set up a law practice in New York and was active in the anti-Nazi movement.[20]

Edith Taglicht was awarded her Doctor of Philosophy on 11 November 1925 from the University of Vienna. However, on 14 July 1942 she was deprived of this hard-earned qualification because, as a Jew, she was not regarded as a fit person to be dignified with an academic degree from a German University. Her doctorate was reinstated thirteen years later on 15 May 1955.[21]

In the *Memorial Book for the Victims of National Socialism at the University of Vienna in 1938*, it states:

> Following the advent of the National Socialist Regime in the year 1938, more than 2,700 mostly Jewish affiliates of the University of Vienna were dismissed and subsequently driven away and/or murdered – lecturers, students and administration employees. Furthermore, over 200 people were stripped of their academic titles.[22]

It was seventy years later, in 2008, that the university publicly acknowledged 'the amount of shared responsibility it bears for this inconceivable atrocity perpetrated against its affiliates'. For the first time the names of all those involved are being collected in a handwritten book.

Herbert Posch has written about the revocation of degrees under the Nazis at the University of Vienna – he uses the term 'akademische ausbürgerung' (academic expatriations).[23] Thomas Mann (1875–1955) used the term in a commentary, and it explains the connection of emigration or escape and the deprivation of German citizenship and the subsequent revocation of academic honours and titles. Mann was a 1929 Nobel Prize winner, but he had received an honorary doctorate from the University of Bonn in 1919. He was abroad in 1933, when the Nazis came to power, and his family advised him not to return home because of his known views. He and his wife went to live in Zurich.

On 19 December 1936, the dean of the philosophical faculty of the University of Bonn, the German philologist and SS officer, Karl Justus Obenauer, wrote to him in Zurich. Apparently, 'he explained that the faculty deemed it necessary to strike him from the list of honorary doctors of the university because of his earlier expatriation. Mann noted this in his diary with only a few words.'

His response was a clear statement against the Nazi state which had long been anticipated from him; he wrote an open letter published under the title 'Ein Briefwechsel' on 15 January 1937, together with the original document. He criticised the 'inhuman, warmongering National Socialist regime'. It had a wide audience, with 15,000 copies sold in three months. It was translated into many languages and published in many foreign newspapers and exile publications between 1937 and 1945.[24]

More than 300 academic degrees – doctorates and Master's degrees – were revoked under the Nazis at Vienna University alone. About 240 of these were for racial or political reasons – the remaining sixty degrees were revoked for criminal reasons.[25] The holders were made aware that these degrees, obtained through hard work and a strict examination process, were not a permanent right but an academic honour which could be revoked for political, religious or sexual reasons.

This was significant, because the status of their degree as a prerequisite for specific professions – doctors, lawyers, civil servants and scientists in various fields – became an existential issue. Without their qualifications jobs could be lost and, consequently, the means to exist. Dr Posch admits that very little is known about many who were affected, but he refers to the philosopher, theologist and cultural scientist, Professor Dr Martin Buber; politicians like the Austrian Minister of Justice, Dr Josef Gerö; and author and founder of the Paneuropean Movement, Dr Richard Coudenhove-Kalergi; as well as famous artists such as composer and musicologist, Dr Egon Wellesz.

The revocation of these degrees was under the 'law on bearing academic degrees' of 7 June 1939, under Section 4 – 'The academic degree conferred by a German University can be revoked … if the bearer has shown himself through later conduct to be unworthy of holding an academic degree.' In effect, those academics who were displaced for being Jewish and who were able to save their lives by escape or emigration could be deprived of their German citizenship under the 'law on the revocation of naturalisation and withdrawal of the German citizenship' of 14 July 1933.[26]

The effect was to ostracise these people and their spouses. Various bodies were involved in this punishment – the Reich ministries of Internal Affairs and Foreign Affairs, together with the various consulates abroad. This made people stateless and in a constant state of emergency while exiled. It is alleged that in some cases pictures of the expatriates were put up publicly, like wanted posters, with a caption, 'If you meet one, kill him'. The official gazette of the Nazi Government published the names of everyone deprived of their citizenship.[27]

In some cases, spouses lost their degrees through what was called 'family liability' (sippenhaftung). There were several cases in Vienna, and an example was Dr Rachel Deutsch who gained her doctorate in June 1914 and was living in Palestine (now Israel) in 1941. She lost her citizenship with her husband, Theodor Deutsch, when he was expatriated. He had no academic degree, but she lost her doctorate. This could also happen to adult children, but they are not aware of any such cases in Vienna.

It is worth noting that the initiative for revoking academic titles from graduates leaving the country came from the German students. Following the publication of the first list on 25 August 1933, the Munich representative demanded the Minister of State for Education & Culture in Munich revoke the academic titles. This was approved and decreed by the Bavarian Minister of Culture on 3 October 1933. Other German states followed suit, and on 17 July 1934, the Prussian Minister of Science & Public Education stated that all exiles were 'unworthy' of a German doctorate. Thus it was, in effect, the SS and the Gestapo who decided who was worthy of an academic title because they decided who would go into exile.[28]

The process was streamlined after 1938 with special committees making these decisions rather than the whole senate having to meet. The names were then published in the *Deutscher Reichsanzeiger*, which rendered the decision legal. The records of the people treated in this matter are quite inadequate, although it is known that hundreds of people were affected.[29]

After the liberation of Austria in 1945, the legal basis for reconferring 'wrongfully revoked doctorates' was made in a decree on 9 July 1945, but it was permitted rather than mandated. The university did not compile lists but merely responded to individual requests as made. Registered National Socialists were banned from obtaining doctorates for five years; however exceptions could be made by the state.[30]

It appears there was some confusion in dealing with the perpetrators and the victims of the Nazis – they were muddled together:

> They were all treated by the same general process but not exactly alike. A first examination of the files showed that convicted National Socialists were consistently quickly pardoned and could expect good will from the University of Vienna and a swift treatment of their applications on reconferral of academic degrees. Apparently this was not the case for victims of the Nazi regime and its justice system.[31]

Very few people had applied by 1955, partly because most people were unaware of the revocation and consequently did not know they needed to apply. For instance the Austrian historian, Gert Kerschbaumer, when writing a biography of Stefan Zweig, enquired from the university when Zweig's doctorate had been reconferred and it was realised it never had been – as he had died in 1941, he was not in a position to apply. So, at a special ceremony on 31 March 2004 all the revocations were nullified and thirty-two names were listed for research into their background.[32]

A particularly interesting case was that of Ignaz Emil Edler von Hofmannsthal, who acquired a doctorate in law on 7 May 1907 in Vienna. In 1938 he fled to Great Britain and then onto Argentina, where he became Emilio de Hofmannsthal. In June 1949 he requested a copy of his doctorate and was told it had been revoked. He did not accept the revocation was legal and consequently refused to apply for reconferral, although the university appears to have ignored his argument. After various investigations on 29 June 1949 the reconferring was approved and a copy sent to him without any comments. He died in 1971 and was buried in Vienna. In fact, his doctorate was reconferred again in 2004, which would not have pleased the internationally well-known lawyer. However he had received other tributes, such as the creation of the 'Emilio de Hofmannsthal Professor of International Law' title awarded at the Hebrew University of Jerusalem.[33]

Additionally, many students who had completed their degrees were not awarded them because of the Nazi decrees. I had the pleasure of knowing Dr Otto Fleming (1914–2007) when I lived in Sheffield. Born in Vienna, after five years of studying medicine at the University of Vienna he was prevented from graduating in 1938, the year of the *Anschluss*. Speaking of his earlier education, he recalled:

> There was sniggering by my schoolmates in primary school whenever the word
> *Jew* was mentioned, particularly around Easter, when we were accused of having
> murdered Jesus. Strangely, while attending Gymnasium I did not experience any
> anti-Semitism. There were some Nazis in my class, but we had no trouble. One
> took anti-Semitism at the University of Vienna for granted.[34]

After serving in the Royal Army Corps as a medical orderly for four years he had to complete his medical training at St George's Hospital in London. He served as a doctor in South Yorkshire for thirty-five years, but was always disturbed by the University of Vienna's treatment of him.

Otto requested that the University of Vienna apologise to those students who were forbidden to graduate in 1938. After refusing for many years, the university eventually relented and apologised, and he and several colleagues were granted their MD (Vienna) in 1999, in an impressive ceremony where Otto spoke eloquently of the loss of dignity and humanity perpetrated for over sixty years on the many students forbidden to graduate and on the many faculty members dismissed from their positions.[35]

Meanwhile, the senate and presidential board of Leibniz University of Hanover unanimously adopted the following resolution:

> The damage to academic positions, degrees and honours based on the Nazi ide-
> ology of political, 'racist', or other discrimination carried out at the Institute of
> Technology, Hannover in the period 1933–1945 represents acts of injustice which
> make a mockery of the law. They stand and stood at the time they occurred in clear
> contradiction to the principles of rule of law which were recognised even then.
> In particular they abused academic freedom, self-administration which safeguards
> this, and the fundamental values of the humanist academic university tradition.[36]

When I asked the university whether there was specific legislation about the withdrawal of degrees, I was told 'the existing legislation was used to justify the measures taken. For example, if a person of Jewish origin emigrated from Germany and lost German citizenship, this included the withdrawal of a doctoral degree.'[37]

An elderly PhD student was the trigger for the Berlin Technical University (TUB) to tackle this issue. Dimitri Stein submitted his thesis on electrical engineering in 1943. A pro-Nazi academic discovered he was of Jewish descent and therefore he was denied the 'Viva' which was obligatory before a doctorate could be awarded. He was forced to go into hiding – aided by a more sympathetic professor. The Nazis murdered his father, so after the war he left for America where he became an academic and later a businessman. In the 1950s he approached the university about getting his degree but was treated very rudely.

In 2006 he was encouraged to try again by a German friend. Horst Bamberg, from the Faculty of Electrical Engineering, said they were shocked when they heard his story and they re-examined his thesis based on 1943 knowledge in the field. Mr Bamberg said, 'We couldn't undo the injustice against Mr Stein, but we did what we could to restore Mr Stein's honour.' Dr Stein said he accepted his doctorate, aged 88 in 2008, 'with a tear in one eye and a smile in the other'. As a result the former president, Kurt Kutzler, initiated the recognition of the university's history under the Nazis.[38]

Ironically, Carina Baganz discovered there was a forced labour camp on the TUB campus from 1941 onwards, with workers initially dealing with the coalyard and transport. By 1944, 140 people were lodged on college premises on the top floor of Building 6 at 29 Franklin Road. There were men, women and children – the youngest was 10 and the oldest was 74 years old. They were engaged in making repairs to the buildings damaged by air attacks and at least one of the labourers was killed.

Their accommodation was only primitive and not suited for long-term use. Ironically, it was located right next to major research institutions which were undertaking secret developments for the Wehrmacht.[39] These workers were not Jews. From 1941 they were prisoners of war from Russia, France and Italy, and later from August 1944 there was an ostarbeiterlager (a camp for slave labourers from the East) of 140 Ukrainians.[40]

A Harvard Medical School professor's colleague raised the issue of a 102-year-old German woman's treatment by Hamburg University over her doctorate in 1938. He told the current dean, Dr Uwe Koch-Gromus, that Ingeborg Syllm-Rapoport had been denied the Viva for her doctorate on diphtheria as her mother was Jewish and she was therefore regarded by the Nazis as mischling. Her mother was Maria Syllm, a pianist. Although brought up as a Protestant, Rapoport's professor wrote a letter on 30 August 1938, saying she had submitted a doctoral dissertation which would have been acceptable 'if the current laws regarding Fraulein Syllm's ancestry didn't make it impossible for her to be allowed to receive a doctorate'. His name was Dr Rudolf Degkwitz and, in 1943, when he objected to euthanasia at the children's hospital, he was imprisoned for seven years but escaped in 1945.

Dr Koch-Gromus was keen to help, but in March 2015 the university's legal department suggested she should merely be given an honorary degree, as her original paper could not be found, she had never undertaken the Viva and she had already acquired a medical degree in the USA. However, neither he nor Dr Rapoport was willing to accept this fudge and it was agreed that she would complete the Viva, seventy-seven years later. This was in spite of her failing eyesight which meant she could not read or use a computer. She therefore had to prepare herself with the help of her family. While she passed the forty-five minute Viva, held in her Berlin home in May 2015, with a performance described as 'brilliant' by the three professors, she commented that the dean 'has made a great effort to show that things are now different in Germany'. However, the degree was only awarded after the Viva through her son Tom's networking, and the university has no policy to award degrees denied to them by the Nazis to other former Jewish students, according to Beate Schäffler.[41]

Commenting on her experience in 1938, Dr Rapoport said, 'My medical existence was turned to rubble. It was a shame for science and a shame for Germany.' She also spoke of the impact of preparing for the Viva. 'Studying made me remember how abandoned and uncertain I felt in 1938. That was covered up, but it's come back recently in my dreams.' Perhaps the insistence on the Viva for an almost blind woman of 102 was a second betrayal?[42]

In Poland, it was reported on 17 December 1934 that there had been disturbances at Warsaw University's medical faculty by medical students who were members of the officially banned National Radical Party (Nara). The Nara students staged demonstrations in the lecture rooms to protest a promise allegedly made to Rabbi Posner by the dean of the university that the Jewish students would no longer have to provide Jewish dead bodies for use in anatomy classes. In the past, access to anatomy classes had been denied to Jewish students on the grounds that they were not providing Jewish bodies to the anatomical institute. The dean is said to have told Rabbi Posner that it was not the duty of the students to provide the corpses.[43] Of course, what the article does not mention is that the desecration of a dead body is forbidden in Orthodox Judaism and therefore the bodies could not have been provided.

Earlier in the year, in August 1934, twenty-four members of Nara had been arrested for operating illegally. The group consisted of students and women who were believed to have been planning proscribed Nara activities on a large scale, particularly anti-Jewish activities. The Naras were an offshoot of the older Endek anti-Semitic group, and withdrew from Endek because it wasn't sufficiently anti-Jewish.[44]

# Numerus Clausus in Hungarian Universities

Hungary had a positive accepting attitude to Jews from Eastern Europe in the nineteenth century and the aristocracy treated them as allies in capitalist development and modernisation. This naturally led to an increase in Hungary's Jews from 127,000 in 1805 to 340,000 in 1850, 625,000 in 1880 and 911,000 in 1910. Their proportion in the population rose from 1.8 per cent in 1805 to 5 per cent in 1910. This was based firstly on immigration, but also a higher birth rate and lower death rate because of better living conditions in the urban areas where Jews lived.

Needless to say, this created antagonism in those missing out on the economic improvement and in 1882 an anti-Semitic party appeared, but its attempts to raise the threat from Jewish world rule in the Hungarian Parliament were laughed at. The prime minister, Kálmán Tisza, stated, 'it is wrong and worthy of contempt to call "base" any race or religious denomination in this country'. This was heartily approved by the parliamentarians. When France was plunged into the frenzy of the Dreyfus case (1894–1906), in Hungary the false accusations against Jews of murdering a Christian girl in the Tiszaeszlár case were thrown out of court.

This 'Golden Era' of mutual advantage between Jews and the Hungarian elite ended with the First World War, which resulted in a much smaller Hungary. The country experienced a Communist revolution in 1918 in the post-war mayhem. Many of the leaders in the democratic and Communist revolutions were Jewish and as in Weimar the idea of the Jews being responsible for the defeat also developed in Hungary.[45]

Consequently, Hungary found itself in a difficult situation after the First World War. Under the Trianon Treaty, it lost a great deal of its territory and was left with a population of 8 million that was mostly destitute. The Jews, who were 6 per cent of the population, were made the scapegoats and, while they regarded themselves as Magyars, Admiral Horthy introduced a law to limit Jewish influence by limiting the number of Jewish students at the universities in proportion to the population. This became an international issue, because of the failure of the League of Nations to compel Hungary to withdraw the law and adhere to the minority protection clauses of the Trianon Peace Treaty.[46]

The Jews in Hungary had been granted full citizenship in 1867 and, accordingly, after 1918 the Jews regarded themselves not as a minority but as Hungarians of the Jewish faith. They stressed their loyalty and desire for full participation in Hungarian affairs and sent an open letter to the Minister of Justice asking for Jewish senators to be nominated to sit alongside the Christians in the Upper House, as had been proposed in 1885. The Jews wanted a proper legal position even though their religion was recognised by law, and in 1895 they had been given freedom of religious practice. It was therefore a great shock when the 'numerus clausus' legislation was first introduced and the debate was acrimonious. It was claimed not to be anti-Semitic but to protect Christian interests which had been eroded by the Jews. After considerable debate the law was passed on 21 September 1920, with fifty-seven votes in favour and only seven against.[47]

After the first shock, Jewish associations in Western Europe began a concerted campaign to get redress from the League of Nations. In November 1921 the Joint Foreign Committee (JFC) of the Board of Deputies of British Jews and the Anglo-Jewish Association, together with the French L'Alliance Israelite Universelle, submitted a petition to the league on behalf of the Hungarian Jews. This was based on various articles of the Trianon Treaty which specified, 'Hungarian nationals who belong to racial, religious or linguistic minorities shall enjoy the same treatment and security in law and in fact as do other Hungarian nationals', and Article 60 of the same treaty which placed the protection of these minorities with the League of Nations. On 30 September 1922, the representatives of Belgium, Spain and China took the matter to the Council of Three which made it a cause célèbre. The Board of Deputies cited Articles 56, 57 and 58 as having been violated by the *numerus clausus*, since Hungary was failing to accord equal treatment to all Hungarian citizens. The French L'Alliance also complained about the law, saying the Jews belonged to a 'different race or nationality', which was untrue because Hungarian Jews were clearly a religious minority.

The Hungarian Government maintained that the law had two aims – to reduce the number of educated working class and to guarantee the rights of minorities. They expressed concern that, with the reduction in Hungary's population, they needed to reduce the number of students who would ultimately be seeking employment in the civil service. There were also concerns about patriotic loyalty because of the Communist activity in the immediate post-war period. The student numbers were to be proportionate to the number of inhabitants of each minority. They claimed the Jews were actually receiving favourable treatment. The league felt it needed more information on admission procedures to decide if the law was being implemented, but it took some two years before the information was made available in August 1924.[48]

The waters were muddied on 1 January 1925 when the two British bodies took the matter to the Permanent Court of International Justice to determine the legality of the *numerus clausus* under Article 14 of the league's covenant which violated Jews' rights. It also affected Jews in other countries who were having to support Jewish students attending foreign universities, and there was a fear that such legislation might be introduced elsewhere. It appears that by 1925, seventy-four Jewish students had gained medical degrees abroad, costing an international Jewish agency $26,000. There were also issues about Hungary recognising such foreign degrees, according to the *New York Times* on 16 August 1925.

The league was still negotiating with the Hungarian Government when the British dropped a bombshell. On 16 November 1925, Lucien Wolf (1857–1930), who in 1917 became the secretary of the JFC and was widely regarded as an expert on minority rights both at the league and in England, admitted that all of the many requests for help had come from individual Hungarian Jews and some Jewish organisations. He therefore felt that the JFC had no mandate to speak on behalf of Hungarian Jews. At the same time, it appeared that some Hungarian-Jewish bodies objected to these foreign interventions and, according to the *New York Times* of 20 December 1925, a resolution was adopted by a large Jewish meeting held in Budapest.

It was felt that permitting such intervention would have diminished their status as Hungarians in the eyes of the Christians.[49] They would also have been leaving their fate to an untried international body instead of negotiating with their government. 'Thus, the Jewish community rejected in principle special treatment, favourable or not.'[50]

As a result, in December 1925, Count Klebelsberg, Hungary's representative, exploited the situation presented by the protests in a presentation to the council in Geneva. He argued that, as the foreign objections had been repudiated, Hungary had no case to answer. However, he explained that the law was temporary until Hungary's economic situation improved after the impact of the Trianon Treaty. He explained that 320,000 refugees had come to Hungary and of these 80 per cent were 'intelligentsia'. He claimed that between the 1910 census and that of 1920 the intelligentsia had increased by 50 per cent, lawyers by 25 per cent, chemists by 33 per cent, magistrates, doctors and other professionals by 50 per cent and state officials by 100 per cent. Because of the economic situation, many public employees were being sacked and it would be absurd to permit students to study for careers which would not exist.

He claimed the law did not affect economic professions but only the liberal professions. He said the law did not apply to schools of technology and economics, commerce, veterinary medicine, art or forestry, nor to teacher training colleges. He claimed that Jews favoured the economic professions. It was therefore a good law, not directed at Jews specifically. In fact, it opened all the universities throughout the country to Jews. After much of the same self-justification, he stressed that 'the Hungarian Christian middle classes were in such an economically precarious situation that their minds were subject to great strain'. Dispensing with the law at this stage could lead to a crisis between the Christian and Jewish communities which the government wished to avoid.

He then explained how they ascertained who was a Jew. Count Klebelsberg explained it was not necessarily based on a person's current religion. It would be determined by his religious status based on state registries. He stated that if a person changed religion to avoid the law, he would still be regarded as Jewish. If the conversion was sincere, the law would not apply.

He produced statistics (which are regarded as reliable) that show that the numerus clausus did not bring a reduction in Jewish students. Accepting annual fluctuations, Jewish attendance in Budapest stabilised at around 7–8 per cent and in provincial universities it was around 12–14 per cent. At Debrecen there was a rise from a low of thirty-one (7 per cent) in 1920–1921, before the law was passed. The following year it was eighty-eight (13.2 per cent). At Szeged University it was very high – 24.7 per cent in 1921–1922, after the law came in, and 19.2 per cent in 1922–1923. At Pécs the figures were a steady 58 per cent in 1921–1922 and 53 per cent in 1922–1923.[51]

Thomas Spira (1923–2005), himself a Jewish refugee from Eastern Europe who arrived in the USA just before the Second World War, commented on these figures. He said that any reduction in student numbers was due more to the diminishing Jewish birth rate. The Roman Catholic birth rate was 23 per 1,000 population, Calvinist 23.1, Lutheran 19.4, Greek Orthodox 20.2, Greek Catholic 33.7, while the Jewish birth rate was only 11 per 1,000 and had been so since the First World War.[52]

It was also noticeable that other minorities were declining in number with few Slovak students and a reduction of German students as well. It is also apparent that Klebelsberg's statements about Jews and the economic professions were incorrect and the statistics he presented to the council demonstrated this. Other aspects of his statement were specious about the philosophy behind the law. However, the council delivered its findings on 12 December 1925 and it was obvious that the protests about outside interference had influenced the body.

De Mello-Franco, the president and spokesman for the Council of Three, announced that the question was whether the law was compatible with Article 58 of the Peace Treaty. He referred to the Hungarians' representative's statements about the law being a temporary measure and that it would be amended with a change of circumstances. 'Therefore the Council recommended regarding the law that the League should not take action at the moment, but await amendment of the law in the near future. Count Klebelsberg accepted these conditions on behalf of his government, a position also adopted by the Council.'

This issue remains problematic and the Hungarian Government's motives are dubious. It never fully implemented the law, perhaps through the recognition of the importance of Jews to the economy. It also achieved acknowledgement from the league that it was fully entitled to jurisdiction over its minorities.

The league missed the significance of the numerus clausus. It did not perceive that the Hungarian Government was challenging its right to interfere in Hungary's internal affairs. The league should have investigated whether minority rights were being violated, not how the law was being applied. It should have looked at Hungary's direct defiance of the Trianon Treaty and its own constitution and laws. The league allowed it to do so with impunity. It also ignored the contradictory actions of including Jews as Hungarians in the census, as desired by the Jews, but then considering them a non-Hungarian minority when expedient. The league should have made it clear to Hungary and other governments that it intended to enforce the treaty instead of shilly-shallying with requests for more information. It therefore condoned such restrictive minority laws. 'This conflicted with the duties and obligations of the League, which had inherited the responsibility of upholding the Peace Treaty provisions from the Great Powers.'

Indeed, this was a memorable event, because for the first time in history an international body had taken collective constitutional responsibility for enforcing international treaties, a task which had hitherto been the exclusive right of individual sovereign states. It was therefore essential for the league to impose its authority firmly in this, its first test case, in order to establish for itself a reputation of prestige and ability in dealing with infractions. By exhibiting weakness and ineptness where firmness and competence were needed, the league surrendered, by default, its authority to impose its jurisdiction in cases of future infractions and violations of international agreements. Thus, in this first important post-war minority test case, the league proved to be unable to uphold the concept of international control over minority affairs, and thus helped to pave the way for more serious violations by other countries in the not too distant future.[53]

The league was happy to accept the Hungarian representative's declaration that the law was merely an exceptional and temporary one until there was a favourable change in the situation resulting from the Trianon Treaty. Some changes were made in 1928 and 1929, but in fact the discrimination continued.[54] I recall my mother, Leona Grunwald, who was born in 1913 in Budapest, telling me that many of the young men she knew were unable to get into Budapest University and went off to Germany instead. This must have been in the late 1920s and early 1930s.

One of the motives for introducing the legislation was said to be in order to decrease the number of graduates because there were too many. However, this was untrue. One commentator said that two new universities at Pécs and Szeged were short of students in the 1920s. They had been moved from Pozsony in Bratislava and Cluj, respectively, after Trianon. A Hungarian professor, Mária Kovács, shows that if the removal of Jewish students was intended to encourage more Christian middle-class children to go to university, it failed. She claims this wasn't the true aim, as the leading politicians wanted to restrict the number of Jews in the arts and the professions. To do this they turned Jews from members of a religious community into an ethnic minority, which according to Kovács was unconstitutional, both formally and substantively.[55]

It does appear that Jews were overrepresented in higher education. In the academic year 1918–1919 there were 18,449 students enrolled, of whom 6,719 were Jewish. One reason for this was that most Jews lived in big cities, rather than in rural areas. In fact, in Budapest 25 per cent of the population were Jewish. More Jews were finishing at the gymnasium and matriculating than non-Jews. In 1910, 18.2 per cent of Jewish men over 18 took the matriculation exams – among Catholics it was 4.2 per cent and among Protestants it was 3.9 per cent. As you needed to have matriculated to enter the university, it is not surprising that the figures seem unbalanced. Apparently, the anti-Semitic Alajos Kovács, head of the Central Statistical Office, was quoted as saying it was 'terrifying'.

Mária Kovács also refers to the percentages for the medical and legal professions – 49.4 per cent of lawyers and 46.3 per cent of physicians were Jewish but these professions attracted only 20 per cent of graduates. The fact that only 4.9 per cent of the 30,000 graduate civil servants were Jewish is rarely mentioned.

All in all, she describes the numerus clausus of 1920 as the first anti-Jewish law in Europe. The creators of the law claimed it was a punishment for Trianon. István Haller, who was Minister of Education in 1920, had a chapter in his 1926 autobiography entitled, 'As Long as there is Trianon there will be Numerus Clausus'.

The political elite of the time thought the Jews should use their influence to restore Hungary's old historical borders. Count Kuno von Klebelsberg said in a speech in the Hungarian parliament, 'Give us back the old Greater Hungary, then we will abrogate the numerus clausus.'[56]

This was obviously a festering sore. At the start of the 1930 academic year on 12 September, there were concerns about the number of Jewish students wanting to apply to the School of Medicine, which was reluctant to admit 'too many' Jewish students. The other schools were accepting more Jewish students. Jewish members of parliament had attempted to negotiate with Klebelsberg, who was then Minister of Education. He responded that the recent Hungarian Medical Congress had complained that there were too many physicians. The current numerus clausus law only permitted 7 per cent of the students to be Jewish, but the Jewish population of Budapest was 20 per cent.

Three Jewish deputies – members of parliament – including Joseph Pakots, who led the Democratic Party, objected to the minister's response. It was reported that:

> They complain that the government has no right to dictate to the students or their parents to adopt professions other than those desired, particularly since the Jewish citizens are paying their taxes and fulfilling all their obligations to the Hungarian state. Hence the deputies insist that the Jewish students are entitled to study at Hungarian universities according to their wishes without being compelled to obtain their education at foreign institutions of learning.[57]

On 13 April 1933 various educational developments were reported. The Bavarian Minister of the Interior, Dr Stutzel, announced that no Jew would be admitted to the medical school of any university in Bavaria. At Leipzig University, no Jewish student was to be admitted for the next five years. Finally, in the province of Baden and in the city of Kiel, all Jewish professors and lecturers were dismissed, while in the government's hospitals, assistants other than those whose immediate departure would imperil the health of patients were also sacked.[58]

The question of the numerus clausus in Hungarian universities was being discussed in the British Parliament as early as 1928. Colonel Josiah Wedgwood asked a question in the House of Commons about the likelihood of the reimposition of the numerus clausus limiting the number of Jewish students admitted to Hungarian universities. Mr Locker-Lampson replied that no information had been received from the British Ambassador in Budapest, but the government would inquire.[59]

The numerus clausus also applied elsewhere. Ignacy Chiger, growing up in Poland early in the twentieth century, had limited career opportunities as Jews were prohibited from certain occupations. He was a highly intelligent man and would have liked to have been a doctor but was prevented by the numerus clausus from studying medicine. He opted for philosophy and history and obtained a doctorate. However, this was done with difficulty – no one would sit next to him. He was fortunate to have a very good friend who was a Ukrainian, who acted like a kind of bodyguard and 'protected him from the young Ukrainian hoodlums who would torment the young Jewish men'.[60] This must have been around 1905 or so and his daughter Krystyna commented, 'it is proof that even before the Second World War, even before the Germans, life was very difficult for Polish Jews'.

Julie Orringer's family were Hungarian and when she discovered her grandparents' story she wrote a novel about it. When she was interviewed in 2011, she said that her grandfather was born in Konyár, a small town in eastern Hungary. He moved to Budapest as a young man and did some work for a magazine which was displayed at a Paris exhibition. A professor at Paris's only private architectural school saw the exhibition:

> When the professor learned that my grandfather wanted to study architecture but couldn't study it in Hungary because of the quota on Jewish students, he arranged for him to study at the architecture school in Paris. A few months after his arrival, however, he lost his scholarship because the Hungarian government passed a law that prohibited sending money to Jewish students abroad. So he had to figure out a way to get by in Paris and stay in school. In 1939, my grandfather was conscripted into the forced labor service in the Hungarian army, lost his student visa and had to return home.[61]

It is important to be aware that strong feelings about Jewish students were displayed elsewhere. In December 1926 the Rumanian Students' Congress, meeting in Jassy, unanimously adopted a resolution calling for a 'numerus nullus' barring Jewish students from the universities and colleges. It was attended by 5,000 students and the military patrolled the city to prevent 'anti-Jewish excesses'. Even on the trains going to Jassy, the students attacked Jewish passengers and several were injured.

However, the congress was chaired by Alexander Cuza, professor of economics at the University of Jassy, who led the rabid anti-Semitic movement among Rumanian students. He was pensioned off by an order of the university senate because he was aged over 70. 'With Cuza's retirement, he will lose his direct influence on the Roumanian academic youth which resulted in so much racial hatred and mob violence, embittering the lives of the Jewish population in Roumania for many decades.'[62] The same report stated that Jewish students had been ejected from the lecture hall of the medical college at the University of Bucharest.[63]

★★★

As a postscript, Godfrey Locker-Lampson (1875–1946), the Undersecretary of State for Foreign Affairs from December 1925 to June 1929, was a member of the British delegation to the League of Nations at Geneva in 1928. His brother Oliver (1880–1954) flirted briefly with Fascism in this country, but became very supportive of persecuted Jews.

> Locker-Lampson was exceptional in how he saved Jews from Germany later on. My grandfather and his family arrived in England a week before the outbreak of war in 1939. They were sponsored by Locker-Lampson after having been rejected by hundreds of other individuals and organizations. My grandfather contacted him because he had a reputation in Germany for going out of his way to save Jews. My family owe him a tremendous debt of gratitude – without his acts of kindness my grandparents would have been murdered along with those relatives who were not lucky enough to leave.[64]

Amongst other Jews he helped were Sigmund Freud and Albert Einstein.

# 12

# PROFESSIONAL EXCLUSION

The whole world is a very narrow bridge; but the essential thing is never to be afraid.

Rabbi Nachman of Bretzlav, Ukraine (1772–1810)

## Nazi Control of Culture and the Chamber of Culture (Reichskulturkammer – RKK)

On 15 November 1933 Joseph Goebbels spoke about the revolution that had taken place and how the individual had been replaced by the community of the people. He was speaking of a cultural revolution and declared, 'There is no art without political bias.' The aim of his revolution was to convert all Germans to the Nazi way of thinking.

Goebbels, as Minister of Popular Enlightenment & Propaganda since 13 March 1933 and a member of Hitler's cabinet, saw his role as the 'spiritual mobilisation' of the German people, mirroring the atmosphere of 1914.[1]

His ministry understood the power of propaganda and also the need for continual popular legitimation of their policies. He understood very well the power of 'stage management' of ceremonies and torchlight parades – what the Roman satirist, Juvenal (AD 55–130 approx), described as 'panem et circenses' ('bread and circuses') nearly two millennia before.

To this was added the personal cult of Hitler, with lavish celebrations of his birthday, renaming of streets and squares after him and, most significantly, the greeting of 'Heil Hitler'. All state employees were to use the greeting on official correspondence from 13 July 1933. The use of the greeting further isolated those not in favour of the regime. William Shirer described in his diary, in September 1934, how brilliantly these matters were managed.

Perhaps the culmination was Leni Riefenstahl's epic film, *Triumph of the Will*, which covered the 1934 Nuremberg Rally. With unlimited resources and a crew of 120 she made a unique film showing Hitler descending from the skies like some god. Not surprisingly, it won an award in Germany but also gold awards at the Venice Film Festival in 1935 and Paris in 1937. Banned in Germany since the war, it remains a classic of documentary propaganda.

Cinema was popular worldwide in the 1930s, boosted by the introduction of sound and colour. Some stars and directors like Marlene Dietrich and Fritz Lang left Germany, but most stayed. However, in 1935 and 1936 the party encouraged filmgoers to question the 'racial and political affiliations of leading screen actors'. One of these was Hans Albers, whose wife, Hansi Burg, was Jewish but he ensured her safety by leaving her in Switzerland throughout the Nazi period. Goebbels was aware of this but took no action because of Albers' great popularity – however, his wife's existence was denied.[2] Joachim Gottschalk, in a similar situation, was not so fortunate. His tragic story appears on pages 442–3.

The control of the German film industry came under the Reich Film Chamber from 14 July 1933 and was run by an official who reported directly to Goebbels. It had ten different departments, covering all aspects of film making and anyone wanting to work in films had to be a member. Financial control came from the Reich Cinema Law 1934, which also precluded scripts that had not been censored from being filmed. These laws gave Goebbels complete control over what films the Germans could see, and Fritz Lang's films were denigrated. The Newsreel Law of 1936 allowed the Propaganda Ministry to control news films as well.[3]

Similarly, to control what Germans heard on their increasingly popular radios, the Reich Radio Chamber was created in the autumn of 1933 and again everyone in the industry had to be a member, including the salesmen. This gave the Propaganda Ministry complete control, as broadcasting had come under governmental control earlier in the year and regional stations came under Nazi control on 1 April 1934. The Nazis approved production of cheap radios called the 'volksempfänger' (people's receivers) available at RM76, or a small one for RM35. That was a weekly wage and it could be purchased in instalments. One and a half million sets were made in 1933, and in 1934, 6 million radios were in use in Germany. By 1939, over 70 per cent of German households had a wireless – the highest level anywhere in the world. They had limited reception so that, apart from in border regions, foreign stations could not be received.[4]

The radio was used as a means of propaganda and Hitler's speeches were broadcast. On 25 March 1933, Goebbels announced that 'radio would be purged' of leftists and nonconformists. Presumably this included Walter Benjamin, the Jewish writer and philosopher, who had found a new career on German radio

where he wrote and delivered more than eighty educational and literary programmes between 1929 and 1932, including special programmes for young
people.[5] Goebbels told broadcasters and radio managers to undertake the task
themselves, otherwise he would do it. Another victim was Jochen Klepper (1903–
1942) whose Social Democratic past, combined with a Jewish wife, made him
very vulnerable to the anonymous denunciation which caused his dismissal in
June 1933 (see pages 443–5).

In the same broadcast Goebbels was quite blatant: 'We make no bones about the
fact that the radio belongs to us and to no one else. And we will place the radio in
the service of our ideology, and no other idealogy will find expression here …'[6]

However, he did not have it all his own way, as Goebbels' plan to incorporate education in his ministry was thwarted by Hitler, who put Bernard Rust
(1883–1945) in charge of an Education Ministry as Minister of Science, Education
& National Culture.

Another battle in the cultural field was with Alfred Rosenberg, who saw his
mission as disseminating his own version of Nazi ideology throughout German
culture. In the late 1920s Rosenberg had been made leader of the Kampfbund für
Deutsche Kultur (Fighting League for German Culture). It was one of a clutch
of specialist organisations created within the party and in 1933 it took on co-
ordination of theatrical activities. Rosenberg was also keen to control the ideology
of music and the visual arts, the churches, universities and intellectual life – these
were all areas Goebbels had wanted to come under the auspices of his Propaganda
Ministry. It was initially a small body with 2,100 members in January 1932, rising
to 6,000 in twelve months, 10,000 in April 1933 and 38,000 in October 1934. They
were responsible for most of the attacks on Jewish and left-wing musicians during
1933 because of the right-wing members of the league. Rosenberg had another
tool – the Nazi daily newspaper, *The Racial Observer*, which he edited.

The rivalry between the two men was aggravated by Hitler's personal taste being
closer to Rosenberg than Goebbels. Rosenberg fancied himself as a writer and
produced numerous works, of which he was proudest of his magnus opus, *The
Myth of the Twentieth Century*. Goebbels described it as a 'philosophical belch'.[7]

Alfred Rosenberg was a 'frightfully confused man', according to the American
psychiatrist, Douglas Kelly, who examined him at the Nuremberg Trials. He said,
'A large part of this confusion lay in the fact that he was unaware that he could
not think straight and he was further befuddled by the fact that he never realised
his intellectual limitations.' William Shirer said he was a 'dimwitted dolt'. Neither
Hitler nor Goebbels had much time for his 'pretentious pseudo-philosophical
theorising'.[8] The fact that this man was in charge of cultural policy in the polycratic
Nazi state reminds me of clever Tom Lehrer's comments on the American Army
having taken the democratic ideal to its logical conclusion by not discriminating
on the grounds of race, creed and colour or even ability.[9]

Rosenberg was born in Tallinn, Estonia, in 1893 and studied in Riga and Moscow, both as an engineer and as an architect. In 1919 he moved from Moscow to Munich and joined the Nazi Party as soon as it was created, having become a naturalised German in 1923. When Hitler was in prison after the Munich Beer Hall Putsch of 9 November 1923, Rosenberg had taken over the running of the party.

> This pioneer of Nazism, who had a particular penchant for lengthy theoretical disquisitions of a pseudoscientific character, also developed a theory of art that explained that Jews were incapable of any real artistic creativity and that their possession of Aryan works of art was therefore an act of usurpation.[10]

Rosenberg suffered because he was a mere party official, while Goebbels was a minister in charge of the Propaganda Ministry. Hitler had little faith in him because of his failings when he was in charge after the unsuccessful Beer Hall Putsch in 1923 in Munich, so he never gave him a government post. Moreover, although he did share 'many of his cruder prejudices, Hitler had almost as low an opinion of Rosenberg's pretentious, pseudo-philosophical theorising as Goebbels did'. Rosenberg was never part of Hitler's inner circle and by the summer of 1933, the impact of the Fighting League was becoming unhelpful.

Goebbels' triumph was to get a decree passed on 22 September 1933, for the creation of the Reich's Culture Chamber (RKK), with him as president. The chamber consisted of seven different individual chambers which covered the divisions already operating within his ministry – literature, theatre, music, radio, film, fine arts and the press. Some, like the Reich Film Chamber, already existed and others were being created – Goebbels got back control of the theatres from Rosenberg in this way. These became monopoly state institutions. Anyone wishing to work in these fields had to be a member of the appropriate chamber and this enabled undesirables to be excluded.

The structure enabled Goebbels to marginalise Rosenberg even further and also present these chambers as cultural self-administration, which was very attractive to the people who ran the chambers and the ordinary Germans working in the cultural arena. In 1937, the Visual Arts Chamber had around 135,000 members – 95,600 were members of the Reich Music Chamber and 41,100 in the Reich Theatre Chamber.

The Reich Culture Chamber was launched at a grand event at the Berlin Philharmonic Hall on 15 November 1933, attended by Hitler himself. Rosenberg's Fighting League lurched on until it fizzled out in 1937. Goebbels still had to contend with Hitler's own interest in visual arts, the music of Wagner, architecture, and films which he watched in his private cinema. There was also Göring, who was in charge of Prussian state cultural bodies, and Bernard Rust, who had responsibilities in the cultural field. Added to this were the trade unions, which were taken over by the Nazi Labour Front, run by Robert Ley, in May 1933. All these bodies bickered and disputed their roles. However, the one aim they all had in common was that Jews and Bolsheviks were to be removed from cultural life as soon as possible. From 1933 onwards, about 2,000 people employed in the cultural spheres left Germany – some because they disagreed with the Nazis, but most because they could no longer earn a living. The Economics Minister, Kurt Schmitt, was opposed to this policy because of the economic implications, but he was soon moved on and by 1935 the purge was complete. Accordingly, German culture faced growing regimentation and control.

Goebbels stated:

> In the future only those who are members of a chamber are allowed to be productive in our cultural life. Membership is open only to those who fulfil the entrance condition. In this way all unwanted and damaging elements have been excluded.[11]

The theatre critic Alfred Kerr fled Germany in 1933 and, after travelling through Switzerland and France, he settled in London in 1935. He had many influential friends – he interviewed Emil Zola, spoke at Ibsen's funeral, wrote a song cycle with Richard Strauss and had been close friends with Albert Einstein, H.G. Wells and George Bernard Shaw. His wife was a Christian who was both a brilliant mathematician and a pianist who wrote two operas. In England his two children achieved great success. Their son, Michael, became the first foreign-born judge since the reign of Henry II and was knighted in 1972, while their daughter, Judith, is famed for her children's books which include *The Tiger Who Came for Tea*, a favourite of mine that I read to my sons.[12]

A manual was drafted which explained how the various subcommittees of the RKK were to operate, and this was available in 1937 as *The Manual of the Reich Chamber of Culture* (1937). The Chamber of Creative Arts' nature and functions were described as follows:

> The Reich Chamber of Creative Art was established as a professional body of public law on the grounds of the law of the Reich Chamber of Culture. Membership in the Chamber is a prerequisite, for the members of the following professions, in practising their professions:
>
> Architects, interior designers, horticulturists, sculptors, painters, engravers, commercial engravers, designers, fine art craftsmen, copyists, restorers of works of art, dealers in works of art and artists, fine art publishers, dealers in prints.
>
> Members of the Chamber must also be: all artists' associations, art associations, associations of fine art craftsmen, institutes for creative art and their faculties.[13]

Other sections of the manual dealt with the chambers for music, literature, motion pictures and radio. There was particular emphasis on music for 'the German people', 'German literature', the 'national socialistic State', with regard to films and, somewhat surprisingly, under-broadcasting – there was concern about the paucity of German listeners to radio compared with 'several great civilised nations'.

> As in other countries, before television the radio was very important to people. Goebbels' ministry recognised the tremendous promise of radio for propaganda. It heavily subsidised the production of the inexpensive Volksempfänger to facilitate sales. By early 1938, the number of radios in German homes surpassed more than 9 million, roughly one for every two German households. Three years later, this figure had risen to almost 15 million, providing 50 million Germans with regular radio reception.[14]

There is no mention anywhere of the thousands of radio receivers Jews were forced to hand in to the authorities in all the Nazi-occupied countries. The receipt my parents got for their radio in Budapest in April 1944 is photo No. 14.

## Jews and the Professions

In Germany Jews never represented more than 1 per cent of the population and their arrival in the professions was comparatively recent. Following the unification of Germany in 1870, Jews were granted equal rights in 1871 but they were not fully achieved.

By 1890 around 50 per cent of the Jews who were in banking and business were doing very well through enterprise and effort. The Jews were unable to become farmers or do manual trades because of the limited opportunities for apprenticeships. Those who went to university found careers in law, medicine, architecture and journalism, but were banned from both the army and the civil service. Some achieved university appointments, but only the baptised could become professors.[15] As society moved toward human rights and social justice the Jews benefitted, so that by 1901–1910 they already accounted for 3 per cent of German university professors.

The defeat in the First World War and the precarious Weimar Republic led the right wing to become increasingly racist and nationalistic. Ten years after the creation of Weimar, all political parties avoided the appointment of Jews to any public office and discussions about the 'Jewish question' became ever more threatening. Like all aspects of the persecution of the Jews, the measures were all perfectly legal and started as soon as the Nazis were elected with 44 per cent of the vote on 5 March 1933.

On 1 April the boycott of Jewish businesses, medical doctors and lawyers took place, having been preceded by the announcement of the creation of concentration camps on 8 March. The Malicious Practices Law (Heimtückegesetz) which prohibited criticism of the regime, was dated 21 March. By July, trade unions and strikes had been outlawed and there were 27,000 political prisoners in concentration camps. However, it is important to note that violence against individual Jews and Jewish businesses had occurred in February and March 1933 prior to the election.[16]

The exclusion from professions was a catastrophe for many Jews, who had perceived themselves as German, because of the financial implications of losing their means of support. Some decided suicide was the only solution. On 3 April 1933, Dr Hans Bettmann, a lawyer, shot himself in Heidelberg Cemetery after being dismissed from the court, and when Professor Jacobsohn was sacked from Marburg University he committed suicide on 28 April 1933. Additionally, many Jewish doctors killed themselves as they were forced out of their posts – especially if they were converts to Christianity.[17]

The misery continued throughout the 1930s, until November 1938 when Dr Emil H., a 73-year-old Jewish doctor, took an overdose of morphine and was investigated by the Hamburg police when his suicide failed. His sister told the police he 'had been depressed over the last few days', not least because, like all Jewish doctors in Germany, he had been forced to close his surgery to non-Jewish patients.[18]

Similar legislation was introduced in other countries: for example, in 1938, when the bill which imposed wide curbs on Jews' participation in Hungary's economic and cultural life was said to be awaiting Regent Horthy's signature. The bill established 'twenty per cent quotas on the employment of Jews in industry, finance, commerce, the theatrical profession and journalism'.[19]

## Teachers

Ernst Loewenberg (1896–1987) was a well-respected teacher in one of Hamburg's state grammar schools. He was soon confronted with the brutality of the Nazis' racial policy:

> In the fall of 1933, a haggard, elderly teacher came to me and explained right away that she had never been at a Jew's, but she did not know what to do. For many years she had been a village school teacher in Schleswig-Holstein ... Now, whilst establishing proof of her Aryan ancestry, she discovered that her father – himself a pastor's son – was racially a Jew. And thus she had been dismissed. Distant friends had taken in the completely destitute woman. Her brothers were abroad. She could not comprehend that she, a German Protestant, had to be helped by Jews, with whom, after all, she had nothing to do. I advised her to leave Germany as soon as possible since there was no other way out. I gave her the money to go to the advisory center. Her passage to the United States was later paid from a general fund and from Jewish quarters.[20]

Even before the Nazis came to power he chose not to apply for the headship, fearing a Jewish headmaster might harm the school's reputation. The new head was Erwin Zindler – a Nazi supporter.

Early in 1934 Jewish teachers, including Loewenberg, were told they would be retired, notwithstanding their status as war veterans. Colleagues who had earlier promised to protest now avoided talking to them. Zindler would not meet them face to face either. Surprisingly, Loewenberg did receive a letter of appreciation from the school administration and was paid a pension.[21] In August 1938 he followed his own advice, left Germany and emigrated to the USA. He died in Massachusetts in 1987.

Edwin Landau (1890–1975), writing about the aftermath of the 1933 boycott, in his despair visited his parents' graves, his grandparents' and great-grandparents'. He spoke to them and 'returned to them everything German that I had received from three generations'. I cried into their graves, 'You were mistaken. I, too, have been misled. I now know that I am no longer a German. And what will my children be?' He wrote, 'the gravestones remained silent'.

Those like him, who were still living, soon had an answer:

My former teacher, who was a popular principal at the girls' Gymnasium and was highly esteemed by the teachers, the pupils, and their parents, soon found out the answer. During the morning hours, as he was teaching, SA men appeared and in the presence of the pupils shouted at him: 'You Jew, get out of here right away! You have no right to teach German children!' He became numb. Many girls began to scream and shouted his name. He, however, said to them: 'Dear children I have taught here for fifteen years. I have always wanted the best for you, have also imparted German culture to you … I shall go from you now, because those in power want it thus. Farewell.' And so he went, and his colleagues followed him with their eyes. That had been the thanks for his selfless work. But he was still to have one joyous experience. In the afternoon many pupils appeared at his apartment with flowers and other small tokens. It was a judgement of a still unspoiled and unbiased youth.[22]

The privations continued apace in the twelve months prior to the outbreak of war. On 1 September 1939, 226 orders, ordinances or additions to laws were issued to make things even harder for Jews.

## Architects

It has been calculated that before 1933 there were over 450 Jewish architects living and working in thirty-five cities in Germany, with around 300 in Berlin. Many of them came from families that had lived in Germany for generations. They tended to be part of the modernist movement and many of their buildings still exist today.

The majority had gone to war for their homelands, whether it was Germany, Austria–Hungary or Russia in the First World War. A few, such as Leo Adler and Harry Rosenthal, were so badly injured that they suffered for the rest of their lives.

These architects had attended a total of eighteen different German-language institutions. Fifty of them studied at the Technical University of Berlin, forty at the Vienna Technical High School, six studied at the Bauhaus and five in Prague. Alexander Klein had already built a successful practice in Russia before he left due to the anti-Semitic activity following the First World War and the Russian Revolution. He went to Berlin in the 1920s and became successful there too.

One-third of these architects had seen their buildings built before 1933 in central Europe, particularly in Berlin, and had published books and articles on architecture. Their buildings influenced the twentieth-century German cityscapes and still do in Berlin, Leipzig and Hamburg. These architects were also members of professional bodies such as Deutscher Werkbund (DWB), Federation of German Architects (BDA), Association of Architects and Engineers (AIV) and the Prussian Academy of the Arts in Berlin.

Yet, despite their productivity and professional stature, their names, with the exception of Erich Mendelssohn and lately Oskar Kaufmann, are rarely mentioned in the architectural literature, their buildings are seldom attributed, and their writings are virtually nowhere to be found, not even in national libraries.

Many of the architects had witnessed or experienced:

> … social exclusion, racist persecution and pogroms in the countries of Eastern and Central Europe. Jochanan Ratner, Eugen Stolzer, Gideon Kaminka and Werner Wittkower all documented their experiences and dealings with anti-Semitism in Germany and Austria. They determined early on that they would no longer submit to these oppressive conditions and therefore made the decision to leave their homelands as soon as possible.[23]

No Jewish architects were represented in the German Architecture Exhibition of 1931 in Berlin. Accordingly, the Central Association of German Citizens of the Jewish Faith (Central Verein – CV), which had been founded in 1893 in Berlin to counter discrimination against Jews in public life, produced a special edition of its weekly newspaper *CV-Zeitung*, entitled 'Architects and Buildings. From Hitzig and Mendelsohn', on 3 July 1931. It stressed the affinity between Jewish creative activity and German culture. An art historian, Dr Max Osborn, described the work of various successful German-Jewish architects and artists of various disciplines. The intention was to refute the widespread smear campaign claiming that Jews lacked culture.[24]

However, on 1 November 1933, Jewish architects were effectively banned from the Reichskulturkammer für Bildende Kunste (Reich Chamber of Fine Arts).

ProfessorVan Pelt from Waterloo University's architecture faculty clarified the situation. He told me that, unlike the legal and medical professions, the proportion of Jews in architecture was quite low. There was therefore less concern about needing to reduce the numbers of Jews. He also drew attention to the monopoly that doctors and lawyers have on their services, whereas architects are competing with contractors, engineers, designers, amateurs and so on.

The architects were designated under the Reichskammer der Bildenden Künste, which also included painters, sculptors, art dealers and garden architects. Initially it was open to all and the Jews were not excluded. Most Jews applying in late 1933 were admitted, but the president of the chamber was entitled to judge the 'loyalty and talent' of the applicants. After Goebbels stated that a Jew was 'in general incapable' to be a 'steward of Germany's cultural heritage' it became harder for Jews to be admitted, according to Volker Dahm, and by 1935 all Jews were expelled from the umbrella Reichskulturkammer and the organisations below.[25] Van Pelt added that architects, whether Jewish or not, had no paid work during the war because no building work took place, except for the military and they had their own architects.[26]

When membership was denied, their academic titles were revoked and they could no longer use the title 'architect'. Two years later a further law excluded 'half-Jews' and those married to Jews. About 500 architects were affected and many left Germany. Over 130 left for Palestine and helped to create the foundations of modern-day Israel.[27]

Others went to North and South America, Australia and New Zealand, South Africa, Cuba, England, Denmark, Sweden, Portugal and Sweden. Of those who remained in Germany, at least seventy were deported to concentration camps and murdered, including fifty-seven men and two women from Berlin.[28] This was thoroughly researched by an Israeli architect, Myra Warhaftig, who died in March 2008 at the age of 78. She had devoted thirty years to researching the architects persecuted by the Nazis and contacting their relatives all over the world.

Warhaftig said of the interwar period:

> Berlin was a living architecture exhibition … After Weimar, Berlin was flourishing culturally. Walter Gropius, Ludwig Mies van der Rohe, and other modernists were looking for a peaceful and social world, and wished to express their ideas in architecture. I think the majority of Jewish architects chose to settle in Berlin to prove that anti-Semitism would no longer play a role in their lives.[29]

Simon Wiesenthal, who later became known as the 'Nazi-Hunter', was born in Lvov (which is now in the Ukraine) in 1908. As a young man he applied to the Polytechnic Institute in Lvov in 1928, but was not permitted entry because of restrictions on Jewish students. He therefore studied at the Technical University of

Prague where, in 1932, he obtained a degree in architectural engineering and got a post in an architectural office in Lvov.[30]

Martin Punitzer (1889–1949) worked in the 1920s in Berlin. In the 1930s, he was persecuted by the Nazis as a Jew and had to emigrate to Chile.

In Budapest at the turn of the century, seventy of the city's 110 architects were Jewish and they developed a distinct style with their identification with Hungarian nationalism.[31] In Vienna, in the 1930s, there were many famous architects and 25–30 per cent were Jewish, according to Richard Bing (1909–2010). Bing was in Vienna in 1930 and he spoke of the blossoming of culture in the post-1918 world and mentioned Sigmund Freud, Oskar Kokoschka the painter, Bing's lifelong friend the art historian, Sir Ernst Gombrich, and the composers Schoenberg and Alban Berg who created the Second Vienna School of the 1920s.[32]

Anna Sondhelm, a Hungarian survivor, said that both her grandfather and father were architects in Budapest. After her grandfather's death, her father continued to practise and made a good living because 'it was a booming regime between the two wars'.[33]

Anna's family stayed put because they were protected as a result of war service (see page 416). She added that before 1944 her father had plenty of work, but:

> … when there was a big competition of [*sic*] of sanatorium or any public building, it was a common fact that Jewish architects couldn't submit their plans under their own name, but always had a goy [non-Jew] whose name was used, you could have been an absolute clot, but he allowed to use his firm's name and he submitted my father's plans and we were sitting at the radio listening who has won the first prize. There was one particular occasion when, my father was specializing at that time in hospitals and sanatoriums and he won first prize.

In Berlin, Myra Warhaftig created considerable current interest in forgotten Jewish architects, thanks to an exhibition held in 2013 organised by the Association for Research on the Lives and Activities of German-speaking Jewish Architects which she founded. The exhibition, 'Berlin 2013 – Destroyed Diversity', highlighted the work of twenty-eight architects with themed city walks. Each building was marked with a label describing the life of the architect and his personal fate, as well as explaining about the building, its history and function. These walks can be followed on a mobile phone app or a printed flyer.

In this way the work, achievements and life histories of these architects, whose lives were disrupted by National Socialist persecution, and the cultural significance of their buildings are demonstrated to the public and contribute to the improvement of Europe's cultural heritage:

The buildings designed by Jewish architects have often undergone structural alterations or conversions since the Nazi area. Sometimes, the current owners or users know nothing about the history of their buildings or the architects. The Association therefore views its activities as helping to redress the injustice – as a means of preserving historical memory.[34]

When I asked whether they intended placing plaques on the buildings, they told me that the signs for the exhibition had been temporary. Some of the buildings already had plaques with basic information. Elsewhere, the association plans to negotiate with the owners about placing plaques on the façade of the buildings.[35] I am grateful to Dr Günter Schlusche for providing information on this project. He is a member of the board of the association and told me that they are seeking funding for a 'Europe-wide research project which compares the biographies of persecuted Jewish architects in central and eastern European countries before and after 1933'.[36]

As this book was almost ready for the publisher, reviews were published of two new books about the greatest architect of his generation, Le Corbusier (Charles-Edouard Jeanneret-Gris 1887–1965), and both highlighted his anti-Semitic views. François Chaslin quotes from a letter written in the 1920s referring to 'Jewish cretins', and in 1925 he drew an ugly caricature of Léonce Rosenberg, the art critic, with a prominent nose. In 1940 he wrote to his mother, 'If he is serious in his declarations, Hitler can crown his life with a magnificent work, the remaking of Europe.' Two years later he wrote to her again, 'Money, the Jews, freemasonry, everything will be subject to the law. These shameful fortresses will be dismantled.' Although he worked with the Vichy Government, Chaslin states, 'The question is why he was not purged when he spent so much time in Vichy, has such detestable things to say and was such a committed admirer of fascism.' Le Corbusier still adorns Swiss bank notes.[37]

The author of the other book, Xavier de Jarcy, told the *Sunday Times*, 'The most shocking thing is not that the world's best-known architect was a militant fascist. It's the discovery that a veil of silence and lies was thrown over this reality.' Perhaps even worse is the view of the leading French architect and Le Corbusier expert, Jean-Louis Cohen, 'that while he may have been anti-Semitic at times, he was no more so than "the average French petit-bourgeois"'.[38]

### Physicians

Jews have a long association with medicine, going back as far as the Babylonian Talmud (written around 500 CE) and continuing all through the Middle Ages into modern times, with major contributions to medicine being made by Jewish practitioners.

One example is Dr Georg Hartog Gerson (1788–1844) who qualified in 1810. He came from a Hamburg family of physicians, with his grandfather, father and elder brothers all being doctors. He was a field surgeon in the King's German Legion at the Battle of Waterloo in 1815 and remained at his post throughout the battle, saving many lives and performing amputations without any anaesthetic other than alcohol.[39]

A recent Nobel Prize winner claimed that many Jews became physicians in Austria because medicine 'was a profession in which Jews in Austria could work with relatively little hindrance from discrimination'.[40]

Jewish doctors were among the first to suffer under Nazi legislation. In April 1933, very soon after their election, the Nazis started to restrict Jewish doctors' activities.

One area in which Jews were a majority was paediatric medicine. Of the 1,418 paediatricians registered in Germany in 1933, 54.5 per cent were considered Jewish and therefore subject to the Nuremberg Laws. As early as the 1900s, the Munich Haunersche Kinderspital was one of the most renowned children's hospitals in the German-speaking countries. Dr Albert Uffenheimer (1876–1941) began working there in 1903, improving the care of mothers and children. He encouraged breast-feeding, which was difficult for many working women who were forced back to work for financial reasons. He was also a pioneer of preventative medicine, called 'sozialhygiene', which is now known as 'public health medicine'.

After serving as a doctor during the First World War, he started his own practice in Munich. In 1925 he was appointed to be director of the children's hospital in Magdeburg, where he continued his paediatric work and maternal public health counselling. In April 1933 he was dismissed from the Magdeburg Children's Hospital and moved with his family near to the Swiss border, where he hoped to see out the war enduring all the humiliations the Nazis inflicted on Jews. In August 1938 he fled to London. He was forced to transfer all his funds from a Credit Suisse account in Zurich to a Nazi-controlled bank, to get approval for his family to emigrate:

> Credit Suisse records show that in December 1938 Dr Uffenheimer contacted the bank from London and instructed it to transfer all the assets in his account to a branch of the Deutsche Bank in Constanze, Germany. Credit Suisse complied with the request, thus transferring ownership of Dr Uffenheimer's life savings to the Nazi Government.
>
> Eventually his family were able to join him and they went to live in Albany, New York. He died there in April 1941 of a heart attack aged 64. In 2001 he was honoured for his medical care of the children of Magdeburg, by having a public square named 'Dr Uffenheimer Platz'.[41]

However, Credit Suisse continued its betrayal of him when his widow attempted to retrieve his funds after the war. In 1949, while admitting that the transfer had not been voluntary, the bank protected itself by stating that as it was ten years since the transaction, it was not obliged to keep the papers. This cruel intransigence prevented his widow from receiving any restitution. It was only fifty-four years later that the Claims Resolution Tribunal came to the aid of the family and ruled that:

> … if the Swiss banks had jointly agreed to refuse to co-operate with the Nazis in the case of such coerced transfers, the Nazis would have had no motivation for torturing victims of Nazi persecution to obtain their consent to the confiscation of their financial resources in Switzerland to use against the Allies.

Compensation was received by the heirs of Dr Uffenheimer in 2003 – seventy years after this kind, caring professional was dismissed from his post simply because he was a Jew. How many of the babies he saved and nourished would be aware of his fate?

Professor Arthur Lippmann was the leading paediatrician at the St Georg Hospital in Hamburg. He was sacked after twenty-six years of distinguished and devoted service to the children of Hamburg. He gained his professorial title for his pioneering use of ultra-violet light on children suffering from tuberculosis. He was respected by his peers in Hamburg and was chosen as one of the five members of the local doctors' council (Ärztekammer). None of this mattered to the Nazis. 'In June 1933 he received his notification of dismissal. Two months later, although a war veteran, he was struck off the register of insurance doctors.' In order to be readmitted, Lippman had to provide written evidence of his military service in a Russian isolation hospital.[42]

In fact, these matters were formalised when the Reich Minister of Labour issued an order on 17 May 1934 banning Jewish doctors, or those related to Jews by marriage, from the various health insurance schemes supported by the government. This included First World War veterans. Dentists were dealt with similarly in February 1935.[43]

Arthur's own son, Rudolf, who was a medical student, committed suicide when he realised he would be unable to qualify as a doctor. His uncle, Leo Lippman, head of the financial administration of the city, gave the oration at his funeral on 13 October 1933:

> He could not bear the fate and defamation that befell the German Jews … he was a German and a Jew, for centuries his ancestors had been settled in Germany. They were bound to Germany with all their hearts. They did their duty as Germans in good times and bad, in peace and in war … You suffered deeply from rejection to be told your help was no longer wanted … You wrote to a friend that what sustained you was the belief that no one could take away from you your feeling of belonging to Germany … in your own words, 'I know I am a German as long as I wish to be'.

Professor Dr Arthur Lippmann died in 1938 in Sydney. In a short time, he succeeded in building up a practice as a consultant for internal diseases. All his spare time was devoted to the new Jewish hospital in Sydney.[44] In 1943, Leo Lippmann and his wife, Anna, committed suicide on 11 June in the knowledge that the next day they were due to be deported to Theresienstadt.

Christabel Bielenberg (1909–2003) was an English girl who, after marrying a German lawyer, Peter, in 1934, lived in Germany with him all through the war. They settled in Hamburg and had three children. As she wrote:

> The Nuremberg Laws did not hit me hard until they walked quietly and with dignity across the threshold of my own front door. Professor Bauer looked after our children. He was a dedicated paediatrician and a busy man, although not a rich one, as he had founded a private children's clinic in Hamburg, and had maintained it during the depression years with as much as of his personal means as he could spare.

Bauer sat up all night with Christabel when her eldest son Nicholas had a fever. The next morning before he left, he asked her whether she wanted him to continue treating the family. She didn't understand. He explained to her that he was a Jew and he had been threatened that unless he handed his clinic over to an Aryan colleague, it would be closed. He had fought it for a year, but had agreed in the interests of the patients.

He also told her that he was no longer a German citizen and he felt she should know that he had received threatening letters, telling him to keep his hands off Aryan children. He told her not to make any more appointments on the telephone. Some weeks later she called at his flat but he was not there. His wife was surrounded by packing cases and she said he had gone job-hunting in Holland. They were not young, but would find something.

The housekeeper who brought in the tea was not young either, because Jews could not employ female domestics under 45. However, she must have been trusted because Frau Bauer said in her presence, 'He loved this country, you see, Frau Bielenberg, something broke inside him when he had to leave his clinic.' Two years later she saw the housekeeper in a tram queue and was shocked to hear that Dr Bauer had died. She said that some people said it was suicide, but she knew his heart was broken. 'They were good people.'[45]

Professionals were not exempted from public humiliation. Frau Haferkamp described the treatment given to her family doctor (hauswartz). She said she did not know that many of the people she saw being mistreated were Jews. She mentioned various local tradesmen and others, but was really upset when she spoke about the doctor:

We had a hauswartz, Dr Stein. We did not know that he was a Jew. My God, I was *furious*, was I ever furious, when I once went to Market Street and, because he was a Jew … [he was] naked, and he had a sign hanging round his neck, 'I am the Jew Dr Stein'.

She began to shout. 'Stark naked down the middle of the street they chased him with the whip. I *saw* it. Sign on him, on it written, "Ich bin Jude Dr Stein". And that was our family doctor.'

She was obviously shocked and said he had not done anything at all, but the people chased after him and nobody helped him:

They just scared the man and screamed at him, 'Out with the Jews, out with these pigs.'… Then I went home and said to my mother, 'Nein, they chased Dr Stein naked down the street.' *Naked*, with a sign covering his stomach, sex organs, 'I am a Jew.' That's what the Nazi swine did.

When asked what happened to Dr Stein she said they took him away and if they had tried to help him, they would have 'beat us dead'.[46]

On 16 March 1937 it was reported that figures released showed that 3,000 Jewish doctors had left Germany in the four years of the Nazi regime. That still left 8,000, but half of them were over 50 and therefore would be unable to emigrate. It was also disclosed that there were fewer than 150 Jewish students registered in all German universities.[47]

Previously, on 5 March 1936, it was reported that hundreds of Jewish mothers were travelling to give birth to their babies in England so they would have British citizenship. Some even risked flying across the Channel to avoid their children being born as second-class citizens under the Nazis. Additionally these children, who were automatically British citizens, could apply on behalf of their parents through agents or guardians, and the British authorities were favourable to such applications. Ironically, in many cases the Jewish mothers were treated by German-Jewish doctors, often by their old family physicians who had left the Reich and set up practice in the UK.[48]

## Lawyers

Photo No. 11 is a well-known picture of Dr Michael Siegel (1882–1979), a Munich lawyer. On 10 March 1933, he had complained to the Munich Police Headquarters when one of his clients was taken into 'protective custody'. The client, Max Uhlfelder, was a Jew who owned a large city-centre store – in fact with a sales area of 70,000 square feet and 1,000 employees it was the second largest department store in Munich. The windows of his store had been smashed on 9 March 1933 by Nazi stormtroopers and Uhlfelder himself had been taken to Dachau. (For Max Uhlfelder's story see pages 237–8.)

The police cut off the bottom half of Siegel's trouser legs and led him through Munich's inner city streets barefoot with a board around his neck saying, 'I will never complain to the police again'. Siegel managed to escape to Peru, but not until 1940. He died there in 1979.[49] The photograph was featured in a book produced by Yad Vashem in 1990 with the briefest of details, stating that Dr Siegel died in Dachau. Subsequently, Peter Sinclair contacted Yad Vashem stating that Dr Siegel was his father and filling in the story.

Dr Siegel and his cousin, Julius, were the senior partners in the family firm, Kanzlei Siegel, founded in the 1890s. Their clients were both Jewish and non-Jewish, including members of the royal Wittelsbacher family who became family friends.[50] So when, on 10 March, Dr Siegel went to Munich Police HQ on behalf of his client, he went as a prominent Munich Jewish lawyer.

Instead of the anticipated normal courteous welcome, he was told to go to a particular basement room full of SA stormtroopers. They beat him up – he lost several front teeth and his eardrum was perforated. Additionally, his trousers were cut off at the knee, revealing his 'long johns' (Munich can be very cold in March). He was then paraded as described above, 'as a clear warning to all who contemplated insisting on *habeas corpus* and other fundamental civil rights'.[51]

Siegel's daughter, Bea (Beate), told me that her father had lost his right thumb as a child on his parents' farm and therefore could not enlist as a soldier, because he could not fire a gun. However, he was appointed as the ski instructor to the Royal Bavarian troops for the duration of the First World War. When he was introduced to King Ludwig III of Bavaria, he asked Siegel, 'So what on earth do you do in summer?' Dr Siegel told him he was a lawyer and after Ludwig was deposed he became a client.[52]

Beate came to England on the Kindertransport on 26 June 1939, aged 14. In photo No. 15, Bea is on the right, the girl in middle was from the Jewish orphanage and the tall girl was called Henny. Her father was an opera singer who was forbidden from performing. The photo was taken by Bea's uncle, Ernst Waldner, who skied out of Germany in 1940 and joined the Yugoslav Army.[53]

She wrote a testimony of the impact on the whole family – his wife, Mathilde, son, Peter, and daughter, Beate. The children were 12 and 8 respectively at the time:

> I was in bed that day with a bit of a cold. My mother was out shopping and I heard the front door open and shut and expected her to come to my room to ask me if I was all right. No one came. ... I got out of bed and went out into the corridor. There, on hooks outside the bathroom, hung my father's blood-drenched clothes.
>
> It was the first time that I was really scared. Children are sometimes afraid of the dark, or of imaginary ghosts or whatever, but this was a real fear, not anything I imagined.

She went down to her parents' room, knocked on the door and opened it cautiously. 'I saw my father pull up the eiderdown to cover his face up to his eyes so I shouldn't see his injuries.' He told her to wait until her mother came home.

It was only years later that she discovered the whole story. After the SA had marched Dr Siegel round central Munich for about an hour they got bored and let him go at the main station, saying, 'Jetzt stirbst du, Jud' ('You are going to die now, Jew').[54] Her father told Beate that he was about to get into a taxi, when a man said he had just taken a photo of him and wanted his permission to publish it. Dr Siegel said he could do what he liked with it and he got into his taxi.

Years later, Beate was living in London with her own family, when her father, a widower, came to visit. Her middle son, Paul, told his grandpa that there was a picture of him in his history book. Beate and her husband were concerned about his reaction. He just said, 'Yes, very interesting.' Beate's husband, Michael, a historian, said, 'I've always wanted to ask you this: What went on in your head at that moment?'

Dr Siegel replied, 'I can answer that. From the moment they started laying in to me, I had only one thought ... I shall survive you all!' Professor van Pelt commented, 'That is defiance, not humiliation.'[55]

It is alleged that the photographer was a professional photojournalist, Heinrich Sanden. Local newspapers refused to publish the photos and he felt they were potentially a danger to him, so he was anxious to get rid of the photographic plates. Through the Berlin agent, he sold the plates to an American press agency, but when they arrived in Washington the writing on the placard was unclear, so it was touched up based on Sanden's rather inaccurate recollections. The photographs were published first on the front page of *The Washington Times* on 23 March 1933, but have been reproduced many times all over the world. Beate told me that the placard said: 'Ich bin Jude und ich werde mich nie mehr bei der Polizei beschweren.' This translates as, 'I am a Jew and I shall never again complain to the Police.'[56]

Dr Siegel secured his children's future and then left Munich with his wife in August 1940. From Berlin they travelled on the Trans-Siberian Express via Moscow to Korea and then Japan. A boat across the Pacific took them to Los Angeles and then Peru. Beate recalls seeing him studying Hebrew texts in Munich while working as a lawyer, which, with other religious knowledge, enabled him to become the acting rabbi of the German-Jewish community in Lima for a time.[57]

The Yad Vashem page updating the story has a splendid photograph of Dr Siegel in September 1971 in Lima. He is wearing the Grosse Verdienstkreuz (Grand Cross of Merit) which he was given on his eighty-ninth birthday by the German President 'in recognition of his services to improving the relationship between the German-Jewish Refugee Community in Lima and the post-war German Republic and also for his services as legal advisor on German and Peruvian Law to the German Embassy in Peru'.[58]

We should remember that these lawyers did not regard themselves as 'Jewish lawyers':

> ... they were German, lawyers and Jews. Many of them had been soldiers during the First World War, others had renounced the Jewish faith and some had been baptized. In the area of jurisprudence, many lawyers of Jewish origin contributed to the development of renowned legal journals and to the establishment of professional organisations. And still there was anti-Semitic propaganda against these 'Jewish lawyers'.[59]

After the Nazi takeover in 1933, Wilhelm Dickmann (1900–1987; later William Dickman), who had been baptised as a child, was considered non-Aryan and was threatened with losing his profession under the Nazi laws. However, since he was a First World War veteran who had fought at the front, he was able to continue practising as a lawyer. He had his own practice in Berlin. On 25 September 1938, around 2 a.m., the telephone rang:

> Hello, I understand that you are going on your vacation tomorrow. I just heard the latest weather report. The weather will change radically later in the morning, so it would be advisable for you to take the earliest possible flight out ...

It was hung up. Dickmann didn't recognise the voice at all, but the warning was unambiguous. He got ready immediately, said goodbye to his sister and gravely ill father – he was not to see them again – and fled to his brother in Copenhagen. At the end of 1938 he travelled to New York on a tourist visa. His German legal degree was not recognised in the USA, so he took on several odd jobs, such as night checker in a restaurant, working twelve hour shifts at night and writing short stories and articles by day under the name William Dickman. In 1939, Dickman won one of eight scholarships granted to European jurists. In 1943 he graduated from the University of Pennsylvania, Philadelphia, and married Ilka Deutsch from Prague.[60]

Fritz Salo Glaser (1876–1956) trained as a lawyer before he joined up in the First World War. In the 1920s he distanced himself from Judaism and became involved in Dresden's bohemian art scene, while he pursued his legal career. He was noted for hosting artistic and musical events and he used to pop into local artists' studios with food. In 1924, he wrote to his friend, Otto Dix, who painted him twice: 'I have always known your art has eternal value.'

In 1933, he quickly lost his right to work as a lawyer and the privileges of being a war veteran. He was also denounced as a Communist because in 1920 he had given a lecture on 'Communism and cultural progress'. As he was unable to work, he started selling his pictures to raise money but destroyed all the records for fear of further difficulties. He was due to be deported to Theresienstadt on

16 February 1945, but was saved by the Allies' bombing of Dresden during the night of 13–14 February 1945, which occurred three days before his deportation. In the confusion, Glaser escaped.

He and his family assumed that his art collection had been destroyed, but in November 2013 several pictures were found in the motley collection of paintings hoarded by Cornelius Gurlitt.[61] Out of the initial twenty-five paintings listed online on 11 November, thirteen were said to be part of the Glaser collection and a lawyer working on behalf of Glaser's descendants said, 'The family, who still live in Dresden, is very happy about the art found and of course they want them back.' The works include one by Otto Griebel, a watercolour called *Child at the Table*, and Conrad Felixmueller's *Couple in a Landscape*.[62]

Glaser had loved the art of his times and had direct contact with 'his' artists. Heike Biedermann, an art historian at the Dresden State Collections, said about 90 per cent of his collection was on paper and 'The prices for works on paper were low, so he managed to buy a large amount of art without having extraordinary wealth'. He owned about forty paintings but his taste was what the Nazis described as 'degenerate'. His position deteriorated as the Nazis squeezed the Jews economically – thus, from 1937 he could no longer work as a tax advisor and from 1938 Jews were banned from selling art.

His situation was aggravated by the imposition of the 'Judenbusse' created by Göring on 12 November 1938, following Kristallnacht, and extorted from the Jews as 'atonement for the hostile stance taken by Jews toward Germans'. A family acquaintance has said that Glaser had to sell two Schmidt-Rottluff paintings, a Klee, a Kandinsky, a Kokoschka and a Nolde:

> He was very cautious with his records because the Gestapo searched his home frequently. He destroyed all evidence of the forbidden art sales and what was left of his collection. After the bombing of Dresden, he left the city and joined his wife and daughter in a farmhouse 10 miles south of Dresden. After the war he carried on working to feed his family and aged 68 he was appointed to a post at the Justice Ministry in Saxony, helping to decide which of Hitler's laws should be kept and which annulled. He died in 1956 aged 80. After his death his family had to sell some of his remaining art for food and accommodation.[63]

Professionals in the Nazi camps were often subject to special mistreatment. Gilbert Michlin commented on the plight of the professional in the camps:

> I was able to survive thanks to my poor father, to whom I shall remain eternally grateful for making me into a tool-and-die maker. As a doctor or an actor, I would have been gassed upon my arrival or else been rapidly eliminated by the terrible work regime that crushed the Jewish inmates who did not have a

'useful' skill. A few doctors and musicians found positions in the camp. Doctors became nurses at the hospital, and musicians made up the camp orchestra. But their numbers were restricted and once the required number was attained, the others were done away with.[64]

Magda Herzberger, from Cluj in Rumania, who was in Auschwitz reiterated the treatment of physicians:

People would think that physicians had privileges, but not all physicians were treated well. Many were treated very badly where I was. Sometimes they would line up physicians in order to persecute them more because they were intellectuals. Some of these guards with very little education now suddenly got power. They hated intellectuals.[65]

She said there was a physician in her barracks and she got worse treatment than anyone else. The guards and the blockältesters were really cruel to her. She concluded, 'sometimes you were better off not to reveal you were a physician'.

The Nazis were so obsessed with the Jews that they wanted to eliminate all signs of Jewish achievement and accordingly, Wilhelm Fric, the Reich Minister of the Interior, ordered the removal of all Marxist and Jewish street names. One eminent example was Dr Nicolaus Ferdinand Haller, who had a fine thoroughfare named after him in the centre of Hamburg.

The Hallers were a prosperous Jewish family who had moved to Hamburg in the eighteenth century. Nicolaus Ferdinand Haller, a prominent patrician and senator, six times Mayor of Hamburg, was baptised, but had married the Jewish daughter of a banker; his father too had been baptised and had married a Jewish wife. His son, Martin Haller, was also baptised – despite Protestant baptisms through three generations, he would nevertheless have been classified as a full Jew by the Nazis, had he not died in 1926. Martin Haller had made a significant contribution to Hamburg's spectacular skyline. He was the leading architect of the Rathaus, the splendid neo-Gothic town hall which dominated the renamed Adolf-Hitler-Platz.[66]

The internationally famous physicist, Heinrich Hertz, who discovered the length and velocity of the electronic-magnetic waves named after him, presented a further problem in Hamburg. Frick was asked to make an exception, but refused. Altogether twenty-two racially impure streets were found in Hamburg.

However, another problem arose with portrait medallions that were prominently fixed inside the Rathaus, which stonemasons had to remove. They represented Salomon Heine, uncle of the poet and a philanthropist; the lawyer and politician, Isaac Wolffsohn; Moritz Heckscher, elected to represent Hamburg in the Frankfurt pre-parliament of 1848; and Heinrich Hertz, again.[67]

There seems something bizarre in the fact that all traces of Jewish dignitaries, even those who were deceased, had to be annihilated and their roles and contribution eliminated. While Jews were being shunned in Germany, it should be remembered that a century earlier Jews and Christians had mixed with each other at the Harmonie Club in Hamburg. In 1829, a young teacher with a PhD, Immanuel Wohlwill, was welcomed as a member of the club, where he met a fellow Jew – Dr Hertz. Wohlwill wrote of meeting the Hamburg elite there for good conversation, a game of billiards, or relaxation with ladies coming for social occasions. Wohlwill was completely at ease: 'The atmosphere of the Harmonie I like very much. Officers, the nobility, scholars and Hamburg citizens all live together here on the most cordial footing.'[68] What would Wohlwill have thought if he could have foreseen the day when Jews would no longer be welcome in that club, or that his grandson, Freidrich Wohlwill, who became a well-known neuropathologist, would be dismissed from his post at the university and the local hospital in 1933?

On 17 July 1942, Dr Heinrich Wohlwill, Freidrich's brother, and his wife received their deportation papers. The night before their departure to Theresienstadt:

> The evening was spent playing Brahms and Beethoven sonatas accompanied by a close non-Aryan family friend. As they made music together they were able to put out of their minds what the next day would bring. The following morning, next to despair, Heinrich tearfully said goodbye to his sister Sophie. He tried to take his old Tyrolean violin with him, but the Gestapo routinely deprived the deportees of anything of value. A faithful elderly maid, Joanna, a member of their household for nineteen years, accompanied Dr Heinrich and Frau Hedwig Wohlwill to the Moorweide assembly point, insisting on carrying their luggage as far as the Gestapo would permit her. Eight years after coming to power, the Nazis had not succeeded in breaking all attachments between Christians and Jews.[69]

Heinrich's 71-year-old sister arrived in March 1943 to find her beloved brother was already dead. Only Hedwig survived to describe the trauma of it all for her grandson.

I found that Immanuel Wohlwill was a teacher of the Hamburgische Israelitische Freischule, founded in 1815. He wrote a pamphlet, dated 31 October 1830, arguing that the freischule's curriculum should be directed toward equipping pupils for emigration. Subsequently, he wrote on 30 April 1833 that their colleague William Leo-Wolf's presence in New York gave him 'a pleasant opportunity, often and successfully, to recommend emigrants to North America'.[70] This seems a most prescient view. This letter was sent almost 100 years to the day before Hitler came to power!

## Scientists

Hitler's attitude to his scientists was particularly bizarre. Some suggest it cost him the war because he got rid of all the scientists with Jewish blood, who then went to work for the Americans and developed their atomic weapons. The provisions of the new legislation, the Restoration of the Professional Civil Service, were applied quite uniformly to the most humble or the most elevated Nobel Prize winners.

The scientists at Freibourg University were vulnerable very soon after Hitler's election when the Nazi students' union put up posters stating, 'Our most dangerous adversary is the Jew and he who serves him. The Jew can think only as a Jew. If he writes German he lies.' When the rektor, von Mollendorf, ordered the removal of the posters he was dismissed, and Martin Heidegger was appointed on 21 April 1933, apparently recommended by his predecessor. He too opposed the posters and prevented a proposed book burning, but had joined the Nazi Party just after his appointment. His political views are still the subject of debate, as is his long-term relationship with Hannah Arendt.

It is interesting to follow the theory of the eminent scientist, Max Perutz, who settled in Britain. He suggested that:

> … without Haber's synthesis of ammonia Germany would soon have run out of explosives in 1915 – the war would have ended, millions would not have been slaughtered, Lenin might never have got to Russia, Hitler might not have come to power, the Holocaust might not have happened and European civilization might have been spared the horrors of the Second World War.[71]

Fritz Haber (1868–1934) is not a household name today, yet he was responsible for the greatest impact on the two world wars of the twentieth century. He was a German-Jewish chemist who developed poison gases, as well as fertilisers which have helped to feed the world.

Chemical warfare is assumed to be a modern creation. In fact, Thucydides recorded the use of arsenic smoke in 425 by the Athenians in the Peloponnesian War. The Chinese are also said to have used something similar around 960–1279, during the Sung Dynasty. Even during the American Civil War of 1861–1865 the use of poison gas against the Confederates was suggested, but Abraham Lincoln stated, 'the use of poison gas should be wholly excluded from modern warfare'.[72]

When the war started, Haber began developing the gas that led Wilfrid Owen (1893–1918) to write the most famous of the First World War poems, 'Dulce et Decorum Est'. The title was based on a quotation from one of the 'Odes' of Horace, 'Dulce et decorum est prop patria mori' ('It is sweet and fitting to die for one's country'). Owen called this 'the old lie', having witnessed the soldiers coughing their lives away from Haber's gas.[73] The 'my friend', chided for telling the lie, was Jessie Pope. Jesse was a female poet writing jingoistic poetry which was intended to encourage young men to enlist. Owen originally dedicated his poem to her, although the dedication was later removed to make it more universal.[74]

Haber developed chlorine gas, used for the first time at Ypres on 22 April 1915 at 6.00 p.m. when the required strong wind arrived. The German troops opened the valves on 5,000 high-pressure steel tanks containing 400 tons of chlorine. The troops most affected by the first attack were the French division from Algeria. Gunner Jim Sutton and Major McDougal were observing from above the gas cloud and 'could hardly have heard the screams, the gasping and choking as the gas cloud rolled across the troops – but they saw the panic – saw the Algerians running for their lives, throwing away rifles as they staggered and stumbled, dazed and terrified, away from the lethal fumes'.

Jim Kiddie of the 48th Canadian Highlanders was celebrating his thirty-fourth birthday that day and had hoped to hear from his mother in Jedburgh. He observed what happened and wrote a report. It was the troops on the left who really suffered:

> In the front-line trenches where the gas was thicker they had no time to run, and not many survived. Rolling over the trenches the gas clouds overwhelmed them so swiftly that men collapsed at once. Lying retching, choking, gasping for breath at the foot of the deep ditch where the heavy gas settled and clung thickest of all, they suffocated to death in minutes. From the support lines fifty yards behind, the troops watched in horror and as the wall of smoke rolled forward to engulf them in their turn, as the wind brought the first wisps of the fumes that clutched the throat and stung the eyes, they panicked and ran.
>
> Fifteen minutes after the gas was first released the German infantry was ordered to don gas-masks and advance. They were prepared for a fight, but there was no one left to fight with. As their guns thundered ahead of them, the German soldiers simply walked through the allied line, over the bodies of the dead, lying sprawled out, faces discoloured and contorted in grimaces of agony. Within an hour the Germans had advanced more than a mile and they had hardly needed to fire a shot.[75]

This exercise was repeated four more times over another two weeks. This gas killed hundreds of thousands of soldiers on both sides. However, Haber did not believe that asphyxiation was worse than blowing a soldier's leg off and letting him bleed to death. His own wife, Clara Immerwahr, one of the first women in Germany to achieve a doctorate in chemistry, was so shocked by his work that on the night of 1 May she shot herself with her husband's service revolver.

The Allies were also outraged, and the leader of the British forces, Sir John French, condemned Germany's 'cynical and barbarous disregard of the well-known usages of civilised war', writing to Lord Kitchener, Secretary of State for War. He added:

> All the scientific resources of Germany have apparently been brought into a play
> to produce a gas of so virulent and poisonous a nature that any human being
> brought into contact with it, is first paralysed and then meets with a lingering
> and agonising death.[76]

Haber worked ceaselessly, conducting further research and expanding his institute. By 1917 he employed 1,500 people, including 150 scientists. This led to
the development of mustard gas in 1917, which was first used by Germany and
then later by Britain and the United States. It had a different technique and
killed by contact, blinding soldiers who got it in their eyes but also killing those
who inhaled it. At a meeting with German chemical industrialists in 1918 Haber
called it a 'fabulous success'.[77]

Haber was awarded the 1918 Nobel Prize for Chemistry for his work on syn-
thesising ammonia. His work resulted in developments in the nitrogen fertilisers
now used in almost every country in the world. Millions of tons of fertilisers are
now produced, worth millions of pounds annually.[78] However, the award was
controversial and other prize winners that year rejected their award.[79]

Carl Bosch was IG Farben's chief executive. Haber and Bosch worked together
and the synthesis of ammonia is known worldwide as the 'Haber–Bosch process'.
When Haber, as a Jew, was forced to resign in April 1933, Bosch was the only
BASF executive to write to him offering support and sympathy. Bosch raised the
subject with Hitler, saying that the persecution of the Jews would harm German
science. Bosch claimed that Hitler replied, 'Then we'll just work for a hundred
years without physics and chemistry!'[80]

Hitler's rise to power threatened Haber, as it did all Jews. When Jewish judges
were removed on 1 April 1933, he realised Jewish scientists might be next. However,
forty years earlier, in 1892, he had abandoned his Judaism in Jena Cathedral and
become a Protestant – a not uncommon act for ambitious academics at the time.
This was reinforced by his second Christian marriage to another Jewish girl.

On 25 October 1917, Captain Fritz Haber, outfitted in military uniform complete with the sword and spiked helmet of a Prussian officer, took Charlotte
Nathan as his wife. The ceremony occurred at the spiritual altar of the German
empire, inside Berlin's Kaiser Wilhelm Memorial Church. According to Charlotte,
Haber refused to have the wedding anywhere else, which meant Charlotte had to
convert to Christianity.[81]

However, the Nazis would not recognise such an action. To them Jewishness
was based on ancestry not religion and therefore his conversion was irrelevant.
'His desire for social status and his loyalty to the national cause' would ultimately
be of no avail.

The new law ordered the removal within six months of all Jews from the
German Civil Service, apart from those who had been soldiers in the First World

War. Accordingly, Haber could have stayed put at his institute. It had been his home, his work and his circle of friends for twenty-two years. In the end he resigned on 30 April, although he allowed until 1 October 1933 for a successor to be found. Max Planck, president of the Kaiser Wilhelm Society, tried to change his mind and approached the Culture Minister, Bernhard Rust, who declared, 'I am finished with the Jew Haber.' Planck then approached Hitler himself and tried to convince him that forcing valuable Jews to emigrate amounted to Germany's 'self-mutilation'. In a 1947 memoir, he recorded that Hitler flew into such a rage that Planck could only leave the room.[82]

When Haber left Berlin on 3 August to visit his son in Paris, he had no idea he would never return to Germany. His health was bad and he died in Basel in January 1934. The Nazis forbade attendance at a belated memorial service in January 1935 and all his efforts for his country were ignored. His insecticide, which was based on a cyanide-based crystal that turned into a vapour when exposed to the air, was stored in the warehouses of the German Society for Insect Control all over Europe. He had thought it would protect human life by destroying insects in flour mills and granaries. In 1924, the product was refined and called Zyklon B.

In the years after his death the world went mad, and camps for killing Jews were created – 'the insecticide became a tool of death on a scale beyond all normal imagination. Members of Fritz Haber's extended family, children of his sisters and cousins, were hauled to those camps and killed, poisoned by the fruit of their famous relative's research.'[83]

Haber's past services to the state counted for nothing in 1933 – he was a Prussian in appearance, a Nazi in attitude. As he lamented in a letter to Chaim Weizmann (1874–1952), a biochemist who became Irael's first president:

> I have been German to a degree which I feel fully only now. I was more than a great leader of armies, more than a captain of industry. I was the founder of great industries. My work opened the way to the great industrial and military expansion of Germany. All doors stood open to me.[84]

Unlike Haber, most dismissed scientists left quietly. The Nobel laureate, James Franck, protested vociferously but found little support from his faculty colleagues. When Franck published an open letter complaining that he and the other Jews were being treated like criminals, forty-two of his Aryan colleagues at Göttingen University responded with a petition branding his letter an act of sabotage and demanding that the dismissals be speeded up.

There is some satisfaction that Germany's first Holocaust professor is to be based at the Goethe University in Frankfurt. It will be located in the 'former IG Farben building, a Third Reich-era industrial conglomerate that made the pesticide that the Nazis used in Auschwitz'. That should concentrate the students' minds and discourage any potential Holocaust deniers.[85]

## Miscellaneous Trades and Occupations

In Berlin, the recently formed central organisation of artisans demanded of the Minister of Economics, Dr Kurt Schmitt (1885–1950), that discrimination be extended to Jewish artisans as it had to the government services and the free professions. The request was refused and the minister rebuked the delegation. It was reported that:

> … the expulsion of Jewish members of the new artisans' association has been prohibited in accordance with the present policy of the government. He warned against the dismissal of Jewish apprentices solely on grounds of their being Jewish and declared that Jews should not be hindered in receiving artisan training.

The ministry sent a communiqué to all bodies of artisans warning against discriminating against Jews. This policy was not supported by most Nazi leaders, but was taken by Dr Schmitt based on his conviction that indiscriminate dismissal of Jews was handicapping trade and industry and was aggravating a difficult situation.[86] Gerald Feldman wrote of him:

> Schmitt shared the belief that Jews were overrepresented within the academic professions, and the role that they played in politics, law and the arts would have to be greatly limited, if not utterly eliminated. He believed, however, that they were entitled to a place in German economic life, and made it into a maxim of his year in office as Reich Economy Minister that there was no 'Jewish question in the economy'.[87]

On 23 January 1942 it was reported in London that an order prohibiting the sale of Czech newspapers to Jews in the Protectorate of Bohemia & Moravia was issued that week in Prague, according to information received by Czechs in London. The shortage of newsprint was given as the excuse. At the same time it was stated that all the Jews in Mlada Boleslav were prohibited from visiting exhibitions, public reading rooms and other similar institutions.

Czechs in London said that the newspaper ban for Jews was another Nazi scheme to drive a wedge between Czechs and Jews in the protectorate. The Nazis had recently resumed their propaganda in the protectorate, blaming 'Jewish underground activities' for the execution of Czechs there. The pro-Nazi Prague newspaper *Ceske Sloco* said, 'Jews are responsible for all Czech tears.' The Czech leaders in London were assured that the Nazi effort to alienate the Czechs from the Jews had failed.[88]

In Spain it was reported on 15 February 1937 that General Franco had entered into an agreement with Germany by which no Jew would be allowed to represent a German firm in any part of Spain. Additionally, it was reported that several German firms in Lisbon had been warned to dismiss all Jewish employees.[89]

In November 1939 Hungarian-Jewish waiters in Budapest were reported as having called on the Finance Minister, Lajos Remenyi-Schneller, about an order which forbade the issue of licences to restaurants employing Jews as waiters. The delegation complained that 600 Jewish waiters had already lost their jobs and another 200, who were currently on army manoeuvres, would not be reinstated on their return. The report ended with a sentence about Jewish taxi drivers being refused licences so that the taxi industry could be Aryanized.[90]

The Nazis experienced the concept of unexpected consequences over the aspect of the Nuremberg Laws that concerned maids in Jewish homes. Apparently it caused:

> ... such great hardship on some 50,000 'Aryan' servant girls, that many of them had appealed to the authorities for permission to retain their positions, and the law was modified to allow them to remain in Jewish households where there were no males over sixteen years of age.[91]

However, on 15 February 1937 in Berlin it was reported that if Jewish employers allowed Aryan salesgirls to wash dishes after lunching with them, they would be tried under the Nuremberg Laws prohibiting non-Aryans from employing Aryan servants, the Federal Court ruled that day. This was the verdict in the case of a sales-girl who voluntarily washed the dishes after lunching with her Jewish employees. The court stated, 'Washing dishes is a part of domestic work in the household.'[92]

On 26 December, the Ministry of the Interior issued an order to the police authorities not to renew the permits of the 30,000 Jewish commercial travellers working in the Reich, on the grounds that 'Jews are no longer politically reliable'.[93]

The restriction on Jews employing Christian domestic maids came relatively late to Rumania. On 17 January 1938 it was reported from Bucharest that a decree prohibiting Jews from employing Christian maids under 40 years of age was announced. This decree, like the German one under the Nuremburg Laws, had been previously announced by the Public Works Minister, Georg Cuza, but it had been repudiated by the premier Octavian Goga, which was surprising as he was an anti-Semite and on 12 January his government had stripped Jews of their citizen-ship. He is alleged to have said, 'The Jewish problem is an old one here, and it is a Rumanian tragedy. Briefly, we have too many Jews.'

Protests against the repudiation were led by Alexander Cuza, who was the father of the Public Works Minister and was a Minister without Portfolio, and this resulted in the approval of the decree. The announcement of the decree stated:

In view of numerous cases where it was found that Jewish employers hire young Christian girls with the object of prostituting them, we decide, firstly, that all Jews are prohibited from hiring and keeping as servants Christian women below the age of 40, secondly that the labor exchanges shall refuse all engagements contrary to the above provisions, thirdly, the director of labor is charged with fulfilment of this decision.

Goga was only in office from 28 December 1937 until 10 February 1938, but in that time he was responsible for the first anti-Semitic laws. In this atmosphere it was also reported that the Federation of Professional Unions, comprising doctors, engineers, lawyers, architects, artist, teachers and other professional men, had decided to petition the government seeking complete 'Romanisation' of the free professions.[94]

Additionally, it was reported in Australia on 24 January 1938 that medical students at Bucharest University had demonstrated to demand that Jewish professors should be removed. They announced that they would boycott lectures by Jews. When interviewed, the new prime minister said, 'For us there is only one final solution of the Jewish problem – the collection of all Jews in a region which is still uninhabited and the foundation there of a Jewish nation. And the further away the better.'[95]

In Warsaw, on 26 May 1938, it was reported that the Union of Landlord Associations had adopted the 'Aryan paragraph' excluding Jews from membership. This was after forty Jewish delegates had walked out in protest against the failure to include Jews in the Praesidium.[96]

## Journalists

Alexander Stille's father was a journalist in Mussolini's Italy. He was a double European refugee – he was displaced firstly by the Russian Revolution and later by Fascism in his adopted home of Italy. He was born Mikhail Kamenetzki (Misha) in Moscow and died as Michael U. Stille in New York. Mikhail's own father, Ilya Kamenetzki, was a dentist, a profession that made him indispensable under any regime, wrote Alexander – ignoring that this did not apply under the Nazis. However, Ilya did well in Italy as his patients included relatives of major Fascists and the mistress of the prominent writer and war hero Gabriele D'Annunzio, who provided him with a protective letter.

After the introduction of the 1938 Racial Manifesto, the Kamenetzki family became 'stateless citizen[s] of the Jewish race', banned from practising professions. The name Ugo Stille was used by Misha as a way of avoiding Mussolini's racial laws and hiding his Jewish name from publication in newspapers. Stille means 'silence' in German, 'and it seemed a good name for a pseudonym'.

He married an American girl, Elizabeth Bogert, who represented all that he loved about the USA, but did not reveal that he was Jewish. She was the daughter of a Chicago law professor 'from a mid-eastern white Anglo-Saxon Protestant' background with the anti-Semitic views of the time. Alexander writes, 'anti-Semitism was a widespread and simply accepted attitude in the world my mother grew up in'.

The attitude of the 'unthinking anti-Semitism' of 'old-stock, upper-class Protestant American families' has been confirmed by one of Varian Fry's colleagues from Marseilles. Miriam Davenport commented that all the high society people were anti-Semitic before the war. She herself 'dated two Jewish boys in the 1930s and was nearly socially ostracised'. [97]

Alexander's mother was angry when she met her father-in-law for the first time at the wedding. Alexander writes that she was revolted by what she saw, 'a Yiddish-speaking Shtetl Jew who had the instincts and manners of an itinerant peddler'. He also records that towards the end of her life she made a shocking confession: 'I thought to myself, Hitler killed six million Jews and he had to spare this guy!' [98]

# 13

# ARYANIZATION – THE THEFT OF JEWISH BUSINESSES

It's not just stolen art. It's a symbol of stolen life.

Dame Helen Mirren, 2015

'Aryanization' was the Nazis' economic theft of businesses from Jews – quite against any rules of natural justice, even though the Hitler regime had legislation in place. It was legalised theft.

Jews no longer had rights to own their own businesses or to sit on the boards of larger companies. The businesses were either stolen or some paltry sums were handed over. In this book there are examples of this vile practice occurring all over occupied Europe, including Jersey. This activity meant that Jews lost their livelihood and means of support. They were unable to find work and therefore, in many cases, became destitute.

A recent exhibition held in Leipzig by the local City History Museum was entitled '"Aryanization" in Leipzig. Driven out. Robbed. Murdered'.[1] This seems a frank assessment of the fate of most Jews during the Nazi regime. In the introduction, the term 'Aryanization' is explained:

The policy promoted by the National Socialists for the 'Aryanization' of German society meant more than just the destruction of a segment of the population which, since the mid-1800s, had played an increasingly important role in the development of German culture and economy. The implementation of this racist policy was characterised, above all, by the vast transfer of Jewish companies and institutions into 'Aryan' hands committed by the Nazi Regime, along with the change of ownership or liquidation of numerous medical practices, lawyers' offices, antique shops, art galleries, banks, department stores and factories. In the end, the methodical confiscation of property took everything of value or which could be assigned a value: houses, land, even synagogues and Jewish cemeteries, along with books, stamp collections, jewellery and art objects of every kind, down to the last silver spoon. Everything was taken from the Jews and ended up in auction houses or in the Nazi coffers, which soon became merely a war chest.[2]

In the foreword to the printed papers of the 2001 Symposium, the bureaucratic nature of the process is described:

> These papers highlight a number of key aspects of the confiscation process. They focus on the seizure of private property such as bank accounts, securities, real estate, household items, and books, as distinct from the so-called Aryanization of businesses. Through a combination of special taxes, blocked accounts, and confiscatory decrees Jews were progressively robbed of their entire private means. Particularly impressive and equally disturbing is the robbers' effort to ensure that property confiscation was carried out by 'legal' means through a vast array of institutions and organizations set up for this purpose. The immensely bureaucratic nature of the confiscation process emerges from the vast archival trail that has survived. Arguments that no one knew about the Jews' fate become untenable once it is clear how many people were involved in processing their property. 'Legal' measures often masked theft, but blatant robbery and extortion through intimidation and physical assault were also commonplace.[3]

Aryanization was applied all over Europe. For example, on 28 December 1941 it was reported that the Aryanization of forty-three large Jewish-owned firms in Paris had been completed as the provisional administrators had been withdrawn. This had been announced on Paris radio.

> Included in the list are some of the large business houses of Paris, such as Brunswick Furs, Cecil Shoes, La Coeur Batave (one of the select department stores), the Grand Maison furniture store of the Boulevard de Sebastopol, and Hundred Thousand Shirts, one of the largest men's furnishing houses:
> Under a recent decree, proceeds from sale of Jewish property after a paying a 10 per cent tax for the benefit of impoverished Jews, goes in the name of the owner:
> The French Government has received the task of collecting a fine of 1,000,000,000 francs imposed on the Jewish community as part of the reprisals for aggressions against troops of occupation, it was also announced.
> Execution of 95 Jews amongst the hostages ordered shot at the same time that the billion franc fine was imposed, was reported earlier this week by the Paris correspondent of the Berne newspaper, *La Suisse*.[4]

Around the same time, Aryanization of Jewish property was being discussed in the Hungarian Parliament and it was reported on 16 December 1941 that it was meeting great difficulties. Deputy Dr Szindley told Count Nikolaus Serenyi, who had served a prison term for anti-Semitic agitation, that Hungary's economic life would be damaged by the implementation of the Serenyi Bill for the rapid exclusion of Jews from trade. Dr Szindley told the parliament:

> The solution of the Jewish question is not exclusively a political question, especially today, when we must consider the economic side of the question, not only in our own interests but also in the interest of the wartime trade of our allies. One could replace all the directors and big traders by Christians, but I am inclined to believe that trade would be damaged by this measure. It is impossible to reform trade so thoroughly by simply setting up a new list of names.[5]

It is significant that Hungary was not occupied by Germany until March 1944, so this was 'home-grown' anti-Jewish persecution.

I will now consider a few companies that were Aryanized.

## The C.F. Peters Music Publishing House

In the nineteenth century Leipzig became one of the leading centres for German music publishing. This helped C.F. Peters, a music publishing house owned from 1900 by Henri Hinrichsen, to become very successful. Hinrichsen became an important philanthropist who sponsored the opening of the Women's College in 1911, as well as a good businessman.

He also purchased a major collection of musical instruments for the University of Leipzig. In 1929 he was awarded an honorary doctorate by the University of Leipzig. Peters was a family business, and from 1931 Henri's sons, Max, Walter and Hans-Joachim, joined the company.

In March 1933, Hinrichsen became a target for discrimination and exclusion by the Music Publishers Association, and relationships with some writers began to change. In 1936 the firm was listed as one of seventeen Jewish music publishers approved by the Reich Chamber of Culture. Max and Walter left Germany, but Hans-Joachim stayed in Leipzig. On 10 November 1938 the firm's premises at 10 Tal Street were ransacked and copies of Felix Mendelssohn-Bartholdy's music were burnt in the company's courtyard.

(For the record, Felix Mendelssohn [1809–1847] was born in Hamburg, the grandson of the Jewish rabbi and philosopher, Moses Mendelssohn. Although Moses Mendelssohn frowned on German Jews converting to Christianity to gain social acceptance outside the ghettos, Mendelssohn's parents baptised their four children, including Felix, into the Lutheran Church. They, in turn, converted to the Lutheran faith in 1816, adding Bartholdy to their surname.)

A year later, on 15 November 1938, the State Commissioner wrote to Dr Hans-Joachim Hinrichsen telling him that the firm had been expelled from the Reichmusikkammer. C.F. Peters was then subject to compulsory Aryanization, organised by SS Leader Gerhard Noatzke, a trustee of the Reich Ministry for Public Enlightenment & Propaganda. In July 1939 the contract created two new partners, Kurt Hermann and Dr Johannes Petschull, the latter becoming the managing director. When Hinkel's letter arrived in November 1938, Hans-Joachim was in Sachsenhausen concentration camp, following Kristallnacht. He had been arrested with his father, but the older man was released after a week in Leipzig Prison. However, his son remained in the camp where the SS amused themselves by torturing the prisoners for six weeks. Many of the prisoners died or suffered serious injuries as a result – punishment, at the whim of an SS officer, was to hang a prisoner by the wrists tied behind his back until he died in agony. Many deaths resulted from such inhuman treatment, hard labour and starvation.

Henri's wife, Martha, wrote to Walter in America on 20 November 1938, after Henri's business, the entire collection of pictures and prints and autographed letters (which included letters from Beethoven, Brahms and Wagner), had been taken from them:

> The dice have fallen. The business was confiscated from us on Thursday afternoon, with immediate effect. None of us may enter the office … I have written of it to you immediately, but I wanted to wait until Hans returned. That seems to be taking a longer time, we have no idea where he has been taken, we only know that he is no longer in Leipzig, it is eight days since they came to fetch him. Ilse and Lotte are in the same state of ignorance about their husbands. Father is finding it terribly difficult to make the decision to emigrate, but it will be impossible to remain here, even he said that this morning. The whole affair is terribly difficult for Father who sees his life's work collapse like this – through no fault of his own … I cannot write in greater detail, I have to be careful because Hans is being held as a sort of hostage, that is why none of you must take any action on account of C.F. Peters.[6]

Noatzke's task was to act as interim custodian until a suitable Aryan purchaser could be found who understood music publishing. The Nazis were keen to keep the company as a profitable music publisher because of the foreign revenue for the Nazi coffers and also as a demonstration of pride in German culture. Noatzke was to review the applicants and complete the Aryanization. Henri found it difficult to cope with this on his own. With enormous courage and at risk of being arrested again, he demanded that Hans be released so they could deal with the compulsory handover together:

He said that unless his son was released, he would not co-operate. It must be credited to his determined stand that the 29-year-old Hans-Joachim was released from the incarceration and tortuous regime of Sachsenhausen. Emaciated and battered, he hid the true extent of his suffering from his mother and father.[7]

Max went to London in 1937, with his non-Jewish wife, and his baby daughter, Irene. He set up his own very successful music publishing business in London. The culmination of his career was when he was elected an Honorary Fellow of Trinity College of Music, London (Hon. FTCL), in July 1965 – the first music publisher to be honoured in the ninety-two years of the awards. The presentation ceremony at the Wigmore Hall, London, also honoured the conductor Sir Malcolm Sargent. Max died prematurely aged 64 on 17 December 1965. However, Irene became the family's chronicler, writing a massive history of the family firm called *Music Publishing and Patronage – C.F. Peters: 1800 to the Holocaust.* In the foreword, Yehudi Menuhin wrote that the book would enlighten 'the general reader who wants to know how destiny and history impinge on the human being'.

Henri Hinrichsen, with his wife Martha, left Leipzig in January 1940 quite destitute. They headed for Brussels and Hans followed two months later. They were unsuccessful in getting to America. Hans-Joachim died in a camp in France in Perpignan later that year; Martha died in Brussels in 1941 and Henri was deported to Auschwitz a year later, where he was gassed on 17 September 1942. After the war, the company was returned to the son, Walter, by the American occupying forces.[8] Walter's daughter, Martha Hinrichsen, told me that in fact the Russians expropriated the company and it was not restituted to the family until 1993 with the Peters Music Library.[9]

Irene also wrote a family history covering the period from burnings during the Spanish Inquisition to gassing at Auschwitz 500 years later. The story covers the martyrdom of ancestor Henrique de Milao who was burnt at the stake in Lisbon on 5 April 1609, aged 81. He had been imprisoned and tortured for two and a half years because as a converso or 'new Christian', as they were known in Portugal, 'he had been found guilty of secretly practising his allegedly heretical religion, Judaism, all his life'. As death approached, he stayed true to his faith:

The flames of religious bigotry and state-ordained terror that consumed Henrique in Catholic Portugal were a cruel foretaste of the terrible end that was to be inflicted upon his descendant and namesake, my grandfather Henri Hinrichsen, 333 years later in Nazi Germany, in the gas chambers of Auschwitz concentration camp.[10]

Thus, a successful family business was stolen from a hard-working, cultured and philanthropic family which itself was destroyed. This is the reality of the Nazis' policy of Aryanization.

Ironically, one of Henri's beloved pictures was in the Gurlitt haul discovered in Munich in 2013. Martha Hinrichsen was contacted in November 2013 and told that one of his drawings had been recovered. She has a letter from her father's lawyer detailing the forced sale of four artworks to Mr Gurlitt in 1940. At the top of the list is Carl Spitzweg's *Playing Piano*, which was in the Gurlitt haul.[11] Martha, who lives in Connecticut, said, 'We'll fight however long we can to get it back ... as we have since 1945 with my grandparents' properties confiscated by the Nazis in 1938–1940.'[12]

## Goldschmidt Bicycles

The Goldschmidt family could trace its family tree back to David Goldschmidt, living in Sulzbürg village in Bavaria in the 1650s where he fathered sixteen children. Early in the nineteenth century his family started an ironmongery business there. Around 1862 the business was moved to nearby Neumarkt by brothers Joseph and Adolf (1848–1899), trading as Goldschmidt & Sohn.[13]

By the 1870s the business was doing well, selling solid fuel stoves of their own manufacture, weighing machines, rails and building materials of all sorts. In 1880, an apprentice, Carl Marschütz, with the help of Joseph, acquired an English penny-farthing bicycle which caused a sensation in the town. The next year, with the help of a cycle mechanic called Pirzer, Carl persuaded Joseph to start making bicycles on the shop premises. This venture was so successful that by 1882 Goldschmidt & Pirzer was flourishing and in 1884 their 'Express' bicycles were so popular they built a large factory on the outskirts of Neumarkt. By 1885, the firm was Gebrüder Goldschmidt (Goldschmidt Brothers), becoming a public company, Expresswerke A-G, in 1896. Ernest Goldschmidt wrote:

> Express bicycles were the first bicycles to be manufactured on the European continent, an achievement in which Neumarkt takes great pride today. Our family's part is also not forgotten, because on the outskirts of Neumarkt there is now a long winding street which is called the Goldschmidt Strasse.

The company expanded by moving to Nuremberg in 1897, and branches were opened in Wels, near Linz in Austria, and also in Munich. The Goldschmidt family were prominent in the local Jewish community and were generous benefactors. The firm celebrated Ludwig's silver jubilee on 1 May 1937.[14] Perhaps the celebration was premature, but the factory had put the town on the map. It is not known when Goldschmidt Strasse was named, but it was there until the Nazis removed it in 1938.[15]

Ernest Goldsmith (1922–2001), born Ernst Goldschmidt in Nuremberg on 19 March 1922, was the middle son, with Fred born in 1921 and Harry born in 1928. His father, Ludwig, son of Adolf, had fought in the First World War and was awarded the Iron Cross. Sophie, his mother, left Heidelberg University in 1914 to become a nurse. She too had a medal for her service in a hospital throughout the war. Obviously both had demonstrated their loyalty to their native land. Their home was on Tiergartenstrasse 66 (now Parsifalstrasse):

> The Tiergartenstrasse house overlooked the park where the Nazi rallies were held and from the balcony the Goldschmidts could watch and hear Hitler's enthusiastic supporters cheering themselves hoarse and saluting their leader as he stood above them on a dais, spectacularly lit by torches against the night sky, telling them (among other things) what a great nation Germany would be if they got rid of the Jews.[16]

Ernest went to the Reformrealgymnasium in Nuremberg, but he was always in trouble for not working hard like his brothers. There was, however, little encouragement as the teachers never gave the Jewish boys good marks. He did learn some English. The Jewish boys did not mix with the Aryans at school because it was not considered good to have Jewish friends, and anyhow they were all involved with the Hitler Youth. The Jewish boys therefore started their own youth club for sporting and hiking activities.

In 1937, just before Ernest's fifteenth birthday, a photographer came to the school to take the annual school photograph. Afterwards he asked if he could take photos of two individual boys. Ernest did not realise he was chosen because he was Jewish, but his father was cross that he had not disappeared like the other Jewish boys. Ernest's photograph was published in Fritz Fink's *Die Judenfrage im Unterricht* (*The Jewish Question in Education*) and then reprinted by Julius Streicher in *Der Stürmer* in October 1937, No. 44. Ernest's photograph was shown alongside one of a fair Nordic boy, whom Streicher claimed represented the true German while Ernest was the alien Jew. *Die Stürmer* had a large circulation and was also posted on street corners, so poor Ernest was often recognised and shouted at in the streets. Accordingly, Ludwig took him out of school and put him to work in the stove factory.[17]

The restrictions on Jews began to increase and Sophie tried to persuade Ludwig to leave Germany, but he was reluctant to become a refugee, knowing the Nazis would not let him take any money with him. However, he did send Fred, his eldest son, to England after he was stoned by some of the boys at his school.

The Goldschmidts' housekeeper lived in the basement of the house with her husband. As she was over 50 this did contravene the legislation on Aryan women staff. On 9 November 1938 (Kristallnacht), she was woken by hammering on the front door:

> It was the Brown Shirts. Threatening to break the door down if she did not let them in, they entered and wrecked the house, breaking up furniture and smashing china. Many of them were young and drunk. Some amused themselves by slashing a feather bed. As they had already broken the windows, the bedroom was soon full of feathers swirling in the wind. Another boy wandered about waving a knife before cutting a gash in the portrait of Sophie's father. It was a terrifying experience. The next morning the SS came to arrest Ludwig but went away when Sophie told them he was not in the house. They did however arrest Sophie's brother Ernst who lived alone and had no one to lie for him. He was sent to Buchenwald where he died.

Ludwig had already decided the family must emigrate after the factory was Aryanized in 1937 – they were forced to sell it for considerably less than it was worth. The bicycle factory had been sold many years before and the firm had returned to making stoves. Netta Goldsmith wrote, 'The fact that the Goldschmidts employed mostly Aryan workers and treated them well made no difference.'[18] He had already applied for visas for England, where he had studied as a young man. Kristallnacht made the move more urgent. He sent the two remaining boys ahead to England, travelling with his friend Sigmund Oppenheimer's three daughters.[19]

In 1998 Ernest was invited back to celebrate the centenary of the first bicycle factory in Europe, and by then the street name of Goldschmidtstrasse had been restored. Ernest was accompanied by Netta and other members of the Goldsmith family. They were well received. No one present was old enough to have been involved in persecution of the Jews and they were clearly embarrassed by the Nazis. The mayor gave a speech saying the bicycle factory had brought employment to the town and put it on the map. Netta met three old men who had worked for the old Goldschmidts. They met every month to chat about their time at Express–Werke and have a few beers – it had been OK, they said.

Ernest missed the country he had been born in, where the customs and food were familiar – he loved potato dumplings, though Netta did not understand why. As he and Netta drove home across Germany, he kept on making detours to visit towns and cafés where he had once stayed or enjoyed a meal with his parents. Many of the restaurants he remembered were still there. He also took Netta to several wine cellars in Bavaria to taste the latest vintage and stock up. Sophie's father had been a wine merchant and the whole family were connoisseurs.[20]

Ernest made a new life in England with a wife, daughter and two granddaughters. He died of pneumonia in December 2001 in Tunbridge Wells.

## The Alligator Leather Goods Company

Adolph and Nathan Schmidt started their leather handbag and travel goods business in Offenbach before the First World War. Offenbach was the centre of the German leather goods industry. After the war they opened six shops in the main German cities trading as 'Alligator', and in 1932 another chain of shops was opened which traded as '5 PS', which stood for '5 price ranges'. At the same time the company opened a factory in London, and three members of the Offenbach team were sent to run the company. This was a wise move as, on 1 April 1933 when the Nazis boycotted Jewish shops, they were targeted and photo No. 16 shows the members of the SA outside a shop with a placard reading:

> Germans, Attention! This shop is owned by Jews. Jews damage the German economy and pay their German employees starvation wages. The main owner is the Jew Nathan Schmidt.[21]

The significance of the wording is that already the Jews were being denied their German nationality – already, on 1 April 1933, you could not be both a German and a Jew.

Members of the family gradually left Germany in the 1930s, particularly after the factories and shops were Aryanized. One couple, Sydney and Barbara Amerikaner, left Berlin in 1938 with their 2-year-old daughter, Franceska.[22] The story I was told appears in Franceska's obituary.

On reaching the border Sydney was arrested.[23] His wife, fearful of what would happen, telephoned Mrs Hermann Göring, who had been a good customer in their shop, and as a result he was released and they managed to get to London. Peter Smith, a member of the family, suggested that Barbara, who was not Jewish, had been an actress, as had Emmy Göring before her marriages. He suggested that was how they knew each other – in any event, their relationship saved Sydney from his intended fate.

The family moved north to Darlington, as the government was offering funds to encourage employers to provide jobs in the north though the Commissioners for Special Areas. The Schmidts chose Bishop Auckland where four factories were planned, and Alligator started producing handbags in August 1938. Unfortunately a good start was sabotaged by a fire which broke out on 19 November 1938 and badly damaged the factory and the adjoining button factory of Ernest & Henry Ltd, also a refugee business.[24] According to the *Northern Echo*, 350 workers were temporarily out of work as a result of the fire, 250 from the Alligator factory.[25] The cause of the fire was not established, but surprisingly the local press did not mention the two factories were run by Jewish refugees, even though there was a great deal on the plight of Jews in Europe in the copies of the *Northern Echo* for late 1938.

## Nivea

The Nivea story was perhaps one of the most interesting cases I found. It concerns Beiersdorf AG, the pharmaceutical company which created Nivea Crème. The firm had been founded by two Jews and a Christian in Hamburg.

Oscar Troplowitz (1863–1918) started work in a pharmacy and, after studying in Breslau and Heidelberg, he gained a doctorate in 1888. He then worked in the pharmacy of his uncle, Gustav Mankiewicz, in Posen. Meanwhile, Carl Paul Beiersdorf opened a pharmacy in Altona, on the outskirts of Hamburg, and a laboratory in Hamburg. He worked with a young Jewish doctor, Paul Gerson Unna, to patent medical innovations to cure skin problems. The success of this partnership led Beiersdorf to concentrate on the laboratory alone. Tragically, in 1890 his 16-year-old son committed suicide and he was so distressed he sold out to Oscar in October 1890. Oscar kept the Beiersdorf name.

Troplowitz was a good businessman as well as a good researcher. Around 1900 he created a paste from a powder that his own dentist gave to his patients to clean their teeth. Troplowitz arranged to have it packaged in tubes to increase its shelf life and thus created the first commercial toothpaste in a tube.

> On Dr Unna's recommendation, calcium chloride was added to the recipe to make the new product effective against infections and inflammations of the mouth. The toothpaste was called 'Pebeco' and its first adverts urged daily dental hygiene. Within five years, Pebeco was Beiersdorf's bestselling product and eventually it became the first to sell more than one million units.[26]

Beiersdorf Pebeco toothpaste was soon sold worldwide. After years of research Troplowitz created Hansaplast, which is known outside Germany as Elastoplast – this development took many years because of the difficulties of creating a plaster that caused no irritation to the skin. His colleague, Unna, developed the standard treatment for skin ulcers, Unna Paste, and a nourishing skin cream which was called Nivea.[27] The name was not new as they had sold Nivea soap since 1905 – the name comes from the Latin for 'snow'.

When the Nazis introduced their boycott of Jewish businesses Beiersdorf was targeted because of the two successful Jews, Troplowitz and Unna – even though neither was still alive. Another Hamburg firm, Queisser & Co., manufactured a rival cream called Lovana. It had never been as popular as Nivea but the owner, Alfred Queisser, thought his hour had come. He launched a new slogan, 'Do not use Jewish skin creams any longer. Lovana is at least as good, cheaper and pure German!' He also had 10,000 stickers produced which said, 'Whoever buys a Nivea product supports a Jewish firm'.

Alfred Queisser was persistent in his efforts, and wrote to 'his esteemed customers' saying, 'our business is 100 per cent Aryan and nationalist'. He would visit pharmacies wearing his NSDAP party badge.[28] However, the campaign failed and Nivea maintained its position, purchased by both Jews and Nazis. Such support for 'the Jewish crème' must have been a source of displeasure to the Nazis.

The virulently anti-Semitic newspaper, *Der Stürmer*, published an attack on Nivea and the Beiersdorf Company in August 1933. The article and a full translation can be seen in Appendix D. This extract gives a flavour of the tone:

> … Beiersdorff was simply crawling with Jews while its travelling salesmen were exclusively German. By employing ruthless business methods and aggressive, typically Jewish advertising campaigns the company elbowed its way to the top of the German market leaving hardly any room for other German firms.[29]

However, the boycott created fear and Jews began to leave the company. Two members of the board resigned, including the chairman, and Unna's son, Dr Eugen Unna, also resigned even though he was, in Nazi terms, only half-Jewish. The financiers M.M. Warburg withdrew their partners from the board and their financial control. A new head, Carl Claussen, was appointed, but Beiersdorf was still not really Judenfrei because he was married to Troplowitz's niece. However, Beiersdorf declared itself 'a German business', and so Nivea and Elastoplast could be freely used.[30] Claussen headed the firm until the mid-1950s. As a result of successfully tackling these problems, Nivea's sales rose remarkably during the 1930s. Between 1934 and 1939 the domestic sales rose from RM14 million to RM26 million.[31]

Troplowitz had always been concerned about his workers' social welfare and was regarded as a model employer. Hours of work were first reduced to fifty-two and then in 1912 to forty-eight without loss of earnings. Women did not lose their employment when they became pregnant, as was then usual; a room was set aside so they could breastfeed their babies. Paid vacations and free warm midday meals were other innovations. A social fund, contributed to in part by the workers, provided additional help in case of sickness, marriage, burial and other costly events. What was unusual was that the workers were given control of decisions, though under Troplowitz's watchful eye.[32]

This was remarkably forward-thinking. In the UK, Marks & Spencer, regarded as the most employee-minded firm for many years, did not provide subsidised lunches until the 1930s Depression. In his memoirs, Lord Marcus Sieff, grandson of one of the founders, Michael Marks, explained that when his father and uncle were visiting a store they saw a salesgirl looking unwell. Although she claimed to be all right, his father made enquiries about her and discovered both her father and brothers were out of work and her wages were inadequate to feed the whole family properly. He wrote:

> Unemployment benefits were small in those days, not enough to keep people above the poverty line, and members of a family like our salesgirl's did not have

enough to eat. Simon and Father agreed that no one who worked for us must go
hungry and they installed kitchens and rest-rooms in every store where a midday
three-course meal cost 6d ...[33]

Troplowitz lived an active and full life in Hamburg. His father, Simon Ludwig
(also known as Louis 1825–1913), was a master mason, who built the synagogue in their hometown Gleiwitz (now Gliwice). It was apparently quite
magnificent, but was destroyed during Kristallnacht.[34] Oscar had wanted to be
an architect but had to leave school early. Once his firm was well established,
Oscar became involved in local politics at the Hamburg Legislative Assembly
and sat on various committees from 1905. He was keen to see improvements in
primary education and road traffic safety, and to increase the number of parks
in Hamburg. Accordingly, he supported the development of the Stadtpark and
was able to influence the changing cityscape.[35] He was very charitable, but not
just to Jewish charities – it is recorded that he supported both the Catholic and
Jewish hospitals.[36]

As he became more successful he devoted more time to fine arts. A Berlin
architect, William Müller, designed a villa for him on Agnesstrasse in 1908. He
gave parties there for artists and intellectuals and began collecting pictures. A trip
to Paris in 1909 introduced him to modern art and over the next few years he
created a fine collection of modern and impressionist art. He was one of the first
private German collectors to buy a work by Picasso, *The Absinthe Drinker*, and also
collected bronze sculptures by Arthur Bock.

When he died of a stroke in April 1918 at the premature age of 55, he owned
ninety works of art in his villa and a similar number at his estate in Westensee.[37]
His will showed he had left twenty-six of his most valuable paintings to Hamburg's
Kunsthalle Museum. These included the Picasso, which had hung above his desk.[38]
This was a remarkable bequest and meant the Hamburg Museum was one of the
first German museums with a Picasso. The gallery's director, Gustav Pauli, expressed
his gratitude for this wonderful gift in 1920, saying:

> The acquisition of these precious paintings enriches the Kunsthalle like no other
> has done in a long time. This donation will ensure that Dr Troplowitz and his
> wife will be remembered with gratitude by all who care about the cultivation
> of art in Hamburg.[39]

Pauli's optimism was quite misplaced. The 7 April 1933 Law for the Restoration of
the Professional Civil Service permitted the dismissal of Jewish individuals or those
who were politically 'unreliable'. Accordingly, twenty-seven museum directors and
professors from art academies were dismissed and Pauli was one of them.[40] He died
in Munich in 1938.

Oscar's Picasso had a chequered history. It was bought from the artist by the writer Gertrude Stein in Paris in 1906 and it hung in the home she shared with her brother, Leo, in Paris until 1913. It was then held by the German gallery owner Daniel-Henry Kahnweiler, who sent it to the Caspari Gallery in Munich. It was here that Oscar Troplowitz purchased it in 1914. Oscar's widow Gertrude died in 1920. Her sister, Valerie Alport (1874–1960, née Mankiewicz), was her heir. Her husband, Leo Alport, was chairman of the Beiersdorf board but died in 1935. The Nazis seized the picture from the Kunsthalle in 1937 because they regarded it as 'degenerate art'. I have been unable to find information on this particular seizure, but there is a description of a similar event at the Kunsthalle in Mannheim:

On July 8 1937, quite without warning, Professor Adolf Ziegler arrived at the Kunsthalle in Mannheim, with two assistants and brandished a piece of paper with Goebbels' signature on it. Professor Ziegler, Nazidom's number-one painter, was known to the opposite faction as 'The Master of the Pubic Hair' for his meticulously detailed nudes. He was authorised by a special order from the Fuehrer to 'secure' all paintings and sculptures of 'degenerate' German art since 1910 that were in the possession of the Reich and of any Laender or individual municipalities.[41]

All confiscated works were taken to a Berlin warehouse and then stored in Niederschonhausen Castle in 1939. The Picasso was scheduled for sale at the infamous Fischer Gallery auction in Lucerne as Lot No. 116 with an estimate of 73,500 Swiss francs, making it the third most valuable picture in the sale.[42] Prospective purchasers were suspicious about the sale, perceiving the proceeds would go into Nazi coffers. The auctioneer, Theodore Fischer, sent a mailing denying these rumours. 'He reassured everyone that proceeds from the sale would go to German museums and would enable them to buy other works. But few believed him.'[43]

The Fischer Gallery sale offered 125 works, at the Hotel National on 30 June 1939. However, the Picasso was not sold. Valerie Alport, who was an avid art collector in her own right, had emigrated to London in 1937. She took out an injunction against both the Hamburg Kunsthalle and the Galerie Fischer and the picture was confiscated in Lucerne. Further legal action was brought against the German Reich. Alport argued that the Picasso had been left to the people of Hamburg and accordingly the German Reich had no authority to sell it. However, in May 1940 the Lucerne District Court dismissed the case.[44]

The auction had been well advertised, causing considerable controversy. *The Burlington Magazine* covered it in its May 1939 section on 'Forthcoming Sales'. The sale was called 'Paintings and Sculptures by Modern Masters: from German Museums'. It is not clear how much the writer knew about the background of the sale, as the article concludes:

All the works mentioned come from German Museums. They were 'purged' on account of their alleged 'degenerate' and 'bolshevist' character. Revolutions have often in the past led to the dispersal of art collections and thus aroused interest in particular schools of art in new quarters. There is little doubt that in the present case new admirers will be found for these rejected works in an atmosphere free from political prejudice.[45]

Following the dismissal of the Alport case, the painting was immediately taken to the German Embassy in Berne. It was sent to Mecklenberg, having been purchased by the art dealer Bernard Böhmer from the German Reich. However, soon it was returned to Theodor Fischer.[46]

Troplowitz's Picasso was eventually bought by the Othmar Huber Foundation in 1942 for 42,000 Swiss francs. Othmar Huber was an optician from Glarus, who in the 1930s started collecting avant-garde artists who were being ostracised by the Nazis. The foundation has owned the painting ever since, but it has been on loan to the Kunstmuseum in Bern since 1979.

When I first read about this picture, I wondered whether it was the same picture that Andrew Lloyd Webber auctioned at Christie's for £34.7 million in June 2010. However, it appears that Picasso painted several pictures of absinthe drinkers and the one Oscar owned was painted in 1902 and is sometimes called the *Bouveuse Assoupie*.[47]

Valerie Alport's son was Erich Alport, the poet. He became a friend of Stephen Spender (1901–1995) when both were students at University College Oxford. Spender came up in 1927 but left without a degree. Spender, whose mother was Jewish, spent the summer of 1929 at the Alport family home in Germany. In an undated letter, he wrote to Isaiah Berlin about Hitler edging closer to power:

> I cannot exaggerate the seriousness of the political situation in Germany. It looks as if the whole system … will break down and that, in December, after another general election, all people of Jewish extraction will be shot, all foreigners will be turned out of the country and all the poor boys will be shipped off to Heligoland or somewhere to break stones.[48]

In 1932 T.S. Eliot sent Erich a draft of Spender's semi-autobiographical novel, *The Temple*, which Faber & Faber were considering publishing. The novel was based on Spender's experiences, including an unflattering portrait of Erich Alport as the character Ernst Stockman. An infuriated Alport reported that he would sue for libel anyone who published the book. *The Temple* was not published until 1988.[49]

Other unflattering remarks were written by the publisher Christopher Hurst, who knew Erich and his mother around 1950 in Oxford. He claimed that Valerie's connection with the family that made Nivea Crème was 'a source of amusement to the many people who despised Erich'.[50] It appears that Erich had several of Gertrude Stein's books in his collection and his college has speculated that this was because 'both were from German-Jewish backgrounds, both were gay, both collected contemporary art'.[51] I wonder whether he was aware that the Picasso painting his mother fought so hard to protect had once belonged to Gertrude Stein?

I must confess to finding some irony in the fact that I started writing about Troplowitz because his company was Aryanized and pilloried after his death because of its Jewish connections. I then discovered that one of his pictures suffered the same fate, even after he had left it to the citizens of his adopted hometown, together with another twenty-five of his finest pieces. Truly he was betrayed twice – both his scientific and commercial ingenuity and his personal generosity to his adopted city counted for nothing in the face of the Nazi onslaught against the Jews.

As he had painted in his youth, Hitler regarded himself as an expert on art especially when the Nazis' developed their concept of 'degenerate art'. In June 1934 Hitler had his first meeting with Mussolini in Venice. It was not a success. Hitler wanted to visit the Biennial International Art Exposition and asked the Italian Ambassador's wife, Elisabetta Cerruti, to accompany him. She recorded the visit in her memoir:

> Italian contemporary art is, of course, modern in theme and execution, precisely the kind of art he despised most. As we walked through the gallery, he did not utter a word, either of praise or condemnation, but disgust was written on every feature of his face. His mood melted into enthusiasm, however, when we entered the German pavilion. There he paused, entranced, before the most atrociously banal paintings, things that looked like gaudy, oil-tinted photographs. He had no understanding of art and was irritated by anything that bore a mark of human feeling or imagination. It was due entirely to his personal intervention that many modern masterpieces from German museums and private collections were later sold at public auction for ridiculous prices.[52]

## Restitution

The fact that these cases were still being raised in the courts in 2015 – seventy years after the end of the Holocaust – shows how powerful the feelings of injustice are for victims, even in subsequent generations. It is also a demonstration of the scale of the Nazis' theft from Jewish collectors.

A 1570 painting by El Greco, *Portrait of a Gentleman*, belonged to a Viennese-Jewish industrialist, Julius Priester. He fled Vienna with his wife in 1938, leaving his collection of fifty paintings with a friend. However, after the *Anschluss* the collection was looted by the Nazis and twenty-one of the works are still missing. After the portrait had travelled round the world it was finally reunited with its rightful owner, who lives in the UK. It had been put up for sale in New York in 2014 but the vendor, an anonymous dealer, returned it to the heirs of Priester when it was demonstrated to have been looted.

The picture's wanderings were caused by an Austrian dealer selling it to a New York dealer in 1954, claiming it was a newly discovered work. Anne Webber, of the Commission for Looted Art in Europe, explained that the dealer's reaction 'was in stark contrast to the attitude of a Swiss trust that had previously held the painting but repeatedly refused to answer requests to discuss it'. She concluded:

> The story of the seizure and trade of this painting over a period of more than 60 years shows how much the art trade has been involved in the disposal of Nazi-looted art and how difficult it is for those who have been dispossessed to find and recover their property.[53]

In April 2015 a film opened about the remarkable Maria Altmann's fight with the Austrian Government for the return of the five Klimt paintings stolen from her family by the Nazis after the *Anschluss*:

> 'They say now Austria was a victim of the Nazis,' Maria says, shaking her head scornfully. 'Believe me, there were no victims. The women were throwing flowers, the church bells were ringing. They welcomed them with open arms. They were jubilant.' Maria was in her apartment when she noticed some Nazis outside, pushing her new car from the garage. Next a Gestapo officer rang the bell and demanded her jewelry. He took her engagement ring from her finger. Adele's diamond necklace was handed over to Hitler's right-hand man, Hermann Göring, as a gift for his wife.[54]

Emmy Göring apparently wore the necklace to Nazi parties; it was never recovered.

The distinguished British actress, Helen Mirren, plays Maria Altmann in a new film, *Woman in Gold*, after the wonderful portrait of Altmann's aunt, Adele Bloch-Bauer, painted by Klimt in 1907. She told the BBC, 'We show in this film the art becomes a symbol of a stolen life and stolen memories.'

Altmann fought all the way to the US Supreme Court to get the picture back in 2006 when she was 89, and she died five years later. The Austrians begged her to drop the case, calling the picture, when it hung in the Belvedere museum, 'Austria's Mona Lisa'. Maria sold the painting in 2006 to Estée Lauder's heir, Ronald Lauder, for an alleged $135 million, at the time the highest price paid for a painting.

There is some irony in the fact that Adele, who predeceased her husband, Ferdinand, aged 45 in 1925, asked Ferdinand in her will to leave the Klimt paintings to the Austrian gallery. However, the Nazis seized them seven years before

Ferdinand's death and Ferdinand's own will from 1945 left the pictures to his heirs, including Maria Altmann.

The film was launched at the 65th Berlin Film Festival in February 2015 and Helen Mirren spoke very emotionally about the story. She said her role in the film puts a spotlight on the slow rate of restitution of Nazi-looted Jewish property. She had visited the Belvedere and seen another Klimt, the haunting unfinished portrait of Amalie Zuckerkandl, who herself was killed at the Belzec extermination camp. Mirren fought her tears as she described how emotional she felt seeing the picture, 'to me that brings all of the whole story together in one image'. She also spoke of the response from the Viennese:

> Vienna was enormously welcoming to us to shoot – there was never any sense of resentment or anger or anything. They said 'we are grateful to Maria Altmann here in Vienna because she made us look at our past in a realistic way and take on board things that we had never taken on board before'.

Anne Webber spoke about a vague estimate of 100,000 looted works still unaccounted for. 'I can tell you that 90 percent of the thousands and thousands of works of art people are searching for still can't be found today. So that gives you an indication of how hard it is to obtain restitution.'[55]

A footnote to the Altmann case is that her American lawyer was Randol Schoenberg, grandson of the famous composer Arnold Schoenberg, who himself 'fled in the middle of the night from Berlin in May 1933 several weeks after Nazi Culture Minister Josef Goebbels announced that Jewish artists and intellectuals had to be expelled from all German universities and cultural institutions'. His maternal grandparents fled after Kristallnacht. Randol continued:

> My grandparents left behind them not only their careers and the cultural institutions that had supported them but also large numbers of their extended families, among them my great-grandfather Siegmund Zeisl [1871–1942], who was later deported from Vienna to Theresienstadt and murdered at Treblinka.[56]

Randol Schoenberg is the president of the Los Angeles Museum of the Holocaust and recalls going back to Vienna with his maternal grandmother, Gertrude Zeisl (1906–1987), when he was a teenager:

> Gamma we called her, was nearly always happy, really never sad, morose, angry or mean. But as we rode the train into Austria she became misty-eyed and said, 'I'll never forgive them for not letting us live here'. She loved her Austrian homeland. She was 33 when the Nazis came and she was forced to flee, on the day after Kristallnacht. To her dying day she thought of herself as an Austrian ...[57]

## Berlin Zoo

Perhaps if one were minded to write an A–Z of Nazism, the Aryanization of Berlin Zoo would be an apt topic. Monika Schmidt, from the Centre for Research on Anti-Semitism in Berlin, reported on her findings in December 2013.

Ms Schmidt discovered that the zoo used to have shareholders who, in lieu of dividends, received free entry to the zoo for their families and the satisfaction of supporting a prestigious social institution. At the time, the zoo was an important Berlin meeting place. In the 1930s there were about 4,000 shareholders, of whom a quarter were Jewish. Ms Schmidt said, 'They were pushed out step by step by the zoo itself, before the Nazi state asked any institution to do those things.' In 1938 the Jewish shareholders were forced to sell their shares back to the zoo, unsurprisingly for less than their value. The zoo then sold the shares to Aryans.

She discovered Jochanan Asriel, now aged 89, whose grandfather was a shareholder. As a boy, Asriel lived close enough to the zoo to go on his bicycle. He said:

> I went there every day in the afternoon, and there was a big coffee house in the open where they served beer. Every day there was another orchestra playing. I remember all the animals, and I remember where they were placed, I don't remember what I ate yesterday, but what I remember from the zoo, I remember very well.

Asriel fled Germany in 1939 when still a teenager and now lives in Haifa in Israel.

The zoo's history was ignored until a retired sociology professor from New York, Werner Cohn, wrote in 2000 asking about his father's shares. The zoo's lawyers' response stated that there was 'neither force, nor compulsion' in the transfer of shares from the Jews to non-Jews, so Cohn put it on the internet. This interested the German media and Monika Schmidt's first investigation was commissioned by the zoo itself. She discovered not only the sale of the shares and the removal of the Jewish board members, but the barring of Jewish visitors to the zoo from 1939. A plaque commemorating the Jewish shareholders was erected in 2011 and the documenting of their lives in a book is being enthusiastically pursued by the zoo.[58]

While the zoo's actions pale in comparison with Nazi atrocities, Johannes Tuchel, professor of political science at the Free University of Berlin, has commented, 'It's very important to see that this discrimination and these Nazi crimes were done not only by *some* people, but in all parts of society'. It demonstrates that nowhere was safe for Jews, with even the city's most simple pleasures being denied.

Lothar (now Larry) Orbach described visiting the zoo one bright sunny day in June 1943 when he was 19, with two friends, one of whom was Aryan:

It was such a glorious day that we decided to stop at the Zoologische Garten, Berlin's immaculate and beautifully landscaped zoo. We looked like three young Germans on summer holiday, slurping on Langanese Ice and wandering among the mothers and children. Everyone was friendly and we exchanged pleasantries about the weather and the monkeys, anything. A hyena screeched, a lion roared. Children of all ages skipped and twirled and chortled around us, their clothes pressed and their golden hair gleaming. They looked so happy and well-cared for.

But where, where were all the Jewish children, on this sundrenched day so perfect for an outing? The zoo suddenly became sinister. Tad and Erika and I looked at each other and could read each other's thoughts: these animals, well fed in their clean cages, are better off than the Jews of Berlin, because the Nazis consider them higher forms of life than us. Wordlessly, we left the park. The chestnut trees were budding and flower boxes outside the apartment windows were sprouting lilies, marigolds, pansies, peonies – but the beauty and normalcy that surrounded me felt like an affront. How could flowers bloom when people were dying?[59]

The spiteful exclusion of the Jews from the zoo reminded me of the 'park bench' ruling. Stefan Zweig wrote movingly about his 84-year-old mother's distress in Vienna:

> ... she was not very good on her legs, and when she took her little daily consti-tutional, after some five or ten minutes' walking with some difficulty she used to sit down and rest on a bench beside the Ringstrasse or in the park. Hitler had not been master of the city for a week before brutal orders were given that no Jew must sit on any park bench – one of those prohibitions obviously and exclusively designed for the sadistic purpose of maliciously tormenting people ... But forbidding an old lady or an exhausted elderly gentleman to rest for a couple of minutes on a bench was reserved for the twentieth century and the man adored by millions as the greatest of his age.[60]

I remember my mother saying how, in Budapest in 1944, her father, Armin Klein, also suffered from the same edict.

It is interesting to contrast the situation at the Warsaw Zoo in 1940, where the director, Jan Zabinski, and his wife, Antonina, hid 300 Jews in the underground pathways that connected the animals' cages. Zabinski was a member of the Polish Resistance and also hid munitions at the zoo. His wife used to play a particular tune on her piano to warn the Jews to remain quiet in time of danger; later she played another tune as a sign the danger was over. In April 2015 a small museum, with Antonina's piano, will be opened at the zoo to honour the Zabinskis, who were recognised as 'Righteous among the Nations' in 1965. Moshe Tirosh, 78, who was hidden as a 3½ year old with his parents, will return from Israel to 'pay homage to the couple that saved my life'.[61] See photos 17 and 18.

## Aryanization of Pedlars in Amsterdam

Aryanization took place at all levels – even market traders were affected. In the early 1930s in Amsterdam peddling was one of the few occupations open to those who had become unemployed due to the depression since 1929. No particular skills were required, nor much start-up capital. Between 1930 and 1935 the number of pedlars rose from 5,475 to 7,184.

On 1 September 1934 the municipal council imposed new conditions, with vendors' licences only available to those who were holding them before September 1933. Additionally, in future there would be a charge. This resulted in a fall in the number of pedlars as they turned to being a standholder (having a permanent stall within the market) or market vendor (unofficial trader dealing in the market area) instead.[62] The numbers of these increased.

| Trade | Date | Numbers |
| --- | --- | --- |
| Pedlars | 1 January 1935 | 7,184 |
| | 1 January 1936 | 5,527 |
| | 1 January 1940 | 3,500 |
| | September 1941 | 2,000 |
| Standholders | 1 January 1935 | 419 |
| | 1 January 1940 | 640 |
| Market vendors | 1 January 1935 | 1,600 |
| | 1 January 1940 | 2,000 |

In 1940 there were six daily markets and four weekly markets in Amsterdam. They sold all sorts of goods: produce, plants, clothing, toys, radios, books, watches, bicycles and musical instruments. The Waterlooplein daily market was located in the Jewish area and, out of the 191 vendors, 181 were Jews. Not far away was the weekly Uilenburg Market, where 288 of the 336 vendors were Jewish. At the other markets Jews and non-Jews were about equal in number.

The Uilenburg Sunday Market was supposed to be a place for the Jewish vendors who have their Sabbath the day before. However, all the Jews I see there also do business on Saturday. You should see them with their cigars in their mouths, strolling along the stands, arrogantly noting the situation of those who are really slaving.

These are the words of Gustaaf Adolf Den Hartog, a Dutch National Socialist, who put himself forward in the summer of 1940 as the spokesman of the true 'slaves' – the Aryan vendors. After three months of the German occupation, Hartog and his comrades thought it was time for some anti-Jewish activity. They chose the weekly Amstelveld Market where they could rely on the support of the vendors who sympathised with their views. Week after week in the summer and autumn of 1940 they attacked the Jewish vendors, spread propaganda and fought the Amsterdam police, causing general disruption. They wanted segregated Jewish markets and the closure of the Uilenburg, which was the best Jewish market.

The local authorities were not opposed to Hartog's National Socialists, but disliked their hooliganism which disrupted law and order in the streets of Amsterdam. Reich Commissioner Dr J.H. Böhmcker had just arrived as Hartog started his activities, so the matter was dealt with by the local municipal council who said, in October 1940, there would be no separation in different markets and the Uilenburg would not be closed because of the cost of paying unemployment benefit to those who lost their stands.

The council did, however, agree to keep separate records for gentile and Jewish traders. 'This was the first time in its history that the council had made a distinction between Jewish and non-Jewish citizens – but it was not to be the last.'[63] In February 1941 Hartog's people, with strong support from Böhmcker, increased the attacks on the Jews. They targeted the old Jewish area with the Waterlooplein and Uilenburg markets. Of the 78,000 Jews in Amsterdam only 7,000 lived in that area, but the anti-Semites saw it as symbolic of the Jewish presence in the city and called it 'Palestine on the Amstel'.

On 11 February there was serious fighting between the National Socialists and the local inhabitants which resulted in Hartog's people being defeated and driven out of the area. However, on 19 February the Order Police (Ordungspolizei) allegedly were shot at by a 'gang of Jews'. Himmler was informed of this 'Jewish insolence' and ordered two round-ups in the Jewish neighbourhood. Accordingly, on 22 and 23 February, 425 Jewish men were arrested. This resulted in a general strike which lasted two days.

Mayor W. De Vlugt announced on 1 March that the Uilenburg Market on 2 March would not take place because of the circumstances. The Germans quickly replaced him with E.J. Voute, who sympathised with the National Socialists. He closed the market permanently in June 1941, meaning that all the Jewish vendors lost their business. Some found new stands at other markets but most were reduced to living on welfare.

On 22 October 1940 a national decree was issued. This had certain 'catch-all' aspects:

Businesses owned by Jews or having one Jewish partner or director, as well as enterprises with predominantly 'Jewish' capital or shareholders were obliged to register. 'Predominantly' did not merely signify the greater part: if as little as one-fourth of the capital belonged to Jews or if Jewish shareholders held half of the total votes, a business fell under the definition of predominantly Jewish 'influence'. Jews were, according to the decree, all persons whose grandparents included three or more or more full Jews by 'race'. Persons with only two fully Jewish grandparents were deemed to be Jewish if they had either belonged to the Jewish religious community as of 9 May 1940, or were married to a Jew as of that same date.

This decree also created the Wirtschaftsprüfstelle (Economic Accounting Office) Bureau for Economic Investigation which basically took over the assets of Jewish-owned business. On 30 November 1940, 19,000 Jewish businesses had been registered, but because of the confusion surrounding the definition of a Jewish company, the date was postponed to 30 December, at which point 20,690 had been registered. By 15 February 1941 the figure was 22,000, of which 65 per cent were in Amsterdam. Across the country 2,500 market vendors and pedlars had been registered, with around 1,700 of them in Amsterdam.

The Nazis then had to decide what to do with the Jewish businesses. The most profitable were taken over by Christians and then sold, with the proceeds transferred to a special bank – the Property Administration & Pension Institute (VVRA). The smaller businesses were not deemed suitable for Aryanization. They were seen as superfluous to the economy, would be liquidated and again the proceeds went to the VVRA.

However, Commissioner Böhmcker had his own agenda. On 25 April 1941, he told the municipal council that he was going to remove the Jewish pedlars' licences and he asked for a list of them. Although the council knew the licensed pedlars, they did not know which were Jewish. Creating such a list would take time, and by July when the annual licence renewals were due, it still had not been created. Accordingly the Jewish pedlars received new licences in July 1941.

Why was the council so reluctant – was it sympathy for the Jews, or anti-German feeling? So far the council had not opposed other anti-Jewish measures. The main reason was the costs involved through a loss of licence fees and welfare payments to be paid to the newly unemployed. For pedlars, these were calculated at 300,000 guilders for loss of fees and 300,000 for welfare payments. For market traders, the figures were 110,000 in lost fees and 540,000 in welfare payments. Böhmcker was delaying because as one of his collaborators stated:

An efficient Aryanization is only possible after having solved the problem of the lodging and the subsistence of the Jews. We have to decide whether we will deport them, or put them in a ghetto or on a reservation.

In general, Böhmcker did not plan strategically – he often announced plans, bullied those who delayed him and then failed to proceed. Sometimes he revoked plans or forgot about them. Thus, the plans for the Jewish pedlars were forgotten until 1942.

Following the September 1941 relicensing there were 2,000 pedlars, of whom 700 were Jews. The only Jewish traders affected were those evicted from the Uilenburg Market. There were 1,000 Jewish vendors working alongside 1,000 non-Jews at the other markets. On 15 September 1941, Himmler's representative, Rauter, announced a ban on all Jewish participation in markets and auctions. This meant the end of Jewish vendors and their customers in Amsterdam's markets.

But Böhmcker had designated three areas for Jews to be concentrated as a temporary measure for the Jewish problem, and therefore Jewish markets would be required in those areas. He persuaded Rauter to exempt them from the 15 September order. Rauter did not object and the council found three sites by 14 October.

In total, 1,000 Jewish vendors applied, but only 600 were required and the rest had to rely on welfare. The pedlars were only allowed to operate in the Jewish areas, so many were deprived of their livelihood. By November 1941, 2,372 Jews were living on benefits. The council and the mayor wanted the Jewish Community to support these people. Until this was possible, he wanted the unemployed put in a compulsory labour camp.

Böhmcker and Voute agreed that 1,600 Jews should sent to a camp in the east of Holland on 10 January 1942. Many people did not answer the summonses and there were difficulties in getting the numbers, which led Böhmcker to forbid all Jews from being pedlars. Sadly, such capricious decrees had the force of law under the Nazis.

He ordered the Amsterdam police to crack down on the illegal pedlars – his own agents were also active on the streets and on 21 March one of them, Inspector Fischer, caught a Jewish pedlar with an Aryan associate, who was arrested with all those still working on the streets. One man was found to be not only breaking Böhmcker's decree but selling inferior apples at more than the fixed price. This man was sent to Mauthausen concentration camp, as was Manus Fransman, arrested by the police on 19 May 1942 for illegally selling fish. The last few pedlars were being forced out of trade after hovering between a meagre income and social benefits since the 1930s.

On 23 July 1942, the Nazis in The Hague agreed that 2,839 itinerant traders' businesses were of no economic importance and their owners were to be liquidated and to report to the SD for deportation. The deportations started in mid-July, but not to the east of Holland. They were officially designated for Germany but Poland was their destination and forced labour was no longer on the agenda.

The Nazis justified Aryanization as a reorganisation of the economy – not theft. But there appeared to be no hurry and by 1945 the Aryanizations were far from complete. However, the Jews, themselves, had all gone.

## Small Businesses

Many small businesses also suffered under Aryanization. Inge-Ruth Poppert née Herrmann (1922–), born in Wolmirstedt to Otto and Regina Herrmann, spoke of the Aryanization of her father's business and how they had to move to Magdeburg in October 1935. Otto owned an apron factory with a non-Jewish business partner called Kurt Jäger in Magdeburg. One day Kurt turned on Otto, saying, 'You bloody Jew! Get out!' (the company was called Herrmann & Jäger Ltd). 'And he just kicked him out and he didn't get a penny.' The details of this event were not documented, but the partnership was dissolved and formally Aryanized in 1936. However, Otto Herrmann received no compensation for his share.[64]

John Rosenthal (1923–) grew up in Cologne, where his parents ran a small haberdashery shop. His mother also sold handknitted dresses. When his parents had finally made arrangements to leave Germany to go to America they tried to sell what had been a successful business. A woman who had been a governess to John and his elder brother, Max, had joined the Rosenthal business. She had been an important part of the family and an album she had made of the boys' childhood, illustrated by her brother, was the only item John had saved from his childhood. However, she betrayed the family. She had joined the Nazi Party and used her party connections to force the Rosenthals to transfer the business to her at a third of its true value. They reluctantly agreed, and were glad to have achieved any sum at all. However, John commented that it showed them 'the force of anti-Semitism from a former trusted family confidante'.[65]

Similarly, Estrea Asseo was arrested in Avignon, France, in 1944. She was betrayed when she bumped into a man called Lucien Blanc while she was in the street seeking food for her family. Blanc had worked for them at their Bouchara fabric shop in Avignon but they had to fire him when sales fell. He had joined the Nazis and although she offered to pay him he refused her pleas and reported her to the authorities. She was arrested, and on the train to Drancy she wrote to her husband that Lucien Blanc had betrayed her – a friendly train employee took the letter for her.

The journey to Drancy took several days. They were in a sealed cattle car, without food or water, hooked onto an ordinary passenger train. They arrived on 13 June 1944. On 30 June they set off for Auschwitz – this time it took five days in a sealed cattle car, with no space to move and again with no food or water. Most of the passengers were gassed on arrival, but a few, including Estrea, were sent to work. After the war her husband ensured that Lucien was arrested by the police and Estrea returned to France in May 1945 to testify at his trial. He was sentenced to death by firing squad.[66]

The Rosenthal Porcelain Company was also a victim of Aryanization because Philipp Rosenthal, who started the company with his wife, Maria, in 1884, was Jewish. Philipp Rosenthal began by purchasing white ware, which his wife hand painted and he sold door-to-door. In 1891, he established a factory in Asch, Bohemia, and began production of his own white ware. From 1897 to 1936, Rosenthal acquired several factories in Germany, and the popularity of patterns like 'Moss Rose' helped the business grow rapidly; by 1939, Rosenthal employed over 5,000 people.

As part of the Aryanization process the Nazis insisted that Jewish trademarks and firm names had to be removed. Göring had first demanded this at a conference on 12 November 1938, pointing out that Aryans who had kept these Jewish designations had been looted during Kristallnacht in error. He stated that the 'names of former Jewish firms shall have to disappear completely and the German shall have to come forward with his or his firm's name … All that is obvious.'

However, German businessmen were not happy because trademarks sold goods and were a valuable asset as part of the normal 'goodwill' on acquiring a business. Although the 'goodwill' of Jews had been eroded, no one liked losing something of value. The businessmen were disgruntled when the decree of 3 December 1938 permitted trustees to remove Jewish firms' names, and then on 27 March 1941 every purchaser of a Jewish business had to change the name of Jewish firms within four months. The minister concerned, the Justice Minister, insisted that all former Jewish owners were removed, whether they sounded Jewish or not. This decree caused a massive response with petitions, correspondence and conferences.

On 18 April 1941, the Rosenthal-Porzellan AG sent a letter to Goebbels asking him to exempt Rosenthal because it was not a question of a name, but the product's symbol (sachbegriff). Philipp Rosenthal had retired in 1933, but the family had never controlled more than 20 per cent of the shares. The name 'Rosenthal' had been a symbol of quality in porcelain for over fifty years. In any event, the name was changed in 1938 from 'Porzellanfabrick Philipp Rosenthal AG' to 'Rosenthal-Porzellan AG'.

The Propaganda Ministry sent the petition to the Justice Ministry with a favourable recommendation. This encouraged the firm to bombard the Justice Ministry with further information that the board (vorstand) had been fully Aryanized by 1933, that the aufsichtsrat (supervisory board) had been cleared of Jews in 1934, that the managing director had died and been replaced by his Aryan widow in the same year, and that the Rosenthal family had transferred its shares to Aryans by 1936.

The Justice Ministry conceded defeat. The order did not apply, because under the decree of 14 June 1938 which defined Jewish businesses, Rosenthal was not deemed to be a Jewish business. The decree stated that a business was Jewish if, in 1938, one-fourth of the shares were in Jewish hands, or on 1 January 1938 a Jew was on the vorstand or aufsichtsrat.

The Rosenthal case was particularly important because the Aryans who took over the firm would have been inclined to place anti-Jewish advertisements in newspapers. There was enormous opposition since, if the firm gave up its name, there was nothing to stop another firm adopting the name and benefitting from its reputation. In the end the Justice Ministry was completely defeated and in September 1941 it was decided to put the issue in abeyance until after the war.[67] Remarkably, after the Holocaust, Rosenthal's son, Philip, returned to Germany where he modernised the out-of-date factories and re-established lost markets.

The Wolff family had a property Aryanized in 1937. The building on 17/18 Krausenstrasse in Berlin was built by Dina Gold's maternal great-grandfather, Victor Wolff, and he ran one of the largest fur businesses in Germany from it. After he died, Dina's grandfather, Herbert Wolff, continued with the business but in the late 1920s Depression it became more of a rental block for other Jewish garment manufacturers. In 1937, Victoria Insurance, the company which held the mortgage on the building, foreclosed. Instead of auctioning the building to get the best price, it was bought at less than the full market value by the Reichsbahn – the German railways, which were to transport millions of Jews to their deaths in the Nazi camps. The chairman of the Victoria Insurance Company, which later was in a consortium insuring the buildings at Auschwitz, was Dr Kurt Hamann (1898–1981). Although not a Nazi Party member himself, he had close ties to those at the top of the party.

Herbert Wolff left for Palestine (now Israel) in May 1933 and his wife and three children followed him to Tel Aviv a few months later. Herbert's brother, Fritz, was a patriotic German and refused to leave. In 1943 he was deported and murdered in Auschwitz. At the end of the war, the property was in the Soviet sector of Berlin, very close to Checkpoint Charlie. Subsequently, it ended up on the wrong side of the Berlin Wall, and the family could not make a claim in East Germany.

Only in 1989, when the wall came down, was Dina able to find the building and start a claim on behalf of her mother and the other inheritors. They were successful in 1996 and the German Government bought the building from the family. It is now part of the Ministry of Transport. This is the first written account of a successful claim of a German property seized by the Nazis.[68]

Finally, the Nazis' Aryanization policy did not appear to have many Aryan objectors, as people mostly fell over themselves to exploit the Jews' predicament. The following presumably comes from a rare voice, a Munich merchant who had been employed as an expert consultant in Aryanization cases. The writer, who described himself as a 'National Socialist member of the SA and admirer of Adolf Hitler', stated in this letter:

[I] was so disgusted by the brutal ... and extortionary methods employed against Jews that, from now on, I refuse to be involved in any way in connection with

Aryanizations, although this means losing a handsome fee ... As an old, honest and upstanding businessman, I [can] no longer stand by and countenance the way many Aryan businessmen, entrepreneurs and the like ... are shamelessly attempting to grab up Jewish shops and factories as cheaply as possible and for a ridiculous price. These people are like vultures swarming down, their eyes are bleary, their tongues hanging out with greed, to feed upon the Jewish carcass.[69]

# 14

# BETRAYAL BY GOVERNMENTS

In our country the lie has become not just a moral category but a pillar of the state.

Alexander Solzhenitsyn (1918–2008), 1974 interview

Mistrust is worse than physical pain.

Lev Mishchenko in his first letter to his girlfriend Svetlana Ivanova, 9 August 1946, from the Pechora labour camp, cited in *Send Me Word*, by Orlando Figes

## Italy's Jewish Communities

On 16 January 1931 the text of the Jewish Communities Law approved by the Italian Government the previous October was published. Under the law, all Jews were forced to become members of the Jewish Community where they lived. They could only cease to belong by a formal act of conversion to another faith or a public declaration that they no longer wished to be considered Jews. The law detailed the way the Jewish Community would be organised within the Italian state and for the first time legalised the rabbis' situation in Italy. It finally achieved the unification of Italian Jewry which had been continuously attempted since 1865.

The law was defended and explained by one of the three Jews on the six-man special commission which drafted the law, Professor Mario Falco, a specialist in religious law at Milan University. The Italian Government wanted the unification of Italian Jewry to fit with the new religious policy it had adopted in 1929, following the concordat with the Vatican.

Most of the existing legislation pre-dated the creation of the Italian Kingdom. This new law meant that religious communities other than Catholic were no longer 'tolerated', but 'officially admitted'. It was the logical extension of Fascist legislation, whose focus was that the activities of all citizens should be controlled by the state and that all associations with practical aims should be under state control.

The leader of the Jewish Community had previously indicated its agreement by sending Mussolini a telegram of thanks in October 1930. However, there were concerns that the state might interfere in the internal affairs of the Jews. Little anti-Semitism existed, except in groups of extreme Fascists which were not supported by the government. However, the Rome correspondent of the *Manchester Guardian* wrote in October 1930:

> … that the Jews who were previously free to associate as they desired are now compelled to form themselves into a Jewish Federation which will 'form one big Union representing all the interests of Italian Hebraism'. With the Fascist passion for grouping and labelling the citizens of Italy, the new law is in keeping, he added, but it also tends to create a racial distinction, of which few Italians have hither to been conscious. If Fascism has any distinctive attitude to Judaism, he wrote, it is hostile, but that is rarely expressed. If it feels in danger this quarter (where none has ever been felt to exist before in Italy), it will be able to 'control' Jews in Italy more easily when they are federated.

Signor Mussolini issued a statement after the conclusion of the concordat with the Vatican:

> I have never used, nor will I ever use, force to close either church or temple, or mosque or synagogue, because it would seem to me an attempt to extinguish the light of the spirit of the ideal. The moral and spiritual power of religion makes it an indispensable part of national life. Wherever there is religious discipline there is also civil discipline.

In June 1929 Signor Mussolini agreed to be interviewed by the managing director of the JTA, Jacob Landau:

> Mussolini contended that that the Concordat has, if anything, improved the position of the Jewish Community in Italy. The Concordat has been widely misunderstood, he claimed. State and Church remain separate as in the United States of America. On the whole, he went on, the Jewish population in Italy is small. We have altogether 60,000 Jews in Italy, of whom 15,000 live in Rome, about 10,000 in Milan, 5,000 in Trieste and about 1,000 in Naples. Here in Italy, he declared, the Jew is free and an equal citizen. He is an Italian. The Jewish Community in Italy is more than 2,000 years old. It is oldest in Europe. The Jew

wept on the grave of Caesar, and has through more than 20 centuries participated in the history of this country in all its vicissitudes.

However, in spite of Mussolini's reassurances, there was considerable concern among the Jews. In particular they were worried about marriages and schools. The schools had all been secular, but now they taught the Catholic tradition of Christianity and parents were concerned that Jewish children going to state schools might be subjection to conversion pressure. They felt that, as these schools were funded from the taxes paid by Jews, they should be entitled to state funding for Jewish schools where their children would be free of Christian pressure.[1]

Professor Mario Falco (1884–1943) was poorly rewarded for his labours. He was dismissed from his position at the University of Milan as professor of religious law because of the racial laws of 1938. Accordingly, with no salary he and his family were destitute. When Milan was attacked in October 1942, they fled to his wife Gabriella's parents in Ferrara, but when Germany invaded Italy on 10 September 1943 they fled to the countryside. Professor Falco died of a heart attack on 4 October 1943 and was buried in the Jewish cemetery in Ferrara. His widow was helped repeatedly by a colleague of Falco's from the university, Professor Carlo Arturo Jemolo (1891–1981), who provided false documents, accommodation and finance for Mrs Falco and her two daughters until June 1945, a month after the liberation of Milan. A well-known jurist, he was a devout Catholic and ardent anti-Fascist and was recognised as Righteous Among the Nations on 13 February 1968, together with his wife, Adele Maria, and their daughter, Adele.[2]

## North Africa

Italy's power extended across the Mediterranean to Libya from 1911 until 1951. Although the Italian racial anti-Jewish legislation was only introduced in 1938, the 38,000 Jews of Libya were initially protected by Marshal Italo Balbo, the Governor of Libya, who lessened their impact and prevented the local Fascists from enforcing harsher anti-Jewish measures. In fact, the Libyan Jews had more to fear from their hostile Muslim neighbours, who tormented them.

Unfortunately, Marshal Balbo died in an air crash in June 1940. Britain, Italy and Germany all wanted control of the region and this affected the Jews. In early 1941 the Italians regained control. Jews with French nationality were sent to Tunisia, while about 300 Jews with British citizenship went to Italy to concentration camps. When Germany took control of northern Italy in 1944, those British Jews were sent to Bergen-Belsen.

Several forced labour camps for Jews were set up in an area 45 miles south of Tripoli. Some 3,000 Jews were imprisoned in Giado on Mussolini's personal orders, while many other Jews were interned in Gharyan, Jeren and Tigrinna. Giado, where they were building military roads, was the worst camp in Libya – 500 Jews died there of weakness, hunger and disease, especially typhus and typhoid fever.

In April 1942, a further 1,750 Jews were taken from Tripoli to forced labour sites at Homs, Benghazi and Derna. Hundreds died from the heat and hunger and also from Allied bombing because the Jews were not allowed to use the air-raid shelters.[3]

June–December 1942 saw even worse conditions for the Jews. Jews were forbidden from property deals with Aryan Italians or Muslims, and they were forbidden to trade with Italy and engage in any activity which could be perceived as affecting the defence of Libya. All Jewish men aged between 18 and 45 were rounded up for forced labour and in August a new camp was created in Sidi Azaz, 62 miles east of Tripoli for the Jews of Tripolitania.

On 9 October 1942 it was decreed that the Italian racial laws were to be implemented in Libya, and on 23 October 350 Jews were deported to Tobruk.

During December 1942–January 1943 the British liberated Libya and the racial rules were repealed. However, in November 1945 there was a three-day pogrom against the Jews – the most vicious in the country's history. One hundred and twenty-one Jews were murdered, many hundreds were wounded, synagogues were ruined and hundreds of Jewish homes and businesses were ransacked and destroyed. This was a terrible shock to the Jews and in many cases it reactivated their sense of Jewish identity. When Israel was created by the United Nations in 1948, 30,000 Jews left Libya to go to their new homeland.[4]

Libya was not the only North African country whose Jews were entangled in the tentacles of the Holocaust. Robert Satloff has researched this subject and it is his view that 4,000–5,000 North African Jews were murdered in the Holocaust. Additionally, 1,200 North African Jews trapped in France were sent to the east to share the fate of European Jews. Satloff noted, 'the Germans and their allies made a significant start towards their murderous goal for North Africa's Jews'. He stated:

> Virtually no Jew in North Africa was left untouched. Nearly 10,000 suffered in labor camps, work gangs, and prisons, or under house arrest. By a stroke of fortune, relatively few perished, many of them in the almost daily Allied bombings of Tunis and Bizerte in the winter and spring of 1943 when the Germans forced Jewish workers to stay at their jobs clearing rubble. But if US and British troops had not driven the Germans from the African continent, in 1943, the 2,000 year old Jewish communities of Morocco, Algeria, Tunisia, Libya and perhaps Egypt would almost certainly have met the fate of their brethren in Europe.[5]

Deborah Lipstadt states that the Arabs behaved like Europeans in the Holocaust – some helped, and others persecuted them or benefitted from the persecution. She does, however, highlight what happened in Algiers. When Vichy officials offered

Algerian Arabs profits if they took over Jewish property, not a single Arab participated, although there were plenty of willing Frenchmen. One Friday in 1941, religious leaders throughout Algiers gave sermons warning Muslims not to take property from the Jews.[6]

Tunisia had 85,000 Jews before the Second World War. There was anti-Jewish feeling in the early days of the war and Jewish homes and shops were attacked. When France fell in June 1940, the Tunisians who longed for independence took it out on the Jews. They wanted race laws imposed but the Governor General, Jean-Pierre Esteva, was sympathetic to the Jews and only imposed some of the Jewish laws. The Italians protected the 5,000 Jews in Tunisia with Italian passports.

Tunisia became the only Arab country directly under German control when it was occupied on 9 November 1942, apparently in reaction to the Allied invasion of Algeria and Morocco. Walter Rauff (1906–1984), who was responsible for around 100,000 Jewish deaths and developed the 'mobile gas chamber', was made Commander of Tunis. His task was to exterminate the Jews, as in Europe. He began by arresting four Jewish Community leaders, including the president on 23 November. On 6 December he replaced the existing community structure with a Judenrät to enforce their orders, as in the rest of occupied Europe. Their first task was to find 2,000 Jews for forced labour – ultimately 5,000 labourers were working in thirty-two labour camps, under very harsh conditions – worse than under the Italians.

Further measures were imposed, with twenty Jewish activists being deported to camps in Europe where they all died. Jewish property was seized and money extorted and the wearing of the yellow star was imposed. The Allies' arrival in Tunis on 7 May 1943, following the defeat of Rommel at El Alamein, saved Tunisia's Jews from further suffering. However, the return of the French was not good news as Italian Jews were arrested as collaborators, but were released after some weeks.[7]

With the fall of France in June 1940, Vichy was dealing with Algeria and Morocco, both French colonies. Algeria had 120,000 Jews and Morocco had 200,000 Jews at the start of the war. It was Marshal Pétain who authorised the creation of the Trans-Saharan Railway on 22 March 1941 – a Vichy initiative. The railway snaked from Oran on the coast of Algeria through the east of Morocco and then back into Algeria. Workers were all interned men and included Poles, Czechs, Greeks, former Spanish Republican soldiers and Jews, and all were treated harshly.[8]

Many European Jews escaped to North Africa, assuming the Mediterranean Sea would be a safety buffer. There were over 1,500 Jews in the French Foreign Legion in April 1940 hoping to fight against the Nazis. However, with the fall of France in June 1940 they were 'demobilised', interned and sent to camps in North Africa. Many of these men were German and Austrian refugees who were in France when war broke out. The law of 4 October 1940 gave the Vichy Government the right to intern Jews inside the unoccupied zone.

A punishment and isolation camp was opened at Hadjerat-M'Guil on 1 November 1941. There were 170 prisoners and nine were badly tortured and brutally murdered. One of the murdered Jews had previously been in a concentration camp in Germany. Following his release in 1939 he had fled to France. When his parents, who were refugees in London, heard of his murder in the Sahara, they committed suicide.[9]

According to Yad Vashem, Pétain's railway was to serve coal mines across North Africa and work camps were created:

> Prisoners were forced to labor in difficult conditions, performing strenuous work, for ten hours each day. They were poorly fed and housed, and lived in terrible sanitary conditions. Tortures and atrocities were inflicted by the guards for the slightest breach of the rules; the internees were not treated as human beings. Many died from beatings; even more died from outbreaks of typhus or just from exhaustion and hunger.[10]

Robert Satloff believes:

> … that of the three countries who brought the Holocaust to Arab lands, the most malevolent by far was France. In Morocco and, especially, Algeria, France implemented strict laws against local Jews, expelling them from schools, universities, and government employment, confiscating their property, and sending a number of local Jewish political activists to harsh labor camps. In some respects, Vichy was more vigorous about applying anti-Jewish statutes in Arab lands than in metropolitan France.[11]

## German Foreign Office Complicit in the Holocaust

An 84-year-old woman, Marga Henseler, a retired Foreign Office translator, caused a furore in 2003 over the German Foreign Office (Auswärtiges Amt, or AA).

A glowing obituary written for Franz Nüsslein (1909–2003), whom she had known in the 1960s, was the cause of her ire. He had been a protégé of Reinhard Heydrich and was responsible for many executions following Germany's annexation of Czechoslovakia in 1938. He refused any reprieves and was responsible for the guillotining of Marianne of Goltz, a Catholic woman from Vienna who was married to a Jew. Her husband had escaped to London, but she could not get away in time. She was involved in a group helping Jews escape. They were betrayed and she was sentenced to death. In prison she acted as an interpreter for the prison wardens with the prisoners.

Marianne knew about her pending execution a few days beforehand. That is why she got hold of poison and took it while in the death cell. The wardens found her in a deep and deathly coma and were scared about investigations on how she got hold of the poison. They thus dragged her in front of the state attorney and she was beheaded in an 'unconscious' state.[12]

Nüsslein, who was on Washington's list of Nazi war criminals, was arrested and sentenced to twenty-five years in prison, but released in the mid-1950s without pardon. He joined the Foreign Service and served for twelve years as the German Consul General in Barcelona. After his death, the Foreign Ministry published a flattering tribute in a 'small internal magazine'. Marga Henseler was outraged that a war criminal could receive such an honour.

Joschka Fischer was the German Foreign Minister at the time and he ordered an investigation.[13] He also asked to be briefed on the protocol regarding obituaries. He discovered it was customary to honour former ambassadors and other leading members of the AA, even if they were known to have had significant roles in the Holocaust. To prevent this reoccurring, Fischer ordered that no further members of the SD, SS or the Nazi Party should be given an obituary. However, this caused a problem because a group of the older generation of diplomats and high-ranking officials in the AA campaigned against this ruling. They argued that:

... among party members there had also been many who had resisted Hitler's regime, claiming further that the AA had been a centre of opposition: the few who supported atrocities and the killing of Jews had been National Socialists and had no adherence to the traditional structure of the AA.[14]

Franz Krapf, who died in 2004, was the first diplomat to die after this policy was introduced and there were many complaints when he did not receive the customary obituary. The explanation given was that Krapf had been a member of both the Nazi Party and the SS. However, post-war he had been at the German embassies in Washington and Tokyo and later West Germany's Ambassador to NATO 1971–1976. Accordingly, a few weeks later:

... a show of solidarity for Frank Krapf popped up in a very prestigious conservative daily *Frankfurter Allgemeine*. A huge advertisement was published in which all the famous veterans of West German diplomacy signed an obituary in memory of Krapf. I think it is not fantasy to connect the sudden solidarity with Franz Krapf with an opportunity to attack Fischer ...[15]

A huge debate followed and perhaps even a revolt in the Foreign Ministry. Fischer said he was shocked it was still an issue in 2004. He admits to having been naïve and realised he needed 'to know what had happened in the German Foreign Ministry during the Nazi period and what happened afterwards'. Fischer convened an international commission of historians to examine the role of the AA and 'take a pluralistic, scientific approach, and, in order not to be one-sided, to be comprised of members not only from Germany, but also from America and Israel'.

Four historians collaborated on the 900 page report, *The Office and the Past*, published in October 2010. The chair was Eckart Conze, a history professor at Marburg University (Germany), and the others were Norbert Frei (Germany), Peter Hayes (USA) and Moshe Zimmermann (Israel). The publishers were overwhelmed by the report's success, when expected sales between 5,000 and 10,000 reached tens of thousands. This generated a huge debate in Germany, especially among the younger generation who were unaware of these facts. One of the main issues was the AA's integral role in the 'murderous machine of the Holocaust', and particularly its involvement in France and Greece:

> Some of you might remember that up until 1943, Thessaloniki was called 'the Jerusalem of the Balkans'. The Foreign Ministry and its representatives in the consulate general were the driving force behind the organisation of the Holocaust there. I personally was not aware of the extent of the Foreign Ministry's close ties to the SS.[16]

Fischer stressed the AA was involved in Nazi policies regarding Jews right from beginning. He calls 'the surrender of these so-called conservative elites to the Nazis and Hitler at the beginning of the 1930s' a very sad picture. Additionally, the postwar situation was depressing:

> Chancellor Konrad Adenauer said, 'If you do not have clean water, you have to use dirty water.' But allow me to be very direct; this water was very foul indeed. The big question for historians will be whether it was possible to do things in a different way.

The commission discovered that there were actually fewer Nazis employed in the Foreign Office during the Nazi period than during the 1950s. There were also many Nazis in the former GDR, usually of lower rank – Fischer said there were many famous names, although he would not give them. He also referred to the false picture of the resistance. If so many people had resisted Hitler, democracy might have had a chance. This was also part of the rearrangement of biographies, and he revealed:

> ... the juridical desk in the Foreign Ministry, which had to deal with aiding Germans in foreign prisons, was in fact a desk used to warn war criminals in

West Germany not to travel to France, Belgium, Italy or wherever they might be arrested, indicted, and convicted.[17]

When Joschka Fischer went to Israel in 2011 he was very honest. He spoke of the difficult situation after the Second World War and Germany's difficulties over its identity after the destruction of German and European Jewry:

> You cannot deny the very fact of the Shoah, of Auschwitz, and of the moral and historical (or also personal at that time) responsibility of some Germans, and the moral and historical responsibility of the whole German people. It was about us, and will continue to be about us. To understand that is very important.[18]

Conze was interviewed at some length by *Der Spiegel* in October 2010.[19] He was quite adamant in his condemnation of the role of the Foreign Office under the Nazis and after 1945. By way of introduction, he said:

> The Foreign Ministry wasn't just somehow involved in National Socialism or even a hotbed of resistance, as was long claimed. From day one, it functioned as an institution of the Nazi regime and backed its policies of violence at all times. After 1945, there was a high degree of staffing continuity within the ministry, and some of its diplomats were seriously tainted.

When asked about the level of activity in the regime's crimes, he elaborated:

> The Ministry contributed, as an institution, to the violent crimes of the Nazis, even including the murder of the Jews. In this sense, one can say that the Foreign Ministry was a criminal organization.
>
> For instance, in 1941 Franz Rademacher, the Foreign Ministry official in charge of Jewish affairs, travelled to Belgrade to meet with local officials, but also with representatives of the Reich Security Head Office – in other words, the SS – to plan and execute the murder of Jews. In fact, he noted on his expenses statement that the purpose of the trip was the 'liquidation of Jews in Belgrade'. Every bookkeeper at the Foreign Ministry knew what was going on.

The interviewer suggested Rademacher was an exception:

> No. Take, for example, Ambassador Otto Abetz in Paris and the head of his political division, Ernst Achenbach, who would later become a politician with the FDP [Free Democratic Party]. They and their staff played an important role in the apprehension and deportation of Jews. When partisans in France killed German

soldiers, the diplomats immediately thought of deporting one or two thousand Jews to the extermination camps in retaliation. The Ministry also played a key role in the abduction and transport of forced labourers to the German Reich. France was one example, and Italy, with Ambassador Rudolf Rahn, was another.

When *Der Spiegel* suggested the Holocaust couldn't have happened without the diplomats, Conze said their co-operation was critical to matters running smoothly. Certainly, 'the Ministry represented the Nazi regime's interests in countries like Greece, France, Serbia and Hungary, and it negotiated with their governments on such matters as the deportation of Jews'. The interviewer asked Professor Conze why so many diplomats were prepared to be 'Hitler's willing helpers'. He replied that many of them saw the Nazi takeover in 1933 as redemption from the Weimar Republic with its 'liberal political order and parliamentarianism'. The Nazis announced they would reverse the Treaty of Versailles and make the German Reich a world power. The diplomats could all sign up for such policies.

The interviewer then queried whether the diplomats signed up for Hitler's racial policies. Conze said:

> A traditional upperclass anti-Semitism was common in top diplomatic circles. Many believed that there was a Jewish problem. The then-ambassador Ernst von Weizäcker [father of former German President Richard Weizäcker] spoke of a 'flood of Jews'. This isn't necessarily the populist-racist anti-Semitism of the Nazi Party. But it did make it easier to participate in the policies of the new Reich chancellor. One out of 10 civil servants in the higher grade of the civil service joined the SS, and 573 of 706 of that higher grade had joined the Nazi Party by 1943.

Many felt the anti-Semitic measures were justified and there was little opposition. Very few resigned – one was Friedrich von Prittwitz und Gaffron, the ambassador in Washington, and Albrecht Graf von Bernstorff, who was in London. Conze referred to 'self-enforced political conformity', which meant diplomats were anxious not to be undermined by others who wanted to be involved in foreign policy. That made them eager to co-operate and they showed great initiative – particularly in spying on emigrants abroad:

> Many emigrants were spied on, including composer Hanns Eisler, the young journalist Stefan Heym and politician Willy Brandt. But we have also found new information about Thomas Mann. He would not have been deprived of his citizenship in 1936 without the initiative of the Foreign Ministry. Mann was in Switzerland at the time, and the Ambassador there – it was Weizäcker – reported to Berlin that Mann had 'responded to the patience of German authorities in dealing with him with derisive remarks', an act that satisfied the legal definition

of 'hostile propaganda against the Reich'. Before then, the Foreign Ministry had warned against depriving Mann of his citizenship, because it would harm Germany's reputation. Now Weizäcker and other diplomats were arguing in favour of this step. The government waited until the Olympics were over before stripping Mann of his citizenship.

The Foreign Ministry was a criminal organisation.

He went on to say that after five years of examining the diplomatic archives it was clear that the Foreign Office had supported Nazi violence every step of the way and had a key role in killing Jews across Europe. He added that claims that the Foreign Office had resisted the will of the Nazi Party were untrue. On the contrary, it often helped the Nazis even before it was asked.[20]

## Reassessment of the Danish Rescue

The rescue of nearly all the Danish Jews is one of the few positive state responses in the Holocaust. It stands with the response of Bulgaria and Albania. In October 1943, Hitler ordered the mass arrest of the Jews of Denmark. Based on new empirical evidence and 100 interviews, the story has recently been reassessed by Dr Sofie Bak, author of *Nothing to Speak of.* The common view was that what the Danish Jews had experienced, compared with the Nazis' murder of 6 million Jews, was 'nothing to speak of', as most Danish Jews had survived.

The Jews of Denmark were not registered, nor forced to wear the yellow star, because the Germans never brought forward the proposal, knowing the government would reject it:

> 'There is no Jewish question in Denmark', were the words of Foreign Minister Erik Scavenius when approached by the top Nazi Hermann Göring in Autumn 1941. Scavenius was willing to make far-reaching concessions to the Germans, but even for him, three issues were out of the question: the death penalty, Danish participation on the German side of the war, and racial laws.[21]

Dr Bak says the rescue of 8,000 Danish Jews being transported to Sweden in a few weeks would not have been possible without the help of their fellow Danes – 'The help was massive, diverse and offered in solidarity. A focus on the personal experiences of the persecuted provides new insights into roles during the flight.'[22]

Herbert Pundik's 1996 memoir recalls:

> My childhood ended when I was sixteen, on the afternoon of Wednesday, September 29, 1943. It happened in my classroom at Metropolitan School, in the

middle of a French lesson. The principal entered the room, interrupted the teacher, pointed at me and to two of my friends, and said, 'Please step out to the hall.'

The courteous tone of his voice made it clear that we were not about to be punished. Then he added, 'If there are other students of Jewish origin in the class, would they step out, too.' The homeroom teacher slipped a few books into his briefcase and joined us. 'We have been warned that a manhunt for Jews is about to begin.' The principal said, 'You'd better rush home. The Germans may come at any time.'

I rushed to my desk and packed my schoolbag. My classmates sat there silently. We were old enough to understand what was happening. We knew that at best we would not see each other again for quite some time. Before I left the classroom, my bench mate pressed a scout's compass into my hand as a going-away present.[23]

Very bluntly, Bak states that 'it can no longer be ignored that money was the hinge on which the whole escape apparatus turned'.

Money was needed to organise the fishermen and their boats and ensure there were enough of them. The price was based on supply and demand – the supply of fishermen was enough to meet the demand, but enough to ensure the price fell as demand dropped, so poor families could afford to go as well. The average price was 1,000 kroner per person. Research has shown that there were some payments of 50,000 kroner, but an average of 10,000 kroner for a family of four people. These higher payments paid for a whole transport, or for poorer Jews who could not pay for themselves. It is also noted that some of these funds were used to establish illegal routes for smuggling 'weapons, letters and members of the Resistance' back and forth between Sweden and Denmark, which assisted Denmark's struggle for liberation. By this time, however, the average price for an illegal crossing was 100 kroner.

This information is meaningless without knowing the value of the Danish krone in 1943. Dr Bak quotes a monthly wage for a skilled worker being 414 kroner and 49 per cent of the Danish Jews belonging to the working class in 1943. She also adds that a new fishing boat could cost between 15,000 and 30,000 kroner. She therefore concludes that the situation would have been hopeless for many of the Jews and that some fishermen earned a fortune at the Jews' expense.[24]

She doesn't moralize over the fishermen's behaviour, as the demands for payment must be viewed in relation to the danger of the crossing, the risks of losing their boat, which would bring a loss of earnings, and the ability to support their families, as well the possibilities of arrest. The payments had to cover these possibilities. However, there was no German policing of the strait between Denmark and Sweden during October 1943. It appears that Werner Best had taken steps to prevent Jews being caught at sea and had all the relevant vessels called into the dockyard for repainting, and not a single boat with Jewish refugees was captured at sea by the Germans.[25]

Werner Best, a senior member of the SS, represented the German Government in Denmark from 1942 to 1945. He was a lawyer and had acted as a judge. From September 1939 to June 1940 he was involved in the mass murder of Polish Jews and intellectuals. He then moved to France from June 1940 until August 1942 where he worked on the exclusion of Jews from French society and tried to put down the French Resistance.[26]

> Those who were caught helping Jews were dealt with in the Danish courts and were even handed over to them by the German police. The first case was heard on 23 October 1943 and the defendants were initially found not guilty, but pressure from the Germans led to a sentence of three months. There were 1,500 German policemen in Denmark on 1 October 1943 but they were not deployed after the round-up of 1 October. The army was passive in spite of instructions to support the police and the German HQ only allocated a small group to dealing with fleeing Jews – they relied completely on Danish informers. Dr Bak writes that roughly half of the 197 arrests were the result of one particularly enthusiastic Gestapo commander, Hans Juhl, in Elsinore – he was a Danish speaker from Flensburg and was nicknamed 'Gestapo Juhl'.[27]

It should not be assumed that the Danish experience was a picnic – the Snekkersten Inn near Elsinore was a pick-up point and the innkeeper Henry Christian Thomsen was a co-ordinator.[28] About 1,000 Jews left for Sweden from here, staying in the inn or nearby while waiting. When too many were waiting, Thomsen got a boat and made several runs himself.

While most people supported what was being done, in the early days a pro-German resident reported the Jewish activities to the police, who made some arrests. Out of sight of the collaborator, the policemen told the refugees to go to the Snekkersten Inn for help. Thomsen was captured by the Gestapo and allegedly tortured at Wisborg, the local Gestapo headquarters, but no evidence against him was found and he was released. He continued in the Resistance but was arrested again in August 1944. He was sent to the Neuengamme camp in Germany, where he died four months later. He was aged 38. In 1968, he and his wife, Ellen Margrethe, were recognised as Righteous Among the Nations.[29]

The escape of the Danish Jews was made possible because of the number of people prepared to help, Sweden's willingness to take the refugees and the amount of money involved. However, the really important factor was the reluctance of the German authorities in Denmark to undertake round-ups of Jews. When local authorities refused to co-operate the Germans gave up. Denmark at the time had no government, but the civil service continued to function.

It is imported to consider why Werner Best made no effort to disrupt the rescue. He wrote a report on the developments which went to Berlin on 5 October:

'As the objective goal of the Judenaktion in Denmark was the de-judaization of the country, and not a successful headhunt, it must be concluded that the Judenaktion had reached its goal.'[30]

The treatment of the Jews' abandoned property, flats, businesses and belongings was exceptional in the history of the Holocaust. On 2 October 1943, the Ministry of Welfare contacted the city of Copenhagen to ask them to safeguard the property of the Jews who had fled. The task was given to the local Social Service agency, who dealt with 1,970 enquiries about empty flats or suspicious circumstances in the city.[31] When they received an enquiry, they visited the home and checked it out. They also made a complete inventory of all the possessions. If it was possible to retain the flat, remarkably, the Social Service agency paid the rent for the duration of the occupation. If that was not possible, everything was put in storage. In all, they paid the rent and associated costs for ninety-seven flats and provided storage for 350 households.

This work of the Social Service was unique, as during the German occupation a Danish public agency managed to protect the abandoned property of the Jews. The rationale behind the work of the Social Service was that the Jews should have homes to return to and the German authorities were evidently aware of this activity. For example, the German security police turned to this agency when they wanted to return keys either handed over by porters and concierges during the round-up on 1 October or collected from the deportees in Theresienstadt.

There was a little damage by the German police, and although there had been some thefts by Danes, these were minimal compared with elsewhere in Europe. Finally, on 3 October 1943, the Social Service received an alarm concerning the synagogue. The Germans had used it as a collection point during the round-up of the Jews and it still exhibited the signs of this. Prayer shawls were thrown over the seats of the chairs and prayer books were spread over the floor. On the elevated area the floor was strewn with cigarette butts, and the wardens' top hats, which were usually kept in a cupboard in the entrance, had been used as footballs and kicked around. The Social Service removed what they assessed to be of value: some Torah scrolls, various silver objects and books. These effects were moved, along with some boxes of items from the Museum of the Jewish Community, to the crypt of one of Copenhagen's old churches with the help of the Museum of Copenhagen. They were restored to a representative of the Jewish Community after the German capitulation.

Although the rescue of the Torah scrolls was well known, it was not so well known that it was the Social Service people who undertook it. By chance they were in the Jewish Community building when two Gestapo men came, and when they left they took a copy of the Talmud and an old candlestick with them. The thefts were reported to the police and the Social Service report noted, 'the stolen goods were returned in the course of a few days'.

Dr Bak concluded that:

> The account of the disrespectful treatment of the synagogue is reminiscent of
> the behaviour of the German occupation forces all over Europe, where Jewish
> property was vandalized and destroyed, but it also tells of the very special occu-
> pation conditions in effect in Denmark, where neither destruction nor theft of
> Jewish property was tolerated.

It is debatable whether the Holocaust ever took place in Denmark, when 95 per
cent of the Jews escaped to Sweden and their property was protected. She concludes that perhaps the action should be called a 'flight' rather than a 'rescue'.[32]

However, two significant issues are the children left behind with Christian
families and the 500 Jews who were sent to Theresienstadt, who feel they have
been ignored. The reasons for leaving the children are various. Some families felt
it would be impossible to lie in the dark overnight waiting for a boat with a small
child. In other cases the Danish fishermen were concerned that the children might
make a noise and draw the Nazis' attention to the crossing. Some of the children
taken were sedated. Other parents left their children because they expected the
war would be brief.

All the survivors said the escape was as clear to them as if it were yesterday –
perhaps because they hadn't spoken about it. On the other hand, the Theresienstadt
survivors did talk and write about their time. The camp was infamous for the Nazi
propaganda film showing a model camp and the Red Cross visit in 1944. Tarabini
Fracapane said, 'It was not a death camp, but people were still surrounded by death,
vermin, horrible living conditions, hard labour, sickness and hunger.'

Steen Metz, whose father, Axel Mogens Metz, died in the camp, is critical of a
2003 book, *In the Shadow of Hitler's Germany* by Hans Sode-Madsens, in which he
writes that none of the Jews who died in Theresienstadt died of starvation. Metz
said his 40-year-old father lost half his bodyweight and died through a combination of malnutrition and being worked to death only six months after arriving.
He emailed the author with the facts, but he was ignored. 'It was a model camp
for one day only.' One month after his father's death, the Nazis allowed the Danish
Red Cross to send food parcels to the Danish prisoners, which gave them items to
barter and reduced the Danish deaths.

Metz says that of the 145,000 Jews sent to Theresienstadt, 32,000 died and a
further 80,000 were sent to extermination camps. Metz and his mother were survivors. It is alleged that Werner Best persuaded Eichmann not to send Danish Jews
to Auschwitz, which was why so many came back – of 470 sent, 412 are believed
to have returned, plus three children born in the camp. While the loss of the total
of 103 Danish Jews is low compared with the rest of Europe, this does not lessen
the trauma of those who suffered and survived.[33]

# Belgium

When Belgium was created in 1830 there were about 1,000 Jews. There was always a large number of immigrants who only stayed for a short period before moving on, so there was a fluctuating Jewish population. There were about 70,000 Jews just before the Holocaust.

Attacks on Jews began in 1933 and the increase in refugees in 1938–1939, following the *Anschluss* and Kristallnacht, aggravated matters. On 25–26 August 1939 there were anti-Jewish riots in Antwerp which were approved by the Catholic newspapers. This eroded the Jews' image and status in the city. According to Lieven Saerens, 'The Jewish public underwent a "stigmatisation" in the eyes of much of the population of Antwerp', and the public did not differentiate between Jews of long standing and recent arrivals. The acceptance of an 'aliens problem' was general and referred to Jews, even though they represented a tiny proportion of the 8 million Belgians. Anti-Jewish feelings existed all over Belgium, but seemed to have a special impact in Antwerp where, for instance, Jewish lawyers were ousted from the Flemish Conference of the Antwerp Bar and the Antwerp Bar Association in May 1939.[34]

There were issues about language within the law because traditionally French had been the language of the courts and the Flemish Conference during the 1930s was promoting the use of Dutch in local courts instead.[35]

Of the Jews who registered in Belgium, 42 per cent were deported. In France it was roughly 25–30 per cent and in the Netherlands roughly 70–75 per cent. However, the regional figures show that 37 per cent were deported from Brussels, 35 per cent from Liège and 42 per cent from Charleroi; in Antwerp at least 65 per cent (9,009 out of 13,779) were deported, which is as high as the Dutch figures.

Just before the Holocaust there were 29,500 Jews in Antwerp, representing 53.8 per cent of the total Jewish population, compared with Brussels with 21,000 Jews (38.5 per cent). It is considered that increasing Flemish nationalism, which was hostile to Judaism and the Eastern European nature of the Jewish community, was responsible. Added to this was Catholic objection to Zionism and the impact the Jews were having in the local diamond industry, as both dealers and polishers. These issues all became more significant in the 1930s when pro-Nazi factions developed within the Flemish nationalist movement.

The Belgian authorities in Antwerp did not initiate anti-Jewish activity but carried out German orders without question or protest, especially when deportations began in August 1942. The leaders, led by the mayor, Leon Delwaide, did not tell the staff the actions were illegal and the police followed the German security police obediently. This study is important because by examining the difference in local situations the generalisation of national approaches is avoided, and while Antwerp was found wanting it is important to note that, when it comes to Righteous

Among the Nations, tiny Belgium has 1,612 – making it third after France and the Netherlands. Belgium also saved more children.

In Belgium in 2012 there was a fracas over the Mayor of Brussels' invitation to a Holocaust memorial event on 2 September 2012. Mayor Freddy Thielmans' original invitation referred to 'a ceremony of official recognition of the participation of local authorities appointed by the occupying power during World War II, in the deportation of citizens of Brussels'. The event was to be the first official recognition by a mayor of Brussels of the municipality's complicity in deporting thousands of Jews from Brussels seventy years ago.

However, the Association for the Memory of the Shoah had complained that the deportees were not all Brussels citizens, but were Jews from all over Belgium, according to their spokesman, Dr Eric Picard. He also pointed out that Germans never appointed the Brussels authorities, they merely kept the elected authorities in place after the German Army invaded Belgium in 1940. The CCOJB (Co-ordinating Committee of Jewish Organisations in Belgium) is the umbrella group representing Belgium's French-speaking Jews and was co-organising the event. Joel Rubinfield, a past president, said the original text was rewriting history.[36]

At the actual ceremony on 3 September, the mayor acknowledged that the registration of the Jews of Brussels by the local authorities helped with their deportation and therefore the municipal authorities were complicit in the result. He said, 'Without this register of Jews, the progressive arrests and the raid of September 1942 would never have had the same impact in Brussels.' Eli Ringer, who represented the Flemish Belgian Jews in the Forum of Jewish Organisations, said this was the first formal recognition of complicity by a Brussels mayor. However, the mayor refused to pass judgement.[37]

A few days later on 9 September, the prime minister, Elio Di Rupo, apologised at a ceremony in the city of Mechelen (Malines) where the first convoys of Jews left on 9 September 1942. Of the estimated 56,000 Jews living in Belgium in 1939, about 25,000 were deported to Auschwitz-Birkenau and only about 1,200 survived. Di Rupo said:

> By assisting in the Nazi policies of extermination, the authorities of the time and the Belgian state failed in their duties. They were complicit in the most abominable crime. I want to now … express the regret and shame that collaboration brought upon us.[38]

The Kazerne Dossin Museum was opened in Mechelen in 1995 on the initiative of Jewish survivors. The site was chosen for Belgium's Holocaust Memorial because during 1942–1944 the eighteenth-century Dossin barracks were a Nazi transit prison for Jews prior to deportation to Auschwitz. It served the same purpose as Westerbork in the Netherlands and Drancy in France. In twenty-eight railway convoys 25,454 Jews and 352 gypsies from Belgium and North France were deported. The majority of them were killed on arrival, while the remaining few were made to work as slave labourers. Only 5 per cent of them survived. They travelled in the same dreadful conditions as the other Jews all over Europe. Simon Gronowski who, as an 11-year-old, jumped from the 20th convoy, which was stopped by Robert Maistriau on 19 April 1943, described the travelling conditions:

> We were packed like a herd of cattle. We had only one bucket for 50 people. How could we use it? How could we empty it? Besides, it would have been impossible to get to it.
>
> There was no food, no drink. There were no seats so we either sat or lay down on the floor. I was in the rear right corner of the car, with my mother. It was very dark. There was a pale gleam coming from a vent in the roof but it was stifling and there was no water to be had.[39]

A 1,100 page report, produced in 2007 for the Belgian Senate about the attitude of the Belgian authorities to the Jewish population during the Nazi occupation, was entitled *Gewillig België – La Belgique Docile* (*Docile Belgium*). It demonstrated that while the persecution of the Jews was devised by the Germans, it was implemented with the large-scale co-operation of the Belgian Government. The Nazi occupying forces could not do it alone because they did not have enough men available. 'The Belgian authorities organised and administered the Register of Jews; they supported the implementation of successive anti-Jewish laws, up to and including individual and collective arrests; and it was the Belgian Government itself that took the initiative in 1942 to start registering Romanies.'

The report said that the least that could be said of the Belgian authorities' attitude to the persecuted Jews was that they showed a lack of courage and 'systematically evaded their responsibilities'. Professor Dan Machman, who is the chief historian at Yad Vashem, commented that while Belgium began dealing with the events of the Holocaust later than many countries, its report is an exception. By 2007 only Rumania, Switzerland and Lichtenstein had completed such investigations. Machman explained one of the reasons the Belgians failed to address the issue earlier was what he called 'the king problem'. King Leopold III stayed in Belgium during the occupation, unlike the government which went into exile in London. This led to queries about his collaboration with the Germans and he abdicated after the war in favour of his 20-year-old son, Baudouin.

Queen Elizabeth of Bavaria, King Leopold's mother, was even recognised by Yad Vashem as a Righteous Among the Nations in 1964 for her intervention on behalf of several hundred Jews with Belgian citizenship – a small minority of the Jewish population at the time. Machman considers that nowadays such an award would be questionable because that intervention for a few Belgian Jews could be perceived as giving the Germans licence to deport all those without citizenship. In total, 25,000 Jews were killed, which was 44 per cent of the Jews in Belgium at the start of the occupation.

The report concluded that 'the Belgian state adopted an obedient approach, and collaborated in a manner unbefitting a democratic country, in various but critical areas, in a devastating policy toward the Jewish population'. In the epilogue, the authors wrote:

> War exposes the soul of the nation. Most of the [Belgian] office-holders retained a certain amount of independence of action even under the occupation. The occupier's power was in hardly any case absolute power. The ability not to carry out certain tasks or not to put certain orders into effect remained in their hands. The significance of this latitude is that at several crucial moments [the Belgian authorities] were required to choose.

The editor of the report was Rudi Van Doorslaer, who claimed the German occupiers needed the collaboration of the local authorities and therefore the power was in the Belgians' hands. Examining the response, the editor said:

> In general, it can be said that the Belgians sacrificed the Jewish community to try to preserve 'normality' and the orderly functioning of the economy. The Belgians were very much influenced by the experience of World War I, but did not take into account the fact that in the second war, the occupation was of a political nature. In World War II the German occupation of Belgium had Nazi and racist characteristics with regard to part of the population, which had not been the case in the First World War.

Van Doorslaer says the team identified three crucial occasions that signified the Belgian authorities' attitude to the Jews. The first was in the autumn of 1940, six months after Belgium surrendered. In November 1940 the Germans ordered all the Jews to be registered. Under the terms of the Belgian Constitution such a register was illegal as it discriminated against citizens according to their religion. It was also a violation of the Hague Convention of 1907, which stated an occupier must respect 'family honour and rights, the lives of persons, and private property, as well as religious convictions and practice'. The order was a problem in the absence of the government, with only senior officials called 'secretaries-general' in charge. After legal consultations, the registration of Jews was allowed. The reasoning was that the Germans had made the order, and if the Jews presented themselves to register, then the Belgians could not avoid the situation – they were merely passive intermediaries.

The Jews were regarded as foreigners, as 95 per cent did not have Belgian citizenship. Van Doorslaer said that much of the Belgian elite was xenophobic and anti-Semitic and the war made them prefer 'the Belgian interest', which did not include protecting Jews who were non-Belgians. The report stated that, paradoxically, 'even though the Jews were the most obvious group harmed by the German enemy, the Belgian authorities related to the Jews as though they were themselves the enemies'.

As elsewhere, registration led to the imposition of a series of instructions and orders aiming to separate Jews from the rest of society. In December 1940 all Jews in official posts were dismissed. In July 1941, the word 'Jew' had to be added to all identifying documents. The report states that from that point 'the transition from passive collaboration to active collaboration was accomplished with great rapidity'. In October 1941, the authorities declared textbooks edited by Jews illegal. In December 1941 Jewish children were expelled from schools and in June 1942 Jews were prevented from working as doctors.

The second crucial moment was in the summer of 1942 when Jews were deported to the east – to Auschwitz. However, there was a distinct difference in the approach of the two major cities with Jewish populations – Brussels and Antwerp. The report states that the Brussels police did not take part in rounding up and deporting Jews. However, in Antwerp the police actively helped the German forces by closing off streets to carry out the deportations. One out of the three deportations carried out on 28 and 29 August 1942 was even managed in its entirety by the Antwerp police, who caught 1,243 Jews and deported them to the death camps. It also appears that less help was offered to Jews in Antwerp than elsewhere in Belgium – few Jews were hidden and little help came from the Church and non-Jewish diamond workers.

Van Doorslaer explained that the difference between the two cities was based on the long-standing division of Belgium between the Flemish north and the Francophone south. He said the Flemish side collaborated more from patriotic and nationalist sentiments. In Brussels, there was a stronger sense of Belgian patriotism and anti-German feeling. In Antwerp there was a strong feeling of Flemish patriotism, with pro-German sentiments. The Flemish had feelings of inferiority going back to the nineteenth century, which still exist and could explain the pro-German bias. They believed the Germans would improve their inferior status within the Belgian state.

The third crucial moment was at the end of the war when the Belgian legal system was working out whether to try collaborators. In the end it was decided that the policemen from Antwerp who participated in the deportation of the Jews would not be tried. It was felt it was too sensitive a topic because if the policemen were guilty then so were their superiors and those above them – this would make the whole system responsible. Accordingly, the report states, 'The Belgian state decided at the end of 1945 that the Belgian authorities bore no legal or other responsibility for the persecution of the Jews.'[40]

## Wannsee Conference, 20 January 1942

It was the Wannsee Conference which finalised the fate of the Jews of Europe and would have included the Jews of England had the Allies been defeated. The typed list presented to the delegates listed the number of Jews to be exterminated in each country – including 4,000 in Ireland and 330,000 in England (presumably they meant the UK mainland) that helped make up the total of 11 million Jews.

The Wannsee Conference House is in an affluent part of Berlin, on the side of Wannsee Lake which boasts the longest inland sandy beach in Europe – first opened as a Lido in 1907. I visited the leafy area in August 2014 and found lovely villas and well-maintained gardens, which were reminiscent of Bournemouth. The Wannsee House is very pleasant, with well-laid gardens and statues. It was built for Ernst Marlier during the First World War and was owned by the industrialist Friedrich Minoux from 1921 until the SS began buying properties in the area and purchased the villa, under cover, to be a guesthouse for SS and SD personnel in Berlin on business.[41] It was bizarre that a meeting to plan the annihilation of 11 million people, who happened to be Jewish, took place in such delightful surroundings. While I was waiting for the bus back to Berlin, I wondered if the local residents had had any idea what was being planned in the neighbouring property.

The meeting was called by Reinhard Heydrich, head of the security police and the SS Security Service (SD), who was in charge of dealing with the Jewish question. Hitler had given Göring, his second-in-command, the power to co-ordinate all anti-Jewish measures. In 1939 he put Heydrich in charge of forced emigration. On 31 July 1941 he wrote to him again:

> In addition to the task assigned to you by the decree of 24 January 1939, which dealt with a solution to the Jewish question by emigration or evacuation in the most favourable way possible under the prevailing circumstances, I herewith appoint you to make all necessary preparations in regard to organisational, practical and material matters for bringing about a total solution of the Jewish question in the German sphere of influence within Europe.[42]

Apparently, the letter had been drafted by Heydrich's department and was put in front of Göring for his signature. Like Chamberlain with his piece of paper, Heydrich used this letter as his authority for masterminding the extermination of the Jews. It was copied to everyone attending the conference and afterwards, on 25 January, was distributed far and wide, making sure everyone understood his significant leading role.[43]

Heydrich was the most senior Nazi leader present and it seems significant that neither Hitler nor Göring was there, almost as though they were distancing themselves from the policy. Eichmann, of all people, at his trial in 1961, appeared to express surprise at the language used. He told the court on 24 July that the discussion of methods of killing was very blunt but not recorded. However, he recalled thinking:

> Look at that ... Stuckart, who was always considered to be a very precise and very particular stickler for the law, and here the whole tone and all the manner of speech were totally out of keeping with legal language.

When Judge Raveh asked him to specify, Eichmann added, 'There was talk about killing and eliminating and exterminating.'[44]

Dr Wilhelm Stuckart (1902–1953) was a Doctor of Law and became a judge in 1930. However, in his role as State Secretary of the Reich Ministry of the Interior, from 1935 he was responsible for the drafting of all the anti-Jewish legislation including the Nuremberg Laws against the Jew. In 1940 he was involved in measures to remove German citizenship from Jews and in 1941 he worked on the proposal to make Jews wear a distinguishing mark. At Wannsee he proposed the compulsory sterilisation of 'persons of mixed blood' – the Mischlinge.

Eichmann also testified that the official part of the meeting was in two halves. The first was when they all listened to Heydrich explaining, and then the second half when:

> ... everyone spoke about the matter all at once, and where the whole time the orderlies kept serving cognac or other drinks, and it got to the stage of alcoholic influence ... all I mean is that, although it was an official matter, but still, it was not a stiff official matter, where everyone is quiet and everyone lets everyone have their say to the end, but at the end everyone spoke at once.[45]

The meeting, held in the dining room, only lasted ninety minutes and then delegates all enjoyed a buffet lunch.

On my visit I felt chilled at being where such a momentous decision had been taken – for all Jews, and consequently for my parents and me. My presence there with another Hungarian survivor was a triumph of sorts, especially as we met a group of Israeli students who were in Berlin for a basketball competition. Their leader explained to them that we were Holocaust survivors and we had our photograph taken with the Israeli students in the house. The attendees from 20 January 1942 must have spun in their graves.

According to the USHMM, not one of the attending Nazis made any objection to the policies proposed. This was not surprising, as the people invited had all previously been involved in anti-Jewish activities. USHMM concluded, 'Never before had a modern state committed itself to the murder of an entire people.'[46]

## James Grover McDonald (1886–1964)

I came across this remarkable man when I was researching the Holocaust rescuers and I have never understood why he is not better known. In the preface to his memoir, *My Mission to Israel 1948–1951*, which covered his time as the first American Ambassador to the State of Israel, he explained his background in Jewish affairs:

> I have been, therefore, actively concerned with Jewish affairs, since the appointment in 1933 to the League of Nations High Commissionership. My acceptance of that appointment grew out of my experience of international affairs in the preceding years when I had been Chairman of the Foreign Policy Association. I had spent much time in Europe, talked much, read more, listened still more. I had met Hitler; and I became convinced that the battle against the Jew was the first skirmish in a war on Christianity, on all religion, indeed on all humanity. And I, a Middle Western American of Scotch and German ancestry, a teacher and student by profession and inclination, found myself increasingly engaged in an active career which gave me the privilege of fighting a good fight. The right of the Jew not only to life but to his own life is in its way a symbol of every man's right. It is in that spirit that I have sought, and continue to seek, to champion this right.[47]

His role at the League of Nations, the precursor of the United Nations, was High Commissioner for Refugees (Jewish and Other) Coming from Germany. It was his meeting with Hitler in 1933 that convinced him of the Nazis' aim to exterminate the Jews. His attempts to help the Jews and other minorities were hampered by both the league's policies and the fact that America was not a member. Additionally, the French and the British governments were not supportive and the post was inadequately funded.

When the Nuremberg Laws were passed in 1935, McDonald realised there would be many new refugees as a result and he decided to resign from his post.[48] However, he chose to write a letter of resignation to the Secretary General of the league on 27 December 1935, with a thirty-four page appendix in which he outlined the background and the issues.

His letter acknowledged that the persecution in Germany was going to impoverish or send into exile hundreds of thousands of Jews and non-Aryan Christians treated as Jews, as well as those Christians who, in conscience, felt they would have to oppose the absolute will of the Nazi state. The really significant fact was that the only charge against these people was that they were not 'Nordic', but 'they cannot escape oppression by any act of their own free-will, for what has been called "the membership of non-Aryan race" cannot be changed or kept in abeyance'.

He also referred to a resolution passed by the Assembly of the League in 1922, which expressed the hope that 'states not bound by specific legal obligations in the matter of minorities will nonetheless observe in the treatment of their own minorities at least as high a standard of justice and toleration as is required by the treaties in question'. That earlier resolution was reaffirmed in 1933 by the assembly, when considering the persecution of German Jews in Germany. Moreover, to avoid any doubts about it covering the German-Jewish situation, the assembly voted, with only Germany dissenting, in favour of a further resolution that this principle 'must be applied without exception to all classes of nationals of a state which differ from the majority of the population in race, language or religion':[49]

> The resignation was followed by a petition which had ten signatories from various international bodies in the US, France and Netherlands. They highlighted the terms of the solemn pledge given to the Principal Allied and Associated Powers at the Peace Conference in June 1919 which the German National Socialist government had by its systematic discrimination and persecution of persons they called 'non-Aryans' violated. That valid and binding undertaking gives the Allied Powers the right and duty to intercede so that this violation will cease. The situation was aggravated by the Nazi Government's deliberately imposing on its neighbours and other states the burden of a refugee problem which is causing international concern.[50]

At the end of his letter, McDonald said that he could not keep silent when he foresaw desperate suffering for Germany's neighbours and 'an even more terrible human calamity within the German frontiers'. McDonald's pleadings concluded:

> When domestic policies threaten the demoralization and exile of hundreds of thousands of human beings, considerations of diplomatic correctness must yield to those of common humanity. I should be recreant if I did not call attention to the actual situation, and plead that world opinion, acting through the League and its Member-States and other countries, move to avert the existing and impending tragedies.

However, as we know from history, his pleadings fell on deaf ears both at the League of Nations and among the individual member states.

In 2004 the 10,000 pages of his diaries were donated to the United States Holocaust Memorial Museum (USHMM) by his daughters and are available for the public to read. The diaries cover the years 1922–1936 and then 1946–1951. He dictated the entries to his secretary at the end of each day.

He was born on 29 November 1886 in Ohio to a German mother, so he was fluent in German. Later at Harvard he became friends with German students and many of them later became prominent in the Nazi Party. He visited Germany regularly in the 1920s and 1930s and his Harvard connections, fluent German and Aryan looks led Nazis to speak openly about their plans for Germany and the Jews. On 4 April 1933, McDonald met two Nazi party officials:

> I looked forward to an informing analysis of the Nazi economic program. Instead, after we discussed it for ten or fifteen minutes, both Daitz and Lüdecke [Werner Daitz and Kurt G.W. Lüdecke] drifted back to the subject of the Jews, which seems to be an obsession with so many of the Nazis ... The casual expressions used by both men in speaking of the Jews were such as to make one cringe, because one would not speak so of even a most degenerate people.
>
> When I indicated my disbelief in their racial theories, they said what other Nazis had said, 'But surely you, a perfect type of Aryan, could not be unsympathetic with our views' ... I had the impression that they really do set unbelievable store by such physical characteristics as long heads and light hair.

He was one of the few people who was clear-sighted about what was happening in Germany and, more importantly, what was going to happen. On 25 November he wrote about his imminent resignation and a meeting with Viscount Robert Cecil, a founder of the League of Nations:

> I then explained to him what I had in mind in connection with my letter of resignation [as High Commissioner] to the Secretary General, that I intended in that to speak with complete frankness about affairs in Germany which are making for the destruction of the whole of the Jewish people and in addition a certain number of non-Aryans.[51]

His diaries also reported the views of various public figures whom he met, such as Cosmo Lang, the Archbishop of Canterbury 1928–1942, who told McDonald just before the Second World War that he believed German Jews had brought on themselves the hatred of Hitler, while Lady Nancy Astor, who had favoured appeasement of Hitler, asked him, 'Did I not after all believe that there must be something in the Jews themselves which had brought them persecution throughout all ages?'

When McDonald met Cardinal Pacelli in 1933, he found him more concerned about Bavarian Catholics than German Jews. This indifference is believed to have continued when he became Pope Pius XII.[52]

Over sixty years later, Eli Wiesel told an audience at the Clinton White House in April 1999 about his views on indifference toward the fate of the Jews in the Holocaust. He spoke about his time in Auschwitz and later Buchenwald and how in all the suffering they assumed the world did not know what was happening:

If they knew, we thought, surely those leaders would have moved heaven and earth to intervene. They would have bombed the railways leading to Birkenau, just the railways, just once. And now we knew, we learned, we discovered that the Pentagon knew, the State Department knew. And the illustrious occupant of the White House then, who was a great leader – and I say it with some anguish and pain, because, today is exactly 54 years marking his death – Franklin Delano Roosevelt died on April 12 1945, so he is very much present to me and to us.

No doubt, he was a great leader. He mobilized the American people and the world, going into battle, bringing hundreds and thousands of valiant and brave soldiers in America to fight fascism, to fight dictatorship, to fight Hitler. And so many of the young people fell in battle. And, nevertheless, his image in Jewish history – I must say it – his image in Jewish history is flawed.

The depressing tale of the *St Louis* is a case in point. Sixty years ago, its human cargo – maybe 1,000 Jews – was turned back to Nazi Germany. And that happened after the Kristallnacht, after the first state sponsored pogrom, with hundreds of Jewish shops destroyed, synagogues burned, thousands of people put in concentration camps. And that ship, which was already on the shores of the United States, was sent back.

I don't understand. Roosevelt was a good man, with a heart. He understood those who needed help. Why didn't he allow these refugees to disembark? A thousand people – in America, a great country, the greatest democracy, the most generous of all new nations in modern history. What happened? I don't understand. Why the indifference, on the highest level, to the suffering of the victims?[53]

The Bermuda Conference of 1943 is in some ways a continuation of the negativity that so frustrated James McDonald in the 1930s. By the end of 1942 the Nazis' intention to exterminate European Jewry had become irrefutable and Jewish organisations were pushing for their governments to do something. There were also millions of refugees in Europe, and so the UK and the USA jointly sponsored a conference intending to resolve some of these issues. It was held in Bermuda from 19 April 1943 and its discussions were secret. After twelve days very little had been achieved.

The Jewish Agency executive was the driving force behind the Bermuda Conference, even though the event was sponsored by Britain and the USA. The agency was acting as an official organisation to form a national home for Jews in

Palestine, but only began to trust reports on the Final Solution in 1942, when the evidence could no longer be refuted.

According to Yad Vashem, the conference was planned by the USA and UK to be ineffective:

> The purpose of the conference, supposedly, was to deal with the issue of war-time refugees. The real reason the conference was called, however, was to shush the growing public outcries for the rescue of European Jewry without actually having to find any solutions to the problem.

Bermuda was chosen for its inaccessibility, which would limit the number of reporters and private individuals who could attend.

The organisers also severely limited the issues that could be discussed. They insisted that the Jewish aspect of the problem not be mentioned, and neither government was willing to discuss the Final Solution. Furthermore, the Americans refused to consider changing their strict immigration quotas to let in more Jewish refugees, while the British refused to consider Palestine as a safe haven for Jewish refugees. They would not even discuss sending food packages to concentration camp prisoners. The Americans also betrayed their lack of seriousness by not send-ing a high-ranking delegation with the authority to make decisions.

The only major outcome of the conference was the decision to open a refugee centre in North Africa. In reality, however, it took more than a year to establish the centre and not a single Jew was saved by the conference.[54]

The British Government had raised 'certain complicating factors' with the State Department in January 1943 which led them to believe in the need for a 'joint effort in dealing with the problem'. The issues raised were:

> (a) The refugee problem cannot be treated as though it were a wholly Jewish problem which could be handled by Jewish agencies or by machinery only adapted for assisting Jews. There are so many non-Jewish refugees and there is so much acute suffering among non-Jews in Allied countries that Allied criti-cism would probably result if any marked preference were shown in removing Jews from territories in enemy occupation. There is also the distinct danger of stimulating anti-semitism in areas where an excessive number of foreign Jews are introduced.
> (b) There is at present always a danger of raising false hopes among refugees by suggesting or announcing alternative possible destinations in excess of shipping probabilities.
> (c) There is a possibility that the Germans or their satellites may change over from the policy of extermination to one of extrusion, and aim as they did before the war at embarrassing other countries by flooding them with alien immigrants.[55]

In spite of these concerns, the UK Government felt something had to be done, but I think the expression of these factors shows a complete lack of understanding of the true situation of the Jews of Europe.

The significance of the British policy on refugees was brought home to me in April 2010 when I spoke at Neath & Port Talbot College, in Wales, about the courage of the Holocaust rescuers. One of the lecturers told me about his father, who served in the British Army in Palestine from November 1945 to May 1947. Apparently he was based on the coast and one day he and his colleagues saw a boat come in full of people, who they could see were in a very poor state. Their orders were not to allow the boat to dock and let the passengers get off. After a while he and some of his chums decided to try to get some of the people off and one night they succeeded. They hid them behind some oil drums and the next day they all escaped. The lecturer said his father had never spoken to him or anyone else about this as they could have been charged. But like the Holocaust rescuers, he did what he felt was right and ignored the government's orders.

One of the ironies of the Holocaust is that even seventy years later, information is still trickling out. I had written this chapter when a report by a panel of historians from the University of Luxembourg was published on 10 February 2015. It had been initiated by the former prime minister Jean-Claude Juncker in 2013, when a list of 280 Jewish children who were transported to their deaths from Luxembourg was discovered. The list created such controversy that Juncker commissioned a study on local complicity during the Holocaust.

Yad Vashem records that 3,500 Jews lived in Luxembourg before the German invasion and 1,945 were murdered in the death camps or on home territory. Very few came back after the war. The 190 page report stated that the country's leaders willingly co-operated with the Nazis in the persecution of the Jews:

> The Luxembourg administrations under occupation were not forced to partici-
> pate in Nazi anti-Semitic persecution under threat. They collaborated once they
> were invited to by the occupier and often fulfilled their task with diligence, zeal
> even – certain heads of the administration did not hesitate to take the initiative.[56]

This was followed in June 2015 by a unanimous adoption of a resolution in the Luxembourg Parliament recognising the suffering of the Jews during the war and apologising for their persecution. The resolution also stated that the memory of the horrors of the Second World War must be kept alive and all efforts were to be made to prevent anti-Semitism developing in Luxembourg. Prime Minister Xavier Bettel stated, 'We must accept responsibility together for this. The fact is that 1,300 Jews were deported from here, Belgium or France and they were all killed. It is a reality for which I apologise directly to today's Jewish community but also to the families.'

Only thirty-six Luxembourg Jews are known to have survived the Holocaust.[57]

# 15

# MEDICAL ISSUES

Of course I am a doctor, I want to preserve life, I would remove a gangrenous appendix from a diseased body. The Jew is the gangrenous appendix in the body of mankind.

Dr Fritz Klein, Auschwitz doctor, in response to the question, 'How can you reconcile that with your [Hippocratic] oath as a doctor?'

The German scientific community and most of its members entered a Faustian pact with National Socialism [NS], trading financial and material support, official recognition and the illusion of professional independence for conscious or unconscious support of NS politics culminating in war, the rape of Europe and genocide.

M. Walker, *Nazi Science*, 1995

On 2 June 1942 reports were received in Istanbul that 30,000 Jews, who had been deported during the winter from Bessarabia and Bukovina into Transnistria, the Rumanian-held section of Soviet Ukraine, had died from typhus. The situation of Jews in Rumania was becoming similar to Poland – the Jews were only receiving half the food ration given to the rest of the population.

The same report referred to an article by Dr Conti, the chief of the Nazi Health Office, broadcast over Berlin radio, which stated that 672 cases of spotted typhus had been registered during the last month among Jews in the Reich territories as compared with 220 such cases among non-Jews and eight cases among Germans. Dr Conti's article was published in the *Berliner Boerzen-Zeitung*. He was known as the 'Julius Streicher' of medical cases because of his ferocious campaign against Jewish doctors and dentists in the early days of the Nazi regime. His mother was the Chief Midwife under the Nazis.[1]

This chapter will discuss doctors' roles in the Holocaust – both the Nazis and the prisoner doctors, who struggled in dreadful conditions and with virtually no tools apart from their skill, experience and humanity to save lives and ease suffering.

Otto Fleming was a GP in South Yorkshire who wrote about his experiences as a student at the Medical School in Vienna. I knew him in Sheffield and he was a charming gentleman. He wrote about the emphasis on medical ethics and how their first lectures were in the Anatomical Institute which had an inscription in large letters above the professor's lectern: '*Primum non nocere* – Firstly, do no harm'.

Among the advice given to the medical students was never to tell patients if they had a fatal illness and still less that they were about to die. It was assumed that the patients could not cope with such information. During the course, Otto attended lectures from Professor Hans Eppinger (1897–1946). He was the head of the first medical clinic in the Allgemeines Krankenhaus, the University Hospital, well known as a researcher and a clinician, but also for his dry and impersonal attitude. One day he brought a patient into the lecture theatre, introducing him to the students with words which Otto remembered clearly sixty years later:

> 'Nephritis can be compared with a tragedy in five acts and' – pointing to the patient – 'this is the final act of the tragedy.' The patient broke down in tears and was obviously distressed throughout the demonstration. We were all shocked by Eppinger's brutal and unfeeling manner and talked about it among ourselves for some time afterwards.[2]

This reference to 'doing no harm' is part of the Hippocratic Oath, dating from the fifth century BC. It had been observed for around 2,500 years by 1933 when the Nazis came to power and, as with so much else, they disregarded those traditional values and a new breed of physician developed.

Elie Wiesel wrote, 'medicine was practised in certain places not to heal but to harm, not to fight off death but to serve it', with a lack of insight or a perverted loyalty:

> Like the fanatical German theorists, Nazi doctors did their work without any crisis of conscience. They were convinced that by helping Hitler to realise his racial ambitions, they were contributing to the salvation of humanity. The eminent Nazi doctor responsible for 'ethical' questions, Rudolf Ramm, did not hesitate to declare that 'only an honest and moral person may become a good doctor'.
>
> Thus, the doctors who tortured, tormented and killed men and women in the concentration camps for 'medical' reasons had no scruples. Human guinea pigs, prisoners both young and not so young, weakened or still in good health, were subjected to unspeakable suffering and agony in laboratories managed by doctors from the best German families and the most prestigious universities …

In Ravensbrück, Dachau, Buchenwald and Auschwitz, German scientists operated on their victims without anaesthesia in an effort to discover cures for obscure
diseases. The researchers let them die of hunger, thirst, cold: they drowned them,
amputated their limbs, suffocated them, dissected their still-living bodies to study
their behaviour and measure their stamina.[3]

So where does the 'brilliant' Professor Eppinger fit in with the Nazis? It seems
that in the 1920s and 1930s he was 'one of the most prestigious and prodigious
investigators in liver disease'. Adrian Reuben never previously wrote to honour
Eppinger because of his 'utterly ethically unacceptable activities as a medical leader,
physician-scientist and human being'.[4]

Eppinger, born in Prague, was awarded his doctorate in medicine in 1902 in
Graz, following in his father's footsteps. Later he moved to Vienna. He had wide
interests, but his work on liver disease was most important. His 'monograph on
liver pathology and therapy was, in its time, the handbook or bible for anyone
interested in liver disease'. However, he was a difficult personality – he was quite
without scruples:

> … he stole case histories from other physicians and had to be supervised while
> watching operations in case he stole the instruments as well. He was banned from
> the university library after being caught cutting pages out of books and jour-
> nals. He stole gallbladders from Wenckebach's laboratory and later, using these
> specimens without due acknowledgement, he published the phenomenon of
> gallbladder edema in patients who died of beri-beri. Eppinger's callous handling
> of his patients was no less honourable or overt.

A theologian, Helmut Thielicke, wrote about the 'cruel, dangerous and demean-
ing treatment he received' from Eppinger in his autobiography. Even members of
the NSDAP in Vienna complained about his brutality to his patients and, also, his
reckless driving.

An ardent Nazi, he did nothing when 153 out of 197 members of the medical faculty in Vienna were sacked after the *Anschluss*, mostly Jews. He fervently
believed in the goals of the Third Reich and many doctors agreed, as 45 per cent
of the profession were members of the Nazi Party – no other profession had so
many. By joining forces with NSDAP he sought to further his own megalomania
for research opportunities and material support. He assisted the prejudiced new
dean, Eduard Pernkopf, in ruthlessly promoting the Nazi ethos in the Vienna
Medical School. Hans even celebrated the first anniversary of the 'cleansing' of
the faculty with an article in the *Neues Wiener Tagblatt*, writing, 'Now that all *disease* has been eradicated, the Viennese School of Medicine can in future dedicate
itself to its great task without inhibition.' Pernkopf became rektor of the uni-

versity in 1943. After imprisonment for two years by the Allies, he completed his magnum opus, *Atlas of Topographical and Applied Human Anatomy*, for which the bodies of almost 1,400 people executed by the Gestapo, mostly for 'political' reasons, were the models.

Eppinger found it natural to undertake research for the German military effort. A major issue for both sides in the war was sustaining crashed airmen and ship-wrecked sailors stranded in the sea for long periods. Both sides were conducting experiments to make seawater potable. The German Air Ministry disputed the use of an additive – the Berka method – versus desalination, which was expensive. Eppinger and Wolfgang Heubner (a pharmacologist from Berlin):

> ... insisted that a controlled trial be conducted to compare the feeding of seawater (plain, Berka-treated, and desalinated) with that of fresh water or complete water deprivation for up to 12 days, to give the best results on whether permanent health impairment or even death might be suffered by the test subjects.

Eppinger recommended that Dr Wilhelm Beiglböck, his Viennese protégé, should undertake the study in Dachau as no volunteers were available so late in the war. The experiments were conducted in the summer of 1944. Reuben describes the experiments as 'monstrous':

> ... but the pitiful descriptions of suffering, including the endurance of a liver biopsy without anaesthesia, do not bear reproducing here, except to mention that the experimental subjects deprived of water would lick mopped floors and other damp objects in crazed attempts to obtain some moisture.

The papers from Beiglböck's trial show that Eppinger was not a mere accomplice but a key protagonist. The defence used various arguments, especially the claim that there was no legal definition of 'crimes against humanity'. Others used were the inevitable – that they were only obeying orders, the Allies were conducting criminal experiments too, the victims were going to die anyway, and there were no guidelines to follow on human experimentation.

However, no country conducted experiments of 'the magnitude, sadism and State-sponsored human degrading policies of the Third Reich. The Hippocratic Oath was certainly recognised in Germany where specific norms for human experimentation also had been established before 1900.' During his trial, Beiglböck's attempts to tamper with his notebooks and his denial of the deaths that people had witnessed were supported by Eppinger's sworn statement. He was sentenced to fifteen years at the Doctors' Trials. Eppinger escaped justice by poisoning himself on the night of 25 September 1946. As a result of the trials the Nuremberg Code was drafted in 1947.[5]

Reuben concluded his article by discussing whether results from such flawed research should be used. He quotes Vivien Spitz, one of the youngest reporters at Nuremberg, who felt that 'no data acquired from unethical heinous experiments should ever be used, by anybody'. This is difficult, because some of the Nazis' work on smoking and cancer was sound and others feel that if the benefit of the research is of such magnitude that it saves more lives than were lost it could be used, while censoring the investigator each time it is used.

Reuben is unhappy with this approach as it makes the victims 'our retrospective guinea pigs, we make ourselves their retrospective torturers'. Harry Becher thought that, although useful information might be lost by ignoring this material, the moral loss to the profession would be greater if it was published. In the 1980s there was an issue when the editor of the *New England Journal of Medicine* refused to publish the results of the Nazi hypothermia studies which were thought to have valid life-saving data.

I would argue that people suffered enormously during those experiments and if they can benefit subsequent generations, that suffering would not be in vain. However, Elie Wiesel asked why so many doctors all over the world have chosen to cross the line, especially given their level of education and the fact they had chosen a 'healing' profession with the commitment to 'doing good and no harm'.[6] Elie's article ends, 'Am I naïve in believing that medicine is still a noble profession, upholding the highest ethical principles? For the ill, doctors still stand for life. And for us all, hope.'[7]

## The Euthanasia Programme

In the autumn of 1939 the German Government established the Euthanasia Programme, under the direction of Philip Bouhler and Dr Karl Brandt. The headquarters of the operation were at Tiergartenstrasse 4, Berlin, which provided the programme's code name – 'Aktion T4'. It was also referred to as '14f13', which was apparently taken from a file number in the relevant office. This programme led to the deaths of some 200,000 German citizens.

The choice of terminology for the programme is consistent with the Nazis' penchant for euphemism. Euthanasia typically means 'mercy killing', and in the 1990s in the United States and other western nations, it became synonymous with 'physician-assisted suicide'. The killing in the T4 program bears little resemblance to contemporary concepts of euthanasia. Another synonym for gassing people was 'disinfection'.

In 1945 the US forces investigating activities at Hartheim Castle, near Linz in Austria, broke open a steel safe and found a book of statistics. It was a thirty-nine page booklet produced for internal use in Aktion T4 covering the six euthanasia institutions in the Reich. In 1968 and 1970, an ex-employee admitted compiling the statistics:

> The bizarre T4 statistics found at Hartheim also provided an exact account of future expenditures saved by killing the disabled. The T4 statistician figured that 70,273 'disinfections' saved the German Reich 885,439,980 RM over a period of ten years. Computing future savings of food, he argued, for example, that 70,273 murdered patients saved Germany 13,492,440 kilograms of meat and wurst – a macabre utilitarianism designed to rationalize the eugenic and racial ideology that created the killing center.[8]

Hitler's rise to power produced a completely new set of definitions. Guided by the overriding principles of racial hygiene, racial purity and national health, the Nazi regime seemed fairly consistently committed to the removal of those unfit to live and/or likely to produce inferior offspring. This was being discussed from 1933, and by 1935 the Nuremberg Laws provided for the forced sterilisation of the unfit. The practicalities of freeing up institutional and hospital places and the relevant staff by removing these people became an important consideration, particularly as the likelihood of war loomed and facilities would be required for the wounded.

Franz Stangl (1908–1971) was born in Altmunster, Austria, the son of a night-watchman. Stangl joined the Austrian police force in 1931, graduating two years later. In 1935 he was transferred to the political division of the criminal investigation department in the small Austrian town of Wels. A year later he joined the Nazi Party and in November 1940 he became the police superintendent at Hartheim.

Far from 'mercy killing', this programme permitted the murder of children and adults deemed mental, physical or social burdens on society – 'life unworthy of life'. There was no specific law, but a bureaucratic structure that permitted medical personnel to transfer certain patients to designated killing centres. Physicians, nurses and orderlies participated voluntarily in the programme, while the patients themselves often pleaded for their lives or tried to flee the hospital. Patients' families were told that their relative had died of natural causes.

Stangl told Gitta Sereny in 1971 that he had had some moral doubts about the murders. Apparently, in November 1940 he visited a hospital run by Catholic nuns in order to locate a keepsake belonging to a murdered child. The child's mother had received notice of the supposedly natural death and the child's toys and other possessions had been returned to her, but a candle she had given her daughter was missing and she wanted it back:

> 'That's why I had to go there: to find the candle. When I arrived, the Mother Superior, who I had to see, was up in a ward with the priest and they took me up to see her. We talked for a moment and then she pointed to a child – well,

it looked like a small child – lying in a basket. "Do you know how old he is?" She asked me. I said no, how old was he? "Sixteen", she said. "He looks like five, doesn't he? He'll never change, ever. But they rejected him." [The nun was referring to the Medical Commission.] "How could they not accept him?" She said. And the priest who stood next to her nodded fervently. "Just look at him," she went on. "No good to himself or anyone else. How could they refuse to deliver him from this miserable life?" This really shook me. Here was a Catholic nun, a Mother Superior, and a priest. And they thought it was right. Who was I then, to doubt what was being done?

'If these people in this mental hospital for children knew what was happening to their patients, then others must have known too: it was known, wasn't it?

'This was the only time I heard anyone "outside" speak of it,' he said stiffly.[9]

The story is gruesome, as was the entire programme. It must have made a significant impression on Stangl, who remembered the details quite vividly over thirty years later. We may accept that his moral qualms about the murder of sick children were laid to rest by a nun and a priest who fervently supported the programme. If these representatives of the Church found it morally acceptable to put handicapped children to death, how could he, as a Catholic, disagree? Not political ideology nor government propaganda, but the moral stamp of approval by clergy played the crucial role in alleviating the pangs of his conscience. However, by 1942 he was running Treblinka, one of the six major death camps in Poland, where he was responsible for the deaths of 900,000 Jews.

It clearly was known of 'outside', as a letter dated 16 May 1941 from the County Court in Frankfurt to the Minister of Justice demonstrated. The local children of Hadamar near Limburg, where one of the six 'institutes' was based, used to shout at the blacked-out buses, 'Here are some more coming to be gassed', and 'The patients are taken to the gas chambers in paper shirts'. The letter continued:

The corpses enter the furnace on a conveyor belt, and the smoke from the crematorium chimney is visible for miles. At night, Wirth's experts, picked by the Berlin Gestapo ... drink themselves to oblivion in the little Hadamar Gasthof where the regular customers take care to avoid them.[10]

Hadamar was the final destination of 15,000 men, women and children between 1941 and 1945. In the first phase (January–August 1941) about 10,000 were killed with carbon monoxide in a gas chamber made to look like a shower room, as was usual. Subsequently, another 4,420 people were killed between August 1942 and March 1945. There was a resident team of physicians and staff who undertook the killing. The victims were:

German patients with disabilities, mentally disorientated elderly persons from bombed-out areas, half-Jewish children from welfare institutions, psychologically and physically disabled forced laborers and their children, German soldiers and foreign Waffen-SS soldiers deemed psychologically incurable. The medical personnel and staff at Hadamar killed almost all these people by lethal drug overdoses and deliberate neglect.[11]

The US forces arriving at Hadamar learnt of these murders, but as they were committed by Germans against Germans on home ground, they did not constitute war crimes. However, 476 forced labourers with TB from Poland and the Soviet Union, which were Allies, had also been killed and these murders came under international jurisdiction.

The head nurse, Irmgard Huber, was arrested but as her testimony that she never killed patients was supported by colleagues and witnesses, she was released. Later the court discovered she selected patients for murder, falsified death certificates and also controlled the drugs used for overdosing the patients. She was rearrested, tried and sentenced to twenty-five years. Later in 1947, a German court tried her with twenty-five others for the murder of thousands of fellow citizens. She was found to be an accomplice in at least 120 cases and received a further eight years. Three of the more senior male staff were hanged on 14 March 1946.[12]

Gitta Sereny also spoke to Stangl's wife, whom she described as 'on the whole of exemplary honesty'. Frau Stangl admitted she had known what was going on and tried to discuss it with her husband, not knowing he was stationed at Hartheim or what happened there. Perhaps it was as well she didn't know?

However, some of the superiors of the Catholic and Protestant Church had a different view to the nun and the priest whom Stangl had met. Their protests reached a climax on 3 August 1941 when Cardinal Graf Galen, the Bishop of Münster, delivered a sermon denouncing the Nazi euthanasia programme:

> It was during that summer too that Hitler, in the course of a trip through Hof, near Nuremberg, where his train was held up when some mental patients were loaded on to trucks, is said to have had the novel experience of being jeered at by an outraged crowd. Whatever the reason, on August 24, 1941 Dr Karl Brandt (as he was to testify later) received verbal instructions from Hitler at his HQ to stop the Euthanasia Programme. There is no written record of the order.[13]

About 30,000 sick and disabled were murdered at Hartheim. Later, Jewish prisoners from Mauthausen camp were also sent there. These were people who could no longer work in the quarries and their records were marked with fictions like 'recreation leave', 'German hater' or 'communist'. Stangl was the deputy office

manager and Christian Wirth, the office manager, later became commandant of
Belzec extermination camp.

It seems that the euthanasia programme was the university education for future
concentration camp commandants. The Nuremberg Tribunal confirmed that the
euthanasia programme was in violation of German penal law – not much comfort
to the families of the 275,000 victims.

Euthanasia victims were chosen on the basis of questionnaires sent to psychiatric hospitals and other German institutions. Based on the information provided,
those chosen to be killed were transported to designated killing centres. Soon after
arrival they were escorted to extermination chambers disguised as showers, killed
by carbon monoxide poisoning and their bodies cremated. Young doctors oversaw
the killings and fabricated natural causes of death notified to the victim's family.

Julius Hallervorden (1882–1965) was the head of the neuropathology department
of the Kaiser Wilhelm Institute for Brain Research from July 1938. He was a distinguished psychiatrist and neuropathologist, and a Nazi. Hallervorden exploited the
T4 scheme to obtain brains for his research. He gave instructions on how the brains
should be extracted from newly killed victims. In June 1945, when interviewed
by Leo Alexander, an American Army psychiatrist from the Office of the Chief of
War Crimes at Nuremberg, he confirmed what he told the T4 killing centres staff:

> 'Look here now boys, if you are going to kill these people, at least take the brains
> out so that the material could be utilised.' They asked me: 'How many can you
> examine?' and so I told them: 'an unlimited number – the more the better'. I gave
> them fixatives, jars and boxes, and instructions for removing and fixing the brains,
> and then they came bringing them in like a delivery van … There was wonderful
> material among those brains, beautiful mental-defectives, mal-formations and
> early infantile diseases. I accepted these brains of course. Where they came from
> and how they came to me was really none of my business.

Hallervorden published scientific articles based on his examination of these brains,
but he was never prosecuted or investigated for working with the euthanasia programme. While he was not as involved as those who planned the programme or
actually opened the gas valves, his research brought him very close to wrongful
deaths. Hallervorden attempted to whitewash his role with Leo Alexander, but he
was instrumental in having the brains extracted and even did it himself on occasions.

Franklin Miller, writing in the *Journal of Medical Ethics*,[14] examined Hallervorden's
complicity in the murder of the T4 victims and argued that he was tied in with
the wrongdoing and therefore was complicit. The first issue is that he did not seek
ethical authorisation for his research. In addition, he had no consent from the victims or their surrogates. Apparently both US and UK law agree that if B solicits or
encourages A to do a wrongful act, aids A in doing it without directly committing

the wrongful act, or fails to prevent A from doing it when B is in a position to do so, then B is complicit with A in the wrongdoing. So Hallervorden was complicit in the sense of being an accomplice in the Nazi euthanasia programme, and bore some moral responsibility for the killings.

It is also alleged that he was involved in selecting particular patients for research. Henry Friedlander wrote:

> During the first 9 months, for example, 56 male and 41 female patients suffering from retardation, epilepsy or brain injuries were delivered to Gorden [a psychiatric hospital] as subjects for research. The subjects were observed and tested at Gorden; eventually they were killed and their brains were removed and studied, with particular attention to a comparison between the anatomical findings and the data collected earlier.

Miller argued that while Friedlander did not mention Hallervorden, he must have been the neuropathologist who examined the brains and:

> ... if so, then he was a knowing participant in research that involved selecting particular patients for investigation followed by their being killed and using their brains for neuropathological research. This would make him a participant in the selection process leading to murder of these patients and thus arguably an accomplice to murder.

This view is corroborated by Robert Lifton, who wrote about Hallervorden's collaboration with a young psychiatrist called Heinrich Bunke who investigated the medical histories of the patients to identify 'those whose brains might eventually be of interest'. This meant Hallervorden was encouraging Bunke in deciding which patients should be killed and was complicit in those killings. This was a true betrayal of his professional status and also of the poor souls whose brains were exploited.

## Euthanasia of Children

Called the 'Children's Operation', it was carried out by the Reich Committee for the Scientific Processing of Serious Genetic Diseases (18 August 1939–April 1945). It was intended to be a progressive Nazi health policy. Three experts were to review each case and then handicapped children were killed individually by specially trained and authorised doctors. The project was run by Ernst Wentzler, who was the Reich Committee expert and was elected chairman of the Association of German Children's Hospitals. The office was based at Wentzler's private paediatric clinic where handicapped children were murdered.[15]

On 18 August 1939, an unpublished decree from the Reich Ministry of the Interior introduced 'mandatory reporting of deformed, etc. newborns'. The reports were to be sent to the PO Box in Berlin for the Reich Committee for the Scientific Processing of Genetic Diseases which was responsible to the Office of the Fuehrer of the Nazi Party. The following were to be reported: idiocy, Mongolism, microcephalus, hydrocephalus, deformations of all kinds, such as spina bifida and paralyses, including Little's Disease. A report form evaluated the child's medical health and development. These same forms were still used in Bavaria in the 1960s and the writer Götz Aly highlighted in a footnote that a ministerial decree (No. 5346 b I) of 30 November 1945 stated, 'mandatory reporting of deformed etc. newborns using the form created in 1939 will continue until further notice'.

The footnote also refers to a further decree, dated 30 June 1958, referring to 'Inquiry on Deformities in Newborns'. It adds:

> Dr Saller of the Institute of Anthropology and Human Genetics of the University of Munich … has requested support from the State Ministry of the Interior for an inquiry on the incidence of deformities in newborns. Health officials are instructed to support Dr Saller in this project and in particular to allow representatives of the Institute to examine files on hereditary illness and midwife reports of deformities.

The footnote concludes with the statement, 'Geneticist Karl Saller was one of a very few German professors who refused to participate in the Third Reich's medical crimes.'

## Medical Experiments in Auschwitz

It appears that when Alma Rosé was first in Auschwitz, she was in 'experimental block', Block No. 10, where Professor Dr Carl Clauberg (1898–1957), a gynaecologist, conducted experiments in sterilisation. However, when it was discovered she was a distinguished musician she was rescued and put in charge of the orchestra (see pages 214–6).

Clauberg was a professor of gynaecology at the University of Königsberg specialising in fertility issues. He joined the Nazi Party in 1933 with the rank of SS-Gruppenführer (lieutenant general). In 1942 he contacted Heinrich Himmler, whom he knew, about conducting sterilisation experiments on Auschwitz inmates. Himmler agreed and Clauberg moved into Birkenau in December 1942, demanding a special block for this important research. In April 1943 he moved into Block No. 10 in Auschwitz, which was very well equipped with 'wards, an elaborate X-ray apparatus and four special experimental rooms, one of which served as a darkroom for developing X-ray films'.

Dr Robert Lifton highlights issues about the funding of Block 10 since, 'As a civilian, Clauberg was an Auschwitz outsider who rented facilities, research subjects, and even prisoner doctors from the SS.'[16] So it is quite clear that the Nazis were making money out of these ghastly experiments, but the participants, apart from Clauberg and presumably any ancillary staff he chose to employ, had no choice about their involvement.

He was very secretive about his processes, presumably to protect his research from competitors. The notorious camp commandant, Rudolf Höss, was very interested and witnessed some injections. He wrote, 'Clauberg informed me in detail on the performance of the operation, but never revealed to me the exact chemical composition of the substance he used.' However, Lifton wrote that the substance was believed to have been Formalin, sometimes injected along with Novocain. Clauberg developed the formula with his assistant, Dr Johannes Goebel, the chief chemist at the Schering pharmaceutical firm.[17]

Clauberg was seeking a cheap, easy method of sterilising women by injecting a caustic substance into the cervix to block the fallopian tubes. The process was meant to involve three injections over a few months, although some women had four or five. Blockages should have developed in the fallopian tubes after about six weeks. A prisoner nurse, Sylvia Friedmann, observed the women for their subsequent symptoms. Many of the women were terrified, but at the same time were fearful of being sent back to the main camp where, according to Marie L., a French prisoner physician, they would await 'death standing in frost, mud and swamps ... without water or care'.

Clauberg encouraged the women to feel safe by telling them that they would not go back to Birkenau, but rather to his private clinic at Königshütte a few kilometres away. This could have been true, because Höss reported that after successful operations, Clauberg planned that every one of the female prisoners would have sexual intercourse with a specially chosen male prisoner to test the success of Clauberg's method. Apparently, 'the course of the war' prevented this stage of the experiment.[18]

The hormonal preparations Progynon and Prolution that he developed to treat infertility were still being used in 1986, as was the 'Clauberg test' for measuring progesterone action. A Czech-Jewish woman called Margita Newmann described her experience with Clauberg:

Dr Clauberg ordered me to lie down on the gynaecological table and I was able to observe Sylvia Friedmann who was preparing an injection syringe with a long needle. Dr Clauberg used this needle to give me an injection in my womb. I had the feeling that my stomach would burst with the pain. I began to scream so I could be heard through the entire block. Dr Clauberg told me roughly to stop screaming immediately, otherwise I'd be taken back at once to Birkenau concentration camp ... After this experiment I had inflammation of the ovaries.

She described how Clauberg's appearance on the ward frightened women, who viewed him with terror and anxiety as 'they considered what Dr Clauberg was doing as the actions of a murderer'.[19]

He appears to have been an unattractive, short, fat man, with a history of violent behaviour to women. None of his colleagues seem to have spoken well of him. However, he had the ability to get the support of Himmler for his project, presenting it as part of the Nazis' perverted ideology and using sycophantic draftings to Himmler. On 30 May 1932 he wrote to him, stating that he (Clauberg) had been told that 'the one person in Germany today who would be particularly interested in these matters and who would be able to help me would be you, most honourable Reichsführer'.[20] Exploiting the Nazis' interest in 'negative population policy', he described the plan to 'evaluate the method of sterilisation without operation … on women unworthy of propagation and to use this method continually after it is finally proved efficient'. Clauberg stated that Auschwitz was the ideal place for 'the human material to be provided'. He even suggested the clinic should be named after Himmler as the 'Research Institute of the Reichsführer SS for Biological Propagation'.

Himmler eventually approved the project and in the letter sent by his assistant, Rudolf Brand, he indicated that he 'would be interested to learn … how long it would take to sterilise a thousand Jewesses'. However, it seems Himmler was being influenced by another Nazi physician – Dr Adolf Pokorny, a Czech ethnic German, retired from military medicine with a high rank.

In October 1941 Pokorny wrote Himmler a letter which Lifton describes as a 'basic document in the ideological corruption of the healer'. Pokorny was writing in response to the concept that 'the enemy must not only be conquered but destroyed'. He wanted to tell Himmler about recent research on 'medicinal sterilisation', in which a particular plant produced permanent sterility. Pokorny was very excited at the vision – 'a new powerful weapon at our disposal'. He explains, 'The thought alone that the 3 million Bolsheviks, at present German prisoners, could be sterilised so that they could be used as labourers but be prevented from reproduction, opens the most far-reaching perspectives.'[21]

Clauberg had unlimited access to his resources – namely the prisoners. It was noted on 9 December 1943 that 'the occupancy of Professor Dr Clauberg's experimental ward is increased by one: 399 female prisoners for research purposes are housed there'.[22]

However, things were not going well and Clauberg was stalling in reporting to Himmler, seeking better equipment and making other excuses. Lifton claims that Eduard Wirths, Auschwitz's chief doctor (September 1942–January 1945), said Clauberg had gone to the dogs, was a severe alcoholic and totally unscrupulous.[23]

Dr Johannes Goebel, who acted as his assistant, was not a physician but was allowed to perform many of the injections. It is not known how many women suffered at these two men's hands – estimates range from 700 to 'several thousand'. The nurse, Sylvia Friedmann, recorded that if a woman died Clauberg showed no interest or reaction and there were many deaths.

As the Red Army advanced, Clauberg moved his project and some of his victims to Ravensbrück camp, and fled to Schleswig-Holstein to join the group of SS leaders surrounding Himmler. Himmler was captured and committed suicide. Clauberg was captured by the Russians in June 1945, tried for war crimes and sent to prison for twenty-five years.

Following Stalin's death, Clauberg returned to Germany in October 1955. He was quite unrepentant, bragging about his work in Auschwitz so much that he was arrested again in November 1955. However, the German Chamber of Medicine, the official professional body, was reluctant to take away his title. It was only when a group of former prisoner doctors from Auschwitz condemned Clauberg by stating, 'such medical practitioners … [who] put themselves at the service of National-Socialism to destroy human lives … are today in a position to practise once more the profession which they have profaned in such a scandalous manner' that the chamber then removed his licence. However, he died suddenly and mysteriously in his prison cell in August 1957. It was believed he was about to reveal the names of the Nazi medical hierarchy and his erstwhile colleagues got to him first.[24]

Margita Schwalbová (1915– 2002) was born in Bratislava. She had been studying medicine but she was stopped before she qualified and undertook various other jobs. She was arrested on 21 March 1942 with about 1,000 other young women under 30.[25]

Margita was working in Block 10 in Auschwitz with Clauberg and Wirths. A French prisoner psychiatrist, Dr Adelaide Hautval, had been assigned to assist Dr Wirths. He was removing 'the procreative organs of healthy young women for cancer research purposes'. Dr Hautval refused to assist him. Dr Wirths expressed surprise and said to her, '… it concerns inferior human beings, completely different from us'.

Dr Hautval replied, 'Herr Hauptsturmführer, I consider you also to be different from me; that still does not authorize me to sterilize you'. She was moved back to Birkenau and they all worried about her future. 'To refuse the execution of an SS-man's order was synonymous with a death sentence.' They put Dr Hautval into the Revier and fed her sleeping pills so that when Dr Wirths visited she was never conscious.[26]

Sonja Fritz, who worked in the same area, wrote about the incident, around February 1943: 'I was present when she declined. She was the daughter of a minister and cited her religion as a reason for her refusal. Many years ago, I saw her again in Paris.'[27]

That was all Schwalbová and Fritz wrote about this courageous woman so, through the wonders of the internet, I discovered her story. Born in France to a Protestant family in 1906, Adelaïde Hautval studied medicine in Strasbourg and afterwards worked in several psychiatric wards. In April 1942, she was living in a Vichy-controlled area in southern France when her mother died in occupied Paris. She asked for permission to enter the occupied zone, but it was refused. She was arrested trying to cross the demarcation line without the correct permit. While awaiting trial in Bourges Prison, she protested about the harsh treatment of the Jewish prisoners. The response was, 'As you wish to defend them, you will follow their fate.' Accordingly, she was sent to Auschwitz, with a group of women prisoners, arriving in January 1943. It is alleged that she had a sign stitched to her coat, 'A friend of the Jews'.

It is not possible to know how many other courageous individuals protested about the treatment of Jews, but in 1941 a Berlin worker reported that a workmate was sent to Wustermark forced labour camp because he 'had expressed indignation and disgust when a column of Jewish workers who were being marched though the factory courtyard were maltreated by the Nazi guards'. [28]

At Auschwitz, Dr Hautval helped hide some women suffering from typhus and tried to look after them. 'Here,' she said, 'we are all under sentence of death. Let us behave like human beings as long as we are alive.' After the confrontation with Wirths she feared some retribution, but was merely advised to stay out of sight and she wasn't punished. After being moved to the Birkenau camp she continued trying to help heal the prisoners. In August 1944 she was moved to Ravensbrück, to be liberated in April 1945. Her health had been permanently impaired but she returned to France and was decorated with the Legion of Honour in December 1945.

In 1963, she came to London for the libel trial of Leo Uris vs Wladyslaw Dering. Uris, in his famous book *Exodus*, had referred to the experiments undertaken by Dering, and others, on prisoners in Auschwitz without anaesthetics and Dering had sued Uris for libel. Dr Hautval was a witness for the defence and the judge, Mr Justice Lawton, in his summing up to the jury described Dr Hautval as 'perhaps one of the most impressive and courageous women who has ever given evidence in the courts of this country'.

Years later, recalling the Holocaust, she stated:

> This unspeakable horror could have been avoided. If only this organised con-
> tempt of humanity, this megalomaniac insanity, had been confronted by a civilised
> world – lucid, courageous and determined to safeguard its primary values.

In 1966 she was recognised as a Righteous Among the Nations, and the next year she travelled to Israel to plant her tree. She died in 1988. [29]

1. Author's mother (far right) with her parents, Rosa and Armin Klein, and sisters, 1932. The photograph was taken to celebrate their twentieth wedding anniversary. (*Author's collection*)

2. Victor and Wilma Deutsch, Otto's parents, on their wedding day in Vienna, 18 May 1920. (*Courtesy of Otto Deutsch*)

3. Otto, his mother and sister Adele the day before he left Vienna on the Kindertransport, 3 July 1939. (*Courtesy of Otto Deutsch*)

4. Nieweg home in Farmsum, Groningen. (*Sara Kirby-Nieweg*)

5. Nieweg teaset. (*Sara Kirby-Nieweg*)

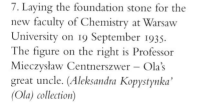

6. Rudi Lek playing his beloved piano in 1999. (*Lek family collection*)

7. Laying the foundation stone for the new faculty of Chemistry at Warsaw University on 19 September 1935. The figure on the right is Professor Mieczysław Centnerszwer – Ola's great uncle. (*Aleksandra Kopystynka' (Ola) collection*)

8. Samuel and Emma Morgenstern in the 1930s. (*Ilse Loeb*)

9. Marcelle Garnier (now Aune) in the 1930s. (*J.J. Aune*)

10. Journalist Philip Mechanicus, who kept a diary in Westerbork camp. (*Jewish Historical Museum collection, Amsterdam*)

11. Dr Michael Siegel paraded through Munich on 10 March 1933, after he had complained to the Munich police about the treatment of his client. The Nazis cut off the bottom half of his trouser legs and led him through Munich's inner-city streets barefoot with a board around his neck saying, 'I will never complain to the police again.' (*Courtesy of Bea Green*)

12. Offenbach book depot. (*Courtesy of Yad Vashem*)

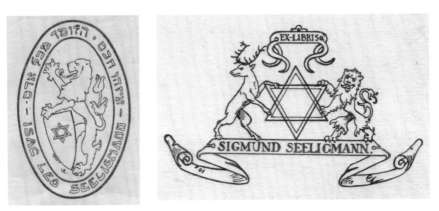

13. Book plates: a) Leo Seeligmann; b) Sigmund Seeligmann; c) David Cohen, who was Chairman of the Amsterdam Jewish Council. (*Ex Libris of Jews in Netherlands Project*)

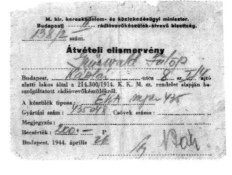

14. Receipt for a radio belonging to Leona and Philipp Grunwald, the author's parents, dated 26 April 1944. (*Author's collection*)

15. Bea Green (right), daughter of Michael Siegel, on Kindertransport train. (*Courtesy of Bea Green*)

16. Boycott day, 1 April 1933, at two of the 5PS stores. (*Peter Smith*)

17. Elephant 'Tuzinka'
at Warsaw Zoo, 1935.
The Nazis took her
to Germany. (*Courtesy
of Warsaw Zoo Archive*)

18. Jan and Antonina
Zabinski, 1945.
(*Courtesy of Warsaw
Zoo Archive*)

19. Valuables from
Berlin in sacks found
in Merkers Salt mine.
(*USHMM*)

20. 1920s JdF poster

21. Janine Webber (4), her brother Tunio (2) and their mother Lipka Monat, 1936. (*Courtesy of Janine Webber*)

22. Nijmegen Synagogue in 1942. (*Courtesy of Regionaal Archief Nijmegen, Fotopersbureau Gelderland*)

23. Photograph of Annelore's mother Maria Knappe, born in 1914, taken in the 1990s. (*Courtesy of Annelore Yasseri-John*)

24. Photograph of Annalore's father Walter Spyra, born in 1911, taken at the same time. (*Courtesy of Annelore Yasseri-John*)

Wirths was from a Catholic family. He came to Auschwitz from Dachau and Neuengamme camps. His 'scientific experiments' were aimed at the early detection of cervical cancer. He never appeared personally at the experiments, which were frequently fatal to the patients. One female witness said, 'He never operated himself … never did … anything … not injections, nothing.' In 1945 he was arrested by the British and committed suicide. Beforehand, he presented a justification that he had prepared when he fled. 'I took pains to help sick prisoners, according to my Christian and medical conscience …'[30]

## IG Farben Experiments in Auschwitz

On 13 October 1942, SS Captain Dr Helmuth Vetter came to Auschwitz. From 1941 to 1944 Vetter carried out pharmacological experiments on prisoners, acting as a camp doctor in Auschwitz, Dachau and Mauthausen camps, testing medicines. Vetter was a former employee of Bayer, part of IG Farben, and he worked 'closely' with his former employer in his experiments. The preparations had various numbers, e.g. B-1012, B-1034 or 3582. The same day, Höss ordered that the families of the SS men within the camp must be immunised against typhus because of the current epidemic. This proved the Nazis had a typhus vaccine, but did not waste it on the Jews.[31]

On 27 January 1943, Dr Bruno Weber and Dr König from Bayer wrote to Vetter to recommend testing the tolerance among typhus fever victims for '3582', which was a nitroacridine preparation. They suggested that if no typhus patients were available, they should try the substance on diarrhoea patients. The Bayer doctors stressed the importance of these experiments for the armed forces. They provided Vetter with additional supplies of medication, both as tablet and granules, and detailed dosage instructions. In fact, Vetter observed the effect of '3582' and Rutenol on fifty typhus patients in the main camp.[32]

A mere twelve days later, on 8 February, Vetter got prisoner Dr Władysław Fejkiel (No. 5647) to prepare a report on the experiments with Farben's 3582 on a group of typhus fever patients. It appears that the fifty patients had not tolerated it well. Fifteen patients (30 per cent) had died, 2.6 per cent at the end of the course of treatment, and 8 per cent during the treatment. Six of those deaths were from weakness of the heart muscle, six from toxic consumption, and two from brain complications and an unknown fever. The report concluded that there had been no 'concrete therapeutic results'.

On the same day, Commandant Höss banned SS members' leave because of ongoing concerns about the typhus epidemic outside the camp. A footnote records:

The mass killings of prisoners infected with typhus as well as the delousings and disinfections that are carried out in the prisoners' quarters, in which the sanitary and hygienic conditions remain unchanged, do not have the success expected by

the SS and cannot prevent a further spread of the epidemic. Although SS personnel and members of their families have been vaccinated against typhus and take
the recommended hygienic precautions, there are cases of typhus even among
them and they spread the disease outside the camp.[33]

## Starvation Research

SS-Obersturmführer Johann P. Kremer MD, PhD, was an associate professor at
the University of Münster, based on a work called 'The Alteration of Muscle
Tissue under Conditions of Hunger'. On 30 August 1942 he went to Auschwitz
to carry out 'research on hunger'. In fact, he was only there for a short period,
leaving on 18 November 1942. His appointment was as a doctor and he was
replacing someone who was ill. He assessed prisoners who were trying to get into
the hospital. He ordered most of them to be killed by phenol injections. For his
research, he selected those who were almost dead from malnutrition – very weak
both spiritually and physically.

While imprisoned in a Polish prison, he described his methods:

> When somebody interested me because of an advanced state of starvation, I gave
> the orderly instructions to reserve the patient for me and to notify me on the date
> on which he was to be killed by injection. At that time, those patients selected
> by me were taken to the block and put on the dissecting table while they were
> still alive. I approached the table and asked the patient about details of interest to
> my research: for example, his weight before imprisonment, weight loss during
> imprisonment, if he had taken medication recently and such things. After I had
> obtained this information, the orderly came in and killed the patient with an
> injection to the heart. I myself never gave a lethal injection.

When he arrived he was given 'strictly secret orders' from the area medical officer,
Uhlenbrock. Kremer kept a journal in Auschwitz from which we can read his
major interests, which seem to be obtaining fresh organs from freshly killed starving
prisoners, and details of what he himself ate and the cost. Sometimes the juxtaposi-
tion of the entries requires what Kremer obviously had – a strong stomach:

> 31.08.1942
> Tropical climate, 38° in the shade, dust and countless flies!
> Food in officers' mess excellent.
> This evening pickled duck liver for 0.40 RM, plus stuffed tomatoes and tomato
> salad. Water is contaminated, so we drink soda water, which is free. First inocula-
> tion against typhus fever.

01.09.1942

In afternoon attended block gassing with Zyklon B against lice.

02.09.1942

3.00 a.m. attended my first Sonderaktion (Special Action). Dante's *Inferno* seems to me almost a comedy compared with this. They don't call Auschwitz an extermination camp for nothing.

05.09.1942

In the morning attended a Sonderaktion from the women's concentration camp. Heinz Thilo, Camp Doctor, was right when he said this is the *anus mundi* (arse of the world).

8.00 p.m. attended another Sonderaktion from Holland. Because of the special rations they get of a fifth of a litre of schnapps, 5 cigarettes, 100 grams and bread, the men all clamour to take part in such actions.

06.09.1942

Today Sunday, excellent luncheon: tomato soup, half a chicken, with potatoes and red cabbage (20g fat), dessert and wonderful vanilla ice-cream.

After the meal met Wirths the new medical officer.

Had now been in camp a week but still had fleas in room in spite of using Flit.

09.09.1942

Very happy because he learns from his lawyer in Munster that he is now divorced. [No information on Mrs Kremer's views.]

Later attended, as the doctor, at corporal punishment of eight prisoners and an execution with small bore rifle.

Received soap flakes and two bars of soap.

20.09.1942

Sunday – heard wonderful concert between 3–6 o'clock – conductor was the director of the Warsaw State Opera. 80 musicians. For Lunch there was roast pork, in the evening baked tench.

23.09.1942

Tonight sixth and seventh Sonderaktion.

Dinner a real feast. There was baked pike, as much as you wanted, real ground coffee, excellent beer and open sandwiches.

03.10.1942
Today fixed fresh living material from human liver and spleen as well as pancreas, also fixed lice from typhus-fever patients in absolute alcohol.

09.10.1942
Sent off to Munster parcel with 9 pounds of soft soap worth 200RM.

10.10.1942
Extracted and fixed fresh live material from liver, spleen and pancreas.

11.10.1942
Sunday – roast hare for lunch – a real fat leg – with dumplings and red cabbage for 1.25 RM.

And so it went on, until he left on 18 November. Kremer was observing the murders and instructing whose organs he wanted from dying, starving people while enjoying amazing food in the officers' mess. He was also sending parcels of basic goods like soap on a regular basis to a Frau Wizemann in Munster. On the day before he left, he noted in his usual methodical way:

> Sent small crate to Frau Wizemann (5th parcel) worth 300RM. Contents: (14 kg!)
> 2 bottles of brandy, vitamin and strengthening preparations, razor blades, washing
> and shaving soap, thermometer, nail clippers, bottle of iodine, preparation in 90%
> alcohol, X-ray plates, cod-liver oil, writing materials, envelopes, perfumes, cotton
> wool, needles, tooth powder, etc. etc.[34]

Natzweiler camp is not well known – it was set up by the SS in 1940 in Alsace and had twenty satellite labour camps. The first executions were held there on 18 September 1942 and it was liberated on 31 August 1944 – in that period at least 25,000 prisoners, Jews and non-Jews, died as a result of starvation, ill-treatment or murder. Members of the French Resistance were also sent there, as well as Polish and Russian prisoners. The meticulous records show that eight civilians from Luxembourg were shot in the camp on 19 May 1944.

I specifically included Natzweiler because of a particularly gruesome plan of Himmler's for a special museum in nearby Strasbourg. On 6 November 1942 he had given support to establishing a collection of Jewish skulls and skeletons at the Reich Anatomical Institute. To provide some exhibits for the museum, though I don't know whether they knew it, seventy-three Jews and thirty Jewesses were chosen at Auschwitz and taken to Natzweiler, where they were measured, weighed and gassed. Afterwards the bodies were sent to the Anatomical Institute. Unfortunately, this sacrifice was in vain as when, on 15 October 1946, Himmler became aware of the advance of the Allies to Strasbourg, he ordered the destruction of the collection, although not the documents – perhaps even he realised the collection might not find favour outside the Nazi Party?[35]

Natzweiler was an experimental centre to perfect the mass killing process to be used in Poland and Germany – but this was in France. Bizarrely, the gas chamber was built inside a disused dance hall in a pine forest. The experiment was ordered by Dr August Hirt, a professor at Heidelberg Anatomy Institute and the University of Strasbourg.

Joseph Kramer was the commandant of Natzweiler-Struthof and lived with his family in a recently built holiday villa, conveniently close to the gas chamber so he only had a short walk to work each day. He had been promoted to Bergen-Belsen. Prior to his hanging in 1945, he gave the British a detailed description of these experiments. He described how, at 8.00 p.m. one evening in early August 1943, he took fifteen women to the chamber and made them undress, telling them they were going to a disinfection room. With the help of some of the SS he pushed them into the chamber and shut the door. He then dealt with the chemicals as instructed and watched through the observation window:

> I noticed that the women continued to breathe for about a half-minute. Then they fell to the ground. When I opened the door after starting the fan in the aeration chimney, I saw that these women were lying lifeless after releasing their faecal matter.
>
> I ordered two SS male nurses to take the corpses to a lorry the following day at about 5.30 a.m. so that they could be taken to the anatomy institute as Professor Hirt had asked.
>
> Some days later, I again took a number of women to the gas chamber and they were suffocated in the same way. Afterwards, I took about 50 men in two or three groups and they were killed, always with the help of the salt I had been given by Hirt.
>
> I felt no emotion in accomplishing these acts because I was bred like that.[36]

These activities at Natzweiler were to receive worldwide media coverage in July 2015 when the remains of some of Hirt's victims were discovered in the University of Strasbourg. An historian, Raphael Toledano, discovered them after years of research and after denials from the authorities. The university's president, Alain Beretz, denied the claims prior to the discovery of the glass containers holding various body parts. The Allied forces who liberated Natzweiler-Struthhof in 1944 had found eighty-six skeletons in Hirt's collection which were sent for burial at the local Jewish cemetery.[37] Toledano was guided by a 1952 letter left by a forensic professor, Camille Simonin, who investigated Hirt's crimes.[38]

The horror increases with Auschwitz women prisoners being 'sold' to Bayer, part of IG Farben, as human guinea pigs for new drugs. This is confirmed in correspondence between Bayer and the Auschwitz authorities found in the Auschwitz files. It dealt with the sale of 150 female prisoners for experimental purposes:

With a view to the planned experiments with a new sleep-inducing drug we would appreciate it if you could place a number of prisoners at our disposal ... – We confirm your response, but consider the price of 200 RM per woman to be too high. We propose to pay no more than 170 RM per woman. If this is acceptable to you, the women will be placed in our possession. We need some 150 women ... – We confirm your approval of the agreement. Please prepare for us 150 women in the best health possible ... – Received the order for 150 women. Despite their macerated condition they were considered satisfactory. We will keep you informed of the developments regarding the experiments ... – The experiments were performed. All test persons died. We will contact you shortly about a new shipment ...

The Bayer company's offer of 170 Reichsmarks for each woman was accepted at Auschwitz. When the first batch died in the experiment, more victims were required. The casual language is remarkable, and the word 'kindly' seems somewhat out of place:[39]

The transport of 150 women arrived in good condition. However, we were unable to obtain conclusive results because they died during the experiments. We would kindly request that you send us another group of women to the same number and at the same price.

## The Entomological Institute of the Waffen-SS[40]

In 1941, Heinrich Himmler, head of the SS and police, ordered the creation of an entomological institute and it was originally surmised that its function was to study insects that inflict harm to humans, particularly louse-vectored typhus. Since then, further investigation suggests that some of the research related to biological warfare.

From summer 1941 to early 1942, Himmler travelled in the east of Germany dealing with the Jewish genocide. That was when he first showed interest in an entomological institute, and on 19 November 1941 he proposed the creation of an Institute for Rat & Pest Control. Over Christmas, Himmler visited the eastern front and he realised the high prevalence of lice among the SS. When he returned to Berlin on 6 January 1942 louse control was on his agenda, as there was an outbreak of louse-born typhus at the Neuengamme camp at Hamburg. There was a constant fear of it spreading to the SS guards and staff.

The fear of typhus was deeply ingrained into most, if not all, leading military personnel at the time because louse-vectored typhus epidemics were a major source of mortality of the German (and other) troops in the First World War and had spread into the civilian population.

Himmler, therefore, had two main aims – to protect his SS troops from insect-borne disease at the front and to protect the SS guards in the camps. He gave very specific instructions as to which insects were to be researched, later adding ants and termites and the defence of humans with 'vaccination improving immunity'. Himmler had some entomological knowledge and knew many epidemic diseases were insect-borne. He also had a phobia about flies. Reinhardt comments that 'the topics on the research agenda were a somewhat bizarre mixture of Himmler's semi-knowledge, personal fears, esoteric views, in addition to genuine concern for his SS troops'.

An additional consideration was the use of slave labour in the arms and chemical industries which brought great financial benefits. The original intention was to use Soviet POWs as the workforce, but the mortality rate was so high, Himmler decided prisoners from concentration camps should be used. This was the infamous Vernichtung durch Arbeit (Annihilation through Work). Accordingly, an insect-borne epidemic could be disastrous to the SS, not to mention the poor prisoners, because of the potential financial loss on their industrial contracts.

The best contender to lead the institute was Professor Karl Ritter von Frisch (1886–1982), who won the Nobel Prize for Physiology & Medicine in 1973 for his work on bees. He was discounted because of a suspect non-Aryan grandmother, and his referee, Professor Gerlach, was suspect because his 'descent also does not seem to be proper'. Eventually in spring 1942 a compromise candidate of doubtful calibre, Eduard May (1905–1956), was chosen. He was not a member of the Nazi Party, but this appointment was not a surprise:

May's appointment parallels other areas of war-and-military-related science in WWII Germany, where the people involved (with very few exceptions) were not the leading researchers in their fields. Himmler especially seems to have given responsibility to people whose careers were on the verge of failing. By providing them with another, seemingly last, chance, they were easy to manipulate. Some became Himmler's most obsessive followers. Did May become one, too?

The institute came under the Ahnenerbe, the culture and education division of the SS that Himmler wanted to develop and exploit to prove his ideas of Aryan superiority in spirit, physical strength and history. Sited on the margins of the camp of Dachau, it was part of the Institute for Applied Defence Science with departments headed by some infamous people. Sigmund Rascher carried out and observed lethal freeze-drowning experiments on live prisoners in Dachau and Professor August Hirt carried out sulphur mustard trials on humans and also chose human subjects to be killed for his skull collection. Professor Claus Schilling, who was executed by the Nuremberg Tribunal, had inoculated prisoners with malaria and his work was the main attraction for creating the Institute at Dachau.[41]

Hitler had repeatedly forbidden the use of biological weapons, even for defensive purposes, presumably because of the risks of retribution. On 30 April 1943, Hermann Göring who, apart from being Hitler's deputy and head of the Air Force, was head of the Reich's Research Council, appointed Kurt Blome to lead a 'cancer research' unit. Apparently this was a code for biological warfare research. This was to be at Nesselstedt near Posen (Poznan).

Blome was the head of the Reich's doctors' association. Göring sent copies of his order to various people, probably including Rudolf Mentzel (head of the advisory board of the Reich's Research Council) and Erich Schumann, a physicist and influential executive of the Army Ordnance Office. Both were interested in biological research, according to Reinhardt. Mentzel had connections with the SS and also funded May's work.

This is confusing, but it is worth noting that: 'At the end of the war, during the Nuremberg Trials, the Allies were stunned by the degree to which the authorities were uninformed of each other's activities.'

It has been suggested that the Entomological Institute was involved in biological warfare research for offensive purposes. However, this is difficult to prove because researchers rely on the documents left after the Nazis and Soviet Army had destroyed papers, and the US Secret Service took others for their investigations. Accordingly, there is no overt evidence of an offensive biological warfare programme at Dachau.

After fiddling about from March 1942, May eventually received a grant classified as 'urgent' from the Reich's Research Council, on 4 October 1943, for 'A study of the habits of insects harmful to humans in order to clarify the questions concerning specific uses and heightened defence against them'. It seems likely that May's main interests in pesticide research and mosquitoes were carried out under this proposal.

In all the research, pesticides were top of the agenda and May's knowledge and contacts in the industry made him an important link for the SS. He reported experiments on spraying malaria mosquitoes from aeroplanes. In a letter dated 23 September 1943, he wrote about the pesticides needed in case of 'biological warfare':

> If the airborne dropping of plant pest insects were to happen on a large scale, and because such actions can be expected from the enemy, the amount of pesticides needed would exceed that which can currently be provided by the industry.

He suggested the use of gesarol, which would only be diluted during aeroplane spraying, which he described as 'an insecticide with an impact on all insects'. The first confirmation of the mosquito research was in a private letter from Georg Ochs to Philipp Gönner on 12 July 1944:

> We try to grow fever mosquitoes in a large scale. We built large flight cages and serve sugar water to male mosquitoes; the ladies receive a rabbit every other night, so they can suck blood. Sometimes we feed these bloodthirsty creatures on our blood, so that they can lay eggs and we get out of our trouble [of obtaining enough insects]. Even the rabbits are caught by us, because we live here at the very margin of the camp ...

Reinhardt draws attention to the fact that May never referred to Claus Schilling's mosquito laboratory in the prisoners' hospital barracks within the closed prisoners' camp. However, Sievers told the Nuremberg Trials that May refused to research on humans.

In a report dated 23 September 1944, marked 'secret', May's comments were ambiguous over whether his research was on the defensive or offensive use of mosquitoes. However, he concluded that of the two types of mosquito used, the *Anopheles maculipennis* females survived longer without feeding and therefore these should be employed.

This wording, particularly in the German original, strongly suggests that May knew about the planned work of mosquito release, he knew about the offensive nature of this research and he made a recommendation based on these trials.

## No Babies Policy

The Nazis introduced a prohibition on Jewish women getting pregnant and giving birth in July 1942. I write this with particular empathy as I was born in July 1944 in Budapest when my mother was a persecuted Jew. The Nazis decided that preventing Jewish babies being born would assist in the extermination of the Jewish race – not entirely an original thought:

> Then Herod, when he saw that he was mocked of the wise men, was exceeding wroth, and sent forth, and slew all the children that were in Bethlehem, and in all the coasts thereof, from two years old and under, according to the time which he had diligently inquired of the wise men.

Matthew 2:16

In the Kovno Ghetto on 24 July 1942, Avraham Tory recorded the following:

> The Gestapo issued an order: pregnancy in the Ghetto is forbidden. Every pregnancy must be terminated. An eighth- or ninth-month pregnancy may be completed. From September on, giving birth is strictly forbidden. Pregnant women will be put to death.

Five days later, Tory noted a circular from the Jewish Council telling physicians and midwives of their responsibilities under the Gestapo order. On 7 August, Tory wrote that SS Sergeant 'Rauca, accompanied by Garfunkel, toured the Ghetto's institutions and noticed a pregnant woman, in her seventh month. Rauca said: "This embryo must perish. If not, it will be taken away from its mother right after birth."' The council, on 8 September, 'issued an announcement about the ban on pregnancies in the Ghetto. From now on, the Germans declare that any pregnant woman will be killed on the spot.'

In early January 1943, council members were questioned by Keiffler, deputy governor of Kovno city, about ghetto statistics, including, 'how many births? ... We answered that ever since last September there have been no births in the Ghetto. That was news to him.'

Of course, the prohibition of births among Jews only confirmed their fate. The Nazis at Kovno could have allowed births and killed off the young ones at the end with their parents. But it would have been doubly wasteful: the children would need to be fed and the parents would expend effort and energy in child-rearing. Such effort and energy of temporarily surviving Jews was required for the war effort, the Nazis would not wish to have the 'distraction' of children in the ghetto.

In the Shavli Ghetto Eliezer Yerushalmi, the Judenrät scribe, noted in his diary on 4 July 1942:

> ... Dr Charny drew the attention of the Jewish delegation to the Order concerning births. The Order was first issued on March 5, 1942. The latest date for authorized births was August 5, 1942. He would extend the date to August 15, 1942. In the event of a birth taking place in a Jewish family after this date the whole Jewish family would be 'removed' and the responsibility would rest with the Jewish delegates ...

A gynaecologist, Dr Joseph Luntz, went to see the Kommandant Hermann Schlöf, who told him quite firmly, 'The order is approved at the highest level and it will be obeyed.' No explanation was offered, but it meant fewer mouths to feed and fewer Jews to kill later. Luntz knew he would not cause a change of view but he managed to extract a concession from the reluctant Nazi, who agreed that no children born before that date would be taken. Luntz went back with a plan to induce births in the women due around the date of the ban. For the rest they had no option but to abort the foetuses. They managed to smuggle some instruments and drugs from the hospital and carried out the plan with no mishaps. Luntz, who survived Dachau, was tortured by what he had done to the end of his days.[42]

Later, on 24 March 1943, it was found that more women were pregnant, which was a threat to everyone in the ghetto. The Judenrät met and reported that the ban was being imposed with great severity in other ghettos – in Kovno all the members of the family had been shot and killed. After lengthy discussion, with great reluctance they agreed to carry out late terminations. Luntz raised the ethical issues of such actions but there was no alternative. Such activity occurred in all the ghettos and of course there is no knowledge of how many babies were aborted – they are not included in the 6 million.[43]

Activities in Auschwitz were recorded by Margita Schwalbová (1915– 2002), a Slovakian Jewish medical student who was unable to complete her studies. She worked in the revier, and wrote about pregnant women and children born in Auschwitz. Schwalbová was deported to Auschwitz on 28 March 1942 in a mass transport from Bratislava and given No. 2675. She worked in various parts of the camp dealing with medical matters and recorded her experiences in a memoir which appears to be undated, but she was aged 79 in 1995.

She wrote about a Dr Bodmann (1908–1945), who was the camp physician at Auschwitz from February 1942. In 1943 he went to Majdanek and later he was at Natzweiler. He ended up as an Allied POW and committed suicide in 1945. Margita described him as about 40 and he looked like 'a meat inspector'. He was 'crude, stern and thought he knew it all'. She said he spoke to the prisoners like servants. Margita wrote that she prepared 'the death certificates of those who committed suicide by throwing themselves into the electrified fences'. One Slovakian girl told people not to work for the Germans because they would be killed anyhow. The guards shot her, and Dr Bodmann said it was a warning to others. 'We were not even allowed to bandage her and had to put her on the ground and let her bleed to death.'

Dr Vetter arrived in November 1942. He was ruthless, and any woman who had a child was gassed with the child. Margita saw someone she knew from Bratislava called Selma Haas. She was 22 and was gassed because she gave birth to a strong baby boy. In 1942 a lot of pregnant women arrived – they tried to hide their pregnancies, but Dr Bodmann aborted every pregnancy regardless of the month – third or eighth. About twenty women were aborted and they all died of blood poisoning. When Vetter first arrived, some of the children were kept alive, but then Berlin ordered that all were to be gassed. Until the spring of 1943 Aryan women and babies were also gassed, but after that it was just the Jews.[44]

When pregnant women confided in them in the first months of pregnancy, the women gynaecologist prisoners terminated them in the hospital and not a single woman died from this procedure. The abortions were done in secret, and women were admitted to the hospital on the basis of other diagnoses.[45]

In contrast, in the Reich, Himmler promoted large families and a high birth rate for German women, with slogans like 'the battle for births of good blood'. He even argued that large families for Germans were a public duty and not a matter for individual choice. Aryan women were therefore not allowed abortions.

Frau Haferkamp, who lived in Oberhausen, eventually had ten children and spoke of the advantages of being a member of the Nazi Party. As early as 1933 she had three children already, with the fourth on the way and the party would help with the children. She got 30 marks per child from the Hitler Government, plus 20 marks 'child aid' from the local city council. That was 50 marks per month for each child. That was often more than her husband brought home. She put it all in separate savings accounts for them, but after the war the accounts were all nullified. This 'kindergeld' was not the only windfall, because when the war came and rationing was introduced she had lots of ration cards. Additionally, parents who were party members did not have to pay the fees for their children to attend high school.[46]

Zabecki described a horrible incident with a Jewish pregnant woman at Treblinka railway station when he was the stationmaster. It involved Willi Klinzmann, a German railwayman who supervised the shunting of the trains. An SS man from the camp was in Klinzmann's flat at the time:

> A frightened, battered Jewess who had managed to get out of the wagon came into the station building. She probably thought she would be safe there. Crossing the threshold of the dark corridor close by the door of the German railwaymen's quarters, she uttered a loud groan and a sigh.
>
> Willi rushed out into the corridor and seeing the woman he shouted: 'Bist du Judin?' [Are you a Jewess?] The SS man rushed out after Willi. The frightened Jewess exclaimed: 'Ach mein Gott!' [Oh My God!] escaped to the waiting room next to the traffic supervisor's office, and fell down exhausted near the wall. Both the Germans grabbed the woman lying there. They wanted her to get up and go out with them. The Jewess lay motionless. It was already late in the evening. As I went out to see to a military transport passing through the station, I shone my lamp on the woman lying there. I noticed she was pregnant and in the last months of pregnancy at that. The Jewess did not react to the German's calls uttering groans as if in labour. Then Klinzmann and the SS man from the camp began to take turns at kicking the Jewess at random and laughing.
>
> After dispatching the train, I had to go into the office again through the waiting room, but I could not do it. In the waiting-room a human being, helpless, defenceless – a sick, pregnant woman – had been murdered. The impact from the hobnailed boots was so relentless that one of the Germans, aiming at her head, had hit too high, right into the wall. I had to go into the office and pass

close to the murderers, since the departure of a train to Wólka Okraglik had to be attended to. My entrance made the criminals stop. In their frenzy they had forgotten where they were and somebody plucked up courage to break in and stop them in their duty of liquidating 'an enemy of Hitlerism'. They reached for their pistols. Willi, drunk, mumbled 'Fahrdienstleiter' [Traffic Supervisor]. I closed the door behind me. The butchers renewed the kicking. The Jewess was no longer groaning. She was no longer alive.[47]

## Nanna Conti (1881–1951) – Chief Midwife, 1933

German midwifery was struggling in the 1920s because there was a fall in birth rates and they were often not paid adequately – additionally, they did not have pensions. In 1933 everything changed because the Nazis wanted increased birth rates and a general improvement in health. All the midwives' organisations were forced to unite under the umbrella, Allgemaine Deutsche Hebammenverband. However, it was not democratic as the chairman was Nanna Conti, who had been appointed by the Home Secretary. Discussion and voting were not permitted. Although the midwives were important for a successful population policy they had no independence and relied on male politicians.[48]

Frau Conti had great power – she was called the 'Führerin' by the midwives. She appointed the federal and local chairwomen and was the chief editor of the professional midwifery magazine – compulsory reading for every midwife. It was the mouthpiece for Nazi ideology on population, working in tandem with compulsory monthly meetings. However, the attendance must have been low because the magazine had constant appeals to attend.

The midwives were to teach their patients to be proud of fulfilling their roles as German mothers and doing their duty to the German nation. They were also to encourage them to give birth to as many children as possible and breastfeed. The midwives were also to spy on the mothers and report newborn babies with disabilities, sick children, miscarriages and abortions.

Of course Jews were not allowed to participate in the midwives' organisation. Firstly, the Jewish editor of the magazine, Professor Siegfried Hammerschlag, was dismissed. He had also written the Prussian midwifery textbook. In May 1933 he was replaced by Professor Benno Ottow, a confirmed Nazi. Hammerschlag managed to escape to Persia (now Iran), where he died in 1948.

In 1938 the first legislation for all German midwives was passed. It excluded Jews from the profession and from 1940 they were excluded from the midwifery schools, together with Mischlinge of both degrees. These regulations were included in the magazine and in the textbooks. The midwifery textbook was revised in 1943, based on Hammerschlag's work, but without reference to him. Mischlinge were covered with 'God created the white man, God created the black man, but the bastard was created by the devil'. The Volljuden (full Jews) were described as parasites, unable to work in productive professions and a danger to the nation's racial purity and health. The person behind this vitriol, which was published by well-known doctors and recommended to every midwife, was Nanna Conti.

There was also a great emphasis on home births, promoted as being more homely to improve family cohesion. In fact, there was concern at the expense of the rising number of hospital births. In 1938 in Berlin 67.5 per cent of births were in hospital and in Düsseldorf it was 80 per cent. Additionally, with war imminent they knew beds would be required for the wounded and they didn't want them cluttered up with women having babies. It is also alleged that in 1935 in Munich midwives were told to 'put aside' disabled babies.[49]

Apparently, the work of Nazi midwives did not cease in 1945. Gina Roitman was born in 1948 in the Pocking-Waldstadt displaced persons camp near the German town of Passau. There were 7,000 people in the American-run camp and most of them were Jews. Her Polish mother, Sula Miedwiecki, met her father in the camp and they married there. Both had lost their first spouses and children in the Holocaust. When Sula was about to have her own baby, she used one of the family's precious ten gold roubles, money intended for their new life in Canada, to get a bed in the maternity hospital in Passau rather than in the camp.

In Canada, Sula continually told her daughter about the newborn babies killed in the camp in 1946–1947. When Sula died, Gina was 28 and eventually she decided to make the trip to Passau in 2004. A writer she had been emailing, Anna Rosmus, convinced her that the babies' deaths were more than rumours. Rosmus was a Passau resident who had caused considerable resentment by researching the city's Nazi past.

In Passau, Gina met Solamon Brunner, a Jewish survivor who knew what happened after the war. He told her that the Americans running the camp noticed that there were a high number of baby deaths. To find out why, they exhumed some of the bodies and found they were killed by someone pushing in on the soft fontanels of the babies' heads. The Americans wanted to avoid panic so worked quickly to find the culprit. They found the same Nazi midwife was present when all the babies died. She was tried quickly and given a life sentence.

Gina Roitman says it was covered up and she thinks that parents didn't know why their babies had died. The midwife's name is not known because they have been unable to find an account of the Nazi midwife's trial, even though a German judge was helping them. Roitman spent some time in Passau – as did Hitler. The SS were trained there and the neo-Nazis held rallies there until 2001. Additionally, the books Anna Rosmus has written keep disappearing from the local library, based in the old maternity hospital.[50]

Nanna's son, Leonardo Conti, was born in 1900 and in July 1939 Hitler appointed him to the euthanasia programme. In 1940 he personally conducted experiments with lethal injections on four to six patients, who died very slowly.

Some had to be given two doses, which led to the Nazis' conclusion that gas was a better alternative killer. He was also involved in experiments on malaria in Dachau and Buchenwald. Of the 1,200 prisoners involved, at least 300–400 died. He was arrested on 19 May 1945 in Flensburg, but he committed suicide on 6 October 1945 by hanging himself in his cell before he could be tried at Nuremberg.[51]

## Deportation from Apeldoornse Bos, 21 January 1943

On the night of 21 January 1943 the Jewish psychiatric centre at Apeldoornse Bos was evacuated specifically on Eichmann's orders. It had been open since 1909 and by the start of the war it had around 900 patients, plus seventy-four mentally challenged children or those with behavioural disorders. With Hauptsturmführer (Captain) Ferdinand Aus der Fünten, who ran the Amsterdam office under Eichmann, in charge the centre was searched, and helpless patients were beaten, abused and loaded first into trucks and then transferred to twenty-five cattle cars.[52]

Dr Jacob Presser (who was responsible for the publication of Philip Mechanicus' diary) witnessed the proceedings and wrote:

They were escorted into the lorries with pushes and blows, men, women and children, most of them inadequately clad for the cold winter night. As one eye-witness later recalled: 'I saw them place a row of patients, many of them older women on mattresses at the bottom of one lorry, and then load another load of human bodies on top of them. So crammed were these lorries that the Germans had a hard job to put up the tailboards.'

From the very start, the patients were thrown together indiscriminately, children with dangerous lunatics, imbeciles with those who were not fit to be moved. The lorries sped to the station, the stationmaster at Apeldoorn who stood by the train throughout …

The earliest arrivals, mainly young men, went quietly into the freight wagons at the front of the train, forty in each. When the stationmaster opened the ventilators, the Germans immediately closed them again.

At first, men and women were put into separate freight cars, but later they were all mixed together. As the night wore on, the more seriously ill were brought into the station. Some wore strait-jackets and they entered the wagons and leant helplessly against the wall of the wagons.

I remember the case of a girl of twenty to twenty-five, whose arms were pinioned in this way, but who otherwise was stark naked. When I remarked on this to the guards, they told me this patient had refused to put on clothes, so what could they do but take her along as she was.

Blinded by the light that was flashed in her face, the girl ran, fell on her face and could not, of course, use her arms to break the fall. She crashed down with a thud, but luckily escaped without serious injury. In no time she was up again and unconcernedly entered the wagon.

In general, the stationmaster stated, 'the loading was done without great violence. The ghastly thing was that when the wagons had to be closed, the patients refused to take their fingers away. They would not listen to us and in the end the Germans lost patience. The result was a brutal and inhuman spectacle.[53]

Apparently the wagons sat there all night, because the report goes on to say that Aus der Fünten asked for nurses to volunteer to go with the train.

Some twenty came forward, Aus der Fünten selected another thirty, the 'volunteers' travelled in a separate wagon, at the back of the train. All of the nurses were offered the choice of returning home immediately after the journey or working in a really modern mental home.

The transport reached Auschwitz-Birkenau on the 24 January 1943, with 921 Jewish patients including children and medical personnel. After a selection sixteen men and thirty-six women were admitted into the camp,[54] the remaining 869 people were murdered in the gas chambers.[55]

Steven Frank's father was a highly regarded lawyer in Amsterdam, married to an English woman. In May 1940, after the invasion of Holland, they pondered fleeing to England to her family with their three sons. However, Frank was the legal advisor on the board of the Het Apeldoornse Bos and he refused to leave the mental patients to the mercies of the Nazis. Sadly he was killed at Auschwitz on 21 January 1943 at the young age of 39 – the very day of this terrible deportation.[56]

Claartje van Aals, one of the Jewish nurses, wrote regularly to her non-Jewish best friend, Aagje Kaagman, living in Utrecht. On 22 January 1943 she wrote:

Today we will go. We don't know where yet and we don't know either what will happen to the people. It is very chaotic. I am writing in the passage and I am ridiculously calm … I have to leave everything behind, I can only take what is absolutely necessary. What will happen to us? I feel like I am drunk. If I wanted to, I could go into hiding, but I feel compelled to go with the people because that is where the heart is … I must stop.[57]

She did not have time to finish the letter.

She had corresponded with Aagje since 1940 and, as she wrote about visiting her father in Utrecht, they may have been school friends. On 22 January 1941 she described seeing a film about Bali and talking to a new male nurse, Jo de Vries, which she had obviously enjoyed. She wrote that she was very busy with nine sick patients. She mentioned that her sister in Amsterdam had said Jews were no longer allowed in cafés. She told her friend to visit her in Apeldoorn soon so they could go out together, because soon it would not be possible. Her sister also said there was hardly any underwear to be had in Amsterdam.[58]

Later, on 9–10 October 1941, she wrote carefully:

> There are things happening to the J … that make us feel awfully frightened. We are all in a crummy, helpless mood. It's just like in Amsterdam though you would not expect that here in Het Bosch.
> … I will be coming to Utrecht October 20 for Dad's birthday. The police don't allow me to stay away longer. Dreadful, eh? Dammit, otherwise I could have come for three days.

The young male nurse had left and others were leaving to go elsewhere. She implied that she couldn't say much because of censors. A few days later, on 13–14 October, she wrote again because she had heard that there were round-ups in Utrecht and she was anxious about her father as she hadn't heard from him for a while. She asked her friend to check up on him and to send her a postcard straight away.[59] Early in May 1942 she wrote, 'Tonight I sewed the Jewish star on my coat. A rotten task, but unavoidable.'[60]

Rudolf Vrba (1924–2006) from Slovakia, one of only five Jews who successfully escaped from Auschwitz, was present when the transport arrived at the camp. The people inside the wagons had been incarcerated since the evening of 21 January and arrived on 24 January – presumably, for two and a half days without adequate sanitation, food or water. He wrote:

> What appalled me was the state of the living. Some were drooling, imbecile, live people with dead minds. Some were raving, tearing at their neighbours, even at their own flesh. Some were naked, though the cold was petrifying: and above everything, above the moans of the dying or the despairing, the cries of pain, of fear, the sound of wild, frightening, lunatic laughter rose and fell.
> Yet amidst all this bedlam, there was one spark of splendid, unselfish sanity. Moving among the insane were nurses, young girls, their uniforms torn and grimy, but their faces calm and their hands never idle. Their medicine bags were still over their shoulders and they had to fight to keep their feet, but all the time they were working, soothing, bandaging, giving an injection here, an aspirin there.
> Not one showed the slightest trace of panic. 'Get them out!' roared the SS-men, 'Get them out, you bastards.' A naked girl about twenty with red hair and a superb figure suddenly leaped from a wagon and lay squirming, laughing at my feet. A nurse flung me a heavy Dutch blanket and I tried to put it round her, but she

would not get up. With another prisoner, a Slovak called Fogel, I managed to roll her into the blanket.

'Get them to the lorries!' roared the SS. 'Straight to the lorries! Get on with it for Christ's sake!'

Somehow Fogel and I broke into a lumbering run, for this beautiful girl was heavy. The motion pleased her and she began clapping her hands like a child. An SS club slashed across my shoulders and the blanket slipped from my numbed fingers. 'Get on you swine! Drag her.' I joined Fogel at the other end of the blanket and we dragged her, bumping her over the frozen earth for five hundred yards. Somehow she clung to the blanket, not laughing now, but crying, as the hard ground thumped her naked flesh through the thick wool.

'Pitch her in! Get her on the lorries!'

The SS men were frantic, for here was something they could not understand. Something that knew no order, no discipline, no obedience, no fear of violence or death. We pitched her in somehow, then ran back for another pathetic bundle. Hundreds of them were out of the wagons now, herded by the prisoners who were herded by the SS, and everywhere the nurses, still working.

One nurse walked slowly with an old, frail man talking to him quietly, as if they were out in the hospital grounds. Another half-carried a screaming girl. They fought to bring order out of chaos, using medicines and blankets, gentleness and quiet heroism, instead of guns or sticks or snarling dogs.

Then suddenly it was all over. The last abject victims had been slung into one of the overloaded lorries. We stood there panting in the chill January air.

The nurses were not allowed to return home or work in a modern mental hospital, because the SS doctor making the selection decided the nurses would share the same fate as their patients. The nurses were loaded onto the lorries and roared off, swaying towards the gas chambers, not a single nurse or patient survived.[61]

Yet another betrayal.

## Lice and Typhus

Living conditions for deported Jews were generally terrible. Lice were a general problem, with people unable to wash either their bodies or their clothes. I recall my mother telling me that we had both had lice in the Budapest Ghetto when I was a tiny baby. However unpleasant that must have been, the big fear was the typhus that lice carried, which was a major killer.

It was reported on 21 December 1941 that, as a result of the typhus epidemic and the large number of wounded Nazi soldiers being brought to Warsaw from the Russian front, there was a shortage of doctors in the city. Therefore the German authorities resorted to employing Jewish doctors and some of them were even ordered to work in German military hospitals.[62]

It was comparatively recently, in 1909, that Dr Charles Nicolle (1866–1936) identified that lice were the vector for typhus. In January 1903, as the director of the Pasteur Institute in Tunisia, he found that typhus was rampant in Tunis and determined to do something about it. In his acceptance speech for the Nobel Prize for Medicine in 1928 he explained how made his discovery.

He observed that many of the Tunisian doctors, particularly in country areas, caught typhus and about a third died. He had to step over bodies of typhus patients as he went into the hospital and the admission staff often caught typhus. However, once the patients were admitted to the ward, they ceased to be contagious. This was because they were bathed and given clean clothes. He surmised it was lice that were the problem. He conducted experiments with chimpanzees in 1909 and confirmed his theory. He also established that it was not necessary to be bitten as they produced millions of powder-like excretions which were contagious.

Dr Weigl of Lvov had, by 1936, developed a vaccine for typhus, but it was a complicated and dangerous process. In the course of his research, helped by his wife, Zofia, he contracted typhus twice. He needed 100 infected lice for each single dose, although later this was reduced to thirty. In 1938 Dr Cox, an American, finally developed a method of producing large quantities of typhus vaccine.[63]

Dr Nicolle had explained that as a result of his work, efforts were made to avoid an epidemic during the First World War. All troops leaving Africa were deloused before arriving in Europe and consequently there was no major outbreak of typhus in Europe, although there was in Russia. This opinion was supported by the Nobel Committee:

> Admittedly it conceded in its report that Nicolle's contribution had been of fundamental importance in combating typhus during the First World War; but since it had not introduced any new ideas nor opened up any new roads of out-standing value to humanity, the members advised against an award. The faculty, however, decided to honour Nicolle with a prize, albeit far from unanimously.[64]

Through force of circumstance, considerable work was done during the Holocaust by Jewish physicians: Bronislawa Fejgin, who perished in the Warsaw Ghetto; Ludwik Hirszfeld escaped from the ghetto and survived on the Aryan side; Jacob Penson, who described kidney failure in typhus (he escaped and was hidden in a village); and Ludwik Fleck in the Lvov Ghetto, who developed the urine antigen diagnosis and prepared a vaccine (he survived Auschwitz and Buchenwald).[65]

Dr Nicolle had concluded his speech with the following:

And this is the ultimate lesson that our knowledge of the mode of transmission of typhus has taught us: Should man regress, should he allow himself to resemble a primitive beast, the louse begins to multiply again and treats man as he deserves, as a brute beast.[66]

The Nazis betrayed the Jews by forcing them to live in conditions which led to the spread of typhus and their consequent deaths. However, as Dr Nicolle foretold, by doing so they betrayed their own brutality.

A report dated 23 January 1942 about the situation in the Warsaw Ghetto stated that an average of 750 Jews were dying each day from the spread of typhus which the Nazi medical authorities 'refuse to check'. The report, which had been received from Poland 'through underground channels', said that mortality among Polish Jews had risen sixteen-fold compared with 1938.

Executed Jews were not included in these figures – more than 1,000 Jewish typhus victims were shot on the orders of the German military authorities. Not only did the Nazi administration refuse medical aid to the Jews in the Warsaw Ghetto, but also, according to the Polish report, they were constantly transporting Jews from all parts of the Reich to the ghettos in Poland to ensure that as many Jews as possible died of typhus. Normally the strain of typhus prevalent in Warsaw was only fatal in one in six cases, but the actual death rate was 40 per cent. This was aggravated by two years of starvation which had lowered the resistance of the Jews.

While all Jewish doctors and nurses in the ghetto were mobilised to work in anti-typhus centres in Warsaw, the Nazis were exploiting the situation and using the spread of typhus to counter the growing sympathy for persecuted Jews, according to the report. The Nazi propagandists were creating agitation among the Poles by accusing the Jews of being responsible for the spread of typhus. Hundreds of posters blaming the Jews for the plague were plastered around Warsaw by the Nazis. They put posters on the ghetto walls which read, 'Jews–Lice–Spotted Typhus. Entrance and Exit Prohibited'.[67]

Gilbert Michlin, a slave labourer for Siemens in Auschwitz, described dealing with lice:

In the evening once or twice a week, after an exhausting day, after the endless roll call, we would have to delay the thing we desperately needed – going to sleep. First we had to delouse ourselves. Each of us had to scrupulously examine his few clothes and his blanket to make certain no lice had latched on. Lice carried typhus and were absolutely banned from the camp. The SS were scared to death of them, scared of being contaminated if an epidemic ever broke out. After this inspection, Bednarek, our sadistic blockältester, examined each and every one of us. Woe to the person with lice.[68]

*The Kovno Ghetto Diary* has many entries on lice, and a fairly long article about how the issue was managed. The diary entry for 16 July 1942 reads:

> The Council imposed the penalty of three days' imprisonment or a ten-mark fine on twenty Ghetto inmates who failed to abide by the instruction of the sanitation department to disinfect themselves of lice.[69]

The diary reports on 15 October 1942 that a commission of Lithuanian doctors came to inspect the ghetto's sanitary conditions. This is followed by a report written by Jack Brauns, whose father Dr Moses Brauns took responsibility for not reporting contagious diseases to the Lithuanian Board of Health. Jack worked alongside his father and, because of the danger to the whole ghetto if the Germans or the Lithuanians had discovered the truth, nothing was written down. Jack wrote the memoir from memory in 1988.[70]

It was important that the outside authorities did not know of contagious diseases within the ghetto because the patients would have been killed. The authorities realised that they had created a breeding ground for typhus in the ghetto – overcrowding, unsanitary conditions, no bathhouse and hunger. People were only allowed 3ft 2in per person, water came from wells and excrement was disposed into cesspools.

The consequences of the Nazis discovering the presence of typhus was demonstrated in a 1941 JTA dispatch:

> More than 1,000 victims of spotted fever in the densely crowded Warsaw Ghetto have been put to death by gas in a new move by Nazi military authorities to check the epidemic of this disease, also known as fleck typhus, which has spread throughout the eastern front area and is taking a heavy toll of German troops, it is learned here today from reliable sources.
>
> The starvation prevalent in the Warsaw Ghetto is one of the chief factors in the extent of the epidemic, since the emaciated Jews are unable to fight off its ravages. At the same time that the Germans resorted to execution to stop the disease, however, they decreased the ration of Polish Jews ...[71]

This chapter has demonstrated the complete callousness of the Nazis to their Jewish prisoners. They literally treated them as so many units to exploit and experiment on without any care or feeling. It is hard to understand how these people, who in many cases were academically qualified, often as doctors, could behave in such an inhumane way. It has also described the courage and ingenuity of those Jews and non-Jews who attempted to alleviate the situation with minimal resources. When they themselves were suffering alongside the people they were treating this feat is remarkable. The pain and suffering experienced by the victims is unimaginable and I believe this was one of the greatest betrayals perpetrated by the Nazis.

# 16

# THE EXPERIENCES OF FIRST WORLD WAR SOLDIERS

My father during World War I was decorated for bravery. This is important in order to understand why so many decent, intelligent Jews did not heed early warnings to leave Germany.

Frank R. Harris[1]

Jews had not previously been encouraged into the German Army, but at the start of the First World War the main Jewish organisations encouraged Jews to join up to show their commitment to their homeland. One hundred thousand Jews fought for Germany in the First World War, including Anne Frank's father, Otto, and Wilfrid Israel's Uncle Richard and his cousin Ernst. They represented one-fifth of the Jewish population, and while 12,000 fell in battle, 30,000 were decorated and 2,000 became officers.[2]

The Association of Jewish War Veterans (RjF) was created by Leo Löwenstein in 1919 and still exists. In 1920 it produced a very poignant poster – see photo No. 20. Its German text can be translated as:

To German mothers
12,000 Jewish soldiers died on the field of honour for the fatherland
Christian and Jewish heroes fought together and rest together in foreign soil.
12,000 Jews fell in battle!
Blind, enraged Party hatred does not stop at the graves of the dead.
German women,
Do not allow that the suffering Jewish mother be mocked in her pain!

The graves of those who fell can still be seen in the Weissensee Cemetery in Berlin – the largest Jewish graveyard in Europe:

An entire section honours the fallen of 1914–18 with rows of little white headstones lined up with military precision. Their occupants were musketeers, grenadiers, telegraphists and officers. The date is 1927. Time is running out, but it is still possible to honour German Jews for having died as patriots for the Fatherland.[3]

Dorit Bader Whiteman visited her father's birthplace in Czechoslavakia, formerly in Austria. Although tombstones had been vandalised or overturned in the Jewish cemetery, there was one tall monument still standing.

It was engraved with a long list an astonishingly long list for such a small village of Jewish men who had fallen during the First World War. When the memorial was erected, surely the Jews felt they had a right to assume that their relationship with the rest of the citizenry had been cemented by the common blood shed?[4]

Marianne Meyerhoff wrote how, in 1914:

… every German synagogue was filled to standing room only, to pray for Germany when Kaiser Wilhelm declared war and asked God for his blessing. The Kaiser told the nation, 'Today, I see before me only Germans.' The Jews of Germany heard that loud and clear. It was certain confirmation from the mouth of their monarch that their constant, historic cycle of oppression and recuperation in the life of the Fatherland had finally brought them as fully-fledged members into the German community. For the moment all differences melted away. A sudden kinship appeared amongst the vast majority of Germans, a full-blown *völkisch Camaraderie* [the whole German people's comradeship] that could be felt in the heart. That brief time is still remembered as special in the life of the nation.[5]

After the war the surviving soldiers, especially the decorated, felt very secure as German Jews, regarding themselves as 'Germans of the Mosaic Persuasion'. They had joined wholeheartedly in the Prussian jingoism of 1914, believing they were an integral part of German culture, but they would eventually be disappointed.[6]

After 1933, they were stunned to realize that they were targets of the Nazi racial laws – that Hitler's diatribes were directed at them. Convinced that there had been some mistake, World War I veterans pinned on their medals and visited local Nazi officials to emphasize their patriotism. In March 1933, the Jewish congregation of Berlin sent a statement to Hitler affirming 'the pledge that we belong to the German people; it is our sacred duty, our right and our deepest wish that we take an active part in its renewal and rise.' As late as 1936, the 'Reich Association of Jewish Front Soldiers' commemorated their fallen comrades from World War I with a ceremony in Berlin that stressed their loyalty to the Fatherland.[7]

Other old First World War soldiers mentioned elsewhere in this book are Ludwig Goldschmidt, father of Ernest, who was awarded the Iron Cross[8] and Ottmar Strauss who had two Iron Crosses – one First Class and one Second Class.[9]

Elisabetta Cerruti (1888–1959), the wife of the Italian Ambassador in Berlin, Vittori Cerruti (1881–1961), was a Hungarian actress of Jewish ancestry. They were based in Berlin from 1932 to 1935, but as the ambassador did not get on with Hitler he was moved to Paris in 1935. In June 1938 they moved again, because the ambassador had been too sympathetic to the French for the Duce.[10]

In her memoirs, she recalled the events of 21 March 1933 when the first official military review of troops since the 1918 defeat took place. Before the marshal took his place on the reviewing stand, he greeted some veterans from the 1870 war – all of a similar age to him:

> Their leader, sitting in a wheel-chair, was a white-bearded patriarch, covered with military decorations. … I was seeking to control my emotion at the touching scene when I heard someone whisper indignantly, 'But that one is a Jew!' The Marshal didn't seem worried. 'All those who had fought for Germany were his comrades, without discrimination. The law of racism was as yet unspoken.'

She continued:

> After the parade, I left Potsdam in the car of an eminent Austrian financier; my husband followed in another car with his staff. That gentleman, a baptized Jew and a man of genius, was completely at ease and very pleased with everything he had witnessed that day. He expressed his hope and conviction that the rumours had been exaggerated and that 'It wouldn't be so very bad after all!'
> Two days later the persecution of the Jews began.[11]

The Boycott Day of 1 April 1933 impacted on former soldiers as it did on all citizens of Germany. Max Plaut, the young administrator of the Hamburg Jewish Community, recalled in 1954:

> … the Jewish shop owners all reacted differently. Tietz was shut. But Max Haak on the Neuer Steinweg offered a reduction of 10 per cent and gave every customer a balloon: he doubled his sales; the communists came and bought so that boycott day here looked almost like a festival; the owner, wearing his Iron Cross first class, stood in front of the shop; discomfited SA with their placards stood around.[12]

Edwin Landau (1890–1975) described his experiences in his small home town in West Prussia. He described the way the SA marched through the town early in the morning on 31 March 1933, with banners declaring 'The Jews are our misfortune'. Later they took up positions in front of the Jewish shops to stop customers entering, including his own. He became quite incensed:

> And for this reason we young Jews had once stood in the trenches in cold and rain, and spilled our blood to protect the land from the enemy. Was there no comrade any more from those days who was sickened by these goings-on? One saw them pass by on the street, among them quite a few for whom one had done a good turn. They had a smile on their faces that betrayed their malicious pleasure.
>
> I took my war decorations, put them on, went into the street, and visited Jewish shops, where at first I was also stopped. But I was seething inside, and most of all I would have liked to shout my hatred into the faces of these barbarians. Hatred, hatred – when had it become part of me? – It was only a few hours ago that a change had occurred within me. This land and this people that until now I had loved and treasured had suddenly become my enemy. So I was not a German anymore, or I was no longer supposed to be one. That, of course, cannot be settled in a few hours. But one thing I felt immediately: I was ashamed that I had once belonged to this people. I was ashamed about the trust that I had given to so many who now revealed themselves as my enemies. Suddenly the street, too, seemed alien to me.[13]

Those who had fought for their native land, like Edwin Landau, were thoroughly shocked by the Nazis' behaviour toward them. The RjF was successful in persuading Reich President von Hindenburg to intervene with Hitler over Aryan limitations imposed on 7 April 1933. Apparently, in a 'gesture of concession' toward the Reich president:

> Hitler agreed to limit the scope of the law, reducing the group of those directly affected. Soldiers who had fought at the front, fathers or sons of those who had fallen in battle, and all veteran government workers who had been given civil servant status before August 1, 1914 were exempted from the purview of the law.[14]

Avraham Barkai, who wrote the above, presumed it would not have been easy to have achieved this concession had Hitler realised how many exceptions there would be. Nazis were convinced that Jews had been shirkers in the First World War and, accordingly, there would be few Jewish veterans to be exempted. He concluded that 'quite a sizable number of Jews were able to continue working in their professions for several years as a result of the regulations governing exemptions'.

However, some were less fortunate. In August 1934 Otto Schneider, a sculptor from Karlsruhe who was a member of the Visual Arts Chamber, discovered that he was not allowed to exhibit his work in Karlsruhe and Baden-Baden because his wife was 'one-quarter non-Aryan'. The fact that he was the bearer of the Iron Cross and described as '50 percent war-handicapped' was ignored.[15]

Perhaps Hitler should have reflected on his own military experience. His commanding officer was a Lieutenant Hess when he was a corporal, and later he, himself, was awarded his Iron Cross, First Class, as a result of another Jewish lieutenant, Hugo Gutmann (1880–1962), who also wore that decoration.[16] Gutmann was from Nuremberg and was nine years older than Hitler.[17] He had a remarkably successful army career and his commendations throughout the war are quite free of anti-Semitism – having been awarded the Iron Cross, First Class in January 1916, after the Battle of Loos. Later, after the Battle of the Somme in October 1916, his commander proposed him for a 'particularly honorific award', for his distinguished behaviour 'beyond the call of duty'.[18]

Thomas Weber read articles in the 10th Army's newspaper where it was quite clear that the Jews were being regarded sympathetically and Germany's mission was to liberate the Jews of Eastern Europe, to 'bring freedom and light to millions of unfortunate people'. He has shown that there were more Jewish officers in Hitler's regiment than Christian and there was no evidence of anti-Semitism.[19]

Weber was a young German academic at Aberdeen University, and spent several years researching Hitler's military career and found discrepancies with what Hitler had promoted so successfully. Hitler's army career was traditionally represented as that of a courageous corporal on the front. Weber has established that he was a private throughout the war – apparently quite an (under)achievement. However, on 4 August 1918 he was awarded the Iron Cross First Class, which he wore all through the Third Reich. Weber found that these awards were often given to back line support staff like Hitler as a mark of long service, rather than bravery. Initially two officers were his fervent supporters, but it was Hugo Gutmann who made the final recommendation and the citation was 'as a dispatch runner he was a model in sangfroid and grit both in static and mobile warfare'. An order had been issued that a higher proportion of Iron Crosses should be given to ordinary troops, but it was the regiment's highest serving Jew who was responsible.

However, Gutmann did not gain much from his solicitous care of Hitler. After the war, he took over his father's office furniture business. As Hitler became powerful he deleted Gutmann's role from his autobiography and disparaged him, saying he had been hated in the regiment. Weber suggests that if Hitler had been such a virulent anti-Semite in 1918, why would Gutmann have proposed him for the Iron Cross?[20]

He was imprisoned by the Gestapo in 1937 in Nuremberg Prison and asked about how Hitler got his Iron Cross. He was looked after in the prison by veteran army colleagues – one guard was a Catholic and told Hugo he hated the Nazis. He brought him food, enabled him to contact his wife and told him the Nazis had nothing concrete against him. This again proves that the regiment was not anti–Semitic and that Gutmann was not despised.[21] He subsequently fled with his family to Belgium in spring 1939. He managed to leave Belgium on 14 May 1940, just before the occupation, with visas received on 9 May. In a 1946 letter to a friend in Germany he wrote:

> In Vichy I could get our emigration permit to Portugal on 28 July. We had wonderful loyal friends among the Frenchmen but the Vichy officials were corrupt beyond any comprehension. We had very influential American help, too. Without the dollars which I took with me when I left Brussels we would not have reached France and would have fallen into the Nazis' hands. Without dollars one couldn't get any stamp in his passport.

In America, he became Henry G. Grant.[22]

Thomas Weber discovered that Hitler spent most of the war as a 'runner' a few kilometres behind the main battle line, often outside the most dangerous area.[23] The heroic soldier seems to have been a figment of Hitler's imagination and Nazi propaganda. Weber concludes his fascinating book:

> The story of how Private Hitler managed to transform himself from a 'rear area pig', shunned by the men of his regiment, to the most powerful right-wing dictator of the twentieth century is thus a cautionary tale for all democratizing and democratized countries. If de-democratization could happen in interwar Germany, it can arguably occur anywhere.[24]

In Hamburg every year representatives of the state and the armed services gathered in the Ohlsdorf Cemetery and honoured the Jewish war heroes. This cemetery is non-denominational, and after the war 105 urns of soil and ash from different camps were placed here in memorial to the victims of the Nazis.[25]

The painter Oskar Schlemmer (1888–1943) was not a Jew. He was a teacher at the Bauhaus School, and was so incensed by the Nazis' 'degenerate art' campaign that he wrote a letter of protest to Minister Goebbels, outlining the development of modern art all over Europe in the years 1910–1914 (1910 is important because works dating from that year could be seized under the 'degenerate art' policy). His letter continued:

> It was in this enraptured mood that we young academy students were surprised by the war. We marched off to battle filled with genuine enthusiasm for a noble cause, for the ideals of art! In the name of my fallen comrades I protest against the defamation of their goals and their works, for those which found their way into museums are today being desecrated.

That was not what they died for! After the war, the survivors, now in their forties, continued their interrupted work in the pre-war spirit, largely oblivious to and uninterested in the political occurrences around them.

These days pictures by both living deceased modern painters are being systematically defamed. They have been branded alien, un-German, unworthy, and unnatural. The political motives ascribed to them are in most cases totally inappropriate. Artists are fundamentally unpolitical and must be so, for their kingdom is not of this world. It is always humanity with which they are concerned, always the totality of human existence to which they must pay allegiance.[26]

Later he wrote to his friend Gerhard Marcks, on 7 December 1937, 'I am cut to the quick for the first time by political events.'[27]

On a recent visit to the Reina Sofia Museum in Madrid, I was delighted to see some of his work, in particular the delightful costumes for his 1920s *Triadic Ballet*, which still look wonderful. Schlemmer died of a heart attack in 1943 at the premature age of 55.

Among the Jews of Magdeburg, it was noted that thirty-six Jewish men gave their lives for their country in the First World War as they saw themselves as German citizens of the Jewish faith. One of the interviewees, speaking about the anti-Semitism of the Weimar period, noted his paternal Uncle Herbert Levy's experience as a veteran of the war:

> One time he was in a Kneipe [local pub] and the discussion centred around what the Jews supposedly hadn't done during World War One and why the Germans had lost the war. Angrily, he pulled his shirt up and shouted at them to come over and take a look at what he 'got' from the war. This is the type of individual he was. Of course the response from those in the tavern was: 'Verzeihung Kameraden!' ['Our apologies comrade!'].

The writer commented, 'What is highly important here is the confidence Levy displayed in knowing that he could defend himself and, conversely, confirmed when those who sought to besmirch the Jewish effort during the war felt honour-bound to offer him their apologies.'[28]

Later things were less good …

Raul Hilberg, who initiated the study of the Holocaust, described his father, Michael Hilburg's, experience in November 1938 when he was arrested and a man with a pistol threw Raul and his mother out of their apartment at a moment's notice. Michael Hilberg noticed a large 'D' against his name. He realised that meant he was destined for Dachau. He told the two Gestapo officers that they could not send him there. When they asked him why not he replied, 'I fought in the World War.' 'One moment, you Jew, where did you fight?' His father recited the locations where he had served. The older man said, 'We cannot send him to Dachau. He is not lying. I was there myself.'[29]

The family escaped the gas chambers and Austria because of a temporary loop-hole in the Nazis' anti-Jewish regulations – Jewish veterans of the First World War could avoid internment if they agreed to surrender their property and leave the country.

Eric Davidson (formerly Erich Davidsohn) was born in 1922 in Hanover. He wrote a brief article about his deportation to Buchenwald with his father Robert, who was born in 1884. The day after Kristallnacht:

> About midday the policeman came again with a man in civvies and told my father and me that we were to be taken to Hamelin prison. My father's protests that he was a war veteran with the Iron Cross, that his brothers had also fought in the First World War and that two of them had been killed were to no avail. We saw that many Jewish men were there already, four or five to a cell. The only consolation I still have from spending that day in the prison is the knowledge that after the Nuremberg trials Nazi leaders (at least those who had been caught and hadn't yet committed suicide) were hanged in that very same prison.[30]

Goebbels ordered that after October 1935 war memorials were not to display Jewish soldiers' names. However, on 14 June 1936 a memorial in the small town of Loge was unveiled showing a Jewish soldier, Benjamin, among the fallen in 1915. It was decided to remove it and replace it with the name of a local soldier who died after the end of the war, but after protests that too was removed.

After Kristallnacht Paul Schmitthenner, the rektor of Heidelberg University, wrote to the Baden Minister of Education on 10 November 1938. He was only appointed in November, so this must have been a high priority for him – perhaps his background as an architect was influential. His interpretation of the situation is noteworthy:

> In view of the struggle of world Jewry against the Third Reich, it is intolerable that the names of members of the Jewish race remain on plaques of the war dead. The students were demanding the removal of the plaque, but this was done out of respect for the German dead. ... I consider the removal of the Jewish names necessary. It should take place in an orderly and dignified way in the spirit of the regulations I am asking for.[31]

The minister sent the letter to the Reich Minister of Education, Bernard Rust, who asked Hitler to determine the issue. On 14 February he announced Hitler's decision that 'Names of Jews on existing memorials would not be removed. Newly erected memorials would not include names of Jews.'

Further humiliation came from 16 November 1938, when Jewish veterans were no longer permitted to wear army uniforms.[32]

Schmitthenner remained as rektor until the end of the war, when he was dismissed without a pension. He had become the most powerful man in south-west Germany's academic culture and in 1940 he became Culture Minister of Baden (in effect, his own boss while still rektor).[33]

During Kristallnacht (9–10 November 1938) there was little consistency in the treatment of First World War veterans:

> Among those who were released – rather than sent to concentration camps – were some men who were veterans of World War One as well as men who could demonstrate that their emigration was imminent. The police exercised a great deal of discretion in such cases, and practices were far from uniform. In Berlin, no Jews were exempted from arrests on November 10, but on November 11 and 12, exceptions were granted to holders of the Iron Cross First Class, those with injuries from World War One, and those with obvious serious illnesses.[34]

Alan Steinweis describes the horrifying experiences the Jewish men who were rounded up after Kristallnacht endured at the various camps. Many were interrogated over what their occupation was and treated according to their popularity. The one thing they were never asked about was military service. 'Notably, the guards never asked the Jewish prisoners about their military experience in the German Army during World War One – a subject that would have been inconsistent with the stereotype of the parasitical Jew.'[35]

About 31,000 Jewish men had been imprisoned following Kristallnacht – 11,000 in Dachau, 9,800 in Buchenwald and 10,000 in Sachsenhausen.[36] However, the purpose had been to encourage emigration, and therefore Reinhardt Heydrich, as Head of the Security Police (Sicherheitspolizei), began issuing orders to release the prisoners in various stages. On 28 November he sent orders to the camp commanders to release Jewish prisoners who had fought in the First World War.

> Heydrich did not explain the logic behind the release of these prisoners, but he did note that he was acting at the request of Hermann Göring. Negative reactions to Kristallnacht had been especially pronounced in German military circles, and the summary imprisonment of Jewish combat veterans in concentration camps must have been an additional irritant. So it might well be that the release of the veterans was the result of an effort at damage limitation on the part of Göring, himself a veteran of the war as well as a severe critic, on tactical grounds, of the pogrom. The veterans – or, more likely, their families – would be allowed to confirm their military record, either by producing their Honor Cross for Service at the Front or by submitting other documentation.[37]

In the small town of Laa an der Thaya, a Jewish community had existed since the thirteenth century. Many of the members of the community fought in the First World War and some of them were highly decorated:

> They were patriots, who were willing to fight and risk their lives for their home-land. Some were badly wounded. Some men never returned from the battlefield. Jewish women also worked for their motherland. There was a military hospital for wounded soldiers in Laa. Most of the nurses worked there voluntarily and quite a few of them were Jewish.[38]

In Hungary, Anna Sondhelm's father had fought in the First World War and received a decoration. In Budapest the rule was that if you had two silver medals you were exempt from wearing the yellow star:

> As it happened, my father was moved to another regiment and he had two docu-ments of the same medal but a non-Jewish friend of my father who was a lawyer said: 'Look, you risk it. It doesn't look like the same medal. It looks like you have been decorated with two silver medals, two different registration numbers and nobody will ever find out because all the documents from Budapest, from the Treasury have been transported to Germany. Risk it. Take the yellow star off. What can happen? And you are being treated as a non-Jew. Stay in the flat and see what happens …[39]

Anna said they took the yellow stars off, trembling because it was illegal, but they risked it and got away with it:

> It was the regulation of the government at that time, after the Horthy Declaration that all Jews, except the exemptions who were exempted from the yellow star can stay in their flat because they count as non-Jews. The special cases like the highly decorated from the First World War and the wounded from the First World War.

It was risky, but they had no problems except one night when the janitor, Babel Bacs, was drunk. She remembered it was horrible:

> Some Arrow Cross people, the Szalasi people came in the house and said: 'Are there any Jews in the house?' And Babel Bacs said: 'Oh no. They were all gone except Mr Scobadi and his family.' I just heard that. He was absolutely dead drunk. 'But they are exempt.' And the chap said: 'That's all right.'[40]

Alexander (Sandor) Weiss was a lawyer in Cluj and the father of Julia, who worked at the Volkswagen factory (see page 213). Julia wrote that her parents let her go back to Budapest in 1944, where she had studied at the Atelier Art School in Budapest 1939–1943. They didn't think they would be affected by persecution as Hungary was not involved in the war at that stage:

> Moreover, my father had fought in the Hungarian army in the First World War and he believed this would protect us if necessary. He believed in comradeship and a positive degree of honour and decency.[41]

Julia and her friend, Uli, were sent to Bergen-Belsen in late autumn 1944 and discovered that her parents were en route for Switzerland on a special transport. The young man who brought them coffee told them there were people from Cluj there. He gave them paper and a pen and she wrote a note to tell them they were still alive:

> My father had been a major in the First World War and always expected to be met with military decency. He went to see the camp's commandant and asked: 'My daughter is here. May I go and see her?' The result: his daughter was sent to Fallersleben. My father, mother and brother were taken out of the special transport and later removed from Bergen-Belsen. My father died in Tröbnitz of meningitis: my mother and brother survived. Uli's parents were also taken out of the special transport. My mother told me that my father's last words were: 'Don't go home until you have found Julia'. It saddens me greatly that my father died. Somehow that is the only thing I feel guilty about it. If he had not received the note, he would not have gone to see the commandant. But what was I supposed to do? I wanted him and my family to know I was alive.[42]

Luise Solmitz was a Christian woman living in Hamburg. Her husband, Fredy, who came from a Jewish family, was a much-decorated pilot from the First World War with the rank of major. She wrote in her diary over 9–20 September 1941 about the new police regulation ordering all German Jews over the age of 6 to wear a yellow 'Star of David'. She went to the city hall to see if the measure applied to her husband. It didn't, because the decree exempted Jewish spouses living in 'privileged marriages', which applied to them because of her husband's war record.[43] Luise was terrified that they would lose their privileges but they already lived a wretched existence and he was shunned by his neighbours.[44] Their daughter was a Mischling and could only marry another Mischling or a Jew.

Erich Narewczewitz (1893–1943) was an Orthodox Jewish teacher who served four years as a soldier in the First World War. He was awarded the Iron Cross, Second Class. However, in 1935 he was no longer allowed to teach in a state school and the pension from his military service was paid reluctantly by his home town. He moved to Frankfurt to work in a Jewish school, but in September 1942 the police department of Frankfurt told the Eschwege Town Council that it could stop the pension payments as he had been 'evacuated'. Sent to Theresienstadt, Erich, aged 50, and his mother, aged 90, died in 1943.[45]

Henk Huffener, in Amsterdam, heard the owner of an Iron Cross, First Class, which was proudly displayed on its black velvet cushion boast, 'I am exempt from deportation.' Henk's plea not to believe it went unheard.[46]

Else Pintus described an incident in Gdansk (Danzig) in the summer of 1941. Mr David, who owned a furniture store, was queuing for food when a woman said that the food was just for Germans. He replied, 'I'm just as German as you. I served four years on the German front.' Someone must have reported this to the Gestapo and although he was ill in bed, he was dragged off by the Gestapo and eight days later he was dead.[47]

Dr Arthur Arndt, who was hidden in Berlin with six other Jews throughout the war, had been awarded the Iron Cross for his services as an army doctor in the First World War. On 16 August 1935, one month before the Nuremberg Laws were passed, he was awarded a Cross of Honour certificate for his work during the First World War. In July 1938 he was told that Jewish doctors were being taken off the medical register and could no longer call themselves physicians or treat Aryan patients. The Jewish doctors were to be known as Krankenbehandler (healers for the Jewish infirm).[48]

Finally, in Hungary all exemptions for Jews, even war heroes, were revoked on 15 October 1944 when the Szálasi Government came to power.

These proud soldiers would have done better to remember the events of 1 November 1916 when, as the war began to go against the Germans, the High Command in the person of the Prussian War Minister, Adolf Wild von Hohenborn, thought the Jews would make a good scapegoat for the Germans' lack of success. It was decided that a census of Jews would show that they were shirking their military duty for the Fatherland. However, because of the Jews' enthusiastic patriotism the Judenzahlung ('Jew Count' or Jewish Census) demonstrated that not only were the Jews serving enthusiastically, but they were volunteering disproportionately for front-line duty. The results of the survey were never published because they did not serve the purpose for which the exercise had been intended.[49]

In the light of this, I was surprised to read that Mark Twain (1835–1910), the famous American writer, had described American Jews as unpatriotic and unwilling to fight for their country in an 1899 essay entitled, 'Concerning the Jews'. His article led to the creation of the Jewish War Veterans of the USA, and they still run a small museum in Washington. However, after checking the statistics of the War Department, Twain found that the Jews had served in a larger proportion than their presence in the population. Twain did have the grace to issue a long retraction and apology.[50]

Rabbi Jonathan Wittenberg wrote about his grandfather, Rabbi Dr Georg Salzberger, a patriotic Jewish chaplain in the German Army during the First World War. The German War Ministry was subject to a barrage of letters complaining that Jews were shirking their duty and were looking for safe jobs well away from the front lines. They were also accused of profiteering from the war. These complaints and rumours led to the notorious 1916 Jewish census about Jews in the forces.

However, the war was seen as a turning point for Germany and its patriotic Jews:

> Many saw the war both as the ultimate test of equality between Christian and Jew and as furnishing its final proof. My grandfather was convinced that the Jewish contribution to the war would never be forgotten; that those who had witnessed Jews fighting, suffering and dying together with Christians as Germans for the sake of Germany would never be able to return to the old antisemitism of the pre-war era. A new age was being born in the trenches, a new awareness that all were brothers together, a new kind of peace, if not between French and Germans, then at least between German Christians and German Jews. This belief would be shaken to the roots by the Judenzähling, the pernicious Jews' census in the autumn of 1916.[51]

Fritz Wachsner, a progressive teacher with a PhD, kept his pride as a First World War veteran right until the end. He adopted the traditional Jewish approach of keeping his head down and hoping it would pass. When his teenage son, Ernest, was attacked by a troop of Hitler Youth who spat at him and called him a 'dirty Jew', he told his father it didn't feel like his country any more. His father responded, 'This is our Deutschland. Even more so when our Deutschland needs citizens who still think. They know very well what they stand to lose without us. We will remain calm in our Heimat homeland. We will keep a low profile and wait and see.'[52]

Many Jews were leaving for Palestine with Nazi encouragement. Ernest, born 1920, tried to persuade his father to leave. His father refused, saying:

> You think we can abandon who we are and what we are. I did not hide from danger in 1915 when my country went to war. Our duty to our country is no less now. It does not need us to cower before bullies. No one can budge us out of our birthright.
>
> Lotte told her daughter, Marianne, that she had agreed with her father, against her brother, 'who saw clearer what the family should do. If only my father had listened.'[53]

He ensured his daughter Charlotte (Lotte) got away with 936 other desperate Jewish passengers on board the *St Louis* in 1939. However, their Cuban visas had been invalidated even before the *St Louis* left Hamburg and after sweltering in the heat of Havana harbour for a week, on 2 June the boat moved off. Sadly, the vast land of America was closed to these desperate Jews and they were forced to return to Europe where Lotte ended up in the transit camp of Westerbork. Her father, however, managed to arrange her abduction from the camp one night and she finally got to safety in Cuba. Often overlooked, the 937 refugees on the *St Louis* were betrayed by both Cuba and America.[54]

Unfortunately, Fritz was unable to arrange escape for himself and his wife, Paula, and on their son's twenty-second birthday, 13 September 1942, they were deported to Riga and murdered by the Gestapo.[55] Marianne Meyerhoff speculated on her grandparents' end:

> The professor, the favourite of his students, among whom were more than a few Nazis, proud soldier in the army of the Kaiser, hears a pounding on his door by his fellow citizens garbed in the same uniform he once wore and with his wife, Paula, is thrown helpless into the street and forced to march in front of their neighbors in a tragic parade through Berlin to the Anhalter train station to be 'sent east' in boxcars as cattle to a sadistic slaughter.[56]

Ernest was found to have been in hiding underground in Berlin and was last seen as the city fell.[57]

The young lawyer, René Cassin (1887–1976), was severely wounded while serving as a First World War soldier. The experience marked him for life. In the interwar years, he represented France at the League of Nations and worked for disarmament. In the 1920s he sought to bring about reconciliation and peace, and he supported the conferences of war veterans. However, Hitler's seizure of power in Germany put an end to such efforts.

Jewish soldiers thought their army service and their proven loyalty to their homeland would protect them from the Nazis. Initially, in some cases it did, particularly after Kristallnacht when many veterans were released from Dachau quite quickly, but in the long run it made no difference. Wounded, decorated and ordinary soldiers all became fodder for the gas chambers in the same way as the non-combatants.

Leipzig had a very large Jewish community before 1933 – most of whom were prominent in its intellectual and cultural life. There were many Jewish doctors whose technical innovations are still used today. The first Jewish doctor in Leipzig was Solomon Hirsch Brugheim (1754–1823). He had to get special dispensation from the state of Saxony to qualify in the town's medical faculty and he was also the first Jew to receive a doctorate from Leipzig University. How shocked would the celebrating Brugheim family have been to know that his advancing footsteps would be halted a mere 150 years later.

Dr Ludwig Frankenthal (1885–1944) had qualified in Munich in 1911. He worked as a surgeon in Berlin until the outbreak of war in 1914, when he volunteered as an army surgeon working in several military hospitals. He specialised in crush injuries to muscles and kidneys, which he called 'crush-syndrome', and in 1916 he published an article on the subject. He was awarded the Iron Cross for bravery – one of the 30,000 decorated Jewish soldiers out of the 100,000 who enlisted.

In 1919 he was invited to work in Leipzig as a surgeon at the University Hospital and he stayed until 1924. His clinical work was not accepted for accreditation, probably down to the anti-Semitism of the medical faculty. In 1929 he married Ilse, one of the daughters of the music publisher Henri Hinrichsen, and they had two sons. In the same year he was made medical director of the Leipzig Jewish Hospital with Dr Pascal Deul. By the end of 1937 he had published fifty medical papers on kidney diseases.

In spite of restrictions on Jewish medical professionals, until 9 November 1938 he was one of the few able to treat members of the Jewish community. When he arrived at the hospital early on 10 November he was arrested and sent to Buchenwald for seventeen terrible days.[58] He was released on condition that his wife arranged their departure within fourteen days and luckily she managed to get visas for Holland. Accordingly, Ludwig was released from Buchenwald on 27 November 1938:

> He was in a terrible condition and couldn't stop crying; he had nightmares at night and complained of terrible pains in his nose. Through her medical connections, Ilse managed to get Ludwig into hospital where he underwent two operations. He was petrified that he would be sent back to Buchenwald; he would not talk about his terrible experiences to anybody for fear of further reprisals. In order to leave Ilse free to make all their emigration arrangements, Ludwig remained in hospital until the family left for Holland on 15 December.[59]

It is also important to record here the financial struggle Ilse had to suffer before they could leave:

> Ilse had to make all the arrangements for the transportation of their household goods to the USA and to pay 100 per cent duty on their value. They had to sacrifice their entire life savings and insurance policies and deposit RM95,000 as Jewish refugee tax. Like all would-be émigrés, they also had to pay Jewish wealth tax, emigration tax, religious community tax, income tax, higher income tax and others. They fled Germany penniless ...[60]

However, their attempts to reach America failed when America entered the war in 1941, and as immigrants in Holland they were vulnerable. On 8 April 1943 Dr Frankenthal and Ilse, with their two sons aged 14 and 11, were 'requested' to enter Westerbork. In her memoir, Ilse explained that this was falsely presented

as a desirable option to former soldiers who had served in the First World War –
although it actually meant transport to Theresienstadt.

They arrived with rucksacks and large blankets – Westerbork had a hospital with
1,800 beds, 120 doctors and other personnel. Dr Frankenthal, employed as a doctor
and a surgeon, worked hard to save patients from transportation. One day, thirteen
women arrived and he was told to sterilise them. He said, 'No', for religious reasons and because of his Hippocratic Oath which insisted on the consideration of
the well-being of the patient. Ilse wrote in her memoirs, which were used in the
Nuremberg Trials:

> The 13 women were sent away, but my husband was told by Slesinger [the Jewish
> head of the camp] that Kommandant Gemmicke had said: 'This refusal means
> gas for him, his wife and children.' But my husband refused nevertheless, quite
> unable to do what was asked of him.

Quite some time elapsed, but suddenly at midday on Sunday, 3 September,
Kommandant Gemmicke announced that on the following morning at 5.00 a.m.,
3,000 people – especially families with children – including the Frankenthals were
to get onto the cattle trucks. They were only allowed to take one rucksack, with less
than they had brought to Westerbork. Even in these circumstances, Dr Frankenthal
could not change his mind about his medical ethics even though so many doctors
under the Nazis did break the Hippocratic Oath.

After two days and two nights on the train they arrived at Theresienstadt, which
was not quite the 'family camp' they had expected. Ilse and Ludwig had to do hard
manual work which they were ill prepared for. Six weeks later, Ilse noted:

> Thousands upon thousands were called up to go to their place of work [a work-
> ing camp that was constantly talked about]. No one talked any more about First
> World War soldiers. The selection was by age group. On 12 October 1944 we
> received our call, packed our rucksacks and the Lager Commandant said to my
> husband, 'Surgeons are needed everywhere.'

With 3,000 others, the four Frankenthals were transported east. On 14 October
1944 they arrived at their destination – Auschwitz. Ilse wrote:

> My husband immediately understood our fate and said goodbye to me forever.
> The order was: nothing was to be taken from the train, no rucksack nor food. Men
> and women separated. It was the last time I saw the two boys and my husband.
> A 'doctor' was standing there selecting people. The boys had to go with their
> fathers, the girls with their mothers. Then old and young were selected. There were
> approximately 200 survivors from the transport of 3,000. Those of us who were

left were driven into showers where we had to stand naked for hours. Everything
was taken from us. I had to hand over my wedding ring and glasses and all my
possessions. All our hair was shaved off. Then we had to stand to attention for 24
hours without any food and in the cold whilst the chimney was smoking.

She said that as she never heard from her husband and sons again, she assumed they
had been gassed on 14 October 1944. Tragically for that family, the transports to
Auschwitz ceased a mere two weeks later on 28 October and the gassing ceased
on 2 November. The SS destroyed the gas chambers on 26 November. It wasn't
until 1948 that Ilse had confirmation that her 58-year-old husband and two sons
aged 15 and 12 had been gassed the day they arrived. Of her husband's eight siblings
only two survived.

Ilse survived five camps and dedicated her life to the memory of her husband
and sons. She wrote:

| | |
|---|---|
| Weiterleben! | Living on! |
| Ludwig, ich lebe! | Ludwig, I live! |
| Ludwig, ich schaffe das! | Ludwig, I manage it! |
| Ludwig, es ist schoen zu Leben! | Ludwig, living is beautiful![61] |

Ilse died on 30 July 1987 in Brunssum, Holland. Her life was a symbol of the tragedy that befell German Jews, whose service to their homeland both as decorated
veterans of the First World War and as valuable medical professionals was ultimately
seen as worthless, as were they, themselves, to the Nazi state.

In one case, I found a woman who spoke about her father's war record. Jeanette
Grunfeld (1921–2013, née Marx) was born in Cologne to a Jewish couple, Salomon
and Marianne Marx. At school the Nazi flag and Hitler's picture were hung in the
classroom. One day Dr Kreitz, a self proclaimed Nazi supporter, started attacking
the Jews with 'vile propaganda' to his captive audience of children. Jeanette was
furious and jumped up:

The teacher told me that all Jews are cowards ... Well, I went out of the school –
I was only 13 years old – pulled my father's decorations off the wall from World
War 1, the Iron Cross and everything from the War, and carried them back to
school. I said, 'Here ... you're a liar, Dr Kreitz! Here's my father's decorations, my
uncle was gassed, one was wounded ... How can you say the Jews are cowards?'[62]

As a result the principal called her in and her mother had to come to the school.
The principal said, 'Look, what you did was right, you did the right thing, but
don't say anything I told you because otherwise I lose my job. But you can't stay
any more.'

After a brief stay in France, aged 17, Jeanette went to England on the Kindertransport and after the war she went to America. Sadly, her parents stayed behind. Her father was paralysed from a beating he received from Nazi thugs who wanted to take his business from him in 1938. He refused and they nearly killed him, leaving him ill for the rest of his life and taking the business anyhow. His family had lived in Germany for 400 years and had not believed Hitler could last. His own brother, Benedikt, saw the light in 1932 and begged him to sell his business and flee with the money.[63]

Finally, Julius Weinberg (1887–1965) was included in the London Jewish Museum's 2014 'First World War' exhibition. His son, Kurt, a child of the Kindertransport, told his story. Julius was born in Werther, in north-west Germany, and worked in his father's cigar factory. He volunteered for the German Army from 1908, and during the First World War served as a sergeant in the Supply Corps. Kurt has reiterated that German Jews were enthusiastic to fight for the Kaiser and their country.

Kurt has photographs of his father in uniform along with his Soldbuch (service record). Julius Weinberg was very proud to have been awarded the Iron Cross (1914–1918) and the Iron Cross (Rhine) medals. When the Nazis rose to power, Kurt explained that his father believed these medals and the fact he was part of the organisation of German-Jewish soldiers would keep him safe. Kurt showed his father's bescheinigung (certification) document which was produced to prove that he had fought in the army. However, even though that document and his Iron Crosses were presented at the police station Julius could not escape persecution, although they might have postponed transportation for two weeks. Julius survived the Buchenwald concentration camp but Kurt felt that he was a changed man.[64]

An interesting sideline to the exhibition is the fact that many of the Jews in Britain had escaped from Russian pogroms or were of Russian ancestry. There was some reluctance to fight with the Russians against the Germans. The poet Isaac Rosenberg joined up because he needed the money. Many felt great gratitude to Britain, and the *Jewish Chronicle* printed a poster in the autumn of 1914. The poster said, 'Britain has been all she could be to Jews, Jews will be all they can be to Britain'. A modern commentator wrote:

> This made me squirm with shame. I thought of the grindingly slow progress of the bill for Jewish emancipation through the Lords and Commons during the 19th century; our failure to provide either chaplains or kosher food for Jewish soldiers on the Western Front; the terrible turning of blind eyes by many in the government to the horrors of the concentration camps; the covert anti-Semitism that simmers beneath the surface of many Englishmen to this day.[65]

I only found reference to one Jewish woman for this chapter, and that was 61-year-old Alina Cavalieri, an Italian Jew, who had won a silver medal for her nursing services at the front during the First World War. As persecution began, she had refused to move or get false papers, claiming she had 'nothing to hide'. That did not prevent her being deported by the Nazis following the round-up in the Rome Ghetto on 16 November 1943, and she was gassed on arrival at Auschwitz on 23 October.[66]

The same transport also took 71-year-old Admiral Augusto Capon (1872–1944), who had commanded a frigate during the First World War. The racial laws of 1938 had forced him to resign his commission. Half-paralysed with an illness from his military service, he had to be carried to the transport. His son-in-law, Enrico Fermi, the nuclear scientist, and his sister, Maria, had offered to hide Capon with some other Jews outside Rome. He refused, thinking his status and the personal letter from Mussolini that he had produced would save him.[67] Like so many others, he was betrayed. He was gassed at Auschwitz on arrival.

# 17

# RACIAL ISSUES

---

If my theory of relativity is proven correct, Germany will claim me as a German and France will declare that I am a citizen of the world. Should my theory prove untrue, France will say I am a German and Germany will declare that I am Jew.

Albert Einstein (1879–1955), in 1929

I'm not really a Jew. Just Jew-ish. Not the whole hog, you know.

Jonathan Miller, Beyond the Fringe, a 1960 revue

---

The Nazis changed centuries of Jewish persecution from religion to race – family ancestry became the issue, rather than religious grouping. The problem that this created was that there was no escape route. Even under the Spanish Inquisition the Jews could, were they minded, escape persecution by converting to Christianity. Even Shylock was offered conversion as a solution at the end of Shakespeare's *Merchant of Venice* to save his eternal soul. The Nazis did not want to save the Jews' souls, they wanted to get rid of them. They therefore did not permit this escape and many people, from families which had converted, were persecuted because of their grand-parentage.

Werner Goldberg is an example. He did not know that his father, Albert Goldberg, was Jewish as Albert had converted to the Lutheran Church in 1900 and his two sons (born 1919 and 1920) were baptised as well. It is suggested that he converted for professional and social reasons, rather than religious belief. He was only 19 and he wanted to be assimilated. He started as a bank clerk in Berlin in 1906 and by 1918 he was a director and accountant in an insurance agency and owned a home in the exclusive Grünewald district of Berlin. He had married a Protestant and for his two sons he hoped for achievement and respect within German society. 'The Jewish identity would be shuffled off, the minority status forgotten.'[1]

At Werner's school there were both Jews and Christians mixing with no problems. His best friend was Karl Wolf – a red-haired lad who lived in the same apartment block. They played together, went to church and had religious teaching at school. When they were 10 they both joined the German Boy Scouts. However, with Hitler's arrival, Albert lost his job under the Law for the Restoration of the Civil Service of April 1933, which expelled Jews from the Civil Service. At the same time, Nazis were being placed in key roles to promote Nazi policies.

Accordingly, a new pro-Nazi headmaster arrived at Werner's school. He aimed to make the school Judenfrei. One day he said, 'All non-Aryans, stand up!'. Werner did not stand up. The headmaster asked him if he was Jewish and Werner said he didn't know. The headmaster said, 'Then I'll tell you: You are not Aryan. So get to your feet.' That evening Albert Goldberg was compelled to tell his son what he had hoped to avoid – that he came from a Jewish home.

However, Werner hung in and, aged 14, he and Karl joined the Hitler Youth. The Boy Scouts had an international flavour with jamborees in other countries, while the Hitler Youth excluded Jews and foreigners. However, originally Mischlinge were allowed to join the Hitler Youth until Himmler became concerned that they were using it to hide their status and to appear politically dependable. Accordingly, leaders of Nazi-related groups were told to expel children of intermarried couples and all Germans married to Jews. So Werner had to leave the Hitler Youth.

By 1934, the new headmaster had got rid of many Jews, but Werner had great respect for some of the teachers and knew they did not support Hitler. One of these was Mr Schenk. One day, Schenk invited the keen cyclists of the class to go on a trip outside Berlin, starting from his home:

> We all stood with our bicycles, ready to roll. And suddenly, a window at the top of the house opened, a flagpole was shoved through the window and an enormous flag with a swastika unfurled. And I stood there, fully perplexed to find that something like this was possible, from someone I had never suspected of being a Nazi, someone I had admired so highly. I began to cry and got on my bike and went home. That was a big disappointment. Now I suspected that inside everyone a Nazi was hiding.[2]

However, Werner still had the Boy Scouts – but, they too, soon had a new leader. One day he called Werner in and very gently he put his arm on his shoulder and said:

> I know, Werner, that you are very attached to this club and have done a lot for it. But you have to understand that for us you are a burden. The Nazis don't want to have any Mischlinge. So I have to ask you to leave. Do us a favor, and quit.

Werner spoke to his chums in the Scouts and was shocked by the results. None of them would support him. He was completely isolated. His father told him to leave: 'If anyone doesn't want you, don't force yourself on them.' At the same time, matters deteriorated at school as Aryan boys were given Hitler Youth uniforms and the girls had League of German Girls' uniforms. Those without uniforms felt left out and even his old chum Karl, proudly wearing his uniform, was avoiding him. He decided to leave school – he had wanted to study medicine, but that was no longer possible. His father just made him finish the school year.

He was apprenticed to a Mr Grohm, an observant Jew who ran a leather clothing manufacturers. Most of his colleagues were Jews or Mischlinge. However, Mr Grohm blamed the thousands of Polish Orthodox Jews who had poured into Berlin after 1918 for the harsh anti-Semitism. His father, desperate for help on losing his job, approached the Berlin Jewish Community but the chairman said he couldn't help him because 'you don't belong to the Jewish Community'. Albert was quite shocked, but Werner philosophically said they probably had plenty of members to help. The Nazis created prejudice which divided families, so that even Werner's uncle – his mother's brother – refused to have anything to do with his Aryan sister.[3]

## Privileged Marriages

The concept of the 'privileged marriage' came out of Kristallnacht, because of the protests from the German partners of victimised Jews who protested directly to high-level officials. One historian, Ursula Büttner, has suggested that it was the prominent Jews from intermarriages who were picked on as victims of that night. These people complained to Hermann Göring and accordingly he devised two categories of intermarriage – privileged and non-privileged or simple.

Privileged marriages were to be those where the wife was Jewish or the couple had at least one child baptised as a Christian rather than enrolled in a Jewish Community. The non-privileged marriages were couples whose Mischlinge children were classified as Jews (Geltungsjuden), as well as childless couples where the husband was Jewish.

The privileged marriages outnumbered the simple ones by three to one because the majority of Mischlinge were baptised. The non-privileged, intermarried Jews would be treated like other Jews, while the Jews in privileged intermarriages would be exempt from the worst aspects of persecution. The classifications were devised to pacify the most influential people just when the Nazis were planning the physical separation of Jews from their German neighbours – when they sent Jews to special designated housing, what were they to do with the intermarried? To attempt to split marriages and families would incur the wrath of the forces behind social and religious sanctions of marriages.

The Rosenstrasse Demonstration took place between 27 February and 6 March 1943 outside the Berlin Jewish Community premises on 2–4 Rosenstrasse. The Germans had rounded up about 2,000 Jews who were mostly married to non-Jewish partners, and any male children of these marriages. The protest occurred because the 2,000 non-Jewish partners feared that the men would be sent to death camps because 10,000 Berlin Jews had already been sent to Auschwitz. The non-violent demonstration in the freezing cold was intended to save their loved ones from such a fate.

At the Wannsee Conference of January 1942, it was originally decided that the issue of Jews in 'mixed marriage' would be postponed until after German victory in the war. Apparently this decision was based on concern that deportation of these Jewish spouses and their half-Jewish children would cause unrest, both among the non-Jewish relations and even among the wider German population.

The last major round-up of German Jews, known as 'Factory Action' (Fabrik-Aktion), took place at the same time as the incarceration of the Jewish spouses at Rosenstrasse. The Germans deported 11,000 Jews to Auschwitz in the first weeks of March alone. However, the Gestapo had always intended to send the Jewish spouses to forced labour camps around Berlin and other cities in Germany. There were about 8,800 in Berlin, and they were regarded as 'exempted'.

Before dawn on Saturday, 27 February 1943 – the Jewish Sabbath, as the Nazis liked to undertake their raids on the Sabbath or Jewish festivals – a massive action was undertaken. Jews were dragged from their jobs and homes and pulled off the streets into trucks and taken to assembly points. The 2,000 at Rosenstrasse were having their papers checked to see if they were 'exempt'. When they did not return home, relatives, mostly women, started to assemble outside the building hoping to find out what was happening. Gradually there were 150–200 people who either shouted, chanted or stayed silent, in spite of being threatened by the authorities. This was such an unusual event that news spread quickly through the country and even to the foreign press.

Those inside Rosenstrasse were naturally anxious and suffered from inadequate supplies of food, sleeping and sanitary facilities. The Gestapo took considerable time reviewing their papers, with the first being released on 1 March and the last on 12 March, although the protest finished on 6 March. Only twenty-five of them were sent to Auschwitz as protective custody prisoners (schutzhäftlinge). However, those released were picked up the next day for forced labour by the German police.

The Rosenstrasse Demonstration took place a month after the surrender of the 6th Army at Stalingrad, when the authorities were concerned that there would be public unrest and turmoil. Some individual Jews from mixed marriages were later deported but, on the whole, the Nazis stuck to the policy agreed at Wannsee. However, the demonstrators outside and their loved ones inside the building could not be sure of this, given the mendacity of the Nazis. The ongoing 'Factory Action' was not an encouraging example, as people were not returning from deportation. Neither were the protestors sure that the German police would not shoot them, as unarmed German civilians, for fear of the impact on the public. Most importantly there had never been a public protest on behalf of the Jews in wartime Nazi Germany – there was no precedent to guide them.

Sadly, the conclusion is that however courageous the participants were in their protest they did not change the Nazis' policy, as they did what they had always planned to do.[4] However, the fact that they were concerned about the PR consequences of harming the Jewish spouses of non-Jews is significant when they had no concerns over harming the Jews.


## Mischlinge

The unpleasant word 'Mischlinge' means literally 'hybrids' or 'mongrels'. The Nuremberg Laws of September 1935 did not actually define who was a Jew. Therefore, an additional decree was made in November 1935 to define the terms 'Jew', 'Aryan' and 'Mischling'.

To be a Jew you had to have at least three full Jewish grandparents. A half-Jew was called a Mischling. However, there were two types of Mischling. If you had two Jewish grandparents you were a Mischling of the first degree, a half-Jew, provided you were not married to a Jew, as of 15 September 1935. A Mischling of the second degree, or a quarter-Jew, was someone with one Jewish grandparent or an Aryan married to a Jew. In 1939 there were 72,000 Mischlinge of the first degree and 39,000 Mischlinge of the second degree still living in Germany.

The Mischlinge issue was important to Hitler. The intention was that Mischlinge of the second degree should be assimilated into the Aryan state, but those of the first degree were to be considered as Jews. The policy was not consistent throughout the occupied territories. Some Nazis suggested, during the winter of 1941–1942, that all Mischlinge of the first degree should be sterilised. However, nothing came of this because the Nazis feared the response of the many Germans who were related to Mischlinge.[5]

Intermarried Jews and Mischlinge – even those who wore the star – were 'temporarily deferred' from deportation. However, once the deportations started the slightest infraction could lead to disaster. Denunciations were more likely to lead to death.

Mrs Böhm was a half-Jew whom the Nazis regarded as a Jew because she was also married to a Jew. She, her husband and newborn son were living with a couple where the man was Jewish and the woman Aryan:

Both Böhms received the Jewish food ration cards and could shop only between 4.00 and 5.00pm. The Böhms, however, needed more food just to keep the baby alive. In an effort to get German portions, Mrs Böhm went shopping one day without wearing the Star of David. Mrs Hensel, the guardian of practices at the local grocer, was watching. She immediately denounced her, and a short while after, the Gestapo arrested Mrs Böhm, leaving behind her husband and small child. 'That was heart-rending to see how she held the child and loved it, before leaving.'[6]

At the Grosse Hamburger Strasse assembly camp in Berlin, the Gestapo had a coloured card index – it was managed by two Jewish women who also registered new arrivals at the camp. Martha Erlich (later Raphael) recalled there were different-coloured cards:

> I still remember that those who counted as Jews by religion and race received white cards if they had no Aryan genealogical background, and that children of mixed marriages brought up as Jews received blue cards. Furthermore, I think that the Jewish wife in a mixed marriage received a yellow card if her children were raised as Jews. There were cards in different colors, but I can no longer remember their details.[7]

## Schutzjuden

The rules about separating Jews from Aryan female servants under 45 was intended to avoid the creation of more Mischlinge, rather than from a moral standpoint. One of the people who protested was the famous philosopher Karl Jaspers (1883–1969), who was married to a Jew. He petitioned various government offices, including the Interior Ministry, for permission to keep his household servant, Erna Baer. He protested that having to release his servant would have disastrous results on his and his wife's poor health and his work. Being childless they had no other help and he hinted that without Erna Baer he might have to stop his 'scientific work'.

So, for people like him a special category was created – schutzjuden – 'Jews protected from Jewish regulations because of their political or scientific usefulness to the state'. The regime needed the courts and the ministries to make their laws on 'Racial Shame' (Rassenschande) respectable. These rules prevented the birth of further Mischlinge but also helped isolate the Jews socially from the Germans, which was important in the goal of concentrating and then expelling the Jews.[8]

When Hitler came into power in 1933, Jaspers was taken by surprise as he had not taken National Socialism seriously. He thought that this movement would destroy itself from within, thus leading to a reorganisation and liberation by the other political forces active at the time. These expectations, however, did not materialise. A professor of philosophy at Heidelberg University, he was one of the few to resist Nazification and was forced into early retirement in 1937.

Because his wife was Jewish, Jaspers was regarded as an enemy of the state. Accordingly, from 1933 he was excluded from the higher councils of the university but he was still allowed to teach and publish. Unlike many other famous intellectuals of that time, he was not prepared to make any concessions to the Nazi doctrines. Consequently, a series of decrees were promulgated against him, including removal from his professorship and a total ban on any further publication. These measures effectively barred him from carrying on his work in Germany.

The couple's friends tried to assist him to emigrate to another country. Permission was finally granted to him in 1942 to go to Switzerland, but this was conditional on his wife remaining behind in Germany. He refused to accept this condition and decided to stay with his wife, notwithstanding the dangers. It became necessary for his friends to hide his wife. Both of them had decided, in case of an arrest, to commit suicide. In 1945 he was told by a reliable source that his deportation was scheduled to take place on 14 April. On 30 March, however, Heidelberg was occupied by the Americans.[9]

Stefan Zweig wrote of the sad situation when his mother was dying in Vienna. She was 84 and was found unconscious one morning in 1938. The doctor said she was unlikely to survive the next night and found a nurse to stay with her. As Stefan and his brother were not in Vienna, his cousin, aged 60, said he would also stay with her so she would have a member of the family with her as she lay dying. Stefan wrote:

> When he began improvising himself a bed for the night in the next room, the nurse came in and said — to her credit, looking ashamed of it — that under the new German laws she was afraid that meant she couldn't stay with her patient overnight. My cousin was Jewish, and as a woman under fifty she wasn't allowed to spend a night under the same roof as a Jew, even to care for a dying woman. By the standards of the Streicher mentality, any Jew's first thought was bound to be to commit an act of 'racial disgrace' with her.

So the cousin, who was not well himself and died a year later, left so the nurse could stay with the dying woman.[10]

Marianne Faithful (*b.* 1946), a singer with a racy reputation as a wild child in the 1960s, revealed that she was the child of a Mischling. Her grandmother Flora was Jewish and by law had to add Sara to her name to identify her religion. Her daughter Eve, Marianne's mother, was defined as a Mischling because Eva's father was a non-Jew. Both women were raped by soldiers from the Red Army who liberated Vienna and became haters of men, which had influenced Marianne for a considerable period of her life, she said.[11]

In his book *Two Cheers for Democracy*, E.M. Forster (1879–1970) makes reference to the Nazis' racial policies. Forster, part of the Bloomsbury Group, was also a humanist and a closet homosexual. Perhaps that gave him insight into those on the periphery of society.

In the same way, Max Glatt (1912–2002), a Berlin Jew incarcerated in Dachau after Kristallnacht, came to England and became a psychiatrist specialising in the rehabilitation of alcohol and drug addicts. Late in life he admitted that he had been 'drawn to helping alcoholics partly because of the way they were stigmatised and made to feel unwelcome'.[12]

Most memorably in 1939 Forster discussed the question of grandparents:

> People who would ill-treat Jews themselves or even be rude to them, enjoy tittering over their misfortunes; they giggle when pogroms are instituted by someone else and synagogues defiled vicariously. 'Serve them right really, Jews.' …
>
> The grand Nordic argument, 'He's a bloody capitalist so he must be a Jew, and as he's a Jew he must be a Red,' has already taken root in our filling-stations and farms. Men employ it more frequently than women, and young men more frequently than old ones …
>
> There is another reply which is more intellectual but which requires more courage. It is to say, 'Are you sure you're not a Jew yourself? Do you know who your eight great-grandparents were? Can you swear that all the eight are Aryan?'[13]

He continues that what he called 'Jew-mania' was the one evil no one foretold at the end of the first war. Although there were warnings, they were not serious and he recalled being in India in 1921 when a colonel lent him the *Protocols of the Elders of Zion* and:

> … it was such an obvious fake that I did not worry.
>
> To me, anti-Semitism is now the most shocking of all things. It is destroying much more than the Jews; it is assailing the human mind at its source, and inviting it to create false categories before exercising judgement. I am sure we shall win through. But it will take a long time.

Agatha Christie (1890–1976), another British writer, appears to have written about fairly unattractive Jewish characters in her crime books. In 1930 she married an archaeologist of Austrian descent, Max Mallowan (1904–1978), whom she accompanied to Baghdad in May 1933 where they visited the museum. The Director of Antiquities was a German, Dr Julius Jordan, who was quite charming to the Mallowans. In his memoirs, Max wrote:

… politically he proved to be no friend, for he was a paid Nazi agent and did all he could to undermine British authority in Iraq. But personally he could not have been more charming; although violently anti-Semitic, he was an excellent musician, and sensitive; it seemed extraordinary that this artistic and cultured man could succumb to the new Hitlerian régime.[14]

Dr Jordan's impact on Agatha Christie was described:

He was an excellent pianist, played Beethoven sonatas for them, and always seemed a gentle, considerate and cultured human being. But, at tea one day in his house, someone mentioned Jews. Agatha noticed that the expression on Dr Jordan's face changed suddenly, 'in an extraordinary way that I had never noticed on anyone's face before'. 'You do not understand,' said the Doctor. 'Our Jews are perhaps different from yours. They are a danger. They should be exterminated. Nothing else will really do but that.'

Agatha was shocked, as it was the first time she came across any hint of what was to come in Germany. He was the first Nazi she had met and later she found his wife was an even more fanatical Nazi. 'It must have been, you cannot help thinking, a salutary experience for Agatha Christie, for the casual anti-Semitic comments which disfigure most of her earlier books are not found in such profusion in those published after the mid-thirties.'[15]

Alfred Pringsheim (1850–1941) came from a wealthy Silesian family with Jewish roots. He studied mathematics and physics in Berlin and Heidelberg, obtaining a doctorate in 1872. He then moved to Munich where he became a professor of mathematics in 1901 and had been elected a member of the Bavarian Academy of Sciences in 1898.[16] He was a corresponding member of the Göttingen Academy of Sciences and also a member in the Leopoldina, Germany's oldest academy of natural sciences.

He considered himself a German citizen who was no longer following the 'Mosaic belief', but that did not save him from the Nazis. In 1878 he had married the Berlin actress Gertrude Hedwig Anna Dohm (1855–1942), whose parents were converts from Judaism to Christianity. They had five children and their youngest daughter, Katia, married Thomas Mann. In his novel *Königliche Hoheit*, the character Samuel Spoelmann was said to be based on Pringsheim. He had an interest in music from an early age and was particularly devoted to Richard Wagner. He corresponded with Wagner and published several arrangements of his work. As a wealthy man, he even gave him significant financial support and also supported the Bayreuth Festival to such an extent he was called a Patron. His granddaughter recorded in her memoirs that he once fought a duel with someone who had insulted Wagner.

Unfortunately for him, he was such a patriotic German that he purchased a considerable quantity of war loans during the First World War and he consequently lost most of his capital after the war. The situation was aggravated by the dreadful inflation of the 1920s, so he was forced to sell part of his art collection and also his marvellous mathematics library containing many sixteenth-century works.

From 1933 to 1939 his life was made impossible as a non-Aryan. He felt too old to go abroad like the rest of his family and, on 1 January 1938 when he was 87, new legislation forced him to change his name by adding 'Israel' (women had to add Sarah). That year, he was forced out of the Bavarian Academy of Sciences by the president Alexander Mueller. Winifred Wagner was unable to help him, in spite of all he had done for her father and the Bayreuth Festival. However, the rektor of Munich University, a neighbour who was a friend of Rudolf Hess, a former pupil who was now a professor of mathematics and even a courageous member of the SS, enabled him and his wife to leave for Zurich on 31 October 1939.

He had built a magnificent home in Munich in the German Renaissance style and with frescoes by Hans Thoma. The house was requisitioned by the Nazis, demolished and replaced by the Nazi Party headquarters. He also had 'one of the greatest of all Italian majolica collections' which was confiscated by the Nazis and sold in London at Sotheby's (7–8 June and 19–20 July 1939). In March 1939 the German Ministry of Trade authorised its export, provided that 80 per cent of the proceeds up to £20,000 and 70 per cent of the remainder was paid to the German Gold Discount Bank in foreign currency. Pringsheim was to receive what remained. Items from his collection can be found worldwide in institutions – the Metropolitan Museum in New York has thirty-seven pieces, the Arts Décoratifs in Lyons twenty-one pieces and there are eighteen in the Fitzwilliam Museum in Cambridge. There is little left in Germany, apart from the three pieces he gave the Schlossmuseum in Berlin. It seems that the Nazis had no desire to expel the Jew's gifts – just the Jew himself.[17]

He died in Zurich on 25 June 1941 and his wife apparently burnt all the papers he had brought from Germany, including the Richard Wagner letters. She herself died a year later.

Annelore Yasseri-John, who lives in Hamburg, was born on 28 November 1935 in Breslau in Germany (now Wroclaw in Poland). The circumstances of her birth are unique to the Third Reich. Annelore's father was Walter Spyra (*b.* 1911). Walter's father, Victor, was Aryan and his mother, Erna, was Jewish. Annelore's mother was Maria Knappe (*b.* 1914), apparently very pretty with lots of admirers, who fell in love with Walter and became pregnant. Accordingly a marriage was fixed for 9 October 1935 in Breslau. The day before the marriage, the Prussian Registry Office informed Walter that the marriage had been stopped because of his two Jewish grandparents and his Jewish mother (Erna).

Consequently, Annelore was classified as illegitimate for the first two decades of her life. She sent her story in German to my friend Hildegard Abraham on 18 February 2014. Hildegard translated it into English and is responsible for telling me about Annelore's extraordinary story.

In 1937 Walter was thrown out of the University of Breslau where he had been a student. Drafted into the Wehrmacht, he was soon dismissed when his origins became known. He was then forced to work for Blaupunkt doing armament work. At the end of 1943 he was deported to a labour camp near Edersee, the dam targeted by the Dambusters. His task was to help rebuild the dam. In 1945 he was liberated from this labour camp by the American troops.

Meanwhile, Maria had lived in a rented room in Breslau up to Annelore's birth. In 1936 with her own non-Jewish mother and her baby, she went to Hirschberg (now Jelenia Gora in Poland) to a two-roomed flat. Maria found work as a book-keeper in a soap factory. Annelore told Hildegard that she remembers her father visiting them surreptitiously during the night with help from friends.

Annelore started school in 1942 in Hirschberg and was registered under her mother's family name. She writes that she became aware when she was very young, about 6 or 7, that her father's surname was different. Her mother would not allow her to participate in the welfare collections at school and she was not to say 'Heil Hitler'. Living opposite them was a family with a boy a year older and he always seemed to be watching what she was doing.

Even as a small child she was sent to Dresden for long periods each year to her father's parents. Maria had three sisters, all married to husbands loyal to the Nazi regime and none of them lived nearby. Her Jewish grandmother had to wear the Jewish star. In all those years, both in Hirschberg and in Dresden, Annelore perceived an oppressive atmosphere – 'insecurity and fear were apparent'. She remembers that in Dresden, often during the night-time, men of the State Security intruded into her grandparents' home and she was woken up by the noisy arguments with her grandfather (Victor) and her grandmother's crying.

She wrote, 'Several times fear drove me out of my bed and when I came out of the bedroom looking for comfort, I was put back to bed very roughly by my grandfather and once he hit me.' It shocked her because he had always been very loving, understanding and forgiving. This behaviour was very puzzling from people who were normally loving and kind to each other, and she wrote, 'I never in later life witnessed loud arguments or angry reaction to strangers by my grandfather.'

She commented that these experiences have followed her through life. Annelore was also haunted by the fearful and conspiratorial actions of her grandmother. When Erna heard that her parents and her sister, Charlotte, had been killed in Auschwitz and Theresienstadt respectively, she created a kind of shrine in the garden where she used to pray each day, taking Annelore with her.

Today, she presumes that because of her grandfather's war injuries, his status as an officer in the First World War and his refusal to divorce or separate from her grandmother, he saved his wife from being sent to a camp. This refusal was probably the cause of the regular nightly visits by the thugs. She has expressed surprise that nothing worse happened and they survived that horrible time. At the end of February 1945 they were evacuated from Hirschberg because of the Russian advance and they managed to get to Dresden, where they stayed with her grandparents until August 1949. From 8 May 1945 Russians lived with them for ten days and then went to barracks outside Dresden.

In September 1945 her father came to Dresden and worked with others to reconnect the city to the electric grid. This was still a very difficult time because the old Nazi civil servants and officials were still in their posts. Apparently, in the Soviet-occupied zone where Dresden was, the Russians were arresting engineers and forcibly taking them to Russia to rebuild Russian industry. He was warned by a friend, and in the summer of 1949 he fled in the middle of the night from Dresden and went to West Berlin. She and her mother followed in August 1949.

Later they were flown by American planes to Hesse in West Germany – it was too dangerous to travel by road. Until 1952 they lived with her father in Kassel in a former barracks which housed refugees and she went to school. In 1952 her father found work in Hamburg working at a TV station and later he worked for the Dutch electrical company Phillips.

In June 1956, twenty-one years after their non-existent marriage, Maria and Walter's marriage was acknowledged to the original date. This resulted in finally making Annelore's birth legitimate at the age of 21. Her sister, who was born in 1947, was also made legitimate. Apparently her parents had tried to get their marriage acknowledged several times before they finally succeeded. Annelore concludes that these experiences meant her family had a very negative, suspicious and cautious outlook on life. Her parents lived out their lives in Hamburg in a very secluded way. She believes this led to her marrying very young (aged 21) to escape, and she was very happy for the first eight years. She has three wonderful sons and now has several grandchildren.

Apparently, Walter's sister, Erika (Annelore's aunt), had fallen in love with a non-Jewish industrialist – she was a tennis champion in Silesia. They were not allowed to marry either – her lover took Walter's parents and Erika into his home in Dresden and got Erika a job as a secretary. They all survived the war and all the bombing in that house. They got married after the war and their daughter, Barbara, was born in 1946.

Annelore said her parents had suffered endless grief and pain which they internalised, and she had followed that pattern in many instances. It was only during her first trip to Israel in 2012 that she talked about her family history for the first time to the Israeli tour guide, Tal Kaizman, and Hildegard. There is no way of knowing how many other people suffered similar experiences under the Nazis, but I think Annelore's story is an extremely important example of the impact of the Nazis' racial policies and yet another form of cruelty and betrayal the Nazis perpetrated without resorting to gas, guns or barbed wire.[18] (See photos 23 and 24.)

In October 1941 Gisela Solmitz watched the first round-up of Jews in Hamburg from the train, and when she went home she told her mother, Luise, an inveterate diarist. She recorded the event in her diary, accepting the party line that they were all immigrants. However, the family should have taken more interest because Gisela was a Mischling. Although her father, Major Friedrich (Fredy) Solmitz, was a decorated war veteran, she was the daughter of a racially mixed marriage according to the Nazis. Her father had been baptised but his parents were Jews, while her mother Luise was an Aryan Christian. The family had already suffered years of discrimination since 1933 and Gisela, aged 21, was full of foreboding.[19]

However, much earlier in 1930 Luise had been enthusiastic about Hitler because she, like many others, believed he would save Germany from the Bolsheviks who were all perceived to be Jews. As early as January 1916 Luise had written about the threat of Jews from the east, which was being exploited. 'I wish that sharper frontier controls were put in place against the Jews from Galicia and Poland, otherwise we will not be able to save ourselves from these people.'[20] Luise became very excited when Hitler became chancellor. Conservative and highly patriotic, Major Solmitz, like his wife, had welcomed the advent of the Third Reich. He even served as an Air Raid Protection League Block Warden in 1933 and found no difficulty dismissing Jews under his authority in accordance with the 'Aryan paragraph'.

However, he found he had to write to the local Nazi Party leader, Peter Schonäu, in early 1934 resigning from the post. Schonäu's hostility to him because of his Jewish background had made Fredy's position difficult.[21]

> True, he felt completely German and had given ample proof of his loyalty to the fatherland, but, with all the vilification of Jews in the street, he could not obliterate the thought that he too was descended from a Jewish family. The future for anyone with Jewish connections was veiled in uncertainty. Some said it was better with Hitler in power forced to act responsibly; others feared the worst.[22]

The 20 May 1933 became an important day in the Solmitz household. Gisela was 13 in 1933 and was a happy young girl doing well at school. She was popular with her peers and her teacher, Fräulein Evers. She joined all the various after-school activities and was a member of the League of German Girls (BDM), wearing the uniform of blue skirt and white blouse with the embroidered swastika. Out of the blue she was given a questionnaire at school with two sections, where her parents either had to confirm her Aryan status or explain about her grandparents. One paragraph had to be crossed out and the form signed by a parent. When Gisela saw her form had the first paragraph crossed out, she thought her father had made a mistake.

Luise was waiting outside her husband's room:

> ... too numb to feel anything. Gisela a 'half-Jew'?' It was a catastrophe. The Solmitz family was no longer to be regarded as part of the German people, but was now identified with a 'race' with whom they had no contact and with whom they shared no beliefs. Both Gisela's parents had been baptized, as was Gisela, and they regularly attended church. What would the future now hold for Gisela on the threshold of adult life? They told their daughter to keep her Jewish descent secret even from her best friends. [23]

She tried to carry on as usual, and Fräulein Evers was 'true to her – an exceptional teacher in Nazi Germany'. Gisela was elected class leader, but without Aryan proof she could not accept – an excuse was found. She remained in the BDM for three years with her dark secret. Her father, the decorated war-veteran pilot, appealed for an exemption based on his war record, proving he was a 'good German' – he even wrote to Hitler. But in the end Gisela was forced out and the once gregarious girl became withdrawn and deeply depressed. No longer a member of the BDM, her thoughts turned to suicide. All this was recorded in Luise's diary and she feared for her 16-year-old daughter. 'We three know with cruel clarity that we are just victims, powerless against whatever is to come.'

> With increasing bitterness and despair, Luise Solmitz chronicled all the humili-ation, her fears for Gisela's blighted youth, the uncertainties of what the future would bring. Some of their best friends broke off contact. Fearful of each suc-ceeding day, they held to one certainty in their lives: the three of them would, if it came to the worst, end their lives together. This was just one family's experience, but there were tens of thousands of families like them suddenly turned into non-Aryans – Germans and aliens, rejected by the bond now holding together the German 'race', the *Volksgemeinschaft*, the people's community. [24]

In 1935, as the Nuremberg Laws were announced, the Solmitzs' fears and reac-tions were all recorded in Luise's diary. On 10 September she recorded that with the introduction of Jewish schools for Jews and half-Jews, Gisela had announced she was leaving school.

On 15 November 1935 the family were glued to the radio to hear the racial laws announcing 'the death sentence of our civic life'. Luise wrote, 'whoever marries my daughter goes to prison and she as well; our domestic help has to be dismissed; we are no longer permitted to hang out our flag ... I may live in my fatherland as a foreigner.'

On 28 October, she wrote of her daughter's despair and how being unable to help distressed her: 'Normally parents are the protectors, helpers and comforters, but we are just as helpless as she is …' However, the Solmitzs' marriage was classified as 'privileged'. On 6 November she recorded:

> Fredy met Dr Rosenstein, our throat specialist; he told him he is still entitled to see insurance patients, but he sits alone during surgery hours. Too old to pass new state exams once more in a foreign country, he is considering Russia where this is not required … Dr R. was a doctor on the front line.

On 15 November more details of the race laws were announced:

> … the Führer can allow exceptions. Gisela is not Jewish but a Mischling, and may with special permission marry a German or a Mischling with only one Jewish grandparent … Fredy is at this moment writing his letter to the Führer. Maybe he will be successful, appointed a civil servant before the war, participated in thirty-three engagements, Iron Cross first class etc.

She was pleased that his pension was secure, but he could no longer vote. She wasn't sure about her own position on her pension or the vote, and as a postscript writes that she is listening to Beethoven's sixth symphony in the darkness of the sitting room …

Major Solmitz never had a reply from Hitler, but on 17 September 1936 a letter was received – delivered by a policeman rather than the postman:

> In the name of the Führer and chancellor I inform you herewith that your application to be freed from the provisions of the supplementary requirements of the Reich Citizenship Law and the Blood Law out of considerations of principle can not be acceded to. The decision is final.

Luise was very low and Gisela again threatened suicide: 'A bitter day'.

A year later, Luise found she was losing her friends because of their fear of being associated with a Jewish household. On 29 September 1937 she wrote:

> A peculiar day which I will never forget. Something has occurred which I could not have thought possible, nothing good, the end of a friendship of forty eight years …
> I visited Lene [name changed] at the institute and said to her I wanted to find out why we had not heard from her and her relatives for such a long time. She replied, 'Let's talk about this frankly. It is best as I am not allowed to visit you. You will know why and that it is not owing to anything personal. I actually continued

to come to you although as a civil servant I was not allowed to. I came to the conclusion that it was impossible. Everyone has enemies and one has to reckon with the possibility this could be used against one. I can understand that this touches you deeply, but other times can come again.' I got up and replied, 'Then we have nothing more to say to each other'… That my oldest blood-related friend and school friend is the first zealously to hide behind a decree so that no one can officially attack her for not acting correctly, and is so weak from a human point of view, that hurts.[25]

When Gisela fell in love with a Belgian engineer working in Hamburg, the officials at the town hall gave good advice – that the young couple should marry in Belgium and Major Solmitz would be able to get help in getting permission to move to Belgium. Times were still hard:

The Solmitzs lived in daily dread that one day the exemptions he enjoyed in a 'privileged' mixed marriage would be cancelled and he would then suffer the fate of all the Jews. His was a wretched existence, shunned by his neighbours. Few remained loyal. Nor could the Solmitzs close their ears to rumours all around – terrible rumours about what awaited Jews deported to the East. But what was happening in Poland surely would not happen here in Hamburg! Jews looked for any good signs. When the rations for Jews began to be curtailed, wounded Jewish war veterans like Major Solmitz received them in full. Aryan husbands, despite their Jewish wives, were serving in the Wehrmacht and their wives received full allowances. The Nazis had no record of brutalising women, children and the old. Surely Germans would never stoop so low?[26]

Fritz Kestler was a German farmer and owned a grocery shop in Ühlfeld. His Jewish wife, Else Rindeberg, ran the grocery shop and was the mother of his four children. She had been expelled during Kristallnacht and was staying with relatives in Nuremberg. Fritz was seeking permission for her to return by applying for a residence permit for her. The response he received from Kreisleiter (County Leader) Seiler, dated 21 November 1938, was blunt. He started by describing Else as 'a full-blooded Jewess', who had repeatedly helped all members of her race, demonstrating 'that she feels that she totally belongs to them'. She also allowed those:

… who wished to buy at the Jew Schwab's to walk through her store and enter Schwab's premises from the back. Your wife has proved thereby that she considers herself a Jew and she thinks she can make fools of the political leadership and the authorities.

I am not astonished that you were not enough of a man to put an end to this, since someone who admits that he has been happily married to a Jewess for twenty-five years shows that he is badly contaminated by this evil Jewish spirit. If, at the time you were oblivious enough of your race to marry a Jewess against the warnings of your parents, you cannot expect today to have the right to ask that an exception be made for your Jewish wife.

He then warned Kestler not to let his wife attempt to return, concluding:

> Your question regarding what should now happen to your wife is of as little inter-
> est to me as twenty-five years ago it was of interest to you what would become
> of the German people if everybody entered a marriage that defiled the race.[27]

Joachim Gottschalk (1902–1941) was a very famous film actor in the mould of Leslie Howard or Frederic March. He married in 1930 and in 1933 had a son called Michael. Unfortunately for all three of them, Michael's mother, Meta Wolff (1904–1941), was Jewish and had been a famous actress until the Nazi regime ended her career. Accordingly, they kept a low profile until he made a very successful series of four films with Brigitte Horney (1911–1988) which made his situation precarious. *The Swedish Nightingale*, made in 1941 and based on the relationship between Hans Christian Anderson and the opera singer, Jenny Lind, was the most famous.

Family and friends had tried to persuade him to leave Germany with his family throughout the 1930s but his film studio wouldn't release him from his contract. In fact, they even tried to get him to divorce his wife. Howard Smith, the veteran American journalist, recorded the events in his book, *Last Train From Berlin*. He described the film studios, Artistenwelt:

> … where a few hard-working, energetic actors and actresses have been waging
> a losing, but none the less inspired battle against the shackles of propaganda for
> years. The story involves Joachim Gottschalk, one of Germany's most intelligent
> and hardest working actors. Gottschalk, a sort of German Frederic March, was a
> born picture-stealer, and made his way to fame against the will of the Propaganda
> Ministry, which deprived him of all publicity in film magazines and newspapers
> …
>
>    As the war proceeded, Gottschalk's popularity grew in Germany, for he seemed
> to have a knack of getting good roles in strictly non-propaganda films, which
> irked the Nazis all the more.[28]

In April 1941, Meta accompanied her husband to the Berlin gala premiere of *The Swedish Nightingale*. Joseph Goebbels, the Nazi propaganda chief, was delighted to meet her and is believed to have kissed her hand. Later he discovered she was Jewish and was furious. Some days later, Gottschalk was summoned to the Propaganda Ministry and told to divorce his wife. Smith asserted:

Goebbels presented Gottschalk with an ultimatum; he was becoming a German institution, he had qualified inadvertently as good propaganda, and he must divorce his wife, or he would be banned from his profession for evermore.

… he was informed that, regardless of his decision, he could no longer live with his polluted family; the Gestapo gave his wife and child one day to pack and join the Jewish exodus to the East.[29]

When he refused, he was told he would be called up into the Wehrmacht and his wife and son would be deported to Theresienstadt in Czechoslovakia. Gottschalk's request to accompany his wife and son was refused. It is believed that minutes before the Gestapo arrived to deport them, Michael was sedated and the gas was turned on, killing all three of them.

The news of his death was blocked by the regime, but it seeped out.[30] The family suffered persecution even after death as Goebbels forbade all the cemeteries in Berlin from burying them. He was concerned that their funeral in the city would lead to a silent protest against the regime at the graveside.[31] As a result the family were buried in the South-west Stahnsdorf Cemetery near Potsdam and his film partner Brigitte Horney attended his funeral with only four other people – all at great personal risk.[32]

The Artistenwelt was incensed and it was said that there was nearly a revolt in the film studios. German women who, in legions of millions, had cried their eyes dry at Gottschalk playing a war-cripple in *Ein Leben Lang*, were horrified. Dr Goebbels and Herr Himmler had under-estimated the fibre of their film-hero, if they had not under-estimated the breadth of his popularity. People said, in one of those little quips that circulate faster than newspapers, Gottschalk killed himself, but he was not the only eminent suicide that day; the other was Goebbels.[33]

In 1957 a bronze sculpture was dedicated to Joachim Gottschalk in the foyer of the Frankfurt City Theatre to commemorate the family's story.[34]

As I typed this tragic story, I thought about little Michael Gottschalk, who was 8 at the time of his death. I thought about the child survivors I know who would have been his contemporaries. He could still have been alive today, enjoying his grandchildren at the age of 82.

Gottschalk was not alone. Jochen Klepper (1903–1942) was a Protestant hymn writer. He was born on 22 March 1903 in Beuthen, then in Silesia and now in Poland. A severe asthmatic, he was taught at home by his father who was a Lutheran pastor. At 14 he went to the gymnasium in Glogau. At university he studied theology from 1922, but he had to help support his family from 1926 and became a journalist. In 1931 he married Johanna (Hanni) Stein, who was thirteen years older than him and brought two daughters into the marriage. She was the widow of a lawyer and all three of them were Jewish.[35]

In 1932 they all moved to Berlin where Klepper became a radio broadcaster. However, when the Nazis came to power, life became difficult for him because of his wife and his former membership of the Socialist Party and he lost his job. As a young man he had dabbled in writing. In 1933 his first novel was published, with another in 1937. At the same time he was writing hymns and between 1937 and 1941, he had three small volumes of hymns and poems published.

By 1939, the persecution of Jews was becoming alarming and the Kleppers tried to get the girls to emigrate for their own protection. In May 1939, 19-year-old Brigitte was able to go to England, but 17-year-old Renate was suffering from diphtheria and had to wait to recover to get a visa. In April 1940 she was baptised – sixteen months after her mother.

In December 1940 Klepper was conscripted into the army but was released after nine months because of his Jewish spouse. As he was released, Renate heard that she was to be deported to 'parts unknown'. Klepper managed to get the deportation postponed for a year, but their attempts to get her into Switzerland, Sweden and the Philippines all failed. In November 1942 Klepper was again conscripted because the restrictions on men married to Jewish women had been lifted in April.

At the beginning of December 1942 Renate, who was now 20, finally received a visa for entry to Sweden. However, the systematic bureaucracy the Jews were continually fighting meant that as the twelve month postponement of deportation had now expired, she was denied the necessary exit visa from Germany. Apparently the decision was personally delivered to Klepper by Adolf Eichmann, who had made the decision himself.

Jochen's sister, Hilde, described what happened the next day:

The telephone rang; it was Hanni's housekeeper. She told me to come quickly, that something terrible had happened … When I arrived, the three corpses had been laid out in Jochen's study. The housekeeper, Frau Dr Panick and two or three in uniform said to me, 'We were still able to fold the hands of the two women. That didn't work with your brother; his arms were already too stiff.' The Kleppers had told the housekeeper that they did not want to be disturbed, they wanted to sleep late; in the meantime she should deliver a pot of flowers to acquaintances as a congratulatory present. When she returned, she noticed on the kitchen door a note in Hanni's handwriting: 'Caution! Gas!' She opened the kitchen door, turned off the gas valve, and ripped open the window. The dead were lying on a quilt on the floor of the kitchen. The two women were arm in arm; their eyes were closed. Jochen's eyes had stayed opened and expressed great astonishment.

The men who took them away in a hearse commented, 'These aren't the first. Already today we've picked up a young woman in Wannsee.' Hilde reported that a neighbour later told her that Adolf Hitler had been enraged over Eichmann's 'incompetent behaviour' in this matter and forbade the announcement of the news of the deaths. Apparently Klepper's works were very popular among the military officers ...

Jochen Klepper had kept a diary and the last entry reads:

> Now we die – But even that is in God's hands – Tonight we go together into death. Above us in our last hours stands the picture of the Blessing Christ, who struggles for us. In whose sight our life ends.

Mixed marriages were still an issue when Jews were incarcerated in Westerbork. Philip Mechanicus, the journalist, chronicled the question in his diary. On 12 June 1943 partners in mixed marriages were summoned and addressed by the Commandant Albert Gemmeker – there were about 300 of them. They were told they could be sterilised and sent back to Amsterdam without a star and a distinctive 'J' on their documents, or face being sent to Poland where they would suffer 'under an inhuman labour system'. Mechanicus commented that there was an irony in the whole situation:

When the Nazis started persecuting the Jews, many in mixed marriages had them dissolved to safeguard both the family and their possessions. Then last year the Germans recognised mixed marriages and even the dissolved mixed marriages with children, so that people were no longer deported and the marriages were no longer broken up. Then the Germans changed their minds and the *dissolved* mixed marriages were flung on the scrapheap, then mixed marriages without children (unless they could show church membership or baptism before January 1st 1941) were broken up and recently partners of mixed marriages with children who wanted to escape the Polish hell were forced to let themselves be sterilised.

The next day, Jews married to Aryans with no children were asked if they were prepared to be sterilised voluntarily and they had to sign a contract – 'the *voluntary* nature of this business had to be clearly laid down – for the benefit of history'. Mechanicus described the dilemmas of two men – one had children and the other didn't. One was Austrian and aged about 60, and the other was from Amsterdam in his thirties. The older man decided to be sterilised because it was too late for him to have children, but later he changed his mind, stating:

> Until now sterilization has only been carried out sporadically on mental defectives to prevent them reproducing themselves, but it hasn't yet been done on healthy individuals. It's not known whether an operation of this kind will cause mental illness later on.

So he refused, with the risk of being sent to Poland. The younger man argued:

> I know that sterilization is contrary to nature and ethically wrong, but I'll get it done all the same and return to Mokum [Amsterdam]. My wife mustn't do work that I could be doing. I must support her.

All the people affected by the issue were discussing it, Mechanicus noted. There seemed to be a view among some of the doctors that after the war such sterilisations might be reversible. However, 'about one thing there is complete agreement: this measure marks the very peak of barbarity'.[36]

On 15 November 1943 he recorded a conversation with a woman behind the prison bars – they spoke through a broken window pane. He asked her what she was doing in there. She said:

> I am an Aryan, a doctor's wife. My husband is half-Aryan, and he's at the Vught concentration camp. My son was in the Labour Service and spoke out rather strongly about it in a letter to my husband. They brought me here with my family out of spite. There was an argument when we arrived and the Untersturmführer: 'Your husband must certainly look like a Jew.' To which I replied; 'You look more like a Jew than he does.' I got a smack from the Untersturmführer. And so I said: 'You're a hero – you'll have to go to the eastern front.' That is why I'm sitting here in this dreary hole. But they won't get me down.[37]

Mechanicus wrote very little about himself and his past. The editor notes that he could not have expected the diary to be published, so he was merely recording events each day. Keeping a diary was forbidden, but the few people who knew kept the secret and it was not discovered. On 18 September 1943 he wrote:

> I have finally handed in to the Applications Office my papers relating to my dissolved mixed marriage with an 'Aryan' child. I was given the assurance that these papers were adequate for me to be sent to Theresienstadt. At all events this means once again that my stay at Westerbork can be extended. A number of divorced partners from mixed marriages departed with the latest transport. The pattern of reasoning is as follows: Jewish fathers and mothers of 'Aryan' children are at present given Theresienstadt as a mark of favour, whereas if Jewish men are found with 'Aryan' women they go to a concentration camp where they are sometimes unlucky enough to be killed.[38]

There is no further information on his ex-wife and child, no mention of their names, no expression of feelings or concern. Perhaps it was a 'normal' divorce rather than one forced by the Nazis' racial policy? We may never know.

Later, on 1 December 1943, he recorded an 'interview with Mr Proosdij, who had come from The Hague in connection with the Aryanization of a number of Jews'. He said it was a friendly interview and he was told to write to Amsterdam for Aryanization. He said he immediately wrote a secret letter to investigate the possibilities, as he knew several people had left already 'as Aryans'. He examined himself in the mirror and decided he could pass as an Aryan, and his name was not even Jewish:

> Why should I not have a try and see if I can leave this squalid place and go about once more as a free man. Relatively speaking. There is no disgrace about passing oneself off as an Aryan, although it is not pleasant to accept a gift from the hands of the oppressor. The main thing is to get out of his clutches.[39]

I was amazed to find the reference to Jaap van Proosdij (1921–2011), as I wrote about him in *The Other Schindlers*. He sent me his story from South Africa, where he had lived since 1951, and we spoke on the telephone. He was a young lawyer aged 21 when he became involved in providing forged documents to 'prove' incarcerated Jews were really Aryans. He was recognised as Righteous Among the Nations in 2003 for rescuing about 250 Dutch Jews – unfortunately Philip Mechanicus was not among them.

Finally, this is not a subject that naturally leads to laughter, but Marta Appel (1894–1980) lived in Dortmund with her husband, who was a rabbi, and had two small daughters in school in the 1930s until they managed to escape. She worried about Nazi indoctrination making school difficult for them and was therefore amazed to see them coming out of school one day 'with shining eyes, laughing and giggling together'.

Apparently, that morning the whole school was assembled in the big hall to hear a talk from an official from the new Rasseamt (Office of Races). The girls had tried to come home but were told they had to stay. The official explained that the Teutonic race, the German one, was the high race, destined to rule the world while one of the lowest races was the Jewish race. Then he started looking round and chose a girl called Eva to come to him. Everyone worried what would happen when he began pointing at Eva:

> 'Look here, the small head of this girl, her long forehead, her blue eyes, and blond hair.' He was lifting one of her long blond braids. 'And look at her tall slender figure. These are the unequivocal marks of a pure and unmixed Teutonic race.'

From all round the hall people were laughing – even Eva was laughing. Then everyone shouted, 'She is a Jewess!'

'You should have seen the officer's face!' Apparently, the principal stood up to bring matters to a speedy end but as the official left everyone was still laughing. Marta was delighted to see her children could still laugh and act like normal, happy children.[40] Her daughters were Doris and Ruth, aged 17 and 18 respectively when they left for America in May 1937. Sadly, Ruth died in 1972.

After I had written this, I saw a report about an 80-year-old New York chemistry professor, Hessy Taft, whose photo as a baby was used to demonstrate the perfect Aryan baby. Her Jewish mother, Pauline Levinson, had taken her to a famous Berlin photographer, Hands Ballin, in 1935. Ballin submitted the photograph, which was personally chosen by the propaganda chief Goebbels as a representation of the ideal Aryan baby. Ballin was quoted as saying, 'I wanted to make the Nazis ridiculous.' The photo was used all over Germany, appearing on posters, cards and the front page of *Sonne ins Haus* (*Sun in the House*) magazine, edited by a friend of Göring.[41]

Mrs Levinson hid her child to avoid the truth coming out if she was recognised. They fled to Latvia and eventually managed to get to America. Hessy Taft presented a copy of the magazine with her photo to Yad Vashem recently, saying although she can laugh about it now, at the time discovery could have caused her death.

Both incidents demonstrate what nonsense the Nazis' Aryan theories were.

Finally, there are references throughout the book to the compulsory wearing of the yellow Star of David with 'Jude' ('Jew') written in the middle. This order was initiated by Goebbels in September 1941. The star had to be worn by every Jew aged 6 and over on their outer clothing, and the punishments for failing to do so were severe. The following year, the measure was introduced in France, Belgium, the Netherlands, Slovakia and other lands under German control. After the Nazis invaded Hungary in March 1944, my mother had to wear one.

The reaction to this edict cannot be gauged, but I found the following report significant. A Jewish worker fled to London and it was reported in December 1941 that there was considerable dissatisfaction with the Nazi Party's constant anti-Jewish propaganda on the radio and in the press. He was a mechanic in a Hamburg factory and was constantly in contact with about 100 other workers. He said that although they all knew he was a Jew, he had no experience of difficulties with his fellow workers; nor did he suffer any indignities or humiliations. Some of his co-workers even remarked that the anti-Jewish laws were 'despicable', he said. Additionally, when the Jews were ordered to wear the 'yellow star of David' one of the factory employees said, 'We, also, ought to wear this thing in order that we might be taken for decent fellows.'[42]

# 18

# CHILDREN

---

Remember the nocturnal processions of children and more children and more children, frightened, quiet, so quiet and so beautiful.

Elie Wiesel – Auschwitz survivor and Nobel Prize winner, 1995, at Auschwitz on the 50th anniversary of its liberation

We have outlived fate and survived survival.

Robert Krell – child survivor and psychiatrist

Men tortured children.
Cleverly. Deliberately. Efficiently.
It was a routine job for them.
They worked hard, they tortured children.

Naum Korzhavin, *Children of Auschwitz*

---

In reading this chapter it is particularly important to remember that of the 6 million Jews killed by the Nazis one-quarter, 1.5 million, were children, who were murdered simply because they had been born Jewish.

Heinrich Himmler, the Reich Leader of the SS from 1929, is identified as being about the only one of the Nazi leaders to expressly refer to the concept of the extermination of the whole Jewish race in words. He made several speeches referring to the need to destroy the whole race – the 'Final Solution of the Jewish Question' ('Endlösung der Judenfrage'). One of these was in the Polish city of Poznan on 6 October 1943. When addressing fellow Nazi leaders, he aimed to convince his colleagues about the policy of genocide:

Perhaps you will have realised that we were faced with the question, 'What should be done with the women and children?' I have decided that our answer to this question must be just as unequivocal, as it is my opinion that it is not right to eliminate just the men – and that means, gentlemen, murder or orders to that effect – and let the children grow up so that they can later take revenge on our children and grandchildren. We have made the difficult decision to wipe this nation off the face of the earth.[1]

Himmler's private life was revealed recently in a unique cache of letters between him and his wife, Marga, and personal diaries from their youth to 1945. This means that there is a 'dense body of documents' from Himmler's private life which is unique among the Nazi leadership. The papers have been studied by Professor Michael Wildt of Berlin's Humboldt University, who comments that while the correspondence might initially appear inconsequential:

> These letters are far from being harmless and banal. The private idylls invoked by these letters stand in stark contrast to the almost entirely unmentioned reality of everyday mass murder, but even this discrepancy fades away when we realise how violence and lack of empathy also shaped the petty bourgeois everyday life of the Himmler family too.[2]

Both were convinced Nazis, having married in 1928, and a daughter Gudrun was born in 1929. In 1933 a foster son, Gerhard, joined the family. Affection and emotion seemed lacking in the correspondence and in some letters Marga expressed her approval of ruthless persecution of 'the enemies of Germany'. Writing about 'lazy' servants, she queried, 'Why don't they put all these people behinds bars, where they have to work until they die?' After Kristallnacht she wrote, 'This Jewish affair, when will that rabble finally leave us, so that we can also enjoy life too?'

Their children were brought up with great strictness, blows were directed at both, but they were much harsher with the boy. By the age of 10, Marga was describing him as having a 'criminal nature'. On Heinrich's advice she ceased calling herself 'mother' when signing her letters to him. Wildt commented that this 'withdrawal of love … was a form of violence that was doubtlessly as effective as a physical blow, in terms of destroying the capacity for empathy'.

Neither of them expressed any doubts about the Nazi policies. Himmler was keen to do his role and do it with 'decency and propriety'. On 4 October he had stated:

> Most of you will know what it means when one hundred corpses lie together, or when five hundred lie there or when a thousand lie there. To have seen this through, and apart from a few exceptions of human weakness, to have remained decent while doing so, this has made us hard. This glorious chapter has never been recorded and will never be recorded in our histories.

Wildt had concluded that:

> He committed mass murder with the same self-certain morality that charac-
> terised how he watched over the lifestyles of his brothers and friends in his
> early years, and the way he raised his own children, a morality that he shared in
> common with his wife in his letters.' This correspondence gives us insight into
> the man who was content to persuade his fellow Nazis that all Jews, even the
> children must be destroyed.

## The Children of Izieu

Two villages close to Lyon have very different memories of early April 1944. Dullin
and Izieu are about 16 miles apart – forty minutes by car. The Germans spent five
days in Dullin looking for Jewish children and the neighbours later spoke about
the armoured vehicles combing the area. In spite of Jewish children hiding there,
they were not found or betrayed. Betty and her little brother, Jacques, were safely
hidden by a courageous peasant couple, Victor and Josephine Guicherd, for nearly
three years.[3]

Ted Morgan wrote of the village of Izieu which had a different experience.
Klaus Barbie (1913–1991), chief of the Gestapo in Lyons, got lucky on 6 April
1944 because he had a reliable informant. Lucien Bourdon was not a native and
lived in Brens, just north of Izieu. He was born in Metz, the capital of Lorraine,
in 1906 when Lorraine belonged to Germany. He therefore spoke good German
as he had attended German schools until he was 12.[4] When France fell in 1940,
many thousands were evicted from Lorraine, so Bourdon came to Lyons with his
wife and rented some land. He was seen drinking with the Germans at the Café
Nevy in nearby Belley. A neighbour, Marcel Bouvier, said that after a few drinks
Bourdon had said the French were not up to the Germans. Bourdon's best mate
was Antoine Wucher who was suspected of collaboration activities such as driving
trucks for the Germans on anti-Maquis operations.

Sabina Zlatin and her husband, Miron, had met in France as young Jews both
fleeing the anti-Semitism of their native Poland. They set up the Izieu Children's
Home. Sabina was a qualified military nurse who was unable to work after anti-
Jewish legislation was introduced. She had volunteered to work at two camps, Agde
and Rivesaltes, where Jews were being interned – the latter housed families. Lois
Gunden was based there (see page 462). Sabina started taking Jewish children into
her home under Vichy, untroubled by the authorities. When the Germans returned
in November 1942 she was told by the prefect that, for safety, they should go to the
department of Ain and see the sous-préfet in Belley (Marcel Wiltzer). By then she
had seventeen children under her protection.[5]

Wiltzer was very sympathetic and helped Sabina find the new home in Izieu which was a former Catholic summer camp. It had large rooms suitable as dormitories and a garden for playing, and food would be easy to find in the rural area. It was almost invisible, being off the beaten track. Wiltzer said they would be safe there as no German had ever come to Izieu, nor any Jews.

They moved the seventeen children and Marcel Wiltzer sent a lorry load of furniture. The local mayor, Henri Tissot, was less welcoming when she paid him a courtesy call. Afterwards, Tissot wrote to Wiltzer telling him the home was Jewish. Wiltzer tore up the letter. Henri Perret, the mayor when Ted Morgan was writing his book, said Tissot was rather brusque but decent. He was just worried about more mouths to feed at a time of hardship and sent the letter merely to cover himself.[6]

Through 1943 the Italians occupied Savoie and the home prospered – at one point there were eighty children there. The Zlatins' friends helped, such as Léon Reifman, a Rumanian medical student who had been studying in Clermont-Ferrand until the anti-Jewish statutes prevented him graduating. He helped run the infirmary on the top floor with his parents and his 27-year-old sister, Sarah, who was a doctor with a 10-year-old son, Charles. Another friend was Leah Feldblum who came from Antwerp in 1940 with her parents. She looked after the smaller children and although she had two opportunities to go to Switzerland in 1943 she chose to stay with the little ones.

The lack of a school in Izieu became a problem, but Wiltzer and his successor, Maurice Silvan, provided a government-paid school teacher to live in and run a school in one room. A 21-year-old novice teacher, Gabrielle Perrier, was sent. The youngsters were keen to learn and some were very good at drawing and writing. Apparently, she told many of them that they would have brilliant futures. Morgan comments, 'The oddest thing about this arrangement was that by delegating a teacher to Izieu who was a government employee, Vichy was helping to operate a home for Jewish children.'[7]

The children lived a life where the war came only over the radio. The home was officially called 'Settlement for Refugee Children from Hérault'. Miron provided a healthy diet by touring the countryside on his bicycle (with trailer) buying whatever he could find. The children made friends, like the German boy, Paul Niederman, who had been chased down the street by members of the Hitler Youth and spent most evenings with Theo Reis. They wondered where their parents were and agreed to meet up after the war. Early in 1944 Paul was 16 and, because he was tall, Sabina was able to smuggle him to Switzerland, but Theo, the same age, was shorter and stayed in the home.

In 1944 there were forty-four children in the home; twenty-one were French and the rest were mostly Austrian, German, Dutch and Polish. The Italians left Savoie in September 1943, only for it to be occupied by the Germans. Some German troops living in Belley scoured the area looking for Jews, paying informants a price per head. The deportation of a Jewish doctor from another village was a warning and made the Zlatins realise they were no longer safe. They wanted to spread the children around and so Sabina sent Léon to see the Catholic bishop, Costa de Beauregard. When he told the bishop they were looking for Catholic homes for the children, he was startled and said, 'Can you for one minute imagine that we would mix Jewish and non-Jewish children?' However, he promised to consider the matter. Apparently a few days later, the Bishop's business card was sent to Reifman. A message was written under the engraved name, 'Regrets that he is unable to give a favourable reply to your request'.[8]

Morgan wrote that had Sabina Zlatin been more suspicious by nature she might have queried two events. The first involved Antoine Wucher, a mechanic who acted as a fixer occasionally at the home. He asked if his 8-year-old son could stay for a while as his wife was ill and he had many other children. Wucher was working all day and couldn't cope. Sabina agreed, but his son was the only non-Jewish child at the home. The other incident was in March 1944, when Bourdon asked if they had a big boy who could help with his crops. Miron Zlatin sent over 15-year-old Fritz Loebmann, who had ID in the name of François Loban. While he was there for a few weeks, Bourdon asked him about the children in the home and Fritz admitted they were all Jewish. Bourdon made him go to Mass on Sunday, saying that people would then think he was a Catholic. At the end of March he sent him back to the home saying the season was over.

On 3 April Sabina Zlatin left for Montpellier for five days as she had found a priest who would take fifteen of the children on 12 April. Léon Reifman returned on the morning of 6 April and, while he was upstairs with his sister, two trucks followed by a convertible arrived. The bell rang for breakfast at 9 a.m., and as he went downstairs he saw three men in civilian clothes talking to his sister. They asked to speak to him but his sister signalled to him and he went back upstairs. Looking out of the window, he saw German soldiers and he jumped out of the window and hid in some thick bushes until nightfall (6 April was a French holiday and so the raid was even more of a surprise).[9]

He then went to see the farmer opposite, Eusèbe Perdicoz, whose employee Lucien Favet had witnessed the raid. Both had seen Lucien Bourdon with the Germans. Perdicoz watched as the children were herded onto trucks – like bundles, he thought. Perdicoz told Léon that the soldiers had expressed disgust at having to do such work. The next day, Léon was taken to hide at another farm about 10 miles away. Perdicoz's daughter-in-law, Juliette, was picking vegetables when the trucks arrived. She also recognised Bourdon. Afterwards, she went into the empty dining room and started to cry because the drinking bowls were still full of cocoa – the children had not been able to have their breakfast.[10]

The son of Wucher, René, the only non-Jewish child, was allowed off the truck and it then set off for Gestapo HQ in Lyon, where they spent the night in Montluc

Prison. The next day they were put on a passenger train to Drancy with the older boys being manacled. Leah Feldblum had French ID but refused to be separated from the children and courageously revealed her true identity to the authorities at Drancy.

On 13 April, Feldblum, the Reifman family and thirty-four of the forty-four children were sent to Auschwitz on the seventy-first deportation train to leave France. Of 1,500 people on that train 300 were under 18. When they arrived at Auschwitz on 15 April 1944, the children were lined up in rows of five with Leah Feldblum in front. An officer asked her if they were her children and she replied, 'This is a children's home.' She was holding onto little Émile Zuckerberg who was only 6 and was a 'fetching' blond lad whom she had been comforting on the journey. However, the officer pulled her away violently and the children were taken in another direction. Morgan wrote, 'That was the last time she saw them, for they were gassed that very day, while she survived to tell the tale. For the rest of her life she would see the children as they were herded away from the Auschwitz ramp.'[11]

Leah survived Auschwitz to go to Israel and, as a grandmother, returned to France in 1987 to testify at Klaus Barbie's trial. She was the only survivor of Barbie's raid and her testimony was poignant:

> And then comes a testimony as shattering as any that has been heard at Barbie's trial. It is spoken by the former supervisor of the children's shelter, a Polish-born Jew who is the only survivor of the Izieu community and who has lived in Israel since the war's end. Lea Feldblum describes how she and her young wards, to whom she was deeply attached, managed to remain together during the three-day train ride from France to Auschwitz, how the children wept and clung to her when Dr Josef Mengele's cohorts conducted the selection of their group, sending Madame Feldblum in one direction toward the work camps, ordering the children the other way, toward the gas chambers. 'I shouted, "These are children, don't separate us!"' Lea Feldblum testifies in a febrile, birdlike voice, speaking a barely intelligible Diaspora idiom that mingles Hebrew, Yiddish, half-forgotten French. 'But they took them away from me and burned them … and the little ones were weeping so …' Her hand clutches repeatedly at the folds of her skirt, as if re-enacting the grasping of the young victims' hands at the end of the fatal voyage initiated by Klaus Barbie.[12]

Leah died two years later, in 1989, having spent her life educating children. The teacher at Izieu, Gabrielle Perrier, said of her, 'All the children were her little pals; she loved them dearly and they felt the same way. The little ones always surrounded her, clambering onto her lap … while she presented each new child to me, her hand gently caressing their heads.'[13]

Miron Zlatin was deported with the older boys on the all-male train of 878 that left on 15 May. It was the seventy-third French deportation train. This did not go to Auschwitz but stopped at Kaunas in Lithuania, where 400 men were sent to Projanowska camp to work in a peat bog. The train then moved on to Tallinn, Estonia, where they were interned in the fortress Reval. Miron managed to send one letter to Sabina – then there was silence.

Sabina Zlatin was sent a telegram in Montpellier: 'Family sick. Sickness contagious.' She rushed to Vichy and the next day, in her nurse's uniform, she saw an important official and asked about the children. He replied, 'Why are you concerning yourself with those dirty kikes?' When she persisted he said, 'Find them yourself.' But it was too late – they were gone and so was her husband.[14]

In 1945 a man came and told her that Miron had been shot on 31 July 1944 – the anniversary of their marriage.[15] She spent the rest of her life working in the memory of the children and promoting human rights. She created the Maison d'Izieu-Mémorial des Enfants Juifs Exterminés on the home's site, opened in April 1994 – the fiftieth anniversary of the raids. She described it as 'a place that would symbolise the denunciation of crimes against humanity'.[16]

Two days after the raid on 8 April, Bourdon's neighbours saw a truck with German soldiers pull up at his house. The furniture was loaded into the truck and Bourdon and his wife climbed in and the truck drove away. They were never seen again. Later it was heard that Madame Bourdon went home to Lorraine, but Lucien was taken to be a guard in a camp. The Resistance caught up with Wucher on 2 August and shot him in front of the cemetery wall in a nearby mountain village.[17]

Bourdon was tried in 1947, but much of the evidence now known was not available at that time and he was only sentenced to 'national degradation for life', which meant he could not vote or enjoy other aspects of being a French citizen.

Madame Zlatin finally realised that Bourdon and Wucher had been in league with the Germans – Bourdon so that he could go home and Wucher for money. They had used Rene and Fritz to suss out the children's home. 'It was a tale of two informers, who had betrayed and sent to their deaths forty-four children for personal gain.' Like poor little Michael Gottschalk (see page 443), many of these children could still have been alive today. Little Émile is described as aged 6 in some sources and 3 in others, but in any event I was born in 1944, the year he died. He would only be a few years older than me.

The footnote to this terrible story is the message sent by Barbie to Paris on the evening of 6 April at 8.10 p.m. It stated:

This morning, the Jewish children's home 'Colonie d'Enfants' in Izieu (Ain) was seized. Forty-one children in all, aged from three to thirteen, were captured. In addition, there took place the arrest of all the Jewish personnel, that is to say, ten persons, including five women. We were not able to find any money or valuables. The transport to Drancy will take place on April 7, 1944.

There were errors in the numbers. There were forty-four children, but three were older boys who were mistaken as personnel.

Morgan analysed the language actually used in German, as the above is obviously a translation. The words used were meant to demean the victims. The word translated as 'seized' was 'ausgehoben' which actually means 'pulled from the nest', and the word 'persons' was not used but instead 'köpfe' which is 'heads', as in 'heads of cattle'. He concludes that, 'the task was facilitated by denigrating the victims through language'.[18]

The case of the Izieu children was notorious. At Nuremberg, Edgar Faure, one of the French prosecutors, used Barbie's message as an example of Nazi war crimes and brought it to court on 5 February 1946. Part of his statement was:

> One can say that there is something even more striking and more horrible than the concrete fact of the abduction of these children and that is the bureaucratic tone of the report, and the conference where several officials are tranquilly discussing it, as one of the normal procedures of their department. All the machinery of the state, that is, the Nazi state, was activated on such an occasion and for such a goal.[19]

Janine Webber was born in July 1932 in Lvov in Poland, to Alfred and Lipka Monat. Her father was born on 6 December 1902 and was an accountant, but when she was born they were running a grocer's shop. Her mother was about ten years younger.

Her father was shot by the Germans almost at the beginning, when the Germans arrived at the end of June 1941. She told me they were moved to the ghetto as soon as the fence was ready, around the beginning of November 1941. Her mother died of typhus in the ghetto. Her uncle, her mother's brother, found a Polish family of Catholic farmers and paid them to hide Janine and her brother, Tunio. Janine does not know how much he paid them. She said her aunt (her mother's sister) sewed some money inside the hem of her dress, but it was taken away by the Polish family.

Janine does not know the date they went to the Catholic family, but her brother was about 7 years old and she was a little over 9. It was outside Lvov, in the country. The daughter of the family was around 18 or 20 and came back one day accompanied by an armed German soldier. They called Janine out and she thought he was going to shoot her. She told me, 'They did not kill me. They killed my brother. The daughter told me they had buried Tunio alive.' She thought that she brought the armed soldier quite soon after they arrived. (See photo No. 21)

Janine was forced to leave the family. She had the name and address of a young Pole. She managed to find him but he was already hiding thirteen Jewish people and she was the fourteenth. She hid in a bunker or hole with the others for a year until her aunt got her some false papers. After the war she went with her aunt and a cousin to France.

In 1956 she came to England and she married in 1958. She has two sons and two grandsons. She became a lecturer, lecturing in French.[20]

Philip Mechanicus (1989–1944), a journalist, was an unusually long-term resident of the Westerbork transit camp and was initially in the hospital because he had been tortured previously. On 5 July 1943 he recorded in his diary:

> In the night a small child kept crying for its mummy and daddy. The patients lay there protesting and cursing. The piping little voice is so penetrating in the stillness of the night. The child has been crying for its mother and father every night for a whole week and the patients have been shouting and cursing every night. Even during the day the child cries for its parents, but then the piping little voice becomes lost in the general hum of heavier voices belonging to the adult patients. There is no sympathy shown to small children here – everyone is too much taken up with his own silent worries. There would also be little point in feeling any sympathy, as sympathy can achieve so little here. Nobody can bring back the child's mother and father, and certainly not at the times when the child is crying for them.[21]

It is impossible to read this without wondering what happened to the poor child and also what happened to the parents who, in turn, must have wept for their abandoned infant – perhaps a cherished firstborn?

Gustav Botkai (*b.* 1936) was born Gusztav Birnfield in Budapest in 1936, into a comfortable middle-class family. His father, Imre, was a musician. He described Budapest as a great place for Jews in the 1920s and 1930s where they were very successful in business, the arts and sciences. However, by the time Gustav was born his parents began to be fearful about the future and in 1938, when he was 2, his parents converted to the Catholic Church. They thought that would protect their future.

In the early 1940s his father, like mine, was called up for forced labour and so, from the age of 6, he saw little of him. In 1943 his parents thought of emigrating to Australia but felt unable to leave the older generation. So instead false identity papers were bought. 'My name was Koretz Thomas, I was born a Catholic and was told not to let anyone see me naked.'[22] Gustav went to the Catholic Church regularly, unaware that he was Jewish. One day on his way back home from church, 'a gang of youths beat me up and told me never to enter a church again, it was not for bloody Jews. Our pretence at Catholicism was over.'

The Germans occupied Hungary on 19 March 1944. Gustav writes that the Hungarians were pro-German and very anti-Jewish. It was the Hungarian anti-Jewish policies which made our fathers liable for forced labour, well before the invasion. Gustav writes:

> … men with batons roamed the streets looking for Jews to beat up and send to concentration camps.
>
> By this time, my parents knew that to be taken away meant something very bad for the Jews, although they had no idea that it meant death camps. They did not want to risk my life so they contacted an agency which offered escape for Jewish children, for a large sum of money. At the last minute they changed their minds. All the children who went with this and similar groups, perished. The agents just handed them over to the Germans and they were taken to concentration camps. None of them survived.

When I asked Gustav for more detail, he replied as follows:

> You asked for more information about the gang that collected Jewish children claiming to take them out of the country in 1944. I was 8 years old and I can only remember my parents discussing the possibility. Later we had a visit from a couple and there was long discussion with them. I was told that I would probably go away. However my parents changed their minds and they did not send me. I do not know if this was a financial consideration or they did not trust them. After the war my mother told me that all the children they collected were handed over to the Nazis and none of them came back. I have no names no documents just recollection.[23]

But for Gustav's parents' change of heart, he would have been another victim of the Holocaust. In his memoir there is a photo of his family celebrating his seventy-fifth birthday in London in 2011 – he has three children and seven grandchildren. None of these would be alive had his parents handed him over to those unscrupulous parasites who exploited and profited from the Jews' fear for the future.[24]

The Kafkaesque Nazi conduct is exemplified by the story of Mrs Prins and baby Machiel.

> A young Jewish woman, Mrs Prins had prematurely given birth to her son while in camp Vught. Following the birth, she was quickly transferred to Westerbork with baby Machiel, who was tiny and wanting. Wrapped in a bundle of clothing to keep him warm he was brought to the camp hospital for observation. Because the mother was unable to breastfeed her baby she was looked upon as useless.
>
> Only breastfeeding mothers could get a '*Sperr*' – an exemption from deportation. Mothers whose babies had died in a diphtheria epidemic continued to breastfeed other babies to secure such a *Sperr*. Accordingly, Mrs Prins, after having recuperated

from childbirth, was put on the first available cattle train to the east for *arbeitsein-satz* – work employment. We all now know what that meant. However, her baby remained behind in the camp hospital to receive extraordinary medical care.

Commandant Albert Konrad Gemmeker, whose reputation was that he 'loved little children so much', immediately ordered an incubator from Groningen. Not only that, he summoned the Jewish Professor van Creveld, who had taught child therapeutics at the university in Amsterdam. Van Creveld was to take care of the baby and Gemmeker charged him with the responsibility to keep the boy alive. Professor van Creveld arrived in Westerbork the same day the incubator arrived from Groningen. Dr van Creveld prescribed a special formula for the baby which needed to be administered every hour because the baby was too weak to suckle. He also suggested the infant be given one drop of cognac with each feed. Bizarrely, Gemmeker immediately ordered a bottle of the finest Hennessy cognac be provided for the child and two Jewish registered nurses to monitor the baby's progress around the clock.

Gemmeker visited the baby daily to ensure that everything possible was done for the child's survival. Machiel gradually grew stronger and started to gain weight. At 5½lb, he was taken out of the incubator and everybody, including Gemmeker, felt that the struggle to keep him alive was won. But, once Machiel weighed in at 6lb the game was over. Gemmeker ordered him placed on the next transport so he could join his mother, who had already reached her destiny.

Having been brought to full strength, by the use of apparently unlimited resources, Machiel Prins set off on his final journey.[25]

## Children in Auschwitz

Claude Romney's father was a doctor in Auschwitz and after he died in 1968, as a result of the typhus he contracted there, her mother gave her his papers about his deportation and articles he had written about Auschwitz immediately after the war. This led her to research the camp and the children who were sent there.

Around 232,000 children were sent to Auschwitz from all the Nazi-occupied countries. Of these, 93 per cent were Jewish and 214,300 of these were murdered on arrival; 41 per cent were Hungarian, murdered in 1944, so I was nearly one of them. Those gassed on arrival were not registered, but 6,700 were, which meant they were allowed to live – for a while. They passed themselves off as old enough to work but most of them did not survive long. When the Red Army liberated the camp on 27 January 1945, only 451 children were still alive.

The prison doctors witnessed the children's suffering and recorded their final words before they died. One of them was Dr Margita Schwalbová from Slovakia, who arrived three days before Dr Lewin. She wrote a book about eleven women whom she knew, all of whom died in Auschwitz. One of them was a 16-year-old Slovak girl called Vera who arrived in the summer of 1942.

Claude said that the passages written about Vera and the other Auschwitz children are among 'the most heart-rending ones written about the camp. At the same time her accounts are extremely poetic.' She called the children 'crushed spring flowers', to sum up the 'cruel annihilation of those young human beings whose lives could have been full of promise'. Dr Schwalbová remembered that:

> No look was more painful than the look in the eyes of the Auschwitz children, their eyes were sad like the darkest night, resigned and yet instinctively troubled. Their eyes no longer asked any questions. I saw in them no 'Why?', only a deeply distressing 'I know'.

And she used the transformation of the look in Vera's eyes, as she stayed in Birkenau, to highlight her tragic fate. At first, her eyes expressed faith and optimism. She had the pure look of a schoolgirl. But as she became acquainted with the cruel realties of the camp, 'the childlike smile in her eyes was extinguished' and her eyes became like those of the other Auschwitz children.

However, Vera then became ill with a kidney disease called nephritis and, although Dr Schwalbová looked after her in the hospital, Vera died. The Slovak doctor could never forget the young girl's eyes 'with her extinguished belief in humankind, her questions silenced by death, those dying eyes, still trusting in their purity, those eyes of an Auschwitz child'.

Another doctor also wrote about the children. Otto Wolken from Vienna was a witness at the Frankfurt Auschwitz trials in the 1960s, and even twenty years after the events he could not control his tears when talking about the children. At this time he wrote an article, 'When I Think of the Children', where his grief is shown in every line. He demonstrated the maturity of the young children because of their experiences and what they had seen.

Jurek, a 9-year-old boy from Bedzin in Poland, told Dr Wolken not to worry about him: 'I'm not afraid of death. Everything here is so horrible that up there it is bound to be better …' Another 9-year-old boy, Karli, from Czechoslovakia, commented to his block elder who had remarked that he was very knowledgeable for his age, 'Yes, it is true that I know a lot, but I won't be here to learn much more. That is why I am so sad.'

A young boy from Kovno tried to comfort the other children with the idea that they would be reunited with their loved ones and would be immortal: 'The world will speak about us.' He turned to the SS men around them, saying, 'There is one satisfaction for me! When you croak, not even a dog will shed a tear after you. And you will have a much more bitter death than us.'

Yet, another boy, Icek, 'small and dark-haired who had been selected by the Nazi doctor to be sent to the gas chamber', had one last wish: 'I would so much like to eat my fill before I die.' He then asked Dr Wolken to find someone who would give him a piece of bread in exchange for his shoes, which were still in good condition.

Professor Claude Romney commented:

> The boys' stories told by Dr Wolken are impossible to forget and if reading them produces this kind of effect, one can only imagine the feelings of those who actually heard those young boys' last words, feelings of unbound pity coupled with complete helplessness because the prisoner doctors in Auschwitz were powerless and could only 'watch with clenched teeth', as one of them, Dr Sima Vaisman, wrote in her memoir.

The last writer quoted is Olga Lengyel who was not actually a doctor but managed to work as one in Auschwitz. Her husband was a surgeon in Cluj in Transylvania and she had helped him in his hospital. She wrote at the end of her book about a group of children who, on 31 December 1944, had to march in a long procession on a snowy road in Birkenau to be bathed in icy water. It was snowing and she called the children 'little snowmen' – 'The children, their rags sprinkled with white flakes, staggered on toward death. They were silent under the blows, silent like so many little snowmen.'

One of the children is mentioned by name – little Thomas Gaston, who was so ill he had to be carried. After being bathed the children were made to stand for five hours in the snow for roll call. Hundreds of them died, including little Thomas Gaston.

I found this piece very hard both to read and to type and cannot conceive why anyone would treat small children in such a manner. Claude Romney wrote:

> This is an extremely moving, an extremely dramatic episode which leaves an indelible impression on the reader. The white colour of the snow symbolizes the innocence of the children but the snow and the cold also brought death to them, transforming them from warm, living human beings to frozen corpses.

Of course it is wrong to blame the snow and the cold for the children's deaths. The snow and cold did not betray them; it was the vicious perpetrators of the Nazis' policies who betrayed and killed them. Dr Schwalbová wrote the Auschwitz children were 'the most pitiful children in the world. They died even faster than the adults from disease, malnutrition or just from not being able to understand the inhuman world that surrounded them.'[26]

Margita Schwalbová ended her memoir of her time working as a doctor in Auschwitz–Birkenau with this story:

One day a transport went to the gas chamber. The selected women had been placed in open trucks and next to them spread-eagled, stood Dr Mengele. A young girl, almost a child, crept up to him, pointed to a woman in the truck – her mother – and asked for her life. She stared at him with large dark eyes. Since Dr Mengele did not move, she asked, 'Don't you have a mother yourself?' Dr Mengele gave a sign to the closest SS-men, and he threw the girl on the truck to the mother. After a while, the transport started for the gas chamber.[27]

As a postscript to this story it seems that Dr Schwalbová herself became ill and was befriended by a nun, Sister Maria Cecilia Autsch, who had come to Auschwitz via Ravensbrück. She cared for Margita when she was sick and depressed and shared her meagre rations with her and others, which was forbidden. She became known as the 'Angel of Auschwitz'.[28]

The 2015 trial of the 'Auschwitz bookkeeper' revealed the fate of another child – a baby. He told the judges in Lüneburg that when he first arrived at Auschwitz in November 1944 he was standing at the ramp when all the Jews had gone and suddenly a baby started wailing:

An SS officer took it by the legs and bashed it against the iron bars of a truck and then threw it into the rubbish on the truck. My heart stopped. I was so shocked that, although I did not have the right to say anything, I told him; 'What you just did, I don't think that's right.'

Mr Groning said that the SS officer replied: 'What do you want to do? Run after the woman and give the baby back to her?'[29]

Laurence Rees, who has made several television programmes on the Holocaust, wrote about the children killed at Auschwitz – 'the more than 200,000 children who perished there and were denied the right to grow up and experience life':

One image stuck in my mind from the moment I heard it described. It was of a 'procession' of empty baby carriages – property looted from the dead Jews – pushed out of Auschwitz in rows of five towards the railway station. The prisoner who witnessed the sight said they took an hour to pass by.[30]

Had the whim of fate been different, my pram might have been among them.

## Lois Gunden at the Rivesaltes Refugee Camp

Rivesaltes refugee camp was based in France near the Spanish border very close to the beach and contained mostly Spanish refugees when Lois Gunden first visited it on 18 November 1941. It housed 8,000 people, 'without adequate food, water, shelter or sanitation; death by starvation or disease was a daily occurrence in the camp'. Lois, a member of the Mennonite Church, was sent from the US to run a children's home called the 'Villa St Christophe' which housed sixty children from Rivesaltes – 12 miles away. The children ranged from toddlers to age 16. Every two weeks or so, a handful of children returned to the camp and were replaced by a new group at the villa.

By February 1942, most of the Spanish refugees were being freed and they took their children from the villa. They were replaced by German, Polish and other Western European Jews. Many of them had fled their homes and taken refuge in France several years before. However, they found themselves embroiled in the anti-Jewish laws of Vichy France, often more repressive that those of the German Nazis. Lois was aware that these children would be traumatised by their experiences and wanted to 'add just another ray of love to the lives of these youngsters who have already experienced so much of the miseries of life'.

However, in early June 1942, the Vichy Government agreed to hand over 50,000 Jews. Those who were in unoccupied parts of Vichy France, such as Rivesaltes, were deported to Drancy, north of Paris, in occupied France. From there they would be deported to Auschwitz. Her colleague, Mary Elmes, visited Lois at the villa on 9 August 1942 and she noted, 'Mary informed me about the return of Polish and German Jews to Poland, where death by starvation awaits them.'

Lois observed that in the deportations in August, September and early October 1942, if children under 16 were not with their parents in the camp they were not sought by the French officials, particularly if they had already met their quota for the transports. Lois therefore realised she needed to move as many Jewish children as possible to the villa.

By this time, she had good working relations with other relief agencies such as the French-Jewish child welfare organisation, Oeuvre de Sécourse aux Enfants (OSE), which worked clandestinely. It moved children from relief agencies' homes and camps to OSE group homes, private homes and Catholic convents, monasteries and schools which would shelter them. Lois Gunden's niece described the informal process as similar to 'the US underground railroad, which helped runaway slaves reach freedom'.

Lois and Mary tried to liaise with local officials to help individual children and generally ensure more humane treatment:

It was the responsibility of local French officials and police to carry out the round-ups and deportations; many of these officials were the same people with whom Mary and Lois had already developed working relationships. In their Department (Pyrenées-Orientales), where enthusiasm for these responsibilities was sometimes lacking, the children sheltered by their groups were often overlooked.

There were issues over getting enough food. The whole of Vichy France faced food shortages over the winter of 1941–1942. The Allied blockade was preventing food coming from North Africa and local officials were concerned that refugee children were getting better access to food than the local children. Throughout the year Lois was in France they experienced uncertainties and she was often encouraged to leave. She wrote, 'if God wants me to return, he will provide a way'.

However, everything changed in November 1942 when US diplomatic relations with the Vichy regime ceased following the 8 November Allied attack on French North Africa. At the same time, on 11 November, Germany took control of southern France and Americans became unwelcome. Lois was stuck in Lyons but managed to provide a plan for the continued care of the children at the villa. However, some months later the German occupiers requisitioned the villa and the children were moved.

Lois was returned to New York on 15 March 1944 as part of a prisoner exchange. In 1958 she married a widower, Ernest Clemens, and acquired a stepdaughter. She died in 2005. She was recognised as a Righteous Among the Nations by Yad Vashem on 27 February 2013 for saving Jewish children.

One of those children was Ginette (Drucker) Kalish, who was born in 1930. Her family had lived in Paris until her father was sent to Auschwitz in July 1942. Her mother and Ginette fled south but were caught and sent to Rivesaltes. It was there that Lois persuaded her mother to let her take Ginette out of the camp. She was initially hesitant, not surprisingly. Ginette told Yad Vashem:

> At the time I was 12 years old and certainly scared but Lois Gunden was quite kind and passionately determined to take me and these other Jewish children out of Rivesaltes to protect them from harm … I remember Lois Gunden being quite kind and generous and she made a special effort to blend us in with the other children. None of the other children were told we were Jewish.

Although far from home, Lois showed great courage, ingenuity and intuitiveness as she rescued children of a different nationality and religion. One morning while the children were out on a walk, a policeman came to arrest three of the Jewish children – Louis, Armand and Monique Landesmann. She told him the children were out and wouldn't be back until noon. He came back and told her to pack the children's clothes and prepare them for travel. She said the clothes were being laundered and wouldn't be dry until late afternoon. All through the day she prayed for 'wisdom, guidance and safety of the three children'. The officer didn't come back and the children were saved.

A young woman in Auschwitz, Miriam Rosenthal (1922–), was four months pregnant when the Nazis tried to trick her into volunteering for a premature trip to the gas chambers. She was born Miriam Schwarcz in Komarno, Czechoslovakia, the youngest of thirteen children to Jacob, a farmer, and his wife, Laura. She had married Bela Rosenthal, her 'Clark Gable', on 5 April 1944 in Budapest.

In a few months, Bela was sent off as a slave labourer and Miriam was sent to Auschwitz. From there she was sent to Augsburg in Germany to work in a Messerschmitt AG factory manufacturing aircraft. However, she was pregnant and beginning to show when two SS men appeared and asked about pregnant women there. They took her on a normal passenger train, which was unusual, with an ordinary German woman in the compartment who said, 'Frau, what is with you? You don't have hair. The clothes you are wearing. What are you, from a mental hospital?' Miriam told the interviewer:

> She didn't have a dream, this German woman, of all the horrible things the Germans were doing. I told her I am not from a mental hospital, I am going to Auschwitz – I am going to the gas. She looked at me like I was crazy, opened her purse and gave me some bread. I ate it so fast. I was so hungry.

Miriam did think she was going to Auschwitz, but instead was sent to Kaufering 1 which was a satellite camp of Dachau. After being tattooed, she was taken to a basement where, to her surprise, she found six other pregnant women chattering away in Hungarian. Apparently they were left alone there and as their babies came they were delivered by another inmate, a Hungarian gynaecologist whose only equipment was a bucket of hot water. A 'kapo' smuggled a stove into the room to keep them warm during the freezing winter of 1944–1945. The Germans, on finding the stove, beat the kapo mercilessly but she replaced the stove the next day.

Miriam's son, Leslie, was the last of the Kaufering 1 babies, born on 28 February 1945. Miriam said, 'He was beautiful, blond hair, blue eyes. An SS came in and was surprised and said he looks Aryan and he asked me if the father was an SS man'.

The American troops liberated Dachau in late April and wept when they discovered the babies. Miriam said goodbye to her 'camp sisters' and went back to Czechoslovakia. Bela also returned, and she saw him running toward her with his sandals held together with string. They went to Canada in 1947 and had two more children. Interviewed in August 2012, just before her ninetieth birthday, she said she still has a recurring nightmare that the SS come and take Leslie away. She smiles as she looks at him. 'He is such a good boy. He visits me every single day. He knows what his mother went through.'[31]

Professor Claude Romney has spoken about her father, Dr Jacques Lewin, who survived almost three years in Auschwitz, working in the camp hospital and laboratory which meant he avoided harsh physical tasks in the freezing conditions of winter and the sweltering heat of summer. He had been deported from France on 27 March 1942, on the very first convoy of 1,100. He came back at the end of May 1945, one of the mere twenty to return. He had survived the 17–18 January 1945 death march from Auschwitz to Mauthausen and then to Ebensee – both notoriously harsh camps. He died in 1968 from the effects of the typhus contracted in Auschwitz.[32]

After he died, her mother gave Claude all his papers and writings about the camp. It led her to research prison doctors and the heart-rending fate of the children sent to Auschwitz.

It is not known how many Jewish physicians died in the Holocaust. It is assumed that it was thousands, as 2,500 names were listed in Poland and 800 were recorded in the Warsaw Ghetto. Of the 243 doctors interned in Theresienstadt, only twenty-seven survived. In the Shargorod camp in Transnitria, Ukraine, twenty-seven Jewish doctors from Rumania were confined, twenty-three became infected with typhus and twelve of them died.[33]

## The Children of Byelaya Tserkov in Ukraine

Belaya Tserkov is a village in Ukraine, 70km from Kiev. The Jewish community there dated back to the late sixteenth century, although it was often attacked. The historian Kruglov said 9,284 Jews lived there before 1941.

In August 1941 the commanding officer of the local garrison of Belaya Tserkov asked for permission to kill the local Jews. The unit that received the order was under SS-Obersturmführer August Häfner. Between 8 and 19 August the Waffen-SS platoon, with the help of Ukrainian soldiers, killed several hundred Jewish men and women by firing squad at a rifle range near the barracks.

The children whose parents had been killed were initially put in a building on the edge of the village. Some of them – three full lorry loads – were taken to the same rifle range on 19 August and killed, but ninety children were left behind in terrible conditions. The next day the Catholic chaplain, Ernst Tewes, and the Protestant chaplain, Gerhard Wilczek, were having lunch together in the officers' mess. A very distraught non-commissioned officer came and pleaded with Tewes to take 'remedial action'. Tewes became a bishop after the war.

Accordingly, the chaplains visited the children and then informed the divisional chaplain of 295th Infantry Division. The Catholic divisional chaplain, Dr Reuss, who became Bishop of Mainz after the war, and his Protestant colleague, Kornmann, went with the other two chaplains to see the children. In the afternoon the senior chaplains went to see the lieutenant colonel of the division who was called Helmuth Groscurth. Dr Reuss' report to Groscurth was dated 20 August. He said that the children were aged between a few months and 5 or 6 years old. They were locked up in the house under deplorable conditions guarded by Ukrainian soldiers. The little ones could be heard whimpering continuously as they approached the house. German soldiers had objected to the situation:

The two rooms where the children had been accommodated ... were in a filthy state. The children lay or sat on the floor which was covered in their faeces. There were flies on the legs and abdomens of most of the children some of whom were only half dressed. Some of the bigger children (two, three, four years old) were scratching the mortar from the wall and eating it. Two men who looked like Jews, were trying to clean the rooms. The stench was terrible. The small children, especially those that were only a few months old, were crying and whimpering continuously. The visiting soldiers were shaken, as we were, by these unbelievable conditions and expressed their outrage over them.

A senior medical officer from the Wehrmacht had visited the children and said water was needed urgently. Dr Reuss said the house was not being supervised by the Germans and the soldiers were free to enter any time.[34] Kornmann's report was quite short, and his main concern was that when he visited the house soldiers standing around outside were very agitated about what they had seen. 'As I considered it highly undesirable that such things should take place in full view of the public eye I hereby submit this report.'[35]

These people produced endless reports within the two or three days after the children's parents were killed and bureaucracy triumphed. All that was done was that the murder was postponed for a day – no one seemed to have the will to do anything to help the children with food and safety, let alone actually rescue them from their fate. The main issue was concern over people finding out about them. There seemed to be general agreement that the Jewish children had to be exterminated.

Accordingly, the die was cast – there was a final wrangle about who should do the shooting. August Häfner, SS-Obersturmführer in the Einzatzgruppen, was told it should be the Waffen-SS, but he protested that they all had young children so it was suggested Häfner's men should do it – and he protested that they too had small children. So Häfner suggested the Ukrainian soldiers should do it and they did not object.

Häfner reported that, on 22 August 1941:

I went out to the woods alone. The Wehrmacht had already dug a grave. The children were brought along in a tractor. I had nothing to do with this technical procedure. The Ukrainians were standing trembling. The children were taken down from the tractor. They were lined up along the top of the grave and shot so that they fell into it. The Ukrainians did not aim at any particular part of the body. They fell into the grave. The wailing was indescribable. I shall never forget the scene throughout my life. I find it very hard to bear. I particularly remember a small fair-haired girl who took me by the hand. She too was shot later ... The grave was near some woods. It was not near the rifle-range. The execution must have taken place in the afternoon at about 3.30 or 4.00. It took place the day after the discussions at the Feldkommandant ... Many children were hit four or five times before they died.[36]

Helga Weiss was born in 1929 in Prague. Her parents were Otto and Irena Weiss. She kept a diary which she illustrated herself. In it she recorded the events as she saw them as a young girl. On 5 October 1941, she wrote about her father's developing cooking skills. She said that it was three years since he had lost his job – he had worked in a bank. Whereas before he couldn't even make tea, now he was making desserts and even whole lunches all by himself. However, the Germans:

> ... came up with a great idea that even the Middle Ages would have been proud of. Conspicuously labelling the Jews. Stars! Bright yellow, with the word JUDE. At school we all boast about whose star is sewn on best. Even though it's not pleasant to have to wear it, we make light of it. In the afternoon, I go for a walk with [my friend] Eva. We count how many stars we meet and compete to see who can count more. We talk gaily and laugh loudly. Let the Germans see that we're not bothered. We put on a cheerful faces and make ourselves laugh. Deliberately, to make them angry.[37]

Helga's comment about the Middle Ages – I wonder whether she was aware at the time that the yellow mark was indeed medieval. It was first introduced in England by royal decree in 1218, to be followed in 1290 by the expulsion of Jews from England. Perhaps she had learnt this at school.

Helga eventually survived four camps, including ten days in Auschwitz which was the worst time. She experienced the dehumanising and depersonalisation of the Nazi conveyor belt entry to camp life. She and her mother arrived at Auschwitz on 4 October 1944, by which time Helga was 15. Fortunately they were kept together on arrival:

> First they led us to the baths, where they took from us everything we still had. Quite literally there wasn't even a hair left. I've sort of got used to the shaven heads but the first impression was horrid. I didn't even recognise my own mother till I heard her voice. But so what, hair will grow back, it's not such a tragedy, as long as we survive. I don't hold out much hope. As soon as we got here, they held us up with a long speech, of which I remember nothing beyond the first sentence, which was plenty; 'Ihr seid in Vernichtungslager!' 'You are in an extermination camp.' Upon which they drove us here, into this building, onto bunks from which we are not allowed to move.[38]

The Volkswagen factory at Wolfsburg had many forced labourers. Sara Frenkel (née Bass) and her sister, Lea, were Jews who worked as nurses there with false papers provided by a Catholic priest. Sara worked in Ward 8 and the forced labourers' babies were looked after there. She became very upset at the death of 360 newborn babies and infants in the factory-owned facility due to neglect. For her, the death of the babies, often just a few weeks old, epitomises the inhumanity of the Nazi system.[39] She described at some length her experiences with these little ones. The patients were the offspring of forced labourers from the Soviet Union and there were usually about ten to fourteen children in the hut:

> It was impossible to separate the healthy children from the sick ones in these huts and child after child died as a result. One day, I needed some sulphate for two babies who were around eight months old, but I was not given any. The nurse in the pharmacy said there was no sulphate available for Ward 8. The children died. There was hardly any medication available for the little ones anyway.

The parents couldn't stop the children being taken away, as they had to work. However, all the hospital patients helped provide food for the children. Life was very difficult as there was a shortage of nappies, medication and everything. They weren't allowed to pick up the children to sing to them and give them a cuddle. 'They went without love.'

In the summer of 1944 the conditions in the hut and the illnesses were so bad that the hut was disinfected and repainted and an 'isolation ward' was set up. The healthy children were put in a different hut in Rühen, known as the 'children's home', but later sick children were put there too – all the children in Rühen died. When the hut was renovated, Sara was asked to go and work there. She refused to accept the posting because it was too terrible:

> That wasn't work, I didn't want to see that. There, the children lay in dirt and the rooms stank of urine and faeces. The place was full of lice and bugs. The food was bad and there wasn't enough water.

She went back to the sister on Ward 8 and said she couldn't stay there.

Speaking in 2004, Sara told the interviewer that twenty years previously (1980s) she and her husband had been visiting the area as her husband originally came from Brunswick. They saw a signpost to Rühen and went to see the children's graves. They found the cemetery and, as it had just been All Saints' Day flowers were everywhere, but the children's graves had nothing and were overgrown and neglected. She and her husband spoke to both Volkswagen and the church, so that a memorial stone was laid which now has flowers on it all the time.[40]

The British Military War Crimes Court tried the senior staff at Rühen in June 1946. Dr Hans Korbel, in authoritative medical charge of a children's home established by the Volkswagenwerk Directorate, was sentenced to death and clemency was rejected. He was executed on 7 March 1947. Matron Schmidt was sentenced to death, which was commuted to life imprisonment, and Sister Bachor was sentenced to five years' imprisonment. Matron Schmidt served eight years in prison, after which she returned to Volkswagen in Germany and, bizarrely, worked there as a social worker.

The press report from the trial, found in the US National Archives, states:

> The charge of which Dr Korbel was convicted alleged that he was concerned, together with the matron, and other members of the staff, in killing those children by wilful neglect.
>
> The conditions in the home were truly appalling. Bugs came out of the walls at night and literally covered the children's faces and bodies. The Home was described by one witness as a living ant hill. Some children had as many as 30 boils or carbuncles, running with pus, on their bodies. They died like flies.
>
> Despite this death rate, Dr Korbel's visits to the Home consisted of a casual weekly inspection; he failed to take any steps to obtain the assistance of a children's specialist though four such were immediately available: he never made any detailed examination or study of a sick infant; no post-mortem was ever conducted upon the body of a dead child; and the death certificates were signed by him with the unscientific and contemptuously casual diagnosis 'feebleness of life'.
>
> The only explanation of such gross neglect was that it was wilful and deliberate, and such an explanation is further strengthened by the callous attitude adopted in the disposal of the dead bodies. These were dumped unceremoniously in a small room in the Home to await removal packed in batches of cardboard boxes, which were then buried in the local cemetery lightly covered with soil.
>
> It was concluded that this wilful neglect was the direct cause of the death of between 350 and 400 Polish and Russian children.[41]

Franciszek Zabecki, the stationmaster at Treblinka Station, recorded two horrible incidents of cruelty to small Jewish children in his memoirs. On the first occasion:

> I saw a policeman catch two young Jewish boys. He did not shut them in a wagon, since he was afraid to open the door in case others escaped. I was on the platform, letting a military transport go through. I asked him to let them go. The assassin did not even budge. He ordered the bigger boy to sit down on the ground and take the smaller one on his knee, then he shot them both with one bullet. Turning to me, he said: 'You're lucky, that was the last bullet.' Round the huge stomach of the murderer there was a belt with a clasp on which I could see the inscription, 'God with us'.

Zabecki did not record the nationality of the policeman, but the second incident concerned a Ukrainian guard. A train had arrived the previous evening but had been kept overnight in Treblinka Station, as was customary. On the following morning the Ukrainian guard:

> … promised a Jewess that he would let her and her child go if she put a large bribe in his hand. The Jewess gave the Ukrainian the money and her four year old child through the air gap, and afterwards with the Ukrainian's help, she also got out of the wagon through the air gap. The Jewess walked away from the train, holding her child by the hand; as soon as she walked down the railway embankment the Ukrainian shot her. The mother rolled into a field, pulling the child after her. The child clutched the mother's neck. Jews looking out of the wagons called out and yelled, and the child turned back up the embankment again and under the wagons to the other side of the train. Another Ukrainian killed the child with one blow of a rifle butt on its head.[42]

Robert Krell is a Dutch child survivor who reflected on the strange attitude to child survivors by adults:

> Surviving children, particularly the youngest, were not considered to have suffered much. Adults who survived the unimaginable torment and suffering accompanied by total comprehension of what was happening assumed that younger children were shielded from the terror. Adult survivors said to child survivors: 'You were so lucky. You probably don't remember anything. You were too young to suffer. Lucky for you, you did not know what was happening.' It was an assumption. It was not mean-spirited. The knowledgeable survivors of the worst could not imagine a suffering comparable to theirs. Fair enough.[43]

He also described the place where child survivors from Buchenwald were collected at Écouis in France. One boy Lulek, aged 8, left quite early to join his brother in Palestine. He was a Polish Jew and had been 2 years old in 1939. Lulek 'had lost the privilege of childhood. He was one of what I have called "elderly children".'

Krell referred to a speech Lulek made in 1994, as the Ashkenazi Chief Rabbi of Israel in Vancouver. He spoke about a meeting he had on 11 April 1983 when he met one of the liberators of Buchenwald, Rabbi Schachter, for the second time. They had met for the first time on 11 April 1945 at Buchenwald. This is what Lulek said in Vancouver:

> Rabbi Schachter was in the first jeep to enter the gates of Buchenwald. The Germans had gone, the gates were still closed and there was a pile of corpses near the gates. I stayed behind the pile of bodies. The gate was broken down and the

jeep entered. Rabbi Schachter was frightened; he could not believe his eyes. He saw eyes watching him, took out his gun and walked around the corpses, where he discovered a little boy with not even one tooth. He understood this must be a Jewish child and gathered me into his arms. Now I was afraid. He was a man in a uniform with a gun. For six years I had seen the uniforms of the SS, the Wehrmacht, of Einsatzgruppen. He saw how frightened I was. First he wept, then he smiled and asked in Yiddish for my name. 'Lulek, in Polish they call me Lulek.' He said 'How old are you Lulek?' I would not have believed it if Rabbi Schachter had not told me this. He was a soldier, a Rabbi and I was less than 8 years old and yet I said, 'I am older than you.' So he asked why I thought so. I answered, 'Because you behave like a child. I haven't laughed or cried for years. I am too strong, too tough. I don't cry any more. So tell me who is older, me or you?'[44]

Krell expressed amazement at the successes achieved by the Buchenwald boys – businessmen, artists, writers, physicians, surgeons, psychoanalysts, plastic surgeons, rabbis, nuclear physicists and, of course, a Nobel Prize winner – Elie Wiesel:

How is it possible that they did not resort to a life of crime or of vengeance? How did they manage to climb back from the abyss? And if so many talented individuals can be counted amongst this small group of surviving children, what talent was lost with the murders of a generation of Jewish children? The music not written, the medicines not invented or discovered, the thoughts not expounded. I often think of those unlived lives. It is our responsibility to remember them.[45]

Esia Baran Friedman (*b.* 1930), who lives in Connecticut, sent me this story about her friend Chaya and her nanny. Esia was born in Vilna – her father was Yitzhak (Isaac) Baran and her mother was Adele (Ida) Szoag Baran. She had a brother, Wolf (now Zev), who was born in 1925. Following the Versailles Treaty, there was conflict between the Polish leaders and Lithuanian leaders over Vilna being ceded to Poland from Lithuania. (The city of Vilnius was called Vilna in the interwar period when it was part of Poland.)

Her father was an administrator in a Russian military hospital and was able to help a Polish Catholic couple who later hid and protected Esia. Her father was fluent in Russian and Lithuanian and acted as a translator mediating between the Russians and Lithuanians. The Lithuanians were still treating the Jews with respect until the Nazi Holocaust:

When the Nazis and their collaborators came to take the Jewish children away, my mother threw me over a wall and told me to run to my father's friends [the Polish couple]. My mother had no idea if the couple would take me in. My mother never knew what became of me until she escaped from a Nazi labour camp and risked her life to look for me! The couple allowed her to stay and the last few months we hid together until liberation. We hid in various locations on the couple's property; the cellar, wooded areas, a garbage bin and behind a closet wall.[46]

Esia described how after the liberation they stayed hidden for a while because they were protecting themselves from the evil people who were still looking for Jews to kill. Eventually they returned to their old home which had been occupied by their neighbours who were Nazi sympathisers. Esia and her mother were the only survivors on their street.

One of the local bakeries was run by the Szczeranski family on their street. The parents were Shimon and Rochl and they had three children – Chaya was the middle child. Esia and Chaya were about 14 or 15 at the time of these events. The family had a nanny called 'Naszcza', which is the Polish for 'nanny'. She walked them all to school and they all spoke Yiddish. The children all spoke Polish, Russian and Lithuanian, but Naszcza only spoke to them in Yiddish. She was about 40 and Esia assumed she was Jewish. Chaya's family were all killed in the forest of Ponary in Vilnius where the Poles, the Lithuanians, the Germans and the Ukrainians slaughtered 70,000 Jews. The Estonians came to help these 'barbarians' liquidate the Vilnius Ghetto by killing the remaining Jews.

Chaya's aunt, Miss Szczeranski, was an engineer working for the Vilnius Electric Company. When the Nazis were approaching, the Russians evacuated their best employees and the entire electric station, complete with generators. She and Chaya's father, her brother, went to Russia but Chaya's father died.[47]

As Esia and Adele were the only Jewish survivors, any mail that came to the street was given to Adele and she replied to the letters as best she could. She then passed the letters to the only surviving rabbi, Israel Gustman. He opened a kehilla (community) and an orphanage for the few remaining children. One of the letters came from Chaya's aunt, saying her brother had died and wondering if anyone from the family had survived.

A year after the liberation, Esia was standing in front of her home and she saw a girl with blond plaits staring at the house. Then she recognised Chaya and crossed the street to greet her:

She looked in a daze, scared and tried to leave. I said, 'Chaya you survived.' She looked at me and I said, 'Chaya, I am Esia Baran and I survived in hiding. Please do not leave.' She replied to me in Polish, 'I do not understand Yiddish', to which I replied in Polish, 'How did you know I was speaking Yiddish'. To ease her fears, I told her that her aunt is alive and looking for her. We hugged and both of us were crying. I asked her how she survived and she told me her story.

Apparently the nanny had saved her. Esia asked how she did that when she was Jewish. Chaya told her the nanny was a devout German Catholic who had converted her to Catholicism and placed her on a family farm owned by a doctor. 'She was made to take care of the animals.' Esia told her she must come and live with her and her mother and become Jewish again:

> She told me she was scared that her nanny will kill her. The Catholic Church killed converts who returned to their roots. We agreed on a date to meet and we would hide her in Rabbi Gustman's orphanage. My mother would provide the food for her and get in touch with her aunt in Moscow ... We were all grateful that Naszcza was a righteous gentile but we did not realize how evil she was.

One day Adele opened the door and was shocked to see Naszcza with two Polish men who were members of the Armia Krajowa. (This was literally the 'Home Army' created by the Polish Government in exile.) They fought with the Jewish partisans but later shot them in the back.[48] Naszcza asked where Anna was. Esia's very courageous mother said to them, 'Are you asking for Chaya who is a Jewish child?' She thanked Naszcza for risking her life and saving Chaya. However, they just asked again, 'Where is Anna?' Esia's mother said she did not know where she was:

> They told us they will kill us. Thank G–d my brother Zev who returned from the front and was ill, awoke and heard the noise. He came out of the bedroom and entered wearing his Russian army uniform jacket and with a gun in his hand. He warned Naszcza and the two men that if they come near his family he will take care of them all. My brother explained to them this is not Poland when you could have pogroms or the Nazis or the brutal collaborators. We never heard any more from the Nanny.

Her mother was making arrangements for them to leave their native land and to get 'out of Europe for good'. At the agency which provided the documents that they required in order to leave, she met up with a school friend called Merel Fuks, who was there with her older sister. They all cried and hugged each other. There was also a very pretty lady watching them and she told them her story:

> She said her niece was found alive and that a little girl wrote her a letter and because of that letter Moscow gave her permission to travel to Vilnius to unite with her niece Chaya Szczeranski. I told her I am the one who wrote the letter. And so more crying, and kissing and hugging.

Her brother, Zev, gave her a lovely ring which she gave to Chaya and told her not to lose touch again. Chaya's aunt took her abroad to either France or Israel, and Esia and her mother fled the Communists, led by her brother Zev. They lost contact.

Finally, a particular child's experience may only be a brief description in a book or journal – I have collected some of these to end this chapter as a way of widening the narrative of children's experiences in the Holocaust. Individual children were treated with great cruelty by Aryans, oblivious of their particularly vulnerable state. George Prochnik wrote:

> My father [Martin] still recalls having asked another boy what time it was in a park by his house and having that boy's father snatch away his child's hand before he could answer. 'We don't tell time to Jews,' the man told his son. My father was all of six years old when he had to process that encounter.[49]

Martin was born in 1931.

Roman Halter (1927–2012) found himself all alone after his family were all killed. He was 17 when he arrived in Auschwitz from where, after ten days, he was sent to Stutthof. He described it as 'more cosy' because there was only one crematorium. He was working as a metal worker, but his main problem was a particularly sadistic female guard who enjoyed kicking the shorter men in the groin with her pointed boots which was extremely painful. Roman managed to make a metal shield, perhaps like a cricket box, which protected him and also failed to clank when hit.[50]

Michal Glowinski's autobiographical story, *A Quarter-Hour Passed in a Pastry Shop*, was detailed in *The Other Schindlers*.[51] However, it is important here because of the way the women treated the little Jewish boy left in the pastry shop by his aunt and their eagerness to report him to the authorities. I asked Marci Shore, who translated Michal Glowinski's book, what she thought about the women's response. She said:

> In general, the women were so anxious presumably because they didn't want to be implicated – that is, to potentially be seen as bearing any responsibility for having been in the presence of a Jew and not reporting him.[52]

An incident took place in Budapest sometime after 15 October 1944, which was noted by Moshe Herczl as symptomatic of 'the spirit and atmosphere of the period':

> As the lines of Jews were driven in the drizzling rain through the streets of the capital toward the race tracks [where the Jews were concentrated] amid the abuse of their fellow citizens, a little girl of four, whose parents had previously been shot, strayed away from the column. An Arrow-Cross man grabbed the little thing and threw her back in line with such vigor that she landed with her face on the muddy pavement, lacerating her skin. The onlooking crowd greeted this feat with laughter, roaring its approval.[53]

Josie Levy Martin, who was hidden by a nun, Soeur St Cybard, went to America after the war with her parents.[54] She suffered for many years because of her parents' dismissive attitude to their experiences:

> It wasn't that we didn't talk about the war. The subject of our suffering was not taboo as it has been in so many other families. My parents, especially Mother, talked often of our lives during The War, but against the more dramatic events of the Holocaust, against the gassings, the crematoria, the unrecognizable bags of bones that rose from tiers of wooden bunks, barely alive, barely human, I think she felt ashamed to make much of what we endured. For years and years her anecdotes always ended with that brisk angry refrain as when she remembered her beloved Rosenthal china, 'Come, let's forget about it … it was nothing.'

It was *not* nothing.[55]

Steven Frank (1935–) was born in Amsterdam, the eldest son of three to Beatrix and Leonard. In autumn 1943 he was sent to Westerbork with his mother and two brothers. Steven was wandering around:

> I found I had wandered across no man's land and had got to the perimeter wire. Here I was set upon by an Alsatian guard dog unleashed by two guards patrolling the wire. I was bitten all over and I can still hear the guards laughing as this little eight year old was being mauled by this dog. Then they called it off and I ran back to the barrack bleeding from all these bite marks. But I had learned my lesson.[56]

Julie Orringer's grandmother gave birth in Budapest in October of 1944 after the Nazi invasion in March 1944. She remembered being terrified as she was in labour in the hospital and pleading with the Nazi doctor not to hurt her baby. 'She said the doctor leaned over and whispered in her ear, "I'm a doctor first", and communicated to her that she was going to be OK and that the baby was OK. But the horror of that is just unimaginable to me.' When Julie had her own baby she looked at her new baby son and was overwhelmed by the thought, 'The set of circumstances that resulted in your being here are so unbelievably fortuitous.' One of the greatest pleasures was to take him to see her grandmother and tell her 'this baby is here because you managed to survive'.[57]

It is appropriate to leave this awful chapter recalling Margita Schwalbová's description of the children in Auschwitz as 'crushed spring flowers', expressing 'the cruel annihilation of those young human beings whose lives could have been full of promise'.[58]

# 19

# OLYMPIANS AND SPORTSPEOPLE

The terrible events of 9 November 1938 (Kristallnacht) were ostensibly the result of the assassination of Ernst vom Rath. However, a similar event had occurred in 1936 which had an altogether different outcome.

Wilhelm Gustloff, the leader of the Nazi Party in Switzerland, was shot dead in his home in Davos by a Croatian Jewish medical student, David Frankfurter (1909–1982), on 4 February 1936. At his trial, Frankfurter claimed he had heard Gustloff state on the telephone, 'The dirty Jews, we'll show them.'[1]

Hitler was furious – he referred to 'international Jewry' directing this crime. However, it was only two days before the official opening of the Winter Olympics. The Nazis were shrewd enough to realise that:

> The games were supposed to showcase the achievements of National Socialism to thousands of tourists and reporters who would be gathering in Germany for the event. Fearing that violent reprisals against Jews might make a bad impression on these visitors, the regime had secretly ordered the police and local governments to take decisive measures to prevent such assaults …

These domestic and international constraints on German actions in February 1936 no longer applied in November 1938. To the contrary, from the perspective of Hitler and other leading Nazis, the shooting of Ernst vom Rath offered a welcome pretext for intensifying the persecution of Germany's Jews.

Gustloff became a martyr for the Nazi cause, with a cruise ship, MV *Wilhelm Gustloff*, and a charitable foundation named after him.[2] The ship was sunk by a Soviet submarine in January 1945 in the Baltic Sea with more than 9,000 civilian refugees on board, which is regarded as the greatest death toll from a single vessel. His wife, Hedwig, who had been Hitler's secretary, was given 'honorary pay' of RM400, which is around $13,000 today.

On 9 April 1936 as part of the Olympic preparations the last of the red-painted
signs saying 'Jews are our Misfortune – Whoever Buys from Jews is a Traitor' were
removed from all public places in Berlin. This was part of the campaign to eliminate
all vestiges of anti-Semitism before the games. In addition, copies of *Der Stürmer*
were no longer displayed in their special boxes and were replaced by *Der Agriff*,
the official Nazi newspaper. However, anti-Jewish attacks would not cease, as evidenced by the attack on Jews over the Phoenix Insurance of Austria controversy
which was covered in Hitler's newspaper, the *Völkischer Beobachter*.[3]

Secret instructions from the Minister for Agriculture, Walter Darre, were sent
to rural authorities to treat Jews politely during the Olympic Games. However,
the instructions emphasise that the 'fundamental German attitude towards Jews
remains unchanged'. Darre was quoted as saying, 'Jewish provacateurs must not get
the chance to create incidents which could add grist to the mills of anti-German
propagandists abroad.' All the anti-Jewish signs were to be removed and the polite-
ness was important 'because the German Government has pledged to the Olympic
Committee to guarantee protection for all Olympic guests.[4]

Later, on 14 July 1936 in Berlin it was reported that Jews were not going to
be permitted to sell 'hot dogs' and other refreshments at the Olympic Games.
According to a police order, such concessions were restricted to the 'politically
reliable'. Licences were required to sell refreshments and the recommendation
of the Nazis' Department of Trade and Artisanship was required. The Nazis
wished to prevent visitors making contact with Jews and other 'politically unreliable elements'.

Additionally, special courses for teaching visitors Nazi theories were to open on
15 July with eminent Nazis speaking, including Hans Hinkel, State Commissar for
Non-Aryan Culture, talking about Nazi cultural policies, and Professor Fischer,
director of the Kaiser Wilhelm Institute of Anthropology, on racial policies. It was
announced that Professor Fischer would 'explain to foreign participants the high
national significance of the much-contested subject of racial science, which, outside
of Germany, has been most often wrongly represented to the public'.[5]

Fred Stein, born in 1928 into a Berlin Jewish family, remembers the Olympics
well as he was 8. He has written about living in Germany until his parents took
him to safety in Australia. He explained the only reason his Jewish school was not
attacked during Kristallnacht was because the caretaker was a non-Jew and he lived
on site with his family. He recorded:

> Prior to Kristallnacht, I have to confess, that for me as a child, I was often
> impressed by the pageantry which the Nazis always staged so brilliantly. Especially
> in 1936 at the famous (or rather infamous) Berlin Olympic Games, the city was
> decorated with banners and thousands of Nazi and Olympic flags. It was very
> inspiring but it was not long before even a child could see clearly the real mean-

ing behind the impressive parades, smart uniforms and the display of flags. It soon became a sinister and frightening experience for me.[6]

After the 1936 Olympics all the tourists and foreign journalists left Germany and the anti-Jewish measures continued without hindrance.[7] The pause in the Germany's anti-Jewish campaign during the Olympics was brief. William E. Dodd, the US Ambassador to Germany, reported that Jews awaited 'with fear and trembling' the end of the Olympic truce.[8]

One English woman recollected her 1936 experiences at the time of London's 2012 Olympics. Dorothy Odam was only 16 when she won a silver medal for the high jump in Berlin – a success she repeated in London in 1948. Her memories were clear, even after seventy-five years. She described Hitler as 'A little man in a big uniform', having sidled up to him at a party that Goebbels had given for the women competitors. She described him 'as a bit of a womaniser'. She also noted that when the German girls relay team dropped the baton, Hitler fell off his seat with rage:

> When we got there, there were Nazi flags everywhere, everyone seemed to be in uniform. It was all very militaristic. We were staying in a large dormitory. The first morning, I was woken up by the sound of marching, and outside there were hundreds of Hitler Youth parading with shovels held like rifles.
>
> When we went shopping we were greeted with 'Guten Morgen, Heil Hitler'. We responded: 'Guten Morgen, Heil King George'. Outside another shop the interpreter told us 'No Jews'. So we all walked in.[9]

They were watched over by three strict German chaperones, though Dorothy now wonders whether they were there to spy on them. She wore her homemade vest and shorts to compete for her event. It lasted for three hours under a blazing sun because of interruptions for other events and medal ceremonies. She recalled the German girls got water from the crowd, but 'we got nothing'.[10]

A troubling postscript was, 'I received a smuggled letter from an inmate of a concentration camp telling me of the atrocities and asking me to take it back to England. I showed it to my chaperone but never saw it again.' I wonder what happened to that poor soul?[11] (Dorothy died on 25 September 2014. See the *Times* 'Obituary' on 29 September 2014 – there is additional material in it.)

The purpose of this chapter is to look at those Jews who reach the pinnacle of their sport as Olympians and with other achievements. However, in all these cases they were destined to be marked out with the yellow star with 'Jude' on it.

The first Jewish victim from the Olympics was not a competitor. Wolfgang Fürstner (1896–1936) is virtually unknown today. He was the former commandant of the Olympic village, who committed suicide on 18 August – only two days after the Olympics finished. The German press were told to say that he had been killed in a car accident but the foreign journalists discovered the truth and broke the story. Fürstner had been found to be a Mischling, but he had done such a good job in planning the Olympics that he was allowed to stay until almost the end of the games even though the arriving athletes saw the commandant listed as Baron von und zu Gilsa instead.[12]

Fürstner was born in Posen to a military father, Captain Ernst Fürstner. In 1914 Wolfgang volunteered as a soldier, becoming a second lieutenant and company commander. He was awarded the Iron Cross, First Class, and stayed in the army until 1920 when he was discharged. He then read political sciences at university. However, he did not graduate and completed a traineeship at the Reichsbank.

In 1925 he married Leonie von Schlick and the marriage certificate cites him as a 'business clerk'. He was not very successful in the civilian world and only felt really at home in the Deutscher Offizier-Bund (DOB) – the monarchist veterans' organisation.

In 1928 Fürstner founded a sports association for the DOB and became its president. In April 1930 he was head of the umbrella organisation of all sports clubs in Brandenburg, and had responsibility for ejecting Jewish athletes and clubs from January 1933. Because of his reputation as an officer with organising ability, in May 1933 he was invited back into the armed services to organise the 1936 Olympic Games.

However, the Nuremberg Race Laws cast a shadow over Fürstner's life because one of his grandfathers had been Jewish. He was, however, confident that his merits as an officer and his sports administration skills would compensate. He was not alone in this view – see Chapter 16.

The blow fell just before the games started, when 370,000 visitors poured through the grounds of the Olympic village and damaged the newly planted flower beds. Fürstner was accused of lacking energy and was downgraded to deputy commander of the athletes' village, although he was still in charge of the whole village each day. During the games anonymous posters began to appear all round the village with the message 'Down with the Jew Fürstner'. The final blow was when his wife announced she wanted a divorce because she could no longer have a successful future with him in Germany. Accordingly, he gave up the fight and shot himself.

*The Sydney Morning Herald*, on 21 August 1936, revealed that he had been found dead with the revolver at his side.[13] He was buried in the Invalidenfriedhof – the Invalids' Cemetery, the traditional military cemetery for the honoured war dead. A new tombstone was laid in June 2002 with the wording 'Suicide as a result of political persecution' by the German Olympic Committee. However, he is still shown as 'Deputy Commandant of the Olympic Village 1936', which is unfair.

As the post-games reports were filed, Hitler pressed on with grandiose plans for German expansion which included taking over the Olympics forever. He apparently told Albert Speer in spring 1937, 'In 1940 the Olympic Games will take place in Tokyo. But thereafter they will take place in Germany for all time to come, in this stadium.'

A postscript to the 1936 games came from Leslie Jeffers, an English policeman who was a wrestler in the British team. On 1 August 1936, as the Führer arrived and was proceeding across the May Field toward the stadium for the official opening of the games, he passed within 7 or 8 yards of where Jeffers stood to attention among his comrades in the ranks of the British team. Fifty years later, the former London policeman is still regretting that he missed such an opportunity. 'If I'd just jumped forward and clobbered him there and then,' he says, 'what an incredible amount of life and trouble I would have saved.'[14]

---

## OLYMPIC OFFICIAL FOUND DEAD

### Aryan Descent Doubted
### Berlin Aug. 20

Captain Wolfgang Fuerstner the former commander of the Olympic Village was found dead with a revolver by his side. Another officer had been placed in command of the Olympic Village before the games after suggestions that had been made that Captain Fuerstner's descent was not purely Aryan.
Captain Fuerstner's percentage of Jewish blood was so small that there was no ground for his anxiety on that score. It is believed that he was a victim of overstrain.
Captain Fuerstner continued the work of organisation of the village and was very popular with the athletes and visitors

---

# The Fate of Olympians in the Holocaust

In spite of pretending to value the Olympic ideals before and during the 1936 Berlin Games, the Nazis managed to kill many of the Olympic medallists in the years afterwards. Among them were three whose successes were at the beginning of the modern games in Athens in 1896. Pierre de Coubertin's aims were influenced by his own aristocratic privileged background. 'Despite the early Olympic message calling for peace and co-operation amongst the youth of the world, the local celebration of the games as expressed in ceremonies leads inevitably to forms of nationalism and nationalist self-aggrandisement.'[15]

Dr Ferenc Kemeny (1860–1944) of Hungary was a supporter of the nascent Olympic movement and a colleague of Coubertin. He was a Hungarian sports administrator and teacher. Kemeny was a founding member of the International Olympic Committee (IOC) in 1894, the first secretary of the IOC and one of the handful of Pierre de Coubertin's colleagues who organised the first modern Olympic Games in 1896. With the founding of the Hungarian Olympic Committee (HOC) in 1895, Kemeny was named as the organisation's secretary. Although he was one of Coubertin's friends, he was still a target of frequent anti-Semitism from other HOC members, which led to his resignation as Hungary's IOC representative and from sports life itself.

It is reported that Kemeny and his wife converted to Christianity prior to Germany's occupation of Hungary in 1944. If true, his reputation as Hungary's most prominent Jewish sports pioneer could not escape him. On 21 November 1944, facing immediate arrest by members of the Nazi Hungarian Arrow Cross Party, the Kemenys both committed suicide.

In 1980, a new sports stadium in the Hungarian city of Eger was named after Dr Kemeny. At the time of the founding of the IOC in 1895, Kemeny was headmaster of the modern school in Eger.

## Skiers

Bronisław Czech (1908–1944) was a Polish skier who participated in three Olympic Games, although he never won a medal. In 1928 he finished tenth in the Nordic Combined, in 1932 he finished seventh in the Nordic Combined and in 1936 he finished seventh in the 4 x 10km relay. He was a graduate of the Central Institute of Physical Education in Warsaw (1934), a coach and a great patriot. During the interwar period he was one of the most popular Polish sportsmen.

Born on 25 July 1908 in Zakopane, Poland, as a 12-year-old he achieved his first sports success in a skiing competition organised in Zakopane, where his prize was a longed-for pair of skis. He won the Polish Nordic Combined championship for the first time at the age of 20, and for the last time when he was 29 (two years before the outbreak of the Second World War). This proves that Bronisław Czech was not a hero of just one competition but he maintained a high level throughout his whole professional career. At that time, he was the only sportsman to become the champion in both the Alpine Skiing Combined and Nordic Combined in the same year (1937), thus proving his versatility.

From 1932, he was one of the first qualified skiing instructors in Poland and was always regarded as a gentleman. During the season preceding the outbreak of the Second World War he was in charge of training at the Kasprowy Wierch School of downhill skiing. His career was stopped by the outbreak of the war. His eminence in his sport led to his arrest at the age of 32 and he was sent to Auschwitz. He was among the first shipment of prisoners and was given camp No. 349. He did not attempt to escape because he did not want to cause problems to other people.

Bronisław Czech refused to train German youths in exchange for his freedom and died on 5 June 1944. His family was informed by a laconic message from the Gestapo. Bronisław Czech's symbolic grave can be found in the Pęksowy Brzyzek National Cemetery in Zakopane. Many streets (for example, in Warsaw, Zakopane, Gdańsk and Szklarska Poręba), more than a dozen schools and the University School of Physical Education in Kraków (1977) were named after him.

## Gymnasts

Three Dutch women have been listed only recently because the Nazis did not list female victims with their maiden names. They were Dutch gymnasts who won gold in the team competitions in Amsterdam in 1928. They were Estella (Stella) Blits-Agsteribbe, Helena (Lea) Kloot-Nordheim and Anna (Ans) Dresden-Polak.

Gerrit Kleerekoper (1897–1943) was the Jewish coach of the Dutch gymnastics team at the 1928 Amsterdam Games, where they won gold. Married with two children, he worked as a diamond cutter. Kleerekoper's team scored 316.75 points, defeating Italy and the United Kingdom.

Many years later, Alida van den Bos, one of the gold-winning gymnasts, explained how important Kleerekoper's contribution was:

> The training for the Olympics always took place at indoor gymnasiums even though the Olympics that year took place at an outdoor stadium. A few months prior to the Olympics, Kleerekoper made us only practise outdoors because he said that you never know how the weather will be the day of the Olympics and that we must be prepared for hot weather or any weather. The practice outside was very good, because we noticed that you have a lot more energy outdoors than needed.

On 2 July 1943 Gerrit Kleerekoper, along with his wife, Kaatje, and his 14-year-old daughter, Elisabeth, were murdered by the Nazis at the Sobibór extermination camp in Poland. Twenty-nine days later, his 18-year-old son, Leendert, was murdered at Auschwitz.[16]

Helena 'Lea' Nordheim (1903–1943) was a Dutch gymnast born in Amsterdam. She won the gold medal with the rest of the Dutch gymnastics team at the 1928 Summer Olympics in her native Amsterdam. She was sent to Camp Westerbork in June 1943, and shortly after she was deported to Sobibór where she was murdered with her husband, Abraham, and their 10-year-old daughter, Rebecca, on 2 July 1943.[17]

Ans Dresden-Polak (1906–1943) was a member of the Netherlands women's gymnastics team at the 1928 Amsterdam Games, the first time women's gymnastics was on the Olympic program. No individual medals were awarded at the Amsterdam Games. At the 1928 Olympics, about half of the Dutch women's gymnastics team was Jewish, but only one member, Elka de Levie, survived the Holocaust. Dresden-Polak was killed at Sobibór with her 6-year-old daughter, Eva, on 23 July 1943. Her husband, Barend, was killed at Auschwitz in 1944.

Judikje 'Jud' Simons (1904–1943) was a member of the 1928 Dutch women's gymnastics team and Olympic gold medallist. After her Olympics career Simons married and, with her husband, ran an orphanage in Utrecht, housing and caring for more than eighty needy children. As the Nazis rounded up Dutch Jews and sent them to concentration camps, Jud Simons and her husband received warning of the occupiers' intentions. But the couple — with two young children of their own — refused to abandon the orphans who depended on them. The Nazis captured Simons and her family, all of whom were shipped to the Sobibór extermination camp and gassed on 3 March 1943. While this story does not have a happy ending, it does show the selflessness displayed by Jud Simons and many like her, who put others before themselves and did good, even in the face of such evil.[18]

The Jewish members of the Netherlands Olympic gymnastics team have been inducted, as a group, into the International Jewish Sports Hall of Fame; they include Dresden-Polak, de Levie, Stella Blits-Agsteribbe, Lea Kloot-Nordheim, Judikje Themans-Simons and their coach.

Lilli Henoch (1899–1942) was born to a comfortable middle-class family. Even in childhood Lilli Henoch developed a passion for sport, particularly track, field and team sports, which was rare for a woman in the 1920s, when these sports were considered unwomanly. Women's track and field athletics were only accepted into the Olympics in 1928, after considerable dispute, although the German Sports Authority for Athletics had, in 1919, called for the creation of a women's section. Similarly, the Berlin Sports Club (BSC), founded in 1895, established a women's track and field section in 1919 which rapidly grew to comprise 120 members. They engaged not only in track and field sports, but also in handball, which was developed as a women's game after the end of the First World War.

Lilli Henoch joined the BSC after the war, and soon became its best athlete and was very versatile. In the 1920s she was the mainstay and captain of the BSC's women's handball team. In addition, she was a member of the club's hockey team, which won the Berlin championship in 1925. In shot-put and discus, she was not only the best performer in Germany, but among the best in the world, several times achieving official and unofficial records in these sports. In 1924 she also became the German long-jump champion and in 1926 she and her teammates achieved a world record in the 4 x 100m relay race.

Not only was she a model sportswoman, but she was also appointed to several honorary positions. She was praised, '... above all, Lilly Henoch, who has won no less than seven German championship titles and three German relay races'. The high esteem in which she was held in the association is evidenced by the fact that even on 18 January 1933, just fourteen days before Hitler was named chancellor, Lilli Henoch was elected chairwoman of the women's athletic section.

We know little about Henoch's attitude to Judaism, but in 1924 she was engaged to train the women's section of Bar Kokhba Berlin.[19] In the process of the 1933 Aryanization of the sports organisations, which was implemented speedily, Lilli Henoch, though still highly esteemed, was, like all Jews, compelled to leave the club and seek a new outlet for her sporting activities. Lilli continued to be active in track and field sports but especially as a handball player. Her team won the Berlin Championship of Jewish Handball Players in both 1935 and 1936.

From 1933 on, Lilli Henoch was also the beloved gymnastics teacher at the Jewish Elementary School in the Rykestrasse. It is, however, impossible to determine how long she continued working at the school, where teaching carried on under increasingly chaotic circumstances until 1942. In any case, the conditions in which she lived deteriorated extremely rapidly from the mid-1930s, in part because of her stepfather's death and the additional worries of earning a living in ever more difficult conditions.

On 5 September 1942 Lilli, her brother and her 66-year-old mother were deported. In a memorial book her name appears together with many other victims of National Socialism listed as 'missing in Riga'. She and her mother are believed to have been taken from the Riga Ghetto and machine-gunned to death by an Einsatzgruppen mobile killing unit later the same year, along with a large number of other Jews. They were all buried in a mass grave in the woods outside Riga.[20]

Henoch's career is remarkable in many respects. Her choice of track and field sports, her achievements and her dedication to her club were exceptional. She could afford this dedication because she was financially secure and independent, which was also atypical.

Alfred Flatow (1869–1942) was a gymnast from Germany who gained three gold medals and one silver in 1896. He was declared 'an enemy of the Reich' and sent to Theresienstadt where he died of starvation on 28 December 1942. His cousin,

Gustav Flatlow (1875–1945), was also a gymnast, winning two gold medals in 1896. He died of starvation at Theresienstadt on 29 January 1945. Recently, a writer, Volker Kluge, found Gustav's grave at Theresienstadt and reported it to his son, Stefan, living in Rotterdam. Apparently Gustav had emigrated to Holland from Germany in 1933. He was betrayed on Christmas Eve 1943 and deported.

A memorial medal was issued in 1987 in honour of Alfred and Gustav Flatlow by the German Federation of Gymnasts. More recently, the boulevard leading to the Olympic Stadium in Berlin was renamed 'Alfred und Gustav Felix Flatlow-Allee, and the German Philatelic Service honoured the two cousins on the highest denomination stamp in a series on Olympic champions.

## Fencers

Dr Herschmann (1877–1942) was one of only three athletes to have won Olympic medals in different sports. He won a silver medal swimming the 100m Freestyle in 1896 and a bronze medal in team Sabre (fencing) at the 1912 Olympics in Stockholm. Coincidentally, Herschmann also served as president of the Austrian Olympic Committee during the 1912 Games, and as such was the only president of a national Olympic committee to win an Olympic medal while in office. For almost two decades (1914–1932) he served as the president of the Austrian Swimming Federation. He was arrested in Vienna and was due to be deported to the Yugoslav concentration camp at Izbica but his transport was rerouted to the extermination camp Sobibór in Poland on 14 June 1942. Sometimes this date is listed as his date of death, but he most likely died in a gas chamber three days later.[21]

Roman Kantor (1912–1943), born in Lódź, Poland, was an Olympic épée fencer. After primary school he went to Paris to finish his education in 1924. He played both tennis and soccer and started to train in fencing. He then went to London and trained under the fencer Lefevre'a 1931–1932 and then went to Germany to train under Gatzera. In 1934 he returned home and joined the Army Sports Club, twice winning the title of City Champion. In 1935 he was Warsaw Champion as part of the Polish victory over Germany. He was killed at Majdanek concentration camp in 1943.[22]

Janos Garay (1889–1945) was a fencer who won three medals for Hungary in the Sabre event. He won an individual bronze and team silver at the 1924 Paris Olympics, and a team gold medal at the 1928 Amsterdam Games. In 1925, Garay captured the Individual European Sabre Championship gold medal and a team Sabre gold medal at the 1930 Europeans. The European Championships were the predecessor to the World Championships, first held in 1937. Garay perished in Mauthausen camp in 1945, shortly before the end of the Second World War.[23]

Oszkár Gerde (1883–1944) was also a Hungarian fencer – he won two Olympic medals in team Sabre in London in 1908 and in Stockholm 1912. He later became an international fencing judge. He had a doctorate in law, and little else seems to be known of him. He was sent to Mauthausen, where he was killed in October 1944. He was one of more than 119,000 prisoners who died in that camp.

Attila Petschauer (1904–1943), another Hungarian, won silver in Amsterdam in 1928 and gold in Los Angeles in 1932. When the labour service rules were brought in, as a celebrated sportsman Petschauer was accorded a special 'document of exemption'. However, during a routine check in 1943 he realised he had left some of his ID papers at home and was soon deported to the Davidovka labour camp in Ukraine. Tragically, one of the people responsible was a fellow member of the Hungarian delegation to the 1928 Games. His name was Kalman Cseh, a colonel in the Hungarian Army who knew Petschauer very well. When they first saw each other Cseh referred to him as 'the Jew' and told his subordinates to give him a bad time. What happened was reported by another Olympian Károly Kárpáte, a Hungarian wrestler who knew them in 1928 and 1936.

He said that one day, when he was digging in temperatures below zero, he saw the guards tell Attila to take off his clothes and climb a tree and crow like a rooster. As he crowed they sprayed him with cold water which froze and eventually he fell off the tree. They took him back to the barracks but he died a few hours later on 20 January 1943, aged 39. Kárpáte was truly shocked by this incident but managed to survive until the Soviet Army liberated the camp shortly afterwards. It is his testimony which ensured Petschauer's story is known.

Robert Markowitz's Hungarian-born grandfather was Attila's cousin, and he grew up in America hearing about his famous fencing cousin. It was only when he himself took up fencing in high school that he discovered more. In 1995 he set up a fencing tournament in Sabre to keep his memory alive. 'It was as if he was wiped off that map. Being a cousin and a fellow fencer and allowing his name to fade into history because there is no tombstone to mark his grave would have been my shame.' The Attila Petschauer Sabre Open competition is a fitting tribute to 'a generous sportsman with a sharp sense of humor' – a tragic victim of the Holocaust who died as a result of the behaviour of a fellow Hungarian team member.[24]

## Footballers

Eddy Hamel (1902–1943) was born in New York to immigrant Dutch-Jewish parents, and returned to Holland as a child. His family lived in the wealthy area of southern Amsterdam, traditionally one of the most cosmopolitan and worldly of European cities, with one of the oldest European Jewish populations. The story is that Eddy and his friends played their football for a small local club on a field next door to Ajax's offices. One day he and his friends decided to kick their balls against the windows of the larger club's dressing room. The players ran out to confront the children, who scattered, but Eddy was caught and was hauled before the trainer. This began his association with the club for whom he would play for more than a decade.

Eddy Hamel played for the 'Men from the Meer' from 1922 until 1930, appearing in 125 matches and scoring eight goals as a right winger. He was the first Jewish player to serve in Ajax's squad, which has had only three more to this day. He also became the first American to appear in the famous red and white. It would be another sixty years before John O'Brien would make the long trek from southern California to Amsterdam.

Edward was very popular with the fans and was loved by the Amsterdammers, especially the Jewish fans who lived in the shadow of the stadium in East Amsterdam. They cheered him on through his eight years of appearances. He always remembered where he came from, and was not shy of his American-Jewish status. He played his final match for Ajax in 1930 and served as a coach for smaller clubs and boys' teams for the next decade. He was the first Jewish player to play for the club: a club whose fans have since embraced Jewish culture and symbolism, often known to chant 'Joden!' or to display the Star of David at matches.

Local Fascist groups assisted in rounding up 'undesirables' after Germany invaded the Netherlands in May 1940. Despite his American citizenship, Eddy was detained as a Jew in late 1942. As Simon Kuper wrote in *The Warm Back of Eddy Hamel*, 'Had he been able to prove his nationality, had he been a better right back, had he played for the Ajax first team more recently than 1930 he might not have been sent to Birkenau but to Theresienstadt, the camp for protected Jews.'

Hamel spent four months doing hard labour at Birkenau. His bunkmate, Leon Green, remembered him as someone whose soul could not be touched – a man who maintained his dignity in even the most unimaginable environment. 'Our conditions were turning us into different people. Not all of us, some remained the same as when they arrived. Eddie Hammel was always a gentleman.'

Eddy Hamel was sent to the gas chambers on 30 April 1943 after a swollen mouth abscess was found during a Nazi inspection. According to Green, when he was called to pass to the group that was being taken to die, he walked past the table calmly, with his head held high. As is often heard in Amsterdam, no Ajacied is forgotten, and Eddy Hamel stays within the heart of Amsterdam and Ajax. There is only one known photo of him, but his memory in his adopted city is indelible.[25]

In May 1922 the Polish national football team narrowly defeated Sweden 1–2 in Stockholm. It was their first ever victory, and on the scoresheet is defender Józef Klotz (1900–1941), whose penalty converted their first ever goal. In the same winning side was Leon Sperling (1900–1941), a left winger with Cracovia renowned for his skilful dribbling and fast feet. They were both instrumental in one of Poland's proudest and most important sporting achievements. Two years later, the men were left out of Poland's clash with Hungary: a repeat of their country's first ever international. Lining up for the opposition, however, was József Braun, a right winger who made a career abroad before later going into management. It is a path followed by Hungarian contemporary Árpád Weisz, international footballer and three-time Scudetto winner, the latter achieved as manager of Italian giants Inter (once) and Bologna (twice) respectively.

In 1941, Józef Klotz was murdered. That same year, his teammate Leon Sperling was shot dead in the Lwów Ghetto. In 1943, József Braun perished in a forced labour camp, and one year before the war's end, fellow Hungarian Árpád Weisz was killed with his family in Auschwitz. All four were rounded up and murdered in cold blood by the Nazis.

Another such victim was Julius Hirsch, the first ever Jewish player to represent Die Nationalmannschaft. A dynamic midfielder known for his powerful left foot, 'Juller' (as he was known to fans) was Karlsruher FV through and through, supporting them as a boy and wearing their colours either side of the First World War. (Incidentally, he lined up alongside fellow Karlsruher Jew and army veteran, Gottfried Fuchs, best known for scoring ten goals in a single game against Russia in the 1912 Olympics. He fled to Canada to avoid the Holocaust.)

During the First World War, Hirsch was awarded an Iron Cross for his service and was considered a loyal patriot. It did not prevent the anti-Semitic persecution aimed at him and his family. The man who had once scored four goals in one game for his country was, in 1933, forced to turn his back on football, and ten years later Julius Hirsch was deported to Auschwitz. Like Inter legend, Weisz, he would never leave.

In accordance with the unforgiving nature of war (and particularly so brutal a war as this), non-Jewish footballers lost their lives, too. Antoni Łyko, a compatriot of Klotz and Sperling who was known as 'the man without nerves' for his composure in front of goal, was shot in the head at close range by an Auschwitz guard in 1941. The Wisła Kraków striker was not Jewish, but a supposed political opponent and Resistance member.

The story of Petea Vâlcov is perhaps more straightforward, even if no less harrowing. Before the war the Rumanian was considered the most gifted player in his country, forming a deadly attacking trio with brothers Colea and Voleoda for Venus București (then the most successful club in Rumania). Things quickly changed. Petea died fighting for the Axis powers, falling victim to the Red Army in 1943. He was 33, Łyko was 34.

A final Jewish footballer was Erno Egri Erbstein.

## Athletes

Janusz Kusociński (1907–1940) was a Polish athlete who won a gold medal in the 1932 Los Angeles Games. Originally a footballer, he only took up athletics in 1928 and joined the Sarmata Club. In 1929 he won Polish titles in the 5,000m and cross-country, and after a year of military service, won the 1,500m, 5,000m and cross-country in 1930 and 1931, adding another Polish title in the 800m in 1932. He set two world records early in 1932, in the 3,000m and the 4 miles, and capped his year by winning the Olympic 10km gold medal. In 1934 Kusociński was second in the 5,000m at the first European Championships and then retired. However, he made a brief comeback, winning the 10,000m at the 1939 Polish Championships.

During the Second World War, Kusociński volunteered for the Polish Army and was wounded twice. Released because of his injuries he served in the Polish Resistance. He was arrested by the Gestapo on 26 March 1940 and imprisoned in the Mokotów Prison. He was executed by the Germans three months later, in Palmiry, near Warsaw. In his honour, the best-known Polish athletics event is called the 'Kusociński Memorial', which has now been held for almost sixty years.[26]

## Combat Sports

### Wrestling

Werner Seelenbinder (1904–1944) was a German wrestler born in Stettin. A well-known German athlete, he competed at numerous international workers' sports events and won the German National Championship several times after 1933. He was active in the Resistance and also a member of the Communist Party of Germany from 1928. Seelenbinder was placed fourth at the 1936 Olympics, where he was allowed to compete in spite of his political affiliations. From 1937, Seelenbinder became active in the underground struggle against Hitler's forces. In February 1942, Seelenbinder was arrested by the Gestapo and sent to a concentration camp, Brandeburg an der Havel, where he was executed.[27]

### Boxers

Heinz Levy (1904–1944) was a Dutch boxer, although he was born in Hanover. He was a furrier by profession but competed as a featherweight in the 1925 Olympics in Paris. He reached the last sixteen. He and his wife, Henriette, and little 4-year-old daughter, Yolanda, were all killed in Auschwitz; Heinz on 31 March 1944 and his wife and daughter on 19 November 1942.

Victor Perez (1911–1944) was a Tunisian boxer who was born in 1911 in the French colony of Tunisia. His father sold household goods in a small shop. His family and four siblings lived modestly, in Dar-El Berdgana, a Jewish quarter of Tunis. Even as a child he wanted to be a boxer and copy his Senegalese idol Louis Phal 'Battling Siki' to win the World Boxing Championship. At the age of 14, he started training with his older brother, Benjamin 'Kid' Perez, in the Maccabi organisation, and two years later he won his first officially staged fight.

Victor 'Young' Perez left Tunis in 1927 to pursue his career in Paris where he met Joe Guez, who became his trainer. In 1930, he won the French Championship in the flyweight class, defeating Kid Oliva from Marseille. On 24 October 1931 he won against the American, Franckie Genaro, to become the Flyweight World Champion and the youngest world champion in boxing history. However, intoxicated by this success, he began to lead a dissolute life and fell in love with the actress Mireille Balin. He neglected training and lost his title to Jackie Brown only one year later. Although he changed to the bantamweight class, Perez was unable to repeat his athletic successes.

Despite the growing anti-Semitism in Paris he thought he was safe, but on 21 September 1943 he was arrested, after being denounced, and was sent to Drancy. He was sent to Auschwitz on Transport 60, on 10 October 1943, and then put in Buna/Monowitz concentration camp as a slave labourer. At first the SS let him train so that he could fight in a show fight for their entertainment against a member of the SS. After that, he was treated like all the other prisoners and he was forced to participate in boxing matches for the amusement of the Nazis. By 1945 Victor had survived 140 bouts in fifteen months and won 139.

Perez was one of the prisoners on the death march that left the camp on 18 January 1945. Victor 'Young' Perez died on the march on 22 January 1945; probably he was shot while trying to escape or died of complete exhaustion. He was 33 years old. The Institut National des Sports in Paris named its boxing arena after Victor 'Young' Perez and put up a plaque in his memory in 1997.[28]

Johann 'Rukeli' Trollmann (1907–1943) was a Sinti boxer from Hanover who became German National Champion. From the age of 8 Trollmann showed great talent in the ring and his reputation would go from strength to strength in his teens when he practised with the BC Heros Hannover and BC Sparta Hannover-Linden. Noted for his speed, agility and surprising power, Trollmann became known as 'Rukeli' which stemmed from the Romani word for tree ('ruk'). As an amateur he won four regional championships and a North German championship. In 1928, Trollmann seemed destined to represent Germany at the Olympic Games in Stockholm but he was rejected because of his supposedly 'yellow, non-German style'. This was to be his first, but by no means last, encounter with racism.

Trollmann turned professional two years later in Berlin as he needed to prove himself to the German boxing authorities. In 1932 Trollmann fought an amazing thirty-two times, but while his box office appeal grew he began to draw attention from the Fascist media who labelled him 'the gypsy in the ring'. When Jews were banned, the light heavyweight title was vacated by Jewish boxer, Erich Seelig, who had fled the country. Trollmann had a shot at glory when he was paired with Adolf Witt on 9 June 1933 in a contest for the unoccupied belt.

Witt was the Aryan who would supposedly make light work of his Sinti opponent. However, the 'Tree' was not going to be chopped down easily. Trollmann dominated the fight for six rounds before the chairman of the boxing authority, by now a member of the Nazi Party, ordered that the judges call 'no decision'. There was such an uproar that the judges had to revoke their decision and declare Trollmann champion. This dramatic success saw an emotional Trollmann shed tears of both sadness and joy in the ring. While he was overjoyed with winning the title, his father William had died of a fatal stomach illness earlier that year.

Hitler was known to be an admirer of boxing and was keen to see his idea of 'the master race' being superior to all others, especially Jews, Roma and Sinti, so the sight of Trollmann succeeding agitated the German leader. Predictably, Trollmann's reign was short-lived. One week later he was notified that he would be stripped of his belt for what boxing authorities claimed to be 'disgraceful behaviour' and 'bad boxing'.

The following month, having been warned to change his flamboyant style and told not 'to dance like a gypsy', Trollmann dyed his hair blonde and used flour to whiten his body before taking to the ring and losing against Gustav Eder. It was a courageous show of defiance against the Nazi regime and would be his last act in German professional boxing.

As the Nazi regime exerted their authority more and more vigorously, the Sinti were given equal status to Jews in 1938 with sterilisation the only way of avoiding being sentenced to a concentration camp. Fearful for his life, Trollmann opted for sterilisation and divorced his non-Sinti wife, in order to protect her and their daughter.

Having served time in a labour camp, he was called up to the German Army in 1939 and served in several countries before being discharged for racial reasons in 1942. That summer, Trollmann was arrested in his home town of Hanover and transported to the KZ Neuengamme concentration camp in Hamburg. Here he was soon recognised by an SS boxing referee and ordered to help train the German soldiers, despite long hours of excruciating labour. This turned Trollmann into a frail shadow of his former self. After other prisoners conspired to fake Trollmann's death, he was transported to Wittenberge in 1943, but his boxing fame soon brought more sinister attention. This time he was forced to fight one of the camp's highest ranking officers, Emil Cornelius, and despite years of brutal treatment under the Nazis Trollmann won. It was to be Rukeli's last stand as a fighter. In an act of cowardly revenge, Cornelius murdered Trollmann in front of the other prisoners during forced labour duties.

Johann 'Rukeli' Trollmann died on 9 March 1944 at the age of just 36. One of his younger brothers, Henry, had been killed four months earlier at Auschwitz. Overcome with grief, their mother, Friedirike, died in 1946. His younger brother, Albert 'Benny' Trollmann, who was also a keen boxer and learnt much from Johann, died of a stomach illness in 1991 at the age of 78 in Hanover.

Seventy years after winning the title, his surviving family members, including his daughter, Rita Vowe, and great nephew, Manuel Trollmann, were given his championship belt and he has been posthumously listed officially as a German Champion at light heavyweight. In the summer of 2011 a temporary memorial was erected in his honour in Hanover and Berlin. It was named *9841*, Trollmann's prisoner number at Neuengamme. Sculpture *9841* is in Viktoria Park, Berlin, fittingly beneath the trees. The artists said that the sloped sculpture aimed to represent the struggle that the great boxer faced with such dignity throughout his career and in his later life against the discrimination and terror of the Nazi regime.[29]

Ben Bril (1912–2003) was born in a poor Jewish section of Amsterdam, Netherlands. He was one of six children born to a fisherman father. Bril began boxing at an early age and made the 1928 Summer Olympics, held in his hometown, Amsterdam. A flyweight, he was only 15 years old at the time – the youngest ever competitor.

Bril was good enough to make the 1932 Olympics, but was barred by the Dutch Olympic Committee because he was a Jew and the committee was led by an anti-Semite. Bril earned a gold medal at the Maccabi Games in 1935. He boycotted the 1936 Olympics held in Nazi-governed Berlin. In 1941, the Nazis began deporting a small number of Jews but these increased with time. Bril was deported to Bergen-Belsen with his wife and son. Amazingly they survived the war, but the rest of Bril's family died in the Holocaust apart from one brother.

Bril became a boxing referee, officiating at fights in the Netherlands, Germany, England and Spain, among other places, with heavyweight contenders such as Henry Cooper and Karl Mildenberger.

Bril, who died in 2003, has been honoured with a movie and a biography in the Netherlands, but there is very little about his life in English. The Ben Bril Memorial, a series of boxing matches, is held every year in October in Amsterdam. Junior Welterweight Barry Groenteman, a native of Amsterdam, has participated in the memorial several times. He said:

> It means a lot to me, Ben Bril is a Jewish boxing legend in the Netherlands. It's an honour for me to carry his legacy. My biggest motivation is to tell our story to the world. I'm a very proud Jewish person and very proud to be a Jewish boxer. It's important for me that in 2014 I will win all my fights. And to keep Jewish boxing in Europe alive.[30]

Nathan Shapow (1921–) from Riga, Latvia, boxed from his boyhood. He honed his skills at local Jewish youth clubs and soon fought in amateur bouts.

As the situation worsened for Latvian Jews throughout the 1930s, Shapow became more political and became a follower of Vladimir Jabotinsky. Latvia was contested ground between Nazi Germany and the Soviet Union. Both countries occupied Latvia in the early 1940s.

While in the Riga Ghetto, Shapow was a member of a group called the 'Strong Ones'. These men stole what they could to stay strong and protect their fellow Jews. At one point, with a crunching straight right, Shapow killed an SS officer who had come to kill him.

Shapow was sent to numerous work and death camps where he avoided certain death many times. He was once saved by a man whom he had known from his boxing days. Shapow's ability to steal food kept him well fed relative to other starving Jews, but he always shared his bounty. In the camps, Shapow was forced to engage in boxing matches with other inmates for the enjoyment of the Nazis. In his book, he claims he was quite successful against even professional fighters because of his tremendous power.

He survived to go to Palestine (Israel) and after independence he fought in the new nation's early wars. By the 1960s, he had grown tired of fighting constantly and took part in a few different professions. Later he moved to the United States, where he still lives.[31]

## Swimmers

András Székely (1909–1943) was a Hungarian swimmer who won Olympic silver (200m breaststroke) and bronze (4 x 200m freestyle relay). In the 1932 Olympics he won a bronze medal in the 4 x 200m freestyle relay event. He was also fifth in his semi-final of the 100m freestyle. Székely died in a Nazi forced labour camp.[32]

Lejzor Ilja Szrajbman (1907–1943) was a Polish swimmer who won the Olympic 4 x 200m freestyle relay. He was born in Warsaw to Jewish parents and became a Polish Olympic freestyle swimmer. After graduating in 1929 he joined the army, serving in the Light Artillery Regiment. He won the Polish Championship in the 400m freestyle (1935) and the 4 x 200 freestyle relay (1938), and was also runner up several times. He represented the Jewish Academic Sports Association in Warsaw (until 1933), then Legia Warsaw.

In addition to swimming he was also a water polo coach. In 1936 he was appointed to the Berlin Olympic team. Together with Kazimierz Bochenski, Helmut Barysz and Joachim Karliczkiem he participated in the 4 x 200m freestyle relay, but the Polish team was disqualified after a false start. Ilja died in 1943 in the Majdanek concentration camp.[33]

Alfréd Brüll (1876–1944) was an extremely wealthy and pioneering Hungarian sports administrator and sponsor. Described as an 'Abramovich of the 1910s', Brüll was president of the MTK (Hungarian Training Club) from 1905 to 1940, when it was disbanded by the Fascists. He had been a soldier during the First World War. Alfréd Brüll was founder and president of the MTK from 1905 until 1944.

He was the greatest and best Hungarian sports leader and patron, with a unique record. Alfréd Brüll was one of the founders of MLSZ (the Hungarian Professional Soccer League). He was the president of the Hungarian Swimming Association, the Athletes Association and the Wrestling Association. He introduced several new sports to Hungary such as sailing and car racing.

It is alleged he was the first person in Hungary to own a car and was the president of twenty-six different sport clubs and the Olympic Committee. The presidency was not a paid job at the time, as the person who was doing the most for the club and who was making the greatest financial sacrifices was chosen to be the president.

The MTK was his life. Their stadium was built only as a result of his negotiations with István Bárcy who was the Mayor of Budapest at the time. Brüll financed the building of the stadium entirely with his own funds at a cost of 150,000 korona and this included facilities for swimming, wrestling and athletics. The MTK tried to cover the cost with MTK shares but he returned them to the club. The stadium is still in use by the club.

Alfréd Brüll got in to the leadership of the MTK in 1903, being immediately elected as the vice president of the club. In two years he became the president, a position he kept until the end of his life. In 1941 in the light of the Nazi persecution he offered to stand down as he could not hold this position because of the racial laws and in the team's best interests. However, the players and the organisation would not accept his resignation. Instead they dissolved the Hungária (the professional team's name) because they did not want to carry on without him. The MTK's amateur team kept going for a short period of time, but soon Hungarian anti-Semitic officials banned it.

Alfréd Brüll fled to Switzerland, but he returned as he was erroneously informed that the hunt for Jews had finished. Alfred Brüll's death has never been clarified. It is most likely that he died in Auschwitz, but there is also information with evidence that his death was cause by Hungarian Nazi officials in Hungary. However, one anecdote says (it is not known whether this source is trustworthy or not) that Brüll got into a discussion with Mengele in Auschwitz, Mengele quoted Shakespeare with errors and Brüll corrected him. Supposedly that was why he was sent into the gas chambers.

A final anecdote (whose authenticity has been confirmed by many witnesses) is that on one occasion he had gone to a training session for the footballers. He noticed that one of the groundsmen was not himself. Brüll asked him what the matter was. He told Brüll that his wife was sick and she needed an operation and he had no money left for it. Brüll replied, 'Aren't you ashamed of yourself? Why didn't you tell me that?' So he reached into his pocket and gave the groundsman 1,000 pengö, which at that time was the average worker's minimum wage for a year. 'We, the MTK fans will remember him with love forever.'[34]

A final comment on sports comes from Philip Mechanicus' diary from Westerbork. On 7 July 1943 he noted what he called 'a sensational event', which was the unexpected deportation of Hartog (Han) Hollander (1886–1943), who was a celebrated football commentator. According to Philip he had been given a cushy job as an administrator at a camp for the SS between Westerbork and Hooghalen. He only got the job because of his international reputation – he had a lot of freedom and privileges.

However, his wife made a careless remark – 'a man ruined by a woman'. As a smart retort to the wife of a German Jew, his wife had snapped, 'Times will change and then we'll make you filthy Boches pay for everything':

> Many other Dutch people think like this, but they don't say so, at least not when German Jews are present. It led to denunciation by a Long-Term Resident and a report to the Obersturmführer who found that Hollander's wife had gone a bit too far. He had them both locked up in hut 51, the prison, a small square building and put them down for deportation … The incident reminds Jews to be humble amongst themselves …[35]

The Dutch records show that Hollander and his wife, Leentje (1886–1943), were sent to Sobibór where they were killed on 9 July 1943. They had a daughter, Froukje Esther, who was born in 1915, and in March 1942 married Adolf Henri Waterman. She was killed at Auschwitz on 28 February 1943 – there is no record of her husband being with her.

Han Hollander was one of the Netherlands' best loved, most celebrated and accomplished sports broadcasters. In fact, when he did the radio commentary for a Belgium–Netherlands football match on 11 March 1928, he became the country's first live sports broadcaster as this was the country's first live sports broadcast. His ability to bring the game to life for distant listeners was the source of his popularity.

After completing his compulsory military service, Han began his career working for a railway company. In 1921, at the age of 35, he decided to make his hobby his work and went to work as a sports reporter for the national daily newspaper, *De Telegraaf.*

Several years later, the AVRO broadcast network was looking for a radio reporter for that historic first live broadcast of the Belgium–Netherlands game. The director of the AVRO recalled his army buddy Han Hollander, who could always keep people on the edge of their seats with his sports stories. He asked Han to do the broadcast and so began his career as a live radio sports broadcaster.

Han Hollander also reported live from the infamous German Olympics in 1936, receiving an award of recognition signed by the Führer himself. When the Germans occupied the Netherlands and introduced their anti-Jewish laws Han Hollander did not go into hiding, believing he would be protected by that certificate of recognition with Hitler's own signature. Sadly, that was a fatal error.[36]

The importance of all these sportspeople is that they were the highest achievers in their field, in many cases holding a unique position in their country. They were honoured by national and international recognition. However, their achievements were of no significance when it came to the Nazi racial obsession. They were all Jews and therefore had to be destroyed with their spouses and their little children. Their sporting success, like that of Jesse Owens, must also have been perceived as an insult to Aryan 'superiority'.

It seems as though some people still have a problem with Jews in sport. Ironically, in the summer of 2015 the European Maccabi Games came to Berlin to take place in Hitler's sports campus which was created for the 1936 Olympics. The 'Jewish Olympics' started in 1929 and the decision to hold the 2015 games in Berlin was controversial among both Jews and non-Jews. Over 2,000 athletes from thirty-six countries participated in nineteen different sports.

The history of Nazism and the 1972 murder of Israeli athletes at the Munich Olympics ensured that security was high, with all being accommodated in the Estrel Hotel with round-the-clock police guards. The need was aggravated by virulent anti-Maccabi internet activity by neo-Nazis and some verbal attacks.[37] Jews were warned not to wander around Berlin wearing visibly Jewish items such as Kippot (skull-caps). Blatantly anti-Semitic remarks appeared in the media and one journalist, Silke Burmester, tweeted about 'these Jewish sports festivals' and asked if it included 'Swastika-throw?'[38]

# YEARNINGS AND EMOTIONAL LOSSES

---

Into my heart an air that kills
From yon far country blows:
What are those blue remembered hills,
What spires, what farms are those?

That is the land of lost content,
I see it shining plain,
The happy highways where I went
And cannot come again.

From A Shropshire Lad, A.E. Housman (1859–1936)

The home land of any heart persists there, suffused with memories and mists not quite concealing the identities and lost lives of those loved once but loved most.

Morning in Norfolk, George Granville Barker (1913–1991)

---

Nazi persecution of the Jews meant ceaseless upheaval for most of them. Families were forced to flee abroad or move to alternative accommodation at home, either as ordered by the authorities or to go into hiding. Ultimately many ended their lives, quite alone, in a death camp with no family, friends or personal possessions. Those who were forced to flee their native land to save their lives had to uproot themselves and their families and move to a new country – leaving a home town they may have known all their lives and where their family might have lived for generations, if not centuries. These moves caused enormous heartache which often lasted a lifetime.

Lilli Aischberg-Bing (1886–1983) wrote about these feelings in 1983 when she was 97 – just before she died on 24 April 1983 in Lima (Ohio). She was referring to their departure from Nuremberg in spring 1939. Her mother went with them because she was 85 and could not have adjusted to life without them:

> When we finally left Germany, my husband, my old mother and myself each $2.50 in his pocket, we were still allowed to send out furniture to America. No silver, no oriental rugs, no piano, no German paintings, no German piece of art. We left behind all the things my husband cherished, his collection of old drawings and etchings, an old family Bible, an early print, old miniatures and his own collection of excavations of prehistoric items. That could be forgotten. But not old friends. The separation of lifelong friends, many of whom I never heard of again.

The Americans would not permit them to enter for some time but, as she noted, 'the English Government was kinder', so they arrived in Southampton on 1 April 1939. They lived in a small, cheap hotel in London which was very cold:

> But I want to explain, coming to a foreign country without friends or connections; by and by a cold loneliness takes possession of your heart. How wonderful it is for you, when you can go and see your old friends or telephone them. Even a little gossip can help to feel at home. Did you ever think how hard it would be to miss them? Yes, it is a sad feeling to be without friends, believe me.[1]

Hédi Fried (*b.* 1924) also wrote very poignantly about the pain of having to leave her home – she was 20 when her family were sent to the Sighet Ghetto in Rumania in 1944. In the period when they were waiting each day for the soldiers to come to deport them, Hédi wandered around the house:

> I went to the piano and struck a few chords, to the bookcase and took out some books. Rimbaud, Villon, Géraldy, you can't come with me. Nor my beloved Hungarian poets, Ady and Arany. At that moment I swore a sacred oath: I shall never bind myself to objects; I shall never weep for material things; I shall never mourn the loss of anything that can be replaced by money. Yet I could not but mourn the jasmine brush in the garden, which sprouted nakedly to the blue spring sky. It was there I used to hide when I wanted to be alone; those flowers had comforted me when I was sad.[2]

She went upstairs:

> I went up to my room and looked around. This room had been my home, that had seen me grow from a child to a teenager, that I must now leave, probably for ever. Even if I come back, I shall not be the same person. When I close the door of this room, it will be for ever.

It was a little attic room with two small windows. Through one window
I looked out onto the garden, with my beloved jasmine bushes, apricot and
walnut trees, and the kennel with faithful old Bodri. We could not take him with
us. The other window gave on to our neighbours, where in an identical loft lived
Geza, my first great love. How many times had I not sat in the window till late
at night and whispered words of love to his shadow? Or just looked at the moon
and sighed longingly?[3]

Helga Weiss (1929–) was also a young girl pondering departure from her home in
Prague. She was almost 12 when she and her parents received the summons. The
man tried to calm them down by saying, 'It's for you today, don't be afraid – after all,
it's only Terezin!' The next morning was 7 December 1941. Helga wrote in her diary:

Five o'clock in the morning. The light is on in the living room; my parents are
also up. My underclothes and dress are laid out on the chair. There are some
notebooks on the desk; probably mine from school. On the doorframe opposite
are hooks for the exercise rings. The piano stands in the corner. My eyes wander
around the room from one object to another. Lying on my back, hands beneath
my head, I etch all these familiar things into my memory so they will never
disappear.

We sit down to breakfast – our last. Today everything, no matter what we do,
is the last.[4]

Helga was luckier than most. She survived four camps – Terezin, Auschwitz,
Freiberg and Mauthausen – to come home to the selfsame flat, and while the
original piano was looted when the flat was ransacked and occupied, a piano sits
in the same place as the one on which her beloved father played Chopin. In 2013,
at the age of 83, she was still living there.

Ruth Schwiening wrote poignantly about her father's yearning for home. She
said Lothar Auerbach (1903–1989) was a quiet man and never spoke about his
past. Lothar had married Hilde in 1933. They had three children. Peter was born
in 1933 and the twins, Ruth and Michael, were born in Silesia in 1935. Ruth was
sent to England on the Kindertransport when she was 3 years and 9 months old
on 2 February 1938, but has no recollection of the journey.[5]

Lothar had been a farmer and had bought a piece of land in Silesia in 1929 and
worked hard on the property, while Hilde spent the week in Breslau earning the
money to help furnish the home. They lived there happily until they were forced
to sell the farm at a loss in 1936 because the new laws forbade Jews to own land. He
took his family to Austria in 1936, prior to the *Anschluss*, where he farmed again
in more primitive circumstances with no electricity and running water and was
happy. The choice of Austria has surprised the younger generation, but without the

benefit of hindsight in 1936 it seemed safe and it was a German-speaking country – people hoped Hitler wouldn't last long. 'I am reminded here of a comment Lothar made in his recollections, that the Austrian rule of Silesia before it was taken over by the Prussians in 1740 was more "laid-back and humane". Lothar much preferred the Austrian style to that of the Prussians.'

The new farm was near Wolfsberg in Carinthia. It is quite a remote area, strongly Catholic and proud of its volkstum (heritage or nationality). After Ruth's visit there after sixty-three years, in 2002, they read about the history of the region. It spoke of the 'glückliche vertreibung' (lucky or happy expulsion) of the Jews of Wolfsberg in 1338, following accusations of 'host desecration'. This was explained in a local newspaper in 1938 when the following was printed:

> Carinthia fought off the Jews, already 600 years ago:
> Villach once had the biggest Jewish population in Carinthia. The first expulsion
> of Jews started in Wolfsberg. Those fellow-citizens who lack an understanding
> for Germany's defensive measures against the Jewish race and who are of the
> opinion that this defence is an unheard-of thing of our time are well advised to
> take a look at the history of the past centuries. They would be taught a lesson;
> they would see that it was necessary and salutary to clip the wings of the Jews
> from time to time in order to protect our own people, who through their hard
> work have cleared the land and made it fertile, from the reckless exploitation by
> the alien Jewish race.[6]

Life changed after the *Anschluss*:

> … almost overnight, but in fact the new masters had merely released a catch
> allowing age-old Jew-hatred, created and sustained by the church over centuries,
> to break into the open and to become not only respectable but a patriotic duty.
> The speed and enthusiasm with which the Austrians applied themselves to the
> task of ridding their country of the Jews and appropriating their possessions was
> astounding, the viciousness as witnessed in the streets of Vienna took even Nazis
> by surprise.

The Auerbachs had to leave behind their land, their house, their animals and all their property. It turned out that the country that Lothar had thought of so highly for its 'humane' approach now regarded them as dangerous 'jüdisches fremdvolk', who had to be expropriated and expelled in order to avert disaster for the true 'volk'. Or had this anti-Semitic attitude in fact been part of their cherished volkstum for a long time, just hidden under a thin blanket?

When Kristallnacht came Lothar was taken to Dachau concentration camp. Ten days later, Hilde and the three children received an expulsion order telling them to relocate to Vienna or emigrate. She decided to go to England via Berlin. Hilde must have struggled with the situation, particularly as she was disabled through childhood polio, but she was very determined. She was only allowed to sell some furniture to pay for the train fares to Berlin. She even made representations to the commander of Dachau to get her husband released. He was released between 27 and 31 December, but never spoke about that time. He had been released on the proviso that he left the country and he was fortunate that Frank Foley of the British Foreign Office helped him get a visa. Eventually he came to England and met up with his family, made a new life and gave his children an education – he was very proud of them.

He was always very grateful to England, but one day he surprised his daughter by saying, 'But this is not my real home!'

She said to him, 'Of course it is, Dad. Here you are safe and with people you love and you are secure.'

'Yes,' he answered. 'But this isn't home!'

His daughter said, 'Tell me about home.'

He closed his eyes and appeared to be transported far away:

Home is to me where the mountains are. Home is where the air is fresh, where the pastures are green and the wild flowers sway in the gentle breeze. Home is where I can hear the sound of the cow bells ringing in the distance, where the horses plough the fields, and in the winter the children ski down the snow-covered hills, laughing and shouting. Home is where I can eat apfelstrudel and real bread. The apfelwein tastes so good and the songs of the villagers who dance and celebrate the end of the harvest echo in my ears. Home is where I can speak my muttersprache. Home is all these things and much more. Home is where my heart and soul are and where I will find peace.

He opened his eyes and awaited a response. Ruth asked him if he wanted to go home and he surprised her by saying it was his dearest wish, but:

Not yet. I'm not ready yet. I owe Britain so much and must repay my debt to a country which, without questioning, took a Jew in with his family and gave them a second chance of life. But one day I want to go home.

Sadly, he died before his dream could be realised.[7] He died in Nuneaton on 2 May 1989 and was buried with his wife, Hilde, who had died on 6 November 1983, in the Jewish Cemetery in Coventry.[8]

Another Austrian, the well-known writer Stefan Zweig (1881–1942), was living in Brazil when he wrote his final work, *The World of Yesterday* (*Die Welt von Gestern*). The translator calls it 'his memoir, a quintessentially humane document and a record of European culture in the late nineteenth and early twentieth centuries, [which] stands as a sane, civilised counterblast to the horrors of war ...'

He and his second wife, Lotte, had committed suicide by the time his publisher received the manuscript in 1942. In it he describes his reaction when, walking down Regent Street in London, he read in the *Evening Standard* in November 1937 about Lord Halifax going to negotiate with Hitler in Berlin and he feared what it would mean for Austria. He said his hands shook as he read the newspaper and, although he had been back to Vienna in the autumn, he immediately got a bus to Victoria to get a flight to Austria the next day. He easily got a flight and packed a few items. His friends were surprised to see him back and seemed oblivious of what was going to happen:

> They invited each other to parties where evening dress was *de rigueur*, never guessing that they would soon be wearing the convict garb of the concentration camps; they crowded into the shops to do Christmas shopping for their attractive homes, with no idea that a few months later those homes would be confiscated and looted. For the first time I was distressed by the eternally light-hearted attitude of old Vienna, which I always used to love so much – I suppose I will dream of it all my life ...

He was distressed at his inability to make his chums understand what was coming:

> On those last two days in Vienna, I looked at every one of the familiar streets, every church, every park and garden, and every old nook and cranny of the city where I had been born with a desperate, silent farewell in my mind – 'Never again'. I embraced my mother with the same secret knowledge that it was for the last time. I turned that farewell glance on everything I saw in the city and the country, knowing it was goodbye for ever. I passed Salzburg, where the house in which I had worked for twenty years stood, without even getting out of the train. I could have seen my house on the hill, with all its memories of past years, from the carriage window, but I didn't look. What was the point? And as the train crossed the border I knew, like the patriarch Lot in the Bible, that all behind me was dust and ashes, the past transformed into a pillar of bitter salt.[9]

Incarceration in a ghetto, particularly the Warsaw Ghetto, meant deprivation of so much taken for granted. Invasion of one's space, being surrounded by many people all the time and the unpleasantness of unwashed bodies – Barbara Engelking interviewed many former ghetto residents. Mary Berg wrote in her diary:

> On the other side of the barbed wire it is full spring. From my window I see young girls with bunches of violets walking along the 'Aryan' side of the street.

I can even smell the sweet scent of the buds opening on the trees. But in the ghetto there is no trace of spring. Here, the rays of sunshine are absorbed by the heavy, grey paving stones ... What has happened to my wonderful spring days of earlier years, happy walks in the park and the narcissus, lilac and magnolia that filled my room? Today we don't have any flowers, or any greenery at all.[10]

Abraham Lewin wrote on 18 May 1942:

I can remember a spring day, also 18 May, several years before the war, which has become engraved in my memory ... I was enthralled by the sea of green, the splendour of the tree-lined avenues and the wonderful radiance of the light, the tranquillity. This is why that morning is so deeply etched on my memory. Where can we find today a patch of green, a tree, a field and the chance to walk without terror over God's earth.[11]

In July 1941 Gita Kron in Shavl, Lithuania, was in her home with her husband, Meyer, and her two small daughters. Antanas Stankus was the captain of the Lithuanian Reserve Corps and a devout anti-Semite. His chaps were given free rein to collect valuables prior to Jews being forced from their homes into the ghetto. The mob were in their home and searching for more loot. She hoped they would be respectful in view of her husband's former status as a manager in the leather factory.

As Gita bowed her head, her eyes alighted on her wedding ring. She sought refuge in her happy memories of 3 May 1934. The scene playing out in her imagination was the vivid recollection of her wedding in the garden of her parents' city home, just a short walk away on Basabaviciaus Street. It might as well have been a world away.

One of the Stankus mob discarded a wine decanter and it crashed into tiny pieces as it hit the hard floor of the kitchen. Gita did not move a muscle, for its shattering had coincided with her recollection of the sound of the wine glass breaking beneath the groom's foot as their covenant was sealed. It was an audible replay of those past cries of 'Mazeltov' that greeted Meyer and his young bride, Gita, when they emerged smiling from beneath the chuppah (wedding canopy). It also shut out the present day crash of furniture upended by the search team.[12]

Stephan Lackner (1910–2000), who was born in Paris, was taken to Germany by his family at the start of the First World War. He was born Ernest Gustave Morgenroth and got his doctorate in 1933 at the University of Giessen. He changed his name in 1935 to the non-Jewish sounding 'Stephan Lackner' and developed a good working relationship with the artist Max Beckman, who painted his portrait in 1939.[13]

Emigrating to America in 1939, he returned to Europe in 1943 as a soldier in a tank crew. Returning to the US after the war, he no longer felt like an exile – his family were Americans with German accents. He began to write in English as well as German and visited Europe often. When he completed his autobiography, he concluded:

Now, at eighty-six, I can't leave California anymore. Occasionally I remember the most deeply touching verses in the *Odyssey*. The hero is stranded far from home, pining 'to see just once again the smoke rising from Ithaca's hills and then to die.' Even this last pleasure was spoiled for me by Hitler's cohorts. The sight of smoke rising from a German chimney cannot evoke nostalgia, but only horror.[14]

Josie Levy Martin's parents moved from their home in Montbron in France for safety. Later, Josie was hidden with a nun and her parents hid elsewhere, surviving to take her to America in 1947.[15] Leaving in a hurry, they could only take necessities. Josie knew the story:

How *Maman* had to leave behind the good furniture, the crystal, the fine Rosenthal china. But worst of all they had to leave the toys. How she longed for those unremembered toys. She imagined entire families of dolls, doll houses, and miniature tea sets. She imagined stuffed bears and bright orange balls. Sometimes she would see herself sitting on the floor, surrounded by the beautiful before-the-war toys.

The village shops did not sell toys. In fact, the only toys she played with were those of her friends. Sometimes she would say:

'Tell me again about my toys in Sarreguemines.' Hearing about them was reassuring; it made her feel that she was more like the other children. It made her feel less like a refugee. *Maman* said there had been a blonde doll with a rose velvet dress, wearing white gloves, but that it had not been taken out of its box because it was fragile. 'Why didn't we bring the doll in Papa's car?' she had asked Maman once, 'Dolls! I had to bring more important things than dolls. It was more important to bring clothes, a few pots and pans. The things we needed to live. It all happened too fast. If there had been time or enough space, I'd have packed my Rosenthal china. That's what I should have packed.'

Her mother would look into the distance and recall her own beautiful things wistfully. Then suddenly her mood would change. 'Forget it! It's all gone. We're here, that's what counts. We mustn't feel sorry for ourselves.' Then Josie would be afraid to ask what she wanted to know most of all – why were pots and pans more important than her doll?[16]

I wonder whether Josie's mother knew that the factory where her precious Rosenthal porcelain was made had its own trauma. It had been Aryanized in the 1930s because Phillip Rosenthal, who had started it with his wife Maria in 1884, was Jewish (see Aryanization – pages 338–340).

In maturity, Josie found a therapist to deal with the child who had haunted her adult life. She was already a mother herself, which had brought the sad child back into her life – perhaps all the bears, dolls, picture books and other toys she had bought were the cause. The therapist said she had to acknowledge the sad child as a person.

One day on Sunset Boulevard she saw a porcelain child's tea set with blue forget-me-nots:

> I bought it for her. We unwrapped it together. She was enchanted! Lovingly, she washed and arranged each piece in a dozen different ways on a glass shelf in a sunny window. She drank real camomile tea from the cups. It might have been a magic potion, who knows?[17]

Hans Freund (1907–1943) was Richard Glazar's chum in Treblinka (see pages 208–10). Born on 18 March 1907, he was deported from Prague to Terezin, and on 8 October 1942 deported from Terezin to Treblinka. A textile worker by profession, he probably died during the revolt in 1943. His wife and son were gassed on arrival at Treblinka.[18]

On a day when one of their colleagues, who had been more their leader, was sent to another part of the camp they all became quite emotional that night:

> … I remember we were lying on our bunks; it was not quite dark. It was very quiet. And suddenly Hans Freund said; 'We aren't human any more …' It was something we had ceased to – or never did was something one just couldn't – think about. Certainly we had never talked about it; regret for the loss of one's sensitivity and compassion was something one just couldn't afford, just as one couldn't afford remembering those we had loved. But that night was different …
>
> 'I can only think of my wife and boy,' said Hans, who had never spoken of his young wife and small boy from the day he arrived: 'I never felt anything that first night after we had come. There they were – on the other side of the wall dead, but I felt nothing. Only the next morning, my brain and stomach began to burn like acid; I remember hearing about people who could feel everything inside but couldn't move: that was what I felt. My little boy had curly hair and soft skin – soft on his cheeks like on his bottom – that same soft

skin. When we got off the train, he said he was cold, and I said to his mother, "I hope he won't catch a cold." A cold. When they separated us he waved to me …'[19]

Werner Cahnman (1902–1980), who described his two months in Dachau in 1938 (see pages 201–3), was forced to leave Germany on his release. He went to England in June 1939 and then onto the US. He had five siblings who included three sisters, Eva, Augusta and Liesolotte. From America he made considerable efforts to help all his siblings leave Germany and I believe they did. His youngest sister, who I think was Liesolotte, wrote a poignant note about saying goodbye to her mother, Hedwig.

Werner had previously described the Jewish family's compulsory moves:

Before the Nazi takeover, we were a happy family living in a beautiful house of 14 rooms on the Sophie-Stehle-Strasse in Neuwittelsbach, the outskirts of Munich. In 1938 we had to move to a three-room apartment on Teng Street. Bent on the separation of German and Jewish populace, the Arisierungsstelle [the Office of Aryanization] issued a decree in April 1939, entitled 'The Housing of Jews and Non-Jews,' which gave them a free hand in ordering the immediate eviction of the Jews from their dwellings. In the winter of 1939 my parents and my youngest sister lived in the Teng Street apartment without heat or electricity. Now they were 'voluntarily' vacating these premises. A friend of my father's offered them a room with a kitchenette (but no bathroom) in the attic of his house on Paul-Heyse-Street. My sister told us about the intimate togetherness of those days, filled with alternating moments of happiness, worry, fear, and love, all experienced in concentrated form. She recalled her departure in these words:

'It was at the door of our tiny place that I saw my mother the last time. I said goodbye to her forever! The separation from this graying, unselfish, and kind woman who stood there without tears and lamentations left a never-healing wound in my heart. She could not get herself to come to the station to see me off. Thus the farewell scene was the last unforgettable picture I have of her!'[20]

His parents had to leave that tiny dwelling in March 1941 and were moved to a makeshift camp on Knorr Street, 7km from the city centre and then to Berg am Laim on the premises of a convent. Although the Nazis forbade them contact with the inmates, one survivor recorded that the nuns 'were generous, helpful, even friendly'. The father, Sigwart, died in January 1942 (or possibly 1941) when all hope of emigration was lost. Hedwig was deported to Piaski in Poland in the spring of 1942 where she died on an unknown date.

Piaski is 21km from Lublin, and in 1921 around 67 per cent of the population were Jews. Piaski was the place where the first ghetto in Poland was created in the spring of 1940. It was meant to be a transit camp for Jews being sent to Belzec and Sobibór but the conditions were so terrible that many people died there, particularly from hunger. Those who survived those horrors were murdered in Sobibór after deportations in July and November 1942.[21]

A flavour of life in Piaski was given by Maxime Rafailovitch, who found herself in the ghetto of Piaski in September 1942. She was born in Warsaw but left before the ghetto was built. She lost her family in the Holocaust and went to America from Paris in 1958. Maxime wrote:

> Starved and tormented Jews of this small town begged the guards for bread and milk for their children. After all, not long ago these 'guards' were their neighbors and some Jews had close relations with the local Christian population. Instead of showing compassion these guards cursed the Jews and menaced them with their rifles. The mob standing outside the wires, ready to loot, mocked the Jews and threw stones at them. Almost everybody in this town knew each other.[22]

Gerta Vrbová (*b.* 1927) was a young girl in Slovakia waiting to hear what her father's farmer friend, Mr Pavelka, had come to tell him that was so important. She had a foreboding that they would have to leave their home very soon:

> Sitting there expecting soon to be told to leave home, I tried to observe and commit to memory all the objects around me: the pictures, the little table and my favourite porcelain figurine of a shepherd with a flute. Somehow I knew that these were my last few hours that I would spend in the house that was my home, and that the familiar objects of my happy childhood would soon be but faint memories quite unimportant in face of things to come. My eyes were watering, although I tried to keep hold of myself and did not allow myself to cry. And yet, in spite of my effort to remember my childhood, and all that mattered to me then, later on when I survived I remembered little of my home.

Her musings were interrupted when her father came, looking defeated, and told her they had to leave that night.[23] (See pages 36–41 for the rest of her story.)

Hardy Kupferberg (*b.* 1922) remembered two special aspects about her childhood in Berlin which others have not mentioned:

> [At the time of the Nuremberg Laws] we had a boat, a motor boat, beautiful motor boat. It was taken away before the cars were taken away. The most awful thing, the absolutely most awful thing, was the law to give up our pets. We always had dogs, always. I was raised with a dog, it was a Great Dane. My father was a

great animal lover. My mother had a bird. And after 1935, after the Nuremberg Laws, every few months came out a different law … The pets was absolutely a terrible thing … As we had to give up our pets, the person who brought the pet had to see how it was clubbed to death … My father had to take the dog and the bird … he was requested to see how it was clubbed to death … And this was absolutely horrible.[24]

Laura Varon (1926–) grew up on Rhodes and was sent to Auschwitz, where her parents were killed. She was lucky that she and her three siblings survived the camps and she now lives in the Seattle area in America. Visiting USHMM in 1993, she was shocked to see that their map showing areas suffering Nazi occupation did not include Rhodes, Kos, Corfu or Crete and so she raised the matter with them. She ended her book about the Jews of Rhodes in the Holocaust:

I've not been back to Rhodes since that day. I fear too much I would hear the whispers of my people in its streets. I fear too much I would stand before our house and see my mother at the door admiring the heavy purses of her Purim-costumed children. But most of all, I've not returned because there is nothing left to return to. There is only the shell of what was. There is only now a foreign place, like so many other foreign places I've been.

But I wonder if the Amora tree still stands and if it still shades young boys and girls, full of today's worries, dreams and hopes. I wonder if fathers still tell stories to their children there and if the gypsies still visit in the summer. I don't know that I'll ever have the courage to find out.[25]

Finally, this memoir was sent to me by Berdina Benning (1921–2013), later Elizabeth Jenkinson, in the early 2000s. She had come to one of the early Holocaust Memorial Day events I helped organise in Sheffield, with her daughter-in-law, Gillie Jenkinson, and sent me this afterwards. It is reproduced as she sent it and with the agreement of her three children:

## Holocaust

### 1941 – *A Town in Holland – Nijmegen*

She caught up with him on her way to school – she was 17 – and he an old man in his long black coat and homburg hat. He always dressed like that. As the rabbi of the town Synagogue, it was his uniform. But breaking the monotony of the black was the orange Star of David, sewn on the sleeve of his coat. She was the daughter of the architect who had built the Synagogue for the local Jewish community and they were friends.

He said: *Don't walk with me, it is forbidden. You will get into trouble.*

Tears pricked her eyes – she said: *You are my friend, I will walk with you.*

The park was ahead: normally she walked through it on her way to school. But now there were signs saying 'GEEN JODEN' – 'NO JEWS'. Parks were too nice for Jews, they might pollute the flowers!!

They walked around the park and he said: *The little ones have come to live with us; THEY won't harm us old ones or the very young … more their leader.* His daughter and son-in-law had gone into hiding, trusting that the grandparents and little grandchildren would be left alone.

She said: *I will come and see you both and play with the children.* And he said: *Take care of yourself, leave us alone for your own sake.*
She touched his arm and said: *School is starting – I must go – see you soon!*

He walked away, his Star of David branding him unclean, like a leper.

She never saw him again: The very old and very young did come to harm, and they were swallowed up in Hitler's … 'final solution'.

The parents of the little ones survived; they were the 'lucky ones?' …

I have been able to establish that Berdina's father, the architect mentioned, was Dirk Andries Benning (1885–1957) who worked with Oscar Leeuw from 1908. Oscar Leeuw was commissioned to design the synagogue built in Nijmegen in 1913 on Gerard Noodtstraat, and later in 1921 the walls and buildings at the Jewish cemetery. At that time the synagogue had about 450 members. Because of its closeness to the German border, when the Nazis began persecuting the Jews in Germany some refugees arrived in the town, so there were about 530 Jews resident in May 1940. Deportations began in the autumn of 1942 and finished in April 1943. Only fifty Nijmegen Jews survived the Holocaust, and most had been in hiding – few came back from the camps.

The synagogue was confiscated by the Nazis and used as a warehouse – both German and Dutch Nazis destroyed its contents. The holy Torah scrolls and other ceremonial items were lost without trace.[26] After the war the fifty Jewish survivors could not afford to refurbish the building. It was sold, and from the 1980s it housed the Nijmegen Natural History Museum. However, even as I write, plans and funding are in place for the museum to move and the synagogue is to be restored.[27]

Oscar Leeuw died in 1944 and it seems that Dirk Benning and his son, Pieter (1913–), then ran the firm as D&P Benning and were involved in the post-war rebuilding of the town.[28] Dirk died in 1957.[29] His daughter, Berdina, who was born in 1921, was Pieter's sister and wrote the piece above. Pieter had a twin, Antonius, who died of leukaemia in 1949. This Christian family hid Jews who were on their way to more permanent hiding places in their attic at great personal risk. Her brothers went into hiding to avoid being sent to work camps in Germany.

Berdina came to England in 1946 to marry a British major, Walter Raymond Jenkinson, who had helped liberate Nijmegen – he was forced to spend the winter of 1944–1945 in Nijmegen when Arnhem proved to be 'a bridge too far'. They lived in South Yorkshire and had three children. She had a good life and was much loved. She died in July 2013.[30]

So far as the rabbi goes – that has been more problematic. In spite of considerable efforts, I have been unable to identify him. The only rabbi in Nijmegen at that time was Rabbi Alexander Salomons. Born in 1890, he was inaugurated as the rabbi in Nijmegen on 25 December 1925. He married Rosie in 1921.

They had to leave Nijmegen on 13 April 1943 to go to Amsterdam, from where he was transported to Westerbork with his wife and four children on 20 June 1943. The children were Louis (born 1923), Sara (born 1925), Sprins (born 1926) and Abraham (born 1930). The rabbi was transported to Sobibór on 6 July 1943 on Transport 70 with his wife and three children, and they were all killed on 9 July 1943. However, his daughter, Sprins, was ill and, bizarrely, she was not deported until she was better. The 17-year-old girl was left behind in Westerbork all alone, only being deported a little while later. She was killed in Sobibór on 23 July 1943.

Isaac Wolf, a teacher and the Chazan (Cantor) at the synagogue, was born in 1888. He came to Nijmegen in 1914 when his son, Heiman, was born. His wife, Joanna, died in 1942 in Nijmegen. Isaac was deported to Auschwitz on Transport 44 on 18 January 1943 and he was gassed on 21 January 1943. His only child was deported to Auschwitz and died on 7 December 1943. Heiman was described as a social worker and married. Isaac Wolf's record notes that his house was cleared on 27 March 1943.[31]

Unfortunately, neither man matched the profile of the rabbi in Elizabeth Jenkinson's memoir.

# 21

# CONCLUDING REFLECTIONS

Is it possible to succeed without any act of betrayal?
Jean Renoir 1894–1979, *My Life and My Films* (1974)

What is betrayal? The *Oxford Dictionary* defines the verb 'to betray' as 'to expose (one's country, a group or a person) to danger'. There are also the connotations of 'breach of trust in the sense of broken expectations'.[1] There is no doubt that the Nazis' behaviour was a breach of trust on every level. It was more than shocking and many of those who had supported Hitler in 1933, thinking he could be managed, were as distraught as the rest of the world when the liberators finally opened up the concentration camps in 1945 to the world's newsreels to reveal what Nazism really meant. Herbert Cremer and Luise Solmitz spring to mind.

The previous chapters have detailed the various types of betrayal experienced by the Jews of Europe and North Africa. There can be no dispute that people were living their normal lives, often literally minding their own business, when they were assaulted by the Nazi juggernaut. We know that 6 million Jews were killed by the Nazis, but I have also shown that we cannot comprehend the numbers of others who were destroyed – the thousands, possibly millions, driven to suicide for fear of what was to come or what was actually happening around them and in the post-Holocaust years.

We know the 6 million murdered Jews included 1.5 million children whose lives were not permitted to reach fulfilment. We cannot begin to imagine what those mites might have achieved; nor the generations to come, whose births were not permitted. The little Jewish girls whom the Nazis murdered were born, like all baby girls, with their reproductive organs storing all the eggs for their entire reproductive lives ahead. When the Nazis killed those little girls, the infinite generations destined to follow were also destroyed.

People all over the world were inspired by Paul Cummins' red ceramic poppies planted around the Tower of London in 2014 to commemorate each of the 888,246 British and Empire soldiers who died in the First World War.[2] Nearly twice as many poppies would be required to commemorate the 1.5 million Jewish children annihilated by the Nazis. To mark the 6 million Jews, nearly seven times as many poppies would be needed.

The soldiers in the First World War knew they might die and were encouraged to write letters to their loved ones, which were only delivered in the event of their death. Captain Harry Cromie, aged 19, wrote to his 18-year-old sweetheart, Vera Vereker, the night before he went into battle on the Somme in 1916. Shortly afterwards, he died and Vera later received his letter, in which he explained his feelings to her:

> By this you will know that I have been killed. I meant to ask you to be engaged to me but when I was on leave I was too frightened to say anything – I loved you very much and would have done anything for you.
>
> Ever your own loving boy.

Vera married another, had children and lived to be 91. She kept that letter all her life and gave it to her daughter, Kate, as she lay dying in 1988.[3] In spite of the terrible tragedy of Harry's premature death, he had a chance to settle his thoughts and tell his sweetheart of his love. Such closure was denied the Jews, cruelly separated on arrival at Auschwitz and sent to the gas chambers thinking they were merely having a shower. Thousands, like my grandfather Armin Klein, were picked up away from their loved ones with no opportunity to express their feelings or say goodbye – their families were left wondering what had happened.

As I wrote in the introduction, I want people to understand what the Holocaust was really like and I hope I have achieved that. The ripples created by the Holocaust pebble in the world's pond still undulate. They probably always will, while Yad Vashem receives 4,000 books on the Holocaust each year.[4]

The betrayal of the Jews by the Nazis was so severe that a whole raft of international law came into force after 1945. However, the occurrence of the Holocaust does not mean that appropriate international law did not exist. The pre-1945 international laws were perfectly adequate to protect everyone from the horrors of the Holocaust – the Nazis just chose to ignore them, as subsequent genocides have ignored the new legislation.

Everything that was done to the Jews and the Nazis' other victims was against the existing laws. We will begin with the pre-1939 international law and then look at the post-1945 situation. On the national level, there is a contract between a government and its citizens, which in many cases is unwritten but in other countries, such as France and America, is clearly stated. In Germany in 1919 a new democratic constitution with the principle of all being equal before the law was approved. The new constitution had some interesting clauses, in the light of later events:

> Article 4 – The generally accepted rules of international law are to be considered as binding integral parts of the German Reich.
> Article 109 – All Germans are equal before the law.
> Article 115 – The house of every German is his sanctuary and is inviolable.[5]

As early as 1920, when Hitler led the National Socialist Workers' Party, they were proposing that existing laws 'should be replaced by a German common law' and the 1919 Constitution should be replaced with laws favouring the Aryan national community.[6] We therefore need read no more to know that the constitution did not meet Hitler and the Nazis' view of the world, and was therefore gradually dismantled. It also explains the early dismissal of the Jewish lawyers and judges in 1933 because they would not have agreed with his proposals. It also explains why Jews had to be prevented from being considered Germans.

Hitler also exploited the loophole of Article 48 which gave the president emergency powers:

> In the event that the public order and security are seriously disturbed or endangered, the Reich President may take the measures necessary for their restoration, intervening, if necessary, with the aid of the armed forces. For this purpose he may temporarily abrogate, wholly or in part, the fundamental principles laid down in Articles 114, 115, 117, 118, 123, 124, and 153.

In the UK, we all know that if we own a home and have maintained our legal commitment to pay the rent or the mortgage, no one can legally remove us from it – in England, we say 'An Englishman's home is his castle'. Perhaps this saying goes back as far as the day King John put his seal on Magna Carta in 1215 – 800 years ago:

> No free man shall be seized or imprisoned, or stripped of his rights or possessions, or outlawed or exiled. Nor will we proceed with force against him. Except by the lawful judgement of his equals or by the law of the land. To no one will we sell, to no one deny or delay right or justice.

Only three of the original sixty-three clauses in Magna Carta are still valid today. These are the first clause guaranteeing the liberties of the English Church; the clause confirming the privileges of the City of London and other towns; and the most famous clause of all as quoted above.[7]

So we know that if anyone takes our property, without our agreement and/or by force, that is theft and we are entitled to have it returned. We also have some expectation that our government will speak the truth. We may anticipate some exaggeration, as the UK Cabinet Secretary Sir Robert Armstrong admitted during the Australian 'Spycatcher' trial in 1986:

> Lawyer: What is the difference between a misleading impression and a lie?
> Armstrong: A lie is a straight untruth.
> Lawyer: What is a misleading impression – a sort of bent untruth?
> Armstrong: As one person said, it is perhaps being 'economical with the truth'.

Armstrong failed to mention that the 'one person' was Edmund Burke (1729–1796), the political philosopher and MP. In 1796 Burke wrote, 'Falsehood and delusion are allowed in no case whatsoever: But, as in the exercise of all the virtues, there is an economy of truth.'[8]

The Jews were told complete and deliberate lies about their future and destinations, what they could take with them, what would happen to them and their families. Even at the very end, when they were told they were going for a shower – in Treblinka, the gas chambers were disguised as traditional Jewish bathhouses with roof tiles made by a manufacturer whose trademark was identical to the Star of David, apparently called a 'Molette d'éperon'.[9] The forensic archaeologist who worked at Treblinka told me:

> I did find multiple tiles like this at Treblinka, some still cemented to foundations. The star is not actually the Star of David as it turns out but rather an emblem of a Polish tile manufacturer. Without a doubt though the Nazis modelled the gas chamber on a Jewish bathhouse and these same tiles can be found in other Jewish bathhouses throughout Poland.[10]

In his afterword to *If this is a Man*, Primo Levi corroborated the archaeological evidence from Treblinka:

> You may wonder why the prisoners who had just got off the trains did not revolt, waiting as they did for hours (sometimes for days!) to enter the gas chamber. In addition to what I have already said, I must add here that the Germans had perfected a diabolically clever and versatile system of collective death. In most cases the new arrivals did not know what awaited them. They were received with cold efficiency but without brutality, invited to undress 'for the showers'. Sometimes they were handed soap and towels and were promised hot coffee after their showers. The gas chambers were, in fact, camouflaged as shower-rooms, with pipes, taps, dressing rooms, clothes-hooks, benches and so forth.
>
> When, instead, prisoners showed the smallest sign of knowing or suspecting their imminent fate, the SS and their collaborators used surprise tactics, interven-

ing with extreme brutality, with shouts, threats, kicks, shots, loosing their dogs, which were trained to tear prisoners to pieces, against people who were confused, desperate, weakened by five or ten days travelling in sealed railroad cars.[11]

I consider the lies that were told to Jews throughout their persecution to be an overwhelming betrayal. The failure to tell people they were about to be killed is unforgiveable because the Jews were entitled to know their lives were about to be ended so they could prepare themselves and, where possible, say their goodbyes. On the Auschwitz ramp families were separated, not knowing that some would be gassed immediately.

A recent controversy in the UK media involved Dr Richard Smith, a former editor of the *British Medical Journal*, who stated that cancer was the best way to die. He elaborated, 'You can say goodbye, reflect on your life, leave last messages, perhaps visit special places for a last time, listen to favourite pieces of music, read loved poems and prepare according to your beliefs to meet your maker or enjoy eternal oblivion.'[12] Everyone has their own 'bucket list' of what they would do knowing death was close. The betrayal of the Jews lay not just in their murder, but in the deviousness of the charade that was played out.

After I had written these paragraphs, by chance I came across Isaiah Berlin's opinion on this topic. It was gratifying that such an eminent philosopher shared my revulsion over the deception. Berlin's friend, George Kennan, the American historian, observed that 'what Berlin loathed about fascism and communism was their moral cynicism, their shared contempt for ordinary human beings. Both were guilty of this in the very way they sought to indoctrinate their adherents and liquidate their enemies.' Berlin replied with emphasis on the most sombre example, 'how Nazi executioners had deceived Jews into peacefully going to their deaths by reassuring them that the cattle cars were taking them towards "resettlement" in the East'.[13] Berlin developed his theory further:

> Why does this deception, which may in fact have diminished the anguish of the victims, arouse a really unutterable kind of horror in us? … Surely because we cannot bear the thought of human beings denied their last rights – of knowing the truth, of acting with at least the freedom of the condemned, of being able to face their destruction with fear or courage, according to their temperaments, but at least as human beings, armed with the power of choice.[14]

Ignatieff wrote that Berlin:

> … came to see there was a continuum of denials of the human right to know one's fate and they could lead, he now saw, to the gas chamber. It was not just the Holocaust that led him to this but also Soviet and Marxist philosophy which

made him defend 'the embattled sovereignty of private judgement and the right of human beings to know their fate and meet it with their eyes open'. Here Auschwitz did play a subliminal part. It was the thought of his own people, indecently deceived, going blindly to their deaths, which turned a theme into a conviction, an idea into a commitment.[15]

## International Action

On the international scene, the impression is often given that there was no legislation to create a contract between citizens over their treatment by an occupying force. This is untrue. Before 1939, there were three Geneva Conventions (1864, 1906 and 1929) which have each subsequently been updated at least once, culminating in their latest versions and the addition of a fourth convention in 1949. There were also two Hague Conventions (1899 and 1907):

1  The first Geneva Convention dates from 1864 and, until it was finally updated in 1949, was known as 'The Geneva Convention for the Amelioration of the Condition of the Wounded and Sick in Armed Forces in the Field'. It protected wounded and sick soldiers on land during the war. One of the articles prohibited 'collective punishments', which was a Nazi favourite, particularly in the camps, with hours-long or even night- or day-long roll calls when the numbers did not tally and escapes were suspected.

2  The Hague Convention of 1899 comprised three treaties and three declarations. The second of these treaties contained the laws and customs of war on land[16] and includes the following important articles:

> Article 23(a): which forbade combatants: 'To employ poison or poisoned weapons'.
> Article 46: 'Family honours and rights, individual lives and private property, as well as religious convictions and liberty, must be respected. Private property cannot be confiscated.'
> Article 47: 'Pillage is formally prohibited.'
> Article 50: 'No general penalty, pecuniary or otherwise, shall be inflicted upon the population on account of the acts of individuals for which they cannot be regarded as jointly and severally responsible.'
> Article 53: 'An army of occupation can only take possession of the cash, funds, and property liable to requisition belonging strictly to the State, depots of arms, means of transport, stores and supplies, and, generally, all movable property of the State which may be used for military operations.'

Article 56: 'The property of the communes, that of religious, charitable, and educational institutions, and those of arts and science, even when State property, shall be treated as private property. All seizure of, and destruction, or intentional damage done to such institutions, to historical monuments, works of art or science, is prohibited, and should be made the subject of proceedings.' [Germany ratified this convention on 4 September 1900.]

3  The second Geneva Convention protected wounded, sick and shipwrecked military personnel at sea in time of war, and dates from 1906, when it was known as 'The Geneva Convention for the Amelioration of the Condition of Wounded, Sick and Shipwrecked Members of Armed Forces at Sea'.

4  The Hague Convention of 1907 consisted of thirteen treaties and one declaration. The fourth treaty, entitled 'Convention respecting the Laws and Customs of War on Land', included all of the articles from the second treaty from the first Hague Convention in 1899 highlighted above. This treaty was ratified by Germany on 27 November 1909.

5  The Red Cross was instrumental in the drafting of the 1929 'Geneva Convention on the Treatment of Prisoners of War'[17] which, when updated for the last time in 1949, became known as the 'Third Geneva Convention'. It was seen as completing the provisions of the Hague regulations. The most important innovations consisted of the prohibition of reprisals and collective penalties; the organisation of prisoners' work; the designation by the prisoners of representatives and the control exercised by protecting powers. The people confined in the concentration camps were not designated as POWs, but they were certainly prisoners *in* a war and the regulations specify a standard of care which could have acted as guidelines for these prisoners. Primo Levi refers to the POWs' right to attempt to escape without retribution in his afterword to 'If this is a Man'.

There was only one fleeting reference to civilians, in Article 81 in Part VII, where it states:

Application of the Convention to Certain Categories of Civilians:
Art. 81. Persons who follow the armed forces without directly belonging hereto, such as correspondents, newspaper reporters, sutlers[18] or contractors, who fall into the hands of the enemy, and whom the latter think fit to detain, shall be entitled to be treated as prisoners of war, provided they are in possession of an authorisation from the military authorities of the armed forces which they were following.[19]

Presumably, at that time they did not foresee that ordinary civilians would require protection.

Despite ignoring international law, the Nazis were happy to exploit it when it suited them. For example, in the Channel Islands on 26 June 1942 it was decreed that all wireless sets belonging to civilians had to be handed into the Germans 'in accordance with article 53 of the Hague Convention'. The Germans' authority to do this was queried in Bulletin No. 1 of the *British Patriots*, in which it stated quite bluntly that Article 53 of the Hague Convention did not give the Germans the right 'to confiscate cycles, wireless sets or any other form of personal property'. All the protests were ignored by the Germans and thousands of sets were surrendered.[20]

Later, in October 1944, there were issues over food when the Germans ransacked the islands for food. John Leale in Guernsey and Alexander Coutanche in Jersey protested that taking food from a captive civilian population was a breach of the Hague Convention. Schmettow, who was the military commander, cited 'military necessity' as the justification.[21]

There were two further relevant conventions in international law that were in place in the pre-Holocaust period:

There was the 'League of Nations Convention on Slavery' – although Germany left the league in 1933, having joined in 1926. The Convention on Slavery was signed at Geneva on 25 September 1926 and came into force on 9 March 1927. The preamble referred to earlier agreements such as the General Act of the Brussels Conference of 1889–1890, which dealt with putting an end to the traffic in African slaves; the Convention of Saint-Germain-en-Laye of 1919 and the General Act of Berlin of 1885. It affirmed their intention to secure the complete suppression of slavery in all its forms and of the slave trade by land and sea, taking into consideration the report of the Temporary Slavery Commission appointed by the Council of the League of Nations on 12 June 1924.

The preamble referred to the desire to complete and extend the work accomplished under the Brussels Act, and to find a means of giving practical effect throughout the world to such intentions as were expressed in regard to slave trade and slavery by the signatories of the Convention of Saint-Germain-en-Laye. It also recognised that it was necessary to conclude more detailed arrangements than are contained in that convention and, most significantly in this context, it was necessary to prevent forced labour from developing into conditions analogous to slavery.

There was also work done by the International Labour Organisation (ILO), in Geneva in 1930, in drafting the 'Convention Concerning Forced or Compulsory Labour',[22] which came into force on 1 May 1932 and was called the 'Forced Labour Convention 1930'.

It is now over eighty years since the convention was agreed. In 2014 it had been ratified by 177 countries, but in 1939 only fifteen had signed up. Germany didn't ratify until 1956 and Austria not until 1960. Accordingly, when David Cohen, the co-chairman of the Amsterdam Jewish Council, protested to the Nazis about the imminent introduction of forced labour, Cohen said forced labour was a violation of international law. He was told by Aus der Fünten, 'We'll decide international law.'[23] Cohen was right, because the Netherlands had ratified the convention some ten years before – but Germany hadn't, and surprisingly America still hasn't.

When we consider the diabolical conditions in which forced labourers toiled under the Nazis, some of the provisions of the 1930 Convention are enlightening. In particular it is salutary to read Article 11, which specifies that only men between the ages of 18 and 45 can be made to work and a medical officer should check that they are fit and inspect their working conditions. Additionally, reasonable numbers of men should be left in the community for normal life to continue, thus, not more than 25 per cent to be taken, and respect for conjugal and family ties should be shown. Article 12 specified that forced labourers should not work for more than sixty days in any twelve month period and should be given a certificate of periods worked. The other articles deal with the hours to be worked and the wages to be paid compared with normal workers.[24]

A fine point is made in *Surviving Hitler*, about the so-called slave labourers, particularly in connection with the IG Farben workers at Auschwitz:

> Historically, slaves, whether in the Roman Empire or the Deep South of the USA, were part of the owner's capital, counted together with property and assets. Their lives were miserable, but they were adequately fed and accommodated, just as farm animals would not be allowed to starve. But slave workers at Auschwitz were worked to death, often within weeks, their numbers immediately replenished from the continuous train-loads of Jews arriving at Auschwitz from all over Europe. The diet of 'Buna soup' meant an average weight loss of up to 9lbs a week for each present. Few could live longer than three months before being sent to the gas chambers at Birkenau. By then they were living skeletons.[25]

## Medical Issues: The Nuremberg Code 1947

The Nuremberg Code came about as a result of the 'Doctors' Trials' at Nuremberg which concluded in 1947. In Chapter 15, and elsewhere, I have attempted to give some idea of the horrific treatment imposed on Jews and others unfortunate enough to find themselves in the Nazis' vicelike grip, such as the ghastly negotiations over the purchase price of the Auschwitz inmates used by IG Farben for their grave experiments (see page 390).

The judges at the Nuremberg Military Tribunals introduced the Nuremberg Code, stating:

Obviously all of these experiments involving brutalities, tortures, disabling injury and death were performed in complete disregard of international conventions, the laws and customs of war, the general principles of criminal law as derived from the criminal laws of all civilized nations, and Control Council No. 10. Manifestly, human experiments under such conditions are contrary to 'the principles of the law of nations as they result from the usages established among civilized peoples, from the laws of humanity, and from the dictates of public conscience'.

The code, as drafted, consisted of ten points (see Appendix V), of which the most important for the Holocaust victims is the first – 'The voluntary consent of the human subject is absolutely essential.'

The issue of ethics with respect to medical experimentation in Germany during the 1930s and 1940s was crucial at the Nuremberg Trials and the related Doctors' Trials. Those charged with these horrible crimes attempted to excuse themselves by arguing that there were no explicit rules governing medical research on human beings in Germany at the time, and that research practices in Germany were not different from those in Allied countries. This is why the Nuremberg Code of 1947 is generally regarded as the first document to set out ethical regulations in human experimentation based on informed consent.

However, new research shows that ethical issues of informed consent for human experimentation were recognised as early as the nineteenth century, when such experiments began. Initially these were mostly done without any consent, under an 'ethos of science and medical progress'. However, some patients were injured during non-therapeutic research which led to public debate on the issue. In 1891 the Prussian Minister of the Interior issued a directive to all prisons that the treatment for tuberculosis with tuberculin 'must in no case be used against the patient's will'.

Detailed regulations about non-therapeutic research were first issued in 1900, following the Neisser case. In 1898 Albert Neisser, professor of dermatology and venereology at the University of Breslau, published the results of clinical trials on serum therapy in patients with syphilis. He had injected cell-free serum from patients with syphilis into patients admitted for other medical conditions. Most of them were prostitutes who were neither told about the experiment nor asked for their consent. When some of them developed syphilis, Neisser concluded that the 'vaccination' had not worked, and argued that they had developed the disease not as a result of his actions but because they were prostitutes. Liberal newspapers published the story and a public debate ensued.

Most academic physicians supported Neisser, but the case was investigated in 1898 by the Public Prosecutor and Neisser was fined by the Royal Disciplinary Court. The court ruled that while he might have thought the trials were harmless, he should have sought the patients' consent. The legal judgement concentrated on the question of consent rather than questionable science.

The Prussian Parliament and the Scientific Medical Office of Health also became involved, and issues such as the imbalance of power between doctor and patient were explored. As a result, in 1900 a directive was issued to all hospitals and clinics stating that all medical interventions, other than for diagnosis, healing and immunisation, were excluded if the human subject was a minor or incompetent in some way, or if unambiguous consent had not been given after a proper explanation of the negative consequences. However, this directive was not legally binding.

In 1931 the Reich Minister of the Interior published guidelines elaborating on the 1900 directive, still emphasising patient consent except in emergency cases. The responsibility for all clinical research lay with the director of the institution and these regulations were actually stricter than the post-war codes of Nuremberg and Helsinki, with the prohibition of experimentation on dying patients and emphasis on the patient's dignity.

> The guidelines of 1931 were not annulled in Nazi Germany when unethical experiments were performed by German doctors in concentration camps. Though no other nation seems to have had such ethically and legally advanced regulations at the time, these did not prevent crimes against humanity by part of the German medical profession.[26]

Thus, the doctors at the 1947 trials who claimed there were no guidelines were being disingenuous. These guidelines did exist and should have been observed, even if the doctors' own training, humanity and compassion failed to direct their behaviour. Additionally, the wider legislation made it perfectly clear that the Nazis would have known that their treatment of the Jews was against international law, as well as normal moral and humanitarian behaviour.


## After the Holocaust

Two Jewish lawyers were responsible for groundbreaking concepts after the war. Raphael Lemkin (1900–1959) was Polish and René Cassin (1887–1976) was French. 'Genocide' was only recognised as a concept after the war as a result of the unstinting lifelong work of Professor Lemkin.

In 1941 when the Nazi horrors began to come to light Winston Churchill said in a radio broadcast, 'We are in the presence of a crime without a name', and this inspired Lemkin to create a name. In 1933 he had referred to 'the crime of barbarity' at a League of Nations conference, but he first used the word 'genocide' in 1944 in a paper called 'Axis Rule in Occupied Europe: Laws of Occupation'.

Raphael Lemkin was born on a small farm in Poland to a Jewish family. He became a lawyer, and in his memoirs he referred to the influence of the Turkish attacks on the Armenians in 1915–1916, anti-Semitic pogroms and other histories of group-targeted violence which led him to believe in the need for legal protection for groups. As early as 1933 he was trying to introduce legal safeguards for ethnic, religious and social groups at international conferences without success.

When Poland was invaded by Germany, he managed to escape to America. In 1942 he went to work in the War Department in Washington. He worked on the preparation for the Nuremberg Trials and he managed to get genocide included in the indictment against the Nazi leadership. He was in Nuremberg for the trials when he learnt that forty-nine members of his own family had been killed in the Holocaust.

However, genocide was still not part of international law and Lemkin fought tirelessly for this in the early days of the United Nations, which replaced the League of Nations in 1945. He was successful on 9 December 1948 with the UN approval of the Convention on the Prevention and Punishment of Genocide. However, he did not stop there, spending the rest of his short life urging nations to pass legislation supporting the convention. When he died he was both exhausted and impoverished by his efforts.[27]

In April 1945, in his paper 'Genocide – A Modern Crime', he explained how he created the word. He wrote that:

> Wiping out whole peoples is not new in the world, it is only new in the civilised world as we have come to think of it. It is so new in the traditions of civilised man that he has no name for it.
>
> [He therefore] took the liberty of inventing the word 'genocide'. The term is from the Greek word *genes* meaning 'tribe' or 'race' and the Latin *cide* meaning 'killing'.

He added that it would 'take its place alongside other tragic words like *homicide* and *infanticide*'.[28]

He also explained that 'mass murder' was not adequate because it did not demonstrate the motivation of the crime – particularly when it was based on racial, national or religious considerations. Previously the term 'denationalisation' was used, but Lemkin regarded this as inadequate because it did not cover the biological destruction but merely implied a loss of citizenship, as with the terms 'Germanisation', 'Italianisation' or 'Magyarisation'. He wrote it would be ridiculous to refer to the Germanisation of the Polish Jews when the Germans wanted to eradicate them.[29]

René Cassin, born 5 October 1887 in Bayonne, France, is considered one of the world's principal advocates for civil liberties. As a wounded veteran of the First World War, he was anxious to use his colleagues as a force for peace. In 1918 he founded a charity for men permanently injured in the First World War, called

'The French Federation of Disabled War Veterans', and he remained the president or honorary president until 1940.

After qualifying as a lawyer, Cassin became a professor of law at the University of Aix-en-Provence and then at the University of Paris. He was a French delegate to the League of Nations from 1924 to 1938. There, he pressed for progress on disarmament and developing institutions to aid the resolution of international conflicts. René Cassin persistently worked on the protection of international human rights, urging the creation of an international court to punish war crimes in 1942. He was a delegate to the United Nations Commission on Inquiry into War Crimes (1943–1945) and frequently served as a delegate for the French Government to the UN General Assembly and UNESCO. Cassin was president of the Hague Court of Arbitration from 1950–1960.

Following the atrocities of the Holocaust, Cassin was part of a team of twelve, chaired by Eleanor Roosevelt, widow of the American president, which drafted the Universal Declaration of Human Rights (UDHR). The UN General Assembly approved the declaration on 10 December 1948, when Eleanor Roosevelt said:

> We stand today at the threshold of a great event both in the life of the United Nations and in the life of mankind. This Universal Declaration of Human Rights may well become the international Magna Carta of all men everywhere. We hope its proclamation by the General Assembly will be an event comparable to the proclamation of the Declaration of the Rights of Man by the French people in 1789, the adoption of the Bill of Rights by the people of the United States, and the adoption of comparable declarations at different times in other countries.[30]

The UN honoured and commended Cassin's work with the Human Rights Prize, and René Cassin was awarded the Nobel Peace Prize in 1968.

Within the process of creating the UDHR there were three further agreements called the International Covenants on 'Economic, Social and Cultural Rights' and 'Civil and Political Rights', which were both adopted in 1966.[31]

We also need to note the Convention on the Prevention and Punishment of the Crime of Genocide 1948.[32] The convention promised to prevent genocide, and it contains three main pillars – the state has the main responsibility for protecting populations from genocides; the international community has a responsibility to help states do this; and, in the event that this fails, the international community must be prepared to take collective action to protect the populations. This is significant because the onus is put on the state to protect its population – as we have seen, most of the Nazi-occupied states manifestly failed to do so, except Denmark, Bulgaria and Albania.

The final post-war creation to be considered here is the creation of the International Court of Justice (ICJ) which was formally established by the United

Nations at the first meeting of its General Assembly on 6 February 1946. The ICJ claims that its origins go back to the Jay Treaty of 1794, between the USA and UK, which laid out ways of resolving disputes by means of tribunals.[33] In recent years we have become used to various leaders of genocides on our televisions appearing in the dock at The Hague for lengthy trials, such as was the case for the Bosnian genocide. These processes are important because modern tyrants now know that there is a superior tribunal that they may have to answer to – atrocities can no longer be committed with impunity, although if we accept the proverb 'the wheels of justice turn slowly', the wheels of international justice turn even more slowly.

I was told that in early January 1945, knowing of the advance of the Russians, Adolf Eichmann planned to kill the 70,000 Jews remaining in the Budapest Ghetto – who included my mother and me, a 6-month-old baby. A combination of SS men and the Hungarian Fascists, the Arrow Cross, were to undertake the massacre.

Raoul Wallenberg had been working with Pál Szalay, an Arrow Cross leader, who was a senior policeman and was horrified at his compatriots' actions. Szalay acted as Wallenberg's spokesman with the German officer, General August Schmidthuber. Pál Szalay was sent to tell him that if the planned ghetto massacre took place, Wallenberg would ensure that after the war the general would be held responsible and hanged as a war criminal. The general, aware of the closeness of the Russian troops, rescinded the orders and thus my mother and I were among the survivors when the ghetto was liberated by the Russians on 18 January 1945. Szalay was the only prominent member of the Arrow Cross who escaped execution after the war. Perhaps knowing that retribution may follow *will* stay the hand of a genocidal killer?

Norbert Wollheim (1913–1998) was one slave labourer who fought back in the early post-war period. Born in Berlin, he was the son of a Jew who had fought in the German Army during the First World War. He was a chartered accountant and tax advisor. In November 1938 he helped establish the Kindertransport scheme, which brought around 10,000 unaccompanied Jewish children to England. In March 1943, he was sent to Auschwitz with his pregnant wife and 3-year-old son – both of whom were gassed. He lost about eighty relatives – all killed by the Nazis. He was one of the 25,000 Jews who were forced to build the synthetic rubber plant for IG Farben at Monowitz – also known as Auschwitz III. He was tattooed with No. 107984.

He described how he endured the nightmare by picking lice off his body, keeping himself clean and finding a razor so he could shave and keep up his morale.[34] He described the conditions in Monowitz when he arrived in 1943 and was taken to the Buna-Werke:

> The buildings, except for those in which the directors and senior foremen worked, were mostly unfinished. As initiation, as was the general rule, we were given only the hardest and most strenuous work, such as transportation and

excavation. I came to the dreaded 'murder detail 4' whose task it was to unload cement bags or construction steel. We had to unload the cement from arriving freight cars all day long at a running pace. Prisoners who broke down were beaten by the German IG Farben as well as by the kapos until they either resumed their work or were left there dead. I saw such cases myself ... I also noticed, repeatedly, particularly during the time when the SS accompanied our labour unit themselves, that the German IG foreman tried to surpass the SS in brutalities.[35]

The shortage of food was also a serious issue:

The ration at Monowitz, for which IG was responsible, consisted of one small portion of bread and margarine in the morning and a ladleful of watery 'buna soup' at midday and evening. On average this pitiful diet gave each prisoner around 1,100–1,200 calories a day, resulting in a weight loss of between six to nine pounds per individual per week. Within three months, most inmates were so weakened by hunger and nutritional deficiency that they were incapable of any sort of labour and were selected for Birkenau. Prisoners assigned to the most physically punishing work used up calories more quickly and succumbed much faster, as did those others who either were too weak to prevent their rations being stolen or had to barter it away to make good some fault with their uniform or pay for some essential item or services. Bartering, eating and repairs all had to take place in the brief period between evening roll call and lights out at nine – also the only time when prisoners, if they were desperate enough, could try to get medical attention for their cuts and bruises and ailments.[36]

Diarmuid Jeffreys, the author, explained further in a footnote:

Officially prisoners were allowed almost no belongings, other than their wooden shoes, underclothes and striped costumes. These had all been worn by others many times before and, never having been washed, were invariably filthy, lousy, tattered and torn. Nevertheless, on pain of a beating or worse from a camp guard, any obvious deficiency – such as a missing button – had to be replaced before it was spotted. How prisoners were supposed to do this without the necessary means is anyone's guess, but somehow they found ways.

After his ordeals, in 1951 Wollheim sued IG Farben, saying it was a matter of principle to him that the Germans should pay him for the two years' work he had been forced to undertake. His desire to study law as a young man had been thwarted by the Nazis' anti-Jewish laws, but he won his case in Frankfurt with three German judges. After they heard his evidence and read the 16,000 page transcript, the judges reached the following conclusion:

The fundamental principles of equality, justice and humanity must have been known to all civilised persons, and the IG Farben Corporation cannot evade its responsibility any more than can an individual ...

They must have known of the selections for it was their human duty to know the condition of their employees. Their alleged total lack of knowledge merely confirms their lack of interest in the lives of the Jewish prisoners for whom they had a duty of care, at least during the time the inmates were in their power. There was a duty to do whatever they could to protect the life, body and health of the plaintiff – which they failed to carry out. For that failure, which was at least negligent, the company is liable.[37]

Although he died in New York aged 85 in 1998, he had highlighted a very important legal responsibility.

This, of course, was the Nazis' cunning plan. They dehumanised and depersonalised their victims – turning them into wild animals. They deliberately starved them to such a degree that death was a release and that cases of cannibalism were found – the Nazis deliberately created the desperation that led someone to eat their dead baby, as occurred in the Warsaw Ghetto.[38] That was the betrayal by the Nazis.

The flurry of international legislation that followed the Holocaust indicates the level of concern over what had been done to people by their captors, neighbours and others. The Nuremberg Tribunal created the Nuremberg Principles which defined a 'war crime'. The International Law Commission adopted these in 1950. A reading of the principles clarifies where the Jews were failed in the years of the Holocaust.

When we wonder why Jews did not leave before it became too late, we need to consider the practicalities of the small businessman who could not uproot his business and go to another foreign country whose language he didn't speak. Many Poles did not even speak Polish well, but with a Yiddish accent, which made it hard for them to hide their Jewish origins. The academics and the Nobel Prize winners had their careers in their heads, often they spoke English and had contacts all over the world – it was thus easier for them to move abroad.

The Nazis betrayed the mores of the civilised world and the tenets of Christianity – loving your neighbour as yourself. They also broke the international conventions that were existing at the time. They passed laws to make their actions 'legal', but they were not because the basic contract of a ruler and the citizen had been corroded and broken.

## Further Genocides

While we have seen that the Holocaust could have been prevented by resorting to international law, we have seen other genocides that have not been prevented by the post-Holocaust developments. The victims of these subsequent genocides were betrayed just as much as the Jews in the Holocaust. We all now know that the proud declaration of 1945, 'Never Again', has proved meaningless.

### Cambodian Genocide, 1975–1979

Youk Chhang is now the executive director of the Documentation Centre of Cambodia (DC-Cam) and a survivor of the Khmer Rouge's 'killing fields'. Youk was 13 when the Khmer Rouge came to power. He became separated from his family and was forced into slave labour. He was nearly beaten to death for stealing rice for his pregnant sister – he saw the horrors and betrayals first hand. His mother lost a daughter and seven siblings, and thirty years later she still searches for them in the hope they survived. Chhang survived by eating whatever he could find – all he wanted was a bowl of rice and one good night's sleep.

The DC-Cam, which he has run in Cambodia for over a decade, is the world's largest repository of information on the Cambodian genocide. It holds hundreds of thousands of documents, photos and films, as well as interviews from survivors and Khmer Rouge members. Like the Nazis, the Khmer Rouge kept excellent records as a measure of their success – a kind of trophy. Chhang said:

> At each time when they kill a person, they document it so they can measure their success one step forward. If they kill two, then two step forward. If they kill five, then five step forward. So to them it's a golden file. But I mean, to us it's a crime against humanity.

DC-Cam has located and mapped nearly 200 prisons and 20,000 mass graves across the country – to Chhang the work is critical to preserving memory and promoting justice.[39]

Chhang has only one photograph of his childhood – it is a black and white snap from his sister, Tithsorye's wedding in Phnom Penh in 1968. Of the eight people in the photo, ten years later only Youk was alive. They were some of the 1.7 million Cambodians, over 20 per cent of the population, who lost their lives between 1975 and 1979. Pol Pot died hiding in the jungle, but none of the surviving senior leaders was tried or punished. Many lived openly in Cambodia without restriction. However, in 2013 five leaders were due for trial using material and witnesses collected by Youk Chhang.

One day, Bou Meng turned up at Chhang's office wanting to tell his story. He was an art teacher with a wife and two young children when, in mid-1977, they were taken by the Khmer Rouge to a prison called Tuol Sleng, known as 'S-21'. He never saw his wife and children again. Months later, one of the guards asked if anyone could paint and Bou raised his hand. He was given a picture of Pol Pot and the director of S-21, Kang Kek Leu (known as Duch), said, 'Paint a picture of Brother Number One. If you don't get it right, I will kill you.' When it was done

Duch approved and Bou was ordered to do more. He was on his fourth portrait of Pol Pot when the camp was evacuated as the Vietnamese advanced.

He was lucky to survive. Of the 17,000 inmates who passed through S-21 only twelve survived. Bou's back is scarred from beatings by the guards, but thirty years later he was anxious to testify. 'If people are convicted and jailed, it will bring justice for my wife and others.'

Pol Pot's surviving relatives threatened Youk Chhang, but he refused to be intimidated. He has also confronted the man who killed his brother-in-law and his niece. The man, Chhoung, told him, 'Decisions came from the top down and I obeyed.' They met several times and Youk realised he was not a bad man, but a man who had done bad things because the revolution offered him a better life and society.[40]

## Bosnia, 1992–1995

Kemal Pervanić, born in 1968, is a survivor of the notorious Omarska camp which was set up by Bosnian Serb forces in the early days of the Bosnian War. The camp, nominally an 'investigation centre', was uncovered by British journalists in 1992, leading to international outrage and condemnation.

Kemal's mother was a Muslim, but Kemal himself says he had no religion and as he was growing up ethnicity and religious beliefs didn't matter. However, after the fall of the Soviet Union political groups started to form along ethnic lines and he noticed some of his Serbian neighbours began looking at him differently. A schoolmate who'd always been a good friend would no longer greet him because he was a Muslim:

> In May 1992, the newly named Bosnian Serb Army began targeting Muslims and my village was attacked. I was captured and taken to Omarska camp where the conditions were terrible; there was very little food, no space to sit, and just two toilets for a thousand people. Luckily I was with my middle brother and this eased the pain. But we didn't know whether the rest of our family members were alive or dead.
>
> A lot of neighbours used this situation to settle old scores. One of the guards was my former language teacher, another was a former classmate. Many times people were taken out and tortured. Some never returned. When I'm asked now, how is it possible for people to turn on those they know so suddenly, I tell them it takes a long time to prepare people for the slaughter of their neighbours.

Kemal has returned to the village in which he used to live in the Prijedor area and reports on the intimate, intra-community nature of the violence and expulsions. Like him, other survivors recount being persecuted by neighbours, schoolmates, even their own teachers:

I spent the whole time in a state of terror, but I knew I needed to suppress my feelings in order to survive. I became able to watch someone being slaughtered like a pig without crying. It didn't mean I didn't care, but extraordinary circumstances make you react in ways you can't explain.

After ten weeks three British journalists came to Omarska and the world's press got hold of the story. As a result, I was transferred along with 1,250 survivors to a camp registered by the International Committee of the Red Cross. The facilities were still terrible but I no longer feared for my life. Finally we were released on condition that we left Bosnia and signed away everything to the newly formed Serbian authority.

Following his release from the camps in December 1992, under auspices of the Red Cross, Kemal arrived in England from the Red Cross reception centre in Croatia in February 1993:

When I first arrived in England I couldn't talk about what had happened. I felt frozen and didn't trust anyone. It wasn't until I heard that my elder brother and parents were still in Croatia, and were being treated extremely badly, that I finally broke down. At my blackest moments I imagined killing my torturers and feeling absolutely nothing as I did it. Such an act I knew would destroy me. What saved me during these years was the support I received from some wonderful people.

Ten years later, I decided to return to my village to ask my former neighbours why they'd taken part in the violence. I managed to meet up with two of my former teachers. One of them seemed full of remorse and said he'd never wanted to participate in the Serb National Project, but the other one I didn't believe. He'd been an interrogator in the camps and had clearly enjoyed the job. He wanted me to say that I forgave him, but at that time I couldn't do that because he showed no remorse.

I went back again to Bosnia, and one day during this trip I recognised a former camp guard hitching by the side of the road. I started laughing. My friend couldn't understand why I was laughing, but what else could I do? I didn't want to swear or scream or get violent. I laughed because I remembered the monster this man had been, but now, hitch-hiking alone on a dusty road, he looked almost pitiful. That's what they call the banality of evil.

People describe these people as monsters, born with a genetically inherent mutant gene. But I don't believe that. I believe every human being is capable of killing.[41]

I interviewed Kemal on 11 April 2013 at the British Library. Kemal told me that, at the time:

People were not mobile and stayed in the same area so we all knew other – in my area of NW Bosnia – Prijedor – they were mostly Muslims and Serbs – we went to school together and later went away together looking for work if it was not available locally.

When his father, Smail, was a child late in the 1940s the area was very poor. Children herded cows together in the fields and one day a Serb child was drowning in the river. Smail jumped in to save him – he was a teenager at the time (he was born in 1936 and died in 2007). The chap he saved was always reminding him that he had saved him, yet before the war (1991–1992) he never once warned them about what was going to happen.

Apparently, in his town an illegal police force had been set up six months before they attacked the Muslims in May 1992. This was initiated by Simo Drljaca, who was a member of the Serbian Democratic Party – just as bad as the Nazis. He was the most notorious of the Serb war criminals. They tortured people for sheer sadism and raped women as policy. Simo was indicted by The Hague – however, he resisted arrest and was killed by the SAS on 10 July 1997.

There was intermarriage in urban areas, but even in his rural village two men married Serb women in the 1980s. Those born in the 1960s and 1970s identified themselves as Yugoslavs and were proud of it. Teachers were the most respected profession in Yugoslavia. Kemal thinks it was because after the Second World War the country was so poor that education was the ladder to improving oneself. Teachers were the real role models for youngsters, yet in the Bosnian war they betrayed their charges.

One interrogated Kemal in the Omarska camp. He recognised the teacher, Miroslav Zoric, who had been one of the nicest guys in the school, but he didn't acknowledge Kemal and he did his best to humiliate him. Kemal had long hair, and Zoric mockingly asked him if he was a male or a female. When he answered his teacher's question about the military training he had received during his national service, the teacher sarcastically responded by saying that Kemal was trained to shell the Serbs, even though the training Kemal received was given mainly by the Serbs.

In 2002 Kemal went to see him because he wanted to know why he had behaved like that. He said he had no choice. Kemal pressed him further, and asked him if he had spoken to his students about it. He said he felt no responsibility, but Kemal said he thought he felt guilty – he became an alcoholic and died young, aged only 50, a few years after this meeting. Kemal said there was no coercion and people who refused were detained for a while, but nothing happened to them and they were released. No Serbs were killed for refusing to take part.

Kemal's brother, Kasim, who was six years older (born 1962), went back to the village in 2003. The whole village had been destroyed but family from England helped him to rebuild the house. He is a sheep farmer now, with good health. There

are forty people there now compared with 720 before the war. When he returned
there Serbs asked him about people who they knew had been killed in the war as
if nothing had happened.

When they had been forced out of their home, the neighbours stripped the
houses and took valuables to a warehouse from where the goods went to Serbia.
A film was made by the local propagandists showing how they stripped houses of
their valuables, cars and agricultural machinery, and later neighbours dismantled
the houses and took away the roof tiles, cables, sockets – everything.[42]

I could have slipped Kemal's story into Chapter 3 and changed the names of the
places, and it would not have looked out of place. We read everywhere of peaceful
communities with different neighbours of different ethnicity living side by side for
generations, if not centuries, and then something happens and everything changes.
The stories are so similar, even down to stripping the properties and sending the
loot back home – it could be Germany or Serbia.

Hilary Clinton, when Secretary of State, was invited to speak at a Genocide
Prevention Conference in Washington. She mentioned a visit to Bosnia shortly
after the Dayton Accord had been signed in 1995. She spoke about a meeting she
had with a group of Bosnians:

> And one Muslim woman told me that when the violence started, she asked a
> neighbor whom she knew well, 'Why are you doing this to us? Why is this hap-
> pening?' She said that their families had known each other for many years, they
> had celebrated together at weddings, they had mourned together at funerals.
> And her neighbour said, 'We were told that if we don't do this to you, you'll do
> it to us first.'[43]

## Rwandan Genocide, 1994

Jean Kayigamba was born in 1963 in the south of Rwanda in Gikongoro. He says
that, even then, 'wanton killing of Tutsis was already taking place' and when he was
3 months old, while his father was in hiding, his mother and he were in danger.
Apparently, 'the killers would snatch baby boys from their mothers and throw
them in the flames of the houses they had just set on fire'. At that time it had been
calculated that around 7,000 Tutsis were killed or missing in that area. The government initiated the killings and then decided when to stop it – the populace obeyed.

Most of the people were killed in a way similar to that used by the Nazis in
Budapest – they were wounded and then thrown in the river. In the days that followed thousands of bodies were seen floating down the Nyabarongo River. Jean's
immediate family survived and rebuilt their lives, but the neighbours hated them
because they lived in a house with a tiled roof instead of a grass-thatched one
like most people and his father was running a small business. People thought they
were better off, and in the years before the 1994 genocide the children of their

Hutu neighbours would tell Jean's siblings that they would kill them and take the house – echoes of Marushka. (See page 37)

As he grew up he was aware of discrimination and a strict quota system. As Tutsis were only 14 per cent of the population, only that percentage of Tutsis were allowed to pursue higher education. In primary school, the Tutsi and Hutu children were continually made to identify themselves, even when they were too young to know. The Hutu classmates called them names like 'inyenzi' (cockroaches) and 'inzoka' (snakes), which was derogatory and humiliating.

When he left primary school Jean couldn't progress because of the quota, but he managed to get a place at the Junior Seminary of Butare which was a Catholic institution. He was shocked to find that even there the discrimination between the two groups continued. Each stage of his education was thwarted by discrimination and when he finally got a university place in 1983 there was continual harassment from Hutus. When he was a year into his MA (1990) war broke out and 8,000 men and women were arrested and imprisoned – they were mostly released after international pressure.

Jean stresses that were three decades of attacks on the Tutsis from 1959 – they were in 1960–1961, 1963, 1967, 1972–1973, 1990 and finally in 1994. There were no repercussions from the earlier attacks, and therefore the attackers of 1994 were confident that they could act with impunity.

Jean exemplifies the situation by writing that his parents had been married in 1959, and his mother's wedding shoes were stolen by one of their Hutu neighbours in the 1963 attacks. His mother could see her wearing them but did not dare claim them back because of the trouble it would cause.

Jean was in Kigali, the capital, when the genocide broke out on 6 April 1994. Life had become difficult for Tutsis since the start of that year. A plane carrying both the Rwandan and Burundi presidents was shot down and both men were killed. A state of emergency was declared and everyone was told to stay indoors – that night the massacres started.

These different genocides have many similarities in the way people responded. In all cases, individuals responded to a call from above to kill people in their area – neighbours and friends whom they may have known well and had previous good relations with. The ethnic or religious differences were exploited and people were treated with unimaginable cruelty.

## Refusal to Comply with the Betrayal

The question of why people didn't fight back or refuse to comply are often raised
with the benefit of hindsight. We speculate on what would have happened had
more people refused to conform to the Nazis. Some of those who did, suffered the
consequences – others, like Wichard von Bredow (1888–1957), did not.

Bredow was the Landrat of the district of Schlossberg in East Prussia and received
notice in November 1938 that he was to order the burning of the synagogue. The
family records the events:

> Wichard von Bredow put on his army uniform and told his wife, 'I'm going to
> the synagogue in Schirwindt, where I want to prevent one of the greatest crimes
> in my district.' When Nazi arsonists arrived at the synagogue, von Bredow was
> waiting for them with his revolver. The group left and the synagogue was saved,
> the only one in the district that survived. Von Bredow was never punished and
> remained the county officer throughout the war.[44]

On 8 September 1942 in the House of Commons, Winston Churchill expressed
his horror at 'the most bestial, the most squalid and the most senseless of all their
offences, namely the mass deportation of Jews from France'.[45]

In the Lyons area of France there were a lot of protests about the deportation
of Jews and the army was asked to help with their transfer. On 29 August 1942
General Robert de Saint-Vincent (1882–1954), Vichy military commander in the
XIV region (Lyon-Grenoble district), was asked by the local police chief to order
his soldiers to initiate mass arrests of Jews and help with the movement of Jews
to the train for deportation. The general refused: 'Never in my life will I lend my
troops for an operation like that.'[46] He was dismissed on 31 August with Pétain's
approval and it was reported in *The Times* on 9 September 1942.

Otto Weidt (1883–1947) was a remarkable German man who employed Jews
in his Berlin brush factory. When one of his employees, Alice Licht, was deported
to Auschwitz, the card she pushed through the floorboards of the cattle wagon
transporting her and her entire family to Auschwitz was miraculously received
by Weidt. He immediately rushed to Auschwitz to try to get her released. She
managed to escape from a forced march, reaching a safe house organised by Weidt.
He disobeyed Nazi instructions to sell all his products to them and sold them
elsewhere, using the funds to buy luxuries to bribe the Nazis to ignore his Jewish
employees. He was a remarkable man – an anarchist and very anti-Hitler, and saved
dozens of Jews in spite of being blind.[47]

Johannes Fest (1898–1960) refused to join the Nazi Party, which cost him his
teaching post. He explained to his young sons why, but they all suffered and his
wife pleaded with him to toe the line for the sake of the family. He refused. His

son, Joachim, wrote about those times and the title of his book, *Not Me*, is taken
from his father's favourite Latin phrase. Fest senior summoned Joachim and his
elder brother into his study in 1936 to explain his position. He made them write
down a Latin phrase, '*Etiam si omnes – ego non*' (in English, 'Even if all others do –
I will not').[48]

Joachim Fest (1926–2006) grew up in this middle-class family in Berlin and his
father was 'a thoroughly civilised and decent man, out of the pages of Thomas
Mann. A headmaster and book-lover, married with five children …'[49] Johannes
sacrificed his job, and the implications for the family were severe. Joachim wrote
of his father, 'One of the most shocking things for him had been to realise that it
was completely unpredictable how a neighbour, colleague or even a friend might
behave when it came to moral decisions.'

By 1936 their neighbours had either resigned themselves to Hitler or were
enjoying the favours offered by the regime. 'Herr Patzek reported, delightedly, that
for the first time he could hear Willi Domgraf-Fassbender and Elly Ney for an
affordable price …' They also had to put up with the block warden (blockwaerter),
Fengler, turning up at whim to check on their Sunday meal – to make sure they
were observing the austerity regulations by eating their monthly regulated hotpot
(eintopf). Apparently it was Goebbels who introduced this measure as the food
in his own home was always austere – perhaps to compensate for his wardrobe of
500 suits …[50]

Like Jews, the Fests had to be careful about everything, because of the constant
risk of betrayal. Surprisingly, fifteen times during the war a disguised voice from a
public call box warned, 'You're going to have visitors!' minutes before a Gestapo
visit. It just gave time to hide a book on Winston Churchill or move the radio
dial to the German station (listening to Allied radio stations brought two years
in prison). After the war Johannes asked Fengler about the warning calls and he
grudgingly admitted it had been him. Asked why, he replied, 'Perhaps, because it
was the decent thing to do.'

Johannes was a lover of fine language:

> I remember the phrase with which, during Hitler's Reich, he had often com-
> mented on some arbitrary decision by insignificant people who had suddenly
> acquired power. It was 'Endure the clowns!' and it soon became a motto with
> proverbial force in our family. At any rate given his propensity for formulae as
> signposts, Father recommended the phrase to us as a guiding principle for the
> coming years, perhaps for the rest of our lives.[51]

The question of why the Nazis attracted so much support will always be discussed.
Fest writes that, like all groups with money who used force, 'it attracted opportun-
ists'. This is confirmed, he claimed, by the mass defections of spring 1933 when

thousands flocked to the party and then its complete disappearance in 1945. No one wants to be associated with a lost cause:

> For years people had ignored the atrocities of the regime and fawned on those in power: senior civil servants, employers, generals and the rest. Each person soothed his conscience in his own way. The conduct of the actress Adele Sandrock will always represent the exception. At 'afternoon tea for the ladies' at the Reich Chancellery, when Hitler burst out with invective against the Jews, she interrupted him: 'My Führer! In my presence not a word against the Jews, please! All my life they have been my best lovers!' But perhaps this was only an anecdote passed on in a whisper. Then one put the Party badge in one's buttonhole. Then one went to cheer along with rest.[52]

The hypothetical question of what would have happened if there had been more Johannes Fests cannot be answered, but research for the book made it clear that the Nazis needed support from local authorities in the occupied countries because they lacked adequate manpower to carry out their plans without it.

Jews who were forced to collaborate, like those drafted into the Nazis' Judenräte, had no choice. Many thought they were helping to alleviate the Nazi excesses. Their role will always be controversial and they could never win. Rumkowski, the leader of the Łódź Ghetto, is dealt with elsewhere (see pages 99–102). Ugo Foà, the leader of the Roman Jewish Community, was criticised for letting the list of Roman Jews get into German hands.[53]

Claude Lanzmann, director of the *Shoah* documentary, has just completed a film about Rabbi Benjamin Murmelstein (1905–1989), who was head of the Judenrät at Theresienstadt and had to deal with Eichmann, who wanted to liquidate the ghetto. In December 2013 Lanzmann, who interviewed Murmelstein in 1975, said:

> I began to understand the fundamental problem of the councils, who were required to collaborate with Germans. They had no choice – no choice at all. The role of 'collaborator' is completely false to describe them and define their attitude.

Lanzmann said he was more and more convinced that Murmelstein had been 'unjustly accused by his Jewish brothers'.[54]

The terrible burden these people had thrust upon them was exemplified by the suicide of Adam Czerniakow (1880–1942), who was made head of the Warsaw Ghetto Judenrät. When the Nazis began liquidating the ghetto he tried desperately to save the children in the orphanage, but failed. He returned to his office on 22 July 1942 and took a cyanide pill, leaving a note saying, 'I can no longer bear all this. My act will prove to everyone what is the right thing to do.'[55]

# Who Counted the Suicides?

As I wrote throughout this book about different Jews committing suicide, I wondered whether anyone had counted the suicides resulting from the Nazis' persecution of the Jews? All the people who were fearful of what was to come, or who preferred to die at home with their loved ones – or abroad like Stefan Zweig. After the *Anschluss* on 12 March 1938, the union was overwhelmingly supported in the April plebiscite, but Jews and Roma had no vote. The suicide rate for the first four months of 1938 in Vienna is recorded as:

|  | January | Februry | March | April |
|---|---|---|---|---|
| Non-Jews | 88 | 62 | 213 | 138 |
| Jews | 5 | 4 | 79 | 62 |

These figures show a marked increase in the suicides of both Jews and non-Jews following the *Anschluss*.[56] Viennese Jews were subjected to severe public violence in the aftermath of the Germans' arrival and hundreds of suicides took place, including the historian Egon Friedell who jumped out of the window when he saw storm troopers trying to arrest someone else in his house. Even in England the press reported, 'More Suicides as Austrian Purge Goes On' in the *News Chronicle*: 'doctors and chemists are pestered by people asking for poisons or drugs to end their existence, which seems to have lost all purpose'.

The Nazis were so pleased with this development that Jews signing documents agreeing to leave were told the 'way to the Danube was always open', and when a Jewish shopkeeper committed suicide with his family in Vienna, the Nazis plastered his shop window with placards saying 'please imitate'. The high rate of suicides of March 1938 was surpassed in November after Kristallnacht. The Nazis recorded a minimum of ninety-one murders, but the suicides may have run into 2,000. Kristallnacht made Jews realise they no longer had a place under the Nazis.[57]

As early as 30 December 1934, Berlin-based Dr Hertha Nathorff wrote in her diary, 'Three more suicides by people who could no longer stand the continuing defamation and spite.' She noted many suicides following the introduction of the Nuremberg Laws. In September 1935 she recorded:

A victim of the Nuremberg Laws! Poor girl. She did not have anything but her relationship with the Aryan man … and now this relationship must be broken off. Therefore she took Veronal. And such cases happen every day.

Veronal was a barbiturate used as a cure for insomnia. Usually, it was the Jewish partner who committed suicide, as the courts treated the Jewish partner more harshly than the Aryan partner.[58] Later, on 4 December 1935, she noted:

Miss G. in the surgery, completely broken. She knows nothing of Jews and Jewry. Suddenly they've dug up her Jewish grandmother! She is no longer allowed to work as an artist, and she must give up her boyfriend, a senior officer. She wants something 'to end it all'. She can only groan pitifully, 'I can't go on living'.[59]

Statistics from Mannheim found that between 1 June 1934 and 1 November 1936 eighty-five Jews were buried, of whom eleven had committed suicide for 'political reasons'. In autumn 1937, there was a report on suicides among Berlin Jews. It was found that in the period 1932–1934 there were 70.2 Jewish suicides per 100,000 population, while among the general population this was 48.8. However, the Gestapo intervened and the suicide statistics were removed from the study.

In Vienna, the first transport left for Łódź on 15 April 1941 and nineteen Jews scheduled for this transport took their own lives in advance. In three weeks the Gestapo reported eighty-four suicides and eighty-seven attempted suicides in Vienna.[60]

It should be noted, however, that the suicide rate among German Jews had been higher than among Christians since before the First World War. Professor Marion Kaplan used the phrase 'social death' to describe how Jews were eased out of German society.[61] This can be compared with Ringelblum's 'the deceased on leave'.[62] As Jews became increasingly marginalised, suicide must have seemed more attractive.

Suicides increased after the introduction of the Nuremberg Laws, when Jews and non-Jews in sexual relationships found themselves in a terrible dilemma as we saw in Chapter 17. It is also clear that many young people were able to flee and that the elderly left behind, perhaps isolated, had few options.

Margarete Schwarzstein was the widow of a doctor living in Berlin in January 1942. One evening a local policeman came to her home warning that she had to disappear as the next day she would be taken to the 'east'. She thanked him for his kindness in coming to tell her and reassured him when he begged her not to tell anyone of his warning as he would meet the same fate if it became known. That night she took several sleeping pills and was found dead the next morning, having left a letter to her children. She was doubly betrayed because she had been convinced that her status as a doctor's widow, with her family having lived in Germany since the mid-seventeenth century, would protect her from the Nazis.[63]

My father, Philipp Grunwald (1910–1955), was a forced labourer rounded up by the Hungarian Fascists in 1943. He managed to survive but was very embittered by his experiences. He would not have any more children after the war because he felt this was not a world to bring children into. My mother always said he felt the world owed him something after what he had been through. Life did not turn out well and in June 1955, when I was 10, he committed suicide.

Suicide has, therefore, always been a fact of life to me and in researching this topic, I was surprised to find how little had been written on the subject of these forgotten victims. When I talk to groups I explain that suicides like my father's are not included in the 6 million Holocaust victims. Neither are the several suicides mentioned in this book. Many Jews carried tablets or poison on their person as an insurance – the writer Walter Benjamin used his when his projected escape over the mountains into Spain was thwarted.

Göran Rosenberg is a Swedish journalist whose father, David, a survivor of Auschwitz, walked into a lake near a mental home on 22 July 1960 and died.[64] He had been rescued from an earlier, similar attempt in April 1960 but he had suffered depression and mental health issues for many years. David left his work voluntarily on 4 November 1959. Later Göran discovered that a colleague had made anti-Semitic remarks about never having seen a Jew working and as a result they had a fight. David was concussed and he suffered from headaches and nightmares.[65] Additionally, his claim for reparations was refused and he was accused of 'pension neurosis' (in German, 'Renten-Neurose') by Dr Lindenbaum, the government's investigator. He stated that David's problems were not caused by his time in Auschwitz, but by his desire for reparations.[66] The theory of 'pension neurosis' was clearly refuted in 2005 – too late for David Rosenberg.[67]

Göran Rosenberg reflected on all Auschwitz survivors: 'Every road from Auschwitz is an individual miracle unto itself, as distinct from the road *to* Auschwitz, which is a collective hell shared by each and every one.'[68]

Recent research undertaken in Israel on Holocaust survivors has shown that the attempted suicide rate among Holocaust survivors is higher than among other elderly people – roughly three times higher. The myth had prevailed that survivors 'were hungry for life' and did not often commit suicide. This was based on a lecture given in 1947 by Dr Aharon Persikovitz, a survivor of Dachau, entitled 'The mental state of the new immigrant'. He stated, 'Holocaust survivors do not commit suicide; they heroically prove the continuity of the Jewish people.' This has been accepted as a national myth with generations of Israeli doctors and educators, according to Yoram Barak.

There has been limited study of the association between those who experienced the Holocaust and suicide. Barak, from the Abarbanel Mental Health Center at Bat Yam in Israel, has researched the field. He found that the first report to look at this topic was in a little known Polish language journal in 1976 which contained an article by Persikovitz. Yoram only found another ten studies in the following thirty years.

In contradiction of the usual canard that, in spite of the terrible suffering in the camps, few people committed suicide, Professor Barak stated that 100 people per 100,000 is a high rate for suicide in normal situations. The rate in the camps was about 25,000 suicides per 100,000, which is one in four. Barak said,

'As far as is known, this is the highest suicide rate in human history. We've learnt that religious people in Auschwitz and other camps made formal application to rabbis in the camps seeking permission to commit suicide [suicide is forbidden in Judaism].'[69]

Some of the sources that he found had interesting snippets, such as the research at the University of South Florida:

> ... at each of the five extermination camps, the Nazis created orchestras of prisoner-musicians, forcing them to play while their fellow prisoners marched to the gas chambers. The suicide rate was higher than that of most other camp workers, except for those working on the death details, whose purpose was the removal of bodies of massacred Jews, who had a higher rate of suicide. Many musicians had been forced to watch helplessly as their friends and families were destroyed.

He also referred to my purpose in flagging up this topic:

> ... another group, whose deaths are related to the Holocaust but not always counted in the totals, comprise the thousands who committed suicide rather than face what they feared would be untold suffering ending in death. In 2006, the European Union financed a project to research these victims; despite religious prohibitions against suicide, it is estimated that in Berlin alone, 1,600 Jews killed themselves between 1938 and 1945.

The paper by Barak also discusses deaths by suicide in the camps, but these would have been included in the figures for deaths in the camp.[70] It is the suicides at home before deportation, and afterwards, which are not recorded as victims of the Holocaust and this is a betrayal of their suffering, fear and memory. But for the persecution, they would not have died prematurely by their own hand.

Even in England, J.B. Priestley, in one of his weekly radio broadcasts, *Postscripts*, quoted from a newspaper article on 23 June 1940. He said:

> ... a German woman – like so many thousands of others, the hopelessly mentally distressed victim of Nazi persecution – had been found drowned in the Thames, and had left the following message, 'I have had much kindness in England, but I decided to leave this world. May England be victorious.'[71]

Marianne Ruth Watt (1928–1962, née Grau) was a German Jew who suffered persecution which later traumatised her. Listed as stateless, she arrived in England from India on board the *Cecelia* in 1948, described as a teacher. She suffered from mental health problems and in June 1962 she went to Beachy Head and jumped to her death. I was unable to establish what influence her persecution had had on her suicide.[72]

Stefan Zweig (1881–1942), the most translated writer of the interwar years from Austria, was one of the most famous of the Holocaust suicides. Perhaps the arrival of the Nazis impacted on him so greatly because of his former privileged life. He wrote about his early life in Vienna:

> Even when Lueger, leader of the anti-Semitic party, became mayor of the city, nothing changed in private social relationships, and I must personally confess that I never felt the slightest coldness or scorn for me as a Jew either in school, at the university or in literature.[73]

Having left Vienna in 1934, the day after the Austrian police searched his house, he simply packed his bags and went to London. He became a wanderer. The upheaval of the Nazis deprived him of his security in his career and his social life. He was also obsessed with fears of ageing. One of his close friends, Carl Zuckmayer (1896–1977), fifteen years Zweig's junior, wrote:

> One of his most peculiar characteristics – perhaps it foreshadowed the tragedy of his later suicide – was his inexplicable fear of aging. I have never seen it so intense in any other person, not even in women. At the time of his fiftieth birthday he fell into a profound depression. That was before the beginning of the reign of terror in Germany …[74]

Zuckmayer described how Zweig invited him to dinner in a small Jewish restaurant in Munich to avoid all the fuss that would have occurred to mark his half-century. After a splendid meal over a glass of brandy, Zweig said, 'You know, we've about had what life has to offer. From now on it's a downhill course.' He added that almost ten years later, a few months before he was 60, in New York Zweig said, 'However the war turns out, there's a world coming into which we won't fit any longer.' Carl remarked that he was healthy and untroubled by the financial worries that 'harassed most of us exiles, but before long we heard the news from Brazil of his suicide'.[75]

Zweig never returned to his much loved home and his collections, which his wife Friederike had packed up and sent to him. He begged Carl not to return to Vienna, telling him it was a trap and he should leave while he could take his possessions rather than running for his life. 'Of course he was right.'

After Zweig's joint suicide with his second wife, Lotte, a fellow émigré from Berlin, Dr Ernst Feder wrote to Lotte's brother about the events in Petropolis, where he and the Zweigs lived. Feder (1881–1964) had been the editor of the *Berliner Tageblatt* from 1910–1931. He left for France in 1933, arriving in Brazil in

1941 where he and his wife, Erna, lived five minutes from the Zweigs. In his letter dated 5 March 1942, written only a few days after the Zweigs' joint suicides on 22 February 1942, he told Lotte's brother of Stefan's depression and the somewhat lonely life they led. He was planning new writing but was thwarted by not having his books with him. One day Zweig described their predicament, 'We are in the part of the boat that rolls the least', but the last time Feder saw them Zweig was very depressed.[76]

Anthea Bell is the most recent translator of Zweig's final work, *The World of Yesterday*. She therefore has insight as 'the close work of translation brings one close to an author's mind', and agrees that the suicides may have occurred because he had 'a sense that whether the war was won or lost, the world of civilised culture in which he had lived and worked was gone for ever'.[77] She also draws our attention to an important but obvious point. Their suicides took place in February 1942, before the full horror of what was to come was revealed. Heydrich's Wannsee Conference, which confirmed the Final Solution of the Jews, was held in January 1942 and he would have been unaware of it:

> Details of the death camps and the Holocaust did not leak out to the Western media instantly by any means, in many cases not until after the war. When Zweig was writing, he describes the fate facing a Jew under Hitler in 1939 – deprived of all his possessions, he would be expelled from the country with only the clothes he stood up in and ten marks in his pocket. It was certainly bad enough, but there was worse to come.[78]

It is clear that Zweig was depressed. The delightful social and successful life he had led in Europe could never be recaptured and his beloved possessions were scattered. Even without knowledge of the horrors to come, his life had lost its purpose and pleasure, as signified by the title of his final work posted to his publisher just days before his suicide.

## Removing the Conversion Option

The Nazis' definition of Jews based on race and their grandparents transformed anti-Semitism. In previous centuries of persecution, conversion provided an escape route. Jews who, in previous generations, sought safety from persecution or even social disadvantage were betrayed by this interpretation. Many were caught up in the Nazi trap, even though they regarded themselves as Christians. Even the vicious tentacles of the Spanish Inquisition, which started with anti-Jewish riots in 1390, encouraged conversion to Catholicism. Only those who refused to convert were expelled in 1492 by Isabella and Ferdinand, who signed the order:

[W]e, with the counsel and advice of prelates, great noblemen of our kingdoms, and other persons of learning and wisdom of our Council … resolve to order the said Jews and Jewesses of our kingdoms to depart and never to return.

It has been calculated that a quarter of a million Jews left at that time. Some went to Portugal, only to be expelled six years later, and most went to the lands of the Ottoman Empire, to Istanbul and Salonika. Others went to Morocco and Syria and Tunisia, to Egypt and Amsterdam and beyond. Tens of thousands of others converted to Catholicism and stayed.

Openly practising Jews did not return in large numbers until the late 1950s, when Moroccan independence led tens of thousands to move north across the Mediterranean. When the Moroccans opened their first Sephardic synagogue in Madrid in 1968, Spain's Fascist Government marked the occasion by issuing an official order revoking the edict of expulsion. Portugal passed legislation in 2013 offering Sephardic Jews citizenship, making Portugal only the second country after Israel to pass a law of return for Jews.[79] Spain has now followed, with a new law approved on 25 March 2015 which would offer descendants of expelled Sephardic Jews Spanish citizenship providing they can demonstrate their link to Jews expelled in 1492.[80]

However, the Nazis removed this option – the escape route. Jews who had converted or were the children of converted Jews still fell into their net because of their grandparents, and therein lay the cunning. The Nazis did not want the alien blood in their citizens – originally they were permitted to leave, but later they were to be destroyed with great cruelty.

The Spanish Inquisition was not noted for its humanity but conversion *could* save Jews. However, many continued Jewish practices in secret – and were called 'conversos'. In Portugal, the converted Jews were called 'marranos' (meaning pigs) and practised Judaism privately in their own homes. However, they had to abandon any obvious identifying Jewish practice, such as circumcision, mikveh and the celebration of any public holiday. When a community member died, a minyan gathered at the home of the family members, but made it appear as if their attendance was just done to console the mourners.[81]

Catholicism did make some inroads into the lives of the Marranos, resulting in a unique combination of Jewish and Christian rituals and terms. For example, Marranos worshipped Saint Moses and Saint Queen Esther and celebrated 'Little Christmas' (which roughly coincided with Hanukkah). Marranos also prayed with a Judaised version of the Lord's Prayer. The phrase, 'I enter this house, but I do not adore sticks or stones, only the G-d of Israel,' was muttered before entering a Catholic Church and is still stated. Many of these Marrano practices are still being performed behind closed doors and shaded windows. In 1920, in the town of Braganca, no child under the age of 12 was permitted to attend religious meetings out of fear of the child innocently exposing their secret faith.

In 1987, David Augusto Canelo, a non-Jew, wanted to write a book about the last Crypto-Jews and was only able to obtain interviews with the community members if he agreed not to use their names. Community members still fear being 'tried' by the Inquisition. In 1991, a French TV crew wanted to film the preparation for the ceremony of matzo for a French documentary. The crew was allowed to tape the ceremony, which was still performed secretly. A knock on the door in the middle of the filming scared many of the participants, despite the fact that the Inquisition had ended more than 150 years earlier.[82]

However, the really important factor is that these people were allowed to survive and it is conservatively calculated that 20 per cent of today's Portuguese population is descended from the Marranos.[83]

The Nazis' racial laws set a trap from which, ultimately, there was only one escape, as millions of Jews discovered.

## Recent Writings

Literature on people's reasons for behaving as they did shows that they were often fairly mundane.

In late 1942 the Ukrainian police were deeply involved in the persecution, spoliation and murder of Jews. Their impetus was a steady income and the desire to conform. The German police, who escorted trains from Italy to Auschwitz fully knowing the fate of the deportees, saw it as desirable work because they got extra days' home leave. It seems, therefore, that extra time at home or some regular money was enough to encourage policemen to participate in genocide willingly. One German reserve policeman, who was asked about guarding the trains to Auschwitz, said he regretted that he had not had the opportunity to do/perform such work 'since the guards were allowed to go back home and they got a few days' leave. It also would have been interesting for me to see what was happening there.' Another article about the Ukrainian auxiliary police (Kharkiv) and German police in Northern Italy found that ideology was not the main incentive for most of these policemen.

Another article compared attitudes to Jews in Poland and France and showed that three types of anti-Semitism – traditional/religious, racist/nationalist and leftist – melded together to lead to the Kielce Pogrom of 4 July 1946 (see page 120–1). It was also found that the people who denounced Jews, turned them in or killed them in rural areas were respected, decent and hard-working men. In France it was found that professional, personal and material interests influenced attitudes to Jews.[84]

The postscript to Faith Matters' remarkable booklet on 'Righteous Muslims' states, 'But most of the personal wickedness of the Shoah was not driven by deep ideology and theological convictions, but on small acts of viciousness, lack of empathy, fear, sadism, ignorance, self-seeking and cowardice.'[85]

## The Barneveld Jews

The Nazis did not differentiate between Jews who had made enormous contributions to their countries, like the Olympians or academics, and those who hadn't. They were all Jews, and as such destined for expulsion or death. The only country which appears to have offered particular protection to certain distinguished people was the Netherlands with its 'Barneveld List'. Stephen Frank's family were promised inclusion on the list.

While more than 102,000 fellow Dutch Jews perished in the extermination camps of Birkenau and Sobibór, these fortunate Barneveld Jews were singled out for survival. Jews were desperate to survive, whatever the means. Some went into hiding while family members were rounded up for extermination. A few managed to escape from Westerbork at the expense of dozens who were placed on the next deportation train. Others, while incarcerated at Westerbork, tried to secure positions of importance that would guarantee, at least for the time being, postponement or perhaps even exemption from deportation to the east. The successful ones were called 'the prominent'. Then there were those who managed to survive this most horrible ordeal using their God-given musical or cabaret talents while others were sent to their death. No matter what, survival must have been on the minds of everyone. Only the more fortunate ones were able to find a way out.

A film, *Ein Gelukkige Tijd* (*A Happy Time*), describes the life of the 'prominent' Dutch Jews and was first shown on Dutch TV on Monday, 18 May 1998. The documentary follows the relatively unknown story of some 700 prominent Dutch Jews, referred to as the 'Barneveld Group'. Most survived the Holocaust. They were interned in a castle near the town of Barneveld in the province of Gelderland from the end of 1942 toward the beginning of 1943. These prominent Jews enjoyed certain protection and even limited freedom while at castle De Schaffelaar because of status and because of connections.

The Barneveld Group was indebted to Frederiks, who was the Secretary General for Internal Affairs in the Netherlands before the war and during the Nazi occupation years. He intervened on behalf of the Barneveld Jews. Frederiks asked Rauter, higher SS and police chief, to guarantee the exemption from deportation for a number of 'well-deserving Dutch Jews'. The fanatic Jew-hater, Rauter, refused to do so. Afterwards, Frederiks visited Schmidt, the representative for the NSDAP in the Netherlands. Schmidt approved the deal because of animosity between Rauter and himself; Frederiks got his wish playing one off against the other.

Frederiks finally got permission from the Nazi authorities to compose a list of 'deserving Dutch Jews'. These, together with their families, were to be exempted from deportation to concentration or work camps. Or rather, it was believed these were concentration or work camps. These aforementioned prominent Dutch Jews included, for the most part, scientists, artists, physicians and industrialists, but others were also added to the list of the prominent. Hundreds of others, however, who hoped for inclusion in this much sought after list were rejected.

While fellow Jews were systematically and unceremoniously hauled from their homes and deported via Westerbork to the death camps, these Jews, known as the Barnevelders, found refuge in castle De Schaffelaar. With the exception of a few elderly people, all of the Barnevelders would survive the war, although, in the end, they too were deported via Westerbork to Theresienstadt.

In Theresienstadt, most received the status of prominence once again and a few were even released into the hands of the Red Cross to be transferred to Switzerland. After the war some, not all, of the surviving Barnevelders understandably felt constrained and remained silent about their time spent in the castle.


## Final points

We have seen that the persecuted Jews under the Nazi occupation had few friends, and even those they had – many personal and long standing – mostly faded into the long Nazi night. Most non-Jews were indifferent to the fate of the Jews but were enthusiastic about getting their hands on the Jews' property – whether it was a valuable art collection or a few old rags of clothes. A Jew could be betrayed for as little as a bag of sugar – a symptom of the poverty of the area, or the worthlessness of a Jewish life?

Those who survived received little support or understanding and struggled to retrieve their lives, their homes and possessions – in Poland, survivors were even massacred. Nazis were allowed to continue their careers in the universities and government departments. The struggle for restitution has continued until the current time, and the recent discovery of the Gurlitt collection highlights the struggle to reclaim treasured art collections almost seventy years after the end of the Holocaust. Survivors mostly died before restitution was available. Most had no justice and have been failed by almost everyone, including the international bodies like the League of Nations, created to protect them.

The reality is that 'never again' has only really been observed by Jews and Israelis. They know that ultimately no one else can be relied upon when Jews are threatened and betrayed. The shadow of the Holocaust is integral to the psyche of Israelis, whether from Holocaust families or not. A failure to understand this is responsible for a great deal of misunderstanding regarding Israel's position since it was created by the United Nations in 1948.

The Israeli politicians who lived through the Holocaust were unabashed in proclaiming their beliefs. When Menachem Begin met President Reagan, he is reported as saying:

> My generation, dear Ron, swore on the altar of God that whoever proclaims his intent to destroy the Jewish state or the Jewish People, or both, seals his fate, so that what happened from Berlin … will never happen again.

This view was reiterated by Begin when he appeared on NBC TV in April 1982:

> If they attack us again we shall hit them; because we will not allow – in our generation of the Holocaust and redemption – Jewish blood to be shed again, while those responsible for its shedding enjoy impunity and even luxury. It happened in the Holocaust. It will never happen again.[86]

Whatever the age of the politician, the Holocaust is always there and influences policy. The current level of anti-Semitism and anti-Israel activity in universities is alarming. Baroness Deech, an influential UK academic, declares:

> Although the UK has spent millions of pounds on Holocaust education for schoolchildren, its impact has not been measured – indeed it seems to have failed in that it has produced a generation who cannot see the connection between Nazi genocide and the obsessive condemnation of Israel today, who cannot see the connection between the result of the unprotected status of Jews in the 1930s and 40s, and their need for one state today to serve as a safe haven. Defending Israel should be the pre-eminent moral imperative for all those who condemn the Holocaust today, and who declare themselves free of anti-Semitism. In particular our universities have become platforms for race hatred under the guise of academic freedom.[87]

This failure to recognise the need and right of Israel to exist, and the derision and demonisation of the word 'Zionist' is tragic for all Jews, but particularly Holocaust survivors. It fires the existential fears Israel holds about a nuclear Iran which has consistently vowed to eradicate Israel and also denies the Holocaust. This is why the BBC's Middle East Editor, Jeremy Bowen's Twitter comment about the Israeli Prime Minister, Benjamin Netanyahu, 'playing the Holocaust card' in his speech to a joint session of the US Congress on 3 March 2015 caused so much offence. What did Netanyahu say to incite Bowen's comment?

> My friend, standing up to Iran is not easy. Standing up to dark and murderous regimes never is. With us today is Holocaust survivor and Nobel Prize winner Elie Wiesel.[88]

He merely acknowledged the presence of a distinguished man, a Nobel Prize winner. To describe this as 'playing the Holocaust card' is despicable. Professor Alan Johnson wrote immediately:

> Mr Bowen's idea is that when an Israeli leader mentions the Holocaust he is being tricksy, manipulative, acting in bad faith, 'playing a card' to get narrow advantage in contemporary politics, not really expressing a genuine thought about the Holocaust itself or a genuine fear about a second, nuclear, Holocaust.[89]

The fact that Bowen shows no insight into what he has said and how painful such a remark can be to a people who experienced the Holocaust and, at the time of writing, face an existential threat from a nuclear Iran shows just how little comprehension he has. A German newspaper covered the story citing the concern Bowen had caused added:

> The controversy surrounding Bowen's offending tweet comes just weeks after his BBC colleague, Tim Wilcox, was accused of anti-Semitism and faced calls for his resignation after he told a French woman that 'Palestinians suffer hugely at Jewish hands as well'. His charge was made as he covered the mass rally in Paris following the deadly attacks on the headquarters of the *Charlie Hebdo* satirical magazine and at the kosher Hyper Cacher supermarket. The woman, who was the daughter of a Holocaust survivor, told Wilcox she feared the resurgence of anti-Jewish persecution as seen in 1930s Europe.[90]

Surprisingly, the BBC's problem with Jews/Israel and the Holocaust started very early. Jonathan Dimbleby has only just spoken out about how his father, Richard Dimbleby, suffered censorship over his report on what was found when Belsen was liberated in April 1945. Although 'Millions listening in Britain could hear the horror in Richard Dimbleby's voice as he stepped past the bodies on the ground at the liberated Belsen concentration camp', Jonathan has now revealed that the BBC initially rejected his father's broadcast until he threatened to resign. In addition, once agreed, the broadcast was cut from eleven minutes to six minutes and edited so that the word 'Jews' was removed, even though most of the victims in Belsen were Jewish. Dimbleby ended the broadcast by saying, 'This day at Belsen was the most horrible of my life.' Jonathan does not recall his father uttering 'a single sentence about the war' to him, but 'I know my father was utterly devastated from talking later to a couple of others with him then.'[91]

   When I speak to groups, the question of Israel/Palestine is rarely raised. If it is, I always say that I am not an expert, but I do know that if Israel had existed in the 1930s there would have been no Holocaust, because the Jews would have had a safe refuge. The fact that French immigration to Israel has increased enormously in recent months in response to anti-Semitic attacks, culminating in the *Charlie Hebdo* and Kosher supermarket murders in Paris in January 2015, underlines the point. In all the heartache over these atrocities and the Danish attacks in February 2015, we must not forget the following:

> In Paris, the cartoonists were killed because of their drawings. The police were killed in the line of duty. The Jews killed in a kosher shop were killed simply for being Jews – just as, three years ago, Jewish children in Toulouse were shot in the head at point blank range for being Jewish children at a Jewish school. That is today's world. That is why we do what we do. That is why Dan Uzan Oliv'sholem, our Danish colleague, did his security duty outside a Saturday night Bat Mitzvah party in the Copenhagen synagogue. He died so that others may live.
>
> Let me tell you about Ahmed Merabet, Lassana Bathilyn and Yoav Hattab. Ahmed was a French Muslim who joined the Paris police so he could lead by personal example. He is the policeman who was murdered by the terrorists as he lay injured on the ground outside the magazine offices in Paris. Two days later, the kosher shop was attacked. Lassana is a Muslim from Mali who worked there. He saved the lives of fifteen customers by rushing them downstairs and into a storage freezer. Yoav was also in the kosher shop. He grabbed one of the attackers' guns, but it jammed and the terrorist shot him dead. Yoav was the son of the Tunisian Chief Rabbi. Lassana and Ahmed were Muslims. Yoav was a Jew. They show how connected, and how complex, the world is today.[92]

It is therefore interesting to read the experience of the Palestinian professor from Al-Quds University forced to resign because of opposition to his trip to Auschwitz with thirty Palestinian students. He was called a traitor by his colleagues and so on 18 May 2014 he resigned, and to his disappointment the university accepted his resignation. Professor Mohammed Dajani had hoped the joint programme with Germany's Friedrich Schiller University and Israel's Ben Gurion University would be constructive. While the Palestinians visited Auschwitz, the Israelis visited a Palestinian refugee camp. When one of the students queried studying the Holocaust, he said, 'Because in doing so, you will be doing the right thing.' This comment has resonances with the Fests' blockwaerter, Fengler, who gave them warnings because it was 'the right thing to do'.

Three years ago the professor had written an article in *The New York Times* with Robert Satloff, 'Why Palestinians Should Learn about the Holocaust'. He wrote that it was essential for Palestinian students to study genocide so that they would be 'armed with knowledge to reject the comparison' between Nakba[93] and the Holocaust. This would make peace more attainable:

> Teaching the Holocaust to Palestinians is a way to ensure they do not go down the blind alley of believing their peace process with Israel is as hopeless as one

would have been between Nazis and the Jews. Discussion of the Holocaust would underscore the idea that peace is attainable.[94]

This book is much longer than originally agreed with my publisher. I make no apology for that – this material needs to be read. I wanted readers to understand what really happened under the Nazis and the depth and breadth of the persecution and cruelty endured by the Jews in the Holocaust.

The proofs were read and the printers alerted when, on 21 November 2015, I read about the haul of Holocaust material discovered in a flat being restored in Budapest. Six thousand three hundred documents relating to a Jewish census held in May 1944, which led to Jews being moved out of their homes prior to deportation, were found plastered in walls. My mother's name may be there.

Accordingly, I conclude with the comment made by Raul Hilberg shortly before his death in 2007. Speaking to an audience in his native Vienna, Hilberg always insisted that much more was to be discovered. 'We know perhaps 20 per cent about the Holocaust.'[95]

*Holocaust Documents Trove Unearthed in Budapest Apartment', the *Guardian*, 21 November 2015, http://www.theguardian.com/world/2015/nov/21/holocaust-documents-trove-unearthed-in-budapest-apartment.

# POSTSCRIPT

The story of Leny Jacobs personifies so much of what I have tried to bring to the reader that it seems an appropriate postscript.[1]

Leny Jacobs (née Melkman) was a young, pregnant Jewish woman in Amsterdam when she wrote to a non-Jewish friend, Theo Westerhof, on 19 October 1942. He kept the letter and it was only on his death in 1991 that it came to light. His son determined to try to find the family of the writer to return the letter. The person he found was Ada – the child Leny was carrying when she wrote.

Leny finished her medical studies in 1936 and signed up at the Faculty for Pedagogy in Amsterdam. Theo Westerhof was the secretary and they must have become friendly as they were of a similar age and both had two children.

In the letter, Leny explains that she could not speak to Theo adequately on the telephone about going into hiding. She is concerned about going into hiding herself with the pregnancy and giving her children up to be hidden while she is still around to care for them herself. She is surprisingly realistic about the future:

> The Jews are to be eradicated and it is such foolishness to think that you will be the only one or one of the few who will not be eradicated. And yet you have to believe in that nonsense because it is the only way to keep one's spirits up. The possibility of winning the race against the end of the war seems to become smaller by the day.

In the end, after the birth of her baby, Leny and her three children all went into hiding in different places. Her husband, Jo, who was 34 at the time, stayed in post as head of the Amsterdam Jewish Council's Medical Services. On 29 September 1943 the entire Jewish Council – including Jo – was rounded up and sent to Westerbork. He was killed on 26 February 1945 in Kommando Ebensee, an annex of Mauthausen concentration camp in Austria. Leny was arrested in January 1944, a year after the birth of Ada, and sent to Westerbork. She was sent to Auschwitz and killed on 28 January 1944.

The three children all survived. Leny's brother and his wife took the two older ones, Bram and Poortje, to Israel in 1957. Jo's sister, Gonnie, brought Ada up and took her to Israel in 1955. It was because Ada had registered her parents' fates with the Dutch-Jewish Community Memorial that the Westerhof family could find her and ultimately return the letter to Ada in late 2010. Ada wrote that she had never known her parents and just had a few pictures of them. Her sister, Tsipora, also wrote how touched they were by their mother's letter.

Their cousin, Dan Michman, who is the head of the International Institute for Holocaust Research at Yad Vashem, arranged for the letter to be donated to the Jewish Historical Museum in Amsterdam. He stated that he appreciates the universal value of his aunt's letter. He considers her exemplary in the intimation of her poignant motherly feelings. More, he indicates that Leny was already, then and much earlier than the general public, painfully aware that the purpose of the Germans was the total eradication of all Jews.[2]

# BIBLIOGRAPHY

Abraham, Henry, *We Remember, 'My Account: Holland 1940–45'* (Leicester: Matador, 2011).

Åkerström, Malin, *Betrayal and Betrayers: The Sociology of Treachery* (New Brunswick: Transaction Publishers, 1991).

Alderman, Geoffrey, *Modern British Jewry* (Oxford: OUP, 1998).

Aly, Götz, Peter Chroust and Christian Pross, *Cleansing the Fatherland: Nazi Medicine and Racial Hygiene* (Baltimore: John Hopkins UP, 1994). Translated by Belinda Cooper.

Aly, Götz, *Hitler's Beneficiaries: Plunder, Racial War and the Nazi Welfare State* (New York: Metropolitan Books, 2006). Translated by Jefferson Chase.

Ambrose, Tom, *Hitler's Loss: What Britain and America Gained from Europe's Cultural Exiles* (London: Peter Owen, 2001).

Assouline, Pierre, *An Artful Life: A Biography of D.H. Kahnweiler 1884–1979* (New York: Fromm, 1991).

Bailey, Brenda, *A Quaker Couple in Nazi Germany* (York: William Sessions Ltd, 1994).

Bajohr, Frank, *'Aryanisation' in Hamburg: The Economic Exclusion of Jews and the Confiscation of their Property in Nazi Germany* (Hamburg: Berghahn Books, 2002).

Bak, Sofie Lene, *Nothing to Speak of: Wartime Experiences of the Danish Jews 1943–45* (Copenhagen: Museum Tusculanum Press, 2013). Translated by Virginia Raynolds Laursen.

Barkai, Avraham, *From Boycott to Annihilation: The Economic Struggle of German Jews 1933–1943* (Hanover: UP of New England, 1989). Translated by William Templer.

Barnett, Victoria J., *Bystanders: Conscience and Complicity During the Holocaust* (Westport: Greenwood Press, 1999).

Bazyler, Michael J., and Roger P. Alford (eds), *Holocaust Restitution: Perspectives on the Litigation and Its Legacy* (New York: New York UP, 2006).

Bielenberg, Christabel, *The Past in Myself* (London: Corgi Books, 1984).

Billstein, Reinhold, Karola Fings, et al., *Working for the Enemy: Ford, GM and Forced*

*Labour in Germany during the Second World War* (New York: Berghahn Books, 2004).

Black, Edwin, *IBM and the Holocaust* (London: Little, Brown & Co., 2001).

Bolchover, Richard, *British Jewry and the Holocaust* (Cambridge: CUP, 1994).

Born, Max, *The Born–Einstein Letters 1916–1955: Friendship, Politics and Physics in Uncertain Times* (Basingstoke: Macmillan, 2005).

Browning, Christopher, *Remembering Survival: Inside a Nazi Slave Labour Camp* (New York: Norton, 2010).

Cahnman, Werner J., *German Jewry: Selected Essays of Werner J. Cahnman* (Transaction, 1988).

Caldicott, E., and A. Fuchs (eds), *Cultural Memory* (Peter Lang: Bern, 2003).

Cerruti, Elisabetta, *The Ambassador's Wife* (London: George Allen & Unwin Ltd, 1952).

Cesarani, David (ed.), *The Final Solution: Origins and Implementations* (London: Routledge, 1994).

Charles, Daniel, *Between Genius and Genocide: The Tragedy of Fritz Haber, Father of Chemical Warfare* (London: Jonathan Cape, 2005).

Chesnoff, Richard Z., *Pack of Thieves: How Hitler and Europe Plundered the Jews and Committed the Greatest Theft in History* (London: Weidenfeld & Nicolson, 2000).

Chiger, Krystyna, and Daniel Paisner, *The Girl in the Green Sweater: A Life in Holocaust's Shadow* (New York: St Martin's Press, 2008).

Child Survivors' Association of GB (ed.), *We Remember: Child Survivors of the Holocaust Speak* (Leicester: Matador, 2011).

Cohen, Frederick, *The Jews in the Channel Islands During the German Occupation 1940–1945* (Jersey: Jewish Heritage Trust, 2000).

Curtis, Michael, *Verdict on Vichy: Power and Prejudice in the Vichy France Regime* (London: Weidenfeld & Nicolson, 2002).

Czech, Danuta, *Auschwitz Chronicle 1939–1945* (New York: Henry Holt, 1997).

Davies, Duff Hart, *Hitler's Games: The 1936 Games* (London: Century, 1986).

Davis, Darien J. & Oliver Marshall (eds), *Stefan and Lotte Zweig's South American Letters 1940–1942* (New York: Continuum, 2010).

Dreyfus, Jean-Marc, and Sarah Gensburger, *Nazi Labour Camps in Paris: Austerlitz, Lévitan, Bassano, July 1943–August 1944* (New York: Berghahn Books, 2014). Translated by Jonathan Hensher.

Duggan, Christopher, *Fascist Voices: An Intimate History of Mussolini's Italy* (London: Bodley Head, 2012).

Eagleton, Terry, *Exiles and Émigrés* (London: Chatto & Windus, 1970).

Engelking, Barbara, *Holocaust and Memory* (London: Leicester UP, 2001).

Evans, Richard, *The Third Reich.*

Feldman, Gerald, *Allianz and the German Insurance Business 1933–1945* (Cambridge: CUP, 2001).

Feldman, Gerald, and Wolfgang Siebel (eds), *Networks of Nazi Persecution: Bureaucracy, Business and the Organisation of the Holocaust* (New York: Berghahn Books, 2005).

Fest, Joachim, *Hitler* (London: Penguin, 1974). Translated by R. & C. Winston.

Fest, Joachim, *Not Me: A German Childhood* (London: Atlantic Books, 2012).

Figes, Orlando, *Just Send Me Word: A True Story of Love and Survival in the Gulag* (London: Allen Lane, 2012).

Fink, Fritz, *Die Judenfrage im Unterricht* (Nuremberg: 1937).

Forster, E.M., *Two Cheers for Democracy* (London: Penguin Books, 1976).

Frank, Steven, *The Young Gardener*, Zachor, 2005.

Fransman, John, *Zachor: Child Survivors Speak* (London: Elliott & Thompson, 2005)

Fraser, David, *The Jews of the Channel Islands and the Rule of Law 1940–1945: 'Quite Contrary to the Principles of British Justice'* (Brighton: Sussex Academic Press, 2000).

Fraser, Robert, *From Kaiser to King: A Family Saga* (Perth, WA: Robert Fraser, 2013).

Fried, Hedi, *The Road to Auschwitz: Fragments of a Life* (Lincoln, NE: University of Nebraska Press, 1996).

Friedman, Max Paul, *Nazis and Good Neighbors* (Cambridge: CUP, 2003).

Friedlander, Saul, *Nazi Germany and the Jews, Volume 1, 1933–39* (London: Weidenfeld & Nicolson, 1997).

Fritz, Sonja, *Block 30 in Birkenau* in 'Criminal Experiments on Human Beings in Auschwitz and War Research Laboratories', Lore Shelley (San Francisco: Mellen Research UP, 1991).

Fulbrook, Mary, *A Small Town Near Auschwitz: Ordinary Nazis and the Holocaust* (Oxford: OUP, 2012).

Gilbert, Martin, *The Atlas of the Holocaust* (London: Dent, 1993).

Gilbert, Martin, *The Righteous: The Unsung Heroes of the Holocaust* (London: Doubleday, 2002).

Gluckman, Ann (ed.), *Identity and Involvement: Auckland Jewry, Past and Present* (1990).

Goering, Emmy, *My Life with Goering* (London: David Bruce & Watson, 1972).

Goeschel, Christian, *Suicide in Nazi Germany* (Oxford: OUP, 2009).

Golden, Dina, *Stolen Legacy: Nazi Theft and the Quest for Justice at Krausenstrasse 17/18 Berlin* (Chicago: Ankerwycke, 2015).

Gordis, Daniel, *Menachem Begin: The Battle for Israel's Soul* (New York: Schocken, 2014).

Grabowski, Jan, *Hunt for The Jews: Betrayal and Murder in German-Occupied Poland.*

Grenville, J.A.S., *The Jews and Germans in Hamburg: The Destruction of a Civilisation 1790–1945* (Abingdon: Routledge, 2012).

Gross, Jan Tomasz, *Fear: Anti-Semitism in Poland after Auschwitz* (New York: Random House Paperbacks, 2006).

Gross, Jan Tomasz, *Golden Harvest: Events at the Periphery of the Holocaust* (New York: OUP, 2010).

Grunwald-Spier, Agnes, *The Other Schindlers* (Stroud: The History Press, 2010).

Gutman, Yisrael, *The Jews of Warsaw 1939–1943* (Bloomington: Indiana UP, 1989).

Hamann, Brigitte, *Hitler's Vienna: A Dictator's Apprenticeship* (London: Tauris Parke, 2010).

Halter, Roman, *Roman's Journey* (London: Portobello, 2007).

Handlin, Oskar, *The Uprooted* (New York: Plenum Press, 1993).

Herczl, Moshe Y., *Christianity and the Holocaust of Hungarian Jewry* (New York: New York UP, 1993). Translated by Joel Lerner.

Hilberg, Raul, *The Destruction of the Jews*, Volume I, (New Haven: Yale UP, 2003).

Hilberg, Raul, *The Politics of Memory: The Journey of a Holocaust Historian* (Chicago: Ivan R. Dee, 1996).

House of the Wannsee Conference, *The Wannsee Conference and the Genocide of the European Jews* (Berlin: DBM Druckhaus, 2013).

Hurst, Christopher, *The View from King Street* (London: Thalia Press, 1997).

Hyde, John Kenneth, *Benjamin Fondane* (Geneva: Librairie Droz, 1971).

Ignatieff, Michael, *Isaiah Berlin: A Life* (London: Chatto & Windus, 1998).

Jones, Geoffrey, *Beauty Imagined* (Oxford: OUP, 2010).

Juers, Evelyn, *House of Exile* (Giramondo: Artamon NSW, 2008).

Kádár, G., and Zoltán Vági, *Self-financing Genocide* (Budapest: CEU Press, 2004).

Kampinski, Marian, *Remember Me* (Bloomington: iUniverse, 2009).

Kater, Michael, *Hitler Youth* (Cambridge, MA: HUP, 2004).

Katz, Robert, *Black Sabbath* (Arthur Barker, 1969).

Kershaw, Ian, *Popular Opinion and Political Dissent in the Third Reich: Bavaria 1933–1945* (Oxford: Clarendon Press, 1988).

Klee, Ernst, Willi Dressen, and Volker Riess, *Those were the Days: The Holocaust through the Eyes of the Perpetrators and Bystanders* (London: Hamish Hamilton, 1993). Translated by Deborah Burnstone.

Kluback, William, *Benjamin Fondane: A Poet in Exile* (New York: P. Lang, 1988).

Knuth, Rebecca, *Libricide: The Regime-sponsored Destruction of Books and Libraries in the Twentieth Century* (Westport, CN: Greenwood, 2003).

Kovács, Mária M., *Afflicted by Law: The Numerus Clausus in Hungary 1920–1945*.

Kurzman, Dan, *The Race for Rome* (New York: Doubleday, 1975).

Lasker-Wallfisch, Anita, *Inherit the Truth 1939–45* (London: Giles de La Mare, 1995).

Last, D. van Galen, and Rolf Wolfswinkel, *Anne Frank and After* (Amsterdam: UP, 1996).

Lawford-Hinrichsen, Irene, *Five Hundred Years to Auschwitz: A Family Odyssey from the Inquisition to the Present* (Harrow: Edition Press, 2000).

LeBor, Adam and Roger Boyes, *Surviving Hitler: Choices, Corruption and Compromise in the Third Reich* (London: Simon & Schuster, 2000).

Lee, Carol Ann, *The Hidden Life of Otto Frank* (London: Penguin Books, 2002).

Lehmann-Haupt, Heilmut, *Art under a Dictatorship* (Oxford: OUP, 1954).

Lester, David, *Suicide and the Holocaust* (New York: Nova, 2005)

Levendel, Isaac, *Not the Germans Alone: A Son's Search for the Truth of Vichy* (Evanston, IL: North-western UP, 2001).

Levi, Primo, *If This is a Man* (London: The Folio Society, 2000). Translated by Stuart Woolf.

Levis, Nicholas and Billstein, Fings and Kugler, *Working for the Enemy* (New York: Berghan Books, 2004).

Levy, Ernest, *Just one more Dance* (Peterborough: Mainstream Publisher, 1998).

Lewin, Abraham, *A Cup of Tears: A Diary of the Warsaw Ghetto* (London: Fontana/Collins, 1989).

Liempt, Ad van, *Hitler's Bounty Hunters: The Betrayal of the Jews* (Oxford: Berg, 2005). Translated by S.J. Leinbach.

Lifton, Robert Jay, *The Nazi Doctors: Medical Killings and the Psychology of Genocide* (New York: Basic Books, 2000)

Lochner, Louis P. (trans. and ed.), *The Goebbels Diaries* (London: Hamish Hamilton, 1948).

Logsdon, Jonathan R., *Henry Ford and His War on the Jews* (1999).

Lovenheim, Barbara, *Survival in the Shadows: Seven Hidden Jews in Hitler's Berlin* (London: Peter Owen, 2002).

Macdonald, Lyn, *1915: The Death of Innocence* (London: Headline, 1993).

McDonald, James G., *My Mission to Israel 1948–1951* (London: Gollancz, 1951).

Mallowan, Max, *Mallowan's Memoirs* (London: Collins, 1977).

Marrus, Michael R., *Origins of the Holocaust Part II*.

Martin, Josie Levy, *Never Tell Your Name* (First Books: 2002).

Matsas, Michael, *The Illusion of Safety: The Story of the Greek Jews During the Second World War* (New York: Pella Publishing, 1997).

Matthaus, Jürgen, *Jewish Responses to Persecution, 1941–1942* (Lanham, MD: AltMira Press, 2013).

Mechanicus, Philip, *Waiting for Death* (London: Calder & Boyars, 1968). Translated by Irene R. Gibbons.

Meyer, B., H. Simon and C. Shütz (eds), *Jews in Nazi Berlin: From Kristallnacht to Liberation*.

Meyerhoff, Marianne, *Four Girls from Berlin: A True Story of a Friendship that Defied the Holocaust* (Hoboken, NJ: John Wiley, 2007).

Michlin, Gilbert, *Of No Interest to the Nation: A Jewish Family in France 1925–1945* (English edition) (Detroit: Wayne State UP, 2004).

Morgan, Keith, and Ruth Kron Sigal, *Ruta's Closet* (London: Unity Press, 2013).

Morgan, Ted, *An Uncertain Hour: The French, the Germans, the Jews, the Klaus Barbie Trial and the City of Lyon 1940–1945* (London: Bodley Head, 1990).

Moseley, Ray, *Mussolini: The Last 600 Days of Il Duce* (Lanham, MD: Taylor Trade, 2004).

Nettles, John, *Jewels and Jackboots: Hitler's British Channel Islands* (St Mary, Jersey: Seeker Publishing: 2013).

Odelberg, W. (ed.), *Nobel: The Man and his Prizes* (New York: American Elsevier, 1972).

Orbach, Larry, *Soaring Underground: A Young Fugitive's Life in Nazi Berlin* (London: André Deutsch, 1996).

Osborne, Charles, *The Life and Crimes of Agatha Christie* (London: Collins, 1982).

Owings, Alison, *Frauen: German Women Recall the Third Reich* (London: Penguin Books, 1995).

Paris, Erna, *Long Shadows: Truth, Lies and History* (London: Bloomsbury, 2001).

Penkower, Monty Noam, *The Swastika's Darkening Shadow* (New York: Palgrave Macmillan, 2013).

Perry, George, *Bluebell* (London: Pavilion Books, 1986).

Perry, Marvin, Matthew Berg, and James Krukones, *Sources of European History since 1900* (Boston, MA: Wadsworth, 2011).

Petropoulos, Jonathan, *The Faustian Bargain: The Art World in Nazi Germany* (London: Penguin Books, 2000).

Prochnik, George, *The Impossible Exile: Stefan Zweig at the End of the World* (London: Granta, 2014).

Rees, Laurence, *Auschwitz: The Nazis and 'The Final Solution'* (London: BBC Books, 2005).

Remy, Steven P., *The Heidelberg Myth: The Nazification and Denazification of a German University* (Cambridge, MA: Harvard UP, 2003)

Richarz, Monika (ed.), *Jewish Life in Germany: Memoirs from Three Centuries* (Indianapolis: Indiana UP, 1991). Translated by Stella and Sidney Rosenfeld.

Ritvo, Roger A., and Diane M. Plotkin, *Sisters in Sorrow: Voices of Care in the Holocaust* (Texas, A&M UP, 2000).

Rosenberg, Göran, *A Brief Stop on the Road from Auschwitz* (London: Granta, 2014). Translated by Sarah Death.

Salomon, Charlotte, *Life? Or Theatre?* (London: Royal Academy, 1998).

Sanford L. Segal, *Mathematics under the Nazis* (Princeton, NJ: Princeton UP, 2003).

Sarfatti, Margherita, *My Fault – Mussolini as I Knew Him* (New York: Enigma Books, 2012).

Schaffer, Kay, and Sidonie Smith (eds), *The Olympics at the Millennium: Power, Politics and the Games* (Piscataway, NJ: Rutgers UP, 2000).

Schlemmer, T. (ed.), *Letters and Diaries of Oskar Schlemmer* (Middletown, CT: Wesleyan UP, 1972).

Schuck, H., and R. Sohlman, *Nobel: The Man and His Prizes* (Grizzell Press, 2007)

Sereny, Gitta, *Into that Darkness: From Mercy Killing to Mass Murder* (London: André Deutsch Ltd, 1974).

Shaler, Tracey L., *Frenchy: I wanted to get back at Hitler* (Bloomington, IN: iUniverse, 2009).

Shapiro, Paul A., and Martin C. Dean, *Symposium*.

Shelley, Lore, *Criminal Experiments on Human Beings in Auschwitz and War Research Laboratories* (San Francisco: Mellen Research UP, 1991).

Shepherd, Naomi, *Wilfrid Israel: Germany's Secret Ambassador* (London: Weidenfeld & Nicolson, 1984).

Shirer, William L., *The Rise and Fall of the Third Reich* (London: Secker & Warburg, 1962).

Shirer, William L., *This is Berlin: Reporting from Nazi Germany 1938–1940* (London: Random House, 1999).

Sieff, Marcus, *Don't Ask the Price* (London: Weidenfeld & Nicolson, 1986).

Siemsen, Hans, *Hitler Youth* (London: Drummond, 1940). Translated by B. & T. Blewitt.

Smith, Howard K., *The Last Train from Berlin* (London: Cresset Press, 1942).

Smolar, Boris, *In the Service of my People* (Baltimore, MD: Baltimore Hebrew College, 1982).

Steinweis, Alan E., *Art, Ideology and Economics in Nazi Germany: The Reich Chambers of Music, Theater and the Visual Arts* (Chapel Hill, NC: University of North Carolina Press, 1993).

Steinweis, Alan E., *Kristallnacht 1938* (Cambridge, MA.: Belknap HUP, 2009).

Stille, Alexander, *Benevolence and Betrayal: Five Italian Jewish Families under Fascism* (London: Jonathan Cape, 1992).

Stille, Alexander, *The Force of Things: A Marriage in War and Peace* (New York: Farrar, Straus & Giroux, 2013).

Stoltzfus, Nathan, *Resistance of the Heart: Intermarriage and the Rosenstrasse Protest in Nazi Germany* (New York: W. Norton & Co., 1996).

Strobl, Gerwin, *The Swastika and the Stage* (Cambridge: CUP, 2007)

Tec, Nechama, *Resilience and Courage: Women, Men and the Holocaust* (New Haven, CN: Yale UP, 2004).

Thatcher, Margaret, *The Path to Power* (London: Harper Collins, 1995).

Tory, Avraham, *Surviving the Holocaust: The Kovno Ghetto Diary* (London: Pimlico, 1991). Translated by Jerzy Michalowicz.

Trunk, Isaiah, *Judenrat: The Jewish Councils in Eastern Europe under Nazi Occupation* (Lincoln, NE: Bison Books, 1996).

Turino, Thomas, *Music as Social Life: The Politics of Participation* (Chicago, IL: University of Chicago Press, 2008).

Unger, Michal, *Reassessment of the Image of Mordechai Chaim Rumkowski* (Jerusalem: Yad Vashem, 2004).

Varon, Laura, *The Juderia: A Holocaust Survivor's Tribute to the Jewish Community of Rhodes* (Westport, CN: Praeger, 1999).

Volkswagen AG, *Surviving in Fear: Four Jews Describe their Time at the Volkswagen Factory from 1943–1945* (Wolfsburg: Volkswagen, 2007). Translated by SDL Multilingual Services.

Vollard, Ambroise, *Recollections of a Picture Dealer* (New York: Dover Publications, 1978).

Vrbová, Gerta, *Betrayed Generation* (London: Zuza Books, 2010).

Vrbová, Gerta, *Trust and Deceit* (London: Valentine Mitchell, 2006).

Warhaftig, Myra, *They Laid the Foundation: Lives and Works of German-Speaking Jewish Architects in Palestine 1918–1948* (Berlin: Ernst Wasmuth Varlag Tubingen, 2007). Translated by Andrea Lerner.

Warren, Andrea, *Surviving Hitle*r, (London: Hodder Children's, 2001)

Wasserstein, Bernard, *Britain and the Jews of Europe 1939–1945* (London: Leicester UP, 1999).

Weber, Thomas, *Hitler's First War: Adolf Hitler, the Men of the List Regiment and the First World War* (Oxford: OUP, 2010).

Webster, Paul, *Pétain's Crime* (London: Pan Books, 2001).

Wegner, Gregory Paul, *Anti-Semitism and Schooling under the Third Reich* (New York: Routledge Falmer, 2002).

Whiteman, Dorit Bader, *The Uprooted: A Hitler Legacy* (New York: Plenum Publishing, 1993).

Yad Vashem, *Encyclopedia of the Holocaust* (New York: Macmillan, 1990).

Zsolt, Bela, *Nine Suitcases* (London: Pimlico, 2005). Translated by Ladislaus Löb.

Zuccotti, Susan, *The Italians and the Holocaust* (London: Halban, 1987).

Zuckmayer, Carl, *A Part of Myself* (London: Secker & Warburg, 1970).

Zweig, Stefan, *The World of Yesterday* (London: Pushkin Press, 2014). Translated by Anthea Bell.

# APPENDIX I

## John Young's Memoir of the Liberation of Bergen-Belsen

In August 1995 I received a letter from a former RAF officer who had been based in Germany, very close to the Bergen-Belsen concentration camp in April 1945 when it was liberated. He wrote:

> Our Padre had been allowed into the camp the day after it was overrun and returned to tell us of horrifying conditions there. Our Commanding Officer agreed that four of us, who had requested permission, could offer to help and also agreed that we could each take a large lorry with us, as we understood transport was desperately required.

He added that in April 1995 he had attended a commemorative event organised by the Imperial War Museum, and told me:

> In conclusion, may I tell you that the Commemoration was not all sadness. In the last few days when the camp was more or less cleared we asked permission to take many children out into a nearby forest away from the camp, where we had music and games and sweets (scrounged from colleagues back at base on sweet ration day). We had a really lovely time with the children and it was so good to see them enjoying themselves away from the horror which had been their home. Fifty years on, at the Commemoration, I met a lady who was one of those very same children. She remembered it quite clearly, having been 15 at the time. As you may imagine, that was quite a moment for me.[1]

I asked him if he had written a memoir and he said he had not. I encouraged him to do so and was delighted when I finally received a copy in 2002. He hadn't given his memoir a title and when I said I needed one for reference he said he'd like 'And there were sweets', in memory of the picnic treat he and his colleagues organised for the surviving children.

John was a 19-year-old solicitor's clerk in 1939, hoping to sign his articles soon. Not wishing to be called up to the army and being familiar with First World War air heroes, he decided to join the RAF Volunteer Reserve in June. He was introduced to Radio Direction Finder (RDF) in a darkened hut on the east coast – the world later knew it as 'Radar'. He joined a mobile radar unit which followed the army and controlled air cover as they advanced over Europe. That was how he came to be based near Belsen.

John wrote that he wasn't sure how much was known about the concentration camps then, although some information came from camps such as Auschwitz which had been liberated by the Russians earlier in 1945. The name Bergen-Belsen, therefore, meant nothing to John until the RAF's padre, Reverend Neil Nye, 'returned one day in very subdued mood and clearly shocked. He told us what the army had discovered at Belsen and we listened, hardly able to take in the enormity of what he was saying.'[2]

As described above, John went into the camp with three colleagues. He described how, even 2 or 3 miles away from the camp, 'we became aware of an unpleasant smell, which, as we arrived at the guarded gates, had become an odious stench'. They were issued with passes so they could come and go freely. John wrote that after all this time he could not really recall what his feelings were when he was taken around the camp, and by now most people will have seen the films and TV programmes showing what met their eyes:

> I can only say that I found it almost impossible to eat or to sleep for days. Because of what I have said, regarding the knowledge of what anyone reading this must now have of the camps, I feel it is unnecessary to go into detailed description, and will content myself with saying that whatever you have read and seen – yes, it was so, and perhaps even worse than can be imagined.[3]

John was not going attempt to describe the entire situation in Belsen, but particular incidents and stories with which he was involved:

> Probably the first impression was almost at the gate of the camp. An enormous pile of boots and shoes, taller than a house and covering more ground. Rotting, stinking leather, no doubt taken from the prisoners as they were admitted in the belief that it would in some way help the war effort. Of course, nothing was ever used and I have since heard that other such mounds were found in other camps.[4]

Work was begun by the army, and medical people rushed in to deal with the enormous task of clearing the foul huts in which so many people had lived and died.

The survivors were divided into four groups. There were those who had died and there were those who could not be saved and just needed to be made as comfortable as possible. The largest group required medical care and a steady diet of good food and there were others who were suffering from malnutrition and would recover relatively easily. However, there were also the children:

> Poor little boys and girls with arms and legs like broomsticks and yet quite cheerful. Some had no doubt been looked after by parents or others who had taken them under their wing. Of course these were the survivors, so many children having died.

After each hut was cleared there followed cleaning, delousing, medical treatment and general rehabilitation. These were done by various nursing services from the forces, the Red Cross, St John Ambulance and other voluntary bodies. People were very dedicated and never showed the horror or shock they must have felt. However, John did recall visiting the old SS quarters which had been turned into a medical centre and finding a young nurse in tears. Her patient was a young lad with a terrible wound on his head. He thought it was the state of the child's head which had upset her, but he discovered she had cleaned, dressed and bandaged the wound only an hour before. Apparently his mother, who was from the Roma, had no faith in the treatment and had replaced the sterilised dressing with a cabbage leaf tied on with a dirty rag. The nurse recovered and started again with the task.[5]

John also described the situation which we are all now familiar with:

> One tragic result of the liberation and sudden increase in food was that it was just too much for these poor starved people and many died simply because their emaciated bodies could not cope with the additional intake. It was soon realised that great care had to be taken in the supply of food until a stage had been reached where the strengthened bodies could absorb a larger quantity.

Other necessities began to pour into the camp – clothing, blankets, medical supplies and other items arrived. But it was difficult to realise how much people had suffered over a long period of time:

> Such everyday things as knives, forks and spoons and the use thereof had in some cases to be learnt afresh as had the fact that it was no longer necessary to fight over food. It is easier to understand if one accepts the fact that it had been years since many had been given reasonable food to eat.[6]

After the cleaning and delousing, everyone was given a blanket and then moved to an area where clothing was available. A choice of clothes and underwear was laid out for the women to take their choice and move on. This proved unworkable, as

after so many years of deprivation the women were arguing, pushing and shov-
ing each other. Instead they were presented with a bundle with one of each item
available and this worked very well.

It is very sad to read what the prisoners had been reduced to by the Nazis'
brutality, but John was very positive:

> … it should be made clear that it appeared that the Jewish people responded so
> much more quickly to the humanitarian treatment than many others. An inher-
> ent tenacity to overcome even the most appalling treatment must have manifested
> itself and I was told that after only a few days of being liberated, some Jews with
> medical knowledge had made their way to the administration offices saying,
> 'Look, I'm OK, now let me help!' That in itself says so much.[7]

John stressed that while the majority of the prisoners were Jewish from Germany,
Hungary, Poland and some from the Low Countries and other countries, there
were also non-Jews such as nomadic or gypsy people and political prisoners from
many countries.

John wrote of an overwhelming sense of sadness in spite of the relief of liberation.
So many had lost loved ones and their future would be tormented by their memories. 'Old folk would move about the camp, slowly and painfully, burdened by all
they had experienced. There was a hopelessness that we who had never known such
terror would never understand.' Only the younger ones seemed to have any hope.

John, still only 24, was in charge of a motley group of POWs who had been
Hungarian soldiers. They were sent to requisition hay from a barn some distance
from the camp. He had trouble controlling them and getting their co-operation
until, firstly, he fired a pistol in the air and, secondly, he bribed them all with a few
cigarettes. The hay was used to stuff thousands of palliasses in place of mattresses.[8]

The camp was full of diseases, including typhoid and typhus, and people were
not allowed to leave as soon as they were liberated. Such a mass exodus would have
caused chaos and spread disease all over Europe. The restrictions must have been
frustrating, as they no doubt wanted to go home, but at least they were now clean,
clothed, fed and generally looked after. John recalled the very strict instructions they
received about keeping themselves as clean as possible by having at least one bath a
day, if not two. If this was not possible, they were to wash all over. They were advised
not to wear tight clothing and were able to abandon their RAF collars and ties.

> It would appear that Typhus lice like to find their way into tightly clothed areas,
> and if there is any dirt in the area in which they bite, that could lead to catching
> the disease. After such cleaning we had to smother ourselves in a 'Talcum Powder'
> known as AL63, the AL standing for Anti-Louse. Even so, I believe that some
> medical people did in fact contract the disease.

In this connection, John described what he called the 'Bathroom Hotel', built by slave labour for the use of the SS. He thought there were twelve bathrooms either side of central passage. The first one had black tiles and fittings, the next one was slightly lighter in colour until the final one which was completely white. He said they were palatial and worthy of a five-star hotel and felt regret for the 'poor starved people who had been forced to build such a place'.[9]

When the old huts were cleared away, replacements were required. Someone had noticed a large timber yard a few miles away with prefabricated buildings like Nissen huts. The short, stout owner was unimpressed by John's request to take some of his huts away and after some argument he turned away with a final 'Nein'. However, John again went to pull his gun from its holster while shouting 'Kommen sie hier!', and the German, whom he nicknamed Otto, went 'wobbly at the knees' and completely changed tack. They loaded up their trucks:

> Being now ready to set off, I tore a page from a small notebook and wrote, 'Two loads of prefabricated huts, taken for use in Belsen Concentration Camp', signed it, adding my rank and RAF. I handed this to 'Otto', saying, 'Hand that to someone, and one day you may be paid for it'. He did not seem to be very convinced. I have sometimes wondered if that scrap of paper ever turned up in an office with a request for payment. I have certainly never been charged for it.[10]

One day, John was given the task of taking two SS soldiers who had been captured while still in the camp over to the town of Celle which was a UK base from 1945–2012. The soldiers were guarded by UK soldiers and were to be handed over to what became the War Crimes Commission. John was surprised to find that:

> Although they were in the SS they were far from being the super beings that these people were supposed to be. They were in fact of low intellect and brutish, one having confessed that pre-war, he had been a burglar in Berlin.

It was ironic that, after some time working at the camp, John and his colleagues were summoned to Wing HQ. As they had volunteered to help, the RAF had become concerned that they might catch a disease or have an accident and then claim a pension from the RAF. They were asked to sign disclaimer forms, which they all did, and returned to the camp.[11]

It was at this late stage that the picnic referred to earlier took place. They took about twenty-five children each time and there were several such events. They went into the nearby forest – 'A beautiful place of glades and grassy areas, shady and cool and smelling so different from the camp.'

They were helped by two or three young women who had a smattering of English and their own language, which helped them communicate with the children. John comments that the young women had done better than most prisoners – they were well fed and very cheerful. The men did not question the situation, but John says they were obviously disliked by the other prisoners:

> What we were not prepared for was the frequently expressed desire to find an eligible and willing, future husband, who would get them to England. Between us we had several proposals of marriage, which we were able to decline, all of us being already espoused.[12]

John returned home eventually and married his girl. He did not go back to do his legal articles and became a salesman and, later, a hotelier with his second wife, Florence. Although he has died since writing to me, Florence was pleased that John's efforts to record his experiences have come to be so useful.[13]

It took a long time for him to put his experiences down on paper. He concluded his thirteen page memoir with some reflections:

> As I have said, memories fade and after 50 years, things are no longer as clear as they were, but I believe that future generations must know of these camps, must know of the millions of human beings who had been tortured, abused beyond all understanding and finally killed. If they know, if they can be made to understand why such evil came about, maybe a repetition can be avoided, although sadly the world of today gives little confidence that it will be so.
>
> And now after all these years, long retired, living in comfort with my wife and family, always trying to keep busy, there are nevertheless those moments when one relaxes and then sometimes, the memories come flooding back. Yes the edges have become blurred, but much remains and I have always been glad that in our very small way the four of us contributed to the truly wonderful work done by the medical people and others in Belsen. I take comfort in thinking perhaps it helped, just a little, to show some of those who survived the Holocaust that compassion of one human being for another had not died in those hell-holes.
>
> It only remains for the human race, to be made constantly aware of the evil which can result from the mentality which created, and allowed the Nazi Party to function in the way which brought such horror to so many millions of people. Generations which are to follow, in all countries, must be taught by all available means about the Holocaust and the conditions which brought it about.

One of the liberators of Bergen-Belsen, Major Leonard Berney, was recently honoured by one of the other girls from Belsen. Nanette Blitz Konig, now aged 84, was at school with Anne Frank. She has lived in Brazil since 1953, and her daughter found Major Berney through his son's Facebook page. Ms Konig had asked him to write to her relatives in London to tell them she was alive, which he did. He visited her in London in 1949 to make sure she was safe. He is now 93, and the family presented him with a silver platter in recognition of his kindness. 'He was absolutely the typical English army officer, an amazing man.' Ms Konig said she last saw Anne Frank about two weeks before she died – they were in different parts of the camp. 'I saw her through the barbed wire. I don't know how we recognised each other as we were both skeletons.'[14]

# APPENDIX II

## Gypsies in Auschwitz

The Nazis were worried by the gypsies, and the ending of the Hungarian deportations meant there was spare capacity in the gas chambers. It was therefore decided to liquidate the whole section in Birkenau, where the gypsies camped. Since 1943 it had accommodated around 23,000 gypsy men and women. They were allowed to live as families and wear their own clothes and did not have their heads shaved, but soon their conditions became the worst in Auschwitz. They were very crowded and lacked both food and water which meant that disease was rampant. They suffered from typhus and a skin disease called 'noma'. Many thousands died – 21,000 out of the 23,000 sent to Auschwitz died there of disease, starvation or in the gas chambers.

Karl Stojka was born into a large gypsy family in Vienna on 20 April 1931. He was arrested at school on 3 March 1943 as part of the mass deportation of the remaining Roma and Sinti families to Auschwitz. He wrote:

> The door opened and in came the caretaker of the school, the headmaster and some men in heavy leather coats: the Gestapo. We all had to jump up and shout 'Heil Hitler!'. Of course I shouted out too, but then they began to whisper with our teacher and she suddenly turned to me and said sadly: 'Come, Stojka Karli, you have to go with them now!' So I took my things and downstairs there was a police car waiting for us along with a lorry that was already full of Gypsies.[1]

In Auschwitz, Karl and his older brother, Mongo Stojka, were separated from their mother and sisters after a selection in Auschwitz where males were sent to Buchenwald and females to Ravensbrück. Both Ceija and Karl Stojka remember being too young for the selection, but in order to save them from the gas chambers of Auschwitz, their mother told one of the guards that they were midgets and embarrassed about their size. They survived to return to Vienna after the war and became successful artists. Karl died in 2003.[2]

The Nazis thought the gypsies 'racially dangerous and asocial'. They wanted to be rid of the gypsies and they suffered more than any group other than the Jews, proportionate to their numbers. The exact figures are not known, but between a quarter and a half a million are believed to have been killed. However, their treatment was very variable:

> … in the Soviet Union, Nazi killing squads murdered gypsies with the Jews; in Romania the extensive gypsy population was not targetted en masse (thousands still died as a result of mistreatment); in Poland the majority of gypsies were in concentration camps; whilst in Slovakia the policy of persecution was enforced unevenly; within Germany itself many gypsies were deported first to ghettos in Poland – 5,000 were sent to Łódź and were amongst the first to die in the gas vans of Chelmno in January 1942.[3]

The Nazis were concerned about the transfer of 'gypsy racial characteristics' into the Aryan population through Mischlinge gypsies. As a result, an 8-year-old girl from Hamburg was, in effect, kidnapped from her home and parents by the Gestapo one night early in 1944. Apparently she was adopted and the people with whom she had lived since she was 10 months old were not her real parents. She was dragged off to go to her real mother. She was just shipped off to Auschwitz with a group of gypsies and abandoned. It was only because one of the block kapos, a woman called Wanda, took pity on her and took her to share her little room in the barracks that she was fine for a while. But one day Wanda disappeared and the little girl, Else Baker, was on her own again. She was fortunate to be saved from the gas chambers and instead was one of the 1,400 sent off to other camps. She went to Ravensbrück, where again she was all alone until September when her stepfather arrived to take her home.

The 8-year-old traumatised child had, like all prisoners released from concentration camps, been made to sign a document promising she would not divulge what she had experienced or seen. She said, 'I think that was the first signature I ever gave in my life.' She went home and after a six month absence Else went back to school 'pretending to be a normal 8-year-old German girl once more'.

It is not known why she was released, because the relevant papers were destroyed by the Gestapo at the end of the war. Perhaps her father's protests that she was fully assimilated into German society were finally accepted. Additionally, he went so far as to join the Nazi Party to demonstrate his loyalty and perhaps that did the trick. However, it resulted in Else being badly damaged. It is certain she would not have survived without Wanda's care because no one else looked after her or showed her the ropes.[4]

# APPENDIX III

## Euthanasia and the Church

Gitta Sereny detailed what the Catholic Church, including the Vatican, knew about the euthanasia programme in advance. Lothar Gruchman claimed that the question of the 'destruction of unworthy life' arose as early as 1933 during discussions on changes to the German criminal code.[1] At that point the German Catholic Church stated quite categorically that any kind of legally sanctioned euthanasia was incompatible with Christian morality.

In 1935 Dr Franz Gürtner, Reich Minister of Justice, firmly opposed a proposal from the Prussian Ministry of Justice for legal euthanasia. However, the wording of the rejection is significant: 'a [judicial] sanction of the destruction of unworthy life was out of the question', but the Nationalist Socialist State was 'already providing against these degenerations in the nation's body by measures such as the law for the prevention of hereditary disease in coming generations, which means these degenerations are in effect in the process of decrease'.

The draft law referred to was the compulsory sterilisation of men and women suffering from hereditary diseases, which was first discussed on 14 July 1933 – six days before the signing on 20 July of the Concordat between the Nazi Government and the Vatican, negotiated by Cardinal Pacelli (the future Pius XII) and signed by Pius XI. At that point the Vice Chancellor Franz von Papen opposed the draft law because Catholics opposed sterilisation.

Hitler did not accept any watering down of the wording of the draft law, but agreed to delay the announcement of the law until 25 July, after the signing of the Concordat. At this point von Papen's concerns proved correct.

A long-time friend of Pacelli's, Father Robert Leiber, wrote to him in August 1933 expressing concerns about several aspects of the Nazi Government which, it is alleged, Pacelli shared at that time. He claimed that Catholics were now fearful of expressing the ideological differences between the Nazis and the Church and some professors were stating that the people must serve the state, rather than vice versa. They were even attributing Catholic origins to the principles of the totalitarian state and using quotations from Thomas Aquinas to support the claim. This was incorrect because the concepts came from Aristotle and were 'totally antique-heathenish', wrote Father Leiber.

He also criticised the final paragraph of the Concordat, which claimed the Catholic Church was free to disseminate its views, as he said this was not possible even in Catholic publications if the views opposed the Nazis. If this was done, the Catholic editor was removed and replaced by a Nazi but the pretence of the journal being Catholic was maintained. He referred to an article of 13 August 1933 by Professor Dr Joseph Mayer, a professor in moral theology at the University of Paderborn, who had written about sterilising the insane in 1927. Mayer was promoting the new law in the 1933 article by interpreting the Catholic view. Lieber said such an article was more harmful than actually advocating the law.

In 1935, a further law was drafted 'to safeguard the hereditary health of the German people', which expanded the original law by legalising abortion where one of the parents suffered from a hereditary disease. This law was separate to the anti-Jewish Nuremberg Laws introduced a week later.

Dr Karl Brandt, who was Reichskommissar for Health and Hitler's person physician, was condemned to death in 1947. He told the Nuremberg Trial that euthanasia had long been on Hitler's agenda. In 1935 he told the Minister of Health, Gerhard Wagner, who was in favour of euthanasia, 'if war came, he would take up and resolve this question, because it would be easier to do so in wartime when the Church would not be able to put up the expected resistance'.

It is therefore clear that Hitler appreciated both the Catholic Church's opposition to euthanasia and also the power of the Catholic Church in Germany. Yet in the early autumn of 1939 Hitler wrote to Philip Bouhler. This note was found after the war in the Ministry of Justice. It is undated, but Karl Brandt's testimony said it was a secret decree made at the end of October 1939 but backdated to 1 September 1939, before the start of the war on 3 September. It stated:

> Reichsleiter Bouhler and Dr Brandt are charged with the responsibility for expanding the authority of physicians who are to be designated by name, to the end that patients who are considered incurable, in the best available human judgement after critical evaluation of their condition, can be granted mercy-killing.

As Hitler had predicted, this was done in the war, but even so they realised the Church would find out and so soundings were taken.[2]

Gitta Sereny met a former Catholic priest, Albert Hartl. He had been a priest for about five years but had always had doubts about his vocation and left around 1933–1934. He joined the party and then the SS. In 1935 he was given the post of

Chief of Church Information at the Berlin HQ of the Reich Security Services
– the SD. He told Sereny that in late 1938 he was told to meet Victor Brack
(1904–1948), who was in charge of the euthanasia programme, in the Führer
Chancellery. Brack told him that many relatives of people with incurable mental
problems wanted Hitler to introduce mercy killings for these people and it was
being considered.

Brack told Hartl that Hitler was currently opposed, especially because he had just
had considerable support from the Catholic Church in Austria with the *Anschluss*,
and he did not want conflict with them. They therefore wanted Hartl to write
an opinion on whether there would be opposition to such a law. Hartl refused
because he did not feel competent to do this. He thought it should be written by
a practising priest who understood Catholic moral doctrine.

He first approached Dr August Wilhelm Patin because he was Himmler's cousin,
but he found his response rather superficial as he suggested there would be no
fundamental opposition. So Hartl turned to Professor Dr Joseph Mayer and went
to see him at the University of Paderborn to explain what was required and inform
him that a fee and expenses would be paid. It took Mayer six months and Hartl
went on the train to collect it. He collected an 'academic' paper consisting of about
100 pages typed on thin manuscript paper, double-spaced. There were five copies.
He read it all the way back to Berlin on the five hour journey and late into the
night once he reached home. Hartl felt he was sympathetic to euthanasia.

Professor Mayer suggested that the whole issue of the mentally ill was based
on 'the error of Christ that the mentally ill were possessed by the devil'. He also
referred to the Jesuit moral system of probability (Probabilismus). He explained
this as:

> … there are few moral decisions which are from the outset unequivocally good
> or bad. Most moral decisions are dubious. In cases of such dubious decisions, if
> there are reasonable grounds and reasonable 'authorities' in support of personal
> opinion, then such personal opinion can become decisive even if there are other
> 'reasonable' grounds and 'authorities' opposing it.

Mayer referred specifically to Thomas Aquinas and, finally, regarding the killing of
the incurably mentally ill, he presented his conclusion – as there were reasonable
grounds and authorities both for and against it, euthanasia of the mentally ill could
be considered 'defensible'.

Hartl said he took all five copies of the opinion to Brack at the Führer
Chancellery the next day, and continued:

> About four weeks later Brack called me in and told me that, since the Opinion
> indicated clearly that a unanimous and unequivocal opposition from the two

Churches was not to be expected, Hitler had withdrawn his objections and had
ordered the Euthanasia Programme to be started.

However, in spite of this, Hartl said he was not convinced. He suggested that they
should advise representatives of both Churches of the Opinion and also small
groups of doctors and lawyers. None of these people made any real comment,
except the Protestant Pastor of Bodelschwingh, who was head of an institution for
the mentally ill. While he said neither yes nor no, he insisted that his own institution was to be exempted. (It is, however, recorded that in the spring of 1940 he and
Pastor Braune, who also ran an institution for the mentally ill, made very articulate
protests against euthanasia.)

Gitta Sereny wrote fairly honestly about her doubts about Hartl, who had a
very dubious career and had been imprisoned in Nuremberg, although he was
cleared in 1949. However, she found herself collecting documents which corroborated Hartl's statements to her. In 1967 there was a euthanasia trial in Frankfurt
where Hartl told his story again. A somewhat elderly Professor Mayer confirmed
what Hartl said, although the opinion had entirely disappeared – none of the five
copies has ever turned up or been used in any of the trials. He was 81 and died
later that year.

Frau Haferkamp, an ordinary German housewife, commented on the earlier
stages of the euthanasia programme. She described her brother-in-law's sister, who
lived in the same house as her, having a sick child. She was 19 but looked 15 and
had become ill through 'a festering in the middle ear'. She lived at a home in Essen,
near Oberhausen, called Franz Hals House. The mother was called Frau von Thiel
and the girl was Anni. One day Frau von Thiel got a letter saying Anni had 'an
inflammation of her lungs' and had been moved to Krefeld about a week earlier.
Frau Haferkamp took the letter to show her husband and he said, 'She's not coming
back. They're gassing them all.' He was right. Apparently when they sent the letter
she was already dead.

Her husband knew about this because they knew a man who sold cards door-
to-door – depending on the time of year, Christmas cards, Easter cards or birthday
cards. He didn't have a proper job, but lived with his sister and was very clean
in his personal habits. One day two policemen came to the sister's home with a
certificate. He had to get a suitcase and they took him away to a home and he was
later gassed. She concluded, 'The man who would not harm a pig.'

She also spoke of a close acquaintance, a Herr Grünewald, whose wife was
Jewish. 'Suddenly it was learned, mother and children can be sent away, Ja, she was
also sent, she never came back. They sent her to the gas chamber.'[3]

Ian Kershaw noted the impact of the euthanasia programme – set in motion
by a secret written order from Hitler shortly after the start of the war. The exact
figure of those killed is not clear because, while the programme was stopped

officially two years later, murders of victims continued, particularly in concentration camps. A figure between 70,000 and 90,000 is considered likely. Ian
Kershaw commented:

> The halting of the 'action' was the direct consequence of the pressure of
> 'public opinion' as the growing unease and opposition became articulated  by
> the hierarchies of both Christian denominations in the most honourable epi-
> sode in the otherwise chequered relations of the Churches with the National
> Socialist regime.[4]

Although prior soundings had been taken about the T4 policy, they had been
misjudged, because when rumours seeped out unrest and alarm were apparent.
Unrest in Württemberg in the summer and autumn of 1940, demonstrated by the
Protestant Bishop Worm's 'weakly formulated protest letter', led Himmler to move
the centre in Grafeneck to Hadamar. However, more forthright letters were sent
by the Catholic leaders to the Reich Chancellery and the Ministry of Justice from
Cardinals Bertram and Faulhaber. The latter wrote to the Justice Minister Gürtner
on 6 November 1940 and:

> … provided hard evidence of what was taking place, spoke openly and categori-
> cally about the immorality of the killing of incurable mental patients and the
> incompatibility of euthanasia with the Christian moral code, and referred to
> 'great unrest', 'rumours' and 'panic' among the population.

Another report in November 1940 from Bavaria referred to the 'laughable' attempt
at a cover-up, pointing out that the notices of death seemed mass-produced – from
the same sanatorium, with the same cause of death. Unaware that the action was
ordered by Hitler himself, the reporter continued:

> Who gave the advice to carry out these measures in this way must have a poor
> knowledge of the mentality of the people (Volksseele). They are all the more
> keenly discussed and condemned and destroy as hardly anything else confidence
> also in the Führer personally … The people reject in their feelings the thought
> that we have the right to gain financial and economic benefit from the elimina-
> tion of national comrades who are no longer capable of working.[5]

The concerns were aggravated by several lunatic asylums in the Bamberg area
transferring their patients, and very shortly their families received letters advising
of the patients' sudden deaths. It appears that the concerns referred more to the
lack of legislation regarding these measures than to the fate of these unfortunates.

The final straw was the protest by Bishop Galen of Munster in his sermon on 3 August 1941 when he attacked euthanasia as a breach of the Fifth Commandment, denouncing the murder of the mentally sick as opposed to both God's laws and those of the German state. Goebbels was clear that at any attempt to get rid of the bishop 'the population of Munster would be regarded as lost to the war effort, and the same could confidently be said of the whole of Westphalia'. He said the Church should not be challenged during the war.

Instead, Hitler gave the order to halt the 'euthanasia action'. It was a victory without parallel during the Third Reich for the force of popular opinion, in a matter which lay not far from the heart of the Nazi racial-eugenic creed of social Darwinism.[6]

# APPENDIX IV

'The Nivea Crème Jews' (from *Der Stürmer*, No. 34, August 1933), English translation by Hildegard Abraham

Beiersdorff & Co., the Hamburg Company that makes the well-known Nivea Crème, was an entirely Jewish enterprise. Many people hold the view that it is a Jewish firm to this day despite all the efforts to restructure it and bring it into line.

For decades mighty Jews used the honest German name of Beiersdorff, the pharmacist from Hamburg-Altona, as a cover. The Jews Troplowitz and Mankewitsch – typical Polish Jews – acquired the small business from Beiersdorff the pharmacist. Later, the Jew Dr Jakobsohn took the helm of the company supported by Jewish board members Senielowski, Dr Unna, Dr Gradenwitz et al. Chairman of the board was the well-known Jewish banker Dr Melchior of the Hamburg banking house of M Warburg. In other words, Beiersdorff was simply crawling with Jews while its travelling salesmen were exclusively German. By employing ruthless business methods and aggressive, typically Jewish advertising campaigns the company elbowed its way to the top of the German market leaving hardly any room for other German firms.

Then came the 30th of January. It was no longer a good idea for so many Jews to remain in the firm. The Nivea Jews knew what to do. They restructured the business and fell into line. All the Jews disappeared and the company assumed an air of good German respectability. They even went as far as obtaining confirmation of this in writing. The Action Group for Independent Artisan Businesses based in Berlin, after careful examination of the ownership and management of the company, certified that Beiersdorff & Co., a chemical firm based in Hamburg, was considered a truly German enterprise.

Beiersdorff & Co. knew only too well how to make good use of this certificate: they shoved it under every customer's nose. Even after the restructuring they conducted the same profitable business as earlier in the Germany of the

Jews and their lackeys. There is just one question: who might the true owners of Beiersdorff be? We are not interested in the management. We regard it as given that they are goyim nowadays.

## Die Nivea Creme Juden

Die Firma Beiersdorff & Co. in Hamburg, die Herstellerin der bekannten Nivea-Creme, war ein ausgesprochenes jüdisches Unternehmen. Es gibt Viele, die behaupten, sie sei es heute noch, trotz aller Gleich- und Umschaltungen.

Hinter dem ehrlichen deutschen Namen des Altonaer Apotheker Beiersdorff haben sich jahrzehntelang pfundige Juden versteckt. Die Juden Troplowitz und Mankwitsch — typische Ostjuden — lausten dem Apotheker Beiersdorff sein kleines Geschäft ab. Nach ihnen kam der Jude Dr. Jakobsohn an die Spitze der Firma. Ihm standen als Vorstandsmitglieder zur Seite die Juden Semielowski, Dr. Unna, Dr. Gradenwitz u. a. Der Vorsitzende des Aufsichtsrates war der bekannte Bankjude Dr. Melchior vom Bankhaus M. Warburg in Hamburg. In der Firma Beiersdorff wimmelte es also nur so von Juden. Ihre Reisenden aber waren ausnahmslos Deutsche. Durch rücksichtslosen Gebrauch der Ellenbogen und durch eine aufdringliche, jüdische Reklame hat sich die Firma den deutschen Markt so erobert, daß neben ihr kaum noch andere deutsche Firmen Platz haben.

Da kam der 30. Januar. Es war nicht mehr ratsam, Juden in so großer Zahl in einer Firma zu haben. Die Nivea-Juden wußten sich zu helfen. Sie schalteten gleich und schalteten um. Die ganzen Juden verschwanden. Die Firma bekam einen soliden deutschen Anstrich. Man ließ sich dies sogar schriftlich bestätigen. Der Kampfbund des gewerblichen Mittelstandes in Berlin bestätigte, daß er die Firma Beiersdorff & Co., chemische Fabrik in Hamburg, nach Prüfung der Besitzverhältnisse und der Geschäftsleitung als deutsches Unternehmen ansehe.

Die Firma Beiersdorff & Co. wußte mit dieser Bestätigung allerhand anzufangen. Sie wurde jedem Kunden unter die Nase gehalten. Man machte nach der Umschaltung dieselben Geschäfte wie zuvor im Deutschland der Juden und Judenknechte. Es fragt sich nun: Wer ist denn jetzt der wahre Besitzer der Nivea-Creme? Die Geschäftsführer interessieren uns nicht. Daß diese heute Gojims sind, halten wir für eine Selbstverständlichkeit.

Der „Stürmer" frißt einen Besen, wenn die eigentlichen Macher in der Firma nicht nach wie vor Juden sind. Juden, die sich getarnt im Hintergrund halten. In dieser Annahme wird man bestärkt, wenn man liest, was der „Fridericus" über die umgeschaltete Firma Beiersdorff in seiner Nr. 19 des Jahrganges 1933 zu berichten weiß. Es heißt da:

„Die Firma Beiersdorff & Co., die in Hamburg sich nicht schnell genug als deutsche Firma umschalten konnte, sieht in Polen ganz anders aus. Dort laufen die Vertreter der Firma Beiersdorff & Co. bei der Kundschaft herum und tun so, als ob die Firma Beiersdorff & Co. unter dem nationalsozialistischen Kurs in Deutschland zu leiden habe. Den jüdischen Kunden erzählen sie, die Firma Beiersdorff sei jüdisch und Herr Dr. Jakobsohn sei ein sehr frommer Jude, der aufs strengste dem jüdischen Ritus nachkomme. Jr. Jakobsohn feiere vorschriftsmäßig das Schabbesfest. Es ständen an jedem Freitag die Kerzen an und es sei infolgedessen kein Grund vorhanden, daß die Polen die Firma Beiersdorff boykottierten, da es sich um eine gut jüdische Firma handle."

Die Reisenden erzählen in Polen ferner, daß Dr. Jakobsohn, eben weil er Jude sei, viel auszuhalten habe.

Das riecht verdächtig nach Greuelpropaganda. In einem berichten die Reisenden sicher die Wahrheit. Daß die Firma Beiersdorff heute noch in den Händen der Juden ist. Die Umschaltung war weiter nichts, wie ein großer Bluff. Das deutsche Volk ist heller als der Jude denkt. Es läßt sich vom Juden nicht mehr hinters Licht führen.

'Die Nivea Crème Juden'. Extract from *Der Stürmer*, August 1933.

The *Stürmer* will eat its hat if the real movers and shakers in the firm are not actually Jews to this very day. Jews who remain in the background, under cover. This suspicion is confirmed when one reads what 'Fridericus' has to say about the restructured Beiersdorff company in his No. 19 (1933) where it says, 'Beiersdorff & Co. which turned itself head over heel into a German firm assumes an entirely different guise in Poland, where the company's representatives give their customers the impression that Beiersdorff & Co. is having a tough time under National Socialism.' They make Jewish customers believe that Beiersdorff is a purely Jewish firm and that Dr Jakobsohn is a very pious Jew following Jewish rituals to the letter. Dr Jakobsohn, they maintain, observes the Sabbath meticulously and lights the candles every Friday, thereby removing any reason the Poles might have to boycott the firm as it is entirely Jewish.

Moreover, the salesmen spread the rumour around Poland that Dr Jakobsohn has to put up with a lot just because he is a Jew.

All this smacks suspiciously of horror stories. However, in one respect the salesmen tell the truth, namely that even today Beiersdorff & Co. is in Jewish hands. The restructuring was nothing but a big bluff. The German people are smarter than the Jew thinks. They will not be duped by the Jew any longer.

# APPENDIX V

## The Nuremberg Code 1947

1     The voluntary consent of the human subject is absolutely essential. This means that the person involved should have legal capacity to give consent; should be so situated as to be able to exercise free power of choice, without the intervention of any element of force, fraud, deceit, duress, over-reaching, or other ulterior form of constraint or coercion; and should have sufficient knowledge and comprehension of the elements of the subject matter involved, as to enable him to make an understanding and enlightened decision. This latter element requires that, before the acceptance of an affirmative decision by the experimental subject, there should be made known to him the nature, duration, and purpose of the experiment; the method and means by which it is to be conducted; all inconveniences and hazards reasonably to be expected; and the effects upon his health or person, which may possibly come from his participation in the experiment.

   The duty and responsibility for ascertaining the quality of the consent rests upon each individual who initiates, directs or engages in the experiment. It is a personal duty and responsibility which may not be delegated to another with impunity.

2     The experiment should be such as to yield fruitful results for the good of society, unprocurable by other methods or means of study, and not random and unnecessary in nature.

3     The experiment should be so designed and based on the results of animal experimentation and a knowledge of the natural history of the disease or other problem under study, that the anticipated results will justify the performance of the experiment.

4     The experiment should be so conducted as to avoid all unnecessary physical and mental suffering and injury.

5     No experiment should be conducted, where there is an *apriori* reason to believe that death or disabling injury will occur; except, perhaps, in those experiments where the experimental physicians also serve as subjects.

6     The degree of risk to be taken should never exceed that determined by the humanitarian importance of the problem to be solved by the experiment.

7 .   Proper preparations should be made and adequate facilities provided to protect the experimental subject against even remote possibilities of injury, disability, or death.

8   The experiment should be conducted only by scientifically qualified persons. The highest degree of skill and care should be required through all stages of the experiment of those who conduct or engage in the experiment.

9   During the course of the experiment, the human subject should be at liberty to bring the experiment to an end, if he has reached the physical or mental state, where continuation of the experiment seemed to him to be impossible.

10   During the course of the experiment, the scientist in charge must be prepared to terminate the experiment at any stage, if he has probable cause to believe, in the exercise of the good faith, superior skill and careful judgement required of him, that a continuation of the experiment is likely to result in injury, disability, or death to the experimental subject.

*Trials of War Criminals before the Nuremberg Military Tribunals under Control Council Law No. 10,* Vol. 2, pp. 181–182. (Washington, DC: US Government Printing Office, 1949).

# APPENDIX VI

## Japanese Atrocities in the Second World War

Laurence Rees wrote of the appalling atrocities committed by the Japanese:

> In China, Japanese soldiers split open the stomachs of pregnant women and bayoneted the foetuses; they tied up local farmers and used them for target practice; they tortured thousands of innocent people in ways that rival the Gestapo at their worst; and they were pursuing deadly medical experiments long before Dr Mengele and Auschwitz ...
>
> They had grown up in an intensely militaristic society. Had been subjected to military training of the most brutal sort, had been told since they were children to worship their Emperor (who was also their commander-in-chief) and lived in a culture that historically elevated the all-too-human desire to conform into a semi-religion. All this was encapsulated by one veteran who told me that when he had been asked to take part in the gang rape of a Chinese woman he saw it less as a sexual act and more as a sign of final acceptance by the group, many of whom had previously bullied him mercilessly. Like the Soviet secret policemen I met, these Japanese veterans attempted to justify their actions almost exclusively with reference to an external source – the regime itself.[1]

Part of the human being appears to derive pleasure from inflicting pain on a person held in their power. This is universal but we need to flag it up. Reading about other cruel persecutions highlights this behaviour. An example are the POWs the Japanese forced to build the railway between Burma and Siam (now Thailand). News of their conditions was only made known in the UK late in 1944 when Sir James Grigg, the Secretary of State for War, made a statement in the House of Commons:

The conditions under which all these men lived and worked were terrible…
many lacked clothing, boots and head covering; the only food provided was a
pannikin [small cup] of rice and about half a pint or less of watery stew three
times a day. But the work had to go on without respite, whatever the cost in
human suffering or life.[2]

The article carried a drawing by Ronald Searle (1920–2011), the cartoonist who
created nasty little pubescent schoolgirls, both at St Trinian's School and riding
ponies. He, himself, was a survivor of the railway ordeal which saw the deaths of
100,000 prisoners, including 16,000 Allied prisoners.[3] He drew what he saw around
him and hid his work under the mattresses of prisoners with cholera, knowing they
would be safe. Much of this work is now preserved in the Imperial War Museum.
This particular drawing shows a severely malnourished prisoner, his ribs clearly
visible, wearing a loin cloth, holding a large rock about his head. Behind him sits
a Japanese guard in a chair holding a bamboo stick with a point in the prisoner's
back. Ronald Searle had written on the drawing:

> To entertain themselves our guards would pick a prisoner at random and force
> him to stand in the sun holding a rock above his head for a long period. A sharp-
> ened bamboo stick was held against his back to discourage him from failing.
> When the rock was dropped the prisoner was clubbed with a pick handle and
> forced to get up again and repeat the performance. Other prisoners were lined
> up to watch. Afterwards the prisoner would be offered a cigarette.[4]

Professor Hugh de Wardener (1915–2013) was serving with the Royal Army
Medical Corps when he became a Japanese prisoner of war for three and a half
years from 1942. In Changi Prison he treated Vitamin B1 deficiency by managing
to get hold of supplies of Marmite – he wrote a report of this success and buried it
in a tin, which he dug up at the end of the war and published in *The Lancet* in 1947.
Later, in another camp, Chungkai in Thailand, he was in charge of a diphtheria
ward and he noticed that those who lay still in bed recovered more quickly. It was
noted that 'It was difficult not to be active when lice and bugs were crawling over
one's skin.'

He may well have known another artist, Jack Chalker (1918–2014), who arrived
sick at the Chungkai camp in March 1943. There, he helped an Australian surgeon,
Edward Dunlop, with designs for crutches and articulated prostheses for the ampu-
tees. He too produced drawings of the appalling conditions which he hid carefully
in the buildings. He was able to take them with him and they helped record the
brutality of the regime.[5]

The conditions in which de Wardener was working would have been familiar
to the physicians of the Holocaust:

There now began the terrible years of imprisonment in various PoW camps. In appalling, insanitary conditions medical officers like him strove in the face of, at best, total indifference and, at worst, active brutality from their captors, to find ways of trying to keep captives, many of them wounded, alive in an ambience where infection and diseases incubated effortlessly.[6]

# APPENDIX VII

## The Hitler Youth According to Adolf Goers

Another aspect of the Hitler Youth (HJ) was provided by Hans Siemsen in 1940. His book is based on what he was told by a 'German Rhineland Aryan youth, with small political consciousness and inclination, who was drawn into the revolutionary ambit of the institution called "Hitler Youth"'.[1] The young man who called himself Adolf Goers, told Siemsen his story. Siemsen said the subtitle could have been 'a faithful record of four years of disillusionment, inflicted upon a German youth by Nazi Germany'.

He described Adolf as a youth from a Rhineland town, where his father was an official. He was 18 when Hitler came to power. He joined the Hitler Youth and became a leader, and described the life of the youth-leaders, 'their ambitions, night life, homosexuality, corruption and embezzlement of funds; the hunt for position and influence, and the double-crossing of leaders by one another'. Goers went with the flow, but lost his position as a leader and found himself facing unpleasant methods of extracting evidence in Columbia House, ending up in an internment camp. When he was released, he fled 'his fatherland' and died in Spain on 23 December 1937.[2]

Goers explained how he came to join the Hitler Youth. He was a very keen sportsman and he was told he could become a physical instructor to 500–600 boys – a 'Sportwart'. He would not have to be a normal member and he was very tempted, especially as so many of his friends were joining. However, he was shocked with his father's response when he asked him if he could join. 'He was furious and said, "Never, so long as I have any say in the matter. No good can ever come of it. You will get thoroughly depraved and demoralised in such company." I was thunderstruck. I had never before seen my father so upset.'[3]

It was during the second half of 1933 that the pressure was on. Previously, boys were coaxed to join but then it became more like compulsion. At his place of work nearly every week there were fresh enquiries pouring into the office asking about the organisations the employees belonged to. They would all have to join the Labour Front, and additionally the men would have to join the SA. However, there were mostly women or older men at the works. The only suitable man was a Catholic who had been beaten up in Munich by the SA, and 'he refused to join'. Goers was too young and was therefore directed to the Hitler Youth, which he had almost decided to join, but he still resented the compulsion.

However, an unexpected development occurred when the head of the firm spoke to him privately:

'Adolf,' he said, 'Do me a favour and join the Hitler Youth. It'll be better for you and better for the firm. You know, of course, that every firm has its SA man. We haven't one. Moreover, we're Jewish. Please join the Hitler Youth. Then at least we shall have a Nazi on the premises. It's best to be on the safe side.'[4]

So Adolf joined the Hitler Youth because he was an apprentice in a Jewish firm. His boss even paid the 150 marks for the uniform for him. He admits it must sound strange but things were at the time. He adds:

SA men of this kind who were workers or employees in Jewish businesses were known as 'Schutz-Nazis'. And it not infrequently happened that a porter or a vanman, just because he was an SA man or even an SA leader, had more authority than the Jewish head of a firm.

His boss had been right – as soon as he joined, he was given promotion at the firm and when he climbed the HJ leadership he found he could do pretty much as he liked at work. 'No head of a business, and certainly no Jewish head, would have dared to administer the slightest reproof to an apprentice who was a leader in the Hitler Youth.'[5]

Goers became disenchanted with the HJ when his chum Willi Schulze was murdered. He says that Willi, who was a leader, was camping with his company in 1934. The boys were not allowed out at night, but the leaders were and they met up with the local girls. Willi was a handsome lad and had more success with the girls than most of the other leaders. However, one day he was found dead outside the village with a bullet in his back. A somewhat older and more senior leader was found guilty of illegal possession of arms – not murder or manslaughter. He was sentenced to serve two months' imprisonment at some future date. In fact, the guilty man never served the sentence and was merely transferred.

Willi Schulze was given a splendid funeral and a company of the HJ was named after him as he had fallen in the fight for Hitler. Goers was told what had really happened by another boy who was there when the body was found:

This was one of the first things that opened my eyes with regard to the Hitler Youth and National-Socialism. It was not so much the murder or manslaughter from motives of jealousy that seemed to me so horrible as the way in which, with the help of the Nazi leaders, the police and the judge, everything was hushed up.

Adolf Goers was too fearful of retribution to give the names of the people involved when he dictated his story to Siemsen.[6]

# NOTES

## Introduction

1 Jack Ewing, 'Letter of Hitler's', *New York Times*, 3 June 2011, accessed 19 Febraury 2014.

2 JTA, 'Threaten "Pitiless Extermination" of Vienna Jews', 3 January 1923, accessed 3 January 2014. The *WM* was the only Jewish daily newspaper printed in German – it ceased publication in 1927 through lack of funds.

3 Joanna Paraszczuk, 'A Revisionist's History', *Jerusalem Post*, 28 April 2011 (http://www.jpost.com/Metro/Features/A-revisionists-history) accessed 23 May 2014.

4 Odelberg, W., *Nobel*, p.562.

5 Kings 21:19.

6 Shimon Samuels, 'The French Bank Holocaust Settlement', in Bazyler & Alford (eds), *Holocaust Restitution: Perspectives on the Litigation and Its Legacy* (New York: New York UP, 2006), p.151.

7 Samuels, in Bazyler & Alford, p.149.

8 Israel Gutman 1923–2013, obituary in *The Times*, 22 October 2013.

9 Renée Fink, emails to author on 3 and 4 January 2013.

10 Dutch Jewish records (http://www.joodsmonument.nl/person/473082/en?lang=en) accessed 24 March 2014.

11 Renee Fink, email to author, 23 March 2014.

12 USHMM, 'Killing Centres', 10 June 2013 (http://www.ushmm.org/wlc/en/article.php?ModuleId=10007327) accessed 14 February 2014.

13 Laurence Rees, *Auschwitz*, p.267.

14 Simcha Jacobivici, 'Archaeology against Holocaust Denial', *Times of Israel*, 31 March 2014 (http://blogs.timesofisrael.com/archeology-against-holocaust-denial/) accessed 1 April 2014.

15 Melanie Phillips, 'Europe's Fascist Fringe is Awakening Again', *The Times*, 3 March 2014.

16 JTA, 'Jewish Groups Decry National Front Election Successes in France', 1 April 2014, (http://www.jta.org/2014/04/01/news-opinion/world/jewish-groups-decry-national-front-election-successes-in-france) accessed 2 April 2014.

17 JTA, 'Latvian School Features "Jew-free" Sign' (http://www.jta.org/2014/05/09/news-opinion/world/latvian-school-features-jew-free-sign) accessed 9 May 2014.

18 Joshua Davidovich, 'Iran's Khamenei "Uncertain" if Holocaust Occurred', *Times of Israel*, 21 March 2014 (http://www.timesofisrael.com/irans-khamenei-uncertain-if-holocaust-occured/) accessed 21 March 2014.

19 Joshua Davidovich, 'Iran Holocaust Cartoon Contest Draws 839 Entries', *Times of Israel*, 7 April 2015 (http://www.timesofisrael.com/iran-holocaust-cartoon-contest-draws-hundreds-of-entries/) accessed 7 April 2015.

20 John Bingham, 'Vicar Investigated over "9/11 Israel did it" Posting', *Daily Telegraph*, 29 January 2015.

21 Dominic Kennedy, 'RSPCA Elects Vegan who said Farming is like the Holocaust', *The Times*, 20 June 2015.


## Chapter 1

1 Simon Sebag Montefiore, 'Kaiser Willy, a Dangerous Clown'. Review of John Röhl's new book on Wilhelm II, *Into the Abyss of War and Exile 1900–1941*, in *The Times*, 1 February 2014.

2 Alan Sked, review of *The Kaiser and His Court: Wilhelm II and the Government of Germany*, (review No. 47) http://www.history.ac.uk/reviews/review/47, accessed 20 April 2014.

3 Daniel Finkelstein, 'Terrifying Telltale Signs, Many Years before Hitler', *The Times*, 9 November 2013.

4 Paul Mühsam, in Monika Richarz, 'Jewish Life in Germany', p.254.

5 Richarz, pp.254–255.

6 Monty Noam Penkower, *The Swastika's Darkening Shadow* (New York: Palgrave Macmillan, 2013) pp.2–3.


## Chapter 2

1 Jupp Weiss, *From the Edge of The Abyss: Family Letters 1940–1946*, p.53. Translated by Gerald Weiss in 2000. I am grateful to David Weiss for sending me these documents in December 2013.

2 Marta Appel, in Richarz, p.352.

3 Ernest Levy, *Just one more Dance*, pp.45–46.

4 Levy, pp.72–73.

5 Wolf-Erich Eckstein, email to author, 29 August 2013. I am grateful to Mr Eckstein for confirming these details.

6 Otto Deutsch, email to author, 25 October 2013.

7 Otto Deutsch, email and telephone conversation with author, 24 February 2013.

8 'Maly Trostinec' (http://ausstellung.en.doew.at/b204.html) accessed 24 February 2013.

9 'Remembering Maly Trostinec' (http://www.erstestiftung.org/blog/remembering-maly-trostinec) accessed 24 February 2013.

10 Otto Deutsch, article in *Community Voice*, magazine of Southend & Westcliff Hebrew Congregation, Autumn 2013.

11 'The Children Britain took to its Heart', Jessica Elgot, *The Jewish Chronicle Online*, accessed 25 August 2013.

12 Otto Deutsch, telephone conversation with author, 17 March 2013.

13 Werner J. Cahnman, *German Jewry: Selected Essays*, p.151.

14 Zeef Eisikovic, *Memories of an Honourable Forger*, unpublished. Translation by Grete Heinz, of a book published only in German. Received 12 September 2013 from Stan Dub of Cleveland, pp.57–58.

15 Alfred Schwerin, 'Memoir' in Richarz, pp.404–405.

16 Alfred Schwerin, in Richarz, pp.404–405.

17 Schwerin in Richarz, p.405.

18 Gilbert Michlin, p.30.

19 Michlin, p.31.

20 Frederico Varese and Meir Yaish, 'Altruism: The Importance of Being Asked' in *Discussion Papers in Economic and Social History*, University of Oxford, No. 24, May 1998, p.3.

21 Varese and Yaish, p.17.

22 Varese and Yaish, p.27.

23 Elaine Sinclair, emails to author, 3 and 15 July 2013.

24 Bundesarchiv, 'The Expulsion of Polish Jews from the German Reich 1938/1938', 10 April 2013 (http://www.bundesarchiv.de/gedenkbuch/zwangsausweisung.html.en) accessed 23 July 2013.

25 Gerta Vrbová, *Trust and Deceit*, pp.10–11.

26 Vrbová, *Trust and Deceit*, pp.12–15.

27 Vrbová, *Trust and Deceit*, pp.19–20.

28 Vrbová, *Trust and Deceit*, p.26.

29 Vrbová, *Trust and Deceit*, pp.27–28.

30 Vrbová, *Trust and Deceit*, pp.15–16.

31 Vrbová, *Trust and Deceit*, pp.16–17.

32 Vrbová, *Betrayed Generation*, pp.18–19.

33 Vrbová, *Betrayed Generation*, pp.20–22.

34 Vrbová, *Betrayed Generation*, p.30.

35 Gerta Vrbová, email to author, 12 April 2014.

36 Lilli Aischberg-Bing Memoir 2002 (http://rjbing.caltech.edu/pdf/lilli.pdf) accessed 23 November 2013.

37 Meyerhoff, *Four Girls from Berlin*, p.113.

38 Meyerhoff, pp.168–169.

39 Bea Green, email to author, 15 January 2015.

40 Bea Green, email to author, 17 January 2015.

41 Peter Sinclair, *From Siegel to Sinclair*, online memoir January 2010 (EN_MU_JU_sinclair_peter_pdf) accessed 24 November 2013.

42 Bea Green, email to author, 16 January 2015.

43 Sara Kirby-Nieweg, *AJR Journal*, July 2013 p.

44 Sara, email to author, 6 August 2013.

45 Sara, email to author, 7 August 2013.

46 Sara, email to author, 6 August 2013.

47 Sara, email to author, 30 November 2013.

48 Sara Kirby-Nieweg, email to author, 13 December 2013.

49 Christine Fischer-Defoy and Judith C.E. Belinfante, 'Life: Biography 1917–1943' in *Charlotte Salomon, Life? Or Theatre?* (London: Royal Academy, 1998), pp.22–25.

50 Laurence Rees, *Auschwitz*, p.255.

51 Curtis, *Verdict on Vichy*, p.24.

52 Richard Cohen, 'Jacques Helbronner', in Yad Vashem, *Encyclopedia of the Holocaust*, Vol. 2 (New York: Macmillan, 1990), pp.653–654.

53 Roman Halter, *Roman's Journey*, p.23.

54 Roman Halter, pp.68–79.

55 Anna Lek, email to author, 10 November 2012, and Marie Rathbone, email to author, 8 December 2012. Anna and Marie are Rudi's daughters.

56 Marie Rathbone, email to author, 21 March 2014.

57 Shackell Pianos, 'The History of the Bechstein Piano' (http://www.shackellpianos.co.uk/bechstein-pianos.php) accessed 13 April 2014.

58 Marie Rathbone, email to author, 29 November 2012.

## Chapter 3

1 Robert Gellately, email to author, 14 July 2012.

2 Yad Vashem, 'Testimony on Ilse Sonja Totzke', emailed from Yad Vashem, 17 July 2012.

3 Meeting with Marta Elian at her home on 13 November 2013. I am grateful to John Andrews for arranging the contact.

4 Dorit Bader Whiteman in Handlin, *The Uprooted*, p.183.

5 Steven Fenves, Interview for USHMM, No. 2616, dated 10 June 2010 (http://www.ushmm.org/information/museum-programs-and-calendar/first-person-program/first-person-podcast/steven-fenves-neighbors-in-subotica) accessed 21 March 2015.

6 Morgan, *Ruta's Closet*, pp.57–58.

7 Morgan, *Ruta's Closet*, p.85.

8 Peter Sinclair memoir, pp.2–3.

9 Agnes Grunwald-Spier, *The Other Schindlers*, 2010, pp.117–120.

10 Henri Obstfeld, email to author, 4 August 2013.

11 Henri Obstfeld, email to author, 18 December 2013.

12 Robert Krell, 'A Little Dutch Boy Returns', address to child survivors, Amsterdam, 21 August 2005. Received from Robert Krell, 9 September 2005.

13 Howard K. Smith, *Last Train From Berlin*, p.132.

14 Smith, p.138.

15 'Reich Working Class Dissatisfied', *The Sentinel*, Chicago, 25 December 1941, p.30 (http://www.idaillinois.org/utils/getfile/collection/p16614coll14/id/1355/index.pdf) accessed 30 December 2013.

16 Hedi Fried, *The Road to Auschwitz: Fragments of a Life*, pp.52–53 (University of Nebraska Press, 1996).

17 Fried, p.59.

18 Fried, p.61.

19 Fried, p.62.

20 This section is based on Henry Abraham, *We Remember, 'My account: Holland 1940–45'* (Leicester: Matador, 2011), pp.3–11, and Max Paul Friedman, *Nazis and Good Neighbors* (Cambridge: Cambridge UP, 2003).

21 Hildegard Abraham, emails to author, 10 and 14 January 2014.

22 John Fransman, *Zachor: Child Survivors Speak* (London: Elliott & Thompson, 2005), pp.45–46.

23 John Fransman, email to author, 28 May 2014.

24 Robert Fraser, emails to author, 26 March 2014.

25 Additional family details from Robert Fraser, email to author, 4 March 2014. Robert has published his family's story in *From Kaiser to King: A Family Saga* (Perth, WA: Robert Fraser, 2013).

26 Keith Morgan, *Ruta's Closet*, pp.48–51.

27 Aleksandra Kopystynska, 'My Life in a Few Words', unpublished memoir dated 20 July 2012.

28 Aleksandra Kopystynska, emails to author, 21 July 2012 and 20 February 2014.

29 Jonathan Jones, 'Fascism or Forgery', *The Guardian*, 25 September 2006, accessed 24 February 2014.

30 Brigitte Hamann, *Hitler's Vienna: A Dictator's Apprenticeship* (London: Tauris Parke, 2010), p.350.

31 Joachim Fest, *Hitler*, p.46.

32 Reinhold Hanisch, 'I was Hitler's Buddy', *The New Republic*, 5, 12 and 19 April 1939, New York.

33 Hanisch, 12 April, p.272.

34 Brigitte Hamann, *Hitler's Vienna: A Dictator's Apprenticeship*, p.359.

35 Hamann, *Hitler's Vienna*, p.359.

36 Hamann, *Hitler's Vienna*, pp.34–37.

37 Ilse Loeb, email to author, 5 December 2010.

38 Hamann, p.349. Warmestuben were literally 'warm rooms' where people could sit and keep warm.

39 Joachim Fest, *Hitler*, p.39.

40 Richard Aronowitz, email to author, 17 December 2013.

41 William Kluback, *Benjamin Fondane: A Poet in Exile.*

42 John Kenneth Hyde, *Benjamin Fondane* (Geneva: Librairie Droz, 1971), pp.17–18.

43 Chiger and Paisner, *The Girl in the Green Sweater*, p.18.

44 Chiger and Paisner, p.31.

45 Aleksandra Kopystynska, unpublished memoir, received 20 May 2013.

46 The testimony in Polish and German (No. 6574) was deposited at the Jewish Historical Institute in Poland. I am grateful to Agnieszka Rezka for forwarding the document and Ola for the translation into English, received 24 August 2013.

47 Agnieszka Reszka, JHI, email to author, 25 February 2014.

48 Ola's email to author, 20 February 2014.

49 Diane Webber, emails to author, 12, 15 and 16 January 2013.

50 Eric Lanuit, *Margaret Kelly Leibovici, AKA Miss Bluebell*, The Lido, Paris, undated biography.

51 George Perry, *Bluebell*, p.120.

52 Perry, pp.122–126.

53 Perry, p.127.

54 Perry, pp.150–151.

55 Lanuit, p.2.

56 Jackie Mesrie (née Bentata), Linda's niece, emails to author, 5 March 2014.

57 Jackie Mesrie, 'An Emotional Journey' in *The Sephardi Congregation of South Manchester Bulletin*, April 2011, pp.47–49.

58 Jackie Mesrie, 'Remembering Linda and the Children' talk at Withington Girls School where Linda was a pupil, 19 Jan 2012.

59 Jackie Mesrie, Withington School essay, p.2 (accessed 14 June 2013).

60 Jackie Mesrie, email to author, 14 November 2013.

61 Withington, p.3, 2012.

62 Perry, Berg and Krukones, *Sources of European History since 1900* (Boston: Wadsworth, 2011), pp.169–170.


Chapter 4

1 Dan Kurzman, *The Race for Rome* (New York: Doubleday, 1975), pp.156–157.

2 Silvia Ross, 'Remembering Betrayal: The Roman Ghetto's Pantera Nera', in *Cultural Memory*, Caldicott and Fuchs (eds), (Peter Lang: Bern, 2003), pp.391–394.

3 Alexander Stille, *Benevolence and Betrayal: Five Italian Jewish Families Under Fascism* (London: Jonathan Cape, 1992), pp.211–215.

4 Silvia Ross, pp.403–404.

5 Klaus Wiegrefe, 'Unpunished Massacre in Italy', *Spiegel* Online, 19 January 2012 (http://www.spiegel.de/international/germany/unpunished-massacre-in-italy-how-postwar-germany-let-war-criminals-go-free-a-809537.html) accessed 26 March 2014.

6 Boris Smolar, *In the Service of my People* (Baltimore: Baltimore Hebrew College, 1982), pp.162–167.

7 JTA, Professor Sobernheim, *Orientalist*, 'German Foreign Office Official Dies at Age of 61', 6 January 1933, accessed 26 January 2014.

8 Steven Frank provided the information about his family.

9 Steven Frank, address for Holocaust Memorial Day on 20 January 2014, London City Hall. Text received 29 January 2014.

10 Frank, 20 January 2014.

11 Steven Frank email to author, 15 February 2013.

12 Steven Frank's address, 20 January 2014. The section is a combination of this document, the Zachor essay and an obituary of Leonard Frank written by Steven's brother, Carel.

13 Howard Boyers DFC, letter to author dated 22 May 1997. The Brodie referred to was Sir Israel Brodie KBE (1895–1979) who was the chief rabbi, 1948–1965.

14 Geoffrey Alderman, *Modern British Jewry* (Oxford: OUP, 1998), pp.281–282, citing a memorandum by Neville Laski on the WJC, dated 6 January 1937, BD C11/10/2 (Board of Deputies Archives).

15 Alderman, p.282.

16 Richard Bolchover, *British Jewry and the Holocaust* (Cambridge: CUP, 1994), p.36.

17 Curtis, p.32.

18 Bolchover, p.72.

19 Bolchover, pp.72–73.

20 Notes of meeting with Kitty Hart-Moxon, 23 June 2013.

21 Kitty Hart-Moxon, emails to author, 14 April 2014.

22 Stuart Jeffries, 'Memories of the Holocaust: Kitty Hart-Moxon', 27 January 2010 (http://www.theguardian.com/world/2010/jan/27/holocaust-memorial-day-kitty-hart-moxon) accessed 19 June 2013.

23 Diane Webber, email to author, 15 January 2013.

24 Diane Webber, email to author, 16 January 2013, contains testimony translated from French by Diane Webber.

25 United States Holocaust Memorial Museum. 'The Holocaust', *Holocaust Encyclopaedia* (http://www.ushmm.org/wlc/en/article.php?ModuleId=10005143) accessed on 4 February 2014.

26 Manfred Landau, telephone conversation with author, 27 March 2013.

27 Manfred Landau, telephone conversation with author, 6 March 2014.

28 Larry Orbach, *Soaring Underground: A Young Fugitive's Life in Nazi Berlin* (London: André Deutsch, 1996), pp.307–310.

29 The report was dated summer 1943, Document 219, but the date could not have been 1943. It must be later because of the contents. Cited in Meyer, Simon and Shütz (eds), *Jews in Nazi Berlin: From Kristallnacht to Liberation*, p.249.

30 Footnote 50 on p.271.

31 Barbara Lovenheim, *Survival in the Shadows: Seven Hidden Jews in Hitler's Berlin* (London: Peter Owen, 2002), p.70.

32 Christian Dirks, 'Snatchers', in Meyer, Simon and Schütz, *Jews in Nazi Berlin: From Kristallnacht to Liberation*, pp.249–267.

33 Carol Ann Lee, *The Hidden Life of Otto Frank* (London: Penguin, 2002), p.96.

34 Ed van Rijswijk, 'The Story of Ans Dijk', unpublished memoir sent to author 14 August 2012.

35 Jewish Virtual Library, 'Alois Brunner' (http://www.jewishvirtuallibrary.org/jsource/Holocaust/Brunner.html) accessed 10 March 2014.

36 Uwe Steinhoff, emails to author, 7 and 8 March 2014. Uwe Steinhoff runs the website for the Muehlberg Camp (lager).

37 Michael Matsas, *The Illusion of Safety: The Story of the Greek Jews During the Second World War*, pp.108–109.

38 Matsas, pp.185–187.

39 Lela Salmona, interviewed by Stephen Isaacs in 1994. Recording made available by Marcelle Black, 17 June 2014.

40 Marcelle Black, email to author, 19 June 2014.

41 http://www.holocaustresearchproject.org/othercamps/greekjewry.html.

42 Laurence Rees, *Auschwitz*, p.145.

43 Rees, p.105.

44 Rees, pp.129–130.

45 Rees, pp.130–131.

46 Michal Unger, *Reassessment of the Image of Mordechai Chaim Rumkowski* (Jerusalem: Yad Vashem, 2004), p.8.

47 Unger, p.9.

48 Primo Levi, 'Story of a Coin' in *Memories of Reprieve*, pp.170–171, cited in Unger p.54–55.

49 *Commentary* magazine, pp.24–25.

50 Unger, p.51, note 127.


## Chapter 5

1 Elizabeth Freund in Richarz, p.418.

2 Freund, in Richarz, p.421.

3 Freund, in Richarz, p.421.

4 Nara was an offshoot of the anti-Semitic party, Endek. Nara left Endek because they were not anti-Jewish enough.

5 JTA, 'Polish Jews are Beaten by Peasants', 11 June 1934, Warsaw, accessed 3 December 2013.

6 *Blackwell Dictionary of Judaica*.

7 http://www.jta.org/1934/08/21/archive/poland-arrests-nara-students-womenindrive#ixzz2mVRDViWD.

8 Lilli Aischberg-Bing memoir, 2002, p.23.

9 Judy Russell, memoir sent to author 3 April 2013.

10 Boris Smolar, p.172–173.

11 Elisabetta Cerruti, *The Ambassador's Wife*, p.148.

12 Nancy Caldwell Sorel, 'When Benito Mussolini met Adolf Hitler', *The Independent*, 3 February 1996 (http://www.independent.co.uk/life-style/when-benito-mussolini-met-adolf-hitler-1317121.html) accessed 19 April 2014.

13 From the collection of the Gratz College Holocaust Oral History Archive, p.4.

14 Chiger, pp.61–62.

15 Richard Chesnoff, *Pack of Thieves* (London: Weidenfeld & Nicolson, 2000), p.26.

16 Magdalena Müllner, *The Jews of Laa: Searching for Traces*, 1996 (http://www.lead-niskor.org/en/page50/page37/page37.html) accessed 15 January 2014.

17 Müllner, p.2.

18 Margaret Thatcher, *The Path to Power* (London: Harper Collins, 1995), pp.26–27.

19 Fay Schlesinger and Sorayi Kishtwari, 'Thatcher and Her Sister Saved a Jewish Girl's Life' in *The Times*, 22 April 2013, p.16.

20 The Bishop of London, the Right Rev. Richard Chartres, 'Oration at Baroness Thatcher's Funeral', *The Times*, 18 April 2013, p.8.

21 Christabel Bielenberg, the *Daily Telegraph* obituary, 4 November 2003 (http://www.telegraph.co.uk/news/obituaries/1445835/Christabel-Bielenberg.html) accessed 12 April 2014.

22 Christabel Bielenberg, *The Past in Myself*, pp.24–25.

23 Christabel Bielenberg, p.111–112.

24 Anna Sondhelm, p.18, unpublished testimony for Yad Vashem, 27 June 1991, 03/6434.

25 Volkswagen, p.22.

26 J.J. Aune, emails to author, 5 February 2013 and 15 February 2014. He is Marcelle's son.

27 J.J. Aune, email to author, 7 February 2013.

28 Aleksandra Kopystynska, email to author, 20 February 2014.

29 Max Dessau, tape for Imperial War Museum, Reel 1, listened to 28 March 2013.

30 Martin Gilbert, *The Boys: Triumph Over Diversity* (London: W&N, 1996)

31 Jan Gross, *Golden Harvest*, p.75–7.

32 Gross, *Golden Harvest*, p.81, cited from Ringelblum.

33 Lance Ackerfeld, 'Emmanuel Ringelblum', JewishGen Inc. website, p.4 (http://www.

jewishgen.org/yizkor/terrible_choice/ter004.html) accessed 24 February 2014.

34 Gross, *Golden Harvest*, p.82 (New York: Random House Paperbacks, 2006), pp.42–43.

35 Gross, *Fear*, pp.40–41.

36 Gross, *Golden Harvest*, pp.44-45.

37 Gross, *Golden Harvest*, pp.84–85.

38 Gross, *Golden Harvest*, p.78.

39 Klee, Dressen & Riess, pp.127–129.

40 Alice Herz-Sommer, obituary in *The Times*, 24 February 2014.

41 Gross, *Fear*, p.68.

42 Gross, *Fear*, p.61.

43 Gross, *Fear*, pp.61–62.

44 USHMM, 'The Kielce Pogrom: A Blood Libel Massacre of Holocaust Survivors' (http://www.ushmm.org/wlc/en/article.php?ModuleId=10007941) accessed 26 February 2014.

45 Gross, *Fear*, p.258.

## Chapter 6

1 'Lawyers without Rights: Jewish Lawyers in Germany under the Third Reich'. Exhibition of National Bar Council and German Federal Bar, June 2010. I am grateful to the National Bar Council for their help.

2 Raul Hilberg, 'The Holocaust: Three Views', *ADL Bulletin*, November 1977, p.1.

3 Douglas Martin, 'Raul Hilberg, 81, Historian Who Wrote of the Holocaust as a Bureaucracy, Dies', *New York Times*, 7 August 2007 (http://www.nytimes.com/2007/08/07/us/07hilberg.html?_r=0) accessed 10 May 2014.

4 Ron Grossman, 'How the Holocaust Happened', *The Chicago Tribune*, 12 November 1992 (http://articles.chicagotribune.com/1992-11-12/features/9204120744_1_perpetrators-victims-bystanders-raul-hilberg-holocaust) accessed 10 May 2014.

5 David Charter, 'British Auschwitz Victim Praises Nazi for Bravery', *The Times*, 25 April 2015.

6 Efraim Zuroff, 'Trial of Former Nazi Oskar Gröning will set a Precedent', i24news, 26 April 2015 (http://www.i24news.tv/en/opinion/69090-150426-the-importance-of-the-oskar-groening-case).

7 Laurence Rees, "Bookkeeper of Auschwitz' Recalls Camp Life with Joy', *The Sunday Times*, 26 April 2015.

8 David Charter, 'Book-keeper Jailed in "Last Auschwitz Trial"', *The Times*, 16 July 2015.

9 Raul Hilberg, 'German Railroads/Jewish Souls', *Society*, Vol. 14, No. 1, December 1976, p.163.

10 Ibid., p.163–172

11 Ibid.

12 Ibid.

13 Ibid.

14 Ibid.

15 Ibid.

16 Yad Vashem, 'The Righteous Among the Nations – Bronchard Family', File 6354, accessed 5 February 2014.

17 Benjamin Ivry, 'Time to Come Clean on Shoah Role' in Foreword, 13 March 2012.

18 Coalition for Holocaust Railway Justice (http://holocaustrailvictims.org/wp-content/uploads/2010/12/SNCF-Invoices.pdf) accessed 7 February 2014.

19 Ivry, p.2.

20 Anne Arundel, wbaltv.com, Baltimore County, 'Holocaust Survivor: Don't Let Train Co. Operate Marc Rails', 3 March 2011 (http://www.wbaltv.com/Holocaust-Survivor-Don-t-Let-Train-Co-Operate-MARC-Rails/-/9380084/8916530/-/view/print/-/4oul9a/-/index.html) accessed 7 February 2014.

21. Maïa de la Baume, 'French Railway Formally Apologizes to Holocaust Victims', *New York Times*, 25 January 2011 (http://www.nytimes.com/2011/01/26/world/europe/26france. html) accessed 6 April 2015.

22. Statement of the Honourable Samuel I. 'Sandy' Rosenberg, 20 June 2012 (http:// holocaustrailvictims.org/wp-content/uploads/2012/06/S.-Rosenberg-Written-Testimony.pdf) accessed 7 February 2014.

23. Jamey Keaten, 'France Agrees to Compensate Holocaust Deportees', 5 December 2014, ABC News, accessed 11 December 2014.

24. Courthouse News Service is a nationwide news service for lawyers and the news media. Based in Pasadena, California, Courthouse News focuses on civil litigation.

25. Joseph Celentino, 'Hungarian Entities Face Trimmed Holocaust Case', Courthouse News Service, 27 August 2012 (http://www.courthousenews.com/2012/08/27/49677.htm) accessed 28 March 2014.

26. Allan Hall, 'Jewish Train Escapers Tortured by Guilt', *The Times*, 17 May 2014.

27. Nechama Tec, *Resilience and Courage: Women, Men and the Holocaust* (New Haven: Yale UP, 2004) p.117.

28. Claire Prowizur-Szyper, 'Looking Backward: A Jewish Woman Fighting in Belgium' (Sifriyat Po'alim, 1981), pp.122–123.

29. Laurence Rees, 'What would the British have done?', 9 April 2012, ww2history.com (http://ww2history.com/blog/ww2-anniversary/what-would-the-british-have-done/) accessed 11 May 2014.

30. Michlin, p.106–107.

31. Michlin, p.57.

32. Isaac Levendel, *Not the Germans Alone: A Son's Search for the Truth of Vichy* (Evanston, IL: North-western UP, 2001) p.209.

33. Levendel, p.225.

34. Steinweis, p.58.

35. Steinweis, p.87.

36. Steinweis, p.46.

37. 'Readings for the Anniversary of Kristallnacht, November 9–10 1938'. From the collection of the Gratz College Holocaust Oral History Archive, p.7 (b.3cdn.net/ gratz/11278d4a084ffd8a3f_z1m6i6fs3.pdf) accessed 14 April 2014.

38. Joachim Krueger, 'Do the Right Thing', in *Psychology Today*, 18 January 2010 (http:// www.psychologytoday.com/blog/one-among-many/201001/do-the-right-thing) accessed 2 April 2014.

39. The Riga Synagogue on Peitvas Street (http://www.jews.lv/en/content/riga-synagogue-peitavas-street-peitav-shul) accessed 18 October 2013.

40. Jan Grabowski, *Hunt for The Jews: Betrayal and Murder in German-Occupied Poland*, pp.101–120.

41. Patricia Treble, 'Poland's Dark Hunt' in *Martyrdom and Resistance*, November/December 2013, p.7, accessed 11 February 2014.

42. Friedrich Klaus-Peter, 'Zygmunt Klukowski' (http://www.aapjstudies.org/index. php?id=89) accessed 12 February 2014.

43. Philippe Sands, 'My Father, the Good Nazi', *Financial Times*, 3 May 2013, accessed 19 November 2013.

44. Andrew Nagorski, 'There's No End Of History', *Newsweek*, 23 January 2000 (http:// www.newsweek.com/theres-no-end-history-158527) accessed 27 February 2014.

45. Fiona Wilson, 'Sons of Top Nazis Confront the Sins of their Fathers', *The Times*, 17 February 2014.

46. Roc Morin, 'An Interview with Nazi Leader Hermann Goering's Great Niece', *The Atlantic*, 16 October 2013 (http://www.theatlantic.com/international/archive/2013/10/an-interview-with-nazi-leader-hermann-goerings-great-niece/280579/) accessed 12 April 2015.

47 Fiona Wilson, '"Lost" Strauss Work Reignites Nazi Debate', *The Times*, 27 May 2014.

48 Laurence Rees, 'What would Britain have done?', 9 April 2012 (http://ww2history. com/blog/ww2-anniversary/what-would-the-british-have-done/#comments) accessed 11 May 2012.

49 Laurence Rees, *Auschwitz*, pp.180–181.

50 Julie Carpenter, 'John Nettles: "Telling the Truth about Channel Islands Cost me my Friends"', *Daily Express*, 5 November 2012 (http://www.express.co.uk/news/ showbiz/356209/John-Nettles-Telling-the-truth-about-Channel-Islands-cost-me-my- friends) accessed 21 May 2013.

51 *Ibid.*

52 David Fraser, *The Jews of the Channel Islands and the Rule of Law 1940-1945: 'Quite Contrary to the Principles of British Justice'* (Brighton: Sussex Academic Press, 2000), p.79.

53 Frederick Cohen, *The Jews in the Channel Islands During the German Occupation 1940–1945*, (Jersey: Jersey Heritage Trust, 2000), p.16.

54 Cohen, p.21.

55 Cohen, p.22.

56 Cohen, pp.42–43.

57 Cohen, pp.80–81.

58 Cohen, p.84.

59 Fulbrook, *A Small Town Near Auschwitz*, pp.19–20.

60 Fulbrook, p.327.

61 Fulbrook, p.1.

62 Fulbrook, p.71.

63 Fulbrook, p.177.

64 Fulbrook, p.277.

65 Fulbrook, p.163–164.

66 Fulbrook, pp.280–281.

67 Fulbrook, p.347.

68 Fulbrook, p.346.

69 Jonathan Yardley, Book Review,1 December 2012, *Washington Post* (http://www. washingtonpost.com/opinions/a-small-town-near-auschwitz-ordinary-nazis-and-the- holocaust-by-mary-fulbrook/2012/11/30/8851e3d4-33dd-11e2-bb9b-288a310849ee_print. html) accessed 23 March 2014.

70 Fulbrook, pp.113–115.

## Chapter 7

1 Kershaw, *Popular Opinion and Political Dissent in the Third Reich: Bavaria 1933–1945* (Oxford: Clarendon Press, 1988), p.363.

2 Boris Smolar, *In the Service of My People*, p. 174.

3 Ad van Liempt, *Hitler's Bounty Hunters: The Betrayal of the Jews* (Oxford: Berg, 2005), p.ix.

4 Liempt, pp.6 and 222, footnote 1.

5 (http://www.yadvashem.org/yv/en/righteous/stories/calmeyer.asp) accessed 22 January 2014.

6 Liempt, pp.10–11.

7 Liempt, p.11.

8 Charles Bremner, 'Dutch Royal Family Returns Painting Looted by the Nazis', *The Times*, 1 April 2015.

9 Liempt, p.12–13.

10 Liempt, p.14.

11 Liempt, p.15.

12 Liempt, p.17.

13 Liempt pp.17–18.

14 Liempt, pp.20–22.

15 Liempt, pp.26–27.

16 Liempt, pp.26–27.

17 Liempt, p.33.

18 Liempt, p.44.

19 Liempt, p.69.

20 Liempt, p.114.

21 Cnaan Liphshiz, 'In Eye of Nazi Storm, Dutch Jews Found Unlikely Refuge', *The Jewish Daily Forward*, 18 May 2014 (http://forward.com/articles/198410/at-the-height-of-world-war-ii-dutch-jews-found-an) accessed 19 May 2014.

22 Herman van Rens' 2013 book is *Persecuted in Limburg*, but is currently only available in Dutch.

23 Philip Mechanicus, *Waiting for Death* (London: Calder & Boyars, 1968), p.119.

24 Mechanicus, pp.172–173.

25 Boris Smolar, *In the Service of my People*, pp.169–170.

26 Chiger, pp.32–33.

27 Richard Chesnoff, *Pack of Thieves* (London: Weidenfeld & Nicolson, 2000), p.29, footnote 3.

28 Notes of meeting with Kitty Hart-Moxon on 19 June 2013, at her home.

29 Sonja Fritz, *Block 30 in Birkenau*, pp.26–27.

30 Danuta Czech, *Auschwitz Chronicle 1939–1945* (New York: Henry Holt, 1990), p.537.

31 Czech, p.542–543.

32 Czech, p.723.

33 Czech, p.812.

34 David Charter, 'Auschwitz Book-Keeper', *The Times*, 22 April 2015.

35 David Charter, 'I Had to Pull Gold from the Teeth of Jews to Survive', *The Times*, 24 April 2014.

36 Gross, *Golden Harvest*, p.121.

37 Friedlander, p.xxi.

38 Gross, *Golden Harvest*, p.121.

39 Gross, *Golden Harvest*, p. xiii.

40 Gross, *Golden Harvest*, p. 6.

41 ARC Treblinka 2005 – accessed 14 February 2014.

42 Gross, *Golden Harvest*, pp.31–33.

43 Gross, *Golden Harvest*, p.35.

44 Footnote 62, *Golden Harvest* p.36.

45 Gross, *Golden Harvest*, pp.37–38.

46 Götz Aly, *Hitler's Beneficiaries* (New York: Henry Holt, 2006), pp.253–255.

47 Prof. Aron Rodrigue, 'The Jews of Rhodes and the Holocaust', lecture at University College London on 21 October 2013.

48 Stephen Gabriel Rosenberg, 'Preserving Cretan Jewry', in *The Jerusalem Post*, 19 November 2009 (http://www.jpost.com/Magazine/Preserving-Cretan-Jewry) accessed 17 November 2013.

49 Rodrigue lecture.

50 Laura Varon, *The Juderia* (Westport, CN: Praeger, 1999), pp.38–39.

51 Laura Varon, 'Testimony About her Family in Auschwitz', Yad Vashem (http://www.yadvashem.org/odot_pdf/Microsoft%20Word%20-%204004.pdf) accessed 10 April 2014.

52 Aly, pp.267–275.

53 Gross, *Golden Harvest*, p.79. The document was translated and made available by Dr Gabriella Etmektsoglou.

54 Gross, *Golden Harvest*, pp.43–44.

55 JTA, 'Vandals Break into Thessaloniki Jewish Cemetery', 30 May 2014, accessed 31 May 2014.

56 Professor Heinz Kuhn, Obituary in *The Times*, 25 June 2013.

57 Frank Bajohr, The Holocaust and Corruption, in *Networks of Nazi Persecution*, Feldman and Seibel (Eds), (New York: Berghahn, 2005), pp.118–123.

58 Bajohr, p.280.

59 Bajohr, p.281.

60 Bajohr, p.281.

61 Jerzy Tomaszewski, 'Polenaktion', *Yivo Encyclopedia*, accessed 18 November 2013.

62 '"Aryanization" in Leipzig', Leipzig City Museum exhibition, p.34.

63 'Jewish Houses in Leipzig 1939–1945', a student project of the Henriette-Goldschmidt School, Leipzig, 2006, accessed 18 November 2013.

64 '"Aryanization" in Leipzig', p.38.

65 '"Aryanization" in Leipzig', p.27.

66 http://www.lesartsdecoratifs.fr/english-439/nissim-de-camondo-742

67 Richard I. Cohen, *The Rothschilds of the East* (http://jewishreviewofbooks.com/articles/264/the-rothschilds-of-the-east), summer 2010, accessed 7 December 2013.

68 'The Camondos: A Saga of Splendor and Tragedy', November 2009 (http://www.french-chicshopping.com/2009/11/the-camondos-a-saga-of-splendor-and-tragedy) accessed 8 December 2013.

69 Sheila Campbell, 'A visit to the Nissim de Camondo in Paris', 11 November 2011 (http://sheilacampbell.com/a-visit-to-the-nissim-de-comondo-in-paris) accessed 7 December 2013.

70 (http://carolwallace.wordpress.com/2011/04/08/pierre-assouline-le-dernier-des-camondo) accessed 6 December 2013.

71 Joan Wickersham, 'Paris and the Ghosts of the Unthinkable', *The Boston Globe*, 24 December 2010 (http://www.boston.com/bostonglobe/editorial_opinion/oped/articles/2010/12/24/paris_and_ghosts_of_the_unthinkable) accessed 8 December 2013.

72 Kate Hedges, 'Musée Nissim Camando', 22 November 2005 (http://nocrowds.blogspot.co.uk/2005/11/musee-nissim-de-camando.html) accessed 7 December 2013.

73 Benjamin Ivry, 'Camondo Splendor', Forward.com, 22 January 2010 (http://forward.com/articles/123207/camondo-splendor) accessed 7 December 2013.

74 Ambroise Vollard, *Memoirs of a Picture Dealer* (New York: Dover Publications, 1978), p.103.

75 Ivry, Forward.com.

76 'The Camondos: A Saga of Splendor and Tragedy', November 2009 (http://www.french-chicshopping.com/2009/11/the-camondos-a-saga-of-splendor-and-tragedy) accessed 8 December 2013.

77 The author is most grateful to Janine and Eddy Webber for providing the English translation from French. Sadly Eddy died in March 2015.

## Chapter 8

1 Maimonides, Mishneh Torah, Laws of Torah 1:8–9i.

2 The librarian (unnamed) of the Sholem Aleichem Library in Radomsko, Poland; quoted in David Shavit, *Hunger for the Printed Word*, cited in Pugliese, *Bloodless Torture*, p.242. Stanislas G. Pugliese, 'Bloodless Torture: The Books of the Roman Ghetto under the Nazi Occupation', Libraries & Culture, Vol.34, No.3, Summer 1999 (University of Texas Press).

3 USHMM, 'Nazi Propaganda and Censorship', p.2 (http://www.ushmm.org/outreach/en/article.php?ModuleId=10007677) accessed 24 December 2013.

4 Janssen and Yacoub, 'In Iraq, a Historic Christian Library Saved from Militants',

Associated Press, 3 April 2015 (http://bigstory.ap.org/article/f9ecd89d18304021af9ee
d7087fe3358/iraq-historic-christian-library-saved-militants) accessed 5 April 2015.

5 'UNESCO Deplores "Cultural Cleansing" of Iraq as Armed Extremists Ransack Mosul
Libraries', 3 February 2015 (http://www.un.org/apps/news/story.asp?NewsID=49982#.
VSE5Boog-P8) accessed 4 February 2015.

6 Pugliese, *Bloodless Torture*, p.242.

7 Christopher Duggan, 'Popular Opinion in Fascist Italy: the Racial Laws in Context',
Powerpoint at Wiener Library, London, 27 November 2013, Slide 3. Also Christopher
Duggan, *Fascist Voices*, p.311. (Professor Duggan sadly died prematurely whilst the author
was completing this book; he was most helpful and kind.)

8 Duggan – Wiener Library Powerpoint, Slide 2.

9 Dreyfuss and Gensberger, *Nazi Labour Camps in Paris*, p.8.

10 Dreyfuss and Gensberger, pp.8–9.

11 Ibid, p.19.

12 Shirer, *The Rise and Fall*, pp.945–946.

13 Shirer, p.945.

14 Interview with Rabbi Meir Schapira, *The Jewish Chronicle*, 29 August 1924 (http://
onthemainline.blogspot.co.uk/2010/08/1924-interview-with-rabbi-meir-shapiro.html)
accessed 28 December 2013.

15 Report on meeting of 19 December 1930, *The Jewish Chronicle* (http://onthemainline.
blogspot.co.uk/2010/08/1924-interview-with-rabbi-meir-shapiro.html) accessed
28 December 2013.

16 Robert Katz, *Black Sabbath* (Arthur Barker, 1969), p.120.

17 Giacomo Debenedetti, '16 Ottobre 1943', cited in *Black Sabbath*, p.123.

18 Pugliese, p.247.

19 Danuta Czech, *Auschwitz Chronicle*, p.512. RSHA transports were organised by
Eichmann's office.

20 Pugliese, *Bloodless Torture*, p.249.

21 History of the IISH, accessed 31 December 2013.

22 Grimstead, 'Documenting Nazi Cultural Looting and Postwar Retrieval', paper at
Cultural Plunder Conference, 19 October 2011, p.2, accessed 31 December 2013.

23 Pugliese, *Bloodless Torture*, p.250.

24 Primo Levi Centre, New York, flyer for 'The Lost Jewish Library of Rome' meeting on
9 February 2015.

25 Elizabeth M. Yavnai, 'Jewish Cultural Property and its Post-war Recovery' in *Confiscation
of Jewish Property in Europe 1933–1945* (Washington DC: USHMM, 2003), p.127.

26 Rudolf Smend, article on Isaac Leo Seeligmann, *Studia Rosenthaliana*, Vol. 38/39,
pp.100–107.

27 Yavnai, pp.137–138.

28 I am grateful to Marit Scharffenorth of Amsterdam for translating the eulogy from
Dutch.

29 F.J. Hoogewoud, emails to author, 31 August and 1 September 2013.

30 F.J. Hoogewoud, 'Dutch Jewish Ex Libris Found Among Looted Books in the Offenbach
Archival Depot (1946)', Leiden, 2001.

31 (http://www.clintonlibrary.gov/assets/storage/Research%20-%20Digital%20Library/
holocaust/theft/Box%20155/6997222-libraries.pdf) accessed 24 February 2014.

32 Seymour J. Pomrenze, 'Offenbach Archival Depot: Establishment and Operation',
USHMM, 30 November 1998, accessed 24 February 2014.

33 Rhys Blakely, 'Leading Libraries Told to Track Down Books Looted by the Nazis', *The*

*Times*, 13 September 2014.

34 Kristian Jensen, letter to *The Times* on looted books, 16 September 2014.

*Chapter 9*

1 Ted Morgan, *An Uncertain Hour*, pp.141–142.

2 Isaiah Trunk, *Judenrat: The Jewish Councils in Eastern Europe under Nazi Occupation* (Lincoln, NE: Bison Books, 1996), p.143.

3 Trunk, p.144.

4 Trunk, pp.144–145.

5 Trunk, pp.145–146.

6 Trunk, pp.147–148.

7 Werner J. Cahnman, 'In the Dachau Concentration Camp: an Autobiographical Essay in German Jewry', *Selected Essays of Werner J. Cahnman*, 1989, pp. 151–158.

8 Alison Owings, *Frauen: German Women Recall the Third Reich* (London: Penguin Books, 1995), Preface, p.xi.

9 Mangel Worsel is sugar beet used as cattle feed from the German – beet is *Mangel* and root is *Wurzel*.

10 Christopher Hammond, George's nephew, email to author, 21 November 2013. I am grateful to Christopher for sending me extracts from George's letter to him from the late 1990s.

11 Christopher Hammond, email to author, 30 October 2013.

12 Yad Vashem, 'The Righteous Among the Nations, British POWs', accessed 1 November 2013.

13 Yad Vashem, 'The Righteous Among the Nations, From the Diary of British POW William Fisher', accessed 1 November 2013.

14 Ibid.

15 *The Journal*, summer 2013, No. 24, pp.63–64 (http://www.thequeensownbuffs.com/ Queens_Own_Buffs/The_Regimental_Newsletter_The_Journal_files/Journal%20 Summer%202013.pdf) accessed 1 November 2013.

16 Martin Gilbert, *Atlas of the Holocaust*, p.34.

17 Marian Kampinski, *Remember Me* (Bloomington, IN: iUniverse, 2009), pp.93–95.

18 *Samuel Pepys' Diary*, entry for 7 June 1665. Tobacco was regarded as having medicinal value against the Plague.

19 Franciszek Zabecki, memoirs 1977, ARC 2005, pp.1–2.

20 Gitta Sereny, *Into That Darkness*, pp.212–13.

21 Sereny, p.213.

22 Sereny, p.214.

23 Rudolf Vrba. He was married to Gerta Vrbová for a while.

24 I wrote about Dora in *The Other Schindlers*, pp.115–116.

25 Nancy Durrant, 'When He Came out of the Camps all he Wanted to do was be an Artist', in *The Times*, 5 February 2014.

26 Laurence Rees, *Auschwitz*, pp.316–317.

27 Danuta Czech, p.59.

28 Jen Singerman, 'Gathering the Voices', *AJR Journal*, March 2014, p.5.

29 Sonja Fritz, *Block 30 in Birkenau*, pp. 18–27, in 'Criminal Experiments on Human Beings in Auschwitz and War Research Laboritories', ed. Lore Shelley (Mellen Research UP, 1991)

30 Julie Nicholson, 'To preserve history and learn its lessons is an essential task', in Volkswagen book, pp.33–38.

31 Timothy Snyder, 'The Auschwitz Volunteer: Beyond Bravery', in *New York Times*, 22 June 2012 (http://www.nytimes.com/2012/06/24/books/review/the-auschwitz-volunteer-by-witold-pilecki.html?_r=0) accessed 3 February 2015.

32 Anita Lasker-Wallfisch, *Inherit the Truth* (New York: St Martin's Pres, 2000), pp.76–77.

33 Lasker-Wallfisch, p.78.

34 Lasker-Wallfisch, p.79.

35 Lasker-Wallfisch, p.85.

36 Lasker-Wallfisch, p.27.

37 Lasker-Wallfisch, p.28.

38 Lasker-Wallfisch, p.33.

39 Lasker-Wallfisch, p.34.

40 Lasker-Wallfisch, p.37.

41 Lasker-Wallfisch, pp.38–39.

42 Lasker-Wallfisch, pp.42–43.

43 Henry Golde, 'Wisconsin Survivors of the Holocaust' interviews, Wisconsin Historical Society, p.52 (http://www.wisconsinhistory.org/HolocaustSurvivors/pdfs/Golde.pdf) accessed 19 December 2013.

44 Morgan, *Ruta's Closet*, pp.86–87.

45 Morgan, pp.88–89.

46 Magdalena Berkovics, interviewed by Gail Schwartz for USHMM on 15 October 2009, accessed 17 December 2013.

47 (http://www.dailymail.co.uk/news/article-2523071/Romanian-state-TV-condemned-Christmas-carol-choir-sang-burning-Jews.html#ixzz200kPUPZM) accessed 20 December 2013.

48 World Jewish Congress, 'ICJP Condemns Anti-Jewish Christmas Carol Broadcast on Romanian State TV', 13 December 2013, accessed 14 December 2013.

49 Hedi Fischer Frankl, 'My Memories of the Holocaust in Zachor', *Child Survivors Speak* (London: Elliott & Thompson, 2005), pp.56–59.

50 Laurence Rees, interview with Toivi Blatt 2003, participant in Sobibór Revolt (ww2history.com) accessed 15 June 2003.

51 USHMM *Holocaust Encyclopedia*, Tomasz (Toivi) Blatt, accessed 15 June 2013.

52 Symi Rom-Rymer, 'People of the Book', interview with Julie Orringer, *Moment Magazine* website, 11 February 2011, p.3 (http://momentmagazine.wordpress.com/2011/02/11/people-of-the-book-interview-with-julie-orringer) accessed 22 April 2014.

53 Solomon Radasky's Story, 'Holocaust Survivors' (http://www.holocaustsurvivors.org/data.show.php?di=record&da=survivors&ke=7) accessed 9 February 2014, p.2.

54 David Weiss, 'Forward and Afterward', April 2011, unpublished memoir sent to author on 5 December 2013.

55 Hans-Dieter Arntz, abstract of book on Jupp Weiss, 27 December 2012.

56 Gerald Weiss, 'From the Edge of the Abyss: Family Letters 1940–1946', memoir 2000, sent to author by David Weiss on 5 December 2013.

57 Madeleine Abramson, 'The Beginning of the Road', *AJR Journal*, December 2013, p.5.


*Chapter 10*

1 Martin Gilbert, *The Kovno Ghetto Diary*, Introduction, pp.xix–xx.

2 David Charter, 'Audi's Nazi Boss Sent Slaves to their Deaths', *The Times*, 27 May 2014.

3 'Siemens Opens Nazi Camp File', Toby Axelrod, 3 March 2011 (http://www.thejc.com/print/46062) accessed 9 October 2013.

4 Toby Axelrod, 'A Holocaust Survivor Stonewalled by Siemens', in *The Times of Israel*, 8 April 2013 (http://www.timesofisrael.com/a-holocaust-survivor-stonewalled-by-siemens) accessed 16 February 2014.

5 Miranda Bryany/Peter Popham – article in *The Independent*, 3 November 2008.

6 Bonstein, Hawranek and Wiegrefe, 'Breaking the Silence', *Spiegel* Online, p.1,

10 December 2007, accessed 18 October 2013.

7 Ibid., p.2.

8 Ibid., p.3.

9 Ibid., p.4.

10 Fiona Govan, 'BMW Dynasty Breaks Silence Over Nazi Past', *The Telegraph* online, 29 September 2011, accessed 18 October 2013.

11 Louis P. Lochner (Trans. and Editor), *The Goebbels Diaries* (London: Hamish Hamilton, 1948), p.58.

12 Lochner, p.xxiii.

13 *Independent*, 3 November 2008, p.3.

14 Richard J. Evans, Obituary for Gerald Feldman, *The Guardian*, 15 January 2008 (http://www.theguardian.com/world/2008/jan/15/secondworldwar.books) accessed 13 January 2014.

15 Aaron Kuriloff, 'Stadium Ends Talks with Allianz, Auschwitz Insurer', bloomberg. com, 12 September 2008 (http://www.bloomberg.com/apps/news?sid=ae12eZK. nqOA&pid=newsarchive) accessed 9 June 2014.

16 Joint Statement of 16 February 1999, report from the Federal Republic of Germany Embassy, London.

17 Smorodsky, 'Nazi Era Slave and Forced Labor Settlement Agreements' (http://www. smorodsky.com/forcedlabor-exec-summary.html) accessed 10 June 2014.

18 Sam Greenspan, '11 Companies that Surprisingly Collaborated with the Nazis'. http:// www.11points.com/News-Politics.

19 Edwin Black, *IBM and the Holocaust* (London: Little, Brown & Co., 2001), p.11.

20 Paul Festa, 'Probing IBM's Nazi Connection', cnetnews.com, 28 June 2001 (http:// news.cnet.com/Probing-IBMs-Nazi-connection/2009-1082_3-269157.html) accessed 30 January 2014.

21 'Hugo Boss Acknowledges Link to Nazi Regime', *New York Times*, 15 August 1997 (http://www.nytimes.com/1997/08/15/business/hugo-boss-acknowledges-link-to-nazi-regime.html) accessed 30 January 2014.

22 Roman Köster, 'Hugo Boss, 1924-1945. A Clothing Factory During the Weimar Republic and Third Reich' (abridged English version) 2011 (http://group.hugoboss.com/ files/Study_on_the_Companys_History_Abridged_Verson_en_final.pdf) accessed 30 January 2014.

23 Avraham Barkai, p.75, citing KZ article of 13 October 1935.

24 Grenville, pp.228 and 286.

25 Transactions of the AES 1918 – accessed 13 October 2013.

26 Dieter Mechlinski, email to author, 12 November 2013.

27 Christie's, Lot 149, Hans Thoma, 2005.

28 Alte Pinakothek, provenance research for Hans Thoma's *Dusk at Lake Garda*, 1906, accessed 10 November 2013.

29 'Sisley in England and Wales', November 2008–February 2009, *Immunity from Seizure*, The National Gallery, London, 'Bridge at Hampton Court 1874' owned by Otto Wolff, p.5.

30 Robin Munro, 'A Nazi-Era Industrialist Makes Good', *The Moscow Times* online, 6 May 2003, accessed 9 November 2013.

31 *Places of Remembrance & Commemoration* – National Socialism in Munich in 2010, p.70 (Landeshauptstadt, Munchen, Kulturreferat, 2010).

32 Münchner Stadtmuseum, 'The Uhlfelder Department Store', accessed 23 November 2013.

33 *Places of Remembrance*, p.69.

34 *Syracuse New Times*, 2001 (http://faithful readers.com/2012/05/10/Oktoberfest) accessed 23 November 2013.

35 Dana Thomas, 'The Power Behind the Cologne', *The New York Times*, 24 February 2002.

36 Adam Sage, 'Chanel Number F-7124: Designer's Wartime Role as German Spy Exposed', *The Times*, 2 December 2014.

37 *Telegraph*, 24 August 2011.

38 *Telegraph*, 5 September 2011.

39 *Independent*, 1 May 2012.

40 Prof. Margo Somerville, email to author, 21 October 2013.

41 Lynda Hurst, 'Decades of Delay: Wages of Nazi Slavery, Groups Jockey for Payment in Race Against Time', *Toronto Star*, 28 August 1999, emailed to author from *Toronto Star* on 31 January 2014.

42 Roger Boyes, 'Former VW Slave Workers Seeking Compensation' in the *Independent*, 17 June 1998.

43 religioustolerance.org.uk, 31 January 2011.

44 *BBC News*, 9 July 1998, accessed 20 October 2013.

45 William Horsley, *BBC News*, 14 February 1999, accessed 20 October 2013.

46 William L. Shirer, *The Rise and Fall of the Third Reich* (London: Secker & Warburg, 1962), pp.266–267.

47 Nicholas Levis, *Working for the Enemy*, Prologue, pp.28–29.

48 Deborah Sturman, 'Germany's Re-examination of its Past through the Lens of the Holocaust Litigation', in *Holocaust Restitution*, 2006.

49 *Wall Street Journal*, 1999.

50 Iwanowa vs Ford Motor Co. (http://www.leagle.com/decision/199949167 FSupp2d424_1453.xml/IWANOWA%20v.%20FORD%20MOTOR).

51 Michael Dobbs, *Washington Post*, 30 November 1998.

52 Melvyn Weiss, p.107 in *Holocaust Restitution*.

53 B.A. Robinson, 'Financial Compensation for Nazi Slave Labourers', 31 January 2011 (http://www.religioustolerance.org/fin_nazi.htm) accessed 20 October 2013.

54 Jonathan R. Logsdon, 'Power, Ignorance and Anti-Semitism: Henry Ford and His War on the Jews' *The Hanover Historical Review* (1999), accessed 30 June 2013.

55 Logsdon, p.28.

56 Michael Dobbs, *Washington Post*.

57 Dobbs, *Washington Post*, p.4.

58 Dobbs, p.6.

59 Joshua Karliner, 'Ford and the Nazi War Efforts: Henry Ford was no Oskar Schindler', 1 November 1998, CorpWatch (http://www.corpwatch.org/article.php?id=4368) accessed 3 February 2014.

60 Billstein, *Working for the Enemy*, p.107.

61 Logsdon, 'Henry Ford and His War on the Jews', *The Hanover Historical Review* (1999), p.27.

62 LeBor and Boyes, *Surviving Hitler*, p.126.

63 ICI Company Profile (http://www.referenceforbusiness.com/history2/19/Imperial-Chemical-IndustriesPLC.html#ixzz33Yh2IJDi) accessed 3 June 2014.

64 Robert Jay Lifton, *Doctors*, p.303.

65 Eva Kor, 'Why Forgiveness is the Best Revenge of All', *The Times*, 25 April 2015.

66 Jozef Paczynski obituary, *The Times*, 2 May 2015.

67 Jeffreys, pp.275–276.

68 Jeffreys, p.277.

69 Sven Keller, email to author, 7 May 2014.

70 Christophe Schult, 'Dr Mengele's Victim', *Spiegel* Online, 12 October 2009 (http://www.spiegel.de/international/world/dr-mengele-s-victim-why-one-auschwitz-survivor-avoided-doctors-for-65-years-a-666327.html) accessed 11 February 2009.

71 Meeting with Kitty Hart-Moxon, 19 June 2013.

72 'The History of the Business with Disease' (http://www4.dr-rath foundation.org/
   PHARMACEUTICAL_BUSINESS/history_of_the_pharmaceutical_industry.htm)
   accessed 1 February 2014.

73 JTA, 'Compliments Do Not Improve Jewish Situation', 10 January 1929, accessed
   10 January 2014.

74 JTA, 'Strict Sunday Closing Imposed on Salonica Jews', 14 January 1934, accessed
   12 January 2014.

75 Hannah Ahlheim, 'Establishing Antisemitic Stereotypes: Social and Economic Segregation
   of Jews by Means of Political Boycott in Germany', *Leo Baeck Institute Year Book*, Vol. 55,
   pp.149–173.

76 JTA, 'Nazi Adherents Flout Schacht on Trade Edict', 17 December 1934, accessed
   5 December 2013.

77 *American Jewish Year Book 5697*, p.365.

78 JTA, 'Jews Forbidden to Sell Newspapers in Hungary', 23 January 1942 (http://www.
   jta.org/1942/01/23/archive/jews-forbidden-to-sell-newspapers-in-hungary-anti-nazi-
   leaflets-in-budapest) accessed 19 January 2014.

79 JTA, 'Huge Crowds Jam German Auction Rooms to Buy Confiscated Jewish
   Possessions', 28 December 1941, accessed 23 December 2013.

80 Brenda Bailey, *A Quaker Couple in Nazi Germany* (York: William Sessions Ltd., 1994),
   p.38.

## Chapter 11

1  Julius Streicher, introduction to *Die Judenfrage im Unterricht* by Fritz Fink
   (Nuremberg: 1937).

2  German Propaganda Archive, Calvin: 'Minds in the Making', 2001 (http://www.calvin.
   edu/academic/cas/gpa/fink.htm) accessed 16 February 2014.

3  Grenville, p.105.

4  *Jewish Forward*, 'Greek School Unearths Diplomas for 157 Jewish Students Killed in
   Holocaust', Forward.com (http://forward.com/articles/190442/greek-school-unearths-
   diplomas-for--jewishstud/#ixzz2piaYvhFd) accessed 19 January 2014.

5  Grenville, p.105.

6  Jonathan R. Logsdon, *Henry Ford and His War on the Jews* (1999), p.27.

7  Emmy Goering, *My Life with Goering* (London: David Bruce & Watson, 1972), p.90.

8  Victor Smart, 'Baldur von Schirach: Reich Youth Leader', HEART Research Project
   2008, accessed 19 January 2014.

9  William L. Shirer, *This is Berlin: Reporting from Nazi Germany 1938–1940* (London:
   Random House, 1999), p.219.

10 See his obituary in *New York Times*, 18 February 2002. He was the moderator for the first
   presidential TV debate between Nixon and Kennedy in 1960.

11 Howard K. Smith, *Last Train from Berlin* (London: Cresset Press, 1942), p.127.

12 Smith, pp.127–128.

13 Smith, pp.126–127.

14 Kershaw, pp. 243–244.

15 Michael Kater, *Hitler Youth* (Cambridge, MA: HUP, 2004).

16 Larry Orbach, *Soaring Underground*, pp.5–7.

17 Orbach, pp.14–15.

18 Orbach, pp.18–19.

19 Christopher Duggan, *Fascist Voices: An Intimate History of Mussolini's Italy* (London: Bodley
   Head, 2012), pp.186–187.

20 JTA, 15 August 1939 – accessed 15 October 2013.

21 'Memorial Book for the Victims of National Socialism' at the University of Vienna in 1938.

22 Ibid., preamble, p.1.

23 Herbert Posch, 'Academic Expatriations at the University of Vienna' (2006), translated into English by Thomas Rennert, received by the author 18 December 2013.

24 Ibid., p.1.

25 Herbert Posch, email to author, 18 December 2013.

26 Posch, p.2.

27 Posch, p.3.

28 Posch, p.5.

29 Posch, p.6.

30 Posch, p.7.

31 Posch, p.9.

32 Posch, p.10.

33 Posch, p.11.

34 Otto Fleming, cited in Dorit Bader Whiteman, *The Uprooted: A Hitler Legacy* (New York: Plenum Publishing, 1993), p.195.

35 R.G. Grainger, 'Otto Fleming', *British Medical Journal*, 19 May 2007 (http://www.ncbi. nlm.nih.gov/pmc/articles/PMC1871790) accessed 2 March 2014. I am grateful to the BMJ for sending me the obituary.

36 Leibnitz University of Hanover, 'Report of the Senate Task Force on the Awarding and Withdrawal of Titles during the Nazi Era', Press Release 13 June 2012, accessed 15 October 2013.

37 Prof. Dr Holger Butenschön, head of the working group, email to author, 21 October 2013.

38 David Wroe, '88-year-old gets Doctorate 65 Years After Passing Exams', *Daily Telegraph*, 21 November 2008, accessed 26 October 2013.

39 Carina Baganz, 'Displaced Scientists', in *Knowledge*, TUB, 11 July 2013, accessed 25 October 2013.

40 Dr Carina Baganz, email to author, 28 October 2013.

41 Beate Schäffler, Hamburg University press office, email to author, 9 June 2015.

42 James Graff, 'Ingeborg Rapoport to Become Oldest Recipient of Doctorate After Nazi Injustice is Righted', *Wall Street Journal*, 14 May 2015 (http://www.wsj.com/articles/ from-nazi-germany-a-tale-of-redemption-1431576062) accessed 8 June 2015. Doctoral awards ceremony for 102-year-old paediatrician, press release from Hamburg University, 9 June 2015, sent to author by Beate Schäffler.

43 JTA, 'Nara Students Row over Corpse Issue', 17 December 1934, accessed 4 December 2013.

44 JTA, 'Poland Arrests Nara Students', 21 August 1934, accessed 4 December 2013.

45 Gábor Kádár and Zoltán Vági, *Self-financing Genocide* (Budapest: CEU Press, 2004), pp.3–7.

46 Thomas Spira, 'Hungary's Numerus Clausus, the Jewish Minority and the League of Nations', *Hungarian Yearbook*, Vol. 4, 1972, Hungarian Institute, Munich, p.115.

47 Spira, p.119.

48 Spira, pp.119–120.

49 Spira, p.122.

50 Spira, p.123.

51 Spira, pp.123–124.

52 Spira, p.124, footnote 33.

53 Spira, p.127.

54 Jewish Virtual Library, 'The League of Nations', accessed 10 January 2014.

55 Mária M. Kovács, *Afflicted by Law: The Numerus Clausus in Hungary 1920–1945*.

56 *Hungarian Spectrum*, a Hungarian high school textbook on the numerus clausus of 1920,

3 March 2013, accessed 10 January 2014.

57 JTA, 'Opening of New College Year Revives Numerus Clausus Question in Hungary', 14 September 1930, accessed 10 January 2014.

58 JTA, 'University Exclusions Continue in Germany', 13 April 1933, accessed 5 December 2013.

59 JTA, London, 21 December 1928, accessed 23 December 2013.

60 Chiger, p.15.

61 Julie Orringer, 'People of the Book', interviewed by Symi Rom-Rymer in *Moment* magazine, 11 February 2011 (http://momentmagazine.wordpress.com/2011/02/11/people-of-the-book-interview-with-julie-orringer/) accessed 9 February 2014.

62 ITA, 5 December 2006.

63 JTA, 'Alexander Cuza, Notorious Anti-semite, is Pensioned off from Jassy University', 9 January 1928 (http://www.jta.org/1928/01/09/archive/alexander-cuza-notorious-anti-semite-is-pensioned-off-from-jassy-university) accessed 6 April 2015.

64 JTA, 'Roumanian Students Demand Numerus Nullus at Jassy Congress', 5 December 1926 (http://www.jta.org/1926/12/05/archive/roumanian-students-demand-numerus-nullus-at-jassy-congress) accessed 11 December 2014.

65 Anthony Cohn, letter to *The Times*, 25 March 2010, accessed 24 December 2013.

## Chapter 12

1 Richard Evans, *Third Reich*, pp.120–121.

2 Evans, p.129.

3 Evans, pp.131–133.

4 Evans, pp.133–135.

5 Ben Mauk, 'The Name of the Critic: On "Walter Benjamin: A Critical Life"', *The American Reader* (http://theamericanreader.com/the-name-of-the-critic-on-walter-benjamin-a-critical-life) accessed 25 May 2014.

6 Evans, *Third Reich*, p.136.

7 Evans, pp.137–138.

8 Chemi Shalev, 'World Awaits Diary of "Grotesque Fool" and Nazi Ideologue Alfred Rosenberg', 12 June 2013 (http://www.haaretz.com/blogs/west-of-eden/.premium-1.529424) accessed 20 May 2014.

9 Tom Lehrer, introduction to 'It Makes a Fellow Proud to be a Soldier' (https://www.youtube.com/watch?v=JoL_rD7CCe4&index=1&list=RDJoL_rD7CCe4) accessed 22 May 2014.

10 Dreyfus and Gensberger, *Nazi Labour Camps in Paris: Austerlitz, Lévitan, Bassano, July 1943–August 1944* (New York: Berghahn Books, 2014), p.8.

11 'Nazi Party Takes Control of All Arts & Culture', 22 September 1933, accessed 25 October 2013, http://www.skepticism.org/timeline/Sept....8681.

12 Sir Michael Kerr, obituary in *The Daily Telegraph*, 23 April 2002, accessed 5 December 2013.

13 Extracts from the *Manual of the Reich Chamber of Culture* (1937), German History in Document and Images, accessed 25 October 2013, p.1.

14 USHMM 'People's Receiver' (http://www.ushmm.org/propaganda/archive/peoples-radio/) accessed 26 October 2013.

15 Ernest Goldsmith, 'Against the Tide' (1988). Unpublished memoir sent to author by Netta Goldsmith, December 2013, pp.5–6.

16 Eagleton, *Exiles and Émigrés*, pp.386–387.

17 Christian Goeschel, *Suicide in Nazi Germany* (Oxford: OUP, 2009), p.97.

18 Goeschel, p.101.

19 JTA, 'Hungarian Anti-Jewish Bill Awaits Horthy's Signature', 26 May 1938 (http://www.jta.org/1938/05/26/archive/hungarian-anti-jewish-bill-awaits-horthys-signature-passed-by-senate) accessed 27 May 2014.

20 Ernst Loewenberg, in Richarz, p.365.

21 Grenville, pp.99–100.

22 Edwin Landau, in Richarz, pp.312–313.

23 Myra Warhaftig, *They Laid the Foundation* (Berlin: Ernst Wasmuth, 2007), pp.10–11.

24 Warhaftig, p.11.

25 Robert Jan van Pelt, email to author, 27 October 2013.

26 Robert Jan van Pelt, email to author, 28 October 2013.

27 Myra Warhaftig, 'Forgotten Architects', *Pentagram Papers*, 37, March 2007 (http://blog.pentagram.com/forgottenarchitects/essay.html), accessed 11 October 2013.

28 Association of Jewish Architects, accessed 11 October 2013.

29 Myra Warhaftig, interview with David Sokol.

30 'Simon Wiesenthal "The Nazi Hunter"', HEART, accessed 15 October 2013.

31 Fredric Bedoire, *The Jewish Contribution to Modern Architecture 1830–1930* – book review.

32 Richard Bing interview with Shirley K. Cohen, June 1998, accessed 25 November 2013.

33 Anna Sondhelm, p.8.

34 Brochure for the exhibition, 'Forgotten German Speaking Jewish Architects', Berlin, 2013.

35 Dr Günter Schlusche, email to author, 3 January 2014.

36 Dr Günter Schlusche, email to author, 18 April 2015. The association's website is www.juedische-architekten.de.

37 Matthew Campbell, 'Critics Knock Down Le Corbusier as Anti-Semitic', *Sunday Times*, 29 March 2015.

38 Gail Taylor, 'Le Corbusier Controversy, Paris, France', in *World Architecture News*, 31 March 2015 (http://www.worldarchitecturenews.com/project/2015/25422/wan-editorial/le-corbusier-controversy-in-paris.html) accessed 31 March 2015.

39 *Jewish News*, 'The Mild Aggressor: The unsung Jewish Hero of Waterloo', 26 April 2015 (http://www.jewishnews.co.uk/the-mild-agressor-the-unsung-jewish-hero-of-waterloo) accessed 28 April 2015.

40 Martin Karplus, 'Spinach on the Ceiling', *Annual Review of Biophysics and Biomolecular Structure*, Vol. 35, June 2006 (http://www.annualreviews.org/doi/abs/10.1146/annurev.biophys.33.110502.133350).

41 Dr J. Rosenecker, 'Albert Uffenheimer: Pediatrician and Public Health Advocate before Nazi Rule', *Israeli Medical Association Journal*, May 2011.

42 Grenville, p.93.

43 Barkai, *From Boycott to Annihilation*, p.56.

44 AJR Information (Association of Jewish Refugees), August 1950, p.6.

45 Christabel Bielenberg, *The Past is Myself* (London: Corgi Books, 1984), pp.30–31.

46 Owings, *Frauen*, p.22.

47 JTA, '3000 Jewish Doctors Quit Reich in 4 Years', 17 March 1937 (http://www.jta.org/1937/03/17/archive/3000-jewish-doctors-quit-reich-in-4-years) accessed 9 March 2014.

48 JTA, 'Reich Jewish Women go to England to Bear Children', 5 March 1936 (http://www.jta.org/1936/03/05/archive/reich-jewish-women-go-to-england-to-bear-children) accessed 5 March 2014.

49 'Lawyers without Rights' (LWR) exhibit, p.5.

50 Peter Sinclair memoir, p.1.

51 Robert Jan van Pelt, 'I Shall Survive You All', in *Prism: An Interdisciplinary Journal for Holocaust Education*, spring 2012, Vol. 4, accessed 22 November 2013.

52 Bea Green, emails to author, 7 January 2015.

53 Bea Green, email to author, 9 January 2015.

54 Bea Green, email to author, 6 August 2015.

55 Robert Jan van Pelt.

56 Bea Green, email to author, 6 January 2015.

57 Bea Green, email to author, 6 January 2015.

58 Yad Vashem, 'Through the Lens of History: Mini Exhibits from the Yad Vashem Collections 2013', accessed 22 November 2013.

59 LWR.

60 LWR.

61 Philip Oltermann, 'Jewish Art Collector's Cherished Works are Among Those in Munich Hoard', *Guardian*, 13 November 2013.

62 *Fox News*, 13 November 2013.

63 Catherine Hickley, 'Nazi Trove Reveals Dresden Holocaust Survivor's Lost Art', Bloomberg, 12 November 2013.

64 Michlin, p.71.

65 Magda Hertzberger in Ritvo and Plotkin, *Sisters in Sorrow*, p.209.

66 Grenville, p.169.

67 Grenville, p.170.

68 Grenville, p.10.

69 Grenville, p.228.

70 Hans G. Reissner, 'A German-Jewish Dream', in American Jewish Archives (http://americanjewisharchives.org/publications/journal/PDF/1962_14_01_00_reissner.pdf) accessed 13 October 2013.

71 Tom Ambrose, *Hitler's Loss: What Britain and America Gained from Europe's Cultural Exiles* (London: Peter Owen, 2001), p.179.

72 Michael Tillotson, 'Chemical Warfare: a Long History of Noxious Weaponry', *The Times*, 2 May 2015.

73 Wilfred Owen's *Dulce et Decorum Est*, British Library Online Gallery, accessed 26 October 2013.

74 Jessie Pope (http://www.poemhunter.com/jessie-pope/biography) accessed 26 October 2013.

75 Lyn Macdonald, *1915: The Death of Innocence* (London: Headline, 1993), pp.192–195.

76 Daniel Charles, *Between Genius and Genocide: The Tragedy of Fritz Haber, Father of Chemical Warfare* (London: Jonathan Cape, 2005), p.164.

77 Charles, p.170, and note on p.281.

78 Schuck & Sohlman, *Nobel; The Man and His Prizes*, p.329.

79 Daniel Charles, p.196.

80 Charles, pp.234–235.

81 Charles, pp.179–180.

82 Charles, p.224.

83 Charles, p.246.

84 Tom Ambrose, *Hitler's Loss: What Britain Gained from Europe's Cultural Exiles* (London: Peter Owen, 2001), pp.178–179.

85 Allan Hall, 'Poison Gas HQ to be Base for Germany's Holocaust Professor', *The Times*, 9 April 2015.

86 JTA, 'Dr Schmitt Rebukes Nazis Demanding Curb on Jewish Artisans', 14 January 1934, accessed 12 January 2014.

87 Gerald Feldman, *Allianz and the German Insurance Business 1933–1945* (Cambridge: CUP, 2001).

88 JTA, 'Sale of Czech Newspapers to Jews Prohibited in the Protectorate by Nazi Order', 23 January 1942, accessed 19 January 2014.

89 JTA, 'Refugees from Reich Ordered to Quit Portugal', 16 February 1937 (http://www.jta.org/1937/02/16/archive/refugees-from-reich-ordered-to-quit-portugal) accessed 10 February 2014.

90 JTA Budapest, 'Hungarian Jewish Waiters Appeal to Government', 6 November 1939, accessed 4 December 2013.

91 Harry Schneiderman, 'Review of the Year 5696 (July 1935–June 1936)' in *American Jewish Year Book*, p.311 (http://www.ajcarchives.org/AJC_DATA/Files/1936_1937_4_YearReview.pdf) accessed 15 October 2013.

92 JTA, 'Washing Boss Dishes After Lunching with Him Barred to "Aryan" Girls', 16 February 1937 (http://www.jta.org/1937/02/16/archive/washing-boss-dishes-after-lunching-with-him-barred-to-aryan-girls) accessed 10 February 2014.

93 *American Jewish Year Book 5696*, p.311.

94 JTA, 'Jews Barred by Official Decree from Employing Christian Maids', 17 January 1934.

95 'Jews Spurned in Rumania', in *The Argus*, Melbourne, 24 January 1938, p.9, accessed 19 January 2014.

96 JTA, 'Landlords' Union Bars Jews', 26 May 1938 (http://www.jta.org/1938/05/26/archive/landlords-union-bars-jews) accessed 27 May 2014.

97 Miriam Davenport Ebel, telephone conversation with author, 17 September 1998. Cited in 'Affected by Atrocity: The impact and motives of Varian Fry, Charles Fawcett and the Emergency Rescue Committee', MA dissertation, Sheffield University, October 1998, p.23.

98 Alexander Stille, *The Force of Things: A Marriage in War and Peace* (New York: Farrar, Straus & Giroux, 2013).

## Chapter 13

1 I am grateful to Leipzig Museum for giving me a copy of the English catalogue.

2 Leipzig Museum catalogue, p.2.

3 Paul A. Shapiro and Martin C. Dean, *Symposium*, foreword, p.7.

4 JTA, '43 Jewish-Owned Firms in Paris Sold to Non-Jews by Nazi Authorities', 28 December 1941, accessed 23 December 2013.

5 JTA, '"Aryanization" of Jewish-owned Business in Hungary Meeting with Great Difficulties', 17 December 1941, accessed 25 April 2013.

6 Irene Lawford-Hinrichsen, *Five Hundred Years to Auschwitz* (London: Edition Press, 2008), pp.138–139.

7 Lawford-Hinrichsen, p.140.

8 Leipzig City History Museum, '"Aryanization" in Leipzig. Driven out. Robbed. Murdered', 2009, pp.24–25. I am grateful to the museum for sending me their catalogue as a gift.

9 Martha Hinrichsen, email to author, 8 June 2014.

10 Lawford-Hinrichsen, p.2.

11 Gamerman and Crow, 'Nazi Art Spurs Search into Family Histories', *Wall Street Journal*, 13 November 2013 (http://online.wsj.com/news/articles/SB10001424052702303559504579196291106825648) accessed 26 May 2014.

12 Martha Hinrichsen, email to author, 8 June 2014.

13 Ernest Goldsmith, 'Against the Tide' (1988), unpublished memoir, pp.8–9. Adolf was Ernest's grandfather. I am grateful to Ernest's widow, Netta, for supplying a copy of the memoir to me on 24 December 2013.

14 Ibid., p.10.

15 Netta Goldsmith, email to author, 1 December 2013.

16 Netta Goldsmith, 'Biography of Ernest Henry Goldsmith' (2011), unpublished memoir

sent to author 3 December 2013, p.1.

17  Ibid., p.2.

18  Netta Goldsmith, emails to author, 29, 30 and 31 May 2014.

19  Netta Goldsmith, email to author, 29 May 2014.

20  Goldsmith, p.6.

21  I am grateful to Peter Smith, a member of the family, for finding these photographs.

22  I am grateful to William and Sally Butchart for first telling me about the Amerikaner family in Venice in November 2014.

23  Obituary of Franceska Rapkin 1936–2001, Jeffrey Kalp, *The London Philatelist*, III:2, Jan/Feb 2002.

24  Herbert Loebel, 'Government-financed Factories and the Establishment of Industries by Refugees in the Special Areas of the North of England 1937–1961', Durham University, 1978 (http://etheses.dur.ac.uk/10025) accessed 5 March 2015.

25  Chris Lloyd, 'A Majestic History', *Northern Echo*, 14 October 2013.

26  'History of Beiersdorf AG', Funding Universe (http://www.fundinguniverse.com/company-histories/beiersdorf-ag-history) accessed 26 June 2013.

27  Grenville, p.15.

28  'Campaign against "Jew Crème"', Bernard Röhl, *Die Tageszeitung*, 18 October 2003. Translated by Hildegard Graham, 17 September 2013.

29  'The Nivea Crème Jews', *Der Stürmer*, No. 34, August 1933. I am grateful to Hildegard Abraham for translating the article into English.

30  Grenville, p.85.

31  Geoffrey Jones, *Beauty Imagined* (Oxford: OUP, 2010), p.146, note 143.

32  Grenville, p.16.

33  Marcus Sieff, *Don't Ask the Price* (London: Weidenfeld & Nicolson, 1986), p.44. Simon was his uncle. 6*d* was sixpence – today's equivalent is just under 3p.

34  Evelyn Juers, *House of Exile* (Giramondo: Artamon NSW, 2008), pp. 80–81.

35  'Portrait of Oscar Troplowitz', BDF Beiersdorf, accessed 23 September 2013.

36  Grenville, p.16.

37  'Portrait of Oscar Troplowitz', BDF Beiersdorf, accessed 23 September 2013.

38  Juers, p.81.

39  'The One Picture that is Missing: Picasso's *The Absinthe Drinker*'. Document sent by Dr Ute Haug from the Hamburg Kunsthalle on 25 September 2013, translated by Hildegard Abraham. See also Note 44 & 46.

40  Jonathan Petropoulos, *The Faustian Bargain: The Art World in Nazi Germany* (London: Penguin, 2000), p.16.

41  Heilmut Lehmann-Haupt, *Art under a Dictatorship* (Oxford: OUP, 1954), p.78.

42  Stephanie Barron, *Degenerate Art* – lists all the works scheduled for sale in the Fischer Auction.

43  Pierre Assouline, *An Artful Life* (Fromm: New York, 1991), pp.257–258.

44  'The One Picture that is Missing – Picasso's *The Absinthe Drinker*'. Article for the Hamburg Kunsthalle Exhibition, 'A Life for Hamburg: Oscar Troplowitz', held in 2013. Translated from the German by Hildegard Abraham.

45  *The Burlington Magazine for Connoisseurs*, Vol. 74, No. 434 (May 1939), p.xvi. I am grateful for help from Barbara Pezzini from the *Burlington Magazine*.

46  See Note 44.

47  Matthew Paton, email to author, 24 September 2013. I am grateful to Matthew Paton of Christie's for his assistance with identifying the painting and telling me about Gertrude Stein's original ownership.

48  Michael Ignatieff, *Isaiah Berlin: A Life* (London: Chatto & Windus, 1998), p.52.

49  (http://alportcollection.wordpress.com/tag/the-temple) accessed 24 September 2013.

50 Christopher Hurst, *The View from King Street* (London: Thalia Press, 1997), p.183.

51 (allportcollection.wordpress.com) accessed 1 October 2013.

52 Elisabetta Cerruti, *The Ambassador's Wife*, pp.148–149.

53 Jack Malvern, 'Old Master Looted by Nazis Given Back to Jewish Family', *The Times*, 25 March 2015.

54 Anne-Marie O'Connor, 'Whose Art is it Anyway?' *Los Angeles Times Magazine*, 16 December 2001, pp.12–16 and p.45.

55 Michael Roddy, 'Mirren Stars in *Woman in Gold* Spotlighting Nazi-looted Art', *Reuters*, 10 February 2015 (www.lootedart.com/R3OJ21837781) accessed 14 February 2015.

56 Randol Schoenberg, 'Whose Art Is It Anyway?', in *Holocaust Restitution* (New York: New York UP, 2006) p.288.

57 Randol Schoenberg, '*Woman in Gold* Premieres in Berlin', 10 February 2015 (http://schoenblog.com/?m=201502) accessed 26 March 2015.

58 Carolyn Beeler, 'Berlin Zoo Seeks Jewish Members Stripped of Shares During the Nazi Era', *News Daily*, 3 December 2013.

59 Larry Orbach, *Soaring Underground*, p.188.

60 Zweig, *The World of Yesterday*, pp.433–434.

61 JTA, Cnaan Liphshiz, 'When 300 Jews Escaped the Nazi Camps by Hiding in the Warsaw Zoo', 23 March 2015 (http://www.jta.org/2015/03/23/news-opinion/world/when-jews-found-refuge-in-underground-warren-at-warsaw-zoo#.VRJrjaIJiAA.email) accessed 25 March 2015.

62 There was confusion over these terms due to the translation. The author of the article, Jos Scheren, clarified it for me in a message on Facebook, dated 13 April 2014.

63 *Holocaust and Genocide Studies*, Jos Scheren, 'Aryanization, Market Vendors and Peddlers in Amsterdam, 2000 (14–3), pp. 415–29.

64 Magdeburg Thesis, p.86 – interview with Poppert, 9 January 1998.

65 John Rosenthal, 'Choosing to Remember', in *Shoah Survivors and Witnesses in Western North Carolina*, pp.2–3.

66 Isaac Levendel, *Not the Germans Alone*, pp.213, 215 and 220.

67 Raul Hilberg, *The Destruction of the Jews*, Volume I (New Haven, CN: Yale UP, 2003), pp.131–133.

68 Dina Golden, *Stolen Legacy: Nazi Theft and the Quest for Justice at Krausenstrasse 17/18 Berlin* (Chicago: Ankerwycke, 2015).

69 Unknown writer, dated 16 April 1938, to IHK Munich, cited by Avraham Barkai, *From Boycott to Annihilation*, p.129.

*Chapter 14*

1 JTA, 'Organising Italian Jewry', 19 January 1931, accessed 19 January 2014.

2 Yad Vashem, 'Jemolo Family' (http://db.yadvashem.org/righteous/family.html?language=en&itemId=4043701) accessed 24 January 2014.

3 Martin Gilbert, *Atlas of the Holocaust*, p.97.

4 Yad Vashem, 'Libya' (http://www.yadvashem.org/odot_pdf/Microsoft%20Word%20-%206407.pdf) accessed 26 January 2014.

5 Robert Satloff, 'Jews in Nazi-Occupied Countries: North Africa', American-Israeli Co-operative Enterprise, accessed 27 January 2014.

6 Deborah Lipstadt's blog, 10 December 2006, accessed 27 January 2014.

7 Satloff – See Note 5.

8 Martin Gilbert, *Atlas of the Holocaust*, p.56, Map 59.

9 Gilbert, p.56.

10 Yad Vashem (http://www.yadvashem.org/yv/en/education/newsletter/25/algeria_

marocco.asp) accessed 28 January 2014.

11 Robert Satloff, *Jews in Nazi-Occupied Countries*, accessed 27 January 2014.

12 Ronnie Golz, Arianne Golz (http://www.rgolz.de/e-marianne.html) accessed 13 January 2014.

13 Joschka Fischer, 'Haunting Obituaries: The German Foreign Ministry's Confrontation with its Nazi Past', speech to Israel Council on Foreign Relations on 3 March 2011, in *Israel Journal of Foreign Affairs*, Vol. 2 (2011), p.75.

14 Markus Bauer, 'Nazi Germany: The myth of the Foreign Ministry', *History Today*, Vol. 61, Issue 9, 2011.

15 Fischer, in *Israel Journal of Foreign Affairs*, Vol. 2, p.76.

16 Fischer, p.77.

17 Fischer, pp.77–78.

18 Fischer, p.78.

19 'Hitler's Diplomats', *Spiegel* Online, translated from the German by Christopher Sultan (http://www.spiegel.de/international/germany/hitler-s-diplomats-historian-calls-wartime-ministry-a-criminal-organization-a-725600.html) accessed 13 December 2013.

20 World Jewish Congress, 'German Foreign Office Complicit in Nazi Holocaust, Historians Prove', 25 October 2010, accessed 10 December 2013.

21 Therkel Straede, 'October 1943: The Rescue of the Danish Jews from Annihilation', Royal Danish Ministry of Foreign Affairs, Copenhagen, 2010, p.8.

22 Sofie Lene Bak, *Nothing to Speak Of*, p.37.

23 Herbert Pundik, 'From the Memoirs of Herbert Pundik', Yad Vashem (http://www.yadvashem.org/yv/en/righteous/stories/related/pundik_memoirs.asp) accessed 3 November 2013.

24 Bak, p.37.

25 Bak, p.38.

26 Yad Vashem, 'Werner Best' (http://www.yadvashem.org/odot_pdf/Microsoft%20Word%20-%206009.pdf) accessed 11 January 2014.

27 Bak, p.39.

28 Per Nelleman Bang, 'The Rescue of Danish Jews in World War II', *The Baltic Eye* (http://www.thebalticeye.com/____TBE073-ELLE.html), accessed 12 January 2014. This website was the only place I found that mentioned that 1–2 October in 1943 marked the Jewish New Year – Rosh Hashonah.

29 Yad Vashem, 'With Fishing Boats to Sweden', (http://www.yadvashem.org/yv/en/righteous/stories/thomsen.asp), accessed 12 January 2014.

30 Laurence Rees, *Auschwitz: A New History* (BBC, 2005), p.216.

31 Bak, pp.39–41.

32 Bak, pp.42–44.

33 Paul Berger, 'Denmark Forced by History to Revisit Heroic Tale of Jewish Rescue From Nazis', *The Jewish Daily Forward*, 27 September 2013 (http://forward.com/articles/184216/denmark-forced-by-history-to-revisit-heroic-tale-o/?p).

34 Dan Michman, 'Why Did So Many of the Jews in Antwerp Perish in the Holocaust', *Yad Vashem Studies*, XXX, Jerusalem, 2002, pp.465–482 (http://www.yadvashem.org/odot_pdf/microsoft%20word%20-%205430.pdf).

35 Sebastian Vandenbogaerde, 'Making the New Order Legal: Het Juristenbad 1941–1944'.

36 JTA, 'Brussels Mayor to Change Text of Invitation to Shoah Ceremony', 14 August 2012, accessed 4 September 2012.

37 JTA, 'Brussels Mayor Apologises', accessed 4 September 2012.

38 'Belgian premier apologises for wartime deportation of Jews', 9 September 2012 (www.ejpress.org/article/61523) accessed 10 September 2012.

39 *BBC News*, 'Escaping the Train to Auschwitz', 20 April 2013 (http://www.bbc.co.uk/

news/magazine-22188075) accessed 10 March 2014.

40 Adi Schwartz, 'How Belgium Sacrificed its Jews to the Nazis', 5 March 2007, Haaretz. com (http://www.haaretz.com/print-edition/features/how-belgium-sacrificed-its-jews-to-the-nazis-1.214634) accessed 15 March 2014.

41 House of the Wannsee Conference, pp.175–177.

42 Ibid., p.71.

43 Ibid., p.67.

44 Ibid., p.129.

45 Ibid., p.130.

46 USHMM, 'The Wannsee Conference and the "Final Solution"' (http://www.ushmm. org/wlc/en/article.php?ModuleId=10005477), accessed 4 January 2015.

47 James G. McDonald, *My Mission to Israel 1948–1951* (London: Gollancz, 1951), p.xi.

48 James G. McDonald, letter of resignation to the Secretary General of the League of Nations, 27 December 1935, London.

49 Ibid.

50 Petition in support of James G. McDonald's letter of resignation, 1936 (BL 20087.b.38).

51 Arthur Berger, 'Papers of Ambassador James G. McDonald', 22 April 2004, USHMM press release, accessed 2 May 2004.

52 Nicholas Wapshott, 'Archbishop of Canterbury "blamed the Jews for excesses of the Nazis"', *The Times*, 23 April 2004.

53 Elie Wiesel, 'The Perils of Indifference', speech at the White House on 12 April 1999 (http://www.historyplace.com/speeches/wiesel.htm) accessed 16 April 2014.

54 Yad Vashem, 'Bermuda Conference' (http://www.yadvashem.org/odot_pdf/Microsoft%20 Word%20-%206001.pdf) accessed 16 April 2014.

55 Bernard Wasserstein, *Britain and the Jews of Europe 1939–1945* (London: Leicester UP, 1999), p.165.

56 JTA, 'Luxembourg Wartime Bosses "Willingly Helped Nazis find Jews"', cited in *Times of Israel*, 13 February 2015.

57 Vincent Artuso, 'Luxembourg Says Sorry to Jews for World War II Government Collaboration with Nazi Occupiers', World Jewish Congress, 9 June 2015 (http://www. worldjewishcongress.org/en/news/legislature-of-luxembourg-set-to-say-sorry-to-jews-for-world-war-ii-collaboration-with-nazi-occupiers-6-2-2015) accessed 10 June 2015.

*Chapter 15*

1 JTA, '30,000 Rumanian Jews Reported Dead from Typhus: Food Ration Halved for Jews', 3 June 1942 (http://www.jta.org/1942/06/03/archive/30000-rumanian-jews-reported-dead-from-typhus-food-ration-halved-for-jews) accessed 15 March 2014.

2 Otto Fleming, 'The Wicked Do Not Always Prosper', *British Medical Journal*, 18 July 1998, accessed 20 March 2014.

3 Elie Wiesel, 'Without Conscience' *The New England Journal of Medicine*, 14 April 2005, translated from French by Jamie Moore (http://www.nejm.org/doi/full/10.1056/ NEJMp058069) accessed 20 March 2014.

4 Adrian Reuben, 'First Do No Harm: Landmarks in Hepatology', *Hepatology*, Vol. 42, No. 6, December 2005, pp.1464–1470 (http://onlinelibrary.wiley.com/doi/10.1002/ hep.21083/pdf) accessed 20 March 2014.

5 http://www.sciencemuseum.org.uk/broughttolife/techniques/nurembergcode.aspx.

6 Elie Wiesel, 'Without Conscience'

7 Ibid.

8 Henry Friedlander, 'From Euthanasia to the Final Solution' (http://www.lbihs.at/ FriedlanderFromEuthanasia.pdf) accessed 15 April 2014.

9 Gitta Sereny, *Into That Darkness* (Pimlico: André Deutsch Ltd, 1974), p.58.

10 Sereny, pp.58–59. 'Wirth' was Christian Wirth who was head of the office at Hartheim. He later became the commandant at Belzec extermination camp.

11 USHMM, Hadamar, 'The Holocaust', *Holocaust Encyclopedia* (http://www.ushmm.org/wlc/en/article.php?ModuleId=10006174) accessed 25 December 2013.

12 USHMM, 'Deadly Medicine: Irmgard Huber', 'The Holocaust', *Holocaust Encyclopedia* (http://www.ushmm.org/wlc/en/article.php?ModuleId=10005143) accessed on 25 December 2013.

13 Sereny, p.59.

14 Franklin G. Miller, 'Research and Complicity: the case of Julius Hallervorden', *Journal of Medical Ethics*, 21 June 2011 (http://jme.bmj.com/content/38/1/53.full) accessed 3 May 2013.

15 Götz Aly, *Cleansing the Fatherland*, pp.184–189.

16 Robert Jay Lifton, 'The Nazi Doctors: Medical Killing and the Psychology of Genocide', 1986, accessed 9 January 2014, nigsh, p.271.

17 The Schering Company amalgamated with the American Plough Company in 1971 and the company merged with Merck (under the name Merck) in 2009.

18 Lifton, p.272.

19 Lifton, p.273.

20 Lifton, p.274.

21 Lifton, p.275.

22 Danuta Czech, p.543.

23 Lifton, p.276.

24 Lifton, p.277–278.

25 Margita Schwalbová, 'They Were Murdered in the Infirmary', in Ritvo and Plotkin, *Sisters in Sorrow*, p.158.

26 Margita Schwalbová, 'Beginnings in Block 30 in Birkenau', in Shelley (ed.), *Criminal Experiments on Human Beings in Auschwitz and War Research Laboratories* (San Francisco: Mellen Research UP, 1991), p.16.

27 Sonja Fritz, *Block 30 in Birkenau*, p.24.

28 JTA, 'German Working Class Reported Dissatisfied with Constant Nazi Anti-Jewish Propaganda', 17 December 1941 (http://www.jta.org/1941/12/17/archive/german-working-class-reported-dissatisfied-with-constant-nazi-anti-jewish-propaganda) accessed 22 March 2015.

29 Jewish Virtual Library, Hautval, Adelaide.

30 Danuta Czech, p.825.

31 Czech, p.253.

32 Czech, p.314.

33 Czech, pp.325–326.

34 Klee, Dressen and Riess, *Those were the Days: The Holocaust through the eyes of the Perpetrators and Bystanders* (London: Hamish Hamilton, 1993), pp.256–268.

35 Martin Gilbert, *Atlas*, p.163, Map 208.

36 Paul Webster, *Pétain's Crime*, pp.247–249.

37 'French University Hands Over Holocaust Victims' Remains', *Forward*, 20 July 2015 (http://forward.com/news/breaking-news/312270/french-university-hands-over-holocaust-victims-remains) accessed 5 August 2015.

38 Alexandra Sims, 'Remains of 86 Jewish Holocaust Victims used for Human Experiments by Nazis Found Hidden in Strasbourg Lab', *Independent*, 19 July 2015.

39 Laurence Rees, *Auschwitz*, p.232.

40 I am grateful to Professor Klaus Reinhardt for sending me a copy of his article on 16 February 2014. 'The Entomological Institute of the Waffen-SS', in *Endeavour*, Vol. 37,

No. 4, 2013.

41 Reinhardt, p.223.

42 Morgan, pp.91–93.

43 Morgan, pp. 96–100.

44 Margita Schwalbová, 'They were Murdered in the Infirmary', in *Sisters in Sorrow*, pp.161–163.

45 http://holocaustcontroversies.blogspot.co.uk/2012/12/pregnant-women-will-be-put-to-death.html.

46 Owings, *Frauen*, p.19.

47 Zabecki, ARC 2005, 'Wspomnienia stare I nowe' (Warsaw: Holocaust Historical Society, 1977) accessed 14 February 2014.

48 Anja Peters, 'Nanna Conti – the biography of Nazi Germany's chief midwife' (2010) (http://www.anja-peters.de/download/Nanna_Conti_Lecture_London_2010_09_16.pdf) accessed 21 April 2014.

49 Norbet Moissl, 'Aspects of Obstetrics in the Time of National Socialism 1933–1945', PhD Dissertation, 2005, p.16 (http://edoc.ub.uni-muenchen.de/4042/1/Moissl_Norbert.pdf) accessed on 18 March 2014.

50 Paul Hunter, 'My Mother, the Nazi Midwife and Me', *The Toronto Star* online, 10 May 2013 (http://www.thestar.com/news/insight/2013/05/10/my_mother_the_nazi_midwife_and_me_documentary_confronts_ghosts_of_past.html) accessed 19 March 2014. I am grateful to Anja Peters for telling me about this story.

51 Janssen-Militaria, 'Dr Leonard Conti' (http://www.janssen-militaria.com/Biography_Leonardo_Conti.html) accessed 18 March 2014.

52 Liempt, p.16. Full details of the horrific evacuation can be found at http://www.holocaustresearchproject.org/nazioccupation/apeldoornsebos.html, accessed 23 January 2014.

53 'Apeldoornse Bos: Deportation of Psychiatric Patients to Auschwitz-Birkenau', by HEART, 2009.

54 Danuta Czech, *Auschwitz Chronicle*, provides the numbers given to those prisoners – the men were given 93297–93312, whilst the women were 31191–31226 (p.311). Those gassed immediately on arrival were not allocated numbers (p.311).

55 Chris Webb and Carmelo Lisciotto, 'Apeldoornse Bos: Deportation of Psychiatric Patients to Auschwitz-Birkenau' (2009) (http://www.holocaustresearchproject.org/nazioccupation/apeldoornsebos.html) accessed 23 January 2014.

56 Steven Frank, *The Young Gardener*, Zachor, 2005, p.42.

57 Last and Wolfswinkel, *Anne Frank and After* (Amsterdam: Amsterdam UP, 1996), p.64.

58 Jurgen Matthaus, *Jewish Responses to Persecution, 1941–1942* (Lanham, MD: AltMira Press, 2013), p.28.

59 Matthaus, p.413.

60 Matthaus, p.318.

61 HEART, p.2.

62 JTA, 'Report on Warsaw, 21 December 1941'.

63 Ludwik Gross, 'How Charles Nicolle of the Pasteur Institute Discovered that Epidemic Typhus is Transmitted by Lice', *Proceedings of the National Academy of Sciences of the USA* (PNAS), October 1996, Vol. 93, No. 20, pp.10,539–10,540.

64 The Nobel Foundation, in *Nobel: The Man and His Prizes* (New York: Elsevier, 1972), p.164.

65 'Medical Discoveries in the Ghettos', *Israeli Medical Association Journal*, May 2011.

66 Charles Nicolle, Nobel Lecture: 'Investigations on Typhus', December 2008.

67 JTA, 'Jewish Mortality Mounts in Warsaw Ghetto', 22 January 1942 (http://www.jta.org/1942/01/23/archive/jewish-mortality-mounts-in-warsaw-ghetto-as-nazis-refuse-to-check-typhus-there) accessed 12 August 2013.

68 Michlin, p.84.

69 Kovno diary, p.111.

70 Ibid., p.143, note 1.

71 JTA, '1,000 Jewish Typhus Victims in Warsaw Ghetto', accessed 21 December 2013.


*Chapter 16*

1 Frank R. Harris, interviewed by Dorit Bader Whiteman in Handlin, *The Uprooted* (New York: Plenum Press, 1993), p.198.

2 Carol Ann Lee, *The Hidden Life of Otto Frank* (London: Viking, 2002), p.15, and Naomi Shepherd, *Wilfrid Israel: Germany's Secret Ambassador* (London: Weidenfeld & Nicolson, 1984), p.26.

3 Erna Paris, *Long Shadows: Truth, Lies and History* (London: Bloomsbury, 2001), p.72.

4 Oscar Handlin, *The Uprooted*, p.198.

5 Marianne Meyerhoff, *Four Girls from Berlin* (Hoboken, NJ: John Wiley, 2007), p. 61.

6 Theo Richmond, 'How German can you get?' in *The Sunday Times – Culture Magazine*, 9 March 2003.

7 Victoria J. Barnett, *Bystanders: Conscience and Complicity During the Holocaust* (Westport, CN: Greenwood Press, 1999), p.99.

8 Netta Goldsmith, 2011 memoir sent to author on 30 November 2013.

9 Dieter Mechlinski made a DVD on Ottmar Strauss. Sent to author December 2013.

10 Margherita Sarfatti, *My Fault – Mussolini as I Knew Him* (New York: Enigma Books, 2012), p.268.

11 Elisabetta Cerruti, *The Ambassador's Wife*, pp.128–129.

12 Granville, p. 83 – interview with Max Plaut, 3 July 1954.

13 Edwin Landau, 'My Life before and after Hitler', in *Jewish Life in Germany*, Monika Richarz (ed.), pp.310–312.

14 Avraham Barkai, *From Boycott to Annihilation*, p.26.

15 Steinweis, *Art, Ideology and Economics in Nazi Germany*, p.109.

16 Grenville, p.30.

17 Thomas Weber, *Hitler's First War* (Oxford: OUP, 2010), p.107.

18 Weber, p.177.

19 Weber, p.176.

20 Weber, pp.214–216.

21 Weber, p.301.

22 'Hugo Gutmann: Escaped Three Times' (http://www.jewishgen.org/yizkor/nuremberg2/nur009.html) accessed 19 April 2014.

23 Georg Bönisch, 'Hitler Biography Debunks Mythology of Wartime Service', 3 October 2011, SpiegelOnline (http://www.spiegel.de/international/germany/a-hero-in-his-own-mind-hitler-biography-debunks-mythology-of-wartime-service-a-749906-druck.html) accessed 19 April 2014.

24 Weber, p.347.

25 (http://www.eclas2013.de/fileadmin/data/headerimg/Ohlsdorf_Guide.pdf) accessed 3 October 2013.

26 Oskar Schlemmer, letter of 25 April 1933, *Letters and Diaries of Oskar Schlemmer* (Middletown, CT: Wesleyan UP, 1972), p.310.

27 Eagleton, *Exiles and Émigrés*, p.14.

28 Michael E. Abrahams-Sprod, 'Life under Siege: The Jews of Magdeburg under Nazi Rule', PhD thesis at the University of Sydney, June 2006, pp.8–10.

29 Raul Hilberg, *The Politics of Memory: The Journey of a Holocaust Historian* (Chicago: Ivan R. Dee, 1996), p.33.

30 Eric Davidson, 'Eric's Story', *AJR Journal*, Nov. 2012, p.4.

31 Saul Friedlander, *Nazi Germany and the Jews, Volume 1, 1933–39* (London: Weidenfeld &

Nicolson, 1997), pp. 392–393.

32 Grenville, p.190.

33 Remy, *The Heidelberg Myth*, p.80.

34 Alan Steinweis, *Kristallnacht 1938*, p.92.

35 Steinweis, p.111.

36 Steinweis, p.108.

37 Steinweis, p.113.

38 Müllner, p.1.

39 Anna Sondhelm memoir, p.14.

40 Anna Sondhelm, p.15.

41 Volkswagen, p.36.

42 Volkswagen, pp.44–45. Fallersleben was the name of the main site of Volkswagen factory. Later the name was changed to Wolfsburg. A satellite factory was created in Brunswick in 1938.

43 Matthaus, p.148.

44 Grenville p.212

45 Kim Narev, Bob Narev, 'Survival – A True Story', published in Gluckman (ed.) *Identity and Involvement: Auckland Jewry, Past and Present*, 1990.

46 Grace Bradberry, 'Surrey's own Oskar Schindler', in *The Times*, 1 March 1999, p.15.

47 Else Pintus, 'The Diary of Else Pintus: The story of a Holocaust Survivor' (1947), unpublished diary translated by Doris Stiefel (née Pintus), June 1998, p.33.

48 Barbara Lovenheim, *Survival in the Shadows: Seven Hidden Jews in Hitler's Berlin* (London: Peter Owen, 2002), pp.24–26. Photo and citation pp.124–125.

49 'Jew Count' (http://en.allexperts.com/e/j/je/jew_count.htm) accessed 3 January 2010.

50 Tom Tugend, 'Museum Tells Story of Jewish Soldiers', JTA, 24 August 2003, accessed 13 March 2015.

51 'Rabbi Jonathan Wittenberg, Chaplain and Patriot', Jewish Renaissance Project, April 2014, p.21.

52 Meyerhoff, p.107.

53 Meyerhoff, pp.108–109.

54 Meyerhoff, pp.175–178.

55 Meyerhoff, p.185.

56 Meyerhoff, p.17.

57 Meyerhoff, p.44.

58 Andrea Lorz, 'Tribute to the Jewish Doctors of Leipzig'

59 Lawford-Hinrichsen, p.142.

60 Lawford-Hinrichsen, p.143.

61 Lorz, 'Tribute to the Jewish Doctors of Leipzig', *Jewish Quarterly*, spring 2006, Vol. 201. Translated by Peter Hold (http://www.jewishquarterly.org/issuearchive/article70c9. html?articleid=186) accessed 18 April 2014.

62 Tracey L. Shaler, *Frenchy: I wanted to get back at Hitler* (Bloomington, IN: iUniverse, 2009), p.40.

63 Shaler, pp.29–30.

64 'Children of the Great War' (http://childrenofthegreatwar.wordpress.com/2014/04/11/here-we-have-kitchener-your-army-needs-you-there-it-was-the-jewish-german-people-were-to-fight-for-the-kaiser).

65 Maggie Fergusson, 'Bitter, Bitter Feelings', 20 March 2014, *The Economist Intelligent Life*, (http://moreintelligentlife.co.uk/blog/jewish-museum) accessed 18 April 2014.

66 Susan Zuccotti, *Under His Very Windows: The Vatican and The Holocaust in Italy* (New Haven: Yale UP, 2000), pp.175–176.

67 Susan Zuccotti, *The Italians and the Holocaust* (London: Halban, 1987), p.104 and p.299,

note 8.

## Chapter 17

1 Nathan Stoltzfus, *Resistance of the Heart: Intermarriage and the Rosenstrasse Protest in Nazi Germany* (New York: Norton, 1996), p.58.

2 Stoltzfus, pp.60–61.

3 Stoltzfus, pp.57–62.

4 USHMM, 'The Rosenstrasse Demonstration 1943', June 2013, accessed 12 March 2014.

5 Yad Vashem, 'Mischlinge, Shoah Resource Center' (http://www.yadvashem.org/odot_pdf/Microsoft%20Word%20-%206504.pdf) accessed 27 February 2014.

6 Stoltzfus, pp.166–167.

7 Beate Meyer, *Jews in Nazi Berlin*, p.329.

8 Stoltzfus, p.73.

9 *Encyclopaedia Britannica*, 'Karl Jaspers' (http://www.britannica.com/EBchecked/topic/301541/Karl-Jaspers/3674/Transition-to-philosophy) accessed 6 April 2014.

10 Zweig, *The World of Yesterday*, p.434.

11 Richard Brooks, 'Faithfull: I Hated Men and Sex', *Sunday Times*, 8 September 2013.

12 Max Glatt obituary in *The Times*, 7 June 2002.

13 E.M. Forster, 'Jew-Consciousness (1939)' in *Two Cheers for Democracy* (London: Penguin Books, 1976), p.31.

14 Max Mallowan, *Mallowan's Memoirs* (London: Collins, 1977), pp.86–87.

15 Charles Osborne, *The Life and Crimes of Agatha Christie* (London: Collins, 1982), p.70.

16 Connor and Robertson, Pringsheim biography, St Andrews Maths Biogs – August 2006 (http://www-history.mcs.st-and.ac.uk/Biographies/Pringsheim.html), accessed 7 February 2014.

17 The British Museum, 'Alfred Pringsheim 1850-1941' (http://www.britishmuseum.org/research/search_the_collection_database/term_details.aspx?searchTerm=alfred&orig=/research/search_the_collection_database/search_results_provenance.aspx&personId=80837&personAssociation=&termDisplay=Pringsheim,+Alfred+Israel) accessed 7 February 2014.

18 Annelore Yasseri-John's testimony dated 18 February 2014, translated by Hildegard Abraham, March 2014.

19 Grenville, p.2.

20 Grenville, p.30.

21 Richard Evans, *The Third Reich*.

22 Grenville, p.57.

23 Grenville, p.97.

24 Grenville, p.98.

25 Grenville, p.136.

26 Grenville, p.212.

27 Saul Friedlander, *Nazi Germany and the Jews, Vol. 1*, p.294.

28 Howard K. Smith, *Last Train From Berlin*, pp.148–149.

29 Smith, p.149.

30 David B. Green, Gottschalk Family Commits Suicide Rather Than Let Nazis Split Them Apart, Haaretz.com, 6 November 2013, accessed 4 January 2014.

31 Gerwin Strobl, *The Swastika and the Stage*, p.124.

32 European Film Star Postcards, 'Brigitte Horney' (http://filmstarpostcards.blogspot.co.uk/2009/05/brigitte-horney.html) accessed 9 April 2014.

33 Smith, p.149.

34 JTA, 'Anti-Nazi Actor Honored', 9 July 1957, accessed 4 January 2014.

35 Joseph Herl, 'The Hymns of Jochen Klepper', *The Hymn*, July 2003, Vol. 54, No. 3, pp.7–8 (http://www.hymnary.org/files/articles/Herl%20The%20Hymns%20of%20Jochen%20 Klepper.pdf) accessed 7 January 2013.

36 Mechanicus, pp.44–46.

37 Mechanicus, p.188.

38 Mechanicus, p.161.

39 Mechanicus, p.201–202. See pages 91–95 in *The Other Schindlers* for Van Proosdij's story.

40 Marta Appel in Richarz, p.183.

41 Adam Withnall, 'Hessy Taft: "Perfect Aryan Baby" of Nazi Propaganda was Actually Jewish', *The Independent*, 2 July 2014.

42 JTA, 'German Working Class Reported Dissatisfied with Constant Nazi Anti-Jewish Propaganda', 17 December 1941.


*Chapter 18*

1 Liempt, p.18.

2 Michel Wildt, 'The Normality of Terror: The Heinrich and Margarete Himmler Correspondence', lecture at the Wiener Library, London, on 3 November 2014.

3 Agnes Grunwald-Spier, 'The Guicherds', in *The Other Schindlers*, pp.69–74.

4 Ted Morgan, *An Uncertain Hour: The French, the Germans, the Jews, the Barbie Trial and the City of Lyon 1940–1945* (London: Bodley Head, 1990), p.268.

5 Morgan, p.264.

6 Morgan, p.265.

7 Morgan, p.266.

8 Morgan, p.267.

9 USHMM.

10 Morgan, p.270.

11 Morgan, p.274.

12 Francine du Plessix Gray, 'Bearing Witness' *The New York Times*, 30 August 1987 (http://www.nytimes.com/1987/08/30/magazine/film-bearing-witness.html) accessed 14 March 2015.

13 Sandy Flitterman-Lewis, 'Women of Izieu', Jewish Women's Archive, accessed 5 January 2014.

14 Morgan, p.272.

15 Morgan, p.275.

16 Morgan, p.270.

17 Morgan, p.272.

18 Morgan, p.271.

19 Morgan, p.272.

20 Janine Webber, emails to author of 2 and 5 December 2013.

21 Philip Mechanicus, p.75.

22 Gustav Botkai, 'Gustav: My Story', personal memoir 2013, received from author 21 March 2013, pp.2–3.

23 Gustav Botkai, email to author, 19 March 2013.

24 Botkai memoir, pp.22–23.

25 'The Holocaust – Lest we Forget: Camp Westerbork' (2009) (http://www.holocaust-lestweforget.com/holocaust-westerbork-medicalcare.html) accessed 8 April 2014.

26 Claude Romney, 'Crushed Spring Flowers', *Vancouver Holocaust Education Centre Newsletter*, 3 August 2007, accessed 21 November 2013.

27 Margita Schwalbová, 'Block 30 in Birkenau' in Ritvo and Plotkin, *Sisters in Sorrow*, p.17.

28 Terry Washington, 'St Angela, Angel of Auschwitz', Catholic Community Forum, April

2000, accessed 21 November 2013.

29 David Charter, 'Auschwitz Book-keeper: I saw SS Murdering Baby', *The Times*, 22 April 2015.

30 Laurence Rees, *Auschwitz*, p.23 and p.376, note 11.

31 Joe O'Connor, 'Pregnant in Auschwitz', *National Post*, 25 August 2012, accessed 20 November 2013.

32 Claude Romney, 'Crushed Spring Flowers', *Vancouver Holocaust Education Centre Newsletter*, 3 August 2007, accessed 21 November 2013.

33 Weisz & Grzybowski, 'Medical Discoveries in the Ghettos: The Anti-Typhus Battle', *The Israeli Medical Association Journal*, Vol. 13, No. 5, May 2011, pp.261–265.

34 Klee, Dressen and Riess, *Those Were the Days* (London: Hamish Hamilton, 1993), pp.138, 141–143.

35 Klee, Dressen and Riess, p.144.

36 Klee, Dressen and Riess, p.154.

37 Helga Weiss, Helga's diary, 2013.

38 Helga Weiss.

39 Volkswagen, *Surviving in Fear*, 2013, p.15 (http://www.volkswagenag.com/content/vwcorp/info_center/en/publications/2013/07/HN_11.bin.html/binarystorageitem/file/VWAG_HN3_Surviving_in_Fear_2013.pdf).

40 Volkswagen, pp.59–63.

41 CBS News, 'Statement on the Trial', press release on the trial of Dr Hans Korbel, undated (http://www.cbsnews.com/news/statement-on-the-trial/) accessed 9 February 2014.

42 Franciszek Zabecki, p.2.

43 Robert Krell, 'The Buchenwald Children and Other Child Survivors', *The '1939' Club*, p.1, accessed 16 August 2005.

44 Krell, p.5.

45 Krell, pp.5–6.

46 Esia Baran Friedman, email to author, 20 February 2013.

47 Esia Baran Friedman, undated memoir in the form of a letter received 4 February 2013.

48 Esia Friedman, email to author, 6 March 2014.

49 George Prochnik, *The Impossible Exile: Stefan Zweig at the End of the World* (London: Granta, 2014), p.112.

50 Roman Halter, p.149.

51 Grunwald-Spier, pp.158–159.

52 Marci Shore, email to author, 25 June 2012.

53 Moshe Herczl, *Christianity and the Holocaust of Hungarian Jewry*, p.244 and p.288, note 183.

54 Grunwald-Spier, pp.49–53.

55 Josie Levy Martin, *Never Tell Your Name* (First Books: 2002), p.198.

56 Steven Frank, unpublished memoir received by author, 29 January 2014.

57 Interview with Julie Orringer, 'People of the Book', 11 February 2011 by Symi Rom-Rymer, *Moment Magazine*.

58 Romney, p.13. See Note 32 on p.618.

## Chapter 19

1 JTA, 'Frankfurter Sobs As Father's Letter is Read in Court', 11 December 1936 (http://www.jta.org/1936/12/11/archive/frankfurter-sobs-as-fathers-letter-is-read-in-court) accessed 12 November 2014.

2 Steinweis, *Kristallnacht*, p.18. I am grateful to my eldest son, Dan Spier, for his assistance with research on this topic.

3 JTA, 'Berlin Preparing for Olympics, Removes Last Anti-Jewish Signs', 9 April 1936

(http://www.jta.org/1936/04/09/archive/berlin-preparing-for-olympics-removes-last-anti-jewish-signs) accessed 20 May 2014.

4 JTA, 'Be Polite to Jews During Olympics', 23 July 1936, accessed 2 March 2014.

5 JTA, 'Hot Dog Vendors at Olympics', 15 July 1936 (http://www.jta.org/1936/07/15/archive/hot-dog-vendors-at-olympics-must-be-politically-reliable) accessed 15 July 2013.

6 Fred Stein, 'Fred Stein, Australian Memories of the Holocaust 2000' (http://www.holocaust.com.au/jn/n_fred.htm) accessed 3 April 2013.

7 Steinweis, *Art, Ideology and Economics in Nazi Germany*, p.113.

8 Jewish Virtual Library, *The Nazi Party: The Nazi Olympics*, accessed 2 March 2014.

9 Alan Hubbard, 'Will Dorothy Light Olympic Flame in London?', *The Independent*, 21 August 2011.

10 insidecroydon.com, 24 July 2010.

11 Alan Hubbard, 'Will Dorothy Light Olympic Flame in London?', *The Independent*, 21 August 2011.

12 Duff Hart Davies, *Hitler's Games: The 1936 Games* (London: Century, 1986), pp. 235–236.

13 *Sydney Morning Herald*, 21 August 1936, p.12. I am grateful to Rob Oxley in Melbourne, Australia, for providing me with a copy of the article.

14 Duff Hart Davies, p.245.

15 Kay Schaffer and Sidonie Smith (Eds), *The Olympics at the Millennium: Power, Politics and the Games* (Piscataway, NJ: Rutgers UP, 2000), p.179.

16 (http://www.geni.com/people/Gerrit-Kleerekoper/6000000015150010895) accessed 30 March 2014.

17 (http://www.findagrave.com/cgi-bin/fg.cgi?page=gr&GRid=46687736) accessed 30 March 2014.

18 (http://www.blog.standforisrael.org/articles/jud-simons-olympic-gold-medalist-and-holocaust-victim#ixzz2uzb6OrOJ) accessed 30 March 2014.

19 Allon Sinai, 'Henoch Remembered for Impact on Sports Humanity', *Jerusalem Post*, 10 April 2013 (http://www.jpost.com/Sports/Henoch-remembered-for-contribution-to-sports-humanity-309304) accessed 30 March 2014.

20 Gertrud Pfister, 'Lilli Henoch 1899–1942', in Jewish Womens Archive (1989) (http://jwa.org/encyclopedia/article/henoch-lilli) accessed 1 April 2014.

21 (http://www.sports-reference.com/olympics/athletes/he/otto-herschmann-1.html) accessed 1 April 2014.

22 http://www.barnesandnoble.com/w/roman-kantor-jacob-aristotle/1108256803?ean=9786138981923.

23 Dr Uriel Simri, 'Jewish Olympic Champions: Victims of the Holocaust', *Journal of Olympic History*, winter 1998, pp.18–19.

24 Steve Lipman, 'In Attila's Memory', *The Jewish Week*, 8 June 2008, accessed 2 March 2014.

25 (thesoccerdesk.com) accessed 2 March 2014.

26 (http://www.sports-reference.com/olympics/athletes/ku/jnusz-kusocinski-1.html) accessed 1 April 2014.

27 (http://encyclopedia2.thefreedictionary.com/Werner+Seelenbinder) and (http://www.berlin.de/2013/en/portraits/selected-portraits/seelenbinder-werner).

28 (http://www.wollheim-memorial.de/en/victor_young_perez_19111945) and (http://www.imdb.com/title/tt2658428/plotsummary?ref_=tt_ov_pl).

29 (http://romediafoundation.wordpress.com/2012/02/06/johann-trollmann-sinti-roma-boxer-who-fought-against-nazi-germany) accessed 1 April 2014.

30 'Ben Bril Memorial', benbrilboxing.com (in Dutch).

31 Shoah Foundation, 'Holocaust Survivor Nathan Shapow Testimony', 1994.

32 (http://store.jewogle.com/andras_szekely).

33 (http://store.jewogle.com/ilja_szrajbman).

34 Information from the MTK Budapest website. I am grateful to Tamás Brodrogi's son for making a special English translation, received 8 April 2014.

35 Mechanicus, p.81.

36 'In remembrance of Han Hollander', 29 May 2009 (http://thru-other-eyes.typepad. com/the_daily_view/2009/05/han-hollander.html) accessed 9 April 2014.

37 Tony Paterson, 'European Maccabi Games 2015: Nazi-built stadium in Berlin to host "Jewish Olympics"', *The Independent*, 28 July 2015.

38 Benjamin Weinthal, 'Euro Maccabi Games Marred by Anti-Semitism in Berlin', *Jerusalem Post*, 1 August 2015 (http://www.jpost.com/Diaspora/Anti-Semitic-abuses-in-Berlin-mar-Maccabi-games-410820) accessed 5 August 2015.

*Chapter 20*

1 Lilli Aischberg-Bing memoir 1983, p.24.

2 Hedi Fried, p.52.

3 Hedi Fried, p.53.

4 Helga Weiss diary, 2013.

5 Jurgen Schwiening, 'Ruth's Story', unpublished memoir received 15 February 2014.

6 'Ruth's Story', p.3 and Appendix 2, p.9.

7 Ruth Schwiening, 'Sehnsucht – A Yearning', *AJR Journal*, January 2014, p.3.

8 Jurgen Schwiening, email to author, 1 March 2014.

9 Stefan Zweig, *The World of Yesterday* (London: Pushkin Press, 2014), pp.429–431.

10 Mary Berg, *Warsaw Ghetto: A Diary* (New York: L.B. Fischer, 1983), p.64, cited in Barbara Engelking, *Holocaust and Memory* (London: Leicester UP, 2001), pp.96–97.

11 Abraham Lewin, *A Cup of Tears: A Diary of the Warsaw Ghetto* (London: Fontana/Collins, 1989), p.77, cited in Engelking, p.97.

12 Morgan, *Ruta's Closet*, pp.58–59. At a traditional Jewish wedding, the couple stand under a cloth canopy, the chuppah, which represents their new home. Towards the end of the ceremony, the groom stamps on a wine glass wrapped in a cloth and everyone shouts 'Mazeltov', meaning 'Good Luck'.

13 'Stephen Lackner', Arts in Exile (http://kuenste-im-exil.de/KIE/Content/EN/SpecialExhibitions/MaxBeckmann-en/Persons/01ThePreExileYears/lackner-stephan-en.html) accessed 20 February 2014.

14 Tom Ambrose, *Hitler's Loss: What Britain and America Gained from Europe's Cultural Exiles* (London: Peter Owen, 2001), p.216.

15 I covered Josie's story in *The Other Schindlers*, pp.49–53.

16 Josie Levy Martin, pp.19–21.

17 Josie Levy Martin, pp.195–196.

18 'Treblinka Death Camp "Remember Me"', HEART 2007 (http://www.holocaustresearchproject.org/ar/treblinka/treblinkarememberme.html) accessed 8 April 2014.

19 Gitta Sereny, *Into That Darkness*, pp.211–212.

20 Cahnman, pp.141–142.

21 Robert Kuwalek, 'Piaski', HEART 2007 (http://www.holocaustresearchproject.org/ghettos/piaski.html) accessed 13 March 2014.

22 Maxime Rafailovitch, 'The End of the Piaski Jewish Community' (http://kehilalinks.jewishgen.org/lida-district/piaski.htm).

23 Gerta Vrbová, *Trust and Deceit*, pp.27–28.

24 Gratz Oral Archive.

25 Laura Varon, p.166.

26 Jewish Historical Museum, 'Nijmegen' (http://www.jhm.nl/culture-and-history/the-netherlands/gelderland/nijmegen) accessed 12 March 2014.

27 JTA, 'Dutch City Pledges $734,000 to Restore Synagogue', 23 August 2013 (http://forward.com/articles/182810/dutch-city-pledges-k-to-restore-synagogue) accessed 13

March 2014.

28 Hylke Roodenburg, Nijmegen Regional Archives, email to author, 14 March 2014.

29 Nederlands Architectuurinstituut (http://zoeken.nai.nl/Zoeken?SearchTerm=benning&s earchType=Person&searchType=Organization&searchType=PhysicalObject&searchType =Project&searchType=Archive&searchType=Publication&searchType=Event&searchType =CMSObject) accessed 12 March 2014.

30 Tony Jenkinson, Elizabeth Jenkinson – Berdina Benning, tribute at her funeral on 9 August 2013, received from the family, 12 March 2014.

31 I am grateful to Sara Kirby-Nieweg and Rob van der Meer of Chabad-Lubavitch, Nijmegen, for their help in finding this information.

*Chapter 21*

1 Malin Äkerström, *Betrayal and Betrayers: The Sociology of Treachery* (New Brunswick: Transaction Publishers, 1991), p.11.

2 'A million memories from his labour of love', Josh Glancy, *The Sunday Times*, 28 October 2014.

3 'Final Love Letter of Doomed Soldier too Shy to Propose', *The Times*, 30 October 2014.

4 Dan Michman, lecture at UCL, 4 February 2015.

5 German History in Documents and Images, 'The Constitution of the German Empire of August 11, 1919 (Weimar Constitution)' (http://www.germanhistorydocs.ghi-dc.org/pdf/ eng/ghi_wr_weimarconstitution_Eng.pdf) accessed 31 March 2015.

6 Ken Rise, 'Hitler and the Law 1920–1945', *History Today*, Issue 60, March 2008. (Thanks to Cheryl Deflorimonte of *History Today* for forwarding the article.)

7 *Magna Carta*, British Library (http://www.bl.uk/treasures/magnacarta/basics/basics.html) accessed 12 April 2014.

8 Gary Martin, 'The Phrase Finder' (http://www.phrases.org.uk/meanings/127700.html) accessed 4 April 2014.

9 Caroline Sturdy-Colls, email to author, 9 April 2014.

10 Caroline Sturdy-Colls, email to author, 4 April 2014. Dr Sturdy-Coll's book on 'Holocaust Archaeologies' has just been published by Springer.

11 Primo Levi, pp.219–220.

12 Hannah Devlin, 'Cancer is the Best Way to Die, Claims Doctor', *The Times*, 2 January 2015.

13 Michael Ignatieff, *Isaiah Berlin: A Life* (London: Chatto & Windus, 1998), p.200.

14 Isaiah Berlin, letter to George Kennan, 13 February 1951, cited in Ignatieff, p.200.

15 Ignatieff, pp.200–201.

16 ICRC 'Convention (II) with Respect to the Laws and Customs of War on Land', and its appendix, 'Regulations Concerning the Laws and Customs of War on Land'. The Hague, 29 July 1899 (http://www.icrc.org/applic/ihl/ihl.nsf/Treaty.xsp?documentId=CD0F6C83 F96FB459C12563CD002D66A1&action=openDocument) accessed 7 April 2014.

17 ICRC, 'Convention Relative to the Treatment of Prisoners of War', Geneva, 27 July 1929 (http://www.icrc.org/ihl/INTRO/305) accessed 11 February 2014.

18 A sutler is a camp follower selling food, etc.

19 'Convention Relative to the Treatment of Prisoners of War', Geneva 27 July 1929, ICRC, accessed 11 February 2014.

20 John Nettles, *Jewels and Jackboots* (St Mary, Jersey: Seeker Publishing: 2013), p.21.

21 Nettles, p.25.

22 ILO, 'Convention Concerning Forced or Compulsory Labour 1930' (http://www.ilo. org/dyn/normlex/en/f?p=NORMLEXPUB:12100:0::NO::P12100_ILO_CODE:C029) accessed 4 April 2014.

23 Liempt, pp.12–13.

24 I am grateful to my son, Ben Spier, for assistance with the international legislation.

25 Warren, *Surviving Hitler*, pp.143–144.

26 Vollmann and Winau, 'Informed Consent in Human Experimentation before the Nuremberg Code', *British Medical Journal*, Vol. 313, 7 December 1996 (http://www.ncbi.nlm.nih.gov/pmc/articles/PMC2352998/pdf/bmj00571-0035.pdf) accessed 4 April 2014.

27 USHMM, 'Coining a Word and Championing a Cause: The Story of Raphael Lemkin', 2013 (http://www.ushmm.org/wlc/en/article.php?ModuleId=10007050) accessed 4 April 2014.

28 Raphael Lemkin, 'Genocide – A Modern Crime', *Free World*, April 1945 (http://www.preventgenocide.org/lemkin/freeworld1945.htm) accessed 20 October 2000.

29 Raphael Lemkin, 'Genocide', *American Scholar*, Vol. 15, No. 2 April 1946 (http://www.preventgenocide.org/lemkin/americanscholar1946.htm) accessed 20 October 2000.

30 Eleanor Roosevelt, speech on ratification of UDHR, in Paris December 1948 (http://www.examiner.com/article/eleanor-roosevelt-speech-universal-declaration-of-human-rights) accessed 12 April 2014.

31 (https://treaties.un.org/Pages/ViewDetails.aspx?src=TREATY&mtdsg_no=IV-3&chapter=4&lang=en and https://treaties.un.org/Pages/ViewDetails.aspx?src=TREATY&mtdsg_no=IV-4&chapter=4&lang=en) accessed 14 April 2014.

32 http://www.oas.org/dil/1948_Convention_on_the_Prevention_and_Punishment_of_the_Crime_of_Genocide.pdf.

33 International Court of Justice, 'The Court – History' (http://www.icj-cij.org/court/index.php?p1=1&p2=1) accessed 15 April 2014.

34 Joseph Berger, 'Norbert Wollheim Dies at 85; Sued Over Forced Nazi Labor', *New York Times*, 3 November 1998, accessed 11 February 2014.

35 Diarmuid Jeffreys, *Hell's Cartel: IG Farben and the Making of Hitler's War Machine*, p.266 (London: Bloomsbury, 2009).

36 Ibid., p.268.

37 Ibid., p.345.

38 Yisrael Gutman, *The Jews of Warsaw 1939–1943* (Bloomington, IN: Indiana UP, 1989), p.110.

39 Jennifer Hyde, 'Killing Fields', survivor documents of Cambodian genocide (http://edition.cnn.com/2008/WORLD/asiapcf/11/13/sbm.cambodia.chhang) accessed 29 April 2013.

40 Brian Eads, 'Youk Chhang's Journey to Justice', 15 January 2010 (http://www.rdasia.com/youk_chhang_s_journey_to_justice_2645) accessed 29 April 2013.

41 Kemal Pervanic, The Forgiveness Project, 29 March 2010 (http://theforgivenessproject.com/stories/kemal-pervanic-bosnia) accessed 22 March 2014.

42 Kemal Pervanic, notes of interview with author, 11 April 2013, at the British Library.

43 Hilary Clinton press release – 'Remarks by Secretary of State Clinton At the Holocaust Memorial Museum Forward-Looking Symposium on Genocide Prevention', Washington, 24 July 2012 (http://www.state.gov/sectretary/rm/2012/07/195409.htm) accessed 11 November 2012.

44 Ruth Leiserowitz, 'Reverberations of Kristallnacht in the East Prussian Province Towns', p.3 (http://www.judeninostpreussen.de/upload/pdf/Leiserowitz_Kristallnacht_engl.pdf).

45 Martin Gilbert, *The Righteous: The Unsung Heroes of the Holocaust* (London: Doubleday, 2002), p.226.

46 Paul Webster, *Pétain's Crime* (London: Pan Books, 2001), p.175.

47 Tony Paterson, 'Tales of Blind Hero who Saved Jews from Nazis Told at Last', *The Independent*, 7 January 2014.

48 Joachim Fest, *Not Me: A German Childhood* (London: Atlantic Books, 2012).

49 Nicholas Shakespeare, '*Not Me: Memoirs of a German Childhood* by Joachim Fest'. Review in *Daily Telegraph*, 14 July 2012.

50 Jonathan Petropoulos, *Art as Politics in the Third Reich* (Chapel Hill, NC: UNC Books, 1999), pp.195–196.

51 Joachim Fest, *Not Me*, p.277.

52 Fest, p.280.

53 Moseley, *Mussolini*, p.50.

54 'The Last of the Unjust', *Pastforward*, USC Shoah Foundation, spring 2014, pp.32–33.

55 'Adam Czerniakow', Jewish Virtual Library (https://www.jewishvirtuallibrary.org/jsource/biography/Czerniakow.html) accessed 9 June 2014.

56 David Lester, *Suicide and the Holocaust*, p.91.

57 Christian Goeschel, *Suicide in Nazi Germany* (Oxford: OUP, 2009), pp.100–101.

58 Goeschel, p.99.

59 Perry, Berg and Krukones, *Sources of European History since 1900* (Boston, MA: Wadsworth, 2011), pp.169–170.

60 Marrus, *Origins of the Holocaust Part II*, pp.670–671.

61 Cited in Goeschel. p.97.

62 See Chapter 5.

63 Hildegard Abraham conversation with the author, 8 January 2015.

64 Göran Rosenberg, *A Brief Stop on the Road from Auschwitz* (London: Granta, 2014), p.317.

65 Rosenberg, p.275.

66 Rosenberg, pp.286–293.

67 Rosenberg, p.296.

68 Rosenberg, p.99.

69 Tamara Traubmann, 'Holocaust Survivors 3 Times More Likely to Attempt Suicide', Haaretz.com, 10 August 2005 (http://www.haaretz.com/news/study-holocaust-survivors-3-times-more-likely-to-attempt-suicide-1.166386) accessed 10 April 2014.

70 Yoram Barak, 'The Aging of Holocaust Survivors; Myth and Reality Concerning Suicide', *Israeli Medical Association Journal*, Vol. 9, March 2007, pp.196–198 (http://www.ima.org.il/FilesUpload/IMAJ/0/45/22847.pdf) accessed 14 April 2014.

71 J.B. Priestley, *Postscripts* (London: Heinemann, 1940), p.18.

72 Obituary for Professor Donald Cameron Watt, *The Times*, 4 February 2015.

73 Stefan Zweig, *The World of Yesterday* (Pushkin Press: London, 2014) p.46., translated by Anthea Bell.

74 Carl Zuckmayer, *A Part of Myself* (London: Secker & Warburg, 1970), translated by R. and C. Winston, p.37.

75 Zuckmayer, p.38.

76 Davis & Marshall (Eds), *Stefan & Lotte Zweig's South American Letters 1940–1942* (New York: Continuum, 2010), pp.189–192.

77 Anthea Bell, Translator's Note in Zweig, *The World of Yesterday*, pp.9–10.

78 Bell, in Zweig, p.10.

79 JTA, 'Portugal Adopts Return Law for Jewish Descendants', 29 January 2015.

80 World Jewish Congress, 'Spanish Lawmakers Vote to Grant Citizenship to Descendants of Expelled Sephardic Jews', 26 March 2015 (http://wjc-website.herokuapp.com/en/news/spanish-lawmakers-vote-to-grant-citizenship-to-descendents-of-expelled-sephardic-jews), accessed 26 March 2015.

81 A 'minyan' is the quorum of ten Jewish men required for certain religious obligations.

82 Jewish Virtual Library (http://www.jewishvirtuallibrary.org/jsource/vjw/Portugal.html).

83 Michael Tuchfield, 'Portugal's Talking Stones', *Esra Magazine*, Issue 171, 2013 (http://www.esra-magazine.com/blog/post/portugal-talking-stones) accessed 11 April 2014.

84 David Silberklang, 'For a Few Days' Leave', in *Martyrdom and Resistance* newsletter, New York Jan/Feb 2014, p.10.

85 Clive Lawton, 'A Final Word' in *The Role of Righteous Muslims* (London: Faith Matters, 2010), p.28.

86 Daniel Gordis, *Menachem Begin: The Battle for Israel's Soul* (New York: Schocken, 2014).

87 Ruth Deech, email to author, 28 February 2015.

88 Benjamin Netanyahu, speech to Congress, 3 March 2015, in *The Washington Post* (http://www.washingtonpost.com/blogs/post-politics/wp/2015/03/03/full-text-netanyahus-address-to-congress) accessed 29 March 2015.

89 Alan Johnson, 'Bowen's Shame over Holocaust Remark', 4 March 2015 (www.thejc.com/print/130987) accessed 24 March 2015.

90 'Another BBC Journalist Under Fire', *The Algemeiner*, 5 March 2015 (http://www.algemeiner.com/2015/03/05/another-bbc-journalist-under-fire-bowen-slammed-for-saying-netanyahu-played-holocaust-card-in-congress-speech) accessed 24 March 2015.

91 Richard Brooks, 'BBC Cut Reference to Jews from Dimbleby's Belsen Broadcast', *Sunday Times*, 7 June 2015.

92 Gerald Ronson, address to CST annual dinner, 18 March 2015. Text sent by email 24 March 2015.

93 'Nakba' is the Palestinian name for the 'Day of Catastrophe' – 15 May 1948, the day Israel was formally created by the United Nations.

94 Yifa Yaakov, 'Palestinian Lecturer Who Led Auschwitz Trip Quits After Backlash', *The Times of Israel*, 8 June 2014 (http://www.timesofisrael.com/palestinian-lecturer-who-led-auschwitz-trip-quits-after-backlash) accessed 8 June 2014.

95 Raul Hilberg obituary in *The Times*, 8 August 2007 (http://www.thetimes.co.uk/tto/opinion/obituaries/article2079983.ece) accessed 20 March 2014.

*Postscript*

1 The author is grateful to Professor Dan Michman for sending this family story – Leny was his aunt, but was murdered before he was born.

2 Dan Michman, Talk at UCL on 4 February 2015, 'What Exactly was the Goal of the Nazi anti-Jewish Enterprise?'

*Appendix I*

1 John Young letter to author, 4 August 1995.

2 John Young, 'And There Were Sweets', unpublished memoir written 1996, sent to author March 2002, p.1.

3 Ibid., p.2.

4 Ibid., p.3.

5 Ibid., p.4.

6 Ibid., p.4.

7 Ibid., p.5.

8 Ibid., pp.6–7.

9 Ibid., p.8.

10 Ibid., p.9.

11 Ibid., p.10.

12 Ibid., p.11.

13 Deborah Gibb, emails to author, 20 December 2013 and 3 January 2014.

14 Billy Kember, 'British Rescuer of Anne Frank's Friend Meets Next Generation', *The Times*, 6 January 2014.

*Appendix II*

1 Milan Gorol, statement on behalf of the Roma, at Holocaust Memorial Day National Event, London, 27 January 2014.

2 Marianne C. Zwicker, 'Journeys into Memory: Romani Identity and the Holocaust', PhD thesis, University of Edinburgh, 2009, p.119 (https://www.era.lib.ed.ac.uk/

bitstream/1842/6201/1/Zwicker2010.pdf) accessed 24 March 2014.
3 Laurence Rees, *Auschwitz*, p.313.
4 Laurence Rees, *Auschwitz*, p.318.


## Appendix III

1 Gitta Sereny, *Into That Darkness*, p.60.
2 Sereny, pp.60–65.
3 Alison Owings, *Frauen*, pp.23–24.
4 Ian Kershaw, *Popular Opinion*, p.334.
5 Kershaw, p.336.
6 Kershaw, p.339.


## Appendix IV

Rees, pp.314–318.


## Appendix VI

1 Laurence Rees, *Auschwitz*, p.14.
2 Clare Makepeace, 'Compensating the Railway Men', *History Today*, April 2014, Vol. 64:4, pp.51–57.
3 David Sillito, 'St Trinian's Cartoonist Ronald Searle Dies', *BBC News*, 3 January 2012 (http://www.bbc.co.uk/news/entertainment-arts-16391857) accessed 29 March 2014.
4 Makepeace, p.55.
5 Jack Chalker obituary in *The Times*, 25 November 2014.
6 Hugh de Wardener obituary in *The Times*, 25 November 2013.


## Appendix VII

1 Hans Siemsen, *Hitler Youth* (London: Drummond, 1940), p.8.
2 Siemsen, p.9.
3 Siemsen, pp.56–57.
4 Siemsen, pp.57–58.
5 Siemsen, p.58.
6 Siemsen, pp.62–63.

# INDEX

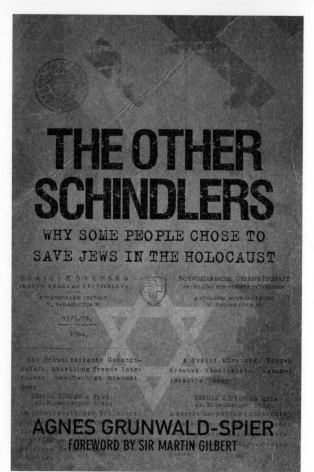

978 0 7524 5967 7